The Breakthrough Years

ALSO BY ELLEN GALINSKY

Mind in the Making: The Seven Essential Life Skills Every Child Needs

Ask the Children: The Breakthrough Study That Reveals How to Succeed at Work and Parenting (author and photographer)

The Six Stages of Parenthood

The Preschoool Years: Family Strategies That Work—from Experts and Parents (with Judy David)

The New Extended Family: Day Care That Works (coauthor with William H. Hooks and photographer)

Beginnings: A Young Mother's Personal Account of Two Premature Births

Children's Books

The Baby Cardinal (author and photographer)

Catbird (author and photographer)

The Breakthrough Years

A New Scientific
Framework for
Raising Thriving Teens

ELLEN GALINSKY

FLATIRON
BOOKS
NEW YORK

This book is a factual presentation of research and related findings, analyses, and conclusions based on the scientific study of adolescence. However, except where noted, many names of research subjects/participants—and especially names of minors—have been changed/anonymized following traditional research protocols and understandings.

Illustrations by Jennie Portnof

Library of Congress Cataloging-in-Publication Data

Names: Galinsky, Ellen, author.
Title: The breakthrough years : a new scientific framework for raising thriving
    teens / Ellen Galinsky.
Description: First edition. | New York : Flatiron Books, 2024. | Includes
    bibliographical references and index.
Identifiers: LCCN 2023037230 | ISBN 9781250062048 (hardcover) |
    ISBN 9781250062055 (ebook)
Subjects: LCSH: Parenting. | Adolescent psychology. | Child development.
Classification: LCC HQ755.8 .G343 2024 | DDC 649/.1—dc23/eng/20230830
LC record available at https://lccn.loc.gov/2023037230

First Edition: 2024

10 9 8 7 6 5 4 3 2 1

To *my grandsons*

As you grew out of adolescence, Antonio, you worked with me
 on the earliest stages of this book.
As you grow into adolescence, Zai, this book is for you and adolescents
 everywhere.
With thanks to Brandon Almy—you have been with me every
 step of the way.

CONTENTS

The Breakthrough Years

INTRODUCTION

"Just Wait"

I remember holding my newborn son in a rocking chair when he came home from the hospital.

A friend who had come over to welcome him to the world was the first to say this to me, soon after admiring him: "Just wait until he's a teenager!"

As a new parent—like any new parent—there were times when I was frantic with worry, especially because my son was born prematurely. What if he wasn't going to be healthy and strong? What if he wasn't going to develop like other children? Now there was a "just wait" decree looming over our future like a jail sentence.

This "just wait" warning was repeated again and again. It seemed as if any time I felt the wonder or the pressure of parenting—exulted in my son or struggled with parenting him—others felt they should warn me about the tumultuous future in store: "Just wait until he's a teenager!"

Well-meaning friends and strangers did the same with my daughter a few years later. At key moments, such as when she pulled herself up on her feet and launched herself out into the world with her first tottering steps, or when she was a defiant preschooler, I'd hear: "Just wait until she's a teenager—see what trouble she walks into then!"

Storm and Stress

More than a hundred years ago, there was no such thing as adolescence as we now know it. For example, many of my relatives in the nineteenth century went straight from childhood into assuming the responsibilities of adulthood.

By the turn of the twentieth century that had changed. Most of my relatives didn't take jobs in their teens; they stayed in school longer and entered the workforce later. During that time, the idea of adolescence as a distinct period of life began to take a stronger hold,[1] and in 1904 the scientific study of adolescence was born with the publication of a two-volume work by G. Stanley Hall.[2] Its focus was on storm and stress. The theme of turbulence—the first formal attempt to understand this unique period of life—has continued to permeate popular perception. Thus, those "just wait" warnings we've heard for so long.

By the turn of the twenty-first century, researchers' focus began to shift away from the perils and toward the promise of adolescence, especially as the tools of science became more precise[3] and as the Positive Youth Development movement spread.[4]

The Promise of Adolescence

We now know that **adolescence is a sensitive period in brain development**—almost as important as the foundational early years. Though the span of years covered by adolescence differs in different parts of the world, its beginning is usually marked by puberty and its ending by the assumption of adult responsibilities, which is in the mid-twenties in the United States. Adolescents so defined make up almost one-quarter of the U.S. population.[5]

During adolescence, **there is heightened brain plasticity with extensive neural change.** Like the early years, adolescence is a time when we're especially affected by the environments we're in.[6]

Decades of research also reveal that there is a set of core attention-regulation skills, called executive function (EF) skills, that are often more important to our school and lifetime success than our IQ or socioeconomic status.[7] These skills emerge during early childhood, and that's when they should be first promoted—the subject of my last book, *Mind in the Making: The Seven Essential Skills Every Child Needs.*

But we can't stop there. Like the early years, **adolescence is a prime time for learning executive function skills.** The superhighways of the brain are under construction during adolescence.[8] The prefrontal regions—central to executive function—develop significantly. There's also improved connectivity between the outer cortical regions (areas linked to cognitive control) and inner cortical regions (areas linked to emotional responses, rewards, and learning).[9]

Researchers call adolescence an age of opportunity and vulnerability[10] because our development can begin to go in a more positive or a more negative direction during these years.

The Societal Challenges We Face

There are many very real challenges that confront us in raising adolescents today. **One is the increase in mental health problems.** In 2021, the Centers for Disease Control and Prevention found that 42 percent of high school students reported experiencing such persistent feelings of sadness or hopelessness in the past year that they couldn't participate in their regular activities, up from 28 percent in 2011.[11] Findings like these are especially alarming because we know that the majority of mental health issues emerge by the time we are twenty-four.[12]

Another challenge is school achievement. School achievement dropped during the pandemic, but it has been historically uneven,[13] and pressures to achieve can be punishing.

Much of public discourse focuses on who's to blame. Has social media changed children's brains? Is it a pressure-filled achievement culture? Is it the divisiveness and loneliness of life today?

This book is quite different from most books and articles you will read about adolescence:

- While most concentrate on one of these challenges or another, this book ties them together.
- While most concentrate on blaming, this book goes beyond who's at fault to concentrate on **breakthrough solutions** that come from the latest science on the brain and psychological development and from young people themselves! It focuses on how we can equip adolescents with environments that meet their needs and promote life and learning skills that help them learn and thrive.

And that's the urgency. **These years between childhood and adulthood are *the time*** where we have opportunities to help set up young people for success now and in the future. These years can be a time when young people begin to discover who they are, what has meaning for them, what they are good at, how they can manage challenges. These years can even be a time of recovery, when it's possible to heal from early adversities. Adolescence is a time of enormous possibility.

My close friend Karen Diamond handed me a note as I was writing this book. On it, she wrote:

What kind of world will we leave our children?

And . . .

What kind of children will we leave our world?

These questions fuel the passion I have in writing this book. It's that simple and that true.

My Research Adventures

I practice a form of science called civic science. In civic science, the people who would traditionally be the subjects of a study become its co-creators and collaborators, drawing on their life experiences to inform the questions that are asked, the study design, and the interpretation of the findings.

In 2015, I began with adolescents from across the United States and abroad, asking 38 fourteen- to eighteen-year-olds in focus groups and interviews: "What do you want to know about your own development? And what do you want me to ask researchers who study adolescent development when I interview them?"* Some said they wanted to know:

Why don't adults understand us?
Why do adults have such negative views of teenagers?

You've probably heard the young people in your life ask questions like: "Why don't you understand me?"

But maybe—just maybe—there's something deeper here than teens merely being teens. That's why I think of research as an adventure. It takes you places you don't know you are going.

I called the study "The Breakthrough Years" because of the enormous promise of these years to shape positive development. It is clear that most of us don't understand normal adolescent development, which in turn seriously inhibits our ability to help young people be and become all they can be.

Over the next years, I interviewed forty-five leading adolescence researchers and read studies by hundreds of others. Their cutting-edge findings and inspiring insights (which for the most part appear in hard-to-access academic books, articles, and journals) are distilled in these pages.

In 2019, our research team** and I conducted a baseline quantitative

---

* My then college-age grandson Antonio participated in some of these focus groups and interviews with me, and his take on what he'd heard was invaluable.

** Our research team includes Brandon Almy, then a doctoral student on adolescent development at the University of Minnesota, now a pediatric neuropsychologist at Helen DeVos Children's Hospital in Grand Rapids, Michigan, and Philip David Zelazo, a developmental social cognitive neuroscientist at the University of Minnesota. Our Families and Work Institute (FWI) team includes Erin Ramsey, Jennie Portnof, and Marline Griffith; they began this work at FWI, were with study of a nationally representative group of 1,666 adolescents (nine- to nineteen-year-olds)* and their parents. The following summer, I conducted qualitative interviews with fifty-six parents and fifty-two of their adolescents from this group, asking them about their take on the initial findings as well as new questions that had emerged.

Then the pandemic happened, and we conducted a follow-up quantitative study with 1,115 of these same parents and their children in August 2020 to see how they were doing. Our team additionally designed a behavioral study that included an assessment of executive function skills with 223 young people (sixth, ninth, and twelfth graders) in nine schools in six states between November 2019 and January 2020.

Among the questions we asked young people in the baseline study was: "What would you like to tell the adults of America about people your age?"

The five main things they want us to know—their messages to adults— align remarkably with the new science of adolescence as well as with parents' hopes and dreams. These messages form both the structure of the book and its unique contributions. Below are a few highlights.

Message 1: Understand Our Development

In response to the open-ended question about what they want to tell the adults of America, **one in five of the young people (21 percent) want adults to know that we don't understand their way of being smart and their development.** Again and again, they wrote: "We are smarter than you think," "Just because we are younger doesn't mean we are less smart," and "We are smart and we need to be heard." They wrote, "Understand me, understand us."

How do adults understand adolescents? In the baseline study, we asked parents an open-ended question to find out more:

When you hear the phrase "the teen brain," or "the adolescent brain," what one word comes to mind?

---

me when I served as chief science officer at the Bezos Family Foundation for six years, and are back at FWI with me again.

* *The Breakthrough Years* defines adolescence as beginning in puberty, which is happening earlier in current generations than in the past. Thus, we began our study with nine-year-olds. Adolescence encompasses the teen years (thirteen to nineteen) but extends until young people assume some of the responsibilities of adulthood. Our study stopped with nineteen-year-olds, but I also share research on older adolescents in their twenties.

We weren't asking about their own child's brain, but about the generic adolescent brain. We found:

- Only 14 percent of parents used *positive* terms, like "exploring," "creative," "fun," or "the future."
- Another 27 percent used *neutral* terms, like "growing" or "changing."
- And 59 percent used *negative* terms, like "forgetful," "stupid," "clueless," "distracted," "know-it-all," or "bratty."

Further insight comes when we look at the actual words that parents use to describe the adolescent/teen brain. The most frequent word? "Immature." It's used 11 percent of the time. That's a remarkable convergence for an open-ended question. Another 8 percent use "un-," "in-," or "not" words, including:

unformed
undeveloped/underdeveloped
unfinished
incomplete
inexperienced
not thinking/not smart

These words indicate that many adults are using an adult yardstick to assess adolescents and are finding them lacking.

Perhaps this conception hearkens back to that earlier era I mentioned, when people moved straight from childhood into adulthood. Perhaps it's because young people can look adultlike, so we assess them based on appearances. Or perhaps our adult experiences cloud our memories of what it was really like to be a teen. There are many reasons.

But young people aren't adults. We wouldn't say that infants are immature toddlers when they experience stranger anxiety in learning whom to trust or that toddlers are immature preschoolers when they say "no, no, no" in learning what they can and can't control. Children at these younger ages are doing exactly what they are developmentally primed to do—what they need to do for their brains to develop.

Yet too many of us seem to think about our adolescents as immature adults, even though they, like younger children, are doing exactly what their brains are priming them to do (and by the way, this was true in earlier eras when there was little societal demarcation of adolescence):

- They are moving further out into the world, so they need to be highly sensitive to social and emotional situations.
- They need to become environmental detectors to determine what's okay and what's worrisome, and to react strongly because their parents aren't necessarily there to help them.
- They need to explore their identities and what it means to be and become them. So they're highly sensitive to what matters to them, and to experiences where they can begin to figure this out.

Our lack of understanding can affect how we respond to and talk with adolescents and can have longer-term repercussions, as this message from a seventeen-year-old girl in our survey reveals:

I wish my concerns, my friends' concerns, and my classmates' concerns could be taken seriously.

I can't count the number of times I have tried to talk to an adult about something that's been causing me pain. (Usually emotional pain.) It's easily dismissed because, "everybody goes through it, you'll be fine." I feel this is an improper, disrespectful, trust-destroying phrase to use. Its variations are equally harmful. Telling me my problems aren't problematic solely because somebody else has experienced the same thing is wrong. It's simply wrong. The same kind of damage is caused by "at least you don't have [fill in the blank]." Invalidating somebody's feelings because their pain isn't critical is the most selfish thing I see in the lives of the people around me. Empathy, sympathy, and love is the proper response. I don't see enough love in the lives of anybody I know. Selfishness is there, even if selfishness [by others] was never the intention.

Because the problems of teenagers are not being taken seriously, we put up a facade. We smile and nod and nod and smile, but inside, there is pain. "That's just your hormones! You'll get over it." "Everybody goes through it." But even if everybody goes through it, nobody should face the problem alone. Why isolate a struggling person? My confidence in my parents has gotten weaker and weaker. I know this is "a rebellious phase all teenagers go through." If "rebellious" means standing up for myself, then I will be rebellious. If it means that my little brothers get to keep their glimmers of hope, if it means my little sisters get to feel loved, then I will keep on being "rebellious." Half a decade of my feelings being disregarded has taken its toll. Half a decade of being told "You're fine" right before I

melt down and cry for an hour has made its mark. A lifetime of "It'll be
better tomorrow" has lied time and time again.

When we understand adolescents and their development, we can talk
with them in more effective ways, as their next message reveals.

Message 2: Listen and Talk *with* Us, Not *at* Us

One in twelve adolescents (9 percent) ask adults to listen and to talk *with*
them. They wrote, "Ask our opinions and *listen to us please!*" And they're
right. When conflicts between adults and adolescents do erupt, the most
effective approach is called autonomy support. This approach:

- Gives adolescents an appropriate measure of autonomy and agency—
  basic developmental needs during these years
- Helps adolescents learn how to resolve problems for themselves,
  rather than have the adults fix problems for them

It's also effective for adults because they set the goal and the ground
rules, and they're helping their adolescent gain skills and experience while
the immediate problem is getting resolved.

Why does this approach work so well for managing conflict? Studies
find that an autonomy-supportive approach aids the development of executive function skills[14] and helps young people thrive[15] by building their own
self-regulation skills (rather than imposing regulation by punishing them,
coaxing compliance, or fixing things for them).

But autonomy support is not enough. Mindsets matter.

A Possibilities Mindset is a growth mindset ("Things can change") plus
self-efficacy ("I can make a change").[16] It's a wondering response (versus
feeling threatened) where we see the obstacles and believe we can figure out
how to overcome them.

Message 3: Don't Stereotype Us

When asked what they want to tell the adults of America, young people
wrote that not all of us are in trouble or doing the things you'd expect people
our age to be doing. For example:

Taking *unhealthy risks*: "We are not all TikTokking risk-takers."

Taking *drugs*: "Not all of us fall under the umbrella of being problematic drug addicts."

Being *entitled*: "We have a lot more to offer the world than many of you see. Sometimes it feels like every adult thinks my generation is nothing more than a bunch of entitled brats that want everything given to them."

Being *troublemakers*: "All kids aren't troublemakers or irresponsible."

Being *addicted to technology*: "We aren't social media obsessed, we aren't extremely self-involved, our phones don't define us, and the internet is not going to be the end of us."

There are two underlying themes in their words. The first is: "Don't judge us all by the actions of a few." The second is: "Don't see us all in such a negative light." In fact, more than one in three adolescents (38 percent)—the largest proportion of adolescents in the study—ask adults not to generalize, make negative assumptions, or stereotype them, but instead to recognize their strengths.

Our study found that age discrimination is more commonplace than one might think. Using a standard measure of discrimination that asks about the frequency of people acting as if they are better than you, treating you as if you aren't smart, and so forth,[17] we found that age is the most frequent reason given for six of the nine types of discrimination among the 73 percent of young people who'd experienced any type of discrimination at least a few times.

It may have always been this way, but what's now clear is that there's a developmental price. Studies show that discrimination because of age (or any other reason) can affect adolescents' physical health, their sleep, and their psychological well-being.[18]

Message 4: We Are Trying to Understand Ourselves and Our Needs

When we hear the words "belonging," "support," "respect," and "contribution," they can slide over us—that is, until we're the ones treated as if we don't belong, don't deserve respect, or can't make a difference in our own way. These are Basic Needs we all have, at all ages—especially during the formative years of adolescence. The concept of Basic Needs is based on decades of research into Self-Determination Theory,[19] revealing how psychological needs are connected with our well-being and thriving.[20] In our studies, we expanded that concept, outlining five needs.

The Five Basic Psychological Needs

1. Caring connections
2. Agency
3. Mastery
4. Identity
5. Purpose

In our baseline study, we tested the extent to which these needs were met through adolescents' relationships (at home, with friends, at school, in out-of-school activities, and online). In the follow-up study, we found that those adolescents whose needs had been met were much more likely to be doing well in school and in life nine months later. "Nine months later" happened to occur during a very difficult and trying time in this country—the COVID-19 pandemic—so it was a strong test of the importance of meeting needs. This finding is especially relevant given what we know about the vulnerabilities of the adolescent years, and the declines our society has been experiencing in the mental health of young people. Meeting these needs helps adolescents thrive!

Message 5: We Want to Learn Life and Learning Skills

Generally, we think of adolescence as the time for learning the academic content that young people will need to know as they begin to take their places in the adult world. That's absolutely essential, but as stated above, executive function skills are foundational for learning, adaptation, and a positive life. These skills are as—if not more—important to our academic and life success and to well-being than our IQ or socioeconomic status. But, as one educational leader recently told me, if he was in a room of superintendents or principals and asked them if they knew what executive function skills are, very few would raise their hands—or if they did, they would associate them with learning struggles like ADHD. This is all the more concerning because a population study in Massachusetts found that EF skills have declined significantly during the pandemic,[21] which may be contributing in major ways to learning losses. This education leader continued, "This is not about some of our children. This is most of our children!"

In this book, I describe EF skills and Life and Learning Skills based on them:

Life and Learning Skills

- Setting and achieving goals
- Understanding the perspectives of others
- Communicating and collaborating
- Problem-solving
- Taking on challenges

To help young people learn and thrive, it is essential that we promote these skills.

The Breakthrough Years is not a typical book about adolescents because it's not a bad-news book, but it's not a good-news book, either. Because I am a parent and grandparent and am always thinking about what to do, I've written it as a real-news book—with news you can use, weaving together the often awe-inspiring wisdom and experiences of adolescents and parents with research- and reality-based principles and strategies for helping adolescents thrive.

I deeply hope that sharing this real news will lead to fewer of us being forewarned, "Just wait until they're teenagers" (as we found 61 percent of parents are), and more of us recognizing these years for the breakthrough years they are.

So, let's begin with the adolescent brain. . . .

1

MESSAGE 1: UNDERSTAND OUR DEVELOPMENT

don't understand how adults don't understand teenagers when they were once a teenager," Ayana, a sixteen-year-old living in Connecticut, told me.

That's always been my main question. I've thought about this for so long. How can adults forget what it's like being a teenager when they were once a teenager and had this same exact thing happen to them?

We'd talk about her experiences with school, friends, and boyfriends. She'd explain how she was different from her parents, then return to her question:

*We **are** different, but I still just don't understand how they can look at me and say, "I understand what you're going through," when they don't.*

Many of us may have had a young person say some version of "you don't understand me" to us. It's a recurrent theme that—because of its frequency, urgency, and impact—deserves to be addressed. It was the driving purpose of the Breakthrough Years study and the foundation of this book.

The Breakthrough Years Study

Young people in the Breakthrough Years study were asked a question that helps us understand what they want us to know:

What would you like to tell the adults of America about people your age?

The 1,666 young people who took this quantitative survey are from all over the United States, ranging in age from nine to nineteen. They live in the mountains and on the coasts, in the deserts and on the plains, in soaring cities and in the countryside around cities and towns. They're high-income, low-income, and in between; they're of all skin hues. Yet, remarkably, many of the words in this nationally representative group in the response to this open-ended question echo each other.*

When they say we underestimate how "smart" they are, they aren't talking about IQ or book-smarts. "Smart" is a stand-in for who they are and how they approach the world.

They say it directly:

We are smart and not bad.
　　—Eleven-year-old boy**

We are smart and try our best, but we still need love.
　　—Nine-year-old girl

We are strong, smart and ready to learn and grow—we need support, love and to be treated like we matter.
　　—Sixteen-year-old boy

I would like to tell them that we are actually smart and we are the next generation that will help this planet.
　　—Fourteen-year-old boy

They say, "Don't assume . . .":

Don't be so judgmental and assume we are dumb.
　　—Sixteen-year-old girl

We are smarter than you [adults] think. We don't get everything right all the time, but nobody does.
　　—Thirteen-year-old boy

They say: "We are *not* . . ."

---

* When quoting Breakthrough Years survey participants, I have very occasionally corrected small typos, added punctuation, or used brackets to add a missing word to make their messages more understandable, but otherwise these statements are as the adolescents wrote them in the survey.

** Adolescents were asked to identify their gender as "male," "female," or "other," and if other, they were asked how they self-identify. I use their self-identifications here and throughout the book.

Give us a chance. Listen to us—we're not as dumb as a lot of you think.
     —Sixteen-year-old boy

*We are not all screwups—a lot of us are smart and try to do the right thing
all of the time.*
          —Thirteen-year-old girl

I was struck by how many times the words "smart" or "not dumb"
appear. In fact, 12 percent—the highest portion of young people in the
Breakthrough Years study in a single coding category for this question—
specifically want adults to know they are smart.*

Another 9 percent want us to "be more patient," as one eighteen-year-old
boy says, and understand they're still learning.

We are difficult, but sometimes all we want is to be understood.
     —Fourteen-year-old girl

*We are young adults finding our way thru life, we should be treated with
respect and hopefully understanding as to what we are going through.*
          —Thirteen-year-old girl

Breakthrough Years Study Finding: One in every five young people
(21 percent) want adults to know that we don't understand their way of
being smart and their development.

What messages are they getting from us that give such frequent rise to
the word "smart"? Maybe we say "that's not smart" when we don't like
something they say or do. Maybe we have low expectations:

*I would like to tell the adults of America that people my age are not "chil-
dren" that should be treated like two-year-olds. We are smart and are more*

---

* Quotes can be coded, or categorized, in multiple ways. For example, "we are not screwups" and
"we are smart" reflect similar yet distinct ideas. When we coded adolescents' responses, we used
the apparent main theme of the response to inform the first code; however, about 26 percent of
the responses received at least two codes or categories. In turning these findings into percentages,
we include all of the relevant responses, sometimes across coding categories, as we do in combining the 12 percent who ask that adults not assume they are dumb and the 9 percent who ask
adults to understand their development. We also have excluded the 19 percent who didn't answer
this question.

intelligent than some think we are. I think that even though we are smaller and have less power than most adults, we can still make a big difference.

　　—Ten-year-old girl

Or a mix of low and high expectations:

I've seen the same phrase everywhere: "Teenagers are treated like children and expected to act like adults." There is this awkward, in-between learning phase we're going through. But let me explain why this hurts. Treating me like a child is upsetting because when I turn eighteen, I feel like I'm supposed to magically turn "adult" and know what I'm going to do with my life.

　　—Seventeen-year-old girl

It's clear that this in-between learning phase isn't well understood by us adults.

How Did We Get Here?

There are many reasons. Adolescents live in a world where they're frequently judged. There's high-stakes testing, where a lot of their future depends on the results. There's social media, where some teenagers curate their images, presenting their lives to seem as perfect as possible, while others feel inadequate and judged.[1] But young people have felt this way before all of this. There's something deeper in society.

For well over a century, most studies on adolescence have focused on the emotional upheavals and vulnerabilities of these years, reflecting long-held societal views of adolescents. The textbook I used as a child studies major[2] in college begins its description of adolescence with the 1904 work of G. Stanley Hall (the first psychologist to study adolescence as a distinct developmental stage), characterizing adolescence as a time of "Sturm und Drang"—storm and stress.[3] And only a few years ago, at a college reunion, my classmates and I attended a lecture on why adolescents make stupid and negative risky decisions, despite seeming to know better.

Has anything changed? Yes. And no.

THE SCIENCE BOOM

Over the past twenty years, there's been an explosion in research on adolescent development, including brain development, often aided by innovative brain imaging technologies and collaborations between developmental researchers and neuroscientists.

In the early years of the twenty-first century, Laurence Steinberg of Temple University and his colleagues began finding a pattern of brain development that they believed helps explain negative risk-taking.[4] Specifically, Steinberg, Jason Chein,[5] and others[6] found that the brain's reward system on average develops more quickly than the cognitive control system.

This was and is an important finding. In its wake, however, an image took hold in the public imagination that researchers and many others have used. Adolescence is like an out-of-control car. The accelerator (the reward system) is well developed and can be pushed to the floor, which is thrilling, but the brakes (the cognitive control system) are faulty because they're not fully developed. The result: risky behavior.

The finding that, in general, the brain's reward system develops more quickly than the cognitive control system has been replicated by the Temple team[7] and many others. But new studies have emerged indicating there's much more to it. In this chapter, I'll share research on adolescence showing that:

- Cognitive control strategies for managing emotions can be taught and learned.
- The reward system is also a learning system that can be harnessed for growth and learning.
- Development isn't set in stone—there are significant individual differences in developmental patterns, and this pattern doesn't apply to many young people.
- Most important, our lack of understanding of adolescent development can affect our children in negative ways.

NEGATIVE AND INCOMPLETE PERCEPTIONS OF ADOLESCENCE PERSIST

The media, including many books, continue to reinforce incomplete and negative images. Between October 16, 2017, and January 16, 2018, FrameWorks

Institute coded and analyzed 249 stories about this age from the top U.S. mainstream media and online news publications. They found that media stories are more than twice as likely to discuss negative influences on adolescents (48 percent) than positive ones (21 percent), "often accompanied by explicit language about the 'riskiness' of adolescence."[8] Influences characterized as negative include peers, gangs, technology, social and entertainment media, and sexual predators.

These messages reinforce existing assumptions—like those "just wait till they're teenagers" warnings I described in the introduction. And so, "over time, these models become ever more deeply etched into culture."[9]

But we now know that this isn't the full story:

> *Experts see adolescence as a period of vulnerability **and** [emphasis added] opportunity, when environments and experiences exert an especially strong effect on development and shape long-term outcomes. Media discourse . . . tells half of this story, focusing only on the threats posed to young people but not opportunities for growth and development.*[10]

I'll explore why these negative stories are so persistent and resistant to change at the end of this chapter. First, let's look at the research that sheds an illuminating new light on adolescent development.

Reflections on Message 1

Think back to a time when you had to move out of your comfort zone as an adult. Perhaps it was moving to a new place, starting a new job, or meeting new people. How did you manage this?

When I ask this question of adults in my talks, here are some of the stories I hear:

Some speak about being brave:

> *I had to summon the courage to take on this project in the first place.*

Others search for meaning:

Thinking on my feet comes to mind. Because I wasn't sure of the customs or conventions at my new organization, I had to look at other people to see how they reacted. I had to listen to the words they used and try to quickly make sense of what was happening so I could respond.

Moving workplaces prompted one person to try to discover the norms in the new culture:

When I was going to a new job, I used self-talk and asked myself questions, like: "Should my boss tell me exactly what to do?" I told myself, "No, that's not going to happen." I need to look to the people who've been there for years to figure out what's expected. I gave myself the grace of not knowing, of asking questions, of exploring, and of realizing it will take time.

Becoming able to take risks helped another manage:

My dad held our large family together for years. When he passed, I couldn't deal with the way the family became, so I decided to move. I had to find new doctors, new stores, and new people to help me. When I was trying to manage all of this, I kept remembering how it felt to be in my old home. That helped me take the risk and try something new.

A man spoke about how much his mindset mattered:

When I have to do something hard, I think about times when a similar experience had gone well in the past. That gives me the confidence to see this as an adventure.

When we move out of our comfort zone, we summon our courage, try to get a quick read on the social situation, think on our feet, explore, and take risks.

For adolescents, this is a phase of life—a yearslong experience of moving out of their comfort zones. This phase is not "complete" once the jolt of the new gradually fades away. It unfolds over a period of years, as they continually form an identity during adolescence (and later in life) and as they adapt to new schools, new people, new situations, and ultimately to adult experiences. The exhilarating, exhausting, exacting process that adults go through when we take a new job, move, or go to an unfamiliar city for a work project *is* the sustained work of adolescence.

The Adolescent Years Are Breakthrough Years

For as long as she can remember, Jennifer Silvers of UCLA has been interested in emotions. She recalls that when she experienced a particularly difficult time as an adolescent—having a problem in school, trying something new, getting rejected by a new crush—it made her feel "nervous," "overwhelmed," and "as if it was the end of the world!" She also recalls that her mother would suggest taking a step back:

> *My mother told me something to the effect of, "Right now this feels like everything, but someday you'll look back and it will seem like just one experience of many." I remember thinking: that must mean that the way I'm looking at the world today will be different when I'm older. It made me wonder what was unique about being an adolescent, particularly since a lot of emotions felt so strong. That was part of what led me to want to study adolescence.*[11]

OVERLY EMOTIONAL + IMPULSIVE + RISKY = ADOLESCENCE?

Imagine that you are slighted at work, someone you care about says something mean, or someone treats you like a child. At any age, we resent having our powerful feelings dismissed. Silvers's mother understood adolescence, which showed in her responses to her daughter. She wasn't confrontational ("Get over it!") or dismissive ("You're blowing things out of proportion"). She accepted her daughter's feelings ("right now this feels like everything") and offered a tool for **reframing** an overwhelming moment ("your perspective might be different someday").

Parents and caregivers like this mother know that how children view and manage emotionally charged situations will change as they grow up, but it wasn't until recently that researchers like Silvers understood more precisely when this happens and how. She has focused specifically on those *when* and *how* questions, looking at cognitive reappraisal—reframing one's interpretation of an emotional event. Her research helps us see adolescence as the *breakthrough years* of dramatic changes it truly is.

REFRAMING TECHNIQUES: ONE SIZE DOES NOT FIT ALL

Initially, Silvers experimented with the emotional regulation techniques used by Kevin Ochsner and the late Walter Mischel,[12] two leading researchers on this subject, finding that one technique that works well with adults—telling people to imagine what they see isn't true (for example, if you see someone with blood on them, imagine it's ketchup or they're acting in a movie)—isn't very effective with children and adolescents, but other techniques are.[13]

Overall, emotional regulation happens in three ways:

> One way is by literally **reinterpreting the meaning** of an event. If I see a man who looks very sick and he's in the hospital, that could be upsetting. But if I were to create a story for myself or say, "He's receiving the care he needs. He'll be better in no time at all," that would be a way of reinterpreting the events.
>
> An alternative way is to use **distancing**, where I'm not relying as strongly on my language skills to change how I feel. I'm simply changing my perspective—taking a step back.[14]

Silvers found that these two ways of reframing—using your imagination to change your perspective—are particularly effective with children and adolescents. There's a third way, too—**fear extinction:**

> If I hear a loud noise after moving into a new apartment building, at first it might evoke a fear response. After I've heard it about twenty times, I might realize it's just steam going through the pipes. The fear has gone away just by virtue of being exposed to it over and over again.

Using brain scanning images from different studies, Silvers's research team found, perhaps surprisingly, that the brain region most associated with fear extinction isn't associated with cognitive reappraisal. Instead, the brain regions activated in cognitive reappraisal are those that:

- Support our working memory and ability to direct our attention
- Help us reflect on what's happening
- Allow us to choose which strategy to use[15]

Managing our emotions at different ages is thus a *deliberate* process of directing our attention to different aspects of the situation, thinking about how we feel about what's happening, and then choosing strategies to try to change our emotions in order to better meet our goals. Managing emotions doesn't just happen—it's an intentional process that needs to be learned over time, which is what Silvers turned to next.

STUDYING THE WHOLE BRAIN IN THE CONTEXT OF EXPERIENCES: BEHIND THE NEW UNDERSTANDING OF ADOLESCENCE

Early brain scanning studies in adolescence focused on individual parts of the brain—for example, studying the amygdala as the site for processing emotions, the hippocampus as the site where memories are stored, the ventral striatum as the brain's reward center, and the prefrontal cortex (the largest part of the brain, behind our foreheads) as the site where plans and decisions are made, impulses are controlled, and self-understanding occurs.

Like the work of many other current adolescence researchers, Silvers's studies don't take a modular view, looking at individual parts of the brain. This older way of viewing the brain parts, she says, is like viewing brain structures "as if they were individual instruments playing their own songs."[16] Rather, Silvers compares the brain in action to "an entire orchestra playing a symphony." Studying brain activity *across regions* is key.

Our brains always operate in the **context** of the experiences we're having. Every one of us navigates the world thanks to split-second interactions within the brain and between the brain, body, and environment where we are continually making adjustments to what's happening. But only recently have we started viewing adolescent behavior within this dynamic, multifaceted, more constructive framework.

HOW ADOLESCENTS LEARN TO MANAGE EMOTIONS

In seeking to better understand the learning process, Silvers and her colleagues combined real-time brain imaging with real-time feedback from young people of different ages about what they're feeling and thinking.[17] In a 2015 study, they asked participants to view upsetting photographs from "close" and "far" perspectives—a refinement of the distancing strategies that are effective with children and adolescents—while they were in an fMRI scanner that took images of their brains as they viewed the photographs. Silvers explains:

We have people look at an upsetting social event—so, somebody getting rejected, somebody getting in a fight with another person—and teach people two different ways to respond.

Sometimes we asked them to imagine that they're very "close"—think about how things sound, how they smell, think about being right there in the room when it's happening.

The other way that we instruct people to respond is to imagine taking a step back and focusing less on their feelings and more on the facts of the situation.[18]

Taking that step back—a "far" perspective—essentially asks participants to use a distancing strategy to regulate their emotions by "turning down the volume dial a little bit on the emotional import of looking at this upsetting event," but without explicitly telling them to try to manage their feelings.

The fifty-six participants were divided into three age groups: ten-to-thirteen-year-olds, fourteen-to-seventeen-year-olds, and eighteen-to-twenty-two-year-olds.[19] They were shown 120 photographs.[20] All three groups report similar levels of negative emotion when viewing negative images from a "close" perspective.[21] But when participants take a "far" perspective, there's a larger decrease in amygdala activity with age. In other words, as adolescents get older, they are better able to regulate their neural activity and distance themselves from the distressing image, a critical aspect of learning to regulate emotions.

Key Finding: Some might think that adolescents are held captive by their emotions and that they can't think rationally until they are in their twenties. In fact, it's not that the prefrontal cortex is impaired but that the skill of managing emotions using cognitive control strategies (like distancing) is being learned, especially during adolescence.

About thirty minutes after showing participants a photograph where they were asked to take a "far" perspective, the researchers showed them the same photo again. This time, the participants were simply told to look at the images. The findings revealed that amygdala response for the eighteen-to-twenty-two-year-olds remained low—but not for the fourteen-to-seventeen-year-olds. Silvers says they had a slightly higher amygdala response to the distressing images the second time around.

This suggests that even though adolescents are learning to manage their emotions, things that are upsetting once may feel a bit more upsetting if they happen again.

Key Finding: The highs in adolescence can be very high and the lows can be very low. Regulating emotions using cognitive control strategies (especially distancing) can be learned in adolescence, but it takes time and experience.

Silvers and her colleagues had one more question: Do adolescents respond to upsetting social images more than to unsettling nonsocial images? So they showed young people images of "bugs, other creepy-crawly animals," and found that young people beginning at age ten were able to regulate their emotions more easily for these than for the social images.[22]

THE CRUCIAL BENEFIT OF ADOLESCENTS' STRONG EMOTIONS

These studies showed that young people *do* learn these cognitive control strategies over time.

Consider this, though. Might there be a benefit to adolescents' having strong emotional reactions? My answer is an unequivocal yes!

Adolescence is a time when young people are learning to move out into the world for themselves. They must learn to find their way and build relationships with increasing numbers of people beyond their families. Because their parents aren't always going to be there to help them, **they need to be highly sensitive to social and emotional situations**—attuned to what's safe and what's not, what's upsetting, what matters to them and to others. Just as infants learn which people around them can be trusted and toddlers learn the scope of their own competence, adolescents learn how to engage socially with a wider world. Ron Dahl of the University of California, Berkeley, talks about what the brain "expects to learn" in childhood and adolescence and it's a wonderful way of explaining development.[23]

The adolescent brain expects to learn to explore, to venture out. It's how young people figure out where they belong and with whom, how competent they are and in what ways, what they can do and can't, who they are and aren't. As the National Academy of Medicine's seminal report summarizing the research on adolescence states:

Adolescent brains are not simply "advanced" child brains, nor are they "immature" adult brains—they are specially tailored to meet the needs of this stage of life [emphasis added] . . . Adolescents must explore and take risks to build the cognitive, social, and emotional skills they will need to be productive adults.[24]

Because adolescence is what researchers call a "sensitive period"[25]—a time when people are especially receptive to learning from specific kinds of experiences—learning to regulate emotions is particularly important during these years.

ADOLESCENCE AS BREAKTHROUGH YEARS

Adolescents' strong reactions to social situations are what I call a **developmental necessity**. Adolescents are learning where they fit in and belong and who understands them. How adults respond matters a great deal; it helps shape how adolescents see themselves.

When Richard Huganir, director of the Department of Neuroscience at Johns Hopkins University, was an adolescent, he wanted to understand his own development—that's what led him to become a scientist. So I asked him to explain how brains work to his seventeen-year-old self. He begins:

A human brain contains about 100 billion neurons or nerve cells—an incredible number. The neurons communicate with each other through electrical signals and form circuits of activity. These patterns of electrical signals create our minds—allowing us to move and respond to environments, have emotions, make decisions, and learn and remember.

When you learn something, those synapses connecting these 100 billion neurons are modified. They change the connectivity—sculpting a new circuit that actually encodes the memory.

Babies are born basically helpless. They have to very rapidly adapt and learn, so there's a lot of synaptic growth. Then, there's a slow progression where the number of synapses decreases over time until about fourteen, sixteen years old.[26]

That's why the early years are foundational. But when synaptic connections peak, it doesn't mean there isn't development—it's a *different kind* of development, where the brain is refining its connections, in a use-it-or-lose-it fashion (meaning connections that aren't used don't remain vital), as well as making new connections.

These refinements occur throughout the brain and in particular in the front part of the brain—the prefrontal cortex—and its connections to the rest of the brain. Beatriz Luna of the University of Pittsburgh and editor in chief of the journal *Developmental Cognitive Neuroscience* points to the importance of linking the amygdala with the prefrontal cortex as well as linking the visual system with the prefrontal area during these years. What's happening, she says, is the further development of executive function skills[27]—important attentional regulation skills, including emotional regulation, that we'll cover in depth in chapter 5.

Jennifer Silvers likens this to a brain under construction, where the connections are both created and strengthened with use.[28] Strengthening involves myelination during adolescence and beyond. Huganir explains:

> *Myelination insulates the connectivity of different parts of the brain, almost like insulating a wire between two different neurons that enhances brain connectivity and brain function.*

With this perspective, we can help adolescents understand that these years are a prime time for learning—including gaining the skills to manage strong emotions. As Silvers says:

> *It seems as though a light bulb is turning on. Children really aren't so good at being able to use this kind of cognitive strategy to turn down their negative feelings and adolescents suddenly seem to have the capacity to do it. They're developing these stronger connections between brain regions that most likely will need to communicate with each other readily for all the years to come.*

Not so long ago, people didn't understand how rapidly the brain was developing during early childhood. With a lot of hard work by a lot of people including me, the importance of the first three to five years of life is increasingly recognized.[29] Now is the time for everyone to understand the importance of the adolescent years as a period of rapid brain and psychological growth—what researchers call plasticity—when young people can learn foundational skills and ways of being that can make a lifelong difference.

What's more, the breakthrough years for adolescents can also be breakthrough years in our evolving relationship with adolescents. That's the journey we will go on together.

PROMOTING A DEVELOPMENTAL UNDERSTANDING OF ADOLESCENCE

We can help adolescents understand that these years are a prime time when brain regions are connecting with each other, when the superhighways of the brain are being built; thus, it's a prime time for learning, including learning how to manage strong emotions. When adolescents act as if an experience is the end of the world, this is normal. As they venture into the world, they need to be acutely sensitive to what's upsetting and what isn't.

Rather than criticizing this developmentally necessary behavior, we can help them learn to balance experiencing emotions and stepping back so they can take on the challenges they face. Taking a "far" perspective can help all of us manage challenging situations—including those moments in our relationships with each other when taking a step back can give us the space to consider more effective ways to respond.

A Learning Spurt

One out of every six adolescents—17 percent—want adults to know they're smart! But what does this mean in their terms?

A NEW VIEW OF THE "RISK AND REWARD" MODEL

Like Jennifer Silvers, Adriana Galván, a professor of psychology specializing in adolescent brain development and dean of undergraduate education at the University of California, Los Angeles, discovered her passion for studying adolescence from her experiences as an adolescent.[30] Galván absolutely loved being a teenager and found a level of autonomy with friends and teachers who encouraged her. There were some cultural clashes with her parents, however. Her parents had emigrated from Mexico and had different expectations than she did about her growing independence, such as when she decided that she wanted to leave California to go to college in New York.

As she puts it, "This was an expression of independence that they weren't prepared for." Because she'd been shy as a child, I wondered what gave her the courage to disagree with her parents on this major issue. Galván attributes it to seeing her friends behave differently with their parents: "They were raised in very typical American homes. It wasn't foreign to them to disagree with their parents. I think that was the model I used to argue my case." Her courage also rested on her passion to figure out who she was on her own terms.

She argued her case quite astutely: she didn't dismiss her parents' point of view, but aligned what she wanted with her parents' values:

> *My parents really cared about education. They recognized that they'd immigrated to this country for me to go to a prestigious college. They were very proud of the fact that I wanted to do that.*

They just didn't want her to go to a college so far away.

Breakthrough Years Study Finding: Galván loved being a teenager, but only about half (52 percent) of parents with thirteen- to-nineteen-year-olds in our study feel that way about their own teenage years. That's something I hope to help improve!

When Galván was in the neuroscience graduate program at Weill Cornell Medical College, imaging studies with adolescents were a new frontier: "There was a lot of focus on brain imaging in younger kids, with much less known about how the adolescent brain develops."

It was, however, well known that adolescents respond more strongly than children or adults to rewarding experiences, leading many researchers, including Galván, to look at how adolescents' reward system connects to their enjoying thrills and seeking negative risks. But Galván eventually took a different path, which she explains to middle and high school students in a TEDxYouth talk.[31]

She first talks about the striatum—the brain region that's a key component of the brain's reward system: "When you receive something that you find rewarding, your striatum is very responsive, and it releases something called dopamine."[32]

Unlike many brain studies that just show study participants pictures of something rewarding, Galván's research team actually gave people something real. "What was it?" she asks the audience.

"Sugar," they shout.

In the lab, the researchers first asked adults and adolescents how much they liked sugar. Adolescents reported liking sugar more than adults.[33] Then the participants had their brains scanned using fMRI imaging (which Galván describes as a "snapshot of the brain in motion") while they were given squirts of sugar water. This activated the striatum of adolescents much more than that of adults. The people who liked sugar more showed the most activation.

To make sure the adolescents' reaction wasn't limited to something like sugar, they tried another reward. "What is something else that everyone likes?" she asks her student audience.

"Money," they answer.

This fMRI experiment included children ages seven to eleven, adolescents ages thirteen to seventeen, and adults ages twenty-three to twenty-nine.[34] As Galván further explains:

> We showed adolescents, kids, and adults pictures of money to see if the adolescent brain responds with greater excitability than the kids' or the adults'. That's, indeed, what we found. If we present a picture of a dollar, for instance, to people of different ages, they all see the same thing, but the adolescent's brain is processing it differently—in a way that motivates them more to try to get that reward.

The same thing happened when they showed images of people being prosocial—helping others.

These findings led Galván and her team to ask a deeper question: What is the meaning of this brain change during adolescence, when young people seem more motivated by rewards? It led her to a broader conclusion:

> At its very core, it's a motivational system that helps us approach things that motivate us and avoid things that we are not interested in engaging with.[35]

WAIT—REWARD-SEEKING COULD BE A *GOOD* THING?

You might think of reward-seeking as teenagers overindulging in sweets or, worse, alcohol. Maybe they're blowing off homework or after-school activities to hang out with friends. We tend to have negative images of reward-seeking, but like Galván, I see this characteristic as developmentally necessary. She explains why:

It makes a lot of sense! During adolescence, we become very motivated to engage, form new social relationships, and pursue passions that we're excited about. **The motivational system during adolescence is helping adolescents explore those new types of opportunities.**

So much of what's written about adolescents focuses on the dark side of their brains' sensitivity to rewards "to explain why adolescents make risky choices, framing this in a way that pathologizes adolescence as a period that we just have to get through—because if we let them, they'll make poor choices," Galván says. But:

The brain simply doesn't work that way! It doesn't have a part that makes you make risky choices. Instead, this reward system helps the adolescent learn!

Furthermore, taking risks doesn't have to be bad. Positive risk-taking can be good for development, as we'll see in chapter 2. Galván's decision to go to New York for college is a great example of taking a positive risk.

A BREAKTHROUGH: A LEARNING SPURT TIED TO DEVELOPMENTAL NEEDS

Many researchers I interviewed had breakthrough moments like Galván's that led them to view adolescence differently.

Key Finding: Adolescents are biologically primed to do what they need to do at this stage of development—explore opportunities and learn about who they are in the wider world!

Ron Dahl describes this as a "learning spurt" in adolescence. "Who would you bet your money on learning a complex new technology faster—an adult, or an adolescent?"[36] he asked me.

No contest—an adolescent.

Dahl says that adolescents can be very flexible learners, especially when their learning is connected to what the brain "expects to learn"—such as questions related to their basic developmental needs, including exploring their identity. He continues:

There's an intense early burst of learning and experimenting with "Who am I in relation to other young people in my world?"

"Rather than talk about a brain region or structure," Dahl says, "let's try a different approach to what kind of learning uniquely happens at puberty":

There's a set of circuits that are particularly important in evaluating information around your goals and your identity in relation to others.

THE VITAL CONNECTION BETWEEN REWARDS, MOTIVATION, AND LEARNING

Galván and Dahl see adolescents' attraction to rewards as connected to the brain's motivational system. Wendy Grolnick of Clark University, a scholar of motivation, defines motivation well:

It's really about why people do the things they do—what energizes and directs their behavior.[37]

Or, as John Bargh of Yale University and Peter Gollwitzer and Gabriele Oettingen, both of New York University, write: "Social psychologists use the term 'motivation' to describe why a person in a given situation selects one response over another or makes a given response with great energization or frequency."[38]

Our motivations can be conscious and deliberate as well as unconscious. Deliberate motivation involves:

- Having a goal that we see as personally valuable
- Putting plans in place to achieve that goal
- Being guided by the expectation that we can actually achieve our goal

For example, suppose you set a goal to exercise more, in order to get fitter and lose weight. If you don't make plans—such as going to the gym, climbing the stairs instead of taking the elevator, or walking more—and if you don't expect that you can stick to those plans, you won't achieve your goal.

Bargh and his colleagues point to another important factor: having constructive feedback throughout the process of striving for goals.

We'll delve much more deeply into this research on goals in chapter 5, when we look at how to support adolescents in developing Life and Learning Skills that can help them thrive, but for now let's look at motivation.

Motivation arises from interactions between multiple brain areas as we engage with life. The Scientific Council at Harvard's Center on the Developing Child writes:

> Motivation is the result of neurons (brain cells) in specific regions sending chemical signals via high-speed neural networks to other regions, creating pathways for future signals to follow. Experiences trigger the release of these chemicals to regions that connect emotions, memory, and the sensation of pleasure or reward.[39]

The brain chemicals most involved are "dopamine, serotonin, norepinephrine, glutamate, and naturally occurring opioids . . . For example, when dopamine is released, it signals to . . . the brain that something important is about to happen—something that we should enjoy or avoid at all costs."

Galván focuses on the role of these chemicals, especially "the primary one"—dopamine:

> Dopamine is very responsive to rewards, but its role in the brain—in people of all ages and all species—is to learn from the environment. I started thinking about how wonderful it is that we have a part of the brain—the learning system of the brain—that is more excitable during adolescence.
> It made me reflect on how we frame the adolescent period of life. Instead of focusing on the negative, wouldn't it be helpful for adolescents, and for understanding adolescents, if we actually appreciate their ability to learn?[40]

Similarly, Daniel Romer of the University of Pennsylvania and his colleagues write about moving beyond stereotypes in adolescent negative risk-taking, pointing to studies indicating that the rise in dopamine activity underlying adolescents' reward-seeking also affects executive function skills, decision-making, reasoning, and memory—in other words, "the ability to exert control over a rewarding experience and to learn from it."[41]

DOES REWARD SENSITIVITY HELP ADOLESCENTS LEARN?

Galván and her colleagues devised a clever learning game to study the adaptive—not just the maladaptive—aspects of adolescents' reward sensitivity.[42] She describes their reframed research question:

> Do adolescents learn better than adults when the things they're learning are rewarding?[43]

Their experiments included forty-one adolescents thirteen to seventeen years old and thirty-one adults twenty to thirty years old. One at a time, they played a game in the lab:

> Participants see a series of butterflies. Each butterfly is presented with two different colored flowers. We ask participants to determine which flower the butterfly will land on. Sometimes it lands on the white flower, sometimes on the orange flower—but over time the participant learns which flower the butterfly prefers.

Each time participants select an answer, they see "correct" or "incorrect" on the screen. As they play, they accumulate information about which flower the butterfly prefers, learning trial by trial through reinforcement. And the findings? Galván says:

> We found that the teenagers learn the associations more quickly and have a higher accuracy than the adults.

Some participants played this game in a brain scanner. As expected, the brain's reward system responded, and the hippocampus—an area involved in what Galván calls "the learning system"—was activated. Most important, though, was how the brain circuitry connecting these systems differed in adolescents compared with adults:

> We found that the way the reward system and the learning system communicate was stronger in adolescents than in the adults!

Key Finding: Adolescents are particularly adept at learning from experience.

This research highlights some critical aspects of how we learn and illustrates the importance of explorative learning in adolescence:

- **Games can spur learning.** In general, people love games where they can match themselves against a challenging task.
- **Trial-and-error learning mimics real-life experience—we learn from doing and practice.** With each round of the game, participants accumulated information, leading them toward greater accuracy.
- **Timely feedback can boost motivation for further learning.** Participants got feedback at every round, which served as a motivator to keep them going.

THE TWO TYPES OF MOTIVATION—DO THEY EVER MEET?

Not all motivation is alike. Intrinsic motivation is doing things for the pleasure or enjoyment we get from doing the activity while extrinsic motivation is doing things for reasons other than this interest and enjoyment. These reasons include doing things because others tell you to, or to get a reward or avoid a punishment—instances when you are doing something because you feel you have to. It also includes doing things because you believe they're important or meaningful, even if they are not fun. You might be wondering, which type of motivation—intrinsic or extrinsic—is stickiest? Well, it depends. Wendy Grolnick says:

> When people do things for pleasure or interest or are behind the things they do for other reasons—when they're active and have purpose—that behavior is much more likely to persist.[44]

Autonomy and agency are key to intrinsic motivation:

> We need to feel autonomous. That concept has been very confusing in the literature. What we mean is that people need to feel "choiceful." They need to feel like they're the owner of their actions and that they're not pushed and coerced.

But what about the many times when things have to be done that aren't inherently interesting? Then you want young people to understand the purpose or value of the activity so they can still get behind it and do it with a sense of choicefulness or autonomy. Adults can help adolescents do this by taking their perspectives, providing rationales for the activity, and not being pushy or controlling. Grolnick says:

> *From my perspective, we start with the idea that people are active—trying to solve problems, trying to increase their competencies. We don't have to teach people to have intrinsic motivation. We just have to set the conditions under which that will flourish.*

What are those conditions?

Gabriele Oettingen, an expert on motivation, defines motivation as "direction times energy,"[45] meaning that if we have a direction *we* want to go in—a goal or wish *we* care about—what we need to add are the energy and the effective strategies to fulfill that wish or goal.

For externally assigned goals (like schoolwork), Oettingen says it helps to make them meaningful, in order to generate the energy to fulfill them. We'll discuss this further in chapter 4.

So, whether the motivation originates from inside or from others, the wish or goal needs to be something we care about—something we feel strongly about, that we value for any number of reasons.

FEEDBACK CAN BE REWARDING AND MOTIVATING . . . OR NOT

Schools and families need to be mindful of keeping intrinsic motivation alive. The Scientific Council at Harvard's Center on the Developing Child notes that overreliance on external rewards such as grades and awards "can lead to a shift from the intrinsic drive to learn to a desire for external recognition and accolades or avoidance of failure or punishment. **While extrinsic motivation may be effective for some in the short term, it is unlikely to last**" [emphasis added].[46]

Feedback was built into the butterfly/flower game: participants saw "Correct" or "Incorrect" on-screen after each round. Unlike, say, grades or points, this immediate feedback helped them figure out how to improve at the game, boosting their intrinsic motivation to learn.

Philip David Zelazo of the University of Minnesota has studied a more elaborate form of feedback with younger children, but its lessons apply to older children, too. In one experiment, preschool-aged children played a game where the rules continued to change, making it challenging to play.[47] This experiment went a step beyond just telling children that they were incorrect, helping them understand exactly why they made a mistake.

Zelazo and his colleagues call this "reflection training": it enables the child to step back and reflect on mistakes. "When you detect a problem and then engage in reflection, you recognize that you can't keep going on autopilot," Zelazo says. "Then you come to a more sophisticated understanding and you effectively resolve the conflict."

We've found that those children who were trained and who now performed better on the task also showed changes in the brain brought about by this relatively brief intervention![48]

So, it's not that we shouldn't give our kids feedback lest we kill their motivation. It's about the kind of feedback we give. **Concrete, timely feedback doesn't interfere with intrinsic motivation.** In fact, it can be motivating. Note that in these experiments, feedback was provided in ways that didn't make children feel inadequate and wasn't about them personally. The feedback was simply informational, designed to help them learn from their experience about how to improve at the task. It wasn't judgmental!

Which brings me back to the judgments we make about adolescents and their sensitivity to rewards. What would happen if we viewed adolescents as Adriana Galván did in her research: focusing not on how their reward sensitivity connects with negative risk-taking but on how it operates in helping them to learn?

Linda Wilbrecht of the University of California, Berkeley, says that this shift is possible, thanks to the new technologies revealing what's happening inside the brain:

*It is easy to focus on the negative and view teenagers as transiently deranged by their biology . . . Yet if you take a closer look at what is going on inside the brain, you might warm with the pride of a grandmother. There is . . . no black hole where the frontal lobes should be. There are neurons there, and they are up to something that looks pretty creative, **smart** [emphasis added], and useful.*[49]

The neurons, she writes, "are hungrily exploring all they can know in the world." That's what we need to understand when adolescents use the word "smart." They're using it in the way that Wilbrecht and Galván are using it. There's a part of their brains that is more excitable than in children and adults and that motivates them to learn.

HOW—AND WHAT—ARE ADOLESCENTS ESPECIALLY MOTIVATED TO LEARN?

During adolescence, young people are particularly motivated to figure out how to navigate their social world, who they are in relation to others, and what their passions are. Galván notes:

> *The motivational system during adolescence is helping adolescents explore those new types of opportunities.*[50]

There's a beautiful symmetry about the fact that it was her own motivation in adolescence to figure out who she was that sparked Galván's passion for adolescence research, and now she's helping us understand that adolescents' reward system fuels their learning spurt and their developmental drive to understand who they are, what their interests are, and where they fit in the wider world. This is the particular form of adolescent smartness that we need to foster.

PROMOTING A DEVELOPMENTAL UNDERSTANDING OF ADOLESCENCE

Remember that when adolescents seem especially motivated or swayed by rewards, we can focus on this as a positive: sensitivity to rewards can make adolescents really good learners! The reward system is also a learning system that can be harnessed for growth and learning.

Rather than criticizing this developmentally necessary phase of life, we can try to understand their form of smartness and give them real-life experiences that build on their intrinsic motivation; that provide supportive, reflective, positive feedback; and that help them dig deeper into exploring the world and in figuring out their interests and passions.

From Developmental Liability
to Developmental Necessity

"What were you thinking?!"

Have you ever said some version of this to an adolescent?

My biggest "what were you thinking" moment happened years ago when I glanced out the window during a work call from home and saw my son drive up our driveway. That might have been fine, except . . .

- He was fifteen.
- He'd never driven our car—only turned the engine on and off!
- Obviously, he didn't have a driver's license!

I threw down the phone and in work clothes (with the requisite high heels) ran up our steep gravel driveway and along the road, consumed with fear. I'd run for about a quarter of a mile when I saw him inching the car back toward home. He was okay. The car, too. My fear dissolved into fury.

I jumped into the driver's seat and asked (probably yelled), "What were you thinking?!"

He said he'd wanted to practice driving in our driveway but didn't know how to put our stick-shift car into reverse, so he had to keep going forward until he could find a place where he could make a U-turn without backing up so he could come home.

Why hadn't he stopped and asked his father or me for help? He said he knew there'd be times when we weren't with him and he'd have to figure things out for himself.

My heart was still pounding. But he was right.

In retrospect, I have even more insight about this experience. My son was using "adolescent smartness"—his need for agency overrode a decision to ask for help. As his mother, I needed to bring my adult smartness—"It's great to figure things out for yourself, but there are times when even grown-ups need to ask for help"—without diminishing his developmental need to make decisions to begin to care for himself.

A "what were you thinking" moment was a catalyst for the "Stoplight Studies," a set of classic studies led by Larry Steinberg of Temple University and his colleagues that captured the public's imagination. They're the jumping-off point for looking at how we can begin shifting our interactions with adolescents by shifting how we view their development, as a group and as individuals.

THE DUAL SYSTEMS MODEL

One of Steinberg's inspirations was his experience as a parent and trying to figure out, as he told me, "why such a smart kid as my son could make such bad choices."[51] He recounts this story in his book *Age of Opportunity*,[52] and repeated it to me. It involved his son and his friends

> *sneaking out of a friend's house at two in the morning to visit a girl in the neighborhood and accidentally setting off the burglar alarm at her house— not realizing that the alarm also sent a silent signal to the police station. The police dispatched a patrol car to the house. Instead of explaining what they were doing, the boys ran and scattered through the neighborhood.*
>
> *When I found out about it the next day, I said, "What were you thinking? You're running in the dark from armed police officers who think they're interrupting a burglary. What WERE you thinking?"*
>
> *He said, "Well, that's the problem. I wasn't."*[53]

Steinberg's personal and professional experience led him and his colleague Jason Chein of Temple University and others to consider the influence of other kids (peers) on making negative risky decisions (something we'll explore further in chapter 2). They adapted a measure to assess this—the Stoplight game, originally called "Chicken." Steinberg says:

> *Stoplight is a video game that mimics a situation that anybody who drives has been in—where you're trying to get someplace in a hurry. You come to an intersection, the light turns yellow, and you decide whether to chance it and run the intersection or put the brakes on.*
>
> *This became our chief measure of risk-taking because we could count up the number of intersections where the participant stopped versus ran the light, and that was a simple measure of risk-taking. We like it because it has some connection to the real world.*[54]

They've used this game in numerous experiments with young people and sometimes adults.[55] Adolescents play this game alone or with friends watching. Steinberg says:

When adolescents are being observed, they take about twice as many risks playing Stoplight as when they're alone.[56]

The researchers also found that adolescents showed more activity in the reward regions of the brain when peers were watching versus when they were playing the game alone, but this wasn't the case with adults.[57] This and many other experiments led to the development of their Dual Systems Model to explain negative risky behavior. Its premise is that the arousal of the reward system and the maturation of the cognitive control system occur on different timetables. This imbalance in development explains why there's a period of heightened vulnerability to risk-taking during adolescence.[58]

We understand that when kids go through puberty, one way the sex hormones affect their brain is by increasing activity of the neurotransmitter dopamine in the brain's reward centers, and that leads to people engaging in more reward-seeking.[59]

The best way to describe this, according to Steinberg, is that "things that feel good—feel even better," leading some young people to do things that feel good, even if they're risky. He found that reward sensitivity peaks during mid- to late adolescence. Steinberg and his colleagues (and many other researchers) have also found that on average the prefrontal cortex, the brain region underlying decision-making and cognitive control, develops at a different rate and doesn't peak until later, not reaching adult levels until one's twenties, although there are many individual differences. Steinberg says:

By the time people are in their late adolescent years, there is much greater connectivity between these systems—more crosstalk. That allows us to put the brakes on impulses that are stimulated by the arousal of the reward system.

Steinberg and his colleagues[60] have tested the Dual Systems Model with an international group of more than five thousand young people ages ten to thirty from eleven countries in Africa, Asia, Europe, and the Americas.

Key Finding: Consistent with their model, the researchers found that on average, sensation-seeking increased between very early adolescence and late adolescence, peaking at age nineteen, then declining. In contrast, self-regulation increased steadily from early adolescence into young adulthood, plateauing between ages twenty-three and twenty-six.

Steinberg describes the Dual Systems Model as a "heuristic"—a simplified model based on findings from many studies. It's important to note that this model has been mostly based on comparing groups of adolescents at the same point in time (i.e., a cross-sectional study design) versus following one group of individuals over time and charting their development as they get older (i.e., a longitudinal study design).

The Dual Systems Model has spurred those who study adolescence in positive ways by sharing important findings and by leading to the testing of the model by many researchers, to academic rebuttals,[61] and to the creation of new models.[62]

It's also led to some critically important advances and victories, such as those Steinberg has championed in the legal system, arguing that adolescents aren't adults and thus shouldn't be tried or sentenced as adults—which has helped countless adolescents be given opportunities to learn from their mistakes and avoid overly harsh punishments.[63]

The interpretations of the findings, however, have led to some unfortunate ongoing misunderstandings (such as that adolescents have impaired prefrontal cortexes). Add to this the historical stereotypes I've mentioned—that adolescents are subject to their raging hormones or adolescence is a time of storm and stress—and it's possible to miss the understanding that this phase of life is *not* a developmental liability but is actually developmentally necessary. In other words, the way the adolescent brain develops is a feature in the design of development, not a bug.

WHAT ARE THEY THINKING? IT MIGHT BE A LOT!

While many researchers I interviewed find that the reward system is at its peak during adolescence, most disagree that adolescents' judgment is necessarily impaired—that they're all gas pedal and no brakes. Remember, the reward system fuels learning, and adolescents can and do learn cognitive control techniques.

Yet parents worry—as I heard whenever I told people I was writing this book. A doctor said she was concerned that her soon-to-be-teen daughter, who's now thoughtful and close to her mom, will freeze her out "because the thinking part of her brain will develop more slowly than the emotional part—that her prefrontal cortex will be impaired and she'll make stupid decisions."

Statements like this have prompted many adolescence researchers to try to correct this misperception of adolescent development. BJ Casey of Barnard College and her colleague Kristina Caudle state that findings of neurobiological research have been simplified for the media and misunderstood.[64] Linda Wilbrecht warns we must be careful that a simplified view of adolescents "doesn't distort how we study and understand them."[65]

THINKING IN HOT AND COOL SITUATIONS

Zelazo has studied executive function skills—sometimes called cognitive control skills—throughout his career:

> Executive function skills provide a foundation for learning deliberately and for adapting to life's challenges. Everything that we want to do deliberately and intentionally requires executive function skills for success.[66]

Executive function skills are formed in the brain's prefrontal cortex and other interrelated regions. Zelazo and other scientists use the terms "hot" and "cool"[67] to describe high-stakes or low-stakes situations. Each makes different demands on our executive function skills. Zelazo and his colleagues found a difference in the development of hot and cool executive function problem-solving skills during the transition to adolescence.[68]

With 102 young people ages eight through fifteen, they administered some tasks measuring cool (low-stakes) executive function skills, such as resisting distractions. Other tasks measured hot (high-stakes) executive function skills, such as gambling. Zelazo says:

> We found that children made bigger gains on the measures of cool executive function and more gradual gains in performance on the measures of hot executive function skills.[69]

Key Finding: When the context isn't stressful, the stakes aren't high, and emotions aren't soaring, adolescents are quite capable of making very thoughtful decisions—that is, they're capable of fully using executive function skills.

Granted, life isn't a lab experiment, but those studying executive function skills have found that adolescents *can* learn to use these skills in "hot" situations during early adolescence, and even before.

That parallels Jennifer Silvers's research: adolescence is a prime time to learn to use executive function skills to manage emotions by stepping back and taking a "far" perspective, plus other strategies we'll discuss later.

WHAT RESEARCHERS ARE LEARNING
ABOUT ADOLESCENT INDIVIDUALITY

Here is one of the most important points: there is a great deal of variety in adolescent development. In her book *Inventing Ourselves: The Secret Life of the Teenage Brain,*[70] Sarah-Jayne Blakemore of the University of Cambridge in the United Kingdom writes that the picture of adolescent development "is more complicated than the stereotype of the reckless and thrill-seeking adolescent suggests."[71]

To look at how different adolescents' brains develop over time, Blakemore, Kate Mills, and their team faced two challenges. They needed multiple brain scans from the same individuals in late childhood, early adolescence, and late adolescence. And they needed scans clearly showing different parts of the brain.

Working in collaboration with Jay Giedd, then at the National Institute of Mental Health, and his colleagues,[72] they found scans from thirty-three individuals that fit their criteria. When they looked at averages, their findings confirmed that the reward systems develop earlier than the cognitive control system. But there were some surprises, which Mills, now at the University of Oregon, discussed with me.

Key Finding: First, these researchers found that some parts of the reward system, specifically the nucleus accumbens, were still changing across adolescence into young adulthood.[73] It's not just the prefrontal cortex that's developing—so is the rewards system.

Second, they found that over time, only half of the sample demonstrated an imbalance in brain growth that fit the average pattern. It was a very small sample, but it indicates that there's a lot of variety in development.

A third finding was particularly surprising. When participants were ages twenty-three to thirty-three in this longitudinal study, they were asked to report on how risky they'd been as adolescents—known as retrospective self-reporting. It turned out there was *no* relationship between those who reported negative risk-taking behavior during adolescence[74] and any actual imbalance in the subcortical structures developing before the prefrontal cortex.

Blakemore's years of research on adolescence led her to write in her book:

One conclusion is that individual differences are just as significant as—perhaps even more important than—averages . . . After all, there's no average teenager.[75]

While averages reveal meaningful trends, examining only averages can obscure deeper insights from research—I call this the "tyranny of the average." It's critical to remember that each adolescent is an individual.

Another research team used a different approach to assess developmental differences. In 2021, Wim Meeus of Utrecht University in the Netherlands and other researchers, including Eveline Crone of Erasmus University, Rotterdam, analyzed a dataset of 7,558 youth ages twelve to twenty-five from the National Longitudinal Study of Youth/Children and Young Adults Study in the United States, in which self-reported data were collected for seven years.[76]

Key Finding: What's clear from this study is that impulse control is just as strong or stronger than sensation-seeking at all ages among close to seven in ten adolescents.

The authors note that there were lots of distinctions between individuals, and that patterns changed as the participants grew older, but this finding is remarkable.

PROMOTING A DEVELOPMENTAL UNDERSTANDING OF ADOLESCENCE

Let's say an adolescent gets emotional about a slight from a teacher or friend. We can be tempted to say, "Stop being such a teenager. It's not the end of the world. Get over it." And we might be surprised if they push back against these words.

When we understand their development, we can respond differently: "You are upset about this. This is the time in life when you are moving out further into the world and your brain primes you to be on the lookout for where you fit in. Now let's talk about your ideas for why you think this happened and what you might do about it."

Let's say it's more than a slight. A friend is mean and rejecting. We can be tempted to say, "Don't put any energy into what this person thinks or does. It should mean nothing to you. You are better than that." And we might be surprised if they roll their eyes or tell us we don't understand.

When we do understand their development, we can respond differently: "I know you care a lot. That's what being a teenager is all about. Right now, you are supposed to be figuring out what kind of friends you want, so of course you care. Let's talk about what you value in friends."

Now let's say there's a whole group involved in severe bullying and mean-kid behavior. We might be tempted to say, "Stand up for yourself. Don't let others treat you that way. Or ignore it." Then we might be surprised if they respond, "I tried that but it didn't work."

When we understand adolescent development, we won't endorse interventions that say "Just say no to bullying" (or smoking, or vaping, or drugs, or whatever). Studies have found that the just-say-no (willpower) approach typically has little to no impact during adolescence and, in some cases, can lead to things getting worse.[77] Effective interventions take into account adolescents' need for some autonomy, involve changing the environment and not just the child, and include them in coming up with solutions.

Understanding their development can make a world of difference.

How We Think About the Adolescent Brain

I was at a neuroscience conference when a tense disagreement among the scientists erupted on what parents think about their adolescent's developing brain. As I listened to the points and counterpoints, I wrote down a question for the survey we were then creating:

When you hear the phrase "the teen brain" or "the adolescent brain," what one word comes to mind?

My hope was that this question would further clarify what adolescents mean when they say: "You don't understand me."

What we found does this and more. It has important implications for adolescents' well-being. Here are four findings of note.

Finding 1: Only 14 percent of parents use clearly positive words or phrases when they think of the "adolescent/teen brain." These include:

Smart, intelligent, focused
Exploring, creative, fun
The future, potential
Busy, active, social
A brain that is still learning

Finding 2: Of the other words, parents are more likely to use negative ones than neutral ones.* Examples of negative words (59 percent) include:

Forgetful, stupid, dumb, clueless
Impulsive, wild, risky
Distracted, confused, jumbled, mush
Sassy, sarcastic, bratty
Know-it-all, smart-mouth, smart-ass
Immature, unformed, undeveloped
Sluggish, lazy, inactive
Drugs, bad decisions, always on screens

---

* In coding words or phrases (an analysis procedure researchers apply in this kind of study), we were very careful that positive and negative words were specifically coded as positive or negative. If there was doubt or ambiguity about the word—as, for example, with the word "puberty"—it was coded as neutral. If neutral words were removed, then 80 percent of the words that parents provided would be considered negative.

Moody
Awkward, goofy, dorky

Examples of neutral words (27 percent) are:

Thinking in the here and now
They don't process like an adult.
Developing
Growing
Complex
Youthful

Unfortunately, this finding isn't unique to the United States. Researchers from the Netherlands asked 164 parents for their free associations with the phrase "teen brain." Parents provided many more descriptions of undesirable behavior (e.g., cranky, rude) than desirable behavior (e.g., responsible, kind).[78]

This finding isn't unique in today's world, either. In 1987, Public Agenda conducted a study called "Kids These Days" and asked Americans what they think of teenagers. In response, 67 percent used negative words, like "rude," "irresponsible," and "wild," while only 12 percent used positive words.[79] It was a different era and a different question, but the statistics are amazingly similar.

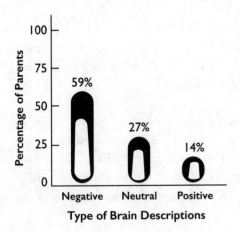

Parents' Descriptions of the Adolescent Brain

Finding 3: Across all categories (positive, negative, and neutral), the most frequent words or phrases parents use to describe the adolescent brain refer to change (35 percent).

Finding 4: Finally, 19 percent of all the words and phrases refer to adolescents as what they are not—namely, mature adults.

Parents use the word "immature" most often (11 percent). In an open-ended research question, this convergence is noteworthy. Other frequent words or phrases, used by 8 percent of all parents, are "un-," "in-," and "not" words, including:

Unformed/primitive
Undeveloped
Unfinished
Incomplete
Inexperienced
Not thinking/not smart
Trapped between being an innocent child and not yet being, hopefully, what we would call a wiser adult
An unformed mind very vulnerable to peer and outside pressures
Underdeveloped brain—they're still growing and don't have the ability to care or comprehend things

For me, this finding says a lot, not only about how we view adolescents but also about how we view our relationships with them. Perhaps because adolescents look more like adults and sometimes speak and act like adults, **we seem to be judging them with an adult yardstick and finding them lacking.**

For me, this goes to the heart of what adolescents mean when they say "you don't understand me." Their brains are not deficient adult brains; adolescents' brains are doing exactly what they should be doing during this distinct phase of development:

- Adolescents are moving further out into the world, so they need to be highly sensitive to social and emotional situations.
- They need to develop a radar for what's safe and what's worrisome because their parents aren't necessarily there to help them, compared to when they were younger. So they need to respond quickly and emotionally to these situations.

- Adolescents are exploring their identities and what it means to be themselves. So they're highly sensitive to experiences where they can explore who they are, what they care about, and what ignites their passion for learning. They learn all of this from new and direct experiences, often in a trial-and-error fashion.

DO PARENTS' VIEWS MAKE A DIFFERENCE
IN HOW ADOLESCENTS FARE?

When we look at the connections between parents' views and adolescents' well-being, the answer to that question is yes. In the study, we assessed the adolescent's own well-being using a number of standardized measures:

- Experiencing positive feelings in the last month (such as feeling happy, brave, calm, joyful) and negative feelings (such as feeling angry, sad, afraid, worried, or lonely)[80]
- Experiencing stress (like difficulties piling up so high that they can't handle them)[81]
- Trying a variety of strategies in order to reach the goals they set for themselves[82]
- Being more engaged with learning at school[83]
- Using better self-control skills during school[84]

To account for demographic differences that may affect well-being, we statistically controlled for the adolescents' age, gender, race/ethnicity, and family income levels.

We found that when parents have positive views of the teen/adolescent brain, their adolescents rate themselves more positively on all of these measures of well-being than do those adolescents whose parents have negative views.

But what about other factors? Might parents who have more conflict with their kids be more likely to see the adolescent brain negatively? Additionally, might these views be affected by the positive or negative views parents have about their own child?

So we conducted a second set of analyses, where we again controlled for the adolescents' age, gender, race/ethnicity, and family income, and we also controlled for the level of parent-child conflict as reported by the parent, as well as negative words that parents used to describe their own child from a list of eight negative terms (like "impulsive/wild," "rebellious," "lazy") and eight positive terms (like "creative," "open to learning and discovery").

All well and good, but you still might say that the data are correlational—you are assessing parents' views of the adolescent brain and their own child's well-being at the same time, so you can't say what causes what.

You'd be right again, but we do have data from the same group of parents and children nine months later. While this still doesn't allow for a causal interpretation (because, for example, we don't have an intervention group and a control group), looking at an association between parents' views and adolescents' later well-being is a strong test of the importance of parental views. In this case, the pandemic happened in between surveys and it was a stressful time for a number of parents and children.

Even with these additional statistical controls and the time elapsed between surveys, we found that the terms parents used to describe the adolescent brain were linked with their children's moods and school engagement.

Breakthrough Years Study Finding: When parents used positive words to describe the teen brain, nine months later, their children reported fewer negative feelings (such as feeling angry, sad, afraid, worried, or lonely) and being more engaged in school.

In sum, then, positive views of the teen brain are associated with positive well-being, which means we should be very mindful about the views we hold.

LAB ←→ LIFE: THE POSITIVE YOUTH DEVELOPMENT MOVEMENT

Over the years, a number of leaders in adolescence research and youth development have led the charge against negative views of adolescents. One of the most eloquent and effective is Richard Lerner of Tufts University, who has been instrumental in creating and championing a strength-based theory of development called Positive Youth Development. The Positive Youth Development perspective, Lerner says, is based on identifying the strengths of adolescents and on putting young people in settings where they can capitalize on these strengths.[85]

It has had another focus, too, as Karen Pittman, co-founder and former CEO of the Forum for Youth Investment and an innovative leader in creating this movement, told me: "We talk about our children as our future, but we don't pay a lot of attention to them in the present."[86]

Adolescents, in particular, are sensitive to and profoundly influenced by the people, places and possibilities they cross paths with. They are eager to make meaning of the broader world, hungry for respect, responsibility, and challenge. If we are not intentional about supporting them in the present, they will fill these needs on their own in ways that could dampen or derail their futures.[87]

Positive Youth Development was designed to change all of this. A team that included Lerner; his wife, Jacqueline Lerner of Boston College; Rick Little, the founder of the International Youth Forum; and Pittman worked on a model to identify and then test adolescents' strengths,[88] which are, in Rich Lerner's words:[89]

Competence: The ability to act effectively, to do the things that are necessary to navigate life well in school, in social situations, and at work.

Confidence: An internal sense of self-worth, a sense of self that you are a person who can act competently at the right time and in the right place—but also knowing that you can't succeed by yourself.

Connection: You need positive connections with family members, with teachers, coaches, mentors, faith leaders, and others—but in those relations, you need to have a moral standard.

Character: You need to know and respect the difference between right and wrong and have integrity—and if you have that character and that connection, and you're confident and you're competent, you'll care.

Caring: A sense of sympathy and empathy for others and the world—and if you then couple that caring with the other Cs, eventually you will be someone who will make a contribution.

Contribution: A sense of purpose. It's planting trees whose shade you will never see.

But don't feel anxious, Lerner writes in his book *The Good Teen*:

If you are reading this list and worrying that your teen doesn't possess these characteristics and [they're] already in trouble—stop! . . . According to my research, your teen already possesses facets of many if not all of the Cs.[90]

Importantly, Lerner knows that young people can't develop these strength-based characteristics alone. They need to be in environments and with people where their strengths are promoted. Lerner's intention is to have adults create environments where three key assets—called the Big Three of Youth Development—exist:[91]

> First, *what young people need in their lives is a competent, caring, and sustained adult relationship—a teacher, coach, faith leader—an adult to guide them and to model for them the importance of being a person of character and purpose.*[92]

Second, in the context of that relationship, young people need to be taught life skills like setting and following through on priorities, delaying gratification, and assuming responsibility. Third, they need opportunities to practice and use those skills autonomously, as leaders.

Being a researcher, Lerner leapt at an opportunity to test this model in 4-H groups, where he and his colleagues believed young people would have experiences that promote Positive Youth Development.[93] Beginning in 2002, the 4-H study included 7,071 young people in the United States ranging from fifth through twelfth grades from forty-two states and 3,173 of their parents in eight waves of data collection—a hugely comprehensive study. The findings (detailed in more than a hundred academic articles) reveal that when young people are in environments with supportive adult relationships and that provide opportunities to learn and use life skills, they are more likely to set and follow through on their goals, to be engaged in school, and to have positive expectations about their own futures.[94]

But there were surprises, as Lerner told me:

> We found that many kids who showed high positive behavior also showed some risk behaviors and, in turn, some kids without high scores in positive development did not engage in risk behaviors.[95]

A major takeaway from this study for me is that Positive Youth Development can be promoted on a large scale. Lerner's studies give me hope that it's possible to reduce the percentages of parents who come up with a negative word when asked to think about the adolescent/teen brain!

Interestingly, Lerner went to college planning to be a coach of good athletes but discovered psychology.[96] In a very real sense, he has coached the field of adolescent development toward a Positive Youth Development approach.

PROMOTING A DEVELOPMENTAL UNDERSTANDING OF ADOLESCENCE

Parents worry. It comes with the territory. But if we let our worries distort how we see adolescents, it can hamper our ability to help them, which in turn can affect them.

We can guard against negative assumptions by remembering what the research reveals: there's a great deal of individuality in adolescents' development, and there are developmental necessities that come with this stage of life. Remember, too, the exuberance, joy, and learning that adolescents can bring to your life.

When we use our understanding of adolescent brain development to refrain from judging adolescents as deficient or immature adults, I'm convinced we'll be able to better appreciate this stage of life for what it is and has to be!

Rethinking Adolescence: From Negatives to Positives and Obstacles

In the beginning of this chapter, we met sixteen-year-old Ayana, who wondered why adults don't understand teenagers even though they were once teenagers themselves. Similarly, I kept wondering why parents with older children warn new parents, "Just wait until they're teenagers," when they may have been warned themselves and disliked it.

I also wondered why 59 percent of us have negative views of the adolescent/teen brain.

Andrew Fuligni of UCLA finds that a negative mindset about teens is hard to dislodge. He says:

I have this talk I give to parents on adolescence. I show the stereotype and then I say, "Look at how they're doing. They're doing a lot better than we did in our generation in so many ways—risky behavior, substance abuse, high school graduation, and college attendance."[97]

I see seven reasons behind our tendency to hold on to negative views of adolescents:

1. **We harbor a necessary protective instinct.** It's part of being human to want to protect ourselves by being ready for the worst. Thus, negative experiences can loom larger than positive ones. It's why bad news sells. But there's a downside: if we only see the negatives, we miss the positive possibilities. And, ironically, seeing the worst can become a self-fulfilling prophecy.

2. **We're afraid *for* them.** Fuligni thinks, as I do, that we sometimes think or fear the worst because we worry about our power to protect adolescents. It is harder to keep them safe as adolescents than when they were younger, especially when the stakes are high and there are few community safeguards.

3. **We're afraid *of* them.** There are probably times when some of us want to cross the street if we see a pack of energetic teenagers barreling toward us. In fact, 12 percent of adolescents in our survey said that people acted as if they were afraid of them at least once within the last year, and of those, 40 percent said that it happened a few times a month.

4. **If they're going to leave home, we have to "break up" with them and they have to "break up" with us.** It seems easier to contemplate our children leaving if we see them as problematic or difficult.

5. **We see their growing up as a sign of our aging.** They can beat us in sports, outmaneuver us on the computer, and eat ice cream without gaining weight. They can create all kinds of possibilities for their future, while we don't have as many opportunities before us. They're a reminder, as one father said, that we're moving up a notch in the generational march from birth to death.

6. **We may find it hard to see their point of view.** Perspective-taking is difficult for adults as well as for children—it's hard to see beyond what *we* know (called the "curse of knowledge") to understand what others know. For example, a number of young people told me that their families didn't support them if they were leaning toward a future where earning money might be difficult (being a musician, writer, or YouTuber, for example). It's understandable—as adults, we want our children to have financially secure futures and this concern may outweigh understanding their dreams. But we can do

both—help them find ways to fulfill their dreams while also helping them find ways to become financially secure.

7. **We use an adult yardstick to judge them and don't fully understand their development.** That's a goal of this book—to help us understand adolescent development and, with this knowledge, change the way we respond to them. Remember how Jennifer Silvers's mother didn't discount her daughter's this-is-the-end-of-the-world feelings after a romantic breakup or a friend's rejection. She was able to understand her daughter's development while also suggesting to her daughter that she might feel differently in the future.[98]

It's important to understand the reasons we hold on to these negative views so that we can let go of them. Framing—how we see things—matters.

Research has found that it takes both a positive outlook *and* a realistic view of obstacles to create change and meet goals. One of the best approaches is an intervention developed by Gabriele Oettingen, whom we'll learn more about in chapter 5.[99] In her interventions, we're prompted to think about a doable change in ourselves that we want to make and then imagine how we would feel after having effectively made that change (imagine the positive future). Next, we seek to understand the critical obstacle *in ourselves* (not in others) that may stand in our way for bringing about the change we want (vividly imagine the obstacle in reality). Then, we make a concrete if-then plan to deal with the obstacle: "*If* that obstacle occurs, *then* I will [find an effective behavior or an effective thought to overcome the obstacle]."

With this kind of balanced anticipation of a positive future and a realistic assessment of the obstacle standing in the way, we can better understand and respond to our adolescents as they develop their abilities and move into the world. And, importantly, we can move away from a largely negative framing of adolescence that has held sway for so long.

2

MESSAGE 2: LISTEN AND TALK *WITH* US, NOT *AT* US

Like many of the researchers I interviewed, Jennifer Pfeifer of the University of Oregon became interested in studying adolescence during her own adolescence. She often wondered then what others were thinking about her—and why. She was fascinated by "the idea that the brain was a window into all the things that made an individual unique."[1]

She recalls "super vividly the first time I ever had an adolescent in the MRI scanner and the first image came up on the screen. I thought, 'Oh, there she is—that's *her*.'"

In time, she realized her view of the brain was incomplete:

I was neglecting the social context that adolescents were developing in. I realized that the action is in the interaction between the brain and its social context. That's what's so fascinating about adolescent development to me!

Social context means the social environments adolescents live in—that is, the important relationships in their lives. A sixteen-year-old I interviewed said it best:

Who I am has a lot to do with everyone I've met.

In *The Extended Mind: The Power of Thinking Outside the Brain*, Annie Murphy Paul takes on the notion that "the mind is a discrete thing . . . sealed within the skull,"[2] a view often expressed by describing the brain as a computer or a muscle. That view has led to ignoring context. In schools, this translates to assessing, grading, and ranking children without considering the environments they're in, including school itself.

Murphy Paul writes eloquently about the "extended mind," meaning that we can only really "extend beyond our limits, not by revving up our brains like a machine or bulking them up like a muscle—but by strewing our world with rich materials, and by weaving them into our thoughts."[3]

When we asked young people in the Breakthrough Years study, "What would you like to tell the adults of America about people your age?" their responses revealed that the "rich materials" in their lives center on relationships—particularly their ardent desire for a shift in how they and adults relate to each other.

As we saw in chapter 1, their first message to us was "understand our development" and "we are smarter than you think." Their second message adds the relationship component: "listen." Here's what they had to say:

We have a lot to offer—please listen.
    —Sixteen-year-old boy

Pay more attention to us, and have more family time to talk to us about what we want and problems we might be facing.
    —Fourteen-year-old girl

We need positive attention and meaningful direction.
    —Twelve-year-old girl

We have new ideas and we are important, we need more attention and inclusion.
    —Sixteen-year-old girl

Not just at home or in school, but out in the world:

We aren't invisible. Pay attention to us at a counter. Don't ignore me.
    —Ten-year-old-girl

Don't ignore kids our age just because we are young. Sometimes we have very important things to say.
    —Fifteen-year-old boy

*We have a voice. We have opinions. We're not all lazy. Listen to us. Talk **to** us, not **at** us.*
    —Sixteen-year-old girl

*We are different but you need to try to understand us and not make us fit
what you want.*
    —Eighteen-year-old boy

*It might be hard to understand teens, preteens but we go through stuff that
might sound dumb, but it is important to us at our age.*
    —Eleven-year-old girl

Each person wants to be heard even if you don't agree with them.
    —Sixteen-year-old girl

Breakthrough Years Study Finding: One in twelve adolescents (9 percent) ask adults to listen, to talk to them—or I would say *with* them, since they're calling for a dialogue, not a lecture.

Their sentiments remind me of the words of the late Daniel Stern, researcher and child psychiatrist from Weill Cornell Medical Center and the Université de Genève, who said that the crux of effective relationships from infancy on is each person feeling "known and understood."[4] "Then you've really done it," he told me. "That's what all of us want."

In this chapter, we'll look at what adolescents and parents can say and do to move closer to each other in understanding. We'll look at relationships with peers and in the digital world as well as the science that underlies a fuller understanding of our children's development.

Reflections on Message 2

Think about a time when you acted differently from how you usually act—differently from the way you see yourself. Why do you think you were acting this way?

When I ask this question of adults in my talks, here are some of the stories I hear:

I was in a work situation where my boss began to have it out for me for reasons that—to this day—I still don't understand. Normally, when people I know call, I can't wait to talk to them. But when I'd see her ID on my phone, my mouth would go dry, my heart would pound, and I would answer the phone with dread, wondering if she was going to be all sunshine and light or whether she'd tell me something else I'd done wrong. I left that job, we "made up," and the toxic thoughts that used to swirl in my mind are no longer there, though I still do wonder how this could happen to me—someone who's usually strong and positive.

A mother of two found herself succumbing to work culture:

I joined a work team that seemed to be ruled by gossip and a lot of it was gotchatalk. I think it came down to us trying to understand what was going on. Since no one could be sure whom to trust and since no one was completely honest with each other, people were constantly trying to analyze each other. I hated gossip in school—and have tried to stay away from it ever since—but I found myself joining in.

The pandemic changed everything for a writer:

Before the pandemic, I loved going out and seeing people. During the pandemic, I lost my appetite for being with people. I was happy staying under my rock and forgetting I like being social. It's really weird that something that was always so much of my life just went away.

She goes on to note:

Dysfunction seems almost contagious. You rather pick at the scabs than buck the tide. If you buck the tide and try to change things—at least where I live, you may get crushed so you adopt the dysfunction, at least publicly, to function.

It is hard to resist the prevailing norms. Another said:

It's the politics of email that gets me. If there's a problem, I know it would be easier to pick up the phone or talk to the person directly. I know we could solve the problem in five or ten minutes, but I send emails, like everyone else, cc'ing everyone to go on record that I am dealing with the problem and to cover my a—.

We tend to think of adolescents as "being led astray" by others, but we adults sometimes do things—small or large—that don't feel like us. All of us are affected by the people we are with, whether those people are our bosses or our co-workers, our neighbors, our friends, or family. All of us are affected by the group cultures we live in.

It's important to look at adolescents and understand that they, like us, are affected by their surroundings, but it's even more important to realize that this is the period in life when they are figuring out "What am I like?" and "What are my values?" We have the opportunity to give adolescents experiences that can help shape the foundation of the identities upon which they will build their lives.

Parents as Brain Builders

Soon after my first study on youth voices, I was invited to help the White House with a conference on adolescents. One of the key topics in our planning discussions was how to address the fact that parents and other adult caregivers didn't fully understand how influential they are in their child's development during the teen years.

That was more than twenty years ago, but there's still a popular belief among some that parents exert, at best, waning influence over their adolescents and that it's all about peers, peers, peers. Brain and other developmental sciences have shown that this assumption is wrong. A review of the scientific literature on parent-child relationships during adolescence from a neuroscience perspective concluded that parents are "highly influential" in adolescents' development, even as young people venture into the wider world.[5]

This review, by Ahna Suleiman, then at the University of California, Berkeley, and now an adolescent development consultant, and Ron Dahl of the University of California, Berkeley, finds that when adolescents have better relationships with their mothers (mothers are studied more than fathers) during adolescence, the "neural responses" in brain regions associated with risk and rewards are "more tempered"—not as reactive—and the responses associated with self-control are better developed.[6]

PARENTS' INFLUENCE ON RISK-TAKING AND SELF-CONTROL

Like many, Eva Telzer of the University of North Carolina, Chapel Hill, initially focused her neuroscience research on negative risk, rewards, and cognitive control. But she came to believe that the Dual Systems Model, discussed in chapter 1—the idea that the reward system matures before the cognitive control system—should be further tested and revised for two reasons.[7]

First, it was clear to her that adolescent development isn't just about these two systems, reflecting the age-old notion of a conflict between emotion and reason. "There're many more neural regions involved," she notes.

Second, she knew that the brain's reward region is much more complex than previously thought. In chapter 1, we looked at Adriana Galván's work pointing to the reward system's essential role in helping adolescents learn. Telzer has gone on to conduct a number of studies to "un-simplify" the story of brain development during adolescence.

THE STOPLIGHT GAME REBOOT—WITH PARENTS IN THE PICTURE

What would happen in the Stoplight game, Telzer and her colleagues wondered, if parents—not peers—were present, observing their adolescents? Remember that in those studies, adolescents took more negative risks when they were being observed by peers. "If parents are present during this game," Telzer wondered, "will adolescents' risk-taking decisions actually decrease?"[8]

Their 2015 study[9] involved twenty-five pairs of fourteen-year-olds and their mothers—a small number, but not atypical for intense, costly brain-scanning experiments at the time. The study participants played the Stoplight game twice, once while being watched by their mothers and once alone.[10]

In this game, the goal was to complete the driving course as quickly as possible in order to win more money. Clearly, a decision to go through intersections was the fastest option—but it carried the negative risk of crashing, which caused a six-second delay. Choosing to stop at an intersection removed the crash risk but resulted in a three-second delay.

As the researchers predicted, adolescents made fewer negative risky decisions when their mothers were present than when they were alone. Mothers are negative risk busters!

The brain scans reflected this, too. Previous studies have shown that a key reward center of the brain (the ventral striatum) is more strongly activated when adolescents are with peers than when they're alone. In this study, brain scans showed that the ventral striatum and the amygdala (a central structure in our brain's emotion-processing system) were less strongly activated when mothers were present during risky decisions. This indicates, as Telzer puts it, that "the presence of moms takes the fun out of being risky!"[11]

In addition, the researchers found that adolescents were more likely to recruit two other important brain regions when they made safe decisions with their moms present:

- The ventrolateral prefrontal cortex, thought to be involved in self-control
- The medial prefrontal cortex, thought to be involved in assessing the costs and benefits of risk-taking, as well as the perspectives of others

The most novel finding of all? Exercising self-control can be rewarding! The researchers found that when mothers were present during safe decisions, there was more coupling between parts of the brain involved in reward and cognitive control, suggesting, in their words, that mothers also "increased the rewarding nature of engaging in cognitive control."[12] So, not only can the reward system motivate learning, as Galván found, but it can also make self-control gratifying.

Key Finding: While some might think that young people have an impaired capacity to use self-control, studies show that parents can affect the brain, influencing how adolescents think and reason about negative risks. Parents can be brain builders.*

Would *any* adult have the same effect?

Telzer and her colleagues pursued that question in a subsequent study[13] in which 23 fifteen-year-olds played the Stoplight game, sometimes with the mother watching, sometimes with a "professor"—introduced as an expert on teenage driving—watching. To ensure that each adolescent had exactly the same experience with the mother and the professor, they followed the same script. In addition, participants saw a photograph of the professor on-screen but never saw her in person.

In the end, mothers' effect on adolescents was more powerful and more

---

* Thanks to Jackie Bezos of the Bezos Family Foundation for coining the phrase "brain builder."

effective than the effect of this unknown adult. The title for this experiment emphasizes its conclusion: "Mother Still Knows Best."

THREE KEY FACTORS THAT AFFECT
PARENTS' POSITIVE INFLUENCE

Telzer and her colleagues wondered how the quality of the parent-child relationship would affect negative risk-taking over time. In a 2015 study,[14] they looked into this, defining quality in three ways:

1. **Frequency of disclosure,** including how often adolescents spontaneously told their parents about their friends, classes, and relationships with teachers
2. **Frequency of family conflict,** including how often adolescents and their parents had arguments or misunderstandings
3. **Frequency of adolescents' feeling supported by their parents,** including how often adolescents felt their parents talked them through difficult moments

The researchers found that these three components of quality are correlated— that is, adolescents who disclose things to their parents more are also reporting less family conflict and more support. Thus, researchers combined these constructs as an overall measure of positive parent-child relationships.

This two-phase study included twenty-three adolescents in the tenth and eleventh grades. They returned to the lab a year and a half later, when the adolescents were in the eleventh and twelfth grades. This time, Telzer and her colleagues wanted to know:

- Do improvements in the quality of the parent-child relationship over time lead to greater declines in adolescents' negative risk-taking?
- If there are changes in the quality of the relationship, are there correlated changes in the brain?

Instead of the Stoplight game, this time the researchers used the Balloon Analog Risk Task (BART). Telzer describes this measure:[15]

The participants see a virtual balloon on the computer screen. Their job is to pump up the balloon. With each pump, they win 25 cents. The larger they pump up the balloon, the more money they win. But if they pump

too much, the balloon explodes, and they lose all the money for that
balloon.

Telzer and other researchers use the BART because other studies have
found that young people who take more risks on the BART are more likely
to take real-life negative risks, like smoking or taking drugs.[16]

The researchers found that the initial quality of the parent-adolescent
relationship wasn't related to how many risks adolescents took, but the
changes in the quality of the relationship over time were.[17] **When the re-**
lationship became more positive over the next year and a half, adolescents
were less likely to take risks on the BART.

Their brain findings echoed the behavioral findings. When parents and
adolescents developed a more positive relationship, there was a decline in activation in the brain's reward system during the BART. In Telzer's words, "the
brain is actually changing how it responds to rewards in a risky context."[18]

But what about negative risky behaviors *outside* the lab?

The research team asked the adolescents in the study about behavior such
as drinking, reckless driving, and unsafe sexual practices. Telzer reports that
better parental engagement was associated with less negative risky behavior.

In still another study, Telzer and her colleagues found[19] that the reverse
was also true: if adolescents' relationships with their parents deteriorated,
the teens behaved in negative, riskier ways.

In both cases, when there were positive and negative changes in relationships, adolescents' risk-taking and brains changed in corresponding ways.

WHAT DO PARENTS SAY?

What's it like to be a parent of a child who's your child's age? If you were
talking to a friend, what would you say?

These were the first questions I asked in the follow-up telephone interviews I
conducted with fifty-six parents who had participated in the baseline nationally representative survey we conducted for the book.

Many used words like "challenging," "hard," or "stressful." Those having
a difficult time at the moment recounted problems—some serious, but most
often battles about social media, homework, keeping the house clean, and
general defiance. Here's Charles, the father of an eleven-year-old daughter
living in New Jersey:

She always—what's the word I'm looking for?—questions authority. It's a good thing. I want her to be an independent woman, but as a parent, it's rather difficult because she's constantly questioning my judgment and not respecting the values I've put in place.

The parents who weren't having a difficult time at the moment gave very revealing answers. Although they generally said that being a parent of a teen was "stressful" or "hard," they continued with a common refrain. Here's Matthew, the father of a fifteen-year-old son, also from New Jersey:

He's a good kid. We're very fortunate. He gets good grades. He's in a high school for gifted kids, and we're very proud of him. He's not in trouble. He's just a good kid, so it's a pleasure.

And Ted, the father of a seventeen-year-old son, from California:

He's not your typical teenager. He's not moody; he does his academics. He's a good kid.

"He's a good kid." "She's a great kid." "He's not your typical teenager." "We are fortunate." There's an underlying assumption here: if negative things aren't happening, we're "lucky."

I wondered: What's the reality? To what degree is adolescence an emotional battleground for parents and their children?

STORM AND STRESS, OR SUNNY SKIES? BREAKTHROUGH YEARS STUDY FINDINGS ON HOSTILITY AND CONFLICT

In the nationally representative baseline study we conducted, we asked parents and adolescents the same questions about parent-child conflict that Eva Telzer uses in her studies:

Parents and their children have disagreements and conflicts from time to time. In the last month, how often did the following happen between _____ [your parent(s) or your child] and you:

1. *Gave each other the silent treatment (purposefully did not talk to each other)*

2. *Gave each other dirty looks or rolled your eyes at each other*
3. *Had a serious argument or fight*
4. *Got very angry at each other*

We asked them to rate the frequency on a 1 to 5 scale, where 1 = "never" and 5 = "almost always." Here's what we found:

- On average, parents reported an overall conflict score of 6.19, and adolescents reported a slightly greater score of 6.42, out of a maximum score of 20 for the four questions, indicating not much conflict.
- Importantly, adolescents and parents generally agreed on how often they got into conflicts—their answers are moderately to strongly correlated.*

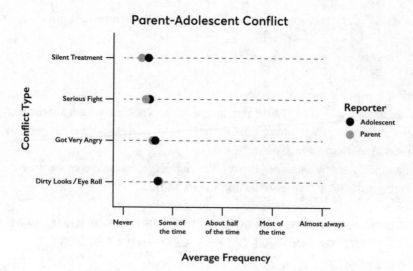

Parent-Adolescent Conflict

Some parents and adolescents said "almost always" for all four conflict questions, while 30 percent of adolescents and 27 percent of parents said "never." With the caveat that averages mask differences, our findings indicate that there's at least some conflict for a majority of families, but most families are not dealing with frequent, nonstop conflict. We saw evidence of increasing conflict with age, but there were no differences in how often male and female adolescents or parents reported conflict. We did find, however, that

---

* The overall correlation between parents' and adolescents' scores is $r = .58$, meaning that they co-occur frequently and thus this is a very reliable association.

different-gender pairs (for example, fathers and daughters) reported experiencing slightly less conflict than same-gender pairs (for example, fathers and sons). Across all four pairings, we found that sons and mothers reported the least amount of conflict.

PUTTING IT ALL TOGETHER: PARENTS AND ADOLESCENTS GETTING ALONG

Ninety-six percent of adolescents in our survey reported getting along at least somewhat well with their parents, with **67 percent indicating getting along "very well" with their parents.** Only 4 percent responded "not too well or "not well at all."

A fairly similar pattern occurred with parents: 98 percent reported getting along at least somewhat well with their adolescents, **with 78 percent indicating they get along "very well" with their adolescents.** Only 2 percent indicated "not too well" or "not well at all."

Breakthrough Years Study Finding: Our data from a nationally representative group of adolescents and parents reveal that conflict is less frequent than we might think. I asked the parents about these findings when I interviewed some of them in the follow-up telephone interviews. One spoke for many when she said, "You mean life isn't what we see on TV?" As we know from the FrameWorks Institute media analysis, this parent is correct: the media overemphasize the bad news.

But just because conflict may be infrequent, that doesn't make it less powerful. Thinking back on my own experience as an adolescent and as a parent, I've found that the aftermath of a fight can linger and reverberate, like earthquake aftershocks.

Judith Warner, author of *And Then They Stopped Talking to Me: Making Sense of Middle School*, explains why conflicts can affect us so profoundly. When middle schoolers experience "awkwardness, painful self-consciousness, and crippling insecurity, in the face of hard and unforgiving peer judgment,"[20] their feelings can spill over onto us and take us back emotionally to our middle school selves.[21] Warner told me:

The kids produce the very behavior the adults most fear and dislike, and then the adults react in ways—or even in anticipatory ways—that bring on more of that behavior.[22]

What does it take to break that negative cycle?

BEST PRACTICES FOR DEALING WITH CONFLICT

The question of how to deal with conflict is one that Nicholas Allen of the University of Oregon pursues in his research on the transition from childhood to adolescence.

Allen is one of the few researchers who study neuroscience and parenting relationships—even though, as he told me, "every time a study's been done, it's shown very strong effects" for the importance of parents in adolescents' lives, and "in many studies, parent-child relationships during adolescence are a bigger predictor of a kid's mental health problems than peer relationships."[23]

Allen thinks one reason for this gap is our buy-in to a "cultural story":

That adolescence is all about peers, and parents don't matter anymore. I'm exaggerating a little, but that's the sense you get sometimes in how people talk about adolescence.

Breakthrough Years Study Finding: Thirty-seven percent of parents feel they have little influence on their adolescent children.

Allen explains why parents' influence outweighs peer influence:

We think that one of the reasons is that adolescent relationships are unstable—they come and go. You make new friends, you lose friends, you make alternative friends. Parents are a constant.

Let's say you have a friend that breaks up with you—a platonic friend or a romantic relationship. The ability to go to your parents and receive some support and advice and care at that time might be a very strong moderator of how kids get on.

To determine what it takes to avoid conflict, Allen and his team "began by studying family interactions 'live'":[24]

We would bring people into our lab and ask them to talk to each other
about specific tasks—like, for example, resolve something that you have a
conflict about or plan a fun activity you want to do together in the future
or reminisce about a time in the family's past.[25]

They videotaped and then minutely examined these interchanges. They
also investigated whether the interchanges predicted adolescents' mental
health over time as well as their negative risk-taking behavior, such as substance abuse.[26] Their comprehensive data included genetic makeup and brain
development. They found that the combination of difficult family environments and genetic risks makes increased problems more likely. On the other
hand, positive parenting reduces the likelihood of problems.

These findings led Allen and his colleagues to identify three key factors
for reducing conflict.

**Lesson 1: When disagreements occur, stay positive and believe the best
about your child.**[27]

Imagine a parent and child disagreeing over an unclean room. Parents
who believe the worst about their child might say:

When you don't keep your room clean, it drives me crazy. You've been
doing this for a long time. You can't seem to improve on it. It's absolutely
unacceptable, but I don't know what we're going to do about it because
I've been asking you about this for ages, and you're not making any
progress whatsoever. I'm really angry.

Conversely, Allen says, parents who believe the best about their child
might say:

Listen, I want you to clean your room, and this is a really important issue
that we need to resolve. I know you can do this because when I've asked
you to do things before, you've been able to turn it around. If we work
together and if we focus on this, I think we can really make some great
progress because you're a great kid, and I love you—but we need to treat
this as an important issue.

**Lesson 2: Enjoy a good time with your child without it becoming derailed
or turning negative.**

When there's an opportunity to enjoy an experience together, keep it
positive and avoid impulses to derail it:

Let's say the family is planning to go out for dinner. And instead of enjoying the fact that they're getting to do something that's going to be fun, the family has an argument about who wants to go where, and then eventually the parent says, "Well, we're not going to go anywhere because nobody can agree, and nobody's going to be happy."

Instead, they might take turns on who gets to decide where they go for dinner.

Lesson 3: When the adolescent is behaving aggressively, don't escalate it.

If your child is saying something nasty to you, don't turn around and be nasty back. Stay calm, firm, and businesslike.

IT'S IN THE DATA: PARENTS MATTER—A LOT!

If ever there was an indication of how much parents matter, it's whether or not adolescents want to spend time with us.

Breakthrough Years Study Finding:
- Only 7 percent of adolescents feel they spend too much time with their mothers and 3 percent with their fathers.
- A total of 72 percent feel they spend just enough time with their mothers and 61 percent with their fathers.
- And 21 percent feel they spend too little time with their mothers and 36 percent with their fathers.

Almost all adolescents want to spend time with us and want even more time, especially with fathers.

I, like you, have read my share of parenting articles disparaging the closeness between parents and kids as overinvolvement and more. But I firmly believe that it's a matter of how we handle that closeness: parents and adolescents can be close and want to spend time together within relationships that enable young people to gain more agency and autonomy . . . or not.

PROMOTING POSITIVE RELATIONSHIPS

There's nothing like a defiant, aggressive adolescent to flip us back into feeling like an aggressive adolescent ourselves, wanting the last word, wanting to make that ungrateful child to whom we've given so much feel our pain. It does take real self-control to step back and remain the grown-up in the room.

It's not only the adolescent who is growing and developing. As parents, we grow and develop, too. Adolescence is a time to learn how to focus on assets—ours and theirs—to look for ways to de-escalate aggression and to resist the temptation to derail a good time. It's a time to look for and admire rays of sunshine, even in those moments when the skies are stormy.

Parenting Strategies: Listening, Understanding, and Creating Shared Solutions

THREE KEYS TO PARENTING ADOLESCENTS

In the Breakthrough Years interviews I conducted following the baseline survey, I asked both young people and their parents about the most important skills and strategies and found a strong convergence. Here are those they most endorsed, in the words of young people:

1. Listen more than you talk.
2. Listen with your "when-I-was-a-child" mind, not just your "now-I'm-an-adult" mind.
3. Create a family problem-solving process where the adolescent has a voice.

Key #1: Listen More Than You Talk

Joshua, a twelve-year-old in California, says that if a parent doesn't listen, the child doesn't want to talk—it's that simple. Listening, says fourteen-year-old Robert from North Carolina, means having an authentic interest in what the child thinks and feels, and *"really* wanting to know more about your kid."

Tim, a seventeen-year-old from Georgia, says listening *before* responding is key:

> *Sometimes you just need someone to listen rather than to discipline or instruct right away.*

Because, says thirteen-year-old David from Virginia, when parents and their adolescents listen and talk with each other, they become closer.

Jessica Lahey, a former teacher and author of the hugely helpful and insightful book *The Gift of Failure*,[28] told me that when she gives speeches in a community, she follows a protocol of speaking to the students first, during the day. At that time, she invites them to email and tell her what they *really* want their parents to know because she will be speaking with parents that evening.[29]

The number one issue she hears is "I'm not some imaginary kid you think you're raising." Lahey says they tell her, "I don't feel seen; I don't feel heard." Her message back to parents is to listen, to know what matters to your child (not just what matters to you). Your children feel you aren't really listening when you are looking at your phone; when you are nodding but not hearing; or when you want to switch the conversation to their achievements versus what matters to them.

Listening more than we talk requires controlling our emotions so we don't jump in to judge, switch to what's on our mind, or resolve things *for* (rather than *with*) our child. Lahey says she's found that parental listening is what sets young people up for success.

Key #2: Listen with Your "When-I-Was-a-Child" Mind, Not Just Your "Now-I'm-an-Adult" Mind

That's also Joshua's insightful turn of phrase. Lucy, the mother of a sixteen-year-old from Michigan, describes it as listening "with your heart—to be able to understand your child's true wants, desires, and needs." It means understanding each child as a unique individual and understanding their stage of development.

How we apply our "now-I'm-an-adult" mind is critical. We need to provide guidance and rules, of course, but we do so with insight into what adolescents are like. This is essential because "no one—an adult or child—wants to be judged," observes Lisette, a soon-to-be sixteen-year-old in Arizona.

She's so right. Only when we feel understood—sensing that we're appreciated, accepted, and belong and that we're being heard—can we open up, learn, and change. Lisette continues:

Maybe you didn't do something that was really good, but if you have a
*sense that parents are on your side and understand, **then** they can counter*
that with wisdom and love.

Fourteen-year-old Robert says being listened to in an accepting way "is very motivating"—a stepping-stone to wanting to "do good."

So, let's look at what listening with our "when-I-was-a-child" mind really means.

- **Read the room.** If your child is withdrawn, seems angry, is "hover-crafting" (hanging around like there's something on their mind), or asks an out-of-the-blue question, they may be asking for a conversation. That's an opportunity not to be missed.
- **Set the stage for a conversation.** This means finding a time or place where there're few distractions or interruptions, like taking a walk, going for a drive, or some other activity where you can fully tune in.
- **Make conversations a predictable and routine part of your parenting.** At all ages, we thrive on routines—being able to count on what's expected and when that will happen. If there's a regular time to talk—mealtime, Friday-night pizza, walking the dog, etc.—with the opportunity to share a rose (a success), a thorn (a challenge), and a bud (a new possibility) or what you're grateful for, it makes open communication a predictable part of your family life.
- **Share without imposing your experiences as destiny.** Listening with your child mind sometimes means talking about your own experiences growing up, but it's important not to assume your experience will be the same as your child's. Hanna, a twelve-year-old from Maryland, wants to talk to her father about middle school but worries that he'll say, "Your middle school is probably going to be horrible because mine was." Rather, she hopes he'll tell her, "My middle school was difficult but yours can be quite different, and let's talk about why."
- **Understand the process of parental growth.** In my studies of parental development,[30] I've found that preexisting expectations—"should," "supposed to," and "ought"—shape our reactions and responses to ourselves and our children, for events as large as the transition to middle school or as small as what your child likes to wear. We use

these expectations as measures of our own success as parents. An unmet expectation can bring anger, sadness, and a sense of loss—but that's the crucial moment when parental growth can take place. If you find that an expectation is tripping you up, ask yourself if it's a realistic expectation. If it is, change yourself to try to live up to it, and if it's not realistic, try to change your expectation to be more doable.

- **Avoid pushing perfection.** Kids will make mistakes, and perfection is an unhealthy standard. Mark, a fifteen-year-old from upstate New York, contrasts two types of parents: those who "want us to always be perfect" and those who help kids aim to be the best they can but don't expect perfection. It's better, he says, if parents recognize perfection is unhealthy and say: "All right, just try to do better next time."

- **Create a two-way safety zone.** Be open so that kids feel comfortable telling you things you may not want to hear, but be clear that you will take action when necessary for their safety.

- **Don't meet aggression with aggression.** Acknowledge what your child is feeling, even when they are expressing emotions in a strong way. If needed, make space to come back to the conversation in a calmer state of mind. Listening to your child's feelings is crucial, but that doesn't mean overindulging their feelings. When you sense that's happening, you can say, "I hear you and I understand. Tell me when you're ready to begin trying to solve the problem."

- **Be consistent, calm, and present.** Especially when you're going through a difficult time, your child will appreciate your efforts to show up consistently. Melinda, whose parents had a contentious divorce, was initially furious at her father and refused to speak to him. He kept showing up. In retrospect, he now says that his decision to keep showing up and to try to manage staying calm when she ignored him turned the tide: "Three years later, this has given me a relationship with my daughter I could never have envisioned."

- **Be open to feedback.** Andrew, a sixteen-year-old from Michigan, suffered a sudden and debilitating onset of anxiety following a hospitalization for infections. Key to his recovery was his parents' openness to feedback—appropriately stated—from him about how they're parenting him. Here's how he tells it:

Sometimes I'll notice behaviors in them that I don't agree with. For example, at one point, I noticed that my mom would try to assign causes to things. If I was grumpy or something, she'd say, "It's because you didn't have enough sleep last night," or "It's because you're not eating right." I was able to tell her what I was noticing and she listened. She's changed and she's not doing that as much. And I think that's really helped.

I remember my own mother's openness to parenting feedback from me, too. My feedback had to be stated respectfully and my mother didn't always heed my views, but she always listened. I think that's one of the greatest gifts she ever gave me.

Developing Perspective-Taking Skills

You might enjoy trying this perspective-taking exercise. Velma McBride Murry from Vanderbilt University and her colleagues use it to help parents/caregivers build their parenting skills as part of an effective parenting intervention they've created in the Strong African American Families (SAAF) program and the more recent e-health program Pathways for African American Success (PAAS).

Close your eyes and recall your ten-, eleven-, or twelve-year-old self:[31]

- What was going on in your mind?
- What were your experiences like?
- What were your relationships with your peers?
- What were you concerned about?
- What were your concerns about your parents and how they reacted to you?

Now, think about your adolescent child and reflect on what you were going through and what your child may be going through:

- How are you responding?
- How do you wish you might have responded, given what you remember about yourself as a child that age?

Ask your child what they need from you to be successful, and share your discoveries with each other.

This exercise is the essence of using the skill of perspective-taking.

Key #3: Create a Family Problem-Solving Process Where the Adolescent Has a Voice

As one adolescent put it to me, if we are the problem, then we have to be part of the solution!

When conflicts arise with our children, it may seem that our aspiration—our north star—for the kind of parent we want to be is light-years away from where we are. That was the case in Ana's family.

Expectations Shape the Course of Parenting

Ana is the mother of four—a twenty-five-year-old son, a seventeen-year-old daughter, and thirteen-year-old twins—in a midsized town in Minnesota. She describes the family she grew up in as severe:

> When I was four, if I was boisterous, or loud, or seen as naughty, I got whipped with a belt. It's normal for a four-year-old to be boisterous, loud, and sometimes even obnoxious. I think my parents had the illusion that if they spanked, they could get me to act in a more adult manner.

Ana's right. When we don't understand and respect the child's stage of development, we may misinterpret normal behavior as abnormal and expect a four-year-old to act like a much older child—or expect an adolescent to be like an adult, as we saw in chapter 1.

Ana said that her husband's family was different from hers: "He came from a very stoic, quiet family and they never got physical." Yet:

> In both families, the child's feelings weren't valued. When I was getting disciplined, my feelings didn't matter. If he got disciplined, his family didn't talk about anything. It was "This is the way it is"—you accept it and move on.

When they married, they worked on what Ana calls "our own traditions so we could raise our kids the way we want." They were united in wanting to listen to and accept their children's feelings. **Ana set a north star: an expectation for herself about how she wanted to raise her children.**

> I told my husband, "I can't have my child go to sleep crying, thinking they're horrible because maybe they colored on the wall or did a kid thing."

Remembering the pain of being hit with a belt and the isolation of having her emotions ignored were catalysts for becoming the parent she wanted to be, but it wasn't enough. Seeing other families whom she considered as role models helped, but it also wasn't enough. Her husband's support helped, but it wasn't enough, either. So Ana found a therapist, who became an invaluable guide.

Ana says the combined support from these sources helped her try to live up to her expectation. Age, too, has helped her be less reactive and more intentional in her parenting.

Ana recognizes that her parents did the best they could with the information they had, so having more information has been a lifeline to her. As a public health nurse, she told me, "I work a lot with child protection and social services. I am constantly going to trainings about how to discipline kids—what works and what doesn't." As a result, she never hit her children.

Recently, her twenty-five-year-old son visited. "I still encourage him to talk about his feelings," she says. During that visit, he told her that although she wasn't raising her fists, she was raising her voice:

"Maybe you shouldn't rant and yell, Mom. It didn't work on me growing up. What makes you think it's going to work with the younger kids?"

She replied: "You know, you're right—you're so right," pledging to have "cooperative conversations" and not yell.

SHARED SOLUTIONS IN ACTION

What Ana calls "cooperative conversation," Joshua, the twelve-year-old from California, calls "open communication":

"Open communication" isn't saying to children "Don't do this. Don't do that." It's listening to what they have to say and being able to take some suggestions from children about how to solve problems.

My term is Shared Solutions,* an approach I've used for years. I find Shared Solutions especially effective with adolescents because:

- It gives adolescents an appropriate measure of autonomy and agency—a basic developmental need during these years.

---

* Special thanks to Sarah Wolman of Lightbulb Learning Lab for suggesting this name.

- It helps adolescents learn how to resolve problems for themselves, rather than have the adults fix problems for them.

It's effective for adults because:

- They set the goal and the ground rules.
- They're helping their adolescent gain skills and experience while the immediate problem is getting resolved.

I'll use an issue in Ana's family—cleaning up the house—as an example. I expect you know the feeling: you come home and find the house a mess because the kids have "forgotten" to do their chores. In the past, Ana tried to solve the problem *for* her children. She says, "We tried charts, schedules, other things. They never worked!"

Rather than give up in exasperation and clean up herself or dole out punishments (no chores = no electronics), she tried a different approach, based on her new expectation of herself—to replace yelling with cooperative conversations.

Step 1: State the Problem and Determine the Goal

The first step in Shared Solutions is describing the problem in a way the parent "owns," then stating a goal for resolution. Here's Ana:

> I explained to my kids how I have to work Monday through Friday—forty hours a week. I don't have time to do everything. It puts a lot of stress on me to have all that responsibility. It's their house, too, and I told them that they can do some things for themselves because they're independent and they'll have to do these things when they grow up.

Importantly:

- Ana framed the problem without blame or criticism (there was none of "you leave the house a mess," "you're slobs," "you're lazy").
- She described the problem from her own perspective, taking responsibility for her feelings: "I don't have time to do everything" and "It puts a lot of stress on me to have all that responsibility."
- She stated her goal—it's essential for her kids to be part of cleaning up because it's their house, too.

- She pointed toward how this would help them be more competent as adults.

It's important to have ground rules in mind for Shared Solutions, such as not blaming or criticizing others, and to share those with your family. I've found it works best in a family discussion or meeting that's removed from the heat of the moment. If emotions are high, you can set a time for a later discussion, saying, as Ana initially did: "I'm upset now, so I am not going to respond. We'll have to talk about it when I calm down."

Because she wasn't listened to as a child, Ana initially overindulged her children's feelings. Now she listens with understanding and she acknowledges their feelings, but she doesn't let them drown in them.

Step 2: Involve Everyone in Generating Possible Solutions

Ana's thirteen-year-old twins and her seventeen-year-old daughter didn't need a family meeting—they divided up the chores and figured out who was responsible for each one.

In my family, Shared Solutions worked best if each of my children brainstormed solutions during a family meeting. I'd make a list of their ideas—no matter how impractical or silly—with no comments. The more solutions generated, the better. Writing them down keeps things from getting personal. If coming up with solutions is hard, briefly discussing wacky solutions may defuse tension. Scaling back the issue to something manageable may also be effective.

Step 3: Consider the Pluses and Minuses of Each Potential Solution

Next, talk about how each solution would work for the parents *and* for the children. If your children have difficulty taking someone else's perspective, they can role-play and pretend to be that person. Again, it's important to use "I-messages"[32] during this discussion—what would or wouldn't work for *you* as an adult—and ask the children to do the same. Abstaining from criticism and expressing confidence that you can figure this out are key.

Step 4: Select a Solution to Try

You can then write down the agreed-upon solution. If none of the solutions on the brainstorm list work, keep going until you come up with a solution that will work for all.

If you think the situation (like breaking a curfew) requires a consequence, you can ask your children to brainstorm with you: "What do you think is a fair consequence if the curfew is broken?" This way, consequences won't be decided in anger, or be unrealistic or irrational. The goal is to try to ensure that consequences will be fair, consistent, and followed.

Step 5: Evaluate the Solution as Necessary, and If It Isn't Working, Return to Step 2

It's critical to see Shared Solutions as a process—as iterative, not punitive. If it doesn't work or if you are at an impasse, you can have another family meeting to come up with another solution and begin the process again. Using Shared Solutions takes practice, but it's worth it because it helps us be the kind of parent we want to be.

LAB ⟷ LIFE: OUR BELIEFS ABOUT ADOLESCENCE AFFECT OUR COMMUNICATIONS

Pediatrician Kenneth Ginsburg of Children's Hospital of Philadelphia and author of a book I see as a treasure, *Congrats—You're Having a Teen!*, knows that what we believe about adolescence shapes how we parent:

> *If you believe adolescents are emotionally out of control—all engine, no brakes—you're going to communicate with them in one way. But if you understand that the emotional part of their brain is brilliant, you're going to communicate in another way, one that respects how intuitive and responsive they can be.*[33]

What I call a developmental necessity, Ginsburg, who founded the Center for Parent and Teen Communication, sees as brilliant, writing that young people are "brilliant at reading social cues and hypervigilant to spoken and unspoken signals."[34]

When parents don't understand this, Ginsburg finds, their children's behavior might anger them or they might adopt a condescending tone, one whose intent is to control or quiet them.[35] With that, Ginsburg says, "you're going to take away the young person's sense of security, sense of agency, sense of confidence. And, of course, they will respond negatively." If you do understand their development, you can be engaging and deeply warm:

> *When you respect young people as experts in their own lives and* **include them in decision-making and problem-solving in a way that's** **authentically respectful,** *they can stay calmer.*

PROMOTING LISTENING, UNDERSTANDING, AND CREATING SHARED SOLUTIONS

Ken Ginsburg's aspiration is having parents know how much and in what ways they matter. That's my aspiration, too.

While writing this book, it was by listening—with my "when-I-was-a-child" mind and my "now-I'm-an-adult" mind—that I could better understand the connections between the research findings and the voices of parents and adolescents to arrive at doable solutions for aiming toward my aspiration.

As you read the chapters to come, I hope you'll find these connections helpful and make more of your own as you think about your own adolescence, the adolescents in your life, and your interactions with young people. Know that every day is a new day with your children and it is never too late.

Adolescence as a Time of Recovery

PUTTING PARENTING STRATEGIES AND COMMUNITY SUPPORTS TO THE TEST

It's never too late to set an aspiration for the kind of parent we want to be, but how much of a difference can we make for children who have had very stressful experiences early in life?

For years, I've heard some advocates for early childhood argue that adolescence is too late. Even the words we use about adversity—"toxic stress," for example—sound lethal. Is recovery from adverse experiences such as abuse or neglect possible during adolescence? If so, how?

The exciting news is that **adversity is *not* destiny.** In their consensus report on adolescence, the National Academies of Sciences, Engineering, and Medicine evaluated programs and interventions that build on the plasticity of the adolescent years, revealing that it's possible to positively affect young people's psychology and physiology to help them thrive.[36] They conclude:

> *While preventing early-life adversities is ideal, research shows that ameliorating and redirecting an unhealthy developmental trajectory remains possible during adolescence and later developmental periods.*[37]

We'll look at what parents and communities can do to offset adversity and the opportunities adolescence offers to do so. There are lessons from this research that can inspire all of us, whatever our adolescents' early childhood experiences have been.

ADOLESCENCE: AN OPPORTUNITY TO
RESET THE IMPACT OF EARLY STRESS?

Megan Gunnar of the University of Minnesota has a unique background in psychology and in developmental psychoneuroendocrinology, which is the study of the relationships among the endocrine or hormonal system, the nervous system, and psychology. While most of her work on stress has focused on young children, increasingly she's turning to adolescence to see if the changes during puberty can lead to changes in how children manage stress.

"Stress," in Gunnar's words, "is when demands on your body—or your expectations of those demands—exceed your ability to handle them."[38] Stress occurs when there's a threat to your physical or psychological well-being.

To understand the impact of stress, let's imagine you realize you're being followed on the street at night. You feel a surge of adrenaline through your body—the fight-or-flight response.[39] Messages speed to the thinking and reasoning brain regions (the cortex) and the emotional and memory regions (the limbic system, including the amygdala and hippocampus). You become laser-focused on what's scaring you: Is this dangerous or not?[40]

Other systems are activated, including the hypothalamic-pituitary-adrenocortical (HPA) system. The hypothalamus and other parts of your brain send messages to your pituitary gland, which activates the outer part of your adrenal glands, the adrenal cortex, to release cortisol and other glucocorticoids.

Cortisol, known as the stress hormone, mobilizes fats and glucose to provide energy to respond to the danger, suppresses your immune system, and changes the activity of many brain regions including those involved in memory and emotion. The effect of the fight-or-flight response is to shift the brain from "think now, act later" to ways of responding that let you "act now, think later." Cortisol then helps to lay down a memory of the threat and response so that the next time you encounter cues about that threat, you will respond faster or, preferably, avoid the threat altogether.[41]

Now, let's say that the person following you turns onto another street. You realize that the danger is over. Along with other changes, the hypothalamus sends messages to your HPA system to throttle down, and your level of cortisol begins to decrease.

The stress system is what Gunnar calls a "fast on–fast off system."[42] It revs up quickly, then tamps down the reaction once the perceived danger is over. But it's known that if stress is prolonged and this system is turned on frequently, it can change how the body and the brain function.

What if stress is severe and frequent in the earliest years and then subsides?

A trip with a research team to an orphanage in Romania in the mid-1990s set Gunnar on a path to answer that question. She saw children in overcrowded and inhumane conditions. Even when their physical needs were met, they weren't able to form relationships to meet their psychological needs, possibly altering their brain architecture in ways that result in atypical biological and behavioral development.[43]

Post-adoption, the adversity subsides—these children tend to be adopted into loving and caring homes. However, the stress responses persist.

Gunnar and her colleagues created a registry of six thousand children adopted from international orphanages worldwide and have conducted numerous studies.[44] They found that **children who experienced deprivation and neglect for two or more years in orphanages with the poorest quality of social care are likely to have a blunted or reduced (hypoactive) stress reaction.** Since stress was omnipresent in the harsh orphanages, Gunnar says that the children's bodies eventually had to dial down their reactions—perhaps nature's way of preserving their brains and bodies.[45] This blunting effect, however, lasts for years after children leave the orphanages, suggesting there's a sensitive period during the early years where a blunted stress response appears to become established.[46]

A hypoactive stress system can make it seem as if children are passive in the face of challenge, but it's more than that. Gunnar and other researchers have found that children with a blunted cortisol reaction are at risk for a number of problems compared with children in similar socioeconomic situations but raised by their biological parents:

> [They] have been found to experience more social and emotional problem behaviors, have greater difficulty understanding social cues, are more likely to experience difficulties in social situations with peers, and have trouble establishing and forming healthy social relationships.[47]

Led by then–graduate student Carrie DePasquale, Gunnar and their team found cascading effects: the young children with a blunted cortisol reaction are less likely to be socially competent,[48] have more problems in regulating their emotions and behavior as kindergartners,[49] and are more likely to be socially anxious as youth.[50]

Importantly, their lab studies have found that the quality of parenting provided to these young children post-adoption in their new homes makes a difference. For example:

- Parents who are **sensitive** and who provide **more structure** are likely to have children with better emotional regulation skills.[51]
- Parents who are **consistent in providing routines** have children who are likely to have better inhibitory control and fewer attention problems.[52]
- Parents who are **supportive** *and* (the "and" here is necessary) who **provide structure and set appropriate limits** are less likely to have children who are socially inappropriate.[53]

Still, the blunted cortisol reaction remains in place for years, leading Gunnar to ask, "If moving the child from an institution into a well-resourced family with parents who score (generally) high in parenting quality doesn't 'fix' the axis, will anything?"[54]

The "anything" she and her colleagues suspected was puberty. They hypothesized that "puberty would open a window when the stress system could be recalibrated."

To find out, they conducted a study with 299 seven-to-fifteen-year-olds, 129 of whom were adopted after being in orphanages as infants and toddlers, and 170 of whom were born and raised by their biological families. Three times over the next two years, they were given the Trier Social Stress Test—"one of the most reliable stressor-tests in the literature."[55]

Reading about the Trier may bring back school memories (or nightmares). Participants are asked to give a five-minute speech introducing themselves to imaginary classmates, stating a few things that would make other kids want to be their friend and a few things about themselves that are not so great.

They have five minutes to prepare and write notes but can't use notes during their speech. If they pause while they are speaking, they are told to "say more about that" or "keep going."

After the speech, participants are asked to do difficult mental arithmetic problems aloud. When they make a mistake, the experimenter says, "Wrong. Start over."

It *is* stressful. I've watched young people rub their hands and squirm during the test. They are asked to spit into a straw five times during their lab visit so the researchers can measure the rise and fall of their cortisol, which takes about twenty-five minutes to peak in stressful situations.

The results? The researchers' hypothesis was correct: "We found beautiful evidence of recalibration!"[56] Gunnar exclaims. Puberty offers a window for the young people to develop new stress responses.

While these data are very hopeful,[57] it's not a completely "happy-ever-after story," Gunnar says.[58]

Their team conducted a subsequent study to find out if the increased (i.e., now normal) cortisol reactivity among these adolescents would mean reduced behavior problems. They looked at externalizing problems, like being oppositional, defiant, and aggressive, and found that increases in stress reactivity were not linked to more oppositional problems or vice versa.

However, there was an association with internalizing problems—depression and anxiety. Increases in reactivity were linked to increases in these problems, and the reverse was also true: internalizing problems was linked with increased cortisol reactivity.[59] But they state that only 3 to 4 percent of these adolescents would be classified as depressed or anxious at a clinical level, where professional treatment would be recommended. Clearly, these adolescents now have to learn to manage their less blunted reaction to stress.

Key Finding: These studies, taken together, confirm that it is never too late—that the results of early and very severe adversity can be diminished. But it takes positive parenting in the early childhood years and in adolescence as the stress system normalizes.

Gunnar's team studied the quality of parenting that was naturally occurring and found that it made a difference for children who'd been adopted from orphanages. But what if there were efforts to identify the most important aspects of early parenting and increase them? That's been a goal of Philip Fisher of Stanford University.

Fisher recognized that parenting children with blunted stress reactions can be challenging because, as he puts it, children remain "closed in"—they are less likely to notice or respond to being nurtured, which in turn makes it harder for parents to notice these "weak signals" from children or to stay positive.[60]

The parenting strategy Fisher's team selected is "serves and returns"—when children initiate an interaction with parents (serves), and parents respond in caring and supportive ways (returns), leading to more positive back-and-forth interactions.[61]

FIND (Filming Interactions to Nurture Development) was designed to make parents of young children aware of the importance of serves and returns and to increase them. Parents videotape themselves with their child; the researchers watch the videos, pinpoint moments where there are serves and returns, and show them to parents via video coaching.[62] Fisher says that the results are "magical": a preliminary evaluation of FIND concluded that increasing awareness and changing behavior are possible and that they're linked to positive changes in parents' own brains.[63] Fisher says:

> We saw changes at the level of brain activation in those areas of the brain around self-control and we know that self-control is one really important part of executive functioning, so it was a very exciting finding.[64]

It's unclear if interventions like FIND would lead to an even happier-ever-after story because they haven't been tested over the long term, but it is clear that change is possible for previously neglected children. If there were ever examples of putting parenting strategies to the test, these are two of them!

LAB ⟷ LIFE: HOW FAMILY AND COMMUNITY COUNT IN RECOVERING FROM ADVERSITY

Another example of putting parenting strategies to the test is the Strong African American Families (SAAF) program and its more recent e-health version, the Pathways for African American Success (PAAS) program. The National Academies of Sciences, Engineering, and Medicine consensus report on adolescence cites SAAF as a compelling example of a program that works with the brain's plasticity during adolescence to overcome adversity to "influence not only behavior but also systemic physiology, ensuring that youth flourish."[65]

Both the SAAF and the PAAS programs were implemented among a population of rural low-income African American families and include young people with their parent/caregiver. One of the sessions, for example, focuses on helping young people deal with adversities they may experience from growing up in poverty and living in a society in which they and their family members experience racial discrimination. The key aspect of this session is how to survive and thrive when facing adversities.

Velma McBride Murry, the co-developer of SAAF and the primary developer of PAAS, says a key question that drove SAAF from its inception in 1995 was "whether being exposed to what we call regulated, communicative, supportive parenting would buffer kids against adversity."[66]

"I was raised by a mother who overcame adversity," Murry says. Orphaned at age eight, "my mother and her two sisters were left without parents. The families in their community raised these girls and raised them to be well-functioning women, who grew up, married, and raised very productive and accomplished children."[67]

It was inevitable, Murry believes, that her mother shared her life lessons with her own children:

I grew up with her instilling in me the fact that you can succeed regardless of the circumstances you find yourself in.

But one doesn't succeed alone. Community counts:

What's most important is being around supportive individuals who can help you survive and thrive.

As a youth worker after college in inner-city Memphis, Murry saw firsthand that it's possible to flourish amid misfortune. While most of these young people were growing up in very challenging circumstances—poverty with all its attendant hardships—many were surviving and thriving as a result of the specific environments they were in. It's like gardening, she says:

When tiny seeds are placed in the ground, they have to be placed in the soil, in dirt and darkness. But if light is shone on them, they will eventually emerge and grow.

Murry launched her academic career at the University of Connecticut, Storrs; she later relocated to the University of Georgia and developed a program of research with Gene Brody and other researchers involving rural African American families and young people living in poverty and encountering discrimination. A key question that framed this line of research from its beginnings in 1995 was: What are the protective processes that help these young people thrive?

They designed a longitudinal study of about one thousand families and were able, in fact, to identify a set of factors (protective processes) that consistently predicted positive outcomes in young people, which they then used to inform the SAAF intervention and the PAAS e-health program. SAAF was tested in a randomized trial with 700 families, with 350 families assigned to receive the program and the remaining 350 serving as the control group.

SAAF begins when children enter middle school, at ten or eleven. Murry describes this as a "developmental turning point" that "provides a time of newness environmentally and socially"—young people experience new rules, new friends, new teachers, and new opportunities.[68] Intervening at such times, before behavioral patterns became more entrenched, can help shape adolescents in positive ways.

Second, the intervention is comprehensive, including both parents/caregivers and their children, first meeting separately, then together.

With parents/caregivers, the seven-session SAAF program focuses on positive (versus punitive) discipline, providing emotional support to children, and active parental monitoring.[69] The parent/caregiver intervention also includes opportunities to role-play that set clear expectations to avoid negative risky situations like alcohol use, strategies for communicating about sex, as well as techniques for positive identity development and for fostering school engagement.

Young people and parents/caregivers learn from the facilitator, from each other, and, in the online PAAS sessions, from avatars programmed to interact with each other. In one PAAS session on pubertal development, for example, an avatar father said he feels uncomfortable when his daughter, who "looks like a woman," wants to sit on his lap, and he's been pushing her away. An avatar parent cautioned him that doing this might be perceived as rejection by his daughter. Another avatar parent suggested that he give his daughter a big hug to demonstrate being a caring and affectionate parent—if that would make him feel more comfortable than having her sit on his lap.[70]

In their sessions, adolescents learn about the importance of respecting and adhering to household rules as a way to avoid situations that could derail their future goals. In addition, they are taught strategies for resisting alcohol and other drugs and for coping with peer pressure. They also learn about selecting friends who can be good role models as well as how to navigate encounters with discrimination so that it doesn't negatively affect them.

After meeting apart, parents and their children come together and practice what they've learned in their separate sessions.

Every aspect of the intervention is designed to improve communication. For example, in the last session, parent and child each write a family creed reflecting strength, growth, and competence and then join together to write a mutual one.

The results? SAAF and PAAS programs improve communication, according to survey reports from both parents and their adolescents. And this improvement in communication is, in turn, linked to preventing negative risky behavior.[71]

Key Finding: Other analyses show that adolescents assigned to the intervention group report better resistance efficacy (assessing and avoiding negative risks) and self-regulation skills.[72] They are more engaged in school, less likely to be negatively affected by exposure to racial discrimination,[73] and more successful academically.[74] Positive physical results include reducing low-grade inflammation, reducing the association between early adversity and prediabetes, and promoting positive brain development.[75]

Given her own history of her mother being raised by the community, it's not surprising that Murry includes a focus on community in the SAAF and PAAS programs. But how, for research purposes, does one define and measure community impact? In this, Murry was inspired by the research on collective efficacy.

THE POWER OF COLLECTIVE EFFICACY

Like Murry, I've been inspired by the collective efficacy research that a 2004 *New York Times* article calls one of the best studies in criminology ever.[76] Collective efficacy is the social cohesion among neighbors and their willingness to intervene with other people's children on behalf of the common good. A few years ago, I sought out Felton "Tony" Earls, now retired from Harvard, one of the creators of this concept, to learn more. He began by describing what led him to it:

> At the beginning of my career as a child psychiatrist in East Harlem in New York, it was very clear that characteristics of the neighborhood—positive and negative—were important in children's lives.[77]

And these weren't just the usual demographic "variables":

> It didn't matter so much what your income level was or what your race/ ethnicity or immigration status was. They could be contributing factors, but it seemed possible that people might even feel insecure in certain kinds of wealthy neighborhoods. It was also conceivable that in a poor neighborhood there was a high level of sharing and social activity, and that children might feel very secure, despite the fact that people didn't have fancy cars, fancy houses, or something like that.

He and Robert Sampson, then of the University of Chicago and now at Harvard, and others selected Chicago for a large-scale study more than a decade long. They hypothesized that collective efficacy would be linked to positive outcomes,[78] which they defined as neighbors trusting one another, sharing common values, and being willing to step in on behalf of the common good—such as supervising children and protecting the public order.[79]

The team compiled a comprehensive neighborhood-level data picture, including wealth, educational level, residential stability, crime rates, racial composition, immigration status, and much more.[80] They made videotapes of the social activity and physical appearance of 343 neighborhoods in Chicago and surveyed about eight thousand community members. Earls describes the kind of questions they asked about collective efficacy:

Let's say a young child needs help to cross a street. Is this the kind of neigh-borhood where it's very likely or not likely that someone would intervene and help that child?

If you saw a child skipping school, spray-painting graffiti, disrespecting an older person—are you likely to hold back or respond to that?[81]

On the basis of these and other questions, each neighborhood was rated on its level of collective efficacy.

Key Finding: In a 1998 report for the U.S. Department of Justice, the researchers summarized their results: in neighborhoods scoring high on collective efficacy, crime rates were 40 percent below those in lower-scoring neighborhoods.[82]

In their research articles, Earls, Sampson, and their colleagues are careful to state that "recognizing that collective efficacy matters does not imply that inequalities at the neighborhood level can be neglected."[83] The study found that collective efficacy did vary by neighborhood and was lower when community members were struggling with issues of poverty and immigration.

Key Finding: "Collective efficacy, not race or poverty, was the largest single predictor of the overall violent crime rate."[84]

This study concluded that there is no such thing as irredeemable "bad" kids. The well-being of every child depends on the child, the family, the school, and the neighborhood, including its collective efficacy.[85]

THE IMPACT OF THE COMMUNITY ON ADOLESCENTS

Murry and her colleagues assess the impact of community by looking at two concepts related to collective efficacy:

- **Community cohesion:** a marker of how much support parents and adolescents feel they have from neighbors and whether they feel they can depend on neighbors if they need help

- **Collective socialization:** a marker of whether neighbors help raise other people's children like their own[86]

I grew up in a community like that, so my husband, Norman, and I wanted this kind of community when we had children. I asked three questions of the people in communities we were considering: (1) Can you be yourself in this community? (2) If you had an emergency at two in the morning, could you comfortably call your neighbors for help? (3) Would they help you, and would you help them? After searching for more than a year, we found a place where people answered yes to these questions, and we've raised our children and grandchildren here. Rarely a day goes by when I'm not grateful for the place I call home for the support it provides to me and to my family.

Murry's studies have found that having a supportive community is especially important for boys. She speculates that perhaps boys seek independence from their families earlier than girls, so they need people beyond their families watching out for them.

Murry and neuropsychiatrist Uma Rao from the University of California, Irvine, are currently assessing the impact of exposure to the PAAS e-health program on cognitive and emotional regulation among adolescents. They are conducting fMRIs on youth before program exposure as well as afterward to see how the program is affecting functioning connectivity in the brain, an attribute that has been linked to better coping skills in risky situations. According to Murry:

> We're seeing incredible shifts in the decision-making processes of the brain through PAAS e-health as young people gain resistance efficacy skills to assess potential risky situations and subsequently decide to avoid them that explain why this program is an important pathway to buffer youth from [various types] of risk. More importantly, we're able to tell how different sessions affect different kids.[87]

In the end, Murry's dream is that this work will advance behavioral interventions as a form of behavioral precision medicine.

PROMOTING PARENTING STRATEGIES

When asked about the most important parenting strategies, adolescents tell us they want us to listen. Both Gunnar's and Murry's research shows that listening is linked to being sensitive and to knowing what is going on in adolescents' lives.

Adolescents also want us to listen with an understanding of adolescent development—to listen with our "when-I-was-a-child" mind as well as with our "now-I'm-an-adult" mind.

Adolescents want us to include them in disciplinary issues as well. Adults should be consistent, set limits, and explain the reasons for disciplinary actions, but they also should involve adolescents in figuring out how to deal with problems so they learn the skills of managing challenges as they grow up.

As Tony Earls says, if we care about the positive development of our children, we must look not only at our individual families but also at the people we surround ourselves with—our communities. Development is always about relationships.

Skill-Building Opportunities: Transforming Challenges into Opportunities for Learning Skills

The three key parenting strategies we just explored in the last section reflect a unique approach to managing challenging moments with adolescents. Here, we'll explore this approach—Skill-Building Opportunities—beginning with why it's unique.

1. **It's based on the knowledge that challenges can become opportunities.**
   Let's take adolescents playing video games and ignoring homework, refusing to clean up, partying, or more serious challenges. Rather than viewing this behavior as a reason to punish, we can see it as an opportunity to teach adolescents skills for learning to manage their own behavior.
2. **It's based on a developmental premise.**
   Adolescents need to feel that they have some choice in how they live. In fact, we all have that need for autonomy and agency, but it's particularly pronounced in adolescents. This approach meets that need.
3. **It's asset-inspired.**
   It focuses not on what adolescents are doing wrong but on the skills that they can use to solve challenges for themselves while working

within boundaries set by adults. In this way, it's very much inspired by the Positive Youth Development movement.

4. **It's solidly research-based.**

This approach is based on a relatively new area of research, Autonomy Support or Autonomy-Supportive Caregiving, and it applies to families, teachers, and all others who work with children and adolescents. We'll begin by looking at the research, briefly with young children, and then more deeply with adolescents.

JUST ENOUGH HELP: HOW AUTONOMY SUPPORT PROMOTES EXECUTIVE FUNCTION SKILLS

Stephanie Carlson is a pioneer in studying autonomy-supportive caregiving with young children, but when I first met her at the University of Minnesota in 2008, she was immersed in studying executive function (EF) skills, a topic we will explore in chapter 5.

Carlson and others have been studying EF skills because, as she says:

There's quite a bit of evidence now that executive function skills in early childhood predict academic achievement later on as well as school attendance, and graduation from college. There are longitudinal studies showing that early executive function skills predict physical health and even financial well-being later in life.[88]

One such study, conducted in Dunedin, New Zealand, followed more than a thousand children—born in the same city in the same year—from birth into adulthood.

Key Finding: The researchers from the Dunedin study found that children (assessed at three, five, seven, nine, and eleven years) with less self-control—an EF-based skill—in their first decade of life had worse health, had less wealth, and were involved with more crime as adults (assessed at thirty-two years) than those with greater self-control.[89] This finding held true regardless of IQ or social class, which usually have a lot to do with how children turn out. It also held true when comparing siblings who grew up in the same families: children with better self-control fared better as thirty-two-year-olds than their sibling with worse self-control.

Given the importance of EF skills seen in this study and numerous others, Carlson wondered, "What helps children learn these skills?" Carlson, Annie Bernier of the University of Montréal, and others began looking for answers, primarily through observing how parents, initially mothers, managed their children's behavior.[90]

Over the years, the researchers have observed three styles of parenting. Carlson explains these in her words:

- *One style is to be overcontrolling, where the caregiver is doing things for the child and not really allowing the child to have much of an active role.*
- *Another style is to be undercontrolling, sometimes called laissez-faire. What this means is to be uninvolved in what the child is doing, not really helping, even when children are struggling.*
- *The third style is what we call autonomy-supportive: recognizing that the child needs to play an active role and work to solve problems on their own, but at the same time letting the child know that you're there to support them and offer help—just enough help—when needed.*[91]

Researchers continue to find that this third approach—**autonomy-supportive caregiving**—is a positive force in children's lives.

You may be wondering: Does this approach make children so used to doing things their own way that they won't listen to their parents?

Just the opposite, actually. Autonomy-supportive caregiving is really about the child or adolescent learning skills to manage their own behavior with the adult giving guidance and setting rules. In fact, studies show that children who receive autonomy-supportive caregiving are more likely to follow the parents' rules, even without being told.[92]

Not only do autonomy-supportive parents foster the EF skills of working memory, cognitive flexibility, self-control, and reflection during the "task at hand, but they also support children's sense of competence and agency by providing children with choices, acknowledging their perspective, and allowing them to feel a sense of accomplishment."[93]

Is it possible that children might be good at EF skills because of the genetics they share with their parent, not just learning? For example, perhaps parents who use autonomy-supportive practices have good EF skills and their children inherit these skills. I was on the research team in a study addressing this question.

Key Finding: Autonomy support was a predictor of children's executive function skills, above and beyond parents' own executive function skills.[94] While these skills might be partly inherited, there was a clear association with autonomy-supportive parenting—and studies show that this can be taught.[95]

SOLVING PROBLEMS *WITH* THEM, NOT *FOR* THEM

Wendy Grolnick of Clark University is a pioneer in studying autonomy-supportive caregiving with children and adolescents. In graduate school at the University of Rochester in New York, she began working with Edward Deci and Richard Ryan on their now-classic research on motivation.[96] They showed that providing external rewards can decrease our internal motivation. She says:

> If someone's doing something really fun and interesting and you start rewarding that person for doing it, their motivation changes.
>
> For example, they're doing puzzles and you say, "We're going to give you $5 for every puzzle you solve." Of course, they do more puzzles because everybody likes money. When the experiment's over and they have an opportunity to do puzzles or something else, the people who were paid no longer want to do the puzzles.[97]

Grolnick thought: "Wouldn't it be interesting to think about motivation from the perspective of parent-child relationships?"

Motivation drives behavior. Grolnick's interest has been in the kind of motivation where people get excited about and value what they're doing, whether their motivation originally comes from within or from other people. "That behavior is likely to persist," she says. "People are much more likely to be happy and have better well-being."

Self-Determination Theory, developed by Deci and Ryan,[98] holds that people are motivated by inherent psychological needs. Like biological survival needs—water and food and shelter—having our psychological needs satisfied enables us to thrive. Grolnick calls them "nutrients required for growth, integrity, well-being."[99] We will explore the importance of meeting needs fully in chapter 4, but here's a brief overview.

Self-Determination Theory identifies three Basic Needs:

- We need to feel **relatedness**: to feel valued and loved, with a sense of belonging versus feeling unimportant and alienated.[100]
- We need to feel **autonomous**: to feel choiceful and behind what we do, versus feeling pressured and controlled.
- We need to feel **competent**: to feel effective and capable, versus feeling ineffective and unable to make things happen to affect our world.

As Basic Needs, feelings of relatedness, autonomy, and competence are not just good experiences to have; their satisfaction is crucial to people persisting at activities and thriving overall. Grolnick says, "There's a plethora of information across the whole range of ages of people, and in many, many different cultures showing that people whose needs are met experience greater well-being."[101]

Grolnick, like others who study autonomy-supportive caregiving, makes it clear that supporting autonomy is "not letting kids do whatever they want. It's not kids going off and doing their own thing." It's helping children feel choiceful.

Grolnick says this means understanding young people, offering choices, and solving problems *with* them, not *for* them. Like Carlson, Grolnick puts being controlling at the other end of the continuum:

Controlling means pressuring people, interacting with them from our own perspective. It's solving problems for children; it's using controlling language, such as "you have to," "you better."[102]

She admits that as parents, many of us use that kind of controlling language because *we* feel pressured and the stakes feel so high. And what better high-stakes example than homework?

In one study, Grolnick and her colleagues studied the impact of how parents help their children with homework.[103] The researchers gave homework assignments to a group of third graders and their parents, telling half of the parents that it was their responsibility to make sure their children learned this information and that the children would be tested on it later; the other half were simply told that this was a task to do together.

Then the researchers compared how the two groups of parents behaved, and it was like day and night. The parents who felt pressure for their child to perform tended to solve the problems for their child and to be more directive; in fact, they were pretty stern compared with the parents who didn't feel pressured to perform. They also found that the children in this group were less able to perform the tasks on their own.

It's evident that when parents feel *they* (not just their children) are being evaluated on their children's homework, they are more likely to solve problems *for* their children, rather than with them. Being autonomy-supportive doesn't just help young people to feel choiceful and accomplished—it actually improves their learning.[104]

The same applies for teachers. As Grolnick points out: "A number of studies show when teachers are more autonomy-supportive in the classroom, children are much more likely to be engaged in learning."[105]

Grolnick conducted her early studies before having children of her own. She watched parents be controlling and thought she would never be that kind of parent. But life has a way of teaching us lessons, and it can be a struggle between going on autopilot and using self-control to do what we think is right.[106]

> When I had my own children, I understood parents in a way that I hadn't before.
>
> I did tie their shoes for them at times when we were in a big rush. I also **felt like** making sure their homework was done right and making them sit there until they did it. I **wanted** to tell them what to wear so that they could look their best. In many cases, I did not follow through on these impulses, but I was surprised at how strongly I felt them!

Not only was Grolnick helping her children learn skills, she was learning skills herself.

In *The Good News About Bad Behavior*,[107] journalist Katherine Reynolds Lewis describes a movement that has grown up around this kind of research that's changing the way parents view "discipline" in the United States. Accordingly, a child's misbehavior is viewed as "a clue to a puzzle that can only be solved with the child's engaged cooperation and as an opportunity to help that child develop an important skill."

That's why I call these Skill-Building Opportunities. We are building our own skills as well as the skills of adolescents.

In reviewing the research over a number of years—especially how researchers like Carlson, Grolnick, and others measure these skills in their studies—I and my team, with feedback from Stephanie Carlson, have identified five foundational strategies we can use to help young people and ourselves promote skills in challenging times.

PROMOTING SKILL-BUILDING OPPORTUNITIES: THE FOUNDATIONAL FIVE

These "Foundational Five" Skill-Building Opportunities can help you develop autonomy-supportive caregiving skills.

1. **Check in on yourself.**
   Try to figure out why you are reacting to this situation as you are. What is the meaning of this situation for you?

   Remember that how we see behavior is how we respond. Our response to our children's challenging moments will set the tone for how they learn to resolve their challenges.

2. **Take your adolescent's view.**
   Try to figure out why your child might be behaving this way, what their goals seem to be, and what they can and can't do, developmentally. Then, respond with this understanding in mind, including how the child learns best.

   This is another way of listening more than you talk and listening with your "when-I-was-a-child" mind instead of only your "now-I'm-an-adult" mind.

3. **Share reasons.**
   Explain your point of view—what is expected and why. You are predictable and share reasons and limits in ways that help your adolescent take an active role.

   A great deal of research shows that children and adolescents are more likely to comply if they understand why they're being asked to do things and how their behavior affects others.

4. **Problem-solve together and provide choices.**
   Invite your adolescent to play an active role by engaging in joint problem-solving (including suggesting choices) versus fixing things for the child.

   This is the essence of Shared Solutions, which provides a problem-solving structure to use when resolving tough issues.

5. **Scaffold.**
   Build on what your adolescent is already doing well, follow their pace, and provide them with a challenge that's hard but not too hard and gives them a chance to develop and use their own Life and Learning Skills.

   We build supports around adolescents' behavior as they learn to do things for themselves.

Try Skill-Building Opportunities. Do they work for you?

Possibilities Mindset

I was sixteen and had recently met Norman, the man who would become my husband. We were just friends then, and he was taking me to his house, unannounced, to meet his family.

As we walked up the porch steps, we crossed paths with my sister-in-law-to-be (I'll call her Kay), rushing down the steps. She sported the teen rebellion look of the day: hair teased high, heavy makeup, very short shorts, and a top that was low and tight.

Hot in pursuit came my mother-in-law-to-be (I'll call her Rose), shouting, "If you dare leave this house looking like that, you'll never—*never*—get back in!"

Kay kept going. Rose stopped, but kept shouting: "Don't even *try* to come home. The doors will be locked!"

Rose noticed me and we were introduced. Her first words to me were about Kay: "She never listens. Does she have any idea what she looks like, dressing like that?"

I don't know what came over me. Maybe it was that my mother and many of my teachers had encouraged my opinions. I also sensed from Rose's vehemence that she'd lost this argument before, and Kay had been allowed to come home. So I asked, "Why'd you say you'd lock her out? I bet you won't."

Rose got quiet. Norman looked surprised. He was even more surprised by her response: "What should I say?" she asked.

She listened to a teenager, I thought. That was impressive.

I can't remember what I suggested. I do remember that Rose listened intently, asked a lot of questions, and said she wanted to try, because what she was doing wasn't working.

But the strife between Kay and her mother continued. They clearly cared a lot about each other. They became even closer after Kay's teen years, and they spent Rose's last years together. But at the moment, they were locked in this battle with no winners, only losers.

Norman would say, "She truly believes she'll make us better by criticizing us. It's probably how she was raised. She's doing what she knows."

I later learned that Norman had been criticized, too. When something went wrong (he dented the car, broke a favorite glass, forgot to do something he'd promised to do), criticism was what he thought he deserved. He'd push me as hard as he could to criticize him. And when I was provoked, I sometimes gave him what he expected but certainly didn't need.

Both patterns—Rose's with Kay, and mine with Norman—helped me to see how easy it is to want to change, and also how our histories can override our good intentions and we get stuck in painful cycles where there are only losers, no winners.

These were the seeds that eventually led to the concept of Possibilities Mindset, which is the belief that change is possible and that you have the efficacy to make that change. It's also a wondering mindset where you see a difficult situation as a challenge, not as a threat.

A Possibilities Mindset

- Things can be different and can get better.
- I try to understand why this happened and what I can do to make things better.
- I believe I can rally and figure out how to handle this.
- A challenge with a child can become an opportunity to bring about change in myself and find solutions.*

It's when we feel that the things we do don't matter—that there's no connection between what we do and how our child responds—that can lead to a loss of hope and an Adversity Mindset, which is the belief that change isn't possible and you couldn't make it happen anyway. It's a non-wondering mindset where you don't focus much on why this situation happened and instead feel threatened.

Adversity Mindset

- Things won't change—this is the way it is going to be in the future.
- I don't focus on the possible reasons why this happened and what's really going on.
- At this point in my life, I don't think I can change or have much of a choice in how I handle this kind of situation.

When I began the interviews for the qualitative study, I didn't expect to find a new concept. I just wanted to better understand what goes through parents' minds when they have a conflict with their adolescents. The more I talked with

---

* Very special thanks to Erin Ramsey, Jennie Portnof, Sarah Wolman, Shawn Bryant, Brandon Almy, and Phil Zelazo for thinking through these concepts together.

parents, however, the more I realized that I needed to go beyond everyday conflicts to the moments when we lose it, so I began to ask parents about that.

By "losing it," I didn't mean falling apart, fighting, yelling, becoming sad, or falling silent, though these things can happen. I meant the moments when we become reactive, not proactive, when we are not the parents we expect or want to be. I began to suspect that these are times when the parenting approaches of Shared Solutions, Autonomy Support, and Skill-Building Opportunities I've written about won't really work by themselves.

My intuition became that there was a view of the world based on specific beliefs and assumptions—a mindset—that mattered. If we could better understand it, we could manage these moments, and maybe then we could use these parenting strategies.

I'll share what I learned in the interviews and the follow-up study that points toward answers.

WHAT LEADS TO LOSING IT?

Ada lives in northwestern Louisiana. She describes her fourteen-year-old daughter Alyssa as "stubborn." When she wants to do something, she won't budge, and that leads to recurrent fights with her mother. In a recent one, Alyssa ran off to her aunt's house, where Ada discovered her and continued the argument until Ada found herself using words her own mother had used with her:

> Next time you leave this house without telling me, I'm calling the police
> and they're going to take you away.

She warned Alyssa: "You do the crime, you do the time."

Fear for Our Child Makes Us More Likely to Lose It

Ada's fear is that her fourteen-year-old is naive about the world, and this fear was stoked when she found out that Alyssa was visiting adult sites online and posting videos of herself dancing on social media. She began monitoring her daughter's online posts and didn't like what she found:

> They're doing these street dances. Nasty dancing, I call them. She'll post
> them on Instagram. I was like, "No, baby. You don't do that." I said,
> "There are perverts out there looking at these." I said, "Think about how
> easy it would be for them to look you up." I told her, "You lift yourself up
> to be somebody you can admire."

Ada sees her daughter as a follower, not a leader. Alyssa just started at a new school, so Ada doesn't know the families of her daughter's friends yet, but they seem quite permissive to her—letting their kids "stay out to any time at night, if they want to." Ada tries to share her life experience as a warning, to prepare her daughter for what the world is like. She also tries to be a role model, but Alyssa doesn't listen:

> She says, "Uh-huh, Mama," but it's like with everything I tell her. If she wants to do it, she's going to do it anyway.

The conflict between Ada and Alyssa about genuinely worrisome issues sheds light on two other elements that can lead us to lose it.

Adult Expectations as Triggers

When Ada told Alyssa that she was going to call the police if Alyssa ever ran away again, Alyssa lashed out at her: "You always want to call the police. For everything!" Ada pushed back:

> No, I don't *always* say I'll call the police. I say, "If you act your age and don't act like a child, I wouldn't have to call the police."

This exchange illustrates another factor that can lock us in conflict with our adolescents. As you saw in chapter 1, we may view adolescents' behavior through the lens of their being immature or deficient adults. Implicit in that view is the expectation that they should act older, but they fall short.

I've mentioned that we use our expectations as a measure of our successes or failures.[108] A clash between expectation and reality can be the impetus for conflict—but also for growth.

Breakthrough Years Study Finding: Twenty-nine percent of parents completely or mostly agree that "when children do things that are wrong,* I feel that at their age, they should know better." Another 42 percent slightly agree.

---

* In the survey, we asked the Possibilities Mindset questions using the same phrase, "when children do things that are wrong," so that parents would have an identical framework for responding. In our new research, we've changed the wording to "when I am in a challenging situation . . ."

Turning Challenges into Opportunities

Lucy, a mother of two from eastern Michigan, has struggled with giving her oldest, Andrew, now sixteen, more autonomy and agency. Standing in the way initially were her expectations of what he should be like. She said, "I was basing my expectations on my experiences of being a teenager myself." But that wasn't working. "The experiences of being a teenage girl and a teenage boy are different. Plus, he's definitely not like I was":

I was much more social. Everything revolved around friends. My son isn't like that. He's very introverted. He has a close group of about four friends, all from elementary and middle school. I kept trying to make him into somebody he wasn't. After a lot of butting heads, I realized I had to change.

We often have a hypothetical "normal" in our minds that can get in the way of our accepting what our children are like. When Lucy realized this—"I think my expectations were set unreasonably"—she was able to begin to let go of them: "At this age, he's his own person."

Reflecting—taking a pause—can enable us to realign expectations with realities, as Lucy did.

Just before he went to high school, I realized that there will be four years, then he's going to be in college. They're not little kids anymore. They're going to be moving forward, and you have no choice. You have to move forward, too.

That's the essence of parental development—our children grow and change, and we have to grow and change, too.

Soon after this realization, Andrew was hospitalized with mono and a strep infection, triggering an onset of anxiety in him. He seemed especially vulnerable. Like Ada, who was fearful about Alyssa, Lucy became fearful about Andrew. Her response was to try to resolve everything for him, leading back to "headbutting."

Lucy came to a second realization—that Andrew had to take a key role in managing his anxiety. It was just before Christmas, after they'd visited a doctor who recommended a gluten-free and dairy-free diet:

Andrew was in tears. He knew why the doctor wanted him to do it, but he said, "I don't think that it's fair. I don't think I'll be able to do it."

We talked and came to a compromise together. He'd do the dairy-free
before Christmas, and add the gluten-free after Christmas. Andrew fol-
lowed the diet for a time, but it didn't change things.

Andrew's anxiety also "caused a lot of issues where he became afraid
of contamination and resisted going to school." Here Lucy set a ground
rule—he had to go to school:

We didn't want him to stay home because we didn't want his anxiety and
compulsiveness to take over. We wanted him to push himself. He had to
develop a lot of gumption and strength to get over the fears. And he did a
good job.

To give him the autonomy he craved, Lucy and her husband asked
Andrew to figure out how to manage school. He developed an impressive
array of strategies, including carrying his school supplies in a foldout folder
so he wouldn't need to touch bare desks.

During the pandemic, Andrew's anxieties surged again as he, along with
the rest of the world, grappled with the fear of contagion from an invisible
virus coupled with near-constant messages of danger:

Another skill he developed: he speaks up for himself. We had the news on
the other day about the coronavirus and the death count, and he said, "Can
we please turn the news off? I really can't handle hearing about that right
now." He was able to set boundaries for himself.

Andrew was not alone in reacting to the news. The findings of a study
about the pandemic and mental health concluded that limiting sensational
news coverage may have helped protect children and adolescents against
mental health problems.[109]

Recognizing adolescents' developmental need for more autonomy and
agency helped Lucy turn away from trying to help by resolving things for
Andrew and toward helping him have opportunities to solve problems for
himself. Even so, as Lucy says, it isn't easy. If we see our child as vulnerable
or as difficult—and if we fear for them—it can be easy to keep trying to fix
things for them.

Breakthrough Years Study Finding: Forty-eight percent of parents completely or mostly agree that "when children do things that are wrong, I want to protect them from failing," while 31 percent slightly agree.

Fear of Being Judged as Parents

Ethan is the father of two sons, ages fifteen and nineteen, living in suburban New Jersey. Ethan says that his oldest son is smart but that things don't come easily for him:

> He was our first child, and maybe we doted over him too much. He had a speech delay, and has epilepsy, but not bad. I don't know if that's impacted him socially or changed his competence.

Ethan recently read an article saying it was important to let your child fail and realized how hard that was for him.

> If he has trouble with a paper, we'll help him instead of having him get a poor grade. I realize that maybe in the long term, it's really not helpful. Yet we still do it. I don't want to see him get a B-minus or a C. Maybe somehow, indirectly, it's a reflection on me if he gets a poor grade.

A B-minus or a C in a course for our child can also feel like a grade for our parenting.

Breakthrough Years Study Finding: Nine percent of parents completely or mostly agree that "when children do things that are wrong, my first thought is I've failed," while 24 percent slightly agree. In addition, 12 percent of parents completely or mostly agree that "when children do things that are wrong, I worry that I'm going to be judged negatively," while 29 percent slightly agree.

Interestingly, Ethan says he wasn't protected from failing when growing up:

My parents didn't do that with me, and it actually helped a lot because I saw where I failed and worked harder to succeed where I was lacking. I know it's not the best thing to do, but I still do it. I don't know why. I'm caught in this pattern.

I asked what it might take to change, if he wanted to. Ethan replied:

I hate to say it. With my oldest son, at this point, I don't think I will. With my younger son, we don't do it as much. Deep in my heart, in the long run, I know he'll be successful, whereas I worry more about my oldest son.

My last interview question with parents was: "What is one of the most important things you have learned in being a parent?" Ethan said:

I'm seeing for myself that I can't do everything for him, that he has to learn to fail. And I'm trying to break free of that as a parent. I've got to be honest—it's really hard.

Ethan was seeing this as helping his son learn to fail, while I see it as helping his son gain skills to manage making mistakes and learning from them.

FEELING THREATENED VERSUS FEELING CURIOUS

While talking to parents unearthed numerous underlying reasons for why we lose it, it was also clear that there was something more. Again, I suspected that there was a mindset—a view of the world—that mattered.

I had an insight when Ada was talking about Alyssa and said, "She could change, but she doesn't want to."

Similarly, Ethan admitted reluctantly that at this point in his life, he didn't believe he could change his behavior with his son.

But then there's Lucy and Andrew. They'd been locked in a no-win conflict, too, but the knowledge of his growing up and the onset of his anxiety had led Lucy to realize that she had to do things differently—she had to see Andrew for who he is, not who she wants him to be, and involve him in dealing with his fears.

So, sometimes things *can* change. What makes the difference?

When I looked at the parents' interviews through the lens of change, it was apparent that:

- **Parents who felt stuck** felt as if they'd tried everything and nothing worked.

- **Parents who *didn't* feel stuck** seemed to have a "wondering" mindset—they wondered about the reasons they or their children may have acted the way they did and they kept trying to figure it out.
- **Parents who became *unstuck*** often began by asking questions. What felt like a threat became a challenge—a doable challenge.

This is important, since feeling threatened versus feeling curious takes place via activity in different networks of the brain. Well-known author and psychiatrist Daniel Siegel of UCLA is eloquent about these differences between threats and challenges. Threats create a "no brain-state" that activates a protective response of fighting or fleeing, while challenges activate a "yes brain-state, when ideal learning can take place."[110]

BELIEVING YOU HAVE THE CAPABILITY TO MAKE A CHANGE

When Rebecca loses it, it's because she feels as if she's hitting a brick wall. She's trying different approaches, but her three teens tune her out. In contrast:

> *When I feel my kids are listening to me, when I feel they're reacting to what I say or doing what I asked them to—that makes me feel incredibly powerful.*

Rebecca is a good example of that something else: **when you believe you have the capability to make a difference, you reconnect with your child.**

Edward Z. Tronick of the University of Massachusetts, Boston, studies the social connection between parents and their children, especially young children.[111] He says it's a process of moving in and out of sync.[112] In fact, Tronick has found that moving in and out of sync with others—repairing a mismatch with a match—is not only normal, it can be a positive learning experience for both parent and child:

When you reconnect, he says, is when you create something new. "If you create something new, you grow."

So, reconnection with your child creates opportunity for growth and learning for both of you. That can lead to a Possibilities Mindset.

My thinking about a Possibilities Mindset has been deeply inspired by the foundational research and insights of Carol Dweck about a growth mindset (things can change) and similarly the research and insights of Albert Bandura about self-efficacy (I believe I can make a change).[113]

There was one parent story that, for me, helped tie everything together.

"A SOFT PLACE TO LAND"

Shannon and her husband have three sons and live in the Midwest. Shannon's journey toward change illustrates the grip that an Adversity Mindset can have and the power of a Possibilities Mindset to loosen that grip. Her journey began with her first child, Patrick:

> *I put way too much pressure on him to do everything right. He was the firstborn. He'd forget his trumpet and I'd go, "Sure, I'll leave work to bring you your trumpet." Or, "You're the star football player and now you're flunking English, so you won't get into college. Let's stay up all night and write that paper"—those kinds of things.*

A hot spot—an unresolved issue—from her childhood was tripping her up, as these issues can for most of us:

> *I realized it was fear-based parenting. I wasn't taken care of very well as a child, so I wanted to take care of Patrick. I was trying to meet my own unmet needs, but in the process, I was telling Patrick he wasn't capable.*

When I asked what helped her, she said she'd turned to spirituality and meditation, but everything came together in an aha moment:

> *Patrick had just graduated from high school. I wanted him to get away from his partying friends. My dad has a company—he could work there.*
>
> *We were in the airport. As he walked away to board the plane, I just lost it. I thought I'd wasted too much time on stuff that didn't matter. At that moment, I thought, "I need to do things differently with him and with my other kids."*

The realization that leads to a Possibilities Mindset doesn't have to be an aha moment like Shannon's. This insight and determination to change can evolve over time. But change does involve making a firm commitment to see and do things differently.

For Shannon—like for Lucy, the mother of Andrew—the impetus was that her son was growing up. Patrick would be leaving home for college that fall. Instead of "wasting too much time on stuff that didn't matter," she thought about the kind of parent she wanted to be:

> I started to think about what I wanted and saw I want to be a soft place to land. I want to show my kids that the expectations in our family are around kindness and contribution, not just performance. Performance matters, but it's not everything.

Shannon faced this issue again with her second son, Brendan. She'd moved away from being a helicopter parent, but there was more to learn:

> Brendan was injured playing football at seventeen and that may have been when things started to fall apart. One day, he came home and said, "Mom, I can't be around these kids talking about their Range Rovers." He had been going to a wealthy Catholic school.

He switched to the local high school, but soon began slacking off. When he turned eighteen, he figured out that school administrators weren't going to call his parents if he didn't show up, so he quit going to school altogether. Every morning was a battle. Shannon would yell at him to get up and go to school. Brendan would stand his ground: "I am *not* going."

> I'd say, "Brendan, you have to get up. You have to go to school." He was totally defiant. He ignored me. I'd get more demanding, but it was crazy for me to think that yelling at him was going to help.

After a couple of weeks of pitched battles, they sat down as a family and decided he could drop out if he got a GED and went to community college. Brendan followed through with a GED, but devolved back into doing nothing. Since he'd been a lifeguard, Shannon suggested becoming a paramedic, but after some community college classes, he told her, "No way am I going to be seeing kids hurt like that in accidents."

> At that point, he was still respectful and cared about what my husband and I think. I realized that if we kept going the way we were going, we might alienate him completely. To me, that was the worst thing that could happen.

I knew someone growing up who was oppositional, a partier. His
family alienated him and he's been living on the streets for twenty years. I
thought, "You know, Brendan could walk away."

It was an internal mindset shift, she says. She had been on a dark path of
feeling angry and scared. It broke her heart that one of her kids wasn't going
to graduate from high school and college. She was afraid that this was going
to be forever, that there was nothing they could do to change him. But she
learned to let go of thinking that she knew what his path should be.

As perhaps you can see, Shannon was in an Adversity Mindset and was
feeling threatened: *Nothing works. Things won't be any different. My child*
won't or can't change. I won't or can't change. I can't make a difference.

Shannon's impetus for change was figuring out what *she* as a parent
wanted to be. She couldn't change Brendan; she could only change herself—
but, in response, things might be different:

I asked myself, what's my point as a parent? I saw that my parenting was
not about Brendan's accomplishments so that I could feel good about
myself. It was about my relationship with him—not what he was doing, but
how we were together.

There were still expectations: that he should be able to turn
unconditionally to his family, no matter what; that he should be able
to go out, sustain himself, care about his work, and care about his
contribution.

I had to pause, and let it go, and begin asking questions. I had to
think of "new possibilities," rather than "He's not doing what I
think he should be doing. He has a life of doom." I had to meet him
where he was rather than assuming he would have the life I had
mapped out for him.

Over the years, Shannon can see that switching to a Possibilities Mindset
is working. Brendan got his own apartment, found a job, and joined a union.
Recently, Shannon saw something she'd never expected to see: her son was
studying for a test that could lead to a promotion at work.

Brendan was motivated to study! It was a moment of joy—a reminder that
I had handled things well, that challenging times pass, and to enjoy the
good times.

WHAT DO THE DATA SAY ABOUT ADVERSITY
AND POSSIBILITIES MINDSETS?

We developed two new scales to assess Possibilities and Adversity Mindsets among parents.* We found that parents mostly agreed with the factors behind Possibilities Mindsets and were more neutral toward the factors behind an Adversity Mindset, but, as expected, there were a lot of individual differences.

We found that:

- A Possibilities Mindset was positively correlated with a measure we used in our follow-up study of Involved-Vigilant Parenting (for example, parents were asked, "When you and your child have a problem, how often can the two of you figure out how to deal with it?" and "How often do you give reasons to your child for your decisions?"). It was also correlated in our follow-up study with a measure we used of Mindfulness in Parenting (for example, parents were asked, "When I'm upset with my child, I notice how I am feeling before I take action," and "I listen carefully to my child's ideas, even when I disagree with them").
- An Adversity Mindset was negatively correlated with these two parenting measures.

That's promising—these mindsets are related to parenting behaviors that have been shown to help children thrive in other studies, including those of Velma McBride Murry.[114]

We also found that the fears parents have when they're in conflict with their kids (that they've failed as parents, that they're going to be judged negatively, that they're losing control, that the children are out to get them, and that children need protection) are highly predictive of an Adversity Mindset.

---

* The **Adversity Mindset** scale consisted of two items rated on a six-point scale: (1) "When children do things that are wrong, I worry that they aren't going to change," and (2) "When children do things that are wrong, I worry that this is the way it is going to be in the future." The **Possibilities Mindset** scale consisted of four items, also rated on a six-point scale: (1) "When children do things that are wrong, I think about possible reasons why they may have acted that way"; (2) "When children do things that are wrong, I see it as an opportunity for me to better understand their thoughts and feelings"; (3) "When children do things that are wrong, I know it is specific to the moment and not a sign for the future"; and (4) "When children do things that are wrong, I see it as an opportunity for me to improve how I handle these situations." Note: we have subsequently revised this measure and are field-testing it.

When we looked at the correlations with how adolescents are doing (that is, outcomes reported by adolescents) in our study, we found:

- A Possibilities Mindset in parents is associated with their adolescents being more hopeful about their futures, while an Adversity Mindset in parents is associated with their adolescents reporting lower positive moods, more negative moods, less hopefulness about their futures, more stress, and more conflict with their parents.
- In addition, we found that an Adversity Mindset in parents shows a somewhat stronger relation to adolescent outcomes than a Possibilities Mindset, suggesting that negative perceptions might have more influence.
- Finally, we found that Possibilities and Adversity Mindsets are not strongly related and they both exist in varying degrees in us. One way to think of this is that each mindset has its own dial, rather than one dial with Adversity at one end and Possibilities at the other. That means that we can shift the way we see challenges either by dialing up Possibilities *or* by dialing down Adversity.

PROMOTING A POSSIBILITIES MINDSET

Our findings from the Breakthrough Years study indicate that mindsets matter. They also indicate that we may be better off in trying to limit the moments when we fall into an Adversity Mindset.

Friendships

It was at a meeting of adolescence researchers and funders that I had an aha moment about adolescent friendships. As an icebreaker, the organizer asked each of us to share an experience from adolescence that affected us positively throughout our lives.

I'd never been asked this question before but had some time to gather my thoughts while others spoke. One researcher told a story about his family:

I had an older brother who had a lot of potential, but his life began to crash and burn in his adolescent years. I realized how easily my path could have followed his path. A couple of different experiences—that inspiring

teacher, the right friends, the right coach, that right lucky experience or
unlucky experience—can drive our entire lives in such different ways.

He is so right about how much these adolescent years can shape our lives. And when he said "the right friends," I thought back to my ten-year-old self.

Against my wishes, my mother had sent me to summer camp. Why should I leave my home in West Virginia, get on a train by myself, and go far away to be with people I'd never met? I was miserably homesick, begging the counselors, the camp director, and my mother to let me come home—to no avail.

While there were clear rules established by the adults, in many ways this camp was run by the kids. The campers had a presiding "camp council" that adjudicated the tough issues—disagreements, broken rules, and so on. "Being bad," on the other hand, was built into camp life in daring but ultimately harmless ways—stealthy raids on counselors, stealing candy from other kids and then sharing the loot at an all-camp candy feast, and the threat of throwing the new campers into the lake on the last day of camp. We were constantly testing ourselves with Outward Bound–type sports and adventures.

Since I was stuck there, I slowly began making friends, particularly with Karen, a girl with long pigtails whose bed was next to mine, and with a "big sister" assigned to me by the camp. Thanks to friends, Karen especially, each day became a little more tolerable.

Over the next few years, I returned to the camp by choice. In my last year, my fellow campers elected me to co-head the camp council. That homesick child from West Virginia learned to do things that seemed unbearably hard and became a teen leader, mainly because of a supportive culture of other kids, within a positive set of traditions and expectations set by adults.

That was my realization at the conference table. And that girl with pigtails? We chose to attend college together as roommates. I was Karen's maid of honor at her wedding, and the first to arrive when her husband tragically died of a brain aneurysm almost forty years later. She was my matron of honor and the first to arrive when my mother died, driving hundreds of miles to be with me. We are there for each other and will be, forever.

With that story and aha moment in mind, I looked at the research on adolescence, asking:

- Can friendships in adolescence be an intentionally positive influence?
- What factors make a positive or negative difference?

What is clear is that the effects of social connections on adolescents are more nuanced than many of us realize.

FRIENDS: FORCES FOR GOOD OR FOR EVIL?

When we think of adolescent friendships, we tend to think of being easily influenced—even led astray—by others. But there's a disparity between what parents say about adolescents in general and how they view their own child.

Breakthrough Years Study Finding: Sixty-six percent of parents with children ages nine to nineteen said that "easily influenced by other kids" is a good description of young people their child's age, while only 29 percent said this phrase describes their own adolescent.

That's a big gap. To me, it also says that with the right culture, other young people can be positive rather than negative influences. That's what I told the group when recounting my camp experience. Can we adults help foster and design an intentional climate for adolescent friendships where the culture is built around a deep understanding of adolescent development—promoting autonomy and agency, support, respect, and competence?

We know that parents are critically important during adolescence—probably more important than some realize—but so are peers. Think back to Jennifer Silvers's research showing how strongly adolescents' brains reacted to pictures of bullying, and the research of Larry Steinberg showing that simply being watched by peers affected whether adolescents took more negative risks when they played the Stoplight game.

The Stoplight game captured adolescents' negative risk choices in the critical moment of decision when a friend is watching. But is it possible that the adolescent's choice in that moment is influenced not just by the fact that a friend is watching but also by other factors within the friendship?

KEY FACTORS IN ADOLESCENT DECISION-MAKING: PEER EXCLUSION AND INCLUSION

Jennifer Pfeifer suspected that simply being around peers in and of itself didn't tell the whole story because it neglects the group environment. What was happening in the group at that moment? What has happened in the past?[115]

In a 2013 pilot study,[116] Pfeifer and her colleagues looked at the immediate social situation—specifically "whether rejection and social exclusion change adolescent decision-making." She says:

> I think it's an important question because rejection is pervasive in adolescence. It's something that adolescents really care about and are concerned about. They want to be accepted by their peers![117]

Twenty adolescents ages fourteen through sixteen were told that they'd be playing online games with two other young people their age who lived in different states. In truth, these peers weren't real—they were created by the researchers so that the study participants would have exactly the same social experience.

To "meet" the peers, the study participants recorded a brief video where they said their name and an activity they enjoyed. They also filled out forms about themselves, including a series of questions assessing their openness or resistance to peer influence.

First, they practiced the Stoplight game without peers watching. Following that, they watched the computer-generated peers each take a turn playing the Stoplight game (to make it feel more like an interaction). Then, the adolescents played the Stoplight game while the two computer-generated peers they'd just met "watched" them.

Next, they all played a game called Cyberball,[118] where the same two peers (shown in animation on a screen) throw a ball back and forth to each other and to the study participant, who is initially included during the first round, then rejected a lot in the second round.

Afterward, the participant plays the Stoplight game again with the same peers "watching" to see how rejection affects the risks the participant takes when approaching yellow lights.

Pfeifer and her colleagues found that after being rejected, the adolescents generally took more negative risks—ran more yellow lights. But not all young people reacted in the same way. Pfeifer explains:

> There were increases in risk behavior after social exclusion for kids who you might characterize as being more susceptible to peer pressure—when they felt excluded, they tended to make riskier decisions the next go-round.

Key Finding: While some might think that being excluded leads to negative risk-taking, this study shows that it's not a cut-and-dried situation. Susceptibility to peer influences also plays a part.

This wouldn't surprise anyone with adolescents in their lives. Both the present circumstances and the adolescent's history determine how much adolescents are affected by rejection.

In a larger follow-up study that included 122 adolescents, ages eleven through seventeen,[119] Pfeifer and her colleagues found that adolescents are more likely to plan to take certain negative risks, like risky drinking, illegal behaviors, and substance use, if they expect that they will be liked more—that is, there will be a social benefit—whereas those who did not see a social benefit were less likely to take these negative risks.

But as always, adolescents differed from each other. Those who had been bullied or treated aggressively by peers saw greater social benefits to taking risks, suggesting that kids who are victimized are more vulnerable to peer influence around negative risk-taking.

HOW DOES THE QUALITY OF PEER RELATIONSHIPS AFFECT NEGATIVE RISK-TAKING?

If you had to describe a positive relationship with a friend from your adolescence, what would you say? What about a negative relationship?

Eva Telzer and her team defined quality as feeling supported and the lack of conflict with friends as central to positive relationships.[120]

They incorporated these dimensions into a 2015 study of forty-six adolescents in the ninth and tenth grades (ages fourteen through sixteen). Each night, before bed, the study participants checked off whether they'd experienced any conflict with their friends, such as arguing with them.

During the same period, they also completed a questionnaire about how much support they'd received from their friends in the past month (for example, "I could count on my friends when I needed to talk," or "My friends showed that they understand me"). They completed the same tasks a year later, at ages fifteen through seventeen.

During both periods, they also indicated how much time they spent with friends. A few months later, they filled out still another form—on how often they'd engaged in negative risky behaviors—and they also played the

BART risk-taking game (which, as you may remember, involves pumping up a balloon on a screen, but if you pump too much, the balloon might explode).

The results showed that young people who had more conflict with their friends took more risks on the BART and reported an increase in real-life negative risky behavior. If they had more supportive relationships, they were less likely to take negative risks, even if they also had more conflict.

Key Finding: While some may think that how much time adolescents spend with friends affects negative risk-taking, this study found that support from friends—not the amount of time spent together—is what matters.[121]

Eveline Crone of Erasmus University, Rotterdam, in the Netherlands, had similar findings from her studies of children over time:

We found that children who have higher friendship quality showed faster development of the medial prefrontal cortex. We interpreted that as when they grow up in a safe environment, that helps their brain development![122]

Breakthrough Years Study Finding: Twenty-nine percent of adolescents reported that their friends are almost always supportive, and 41 percent said most of the time—totaling 70 percent. Another 16 percent said about half the time, with 11 percent reporting some of the time and 3 percent never.

WHAT ABOUT ROMANTIC RELATIONSHIPS?

Ahna Suleiman spent years running school-based health clinics and conducting health interventions. Despite the fact that romantic relationships were top of mind for young people and the latest CDC figures indicate that 21 percent of high schoolers are sexually active,[123] there was surprisingly little research on this topic.[124] So she conducted a study of forty adolescents between the ages of fifteen and nineteen, asking them to reflect on their romantic relationships as well as studying their implicit attitudes about dating and sex.[125]

She found that there were many reasons adolescents formed romantic relationships, but—perhaps surprisingly—the young people in her study hadn't thought much about the characteristics of someone they want to date. She also found that while parents may set rules about dating—"do this, don't do that"—they may not ask questions that prompt deeper thinking about the characteristics of dating partners. This finding presents an opportunity for adults to ask our children: "What matters to you in a relationship?" Or "What do you love about this person?" Suleiman says if we don't help them think about their values, we're missing a big opportunity.

FRIENDS' INFLUENCE VERSUS PARENTS': GETTING A CLEARER PICTURE

Perhaps one reason we focus mainly on the "dos and don'ts" when talking to young people about dating is that we're held captive by the view that other kids lead our kids astray and we focus on protecting them. Eva Telzer, Kathy Do, and Ethan McCormick of the University of North Carolina, Chapel Hill, decided to investigate friends' influence versus parents' influence head-on in a 2020 study[126] involving thirty-nine adolescents and their parents that asked:

1. How do young adolescents, twelve to fourteen years old, balance being themselves—staying true to their views—and fitting in with others, especially when there are conflicting attitudes?
2. When do they shift their attitudes?
3. If they shift, are they more influenced by parents or by peers and are they more likely to shift toward positive or negative views of behavior?

The researchers intentionally selected this age group because others have found that twelve-to-fourteen-year-olds are especially open to their experiences. In the study, they first asked the adolescents and their parents to rate a list of more than a hundred everyday behaviors, covering positive behavior (working hard in school, volunteering) and negative behavior (smoking a cigarette, cheating on a test) on a scale from 1 (very bad) to 10 (very good).

Two weeks later, the adolescents returned to the lab and were introduced to a peer through a photograph and a taped recording. In actuality, this peer was created by the research team to match the study participant—same age, same race/ethnicity, same gender.

The experiment itself took place in a brain scanner. The participant was shown a screen where each behavior, one at a time, was listed—for example, drinking and driving. Above it, they saw their parent's and the peer's ratings for this behavior, and they were asked to rate it again. You can see the possibilities: the participants could assign a rating similar to the one they made two weeks earlier (they weren't shown their previous rating), or they could be influenced by their parent's or the peer's ratings.

Prevailing wisdom would say that they would be affected by their parent's or peer's views, but that wasn't necessarily the case. The researchers found that 65 percent of the time, the participants' ratings didn't change over the two weeks, suggesting that they stayed true to what they actually believe, even in the face of conflicting opinions from others.

Those who shifted to be more like their peers were likely to shift in a positive direction—to rate something that was positive (like doing volunteer work) even more positively than before when the peer gave it a positive rating. The researchers also found that peers' ratings were not more influential than those of parents.

Key Finding: While peers are typically seen as a negative influence, this study reveals that adolescents are more likely to be influenced in positive ways, not negative ways. Although 66 percent of parents in the Breakthrough Years study report that "easily influenced by others" is a good description for young people their child's age, 65 percent of adolescents in this study actually held firm in their original beliefs when put to the test.

ONCE AGAIN, THERE ARE INDIVIDUAL DIFFERENCES

Do you have more than one child? If you do, like I do, you'll probably tell me how different these children are from one another, starting even in the earliest days. Mine certainly are. Pediatrician Jack P. Shonkoff of Harvard University says that "science is screaming this fact":

If children live in the same environments and share the same conditions, do
they all end up with the same life outcomes? Of course not. Some children are
more sensitive to what's going on around them, some roll with the punches.
Some kids get sick more, some kids get sick less. All in the same family.[127]

Shonkoff says that "science is beginning to explain this commonsense
observation at the molecular level—understanding how similar experiences
interact with each child's unique genetic potential, which, in turn, is continu-
ously shaped by the ongoing experiences and personal relationships children
have as they develop over time.

We've seen that some adolescents are more susceptible to peer influence
than others in the studies I've been describing. Eva Telzer and her team have
explored the research on whether there are neurobiological biomarkers that
can help explain these differences. They find promising evidence from psychology, biology, genetics, and neuroscience. It's a new area, they write, one
that researchers are just beginning to "unpack."[128]

Their team is doing a number of studies on this subject[129] and they've
begun to classify adolescents into those who are highly sensitive to their environment at the neural level and those who aren't, based on brain scans.[130]
They've found that those adolescents who are low in sensitivity are less affected when exposed to prosocial and antisocial peer groups. The opposite
is true for those who are highly sensitive: if they're exposed to antisocial
norms, they'll be more likely to engage in more of that behavior, but if they
are exposed to prosocial norms, they'll be more likely to behave prosocially.
This is not bad news, Telzer concludes. In fact, it's very good news:

Heightened neural sensitivity does not place adolescents at risk. Most
importantly, being highly sensitive can actually allow youth to thrive if
they're in the right environment. This—I think—is key.[131]

You may have heard the terms "orchid children" (those highly influenced
by their environments) and "dandelion children" (those less influenced)[132] to
describe these differences in children, but I am wary of assigning children to
groups, even given the research from Telzer. I know how easy it is for people
to see a child in one group (an orchid, for example) and then to think "once
an orchid, always an orchid," but that's not necessarily so. Longitudinal
research on temperament by the late Jerry Kagan of Harvard University did
indeed find that some children are more reactive to their environments than

others in infancy—they become physically agitated and distressed by new experiences so they tend to behave in a reserved manner until they become comfortable. But they don't necessarily stay that way. Kagan told me, "I start with twenty out of one hundred of these infants; at adolescence, seven will be very introverted." The other thirteen will look average, but not highly bold and outgoing. **Biology**, he said, **is a "push," not a determination.**[133]

Jay Belsky of the University of California, Davis, takes on the issue of orchid and dandelion children directly.[134] First, his studies show that not all aspects of the environment have the same effects on different children. Second, he's found that the overwhelming majority of young people are not like orchids (perhaps 7 percent are) or like dandelions (he puts it at 10 percent). Most are what he calls mosaics.

The trick is not to let a characteristic define children or to put them into ironclad boxes with labels but to understand that there isn't just one way to be, and that differences—or mosaics, as Belsky puts it—are normal.

PROMOTING POSITIVE FRIENDSHIPS

Like with much research, studies of friendships in adolescence often seem to conclude with "it depends." Whether adolescents are susceptible to negative or positive influences from their friends *depends* on their biology and their neurology, their past histories and their current circumstances. And it *depends* on the adults in their lives.

While we can't do anything to change the events of the past, we can do everything about the present and the future. We've already talked about parenting and problem-solving strategies, Skill-Building Opportunities, and Possibilities Mindsets that we can use. We can also help create **the right environments** with friends where there are risks—positive risks—that help adolescents feel choiceful and supported to set and reach their goals. That's what we'll look at next.

Positive Risks

On a school camping trip, twelve-year-old Ingrid's best friend urged her to do something risky. It happened when Ingrid and a group of girls were playing tetherball outside the cabin that she, her best friend, and the "popular girls" shared:

> *My best friend comes out of the cabin with all the popular girls and whis-*
> *pers to us,* "Come on, we're going to the boys' side of camp."
> *I'm like,* "What?"
> *She's like,* "Come on, they're all doing it."

Ingrid had seconds to decide. It wasn't a big negative risk, as risks go, but for Ingrid, it mattered.

> *I'm like,* "You could get expelled. I'm not doing that."
> *She's like,* "Come on, it'll be fun."
> *I'm like,* "Absolutely not. You shouldn't do that, either."

Her friend pushed back:

> *She said,* "Live a little."
> *I'm like,* "I will live a little, but I will not go to the boys' side of camp."

Ingrid was able to make a quick decision because her father had talked with her before the class trip, outlining possible temptations and consequences, including expulsion.

Ingrid tried to reason with her best friend, but she went anyway, Ingrid thinks, because she wanted to fit in with the popular girls. Ultimately, nothing happened because an adult was standing guard at the boys' side of the camp. When the girls saw him, they ran back.

Ingrid could reel off the repercussions of doing something risky because she'd thought them through in advance. If she was expelled, she might have to switch schools, lose her close friendships, and carry an expulsion on her school record. She said to herself, "Why would I risk everything just to go to the other side of camp?"

Ingrid's relationship with her father is a trusting one. She describes him as a "strict parent" but sees him as on her side. Yet it was more than having a quality relationship:

- **Her father had helped her think about possible scenarios and consequences**—a tactic that a number of adolescent parenting programs foster. Importantly, too, he'd done so in a realistic way, without dramatic exaggerations.

- **She's had opportunities in her life to do positive things that are equally thrilling, scary, and "risky."** Taking a drama class gave her an exciting chance to challenge her fear of acting onstage. She'd been terrified but performing was also gratifying, so she'd practiced with her drama teacher and with the other students until she became able to stand in front of an audience and sing and dance. Because Ingrid had taken these positive risks in her life, she had less of a need to take a negative risk.

Let's assume that many adolescents need some experiences that are thrilling, scary, exciting, where they're testing themselves.[135] These experiences and the environments that provide them can help them grow and learn.[136] So the question becomes: What kinds of risks will lead to learning and growth, and how can we help to provide those? That—plus new insights into the internal and external factors that motivate and shape adolescent risk-taking—is what we'll explore in this section.

FIRST, LET'S REDEFINE "RISK"

I thought hard about saying "positive risk." I have wise colleagues who think that the word "risk" can trigger such negative and false assumptions about adolescents as harmful risk-takers that it is not worth using the word.

I decided in the end to stick with "risk" but to try to expand its meaning by including the times in life when a risk is positive. So let's look at risk with a new lens.

Simply stated, a risk is an action with an uncertain result—good, bad, or neutral. Natasha Duell of the University of North Carolina and Larry Steinberg of Temple University[137] define risks as entailing *rewards* (the possibility of gain) and *costs* (the possibility of loss). The size of both can vary, maybe neither happens, and achieving the rewards or paying the costs is uncertain. Adriana Galván of the University of California, Los Angeles, adds that since you don't know what will happen, you have to trust your own ideas, so you're vulnerable.[138] Daniel Siegel writes in his book *Brainstorm*: "Risk breathes new life into rigid ways of doing things."[139]

LEARNING TO BE BRAVE

Since adolescents take more risks than younger children or older adults, some have assumed that they believe they're more immune to danger. Why else would they want to watch scary movies or go on terrifying amusement park rides? But that explanation turns out to be untrue. Ron Dahl of the University of California, Berkeley, has found that the hormones of puberty, including testosterone, appear to increase the activation of fear circuits in the brain, making them *more* reactive to threat, not less.[140]

And in fact, Dahl and his colleagues have noted that this has been an enduring paradox in the research.[141] Studies show that adolescents are quite often aware of the consequences of doing dangerous things,[142] such as swimming with sharks or jumping off a roof—though they may take longer to consider their answers than adults.[143]

So, if they know (or are told) better, *why* do they still take risks, even dangerous ones? In a study of hormonal changes and brain development over time, Dahl and his colleagues realized that this paradox makes perfect sense:

> As these hormones—testosterone and the other hormones of puberty—go
> up, the capacity to activate reward and excitement goes up, too.[144]

Dahl and his colleagues have been researching "how the two sets of circuits—the fear and the reward excitement circuitry—interact more as puberty occurs."[145] He continues:

> Kids want the feeling of thrills. You can't have a thrill without fear. They
> don't go on roller coasters and watch horror movies because they're
> fearless. They do it because they like thrills.[146]

Dahl sees what researchers have called sensation-seeking—"the tendency to seek novel and thrilling experiences[147]—as adaptive because it enables young people to learn to face fear. In essence, they learn to be brave. He references Mark Twain in observing that courage is mastery of fear, not absence of fear.[148] Dahl says:

> This idea of overcoming our fears is something that's admired across
> all cultures. Heroes are basically people who can be brave in important

*circumstances—whether it's a firefighter or a soldier or an everyday hero
helping others. Being brave is a valued quality.*

**How do you learn to be brave? Not by being fearless, but by learning
to do the right thing even when you're afraid** *[emphasis mine]. How do you
do that if you don't practice?*[149]

That's just what Ingrid was doing when she practiced hard to overcome
her fear of performing onstage.

Key Finding: While some think adolescents are immune to fear, that's not
so. Adolescents can feel fear intensely, but they're driven to learn to overcome it, to try to be bold. This can be seen as a developmental necessity.

DO INDIVIDUAL ADOLESCENTS
DIFFER IN SENSITIVITY TO REWARDS?

Because of the variations in individual development, Eveline Crone wanted
to conduct longitudinal studies—to follow the same children as they grow
up. It's an expensive proposition in neuroscience, but, as she says, "If we
truly want to answer developmental questions, then we need longitudinal
designs!"[150]

Crone's dream became a reality in 2011. The Braintime Project began
following 299 adolescents spanning the adolescent years, ages eight through
twenty-five, at the beginning of the study.

In a study using this sample, led by Barbara Braams, then a doctoral
student of Crone's at Leiden University[151] (and now at Vrije Universiteit,
Amsterdam), researchers included 254 of those young people. They focused
on the nucleus accumbens (NAcc), an important region in the brain's reward
circuitry. This area of the brain's ventral striatum is also very sensitive to hormonal changes, like changes in testosterone. The researchers were looking
for age-related changes in NAcc activity in puberty (including as a function
of testosterone levels), so the participants were assessed at the study outset
and then two years later.

At both checkpoints, participants played a gambling task in the scanner
and took the balloon BART test that we've discussed. Testosterone samples
were collected through their saliva. The researchers found that testosterone
levels showed a sharp increase for boys and a more modest increase for girls

starting at approximately age ten. For girls, testosterone levels stabilized at about age fifteen and for boys at about age eighteen, suggesting not only a steeper but also a prolonged trajectory of testosterone change in boys than in girls.

As expected, the researchers found that adolescents became increasingly sensitive to rewards as they entered puberty (as shown by NAcc activation). This sensitivity peaked in mid-adolescence, at about ages fifteen through seventeen. But two other findings were more surprising:

- Not every adolescent was a negative risk-taker. Some increased in risk-taking; others *decreased*.
- Individuals with higher testosterone levels—both boys and girls—showed higher activity in the NAcc in response to rewards.

As expected, there are individual differences in sensitivity to rewards and to risk-taking among adolescents and testosterone level is yet another factor that can make a difference.

But that's not the whole story.

CULTURE AFFECTS RISK-TAKING, TOO

In cultures worldwide, adolescents respond differently to brain development and hormonal changes in the transitional period between childhood and adulthood. And, interestingly, there's a connection with testosterone.

So, exactly what does testosterone do? Dahl's conclusions are insightful:

It's a hormone that activates social motivations—seeking social bonds and learning about and seeking social status. This is a really interesting story![152]

Testosterone is elevated in babies as they form important relationships with their caregivers. Then it drops and stays low until puberty, when it rises again, first in girls because they begin puberty earlier, then in boys. While testosterone elevates sensation-seeking—thus providing young people with new opportunities to learn to be brave—Dahl says it also plays another role in adolescence:

Testosterone sensitizes individuals to be motivated to figure out how to be admired—and to be very sensitive to being diminished or disrespected.[153]

One of his favorite stories of how being admired varies across cultures comes from a conference he participated in with the Dalai Lama. The American researchers were discussing the role of testosterone in the United States as adolescents transition to middle school, where being admired involves fitting in and social status. According to Dahl, the Buddhist monks told the conference participants that in the monastery, the boys compete over being kind and compassionate, because that's the way to be admired in that setting.

The social context dramatically affects brain systems and behavior. For example, if assertiveness is more admired for boys than girls, you would see this expressed in behavior. Biology drives young people of all genders to search for their niche, but culture shapes how this is expressed.

WHAT'S THE PREVALENCE OF NEGATIVE RISK-TAKING IN THE UNITED STATES?

The Youth Risk Behavior Surveys by the Centers for Disease Control and Prevention (CDC) have tracked negative risky behavior among U.S. high school students since 1991.[154]

Their 2019 data show that the typical prevalence hovers around 5 to 9 percent for rarely or never wearing seat belts (5.9 percent), driving after drinking (5.5 percent), and smoking cigarettes (8.8 percent).[155]

Below are their most recent data on substance abuse, comparing 2011 and 2021 (note: "currently" is defined as at least once in the last month).[156]

The Percentage of High School Students Who:	2011 Total	2013 Total	2015 Total	2017 Total	2019 Total	2021 Total	Trend
Currently drank alcohol	39	35	33	30	29	23	▼
Currently used marijuana	23	23	22	20	22	16	▼
Currently used an electronic vapor product†	—	—	24	13	33	18	◇
Ever used select illicit drugs	19	16	13	13	13	13	▼
Ever misused prescription opioids‡	—	—	—	14	14	12	▼
Currently misused prescription opioids§	—	—	—	—	7	6	◇

†Variable introduced in 2015.
‡Variable introduced in 2017.
§Variable introduced in 2019.

◇ No change

▼ In right direction

Source: CDC, "Youth Risk Behavior Survey: Data Summary and Trends Report: 2011–2021."

What's important to note is that a number of these negative risky behaviors have declined over time, revealing that changes within the U.S. culture seem to be affecting adolescents' behavior.

WHY DO ADOLESCENTS TAKE RISKS?

As we've seen, a number of adolescence researchers have shifted their views about risky behavior,[157] including Eveline Crone:

We saw reward sensitivity in almost all adolescents in my studies, but the actual risk-taking behavior—the reckless, thrill-seeking, rebellious risk-taking behavior—we only saw that in a small percentage of the adolescents. I thought, "Why do they have this reward sensitivity when only a small percentage engages in excessive risk-taking?"[158]

This led Crone to a breakthrough moment:

I now think that it helps you to be explorative, to look at different options and seek out different alternatives, to find your way in new social worlds.

Key Finding: Reward sensitivity has typically been seen as leading to negative risks, but now it is increasingly also seen as enabling adolescents to explore, develop new friends, find new interests, and try new things—all developmentally necessary.

BEYOND "THE ANGEL ON YOUR SHOULDER": A NEW MODEL OF ADOLESCENT DECISION-MAKING

Jennifer Pfeifer and Nick Allen are among those who have challenged the narrative that adolescent development should be seen as a battle between the reward system and the cognitive control system.[159] Pfeifer says:

It's not that these self-regulatory networks are like the angel on your shoulder.[160]

Self-regulatory networks can enable you to plan how to achieve any kind of goal, including, she says, "goals that adolescents' parents might not approve of." Similarly, the ventral striatum—a key part of the brain's reward system—is involved when young people make selfless choices that serve others. In fact, both of these systems can help young people achieve greatness or mischief:[161] the two don't need to be in conflict with each other.

It's rare to talk to a group of people about adolescence without someone naming the conflict between the so-called lizard brain (the emotional brain) and the wizard brain (the cognitive control system). Although educators tell me they try to ensure that the lizard brain is not seen as bad or primitive and the wizard brain is not seen as good or advanced, when I hear people using this analogy, they tend to simplify these concepts, pitting emotion against reason as a key theme in adolescent development. It is very clear that new models that follow the science are much needed.[162]

That's exactly the challenge that Pfeifer and Elliot Berkman, also of the University of Oregon, have taken on. The resulting model they created has several distinguishing features. First, since many parts of the brain are involved when adolescents make decisions, they describe their model as "unified."[163] Pfeifer explains:

> By unified, I mean that there's actually one system in the brain that we know integrates all these different inputs—all these values that your brain is calculating about how different behavioral choices might serve your different and potentially competing goals.

Although others may see decision-making as either-or choices, emotion versus reason, it's more complex than that and this model recognizes this.[164]

Second, when adolescents make decisions like whether to study or go to a party, they weigh various value inputs (for example, how they would fit in with the people at the party, the chances of a good time, the downsides of not studying, and so forth). Importantly, all of these various value inputs influence their decision-making options. This is why Pfeifer and Berkman call this a "value-based model."

Third, in making decisions, adolescents are exploring who they are and who they want to be. They are, in Berkman's words, "trying out different identities." This model is based on the developmental necessity of exploring their identities.[165] In effect, the model moves away from an adult perspective of adolescence where young people are incomplete adults toward an adolescent perspective rooted in their need to explore, learn, and figure out who they are.

Key Finding: Adolescent decision-making has been seen as a struggle between the emotional and rational parts of the brain, but new studies point to a complex interplay between many parts of the brain that is driven by what matters to adolescents as they explore their values and identity.

NOW, ABOUT POSITIVE RISKS . . .

We know that the attraction to rewards increases in adolescence. Since this attraction to rewards can help adolescents explore and understand the possibilities open to them, and since this attraction can be instrumental in helping adolescents shape their identities, what if adolescents were offered many positive risk-taking experiences in the right environments that helped them create their identities?

In a 2019 article,[166] Natasha Duell, now a postdoctoral student at the University of North Carolina, and her doctoral advisor, Larry Steinberg of Temple University, report that a search of the literature yielded only three studies on positive risk-taking, compared with thousands of studies on negative risk-taking. Let me emphasize that: *only three studies on positive risk-taking!* These three studies reveal that the same young people who are more likely to take positive risks are also more likely to take negative risks, possibly because they're more drawn to risk in general.[167]

If young people were offered more opportunities for taking positive risks, might that help channel their drive to take risks in constructive ways? In 2020, Duell and Steinberg continued their inquiry with a study of 223 adolescents, ages sixteen through twenty.[168] Their measure of positive risk-taking included:

- **Activities**, like taking a class where the adolescent knows nothing about the subject or it seems challenging
- **Actions**, like standing up for what they believe is right even though someone might disagree
- **Relationships**, like starting a friendship with someone new when they're not sure how their other friends would react

They found that both positive and negative risks are associated with higher sensation-seeking, but positive risk-takers aren't likely to be impulsive or score poorly on the BART or the Stoplight task, and they are more engaged in school.

That's an important finding and goes a long way in defining what the right environment can be. And those environments can be at home, in the community, and in schools. "Schools," Duell says, "could provide opportunities for students to take positive risks through extracurricular activities like sports, theater, student journalism, and student government. Similarly, schools could also offer the opportunity to take advanced classes and more chances for class participation."[169]

THE GOOD, THE BAD, AND THE FUN

In 2016, Eva Telzer surveyed existing research on the limbic system that underlies reward sensitivity. While the older view is that this system is related to increased risk, Telzer emphasizes that this system can also be related to *decreased* risk-taking behavior.[170]

This finding promotes a more constructive view of adolescent development:

> *It challenges the widely supported model of adolescence as a period of heightened vulnerability by suggesting that traditionally negative behaviors like risk-taking could foster positive development if those risks are taken to benefit others!*[171]

There's more. In 2020, Telzer and Crone and their colleagues published a study on risk-taking and positive—that is, prosocial—behavior.[172] Led by Neeltje Blankenstein of Leiden University, this study followed 210 adolescents in the Braintime Project, the longitudinal study mentioned earlier.

Their measure of prosocial behavior included how often the young person did any of the following:

- **Sacrificed their own goals to help a friend** or peer with their goals
- **Helped a friend find a solution** to their problem
- **Gave money to a friend or a peer** because they really needed it

Summarizing the findings, Telzer says that both positive and negative risk-taking "tend to be predicted by a similar behavioral trait."

What's that trait? It's not just sensation-seeking—it's fun-seeking!

These researchers define fun-seeking as the desire for rewards and the willingness to pursue rewards that are fun. For example, "I am always willing to try something new if I think it will be fun."

Helping others is rewarding and can be fun. Eva Telzer shares these new conclusions with excitement:

> *Adolescents are especially well poised to take risks with the broader goals of helping others. For example, teenagers today are taking extreme personal risks to stand up against racism, climate change and gun violence!*[173]

I bet you can think of many examples, from the young people standing up to gun violence after the Parkland school shooting to the young people of all ethnic and racial groups who are standing up to racial injustice and climate change. And it doesn't have to be a big thing like that. When my close friend Penny Armstrong and I worked on community projects in high school, we were taking positive risks.

Key Finding: All risks aren't negative. Positive risks can benefit the individual and can benefit their communities.

LAB ←→ LIFE: THE ASPEN CHALLENGE

> *It's always good to step out of your comfort zone. When I push myself to go out of my comfort zone, it just makes everything so much better. It gives me more confidence in myself.*[174]

That's how Dominique Gordon, a Philadelphia high school student, describes her experience with the Aspen Challenge. The Aspen Challenge exemplifies a program that provides adolescents with positive risks. As program director Katie Fitzgerald says, it "provides a platform for young people to create solutions to some of society's toughest problems."[175]

Since its founding in 2012 by the Aspen Institute and the Bezos Family Foundation, the Aspen Challenge has formed partnerships with urban school districts, each for a two-year cycle. Twenty high schools in the selected district are invited to participate, with each school forming a team of eight students and two educators serving as coaches.

Not only is there an intellectual risk in the Aspen Challenge but there's a social risk since the students come from different grades and don't necessarily know each other. There are seven steps in this eight-week process:[176]

1. **Build empathy.** The students learn about their community and its challenges.
2. **Get inspired.** The twenty teams gather at a community-wide forum where local and national thought leaders challenge the teams to come up with solutions to a specific problem in their own community.
3. **Design a solution.** Teams have one week to select a challenge and begin drafting a vision and setting goals. For example, a team in Washington, D.C., selected the lack of community playgrounds for children; a team in Chicago selected the fact that city street lighting blocked out the night sky; and a team in Louisville, Kentucky, selected the lack of mental health resources for students.
4. **Give the solution a voice.** They receive coaching in how to present their solution to community stakeholders.
5. **Outreach and community engagement.** The teams engage their communities through events, meetings, and media. In Chicago, for example, teams working on the night sky issue met with the mayor to discuss solutions.
6. **Present and compete.** The teams present their solutions to a panel of distinguished judges, who select winners based on "creativity, feasibility, sustainability, and teamwork."
7. **Reflect and grow.** The twenty teams meet to reflect on what they've learned about leadership from this experience.

Participating districts to date have included Los Angeles; Denver; Washington, D.C.; Chicago; Philadelphia; Dallas; Louisville; and Miami.

Since its founding, local and national thought leaders have issued a number of very compelling challenges. In the 2019 cycle in Louisville, for example, Jenara Nerenberg, a journalist from the Greater Good Science Center at the University of California, Berkeley, challenged students to remove the stigma around mental health. The team from Jeffersontown High

School in Louisville created a podcast called *The Umbrella of No Judgment* through which students can anonymously share mental health stories. They also displayed positive messages and affirmation boards throughout the school.[177]

John Dugan of the Aspen Institute is evaluating the Aspen Challenge as part of his rigorous ongoing leadership studies. He and his team have found that in just eight weeks, the participating high school students make gains in the leadership outcomes they measure that equal or exceed the gains made by a comparable group of older students in a full year of college.

A four-year follow-up study further reveals that this experience has a durable impact: participants continue to make gains in leadership efficacy (the belief they can succeed) and social perspective-taking and are more likely to participate and take leadership roles in student and community organizations.[178]

Devyn Williams, a high school student from Louisville, illustrates the power of taking positive risks when he says:

> By going through the Aspen Challenge, I . . . think that I'm more able to go through adversity . . . it taught us persistence and it taught us dedication . . . And it's something that I'm going to take with me for the rest of my life.[179]

Obviously, not every community can participate in the Aspen Challenge, but community leaders and teachers can be inspired about what it means to create "the right peer environment," where young people thrive, and adapt their activities and assignments in this way.

PROMOTING POSITIVE RISKS

If you have adolescents in your life, what kind of positive risks can you help them take to constructively channel their energy and daring drive and steer them away from negative risks? Are there risks that can provide fun and challenge? Are there risks that can benefit others? If more of us did this, what a better world it could be!

The Digital World

When I speak to groups—no matter the audience or topic—I'm asked, "What do you think about screen time?" Then, without pause, people launch into a litany of potential dangers: bullying, addiction, predators, mental health problems such as anxiety and depression, a distracted or superficial generation who can't connect or communicate with real people or understand complex issues—to name just a few.

Adolescents today have grown up in the digital world. Since 2014–2015, there's been a 22 percent increase in those reporting having access to a smartphone (95 percent now, 73 percent then), according to a 2022 Pew Research Center study of thirteen-through-seventeen-year-olds.[180] The proportion who say they use the internet about once a day or more also increased, from 92 percent to 97 percent during that time. A 2021 Common Sense Media study found that in 2019 and 2021—years that included the pandemic—the total amount of daily screen usage jumped from 4 hours 44 minutes to 5 hours 33 minutes for eight-to-twelve-year-olds and from 7 hours 22 minutes to 8 hours 39 minutes for thirteen-to-eighteen-year-olds.[181] Researchers Mitchell Prinstein, Jacqueline Nesi, and Eva Telzer share this shocking—to me—news:

> *Epidemiological data suggest that adolescents may spend more hours each day communicating with peers via electronically mediated platforms than they do sleeping, attending school, or interacting with adults.*[182]

Until recently, there've been few child development issues where research results and adults' concerns have appeared to clash more fiercely, but research is beginning to catch up.

Teachers worry. For example, although 77 percent of more than two thousand middle and high school teachers surveyed by the Pew Research Center in 2012 saw the internet as having a mostly positive impact on their students' research habits, they were concerned about what it was doing to adolescents' cognitive development:

- Eighty-seven percent felt that widespread internet use was creating an "easily distracted generation with short attention spans."[183]
- Eighty-six percent reported that "today's students are too 'plugged in' and need more time away from their digital technologies."

- Sixty-four percent stated that today's digital technologies "do more to distract students than to help them academically."

And these were teachers of high-achieving students from Advanced Placement classes and National Writing Project communities!

Parents worry, too. Media headlines call for a "digital detox"[184] and report that parents are hiring coaches to pry kids away from their screens. Books and TV shows expound upon perceived dangers, asking, "Are we in a crisis with our kids?"[185]

A NUMBER OF OVERVIEW STUDIES SAID "DON'T WORRY"

The National Academy of Medicine's 2019 scientific consensus report on adolescents—*The Promise of Adolescence*—said there was little cause for concern, at least as far as was known at the time:

> *Notwithstanding the many worries . . . about the possible detrimental effects of social media consumption on overall adolescent well-being, strong evidence documenting such effects has not yet emerged.*[186]

Amy Orben and Andrew Przybylski of Oxford University reached a similar conclusion after applying rigorous statistical controls to the datasets of three large-scale studies consisting of 17,247 students. These datasets included time diaries chronicling screen time (i.e., did an adolescent use a screen in the last thirty minutes, hour, or two hours), as well as general use (i.e., responding to a non-time-based question about usage in general):

> *The study found little substantive statistically significant and negative associations between digital-screen engagement and well-being in adolescents.*[187]

In yet another large-scale study, with over 355,000 adolescents, the correlations with the kinds of risky behaviors we've talked about previously, such as substance use or fighting, were much more negative than technology use across all three studies. Placing screen time in the context of non-risky activities provides the most telling example:

> *The association of well-being with regularly eating potatoes was nearly as negative as the association with technology use.*

Eating potatoes! The report went on to say that "simple actions such as getting enough sleep and regularly eating breakfast have much more positive associations with well-being than the average impact of technology use in all datasets."[188] The authors summarize the results of their analyses:

> The evidence . . . suggests that the effects of technology might be statistically significant but so minimal that they hold little practical value. The nuanced picture provided by these results is in line with previous psychological and epidemiological research suggesting that the associations between digital screen-time and child outcomes are not as simple as many might think.

On the other hand, the surgeon general of the United States, Vivek Murthy, issued a 2023 advisory on social media, stating that social media can cause harm to the mental health of adolescents.[189]

What's real? How concerned should we be? This section will address three key questions, notwithstanding the fact that research in this area is continuing to change.

A NEW NAME FOR NEW STUDIES: DIGITAL MEDIA

To begin, exactly what is being studied? Is it screen time or social media consumption—both of which focus on time spent online? Eva Telzer says, "If you wanted to understand the impact of nutrition on children's development, would you just look at how much time they spend eating?"[190] No, of course you wouldn't.

Accordingly, the name used to describe newer studies is changing. Nesi, Telzer, and Prinstein write that there's a growing body of research aiming to move away from the concept of screen time and "instead consider *how* and *why* digital media use may alternatively promote or undermine adolescent mental well-being."[191]

SO, HOW DO THE REALITIES OF THE DIGITAL WORLD AFFECT ADOLESCENT DEVELOPMENT?

In many ways, interacting in the online world is quite different from interacting in the offline world:

- The digital world is public and the audience can be large.
- It's permanent: it's hard to erase a post.

- It's often missing interpersonal cues and clues.
- It's created in response to a specific context (a time, place, or experience) but can be interpreted without an understanding of that context.
- It has built-in feedback mechanisms with "likes" or comments.[192]

As such, the digital world is affecting key developmental processes in ways that have the potential of being for better and for worse:

- **Identity exploration.** Adolescence is a time for exploring identity, for asking, "Who am I?" and "Who do I want to be?" On the positive side, the digital world offers a much larger world to explore. On the negative side, many adolescents (and adults) curate what they post, presenting images of their best selves living their best lives. Additionally, advertising and media companies promote perfect bodies. These online images and constantly curated content have the potential to harm adolescents' images of themselves by presenting unrealistic or unattainable standards.[193] Logan Lane, a Brooklyn teen who ultimately gave up social media, recalls, "I was just blatantly unsatisfied with myself. I was constantly seeing something better that I could be, someone prettier, someone more artistic, and I developed this level of shame about who I wasn't."[194]
- **Imaginary audiences and attention.** Adolescents tend to carry imaginary audiences in their minds, as David Elkind of Tufts University noted decades ago, imagining that people are looking at and evaluating them.[195] Online, imaginary audiences easily become real people, known and unknown, who comment, "like," or share adolescents' posts, with varying repercussions.
- **The need for autonomy and agency.** Adolescents have a basic need to feel they have some choice in what they do (autonomy) and that they can effect change (agency). The online environment can become one way these needs are met.[196] On the other hand, the major media sites young people use (YouTube, TikTok, Instagram, and Snapchat, according to the Pew Survey)[197] are businesses. Their purpose is to sell, and they have incredible access to young people. Adolescents don't like to be manipulated and the knowledge that these sites use algorithms to capture data about them in order to convert them into consumers, as well as keep their attention on the app (e.g., infinite scroll), often doesn't sit well with parents and with adolescents.[198]

- **Self-disclosure.** Self-disclosure—where adolescents share personal information or secrets about themselves with others—can be a building block for finding belonging in personal relationships. In a study of 125 girls in the fifth and sixth grades,[199] Jennifer Pfeifer found that in-person "sharing about oneself is a way of strengthening relationships and deepening intimacy in all kinds of close relationships"; moreover, these stronger relationships can buffer adolescents against mental health problems.[200] What happens when these relationships are online? And what if adolescents get shunned when they share more personal perspectives? In the future, are adolescents going to want the public to have access to their online teenage selves?

- **Social status and feedback.** During adolescence, hormonal and other biological changes elevate the power of social relationships, the social status and respect they impart, and acceptance and rejection.[201] In the online world, there are quantifiable ways of assessing status and belonging—by the number of "likes" and by whom—giving these developmental processes new potential for good and for harm.[202] Eva Telzer has found that some adolescents are neurobiologically more sensitive to peer influence and status than others, and for them, these online dynamics can have an even stronger sway.[203]

- **Finding people "like me."** Adolescents who feel lonely, different, stigmatized, or ostracized in the offline world can find online friends. Prinstein, Nesi, and Telzer write that this can provide "resource sharing, and emotional validation that is much harder to access otherwise."[204] Conversely, behind many school shootings are stories of how a young person with seething and vengeful anger found an online community to further ignite their rage.

When facing these issues, how often have you felt, "I didn't grow up with this, I'm not sure how to deal with it"? It is a new world, raising many new concerns, which we will explore by looking at what the research says on three key questions.

Question 1: Will Digital Media Harm Young People's Well-Being?

This is a central concern that many families, professionals, and policymakers have. I begin with some older studies because they illustrate the necessity of going beyond time spent on media, though that's where Ethan Kross of the University of Michigan began more than a decade ago. He recounted this when we spoke:

Social media has provided us with a world of new questions. This is a new way in which human beings are beginning to interact. How often do you get to say that in one's lifetime we're living through a time in which the very way we interact as a species is fundamentally shifting? To me, it is a mindblower![205]

When Kross and his colleagues looked at the literature, they found most studies were cross-sectional (conducted at one point in time) and asked young people (typically college-age students) how often they used social media and how they felt after. Overall, the results from a number of studies were, unsurprisingly, contradictory: a third found positive results; a third, negative results; and a third, "it depends."[206]

The Kross team concluded a different methodology was needed. In a 2013 study,[207] eighty-two college-age people were sent text messages (called experience sampling) about their usage of Facebook (the major platform at that time—but if the study were conducted today, it might be about You-Tube, TikTok, or other platforms), their non-Facebook interactions with others, and their moods between morning and midnight, five times a day for fourteen days. Before and after experience sampling, participants completed questionnaires on well-being and life satisfaction. The findings revealed a pretty clear pattern. Kross says:

The more you use Facebook, the more your positive mood drops, the worse you subsequently feel![208]

That study confirmed parents' fears and made headlines. But Kross didn't believe social media use was that simple. They'd found, for example, that people use social media in different ways. He suspected this might matter:

*You can use Facebook **passively**—just scroll through your news feed and people's profiles and see what's going on, keeping track of your relations and your social networks. Or you can use it **actively**—to communicate with others, exchange messages, post information.*

This research team predicted that passive usage would be linked to lower well-being. In his 2015 experiments,[209] eighty-four college-age students were asked to use their own Facebook feeds passively or actively for ten minutes. Afterward, participants were reassessed, asked how connected to others they felt and how their lives seemed compared with others. Finally, they received a questionnaire at nine p.m. that night.

Kross's predictions were accurate—the young people who used Facebook passively reported lower well-being. In a second experiment to find out why, eighty-nine college-age participants were texted five times daily over six days. In addition to the questions in the first study, they were asked, "How envious have you been of others since we last asked?"[210] Two findings stand out to Kross:

> First, we found that the majority of the time people are on Facebook, they're using it passively.

In fact, participants used Facebook passively about 50 percent more than they used it actively. He continues:

> Number two, passively using technology leads to more feelings of jealousy, which explains how passive Facebook usage leads people to feel worse over time.[211]

Key Finding: Simply using social media isn't what affects college students' well-being: how it's used also matters. These studies show that using social media passively can negatively affect young people's well-being.

Although this study provides an important distinction between active and passive usage, I expect that if it were conducted today, researchers could and should be more nuanced about what being "active" on social media means. There is a world of difference between posting curated images of your best self and using social media in creative and expressive ways. In addition, today's researchers would and should look at the impact on adolescents of different ages.

A key question that researchers are pursuing today is about causality, especially in the wake of the 2023 release of data from the CDC's Youth Risk Behavior Survey, which reveals that in 2021, 42 percent of high school students reported experiencing persistent feelings of sadness and hopelessness, up from 28 percent in 2011 (findings that I discuss in chapters 4 and 5).[212] A number of people see the strong possibility of causal links between social media use and these mental health declines, including Jean Twenge, professor of psychology at San Diego State University and author of *iGen*,[213] and Jonathan Haidt, a professor at New York University and co-author of *The Coddling of the American Mind*.[214] Especially troubling is the fact that the decline in mental health parallels the spread of digital technology around the world.

If pushed to give a simple yes/no answer, Jacqueline Nesi of Brown University writes, "Social media **alone** [emphasis added] does not cause mental health issues"; however, studies are showing correlations. Nesi continues: "There is a statistically significant (but very small) association between more time spent on social media and worse mental health." Other things matter a lot, too, such as who the teens are and how they use social media.[215]

A recent research analysis of twenty-five research reviews (we're at the stages where differing reviews need an overview) states that the picture is mixed. Most reviews conclude that the links between social media and adolescent well-being are weak or inconsistent, though some find that the links are worrisome.[216] They make the point that even a small effect can impact many young people.

Surgeon General Murthy acknowledged this mixed picture when releasing his May 2023 advisory, writing that while the effects of social media on adolescents' mental health are still not fully understood and that social media can be positive for some adolescents, the public needs to know that "there are ample indicators that social media can also have a profound risk of harm to the mental health and well-being of children and adolescents."[217]

The American Psychological Association weighs in with more caution, writing in a May 2023 consensus statement: "the effects of social media likely **depend** [emphasis added] on what teens can do and see online, teens' pre-existing strengths or vulnerabilities, and the contexts in which they grow up."[218] In addition, they emphasize that the impact of social media depends on age—the risks are greater in early adolescence than in later adolescence.

They, like others, say that social media is not the only contributor to mental health declines, writing that "insufficient sleep is associated with disruptions to neurological development in adolescent brains, teens' emotional functioning, and risk for suicide."[219]

When considering adolescents' mental health, I remain concerned that so few researchers and policymakers are paying attention to parental job stress as a factor. This is a long-standing concern of mine and one I've worked hard with employers to address. In 1999,[220] we found that if given one wish to improve the impact of their parents' job on their lives, the largest proportion in a nationally representative study of third through twelfth graders wished that their mothers (34 percent) and their fathers (28 percent) would be less tired and stressed. We repeated this question in the Breakthrough Years study and again found the largest proportion of adolescents (40 percent) wishing that their parents* were less tired and stressed.

Breakthrough Years Study Finding: We find that when adolescents report that their parents are stressed, they aren't faring as well on all the well-being outcomes we measure.

These data indicate that other factors beyond social media need to be taken into account when thinking about youth mental health. Thankfully, Eva Telzer and her colleagues have launched longitudinal studies, beginning with children in the third grade, and are using rigorous methodology, including brain scans.[221]

I asked Telzer, knowing what she knows now, how she would handle the digital world when her own child becomes a teen. She responded that she doesn't see the digital world as uniformly bad or good, so "I don't know that I would necessarily resist my child using social media." Instead, she told me, she would have conversations about how to use it in an adaptive way and to watch out for "algorithms that suck you in and take you into a black hole of content."

Question 2: How Does Digital Media Affect Young People's Learning?

Since facts are now at our fingertips, will our capacity to remember—which is key to cognition—be affected? Betsy Sparrow, then at Columbia University,[222] and her colleagues tackled this question by asking undergraduate students to read forty memorable trivia statements, like "an ostrich's eye is bigger than its brain." The participants were then asked to type these facts into the computer. Half believed the computer would save what was typed. The other half believed their typing would be erased. Half of each group was also explicitly asked to remember these trivia facts.

All the participants were then asked to write down as many of the statements as they could recall. Those who believed their typing would *not* be saved remembered the most information, regardless of whether they were

---

* While it appears that the percentage is increasing, we can't directly compare these findings because the Ask the Children study in 1999 asked about mothers and fathers separately and the Breakthrough Years study in 2019 asked about parents without differentiating between mothers and fathers.

told to memorize it or not. Those who "thought they could later look up the trivia statements," the researchers write, "apparently did not make the effort to remember" them.[223] In another experiment in this series, the researchers found that the study participants recalled the folder names better than the facts themselves.

Indeed, Kate Mills, a neuroscientist at the University of Oregon who has written two excellent reviews of the impact of the digital world on young people,[224] says that findings such as these suggest that young people are adapting to new technology:

> *That might signal a change in a cognitive ability—maybe we're better these days at figuring out where to find information rather than memorizing everything.*[225]

Key Finding: While we may think the near-constant accessibility of the internet harms memory, the impact of the internet seems to depend on our expectations—whether we need to remember information or instead remember how to find this information.

While a quick smartphone search may help with memory recall, there are many other ways phones and media can get in the way of studying or completing tasks. In a 2018 Common Sense Media survey, only 31 percent of young people reported silencing their phones all of the time when doing homework; 31 percent did so some of the time; 37 percent said they hardly ever or never do. Yet, by their own admission, 57 percent strongly or somewhat agreed that using social media often distracts them when they should be doing homework![226] Is media multitasking harmful or not? Or are adolescents uniquely able to switch between different task demands?

One of the researchers working on some of those studies was Melina Uncapher. As an adolescent, she'd wanted to be a neurosurgeon or a neurologist so that she could "help cure memory disorders," a dream that took hold as she watched her grandmother suffer from a variant of Parkinson's disease.[227]

As she was prepping for the medical school admission test, a neighbor, who happened to be a neurosurgeon, leaned over the fence and said, "If you really want to honor your grandmother's legacy, you'll help build a knowledge base rather than become a practitioner." Instead of enrolling in medical school, she went to graduate school to study neuroscience.

Her commitment to her grandmother's legacy led her to write her dissertation on divided attention during learning. There she discovered an intriguing finding:

> There's some great work showing that if your attention is divided, it may
> actually not be the hippocampus that's picking up that experience and
> transforming it into memory, but rather one of the other learning systems
> of the mind, which is a less flexible learning system. Therefore, you would
> learn it differently—not as richly and often not as long-lasting.

Just as Ethan Kross recognized that social media is changing the nature of how people interact with each other, Melina Uncapher recognized that social media is changing how people pay attention. Despite her worries about media multitasking, she does note that most people do it.[228]

With Anthony Wagner of Stanford University and other colleagues, Uncapher, then at Stanford, wrote a series of research reviews on media multitasking in 2016,[229] 2017,[230] and 2018.[231] In the 2018 review, she and Wagner report that although the data are sparse and findings are mixed, there seems to be enough evidence that heavy media multitaskers (measured differently in different studies, so there's no real standard except perhaps that they multitask more than others their age) in adolescence and in adulthood may have more difficulty staying on task or returning to a task when they get distracted.

In a study of Stanford undergraduates,[232] Uncapher and her colleagues found that chronic multitaskers were more reactive to distracting information and had a harder time staying on task. She has extended this research to children in grades three, five, and seven, where she and her colleagues found that media multitasking was correlated with lower skills in working memory capacity but not with the capacity to filter out distractions.[233]

Key Finding: There are some red flags suggesting that chronic media multitasking may negatively affect learning skills. Until we know more, Uncapher says, it may be prudent to limit multitasking.

And Uncapher herself? She is now chief of research and development at AERDF (Advanced Education Research and Development Fund), a national nonprofit education research and development program designed to address intractable teaching and learning challenges that disproportionately affect students experiencing poverty[234]—doing work that honors her grand-mother's legacy.

Question 3: What Can Parents Do to Manage the Digital World?

In one study pursuing this question, Laura Padilla-Walker of Brigham Young University and her colleagues followed 681 adolescents and their mothers for two years, beginning when the students were thirteen. They identified four strategies parents use to manage media:[235]

- **Restrictive media monitoring** is used to control media use by setting rules about the kind of content children can access or by limiting the amount of time children spend on media.
- **Active media monitoring** is used to help children become wise consumers of media by promoting their learning and critical thinking.
- **Media co-use** covers the third and fourth strategies, which involve co-viewing, co-listening, and co-reading. There is **connective co-use** (where the intent is to connect with and talk with children about the content) or **passive co-use** (for example, parents and children watching the same television show at the same time but not discussing the content).

In addition to measuring the time adolescents spent on their screens, the researchers asked them to name their three favorite television shows and video games, and independent raters assessed the level of violence in the content.

Their results indicate that mothers rarely use only one monitoring strategy—different situations call for different strategies. Thus, the researchers focused on the *predominant styles* that mothers used. Results indicated that active media monitoring and connective co-use are linked with lower media use as well as with less aggressive and more prosocial behavior. The researchers comment that being restrictive doesn't seem as effective at decreasing media use, likely because it conflicts with adolescents' desire for autonomy.[236]

Below, I share an evidence-based initiative that promotes constructive media use.

LAB ←→ LIFE: APPLYING MORE THAN
COMMON SENSE TO MEDIA USE

As a parent and longtime children's advocate, Jim Steyer saw that technology was altering how children are raised—in essence, they have another parent. His 2002 book, *The Other Parent: The Inside Story on Media's Effect on Children*,[237] was written as a call to action.

In 2003, Steyer took action himself, creating the nonprofit Common Sense Media, which centers on a website featuring media reviews. Linda Burch, a co-founder, recalls the early days as a time when parents needed "nutritional-like" labeling for media and help in assessing which movies, TV shows, video games, and books to share with their kids.[238] As their tagline now states, "Reviews for what your kids are into (before they get into it)."[239] The public was immediately receptive because they saw a need to protect kids. Burch, who became the chief strategy and development officer, says the organization's focus is broader:

> *Our goal was to give parents, teachers, and kids themselves the confidence and skills to navigate a rapidly evolving tech and media world in healthy and responsible ways.*
>
> *When we gave talks at schools, I'd typically follow the law enforcement person who'd just gotten parents panicked about predators and about what media and technology would do to their kids' brains. Then it was my job to say, "You really need to embrace your kids' lives, to understand how important media and technology are in it, and make some decisions together as to how to make it positive."*[240]

A national survey of families that they conducted revealed that parents wanted objective advice—not advice from a moralistic or overly protective perspective. "Every family's values are different and every child is different," Burch says. Common Sense Media's goal is to provide the right kind of information so families can figure out what's best for them. They now reach 125 million families a year.

Another pillar of their work is a digital citizenship curriculum for schools. Again, Burch says, the tenor of the times centered on protecting kids from danger, but their approach has been about helping kids gain skills for the digital world.

In creating the curriculum, Common Sense didn't just rely on common sense—they brought a strong research perspective by partnering with Howard Gardner at Harvard's Project Zero and other researchers. Today the curriculum is taught by one million teachers in 102,000 schools around the world.[241]

PROMOTING POSITIVE USES OF THE DIGITAL WORLD

Few other child development issues elicit more concern than the digital world. Some young people have taken matters into their own hands and are starting groups to combat social media (see chapter 5 on the Luddite Club and Tech(nically) Politics). It is something that we all—adults as well as young people—need to address to ensure that it doesn't harm young people. We can turn our concerns into Skill-Building Opportunities:

- **Connections:** Find ways to connect adolescents' interests to people they'd like to meet or subjects they'd like to explore.
- **Creativity:** Rather than being consumers of media, help them become creators of media, making videos or art, developing games, and collaborating with others on how to improve their communities.
- **Contributing:** There are so many ways to use technology to contribute, such as tutoring others online, teaching something they love to others, or solving community problems.
- **Control:** For some adolescents, media feel addictive—and that's not surprising; developers have designed it that way. Rather than relying on setting rules and time limits (restrictive media monitoring), we can work with our kids to come up with shared family rules and a family media plan. And rather than battle their demands for more and more time, we can help them reflect about what helps them use self-control and transition to other activities, using a process like Shared Solutions, described earlier. In these ways, we are being active media monitors.
- **Conscious Role Models:** Our own use of social media in the presence of our children should be considered. The American Psychological Association report states that there is evidence that our use of social media (for example, not paying attention to our kids because we are using social media) can affect adolescents' usage.[242]

- **Wise Citizenship:** We can help our adolescents become wise citizens of the digital world by discussing the benefits and risks of social media, the importance of protecting their personal information in age-appropriate ways, and how to take action against cyberbullying or inappropriate content or contacts.[243]
- **Turn-off Times:** Families have found it very freeing to have some tech-free zones when they go digital free, such as at dinnertime and an hour before bedtime. Tiffany Shlain, a media creator herself, practices tech-free times or what she calls "24/6" in her family, with all screens turned off one day a week. Her eponymous book shares the successes of this approach.[244]

As wise citizens of the digital world, it's important for us to encourage adolescents' unplugged interactions and interests offline. Over the years, our research has found adults who are thriving aren't work-centric—they are dual or multicentric, with a number of interests.[245] We need to help children be multicentric, too.

Working Toward a Kinder World

There's something powerful about asking people for *one* wish to improve their lives—because wishes reveal what matters, sometimes in surprising ways. For this reason, we've asked about wishes in most of our studies. In the current study, we asked adolescents:

If you had one wish (besides having a lot of money) that would improve the lives of people your age, what would that wish be?*

Their answers are mainly about how people treat each other.

WISHES: BREAKTHROUGH YEARS STUDY FINDINGS

The largest proportion of adolescents wish for a more peaceful, more accepting, and kinder world. In fact, 20 percent wish others would "be kind":

---

* The exact wording of this question (specifically excluding money as a potential wish) was suggested by young people I interviewed before conducting the study.

People would get along with each other.
   —Sixteen-year-old boy

It would be for everyone to treat each other with respect even though you may hate that person.
   —Twelve-year-old girl

To be kind to everyone and give them all an equal chance no matter who they are.
   —Ten-year-old girl

They specifically mention not gossiping or judging based on looks or popularity, and call for an end to bias and discrimination, and less bullying:

To not belittle or talk about people. Just be nice.
   —Seventeen-year-old boy

That people would like everybody (like as a crush) no matter what race, weight, height, skin tone, hair, acne, or anything.
   —Eleven-year-old girl

I would wish for everyone to know that they are all equal. So that no one was ever mean to others and there would no longer be any racism or discrimination.
   —Ten-year-old boy

I wish hate would just disappear.
   —Nine-year-old boy

FIRST OF ALL DON'T EXPECT KIDS TO ALWAYS WANT MONEY!!!! IT IS VERY RUDE! But, I would like kids [to] like me or the world to have world peace.
   —Nine-year-old boy

I wish there was a way that bullying could be outlawed and stopped. Everybody should be able to live like they want to and not be made fun of.
   —Sixteen-year-old girl

Breakthrough Years Study Finding: Twenty percent of adolescents wish for more niceness, kindness, and civility to improve the lives of people their age. An additional 4 percent of adolescents wish that bullying would end, and that there would be "bully-free spaces."

Another 4 percent make the same wish as their "message to the adults of America"—"listen to us, understand us":

I'd wish that older people would try harder to understand my generation. We have so much more stuff thrown at us through social media and television that they have no idea what we really think about.
    —Seventeen-year-old boy

I would wish for an unlimited amount of wishes. But if I had to choose one it would be that adults start listening to us when we say that there is something wrong.
    —Fourteen-year-old girl

The common theme in adolescents' wishes is a longing for us to treat them and each other well. In a sobering finding, in the interviews I conducted for the qualitative study, some said they don't think change toward more civility is possible. That's worrisome, since adolescents are often the fuel behind societal change; it's a good way to channel their drive for positive risks and to make the world a better place.

Although it's unclear how pervasive this view is, I can certainly understand it from my own experience over the past years. As the political discourse in our country has become more hateful, more unforgiving, and more violent, adults, too, wonder if civility is possible. Yet to give young people the world we want them to inherit, we have to try, and there are efforts that provide hope.

LAB ◄──► LIFE: CHANGING THE CULTURE OF CONFLICT

Improving civility isn't just about personal change. It depends not only on what we do but also on how others respond. This kind of change requires altering community-wide patterns of behavior, "one of the most elusive and important goals in behavioral science," write Elizabeth Levy Paluck of Princeton University, Hana Shepherd of Rutgers University, and Peter Aronow of Yale University.[246]

Laws can be a "top-down" way to produce community-wide change, but what about voluntary change? Paluck and her colleagues note three different approaches:

- **One person at a time.** This approach reaches individuals through persuasive messages, environmental cues (such as signs stating "Children Playing, Drive Slowly"), and peer influence (spokespeople echoing the message).
- **Large-scale campaigns.** These are designed to reach a large portion of the population. One of the more successful examples in my experience is the Designated Driver Campaign, which began in Scandinavia, spread to Canada, and was brought to the United States by Jay Winsten of Harvard University. Winsten attributes the success of this campaign to having a consistent and widespread message, including public service announcements and depicting examples of designated drivers in 160 prime-time shows. The right message—and messengers—were critical, Winsten says. It was important that the designated driver not be positioned as a party pooper or as throwing a wet blanket on the evening:

Rather, [they] had to be positioned as an integral, important and popular member of the social group—that they were each taking their turn, protecting their friends.[247]

This 1980s campaign is credited with a substantial decline in traffic deaths.[248] But it's not easy to raise the funds for a comprehensive campaign in today's diffuse media market. Which leads to a third approach:

- **The right messengers, the right messages, in the right places.** Paluck, Shepherd, and Aronow used this approach "to seed a social network with individuals who demonstrate new behaviors, and to rely on processes of social influence to spread the behavior."[249]

This research team had previously found that adolescents whose behavior is more likely to be "noticed" by their peers—social influencers—have an outsized impact and can alter a culture of harassment.[250] They followed up with an intervention in fifty-six New Jersey middle schools to change the culture of conflict to a culture of civility with 24,191 students.[251] Schools were randomly selected to be intervention schools or control schools (i.e., business as usual with no intervention). The researchers highlight several key contributors to their success.

First, they identified these effective messengers (the social influencers). They surveyed everyone in each school, asking them to nominate up to ten students they'd chosen to spend time with in the last few weeks—in or out of school, or online. "Using student social networks to choose the peers," Paluck states, was "the real innovation here." They note that if adults had selected the messengers, they might have chosen the good kids, but when students chose, some of the leaders they selected are "right smack in the center of student conflict":

These are the students whose behavior gets noticed more.[252]

In the intervention schools, they selected a group of students and randomly assigned half of that group to participate as a "seed group" (i.e., the group seeding change) in the anticonflict intervention. A random number of social influencers ended up in each seed group, enabling the researchers to test the impact of groups with more social influencers versus fewer. The seed groups received Roots training, an anticonflict program offering training in dealing with student conflict and templates for messaging campaign materials.

A second factor of importance was **having influential adults on board**. The governor of New Jersey had recently required all teachers to have antibullying training, but there was no funding for it. This project enabled schools to comply with the mandate and thus the school leaders were on board.

The third factor of importance was **involving students in the process**. Paluck says that the best way to change social norms for young people is to have students speak in their own voices—a "grassroots approach can be very powerful."[253]

Throughout the school years, the seed group in each intervention school launched messaging campaigns. One campaign, for example, used posters with the hashtag "#iRespect," highlighting the stories of intervention group students. Another gave rubber wristbands to students caught doing something great like intervening in a conflict. That active recognition truly was a culture changer, the authors write, by countering students' perception of conflict as "normative within their school's social network" and thus changing their tendency to "perpetuate and tolerate" it.[254]

There was also a "Roots Day," when students were encouraged to sign statements promising that they'd do something nice for someone in their school.

Thanks to this intervention, student disciplinary reports went down by 25 percent in the intervention schools compared with the control schools. The effects were stronger when seed groups had more social influencers. Conclusion? Social influencers can change the culture of conflict.[255]

"Just be nice," a seventeen-year-old boy wrote in the Breakthrough Years study survey. It may sound pie-in-the-sky, but this intervention shows it can be done.

OTHER WISHES

The main other wishes by adolescents were about making the world safer. Seven percent wished for housing, food, and jobs for those in need:

Everybody would have enough to eat and some warm place to sleep.
   —Seventeen-year-old boy

I wish I can help all kids have things like me like clean water.
   —Thirteen-year-old boy

If I had one wish that would improve the lives of people my wish would be to get a good job that helped lots of people.
   —Nine-year-old girl

Twelve-year-olds are smarter than people think. I would wish for more activities for my age group to be involved in, like conservation. Groups and activities are mostly focused on under ten and over fifteen years old.
   —Twelve-year-old boy

Another 5 percent wish for cures for physical and mental illnesses:

I wish we could end cancer, world hunger and have great education for all the youth.
   —Fifteen-year-old girl

Good health because it sucks being sick.
   —Fourteen-year-old girl

To give kids who are hard of hearing like me hearing aids so they can talk like me.
   —Ten-year-old girl

End world complications that take the lives of children every year.
   —Twelve-year-old boy

Breakthrough Years Study Finding: Seven percent of adolescents wish for addressing physical needs—food, water, shelter, and jobs—while another 5 percent wish for an end to diseases like cancer.

Other wishes are for the health of the planet, for the weak and unfortunate to have better lives, for everyone to have caring parents, for everyone to have an opportunity to learn, for good mental health and an end to depression, and arts for all.

Does this sound too altruistic? Possibly. There are also some adolescents who wish they were more physically attractive, had a romantic partner, and were more popular. There are some who wish not to have to go to school or have homework, to have bigger houses or a car, to have lots of wishes and gift cards, and to have more money for themselves. This group, however, represents only 7 percent of the wishes. The majority of the wishes are a call for changes that benefit themselves *and* others.

With all this energy for social change, there's so much room for young people to take steps to create the world they want to live in with the help of adults! That's what Hope did.

HOPE BRINGS HOPE

When her high school classes switched to an online platform during the pandemic, Hope,* then a high school junior from the Los Angeles area, was impressed by how quickly her teachers adapted:

I was inspired by my teachers—how they continue to keep us engaged online.

---

* Hope is Hope Shinderman, now a college student, whom I interviewed on April 11, 2020.

She also saw something else—the family lives of her teachers as they tried to teach other people's children *and* care for their own children—and realized that some of her teachers' children were getting short shrift. She saw teachers whose kids only had two and a half hours of classes a day—and many had long stretches of boredom:

> *My teachers were providing us with a quality online education but they'd lament that their own children weren't receiving a quality education, if they received any at all.*

Finally, she saw how stressed her teachers were:

> *They were really feeling the effects of the pandemic.*

Shortly before spring break in 2020, Hope had an idea: What about offering free online tutoring and group enrichment opportunities to her teachers' children—and to other parents whose children might need it? She says:

> *I thought this could ease the burden on teachers, provide academic support and social connections for the children, and create some consistency in the lives of the children.*

Because Hope has had learning challenges, she knows how important consistency is for children, how hard spring break can be because school routines disappear, and how important it is to teach in the way that children learn best.

No stranger to community activism, Hope had been involved in several committees and organizations locally. But she'd never started anything herself—until now!

She contacted four other classmates, inviting them to be tutors. Those classmates invited others. If Hope and her classmates didn't know a prospective tutor, they interviewed them, asking how they liked to learn and teach.

Next, they recruited families whose children might benefit from tutoring by older students. To spread the word, Hope and the other tutors reached out to their teachers, to organizations they knew, and to their places of worship.

Within five days, they had thirty-two tutors and two hundred children. Here's how it works:

- The tutoring is free, but they do ask families—if they can—to donate to their GoFundMe initiative to help close the digital divide.
- When families contact Hope, she and others get in touch with all the tutors, saying, "We have a fourth grader interested in Spanish, math, and biology. Can anyone take him on?"
- Within minutes, she says, she has a volunteer. Then she writes to the parent, introducing parent and tutor by email "so that the two of you can connect and schedule some sessions."
- Before the tutoring officially begins, the tutor, parents, and child schedule a fifteen-minute introductory video meeting to talk about what the students want to learn and how they learn best.

Hope talks about wanting to "unlock every student's potential," "make learning enjoyable for all students, especially those who have been excluded like neuro-diverse students or English-language learners," and "to create safe places where everyone can learn." These tutors seem to be doing everything they can to walk the talk.

For example, working with a sixth grader on essay writing, Hope helped him learn skills, like annotating what he reads, making an outline, selecting evidence to support his argument, then writing and rewriting until he gets it right. She's careful not to do anything *for* him, but to ask guiding questions so "he can do things for himself when I'm not there."

After a rocky start tutoring a third grader in Spanish, Hope figured out that vocabulary was more fun if they made it into a game where the student had to guess the words. And a group class she's teaching on women in history focuses on women from very diverse backgrounds who've been change-makers.

The name they selected for this endeavor, Bored of Boredom, turns out to be fitting, since the emails Hope receives from families testify that their children are now more fully engaged.

And all of that happened during spring break 2020. When their own classes resumed, Bored of Boredom continued:

The tutors are continuing to work with their students at lunchtime and after school. It's inspiring to see how dedicated they are. They're giving the time they have to make others' lives better.

"It's like my name," she says. "I like to bring hope."

Hope is now in college in New York City, and the baton has been passed from the group of five passionate high schoolers to an organized initiative with the help of their parents and other adult friends. More than a thousand volunteers now serve several thousand children. I asked Hope what led her to take a positive risk in creating Bored of Boredom during the pandemic. She said:

I've grown up in an environment and family that really prioritizes healing the world. Essentially, I learned that, whenever I could take action to alleviate suffering, I needed to do so. Whether I'm helping one or one thousand people, I'm still lessening the net suffering in the world.

What advice would she give parents?

I think that leading by example is imperative. If a person doesn't see others taking action, then they're less likely to see it as feasible or normal.

Additionally, it is crucial for parents to maintain a positive attitude. If children and teens are routinely told that they won't have an impact or that their actions don't matter, they're less likely to act. Parents ought to emphasize the fact that any small kindness has an impact on lessening the net suffering in the world.[256]

PROMOTING A KINDER WORLD

A ten-year-old wrote: "Stop hating each other. Just stop!" When I've shared that quote with colleagues and friends, many dismiss this call for change as naive. When we dismiss it, we are disrespecting adolescents.

If we don't try to stop conflict, nothing will change.

But if we try—take one small step to look for kindness and be that kindness, whether it's directed at one person or one thousand—we'll be on our way toward a kinder world. In the process, we'll be setting an example for adolescents, respecting the values they believe in, and empowering them to live these values in their lives.

Rethinking Adolescence: From a Portrait to a Landscape

"He won't be different," the school principal said to Edith in response to her request to move her son to a different classroom.

"I believe he will," she said. "This isn't the way he acts at home."

"We never move children," another administrator told her. "We don't want to set a precedent."

It bothered Edith that her child was suffering because of a precedent that didn't make any sense. Her son had gone from an energetic fifth grader to a listless, despondent one. He was throwing up most mornings before school. "He's being manipulative," some told Edith.

"But kids can't like throwing up," she recalls thinking.

Finally, in both confusion and desperation, she pulled him from the school and found another school nearby where she could enroll him. "He won't change" were the parting words from the old school.

The first day at the new school, his grandmother picked him up and asked about his day. "You know," he said, "the kids here actually like going to school." "Really?" she said. "Why?"

"In my old school, if you made a mistake and if they'd been allowed to have guns, they would have shot you," he answered. "In this school, it's okay to make a mistake."

It wasn't an overnight turnaround. It took months for him to believe that a teacher could be on his side and that he wouldn't be humiliated by the teachers and by the other kids for making mistakes or not knowing an answer.

Three years later, as he was graduating from eighth grade and moving to another city, he spoke in the school assembly, thanking the teachers and his classmates. "They thought I wouldn't be different in another school," he said. "But I was."

THE LURE OF INDIVIDUALISM

Have you ever wondered why most articles in the newspaper, spots on TV, or social media posts begin with a story of an individual? This is what's called a "portrait." These stories of individuals draw us in, make us want to keep reading or listening.

Individualism—the notion in psychology that we are each independent and self-reliant—is a cultural value in the United States. Individualism reverberates throughout the way we frame our experiences. We talk about individual heroes who succeed because of their character and grit.

We also tell stories of individuals who falter and fail. When some of these heroes get back up on their feet, it's on their own. They "pull themselves up by their bootstraps." They are "comeback kids."

We use this framing as a filter for understanding our world. When something goes wrong, it helps us explain causes, like in the case of Edith's son having a hard time in school. The school saw him as recalcitrant, resistant, spoiled. The blame probably extended to Edith, a single mother who worked long hours in her job to support her child. She said, "They keep looking at me as if I was doing something wrong."

Framing things in terms of the individual can cause us to lose sight of something very important. While many stories in the media, in our history, and in our folklore begin with portraits, the best stories weave in, alongside the portraits, what's called the "landscape." That's the context—the social, psychological, and physical environment—in which the individual's story unfolds. It's there that the hero learns crucial lessons, becomes strong, or rebounds from failure. In Edith's situation, the context was the school environment—the teachers, the administrators, the other students.

I heard stories like Edith's from so many others. Where there was a mismatch between an adolescent and a teacher or an adolescent and a school, the blame was put either on the adolescent and family or on the teachers and school. **But unless we look at both the portrait and the landscape together— the individual and the context—we have an incomplete understanding.**

There may be no better example of the importance of context in child development research than the Marshmallow Test,[257] the classic experiment created by the late Walter Mischel and his colleagues. Four-year-old children in this experiment are given a choice between one marshmallow now and two marshmallows later if they can wait as long as up to fifteen minutes. "The longer the young children were able to wait at age 4," Mischel explained, "the better the SAT scores, the better their ability to control themselves and to pursue their academic and other goals successfully."[258]

If that's all you examine—what the individual child (and later the adult) does—then it looks like the story of success begins and ends there. But as it turns out, it's not just the child's self-control that affects how long children wait. It's the context, too. If the person offering the marshmallows demonstrates that they are unreliable (promising some toys for the child to play with that they don't deliver on), children wait for an average of about three minutes compared with about twelve minutes if that person is reliable.[259]

In this chapter, we've seen similar research indicating how much families, friends, and social media can shape the behavior and attitudes of adolescents. And we've seen that change is possible in each of us and all of us. We've also seen that what seems almost intractable—the culture in schools—can change, too.

We know we can change ourselves, as difficult as it can be. We also know we can't force others (our teen) to change. But we *can* change the context, the environment. So, when things are tough, maybe we don't have to feel we're out of options. Maybe we just haven't yet found the right match of context-to-individual that works.

Paying attention just to individuals or just to the context won't work; paying attention to the individual and the context together is the path to much greater success.

3

MESSAGE 3: DON'T STEREOTYPE US

The first message from adolescents—understand our development/we are smarter than you think—is part of a much larger message: don't stereotype us.

Here's what they want us to know about who they are—and aren't:

They want to be valued and respected as an age group:

We are people, too.
>—Sixteen-year-old girl

We aren't less respectable than you. We aren't less than you. We are just as valuable people as you.
>—Twelve-year-old boy

We are underestimated because we are underaged.
>—Eleven-year-old boy

They want us to know they aren't all lazy:

We are not all lazy and crazy.
>—Sixteen-year-old boy

We are trying hard.
>—Twelve-year-old boy

We are hard-working and we care about the future.
>—Twelve-year-old girl

They also want us to know that most of them aren't self-absorbed, disrespectful, weak, social media–obsessed troublemakers:

Don't think we are all druggies or selfish and self-centered. Many of us are loving and caring about others and those less fortunate than we are.
        —Thirteen-year-old girl

We aren't a bunch of snowflakes. That's rude and unkind.
        —Seventeen-year-old girl

That we aren't as addicted to our phones as you think we are. We also have stuff going on so be patient with us please.
        —Fifteen-year-old girl

We have a lot more to offer the world than many of you see. Sometimes it feels like every adult thinks my generation is nothing more than a bunch of entitled brats that want everything given to them.
        —Seventeen-year-old girl

We're not all TikTokking risk-takers, to put it lightly. Hell, I barely use social media.
        —Eighteen-year-old boy

Don't judge all of us by the actions of a few.
        —Sixteen-year-old girl

They say they are responsible, strong, and fun:

We are responsible and trustworthy.
        —Sixteen-year-old girl

We can accomplish things and be responsible but recognize fun must be a part of our lives.
        —Seventeen-year-old boy

Breakthrough Years Study Finding: More than one in three adolescents (38 percent)*—the largest proportion of adolescents in this study—ask adults not to generalize, make negative assumptions, or stereotype them, but instead to recognize their strengths.

---

* Overall, this finding combines six coding categories from the survey, such as "We are not dumb," "We are not lazy," "We are not bad," and others.

The sheer number and the passion of these messages reveal an issue that we, individually and collectively, need to pay attention to: our conceptions of adolescents.

Reflections on Message 3

Think of a time when someone made an assumption about you because of the way you look or sound, or because of your background. What do you remember? How did they treat you as a result? How did you react?

The issues in adolescents' lives carry some parallels with our lives, too, so it is important to ground our thinking in those commonalities.

When I ask these questions in speeches to adults, I find it takes some back to their early experiences when other people's assumptions struck sharply at the core of who they were. A woman in her fifties remembers a time when she was seven or eight:

My mother picked me up from school but I had to go to the bathroom first. I walked into the bathroom and someone came after me—a woman I'd never met before. I didn't know who she was, and she had no idea who I was. She was so angry that there was a boy in the women's bathroom. She said she was going to call the principal.

It was so frightening—I remember a full-body flush of embarrassment. It was like I'd walked into a classroom naked.

I ran out to my mom. I couldn't find the words; I couldn't find my voice. My mom had never seen me like that before. She said, "What happened?" and I told her, "I don't know what I did wrong. This woman said I was a boy and I tried to tell her I wasn't a boy."

My mom went into full mom-mode and marched into the bathroom with me, yelling. The woman backed down. My mom then took me into her arms and let me cry and said, "You are the most beautiful person I've ever met. Don't ever let anyone ever tell you otherwise."

Because of the explosion, everyone in the school heard about it and everyone wanted to talk about it. I didn't want to have any part of that. I just wanted to be left alone and go to the bathroom.

Even now, when I tell this story, I get teary. It's the way I look—I look androgynous. I am very clear about what I am. I am a woman.

For another woman, it was the way she sounded:

When I came to the United States from England, I was eleven, turning twelve, and was starting junior high school. All of the kids had gone through the previous grades together. The first day of school, I walked in and was put on the spot to introduce myself. The whole class burst out laughing because of my British accent.

I ran out of the classroom and all the way home and cried. I was mortified that they laughed at me. I was like, "I don't want to go back," but I had to go back. The next day, everyone would say, "Say something, say something."

For some, their memories are current and include assumptions about gender:

At work, the assumption usually is that I'm the errands person. It makes me question: "Did I do anything to make that happen?" I try to keep calm, but it does really get you down.

For others, it's their skin color:

*When you hear my voice and when you see me, it's different behavior. They love my voice and act one way and then they see me—they see my skin color—they see **me**, it's at a different level.*

Or assumptions about them as an employee that they can't seem to live down:

Where I work, there are negative assumptions that float around and stick—this one's too controlling, that one's not too smart, the other one's a micromanager. In all of us, it creates feelings of being on guard, all the time.

When assumptions are made about who we are—our identities and our group belonging—and when these assumptions feel mistaken, constricting, or harmful, they can elicit embarrassment, mortification, a sense of being naked, of doubting, of getting us down, of having to be on guard. These feelings remain powerful, even in recalling them. That's why stereotyping and discrimination touch us, get under our skin, even affect our biological health.

THE ORIGINS OF ISMS

When my children and grandchildren were babies, I loved playing "imitation games" with them—smiling, shaking my head, making silly faces, and delighting when they'd copy me.

We see babies imitating all the time. When they get their hands on the TV remote or our cell phone, they typically mimic adults' behavior. But how does a baby "know" what to do—really know which part of their bodies to use when they copy us picking up a cell phone with our hands or shaking our heads?

To talk about how we—adults and adolescents alike—view adolescents, we have to understand how very young children begin forming conceptions of themselves and others. It starts way back with babies taking their cues from us through imitation.

Andrew Meltzoff is one of the researchers who's been instrumental in helping us understand how young children form these conceptions.[1] He developed a theory called "Like Me Development"[2] and began seeking the neural underpinning of this behavior with seven-month-olds.[3] Here's what he found:

When we touched the baby's hand, we were able to find a particular area in the baby's brain that became active, or lit up, often called the "hand region."

The really interesting thing is that when a baby simply watched an adult's hand being touched, the very same neural region became active in the baby's brain.

This means that the infant brain is already comparing self to other, before the child can produce language or verbally label body parts. The infant is already able to tell my hand is like your hand, my foot is like your foot, my lips are like your lips.

This has profound implications for the development of social relationships. The infant knows, "You are like me and I am like you." This is an important building block for interpersonal connections and a sense of belonging.[4]

Starting from infancy:

- We are primed to pay special attention to people who are like us or with whom we interact a lot, and to sort people into categories.[5]

And:

- We are primed to make judgments about these similarities and differences.[6]

I use the word "primed" purposely. This is normal brain development—something it seems we're wired to do.

SOCIETAL VIEWS SHAPE YOUNG CHILDREN'S VIEWS OF OTHERS AND THEMSELVES

"Kids pay attention, not only to who's like me, but how society treats others who are like me," Meltzoff says. "That's where preschool and elementary school children and stereotypes begin to intersect."[7]

Meltzoff and Allison Skinner of the University of Georgia found that young children "catch" others' views by watching how people interact. They prefer the people we act warmly toward versus people we reject or interact with in a cold way.[8]

They also pick up on what others think of "their" group. Meltzoff says:

If you're a little girl, you've already built the "like me" class that the females out there are like me, in a gender sense; now you're paying quite close attention to how society treats those like me.

You're drawing lessons and inferences: You look to others in society for information and guidance.[9]

For example:

If you're a girl and people in your culture are constantly conveying the idea that girls don't do math, you could draw the social inference, "Well, maybe I shouldn't do math if I want to fit in."

SOCIETAL VIEWS CAN BE ALTERED

Meltzoff has found that girls adopted these societal judgments about girls and math and science in their very early years—but importantly, they can be changed. He and Allison Master of the University of Houston found that if preschool girls learn that people like them *are* very interested in math and science, they persist longer and do better in math and science activities:[10]

> *Having children and adolescents believe that they're part of a social group that has this interest in math, science, and technology is highly motivating for their learning, their educational choices, and their aspirations for the future. All people want to feel that they "belong"; it's a fundamental motive even for children and adolescents—maybe even especially for them.*[11]

CASTE

One classification that societies make is what Isabel Wilkerson and others call "caste." In her book of the same name, Wilkerson compares caste to the architecture of a house. America, she writes, has a caste system that is "as central to its operation as are the studs and joists that we cannot see in the physical buildings we call home. Caste is the infrastructure of our divisions. It is the architecture of human hierarchy."[12]

What is caste? In Wilkerson's words, it is "a fixed and embedded ranking of human value that sets the presumed supremacy of one group against the presumed inferiority of other groups."[13]

Every society has rankings. These determine who has more or less access to power and resources. The categories used for rankings could be race, ethnicity, religion, place of birth, language, and so on. If you look at the categories used through the lens of history, they can seem arbitrary.

Wilkerson differentiates between caste, which is based on outward manifestations of things we cannot change about ourselves (like skin color or hair texture), and class, which is based on things we can change about ourselves (the way we talk, the clothes we wear, etc.).

How do children learn these hierarchical rankings? Again, Wilkerson's analogy is unforgettable:

> *As we go about our daily lives, caste is the wordless usher in a darkened theater, flashlight cast down in the aisles, guiding us to our assigned seats for a performance.*[14]

Not only is it about power, resources, who is worthy of them, and who gets them or not, but it's also "about respect, authority and assumptions of competence—who are accorded these and who are not."[15]

And these—belonging, respect, autonomy, and competence—as we will discuss later, are basic psychological needs for us all.

HOW ISMS HAPPEN

So, while it's normal to look for how we're different from and the same as others and to classify ourselves and others into groups, problems arise when these differences become laced with assumption and negativity. This can become the basis for sexism, racism, ageism, and other isms. Isms arise when groups of people are seen as inferior to others by individuals, institutions, and the culture as a whole.[16]

In the sections that follow, I'll show that there's another "ism" that can do damage, including health damage, to our children: teenism.

Teenism affects us all. We were once adolescents, growing up under perhaps limiting assumptions. If we have children, they have been, are, or will become adolescents. And they are or will become the adults who make the decisions about the future of our world. Thus, the negative stereotypes we hold about adolescents as a group can potentially harm them, and in doing so, harm us, too.

Are Adolescents Stereotyped?

Almost all of the parents and the adolescents I interviewed for the qualitative study said a resounding yes.

Hank, a father of six from Georgia, echoed others when he told me:

> I think there're stereotypes at all levels: "The kids do crazy things," or "The kids are driving too fast through the neighborhood." But that's always been the way adults talk about kids.

Nancy, the mother of an eighteen-year-old from Oregon, said these stereotypes are widespread, and she worries about their impact:

> It's normal to hear them from friends and family. I even hear them on TV programs: all teenagers drink, all teenagers sneak out. Parents are just

expecting it. I think that's dangerous because kids do what they're expected to do, in my opinion.

As you know, more than one-third of adolescents in the quantitative Breakthrough Years study said, "Don't stereotype us." This was amplified in the qualitative interviews with young people. Fifteen-year-old Brittany from Virginia told me:

I feel like many people view teenagers in extremes, like you're all one thing, which isn't true. There's definitely a middle ground. I walk that middle ground all the time. There are a lot of really good kids.

From the very start of this research, it was evident that being stereotyped was on adolescents' minds. When I asked the young people in focus groups/ interviews when I first launched these studies what I should ask researchers on adolescent development, there was a discussion that really stood out. One said:

Look at us—we're not what comes to mind when you ask an American adult to think of the typical teenager.

Recalling the six-word memoirs he had composed in school, this adolescent said:

I would be interested to see what six words do come to mind.

From that discussion the idea emerged that I should ask researchers what three words come to mind for typical adolescents—the adolescents they study—and three words for stereotypical adolescents.

So I asked and found a sharp contrast between these two descriptions:

The most frequent words the researchers used to describe the **stereotypical adolescent** tended to be **negative:**

Moody/overly emotional
Makes risky decisions
Selfish/self-centered
Impulsive/wild
Rebellious
Awkward

Easily influenced by other kids
Lazy

The most frequent words the researchers used to describe the **typical adolescent** they've studied tended to be **positive:**

Motivated
Creative
Fun
Curious
Social
Excited by life
Open to discovery and learning
Hardworking

JUST HOW ENTRENCHED ARE NEGATIVE STEREOTYPES ABOUT ADOLESCENTS? OUR TOP FINDINGS

I made a list of the researchers' most frequent positive and negative words—sixteen in all. Then, in the Breakthrough Years baseline survey, we asked parents to respond to these words in a number of ways:

Which of the following words or phrases would best describe young people who are your child's age?

And:

Which of the following words or phrases would best describe your child?

They could select all the words or phrases they wanted. Here's what we found, in order of the frequency of parents' responses:

Finding 1: Negative stereotypes exist—there's often a gap between what parents say about *their own* adolescents and adolescents their child's age.

- **Easily influenced by other kids.** Sixty-six percent of parents of adolescents say this phrase best describes young people their child's age, but only 29 percent say their own adolescent is easily influenced by other kids.

- **Moody/overly emotional.** Fifty-two percent of parents say "moody" and "overly emotional" describe adolescents their child's age. By comparison, 42 percent describe their own adolescent this way.
- **Selfish/self-centered.** While 43 percent of parents indicated that "selfish/self-centered" is a good description of adolescents their child's age, 20 percent describe their own adolescent that way.
- **Awkward.** Thirty-seven percent of parents describe adolescents their child's age as awkward, whereas 23 percent say their own adolescent is awkward.
- **Lazy.** Forty percent of parents see adolescents their child's age as lazy; 28 percent see their own adolescent as lazy.
- **Wild/impulsive, rebellious, makes risky decisions.** Of young people their child's age, 39 percent of parents say "wild/impulsive," 36 percent say "rebellious," and 32 percent say "makes risky decisions" are good descriptions, compared with 17, 14, and 12 percent, respectively, saying that about their own child.

The pattern is clear. Parents hold more negative views about adolescents their child's age than they do about their own child. This is where stereotyping comes in. A stereotype is a set of generalizations (e.g., beliefs, expectations) about the qualities and characteristics of the members of a group or social category. These generalizations are often exaggerated, negative rather than positive, and resistant to revision even when people know individuals with qualities that don't fit the stereotype.[17]

The sample in this study is nationally representative of parents with adolescents ages nine through nineteen. This means it represents individual parents' views about their own child *and* it includes other parents' view of their children. Taken together, these views can be seen as representing how parents see adolescents these days.

As one example, look at the negative terms related to risk-taking in this study—"makes risky decisions," "rebellious," and "wild/impulsive." As we've seen, these are widespread concerns in the media, in books, and among researchers. Not very many parents use these terms to describe their own child—12 percent for "makes risky decisions," 14 percent for "rebellious," and 17 percent for "wild/impulsive." Yet when describing adolescents in general, those percentages jump to 32, 36, and 39 percent, respectively.

Putting this information into a bar graph showing the gaps between what we think of adolescents in general compared with what we think of our own adolescent is a sure sign that negative stereotypes exist!

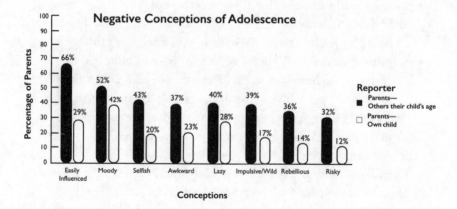

While we need to do everything we can to reduce unwise, dangerous behavior in adolescents, that doesn't mean we should automatically assume the worst of all of them as a group. As Nancy, the parent from Oregon, says, others talk about "all" teenagers drinking, "all" teenagers sneaking out. "Parents are just expecting it."

Finding 2: Regarding positive attributes, parents for the most part are more likely to see their own adolescent as having positive attributes than they are to see other adolescents that way—thus, stereotyping still shows up.

- **Curious.** There's a one-to-one match here, with 62 percent of parents selecting "curious" as describing adolescents their child's age, exactly the same percentage as those who see their own adolescent as curious.
- **Social, fun, creative, open to discovery and learning, excited by life.** The percentages begin diverging here. Parents are more likely to see their own adolescent as having these positive attributes than other children their child's age.
- **Motivated, hardworking.** Nowhere are stereotypes more prevalent than in parents' views here. Twenty-two percent see other children their child's age as "motivated" and 16 percent see them as "hardworking." In contrast, 37 percent of parents see their own adolescent as "motivated" and 44 percent characterize them as "hardworking."

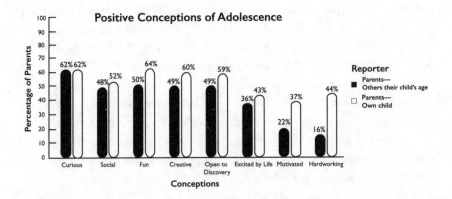

Our study puts numbers on something we've long understood about our conceptions of adolescence. As Hank, the father of six from Georgia, says, "That's always been the way adults talk about kids."

Do these stereotypes carry a cost to adolescents, or to our relationships with them? The next sections explore our findings.

The Impact of Teenism

The summer before my senior year in college, I worked for a West Virginia agency conducting a study of teens and their families. This project, funded by a federal grant, was seen locally as a thank-you from President John F. Kennedy to West Virginia—for the primary where Kennedy captured the Democrats' nomination for the presidency. He returned as president on a rain-soaked day in June 1963 to celebrate the state's centennial. I was one of those standing in the sheets of rain as he famously said, "The sun does not always shine in West Virginia, but the people always do."[18]

That was the West Virginia I knew growing up. That was the West Virginia of my family and friends.

And that was the West Virginia I saw daily, traveling the hills and hollows of Kanawha County to interview teens and their families for my summer job. While many families had experienced crippling poverty, many had strengths. It was clear, though, that a number of my out-of-state colleagues saw the people of my state differently than I did. At staff meetings, they talked openly and critically about them. I remember thinking that seeing homes in need of repair or hearing an "Appalachian" accent may have blinded them to the circumstances that kept these families in poverty and to their resilience despite hardship. They didn't talk about how children without store-bought toys created their own playthings from nature, or how families came together to care for each other when troubles arose. Of course, not all families were this way, but enough were. It felt as if the circumstances and strengths of these people weren't always seen or understood.

This experience sensitized me to place-based stereotyping. Later, as a teacher, I heard colleagues regularly say derogatory things about parents in the teacher lunchroom. I came to call this "parentism" and did a number of studies exploring why it happens and what makes a supportive parent-professional relationship possible. Still later, when I had children, I was watchful. If there was any chance my children might be labeled negatively, I did everything I could as a parent to prevent it from happening.

So, when I began the journey that became this book, I was especially drawn to adolescents' requests that I look at what I've come to call "teenism."

Underlying teenism are both conceptions and stereotypes of adolescents. Conceptions are views of what adolescents are like. Some can also be stereotypes—negative beliefs about individuals based on their membership in a group of people, in this case, their agemates.[19]

DO STEREOTYPES OF ADOLESCENCE AFFECT ADOLESCENTS?

Given the importance of age stereotyping to adolescents themselves, there are surprisingly few studies on it. Christy Buchanan (now of Wake Forest University) and Grayson Holmbeck of Loyola University, Chicago, are rare exceptions. In the 1990s, they developed a scale to measure stereotypes by asking college students and parents to describe the stereotypical and average adolescent and then testing these words with college students and parents of middle school students.[20] The result was a Stereotypes of Adolescents scale.

Buchanan's next question: "Can expecting storm and stress increase real or perceived storm and stress?"[21] She and Johna Hughes, then of the University of North Carolina, Chapel Hill, speculated that if parents expect negative behavior, they might overreact, consider negative behavior inevitable, or focus on behavior that fits their expectations and ignore behavior that doesn't.

They assembled a sample of 270 adolescents in the sixth and seventh grades and most of their mothers (255) from two public schools in the southeastern United States. Mothers were asked about their expectations for their children, using questions from the Stereotypes of Adolescents scale— for example, if they expected their child to take negative risks, test limits, or be rebellious, reckless, stubborn, rude, impulsive, restless, or selfish. Mothers were also asked questions about their child's behavior problems, using a well-established measure.

The sixth and seventh graders were asked very similar questions, rating how well each of fifty-seven statements described them during adolescence. They also reported on their own behavior problems, their susceptibility to peer influence, and their closeness to and conflict with their parents. One year later, when the children were in the seventh and eighth grades, both the adolescents and mothers were reinterviewed and resurveyed.

Buchanan and Hughes had hypothesized that when mothers and adolescents expected more negative risk-taking and rebelliousness during adolescence, there'd be more risk-taking and rebelliousness reported by the adolescent.

But you might wonder: Wouldn't children's behavior problems and their conflict or closeness with their parents at the beginning of the study affect the results one year later? You'd be right. So the researchers statistically controlled for these and for demographic factors—that is, held them constant in their statistical analyses.

The study results, even with these controls, confirmed their hypothesis—not to an overwhelming degree, but parents' views were predictive of their children's later behavior problems.

Key Finding: Expecting a difficult time when children become adolescents is linked with actual difficult times later on, somewhat over and above what the child's prior behavior before becoming a teen might suggest.

REBELLIOUS OR READY FOR RESPONSIBILITY? CULTURAL CONCEPTIONS OF ADOLESCENCE MATTER, TOO

Sometimes it takes a clash between how we view the world and how others view it to prompt us to rethink what's true. It happened for me when I encountered the clash between my views of West Virginians and the views of others. It also happened for Yang Qu of Northwestern University during graduate school at New York University. He grew up in China, and was struck by the discrepancies between how adolescents are seen in the United States and in China.

In the United States, research focused on adolescents moving away—separating from—their families, being influenced by their peers, and behaving in "rebellious and irresponsible" ways.[22] He says:

It is just totally different from Chinese or East Asian culture. In East Asia, adolescence is actually a time that adults and society expect you to take on more responsibility.

Because adolescence is viewed as the first step toward adulthood, young people in East Asia are expected to work hard in school and fulfill their obligations to their parents:

All the cultural forces guide East Asian children toward more responsible pathways.

These and other striking differences led Qu to question how cultural conceptions of adolescence, especially stereotypical views of adolescents as being rebellious and irresponsible, affect young people's school engagement. He focused on school engagement as an outcome because it's obviously important and because U.S. and Chinese adolescents show such different patterns:

We know from a lot of research that American adolescents show declines in school engagement when they enter the middle school.

In contrast:

Our own prior research shows that Chinese children either maintain or show an increase in their school engagement during the middle school years.

In the United States, Qu and his colleagues recruited 203 seventh-grade students from Illinois to participate in this study on the drivers of school engagement.[23] In mainland China, they selected 194 students of the same age from Shandong Province, a province Qu says is "exposed to typical Chinese culture." He says they "intentionally selected this age group because we wanted to make sure we capture their [views] when they first enter the adolescent years."[24]

These students were surveyed in the spring of their seventh-grade year and again in the fall of their eighth-grade year, using open-ended questions (i.e., with no suggestions or prompts that might influence their responses).

Seventh graders were asked to list whatever came into their minds about the attitudes and behaviors of teens that they saw as typical.[25]

Then they completed a questionnaire, where they were asked to rate thirty items on whether that attitude or behavior was "more true before the teen years," "equally true before and during the teen years," or "more true during the teen years."[26]

From their findings and the prior literature, the researchers identified four potential "drivers" of school engagement:

- **Individuating from parents:** Both Chinese and U.S. children see the teen years as a time of separating from parents, but U.S. children are more likely to characterize the teen years this way.
- **Family responsibility:** U.S. children see family obligation as more characteristic *before* the teen years, while Chinese children see it as more characteristic *before* and *during* the teen years.
- **School disengagement:** U.S. children see school disengagement as more characteristic *during* adolescence, while Chinese children saw school disengagement as more characteristic *before* the teen years.
- **Peer orientation:** Both U.S. and Chinese children characterize the teen years as a time of peer orientation, but U.S. children more strongly see the teen years this way.[27]

To measure engagement, the researchers asked the study participants about strategies for doing their schoolwork—for example, asking how true it was that "If I get confused about something at school, I go back and try to figure it out."

Key Finding: The researchers found that adolescents' view of adolescence as a time of becoming more independent from parents and less engaged in school in the United States was associated with using fewer school engagement strategies over time than young Chinese people.

In the words of the researchers, "Culture shapes youth's conceptions of adolescence in the United States and China, which contribute to differences in youth's engagement in school over this phase in the two countries."[28]

CAN NEGATIVE STEREOTYPES OF ADOLESCENTS
AFFECT BRAIN DEVELOPMENT?

That was a logical next question for Qu.[29] Twenty-two of the students who participated in the study in the seventh grade in the United States underwent brain scans in the eighth and ninth grades while completing a task that assessed cognitive control.[30] Although the researchers looked at the whole brain in their analyses, they ultimately focused on the prefrontal cortex, which continues developing in adolescence and is directly involved when young people manage their behavior, including avoiding negative risk.

The cognitive control task they used specifically assesses executive function skills—the Go/No-Go task. On the computer, study participants see letters, one at a time, and are asked to press a button (i.e., "go") every time a letter appears—except for the letter X, when they are asked not to press the button (i.e., "no-go"). It takes inhibitory control to turn off an automatic response and not press the button when an X appears.

Adolescents also reported on their negative risky behavior in the eighth and ninth grades, such as stealing, drinking, smoking, and hanging around with others who got into trouble.

The study team found that adolescents who saw the teen years as a time of being more irresponsible in their family life (such as being disrespectful to parents, rarely complying with family requests, and not caring about meeting family obligations) were more likely to show longitudinal increases in their ventrolateral prefrontal cortex activation over time during the cognitive control task, suggesting that they needed to work harder at regulating their impulsive behavior.

Qu says:

> *The findings suggest that the stereotypes that children hold when they first enter the adolescent years play a role in their brain development over time.*

Importantly, the scan findings correlated with the adolescents' reports on their own negative risky behavior—that is, if they showed increases in their ventrolateral prefrontal cortex activation, they were also more likely to show increases in risk-taking behavior over time.

Key Finding: It's a small sample and a first step—but this study points to the fact that holding stereotypes of young people might affect adolescents' behavior and brain development.

DOES COUNTERING NEGATIVE STEREOTYPES PROMOTE POSITIVE BEHAVIOR IN ADOLESCENCE?

These results led Qu to ask: Can negative stereotypes be changed into more positive views? Would more positive beliefs then change young people's behavior? For this study, Qu and his colleagues focused on Chinese adolescents in Shanghai:

> *Since Shanghai is the most westernized city in China, children there are exposed to both East Asian views and Western views of teens, so maybe their stereotypes of adolescence are flexible and open to change.*[31]

The researchers developed counterstereotyping interventions that discredited the idea that teens are irresponsible.[32] In one experiment with 319 seventh graders in China, students in the intervention group were given a passage to read that said that while young people are often portrayed by the media as rebellious and irresponsible, this depiction is inaccurate for many teens, who can be quite responsible. In the next phase, the study participants were given a single sheet of paper. In the control condition, they were asked to write about typical teen behavior at home with their families and at school. In the experimental condition, they were asked to write down examples they'd observed of teens doing responsible things at home, with their families, and at school. This activity is called "saying is believing"[33] in mindset interventions: when you state something to someone else, you are more likely to believe it's true.[34]

Following those exercises, the original experimenters left and a new group of experimenters came into their classrooms and told students in both the intervention and control groups that there would be a five-minute break during which they could work on an English word-search puzzle.[35] Students were also given daily reports to complete for each of three days that asked questions about their academic engagement for that day—for example, whether they'd "listened very carefully in class" and "tried hard to do well in school." In addition, they were asked about their negative risk-taking for that day, such as "cheated on an assignment or exam" and "hung around with kids who get in trouble."

Key Finding: In this study, not only did young people in the counter-stereotyping intervention perform better on the word puzzle but their academic engagement was higher.

This study spanned three days and was conducted in China, but Qu sees it as holding a lot of promise for the United States. The journey continues for him. He's planning to conduct a larger and longer-term intervention in the United States.

As I talked with Qu, I kept thinking of the young people in the Breakthrough Years study passionately asking adults not to stereotype them. It's so important to them, yet so few researchers are pursuing this subject. When I told Qu that I'm grateful he's asking these questions, he replied:

> Since stereotypes can affect how young people navigate the teen years, I do think our field should pay more attention.

So do I.

The Disruptive Effects of Discrimination

"In sixth grade you're like, 'Yay, I'm in middle school,'" Joshua, now twelve, remembers. When seventh grade happened, he was like, "Gosh, this is not what I wanted."

Why?

> Because seventh is usually the year everybody hits puberty, which nobody likes. Because if you sound different, look different, or have pimples, you get made fun of.

When we think about discrimination—the prejudicial treatment of individuals because of the groups they belong to—we rightly tend to think of race/ethnicity, gender, religion, or age as it applies to the elderly. We rarely think of treating young people in prejudicial ways when they hit puberty because they sound different, look different, or have pimples. But the adolescents I interviewed—though they didn't call it discrimination—told me many stories where that happened to them by different kinds of people.

For Lola, twelve, from Nevada, it was people in general. Because she matured early and looked older, people thought she looked mean and treated her like a mean girl. She told me she had to work hard to counter those assumptions from people in stores, on the street, even from people she knew:

I show them I'm not like that and not all people are like that; and that they shouldn't be judging or treating people poorly because of their looks.

For Tim from Georgia, now seventeen, it was the people in his church. He'd volunteered in Sunday school classes with young children since he was young himself and cared a lot about teaching, but when he became a teenager, parents began acting as if they didn't want him around their young kids:

Maybe because I'm a guy. I'm big. Not fat. I'm tall and muscular. So, they began to act like they felt uncomfortable or I didn't belong doing that.

So he stopped volunteering.

If we heard these stories in everyday conversations, we might dismiss them as "everybody goes through this—get over it." But since we know discrimination can have repercussions, we need to know more.

Andrew Fuligni of the University of California, Los Angeles, heard stories about age discrimination from young people in his studies, and fortunately for all of us, he didn't dismiss them. Coming from a family that immigrated to the United States, he had been studying ethnic and racial discrimination, beginning in New York City, where he and his colleagues found that children from ethnic minorities (specifically African American, Chinese, Dominican, and Russian families) were uniquely aware of the stigma attached to their backgrounds at young ages.[36] This stigma spilled over into school: all children who felt that their group was of a lower status were less motivated academically—that is, unless the children (whatever their background) felt they belonged in their school.

When he moved to UCLA, Fuligni continued to study discrimination and found, as the title of a 2010 article states, "discrimination hurts."[37] In this study of 601 twelfth graders from Asian, Latin American, and European

American backgrounds, students filled out daily diaries and reported on their experiences with discrimination. The researchers also collected information about the students' self-esteem, depression, and physical well-being, and the schools provided access to the students' grades.[38]

Discrimination doesn't happen every day, Fuligni learned:

> When you ask about the actual frequency of experiencing overt hostile or unfair treatment because of race or ethnicity, these reports tend to be fairly infrequent.[39]

Even so, discrimination was "very consequential."[40] Young people who'd experienced discrimination by both adults and peers were more likely to have lower grade point averages, lower self-esteem, more symptoms of depression, and more physical problems such as headaches, stomachaches, and feeling tired for no reason.[41]

In subsequent studies, Fuligni and his colleagues looked at discrimination on the basis of gender, weight, height, *and* age.

What led to their asking about age? I wondered. He told me he'd been listening to the students in his in-depth qualitative studies and to his own children:

> They feel that simply because they're a teenager, society has particular views of them. They really bristle against that. They find that oppressive and unfair![42]

AGE DISCRIMINATION SCORES HIGH

In this study from 2016, Fuligni, Virginia Huynh, a former graduate student now at California State University, Northridge, and their colleagues used the Everyday Discrimination Scale, developed by David Williams of Harvard University.[43] Two hundred and ninety-two tenth- and eleventh-grade students from four public high schools in the Los Angeles area were asked:

> In your day-to-day life, over the last twelve months, how often have any of the following things happened to you?[44]

The experiences included being treated with less respect than others, people acting as if they thought you weren't smart, or people acting as if they were afraid of you. After asking about each type of discrimination, they asked students why they thought this had happened—listing a number of possible reasons, including age.[45]

Perhaps surprisingly (because so few researchers have asked about age), **age discrimination scored high.**

Key Finding: In the words of Andrew Fuligni: "The students attributed unfair treatment to their age at very high rates—almost, if not just as high—as they attributed to their ethnic or racial background or their gender. That was very striking to us!"[46]

DISCRIMINATION CAN "GET UNDER THE SKIN"

The main purpose of a follow-up 2016 study was to look at the links between discrimination and biological measures of health and well-being,[47] specifically "its relationship to the rhythm of cortisol output during the day, which is one indicator of the body's stress response." They assessed cortisol output over three days of the 292 tenth and eleventh graders:

> We provide swabs that they're supposed to use during the week. They're given very explicit instructions to put them in their mouth, chew on them for a while, and then put them back into the vial. We also remind them with text messages so they would do it on a timely basis . . . a few times in the morning, once around dinnertime, and once before bed. The swab extracts their saliva, which we assay for levels of cortisol.[48]

They found a connection.

Key Finding: As the researchers summarize in their journal article: "Everyday discrimination occurred relatively infrequently, but adolescents who perceived higher rates of such unfair treatment evidenced elevated levels of cortisol across the day."[49]

This is one of the few studies that have asked adolescents *why* they think they experienced discrimination. But in the end, the reasons were less significant than the fact that it occurred:

Our results indicate that attributions may not matter as much as the frequency of any type of discrimination. Although attributions to age and race were most common, there was no clear pattern associated with the type of attributions and the cortisol parameters.[50]

As Fuligni told me, these findings indicate "that in many ways this experience is 'getting under the skin of these youth,' and, in turn, could potentially have some health consequences down the line."[51]

Elevated cortisol in adults is linked to psychological problems such as depression and physical problems including cardiovascular disease. It's increasingly understood that these problems begin much younger than previously believed.[52]

DISCRIMINATION AND SLEEP

Expanding their studies beyond the waking hours was the logical next step. The Adolescent Development Lab that Fuligni directs at UCLA has studied sleep for years. Fuligni calls sleep a "biological necessity":

- **Sleep is restorative:** "Biologically, we need it as a restorative process."
- **Sleep regulates bodily processes:** "Sleep is important for the regulation of multiple body processes, whether it be inflammatory processes or growth processes."
- **Sleep is critical to learning:** "What's going on during sleep may be fundamental to learning—cognitive, factual learning, but also emotional learning."[53]

Richard Huganir of Johns Hopkins University and his colleagues have conducted studies of mice that further explain the importance of sleep to learning. During the day, they found, the synapses in the brain get larger, while during the night they get smaller.[54] Huganir explains:

What we think is occurring is that during the day you're learning a lot of things, you're gaining information; your synapses are getting stronger, but then to learn the next day, you have to reset the whole system. You have to decrease the excitability, decrease the size of the synapses. This is involved in consolidation of memory.[55]

This means that sleep is linked to learning in ways we didn't previously understand. Huganir jokes that the saying "sleep on it" is scientifically valid:

We think the normal sleep process—having a good night's sleep—really helps consolidate memories from the previous day and enables you to recall them. This has been a major discovery!

Discrimination can interfere with sleep, Fuligni finds, because it promotes elevated arousal:

For us to have a good night's sleep, we need to minimize threat and arousal and maximize safety and security. Discrimination works against that.[56]

This is particularly important in adolescence, because, as the researchers write (and as we've seen):

Adolescence is a period of increased sensitivity to social evaluation, contributing to teenagers' vulnerability to social experiences that can undermine their feelings of safety and belonging.[57]

The 316 participants in this study were from the same sample of tenth and eleventh graders in the cortisol study. Specifically, the researchers wanted to know:

- How are ethnic, gender, age, and height or weight discrimination associated with adolescents' sleep duration, variability, and quality?
- Do loneliness and perceived stress make a difference in the connections between discrimination and sleep?

Since bringing participants into a sleep lab (the ideal way to measure sleep) wasn't feasible, the researchers gave each participant an ActiGraph watch that measures physical activity, sleep, and movement and asked them to put it on before going to bed at night:

They're supposed to push a button on the watch to indicate that they're going to sleep. If they get up during the night, they push a button to let us know the higher frequency of movement is because they're getting out of bed. Then, they hit the button when they wake up and they're done sleeping.[58]

These watches are like sports watches but more sophisticated:

*Based upon the estimates of movement from the watch, we figure out
what time they went to bed, how long it took for them to fall asleep, sleep
duration, and how often they woke during the night.*

The participants also answered many questions about their sleep and completed questionnaires about everyday discrimination, loneliness, and stress.

The researchers found that discrimination for ethnic and nonethnic reasons (gender, age, height, or weight) affected the quantity and quality of the adolescents' sleep. Interestingly, if young people reported being discriminated against because of their ethnicity, they were more likely to feel lonely, which in turn affected their sleep. If they reported discrimination for nonethnic reasons (gender, age, height, or weight), they were more likely to feel lonely and stressed, which similarly affected their sleep.

Key Finding: Discrimination affects the quantity and quality of sleep. In this study, the association between discrimination and sleep was due in part to feelings of loneliness and stress.

IT'S MORE THAN JUST TELLING OURSELVES "EVERYBODY GOES THROUGH THIS—GET OVER IT"

As I write this, I recall some of the people I interviewed who said discrimination doesn't matter, like sixteen-year-old Tim:

*I usually just try to avoid the people who stereotype me because their
opinions don't really matter to me. If you're that closed-minded, I don't
care.*

Helping individuals learn and apply coping and resilience strategies is a good start. But it's not enough. As the Adolescent Development Lab team at UCLA notes on their website in sharing their study results:

*Our work joins emerging research from other labs to suggest
discrimination is a very real experience for adolescents that can have a*

*negative impact upon their development. Although it is important to study ways to help youth cope with discrimination, it is equally imperative to prevent adolescents from experiencing such unfair treatment due to their race, ethnicity, gender, **and age** [emphasis added] in the first place.*[59]

Make no mistake: I'm all for learning to take on challenges, which I see as an essential Life and Learning Skill. But one way we develop that, as my research and the research of many others shows, is through our social connections. We are by nature social. Community helps us to know and become who we are. Stereotyping and discrimination hurt us in ways we're only beginning to understand. For our own and our children's future, we can do better.

Everyday Discrimination: Hidden in Plain Sight

When I asked parents in the qualitative study whether their children experienced discrimination, those who said yes pointed to discrimination for gender, race, and sexual orientation:

- A daughter isn't taken seriously in sports.
- A gay teen is bullied at school and no one steps in to help.

Unless it happens to you, discrimination can be hidden in plain sight. But if or when it occurs, it's glaring, as it's been for Diane, an African American single mother living in Georgia with twelve-year-old Winston and ten-year-old Charles.

Her children have experienced discrimination a number of times and they've watched it happen, like the time Diane's ex-husband was visiting and they were going across the street to a store for snacks when a police car pulled up.

The officer's like, "Okay, we have a warrant out. We're going to take you in."

So, my ex is like, "Well, what is the warrant for?"

The officer began to try to handcuff him:

My ex is like, "No. Can you tell me what it's for and then cuff me?" The officer was like, "No. It doesn't really work that way."

Things began escalating quickly:

The officer got on his radio and says, "I'm at such and such address. Suspect resisting."

Next thing you know, another car comes out of nowhere and speeds to the house. That officer gets out. His gun is already drawn when he comes out.

He wheels toward Diane:

He pointed the gun at me and then pointed it at my ex, screaming, "Get on the ground. Get on the ground. Don't resist."

He's like, "I'm not resisting. I asked a question."

The second officer then turned on the first officer, demanding:

"Why'd you give him a chance? You should have tased him or pulled his hands out or something."

The first officer on the scene was like, "Well, he was cooperative. I didn't want to do that."

The second officer was like, "You don't give them that many chances. Pull out your taser."

The officers handcuffed her ex and put him in a patrol car for, as it turned out, driving with an expired license. Winston and Charles were very rattled:

When I got inside, they were like, "Momma, are you okay? Was that a gun?" I was like, "Yeah, a gun. It was crazy."

Diane knows she has to help her children deal with other people's assumptions about them because they are Black, but now that her children are becoming teens, she also has to help them deal with assumptions because of their age. She saw a local news story that frightened her. It was about teenagers walking through a neighbor's yard and getting shot at.

One of her own neighbors recently posted "No Trespassing" and "Private Property" signs, prompting Diane to show her twelve-year-old these signs and to try to talk to him about not cutting through their property as a quicker route to get to the store. When he didn't take it seriously enough, Diane got forceful:

> *"Our neighbor has signs up that say, 'No Trespassing.' If you go there, you're violating his property. There're no questions asked until after the fact. And after the fact means you can be shot in the leg or you can be dead."*

Some people refer to discussions with adolescents about sex as "the talk." But for children of color, "the talk" can include how best to respond to encounters—with the police, neighbors, or strangers—where assumptions are made about their intentions, and parents have to try to help their children navigate these interactions safely.[60]

AGE DISCRIMINATION?

When I asked parents I interviewed in the qualitative study if their children experienced age discrimination, most said no, except for those parents, like Diane, for whom the kind of treatment their children faced for other reasons amped up when their children became teenagers.

In general, we tend to connect age discrimination with elderly people. Here's Ethan, the father of two sons from New Jersey:

> *I've seen workplace discrimination with elders not able to get a job. But with kids? No.*

When I asked young people themselves, most didn't connect the term "age discrimination" with their experiences, though they could readily talk about gender and racial discrimination.

Without connecting it to "discrimination," however, they told stories about being treated unfairly because they're teenagers. Jessica, age fifteen, said, "If one person makes a bad decision, then all of us are seen as making bad decisions. I am not fifteen and pregnant. I hold myself to a high standard and I wouldn't do that stuff because I know better."

Yet discrimination follows them. Jessica recounted going to a makeup store for a girls' day at the mall:

> *We walked in, and the lady asked us if there was anyone over eighteen with us. I told her, "No. It's just us." She told us we weren't allowed to*

be in the store and kicked us out. We hadn't done anything. We simply stepped foot in the store. It really angered me because I wanted to shop for makeup. I hadn't done anything to make her think that I couldn't be in the store.

When asked why she thinks this happened, Jessica says:

We're teenagers. People think we are up to no good. Seeing us put an unsettling feeling in that lady's stomach—that's at least what I like to think.

In the Breakthrough Years survey, we asked adolescents about discrimination, using the Everyday Discrimination Scale developed by David Williams of Harvard University[61]—the same measure that Andrew Fuligni and his team used in their studies.

Finding 1: Overall, nearly 73 percent of adolescents had experienced one or more types of discrimination in the last year.

- People acted as if they were better than you (61 percent)
- Being called names or insulted (41 percent)
- People acted as if they thought you were not smart (37 percent)
- Being treated with less respect than other people (37 percent)
- People acted as if they thought you were dishonest (28 percent)
- Being threatened or harassed (19 percent)
- Receiving poorer service than other people at restaurants or stores (15 percent)
- People acted as if they were afraid of you (12 percent)
- Being followed around in stores (10 percent)

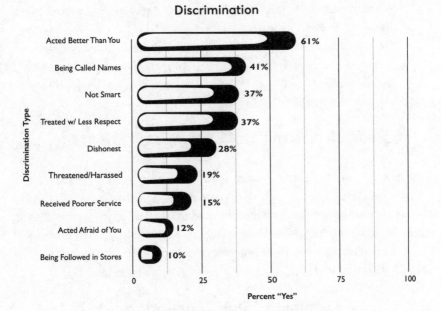

Discrimination

Finding 2: Of all the adolescents who'd experienced discrimination, age discrimination tops the reasons why they think it occurred.

We asked adolescents who'd experienced any of the nine types of discrimination at least a few times why they thought this had happened—what the main reasons were. They had eight reasons to choose from, including gender, race or ethnicity, sexual orientation, and the kids they hang out with. For six of the nine types of discrimination, adolescents selected age more than any of the other reasons.

Finding 3: Discrimination is associated with lower well-being.

Based on the number of times adolescents reported being discriminated against, we divided the study participants into three groups: one that experienced none of the nine types of discrimination in the past year (27 percent), a second group that experienced one to three instances (39 percent), and a third group that experienced four or more instances (34 percent).

We then compared the groups while controlling for demographics to allow for a better interpretation of possible differences among them, though as you know, correlation doesn't mean causation. We found:

- The adolescents who experienced one to three or four or more instances of discrimination reported lower school engagement, lower positive moods, more negative moods, more stress, and lower hopeful future expectations than those who didn't experience any discrimination.

- The adolescents who experienced four or more incidents of discrimination reported lower grades than those who experienced no discrimination.

PROMOTING POSITIVE CONCEPTIONS OF ADOLESCENTS

Although we may not be paying attention to age discrimination, it can be consequential—just like other types of discrimination. It was young people who told me that I should pay attention to "teenism." As a result, I hope that more of us will take teenism seriously and address it so it—like other isms—will no longer be hidden in plain sight.

Rethinking Our Conceptions of Adolescence: From Averages to Individuality

If we know that stereotyping adolescents can cause them harm, why do we do it?

We stereotype because we're drawn to see the world as "like me"—but the conceptions we form can be changed.

Studies show that infants are drawn to people like themselves.[62] This, as we've discussed, is called "Like Me Development."[63] Studies also show that young children aren't blind to color, gender, or other characteristics. They assign labels to groups they're in and not in—for example, "Girls like me aren't good at math." They absorb clues from the surrounding culture, even when we may think they're not noticing.[64] But we also see that negative labels can be changed. Girls "like me" can be good at math.[65]

We stereotype because of a bad-news bias and the challenge of holding multiple perspectives—but we can learn to look for positives and find the humanity we share.

We stereotype adolescents for many of the same deep-seated protective reasons that we're drawn to bad news—which involves protecting ourselves from difficulties. We also stereotype because it's challenging to understand others' perspectives, but we can learn these skills for our benefit and the benefit of our adolescents.

We stereotype because we worry about what's "normal" and to create simpler stories from complex realities—but what does "normal" mean, and how often do such comparisons help?

Just as adolescents ask themselves, "Am I normal?" parents also ask, "Is my child/Is my child's behavior normal?"

In our family, there's a story about normalcy that's become lore. My daughter found out via the internet that her friend's toddler could count to two hundred in Japanese. While this was remarkable because this little girl had no Japanese in her background, it was particularly remarkable to Lara because her son, my grandson, was barely counting to twenty in English at that age.

My refrain to such stories became "Remember Oliver." A classmate of my children, Oliver was doing twelfth-grade math in fourth grade. But subsequently, Oliver faced real challenges in life—so the moral of the story is that being able to count to two hundred in Japanese at age two or to do high school math at age nine isn't the singular ticket to a perfect life—nothing is.

But every parent wonders at times: "Is my child normal?" In trying to figure that out, we look at averages—even as we want our children to be above average.

Seeking normalcy (which is largely based on perception) and averages (which is a mathematical concept based on data) has its pluses. It can help us anticipate what to expect as children grow and change. That's why the pediatric ages-and-stages charts can be so helpful. But seeking normalcy and averages has serious downsides, too.

First, it's common to put anyone seen as below average into a deficit or disability category. David Rose, a neuropsychologist and educator from Harvard University and CAST, has pioneered a concept called Universal Design for Learning, a curricular approach that works for all kinds of learners. Rose notes that what's seen as normal or average can depend on the context. In his talks, he tells a story about his wife, Ruth:

> One of the anomalies of Ruth is that Ruth has perfect pitch.[66]

She is able, Rose says, to hear a musical note on any instrument and recognize, identify, and repeat it, unlike himself:

> I, in spite of twelve years of music lessons, don't have that and most of you don't have it either. It's fairly rare—estimated at about one in four hundred people.

Rose shows images of the brains of people with and without perfect pitch. The differences are dramatic. He likens the brain of someone with perfect pitch to a superhighway with many connections. The brain of someone without perfect pitch—like him—is like a country road: there are many connections, but they're less direct and slower. He then asks, rhetorically, who has the disability? His wife would say he does:

> She feels—and has since the very first time we sang together—that she has married a very disabled person, because I can't sing on pitch with her.

But this judgment depends on where they're singing. Rose and his wife attend church together (although she usually sings in the choir):

> The congregation has people like me. We all have what's called relative pitch—so we're singing along with the organ as best we can, and not all of us are very close to the right pitch.
>
> When singing in the congregation—not the choir—Ruth actually has a very significant disability. Since people are singing on quite different pitches, she's confused.

It's a wonderful example of how context defines what's normal, and the context can change. That's increasingly recognized, as people who've been seen as having disabilities are calling for recognition of widespread learning differences, or neurodiversity.*

That's the second downside—that focusing on normal or average obscures the variety in growth and development. Just look at a class photograph of seventh graders—it's clear they mature at different rates. Yet sometimes I think that our educational system expects all seventh graders to be able to know and do exactly the same things. I call that "the tyranny of the average."

As to adolescence, we've seen that there are different patterns in the development of the brain's prefrontal cortex and the rewards systems.[67] And remember that Sarah-Jayne Blakemore has concluded: "Individual differences are just as significant as—perhaps even more important than—averages. . . . After all, there's no average teenager."[68]

A third downside of focusing on normalcy and averages is that it's an inadequate way to measure growth. Rich Lerner, the pioneer in Positive Youth

---

* See www.understood.org as an example of the recognition of diversity in learning.

Development whom we met in chapter 1, has done a complete turnaround in how he conducts research on development.[69] To demonstrate his breakthrough, he first shows the results of mapping the development of the skill of being goal-directed for children from the fifth to the twelfth grade. Putting all of those kids together into an average is very close to a flat line.

Next, he shows the average changes over time for fifty-nine of these children. There the flat line goes up and down a little.

Finally, he shows how each individual has changed over time. That figure shows a multiplicity of up, down, and sideways lines. He says:

This is what adolescent development is like. Adolescence is like the ups and downs. No kid in this group is represented by the average.

What if we focused more on how individuals change over time rather than the hypothetical average? If we did, we could begin to move from just seeking averages to a more balanced view that includes the very real and normal individual variations in development over time. I believe it would take us far toward seeing adolescents as they are urging us to see them: as the wonderfully complex people they are.

4

MESSAGE 4: WE ARE TRYING TO UNDERSTAND OURSELVES AND OUR NEEDS

Adolescents tell us we don't fully understand this unique stage between childhood and adulthood. They also acknowledge and share what they're trying to understand about themselves:

We may seem like we're going through a phase or something, but we are actually learning more about ourselves and others.
    —Ten-year-old girl

Through their experiences and relationships, they're learning about who they are and where they fit in and belong:

Most of us are trying to graduate, navigate through the difficulties of high school like passing class, fitting in, and social standing. We are also still trying to figure out who we are and who we want to be.
    —Seventeen-year-old girl

They ask for patience, support, and respect:

We're growing daily and we need all the love and support no matter what it is.
    —Nine-year-old girl

Give us a chance to figure out things.
    —Eleven-year-old boy

Just because I'm young and inexperienced in doing things, we don't get the respect.
    —Fifteen-year-old boy

They ask for autonomy and agency—to have more of a say in figuring things out and taking action:

Let us be more independent and make our own decisions. We need to learn to find our own way.
    —Fifteen-year-old boy

I wish I could tell them that children my age can do things, and we just need to be given the choice! I wish I could tell them to give us a chance and/or more to do.
    —Twelve-year-old girl

Ultimately, they're trying to understand what it means to be themselves now and in the future while trying to make sense of the world's future at a confusing time:

My generation would like more acceptance and respect from our adults. After all they were once our age and wanted these same things. The difference is that my generation is exposed to more advanced knowledge than our adults when they were our age. Technology is more advanced and security is more at risk for us. Our global warming is a threat as well as terrorism. My generation worries about what kind of future we will have.
    —Seventeen-year-old boy

What is important to us, we are a group of people with lots of challenges, like education, employment, health, religion, and sex. We are in a stage that if we do not [do] what is right we could be in the wrong path for several years until we get the sense of our actions either good or bad. But if we receive support from grown-ups that journey will [be] more easy knowing what we are doing goes according to our society expectations.
    —Sixteen-year-old girl

A number of them write about wanting to contribute to improving the world:

We aren't as lazy as you portray us to be. We are just trying to figure out this world and how we can make a difference.
    —Sixteen-year-old girl

We like to learn and want to get involved in making a change.
—Sixteen-year-old girl

These are big questions: identity, autonomy, purpose, and contributing. They are questions we all ask as our lives continue to unfold. Adolescents are on this journey, too. These are the basic psychological needs we'll explore in this chapter.

Breakthrough Years Study Finding: Nearly one in four adolescents (24 percent) ask adults to understand their needs.

Reflections on Message 4

Think of a time when you—as an adult—were in a challenging situation. Perhaps it was a new place or a situation where people treated you differently than you thought you should be treated. What did you think? How did you feel?

We've heard from adolescents that it is important for adults to meet the Basic Needs in their lives. But this is not just about adolescence, as you'll see from a sampling of the stories I've heard in the talks I give to adults. For one person, it is about competence:

I moved to a different team at work. In my old team, we were open to ideas, but this team wanted to stay with the status quo. Whenever I'd come up with a new idea, it would be dismissed. I felt like I wasn't being trusted, that I wasn't thoughtful or even an expert in my field. I started to doubt my own competence, which is crazy, because I know who I am and I am really good at what I do.

For another, a lack of autonomy couldn't compensate for the other things a job offered:

I've thought a lot about why I left my job because, from the outside, it was a great job—with a company that paid well, had good benefits, and really smart people. Whenever I told people where I worked, they looked impressed. But inside, it felt different. Even though I had a title that should have given me responsibility and autonomy, the people above me mapped out the company plan and my job was largely to execute. It was like driving a BMW but I had to be given permission for wherever I went. My new job is like driving a Hyundai but I can decide where I'm going, and I've never been happier.

A lack of respect to a colleague affected still another's sense of identity:

One of my close colleagues at work endured two years where she lost her mom, she almost lost her husband, and her health was starting to go. She was in dire straits and needed to take some extra unpaid time off. The place where we work would not accommodate her; they would not be generous for someone who had given so much, for many years. They let her go. They saw her as replaceable. They were like, "We can hire another person like her. There are thousands of people like her." I took this job wanting to be part of that organization and wanting to trust them. But when I saw how they treated my friend—their complete lack of valuing and respecting her—I checked out. I don't belong in a place that treats people this way.

Belonging at school matters not just to children but also to their parents:

My son has ADHD and we got him the services he needed and an IEP. When I went to the parent conference, I could see the teachers were being defensive. They started to tell me all the things that were wrong with him, all the things he couldn't do. I could feel it building up in me and I finally burst out, "You just don't like him, do you?" A few years later, when my son was graduating from high school, one of those teachers came up to me and apologized. He said, "You were right to say that to us—the way we were talking about your son." I told him, "You know, parents just want to feel that they belong and that their child belongs—then we can work together."

When we hear the words "competence," "identity," "autonomy," "respect," and "belonging," they can slide over us: "Oh yeah, belonging . . . identity." That is, until we're in situations when we're treated as if we're incompetent, don't deserve respect, don't belong. That's when we begin to realize that these are Basic Needs we all have at all ages—especially during the formative years of adolescence.

A Radical Idea

I was speaking to a group of educators, talking about adolescents' Basic Needs for autonomy, competence, belonging, and contribution. They'd heard these words many times—perhaps so many times that the words had lost meaning.

So I stopped and asked them the question I just asked you: to think about a time when they—as adults—were in a challenging situation, perhaps a new place or a situation where people treated them differently than they thought they should be treated. I asked them to share their stories.

And the stories came. An urban district superintendent told of first coming to the United States and finding the English he'd learned in his country's English classes was insufficient to understand what people were saying, especially idioms—like "put a pin in it" or "ice out"—or slang. He said he used every clue he could to figure out what people were saying. He'd been so competent in his own country, and here he felt stripped of what he'd worked so hard to achieve.

A rural district superintendent spoke of going to a doctor about a persistent pain in her leg. The doctor spoke to her condescendingly, accusing her of not seeking help soon enough, giving her a list of dos and don'ts for her recovery, and then acting like she couldn't follow directions. "I felt like I was a child," she said.

A suburban principal spoke of the sudden, unexpected loss of a valued teacher in his school who was hit by a car while walking at night. "I was a stranger to that kind of grief," he said. "I just saw gray." Everything was devoid of color and meaning until he had the idea of approaching the school community and asking them to make their neighborhoods safer for walking. By coming together, his and others' grief wasn't lessened but was rechanneled into contributing.

Through telling and listening to each other's stories, the ideas of autonomy, competence, belonging, and contribution weren't just tired words anymore. They were themes they could understand anew, in their own lives as adults.

One said, "You don't really know what you need until it's gone."

It's like *Fish Is Fish*, I said. As child development people, many knew that children's book by Leo Lionni.[1]

If you don't know the story, it's about Fish and Tadpole, who grow up in a pond together. They're always together, best friends, until Tadpole sprouts legs and ventures out of the pond onto land. He returns to the pond with glorious descriptions of land. Fish yearns to see for himself. So he heaves himself out of the pond but, of course, he can't breathe. Frog eventually rescues Fish with a push back into the pond, where Fish discovers that his world "was certainly the most beautiful of all worlds."

Fish took his need for water for granted, until he didn't have it. The book's conclusion: Fish is Fish and Frog is Frog. The educators' realization and my conclusion: we may not recognize what we need to thrive until it's gone.

It's actually quite a radical idea. We're used to the idea that we need food, water, and shelter to survive, but I would guess that most of us aren't used to the fact that we have basic psychological needs and that those needs must be met for us to thrive. Belonging sounds like a nice-to-have, not a must-have.

This concept isn't at all radical in Self-Determination Theory, where there are decades of research showing it holds true. Wendy Grolnick of Clark University, a scholar of Self-Determination Theory, uses the comparison between physiological and psychological needs. Food, water, and shelter are the nutrients required for bodily health and safety; ingredients we need to survive:

> But you can also think about needs as psychological. Psychological needs are nutrients required for growth, integrity, well-being.[2]

When these needs are met, we can do more than survive. We can grow, have better well-being, and thrive. When these needs are not met, it can lead to less positive outcomes, such as increased mental health concerns.[3]

WHAT ARE THE NEEDS IN SELF-DETERMINATION THEORY?

Self-Determination Theory is a very robust theory of human motivation conceptualized by Edward Deci and Richard Ryan from the University of Rochester[4] and tested over many decades. In fact, this broad theory encompasses six "mini-theories" on motivation, relationships, and goals. One of these six mini-theories is Basic Psychological Needs Theory, which addresses how psychological needs are connected with our well-being.[5] This mini-theory is most relevant for this part of the book, as we'll be considering what happens to adolescents when these needs are met or unmet across the different environments they're in. Grolnick beautifully summarizes[6] the needs in Self-Determination Theory, which you may recall from my quoting her earlier. The first need is **relatedness**:

> *We need to feel connected or related to other people. We are social human beings and need to feel valued and loved and connected.*

The second need is **autonomy**:

> *We need to feel autonomous. What we mean is that people need to feel choiceful. They need to feel like they're the owners of their actions or behind what they do; that they're not pushed and coerced.*

Grolnick notes that the concept of autonomy has been confusing. Some people see autonomy as being independent or separate from others, but in Self-Determination Theory, autonomy depends on relationships where people feel that they're not controlled and have choices.

The third need is **competence**:

> *We need to feel competent. We need to feel like we're able to affect things, to affect our world. We just don't do well as human beings when we feel incompetent, helpless, and unable to do things.*

THE FIVE BASIC PSYCHOLOGICAL NEEDS OF ADOLESCENCE

In the book so far, we've seen that adolescents are neurobiologically primed to respond strongly to:

- Rewards and novelty
- Being included or excluded
- Wanting some say or autonomy in what they do
- Being respected and seeking social status
- Trying to figure out who they are and what matters to them*

---

* This list is inspired by my own reading and research and by the many speeches I have heard given by Ronald Dahl of the University of California, Berkeley.

Many of these responses were described by researchers before the advent of neuroimaging; however, the thoughtful and clever experiments we've seen so far begin to reveal that there are neurobiological underpinnings to these ideas. Drawing from others' research and my own, I've come to see more than three psychological needs as foundational in adolescence—and in life. I group these basic psychological needs into five categories:*

Caring connections
Agency
Mastery
Identity
Purpose

What Are the Characteristics of the Five Basic Psychological Needs of Adolescence?

- **These Basic Needs can be further defined and grouped together.** When adolescents feel they belong and are supported, they can feel connected (**caring connections**); when they are given some autonomy and treated with respect, they can become rightful owners of their own actions (**agency**); when they are encouraged to handle challenges in ways that develop competence, they can feel effective (**mastery**); when they can address questions about who they are, they can build their sense of identity (**identity**); and when they have opportunities to explore what's meaningful to them and contribute to the greater good, they can begin to develop a sense of direction in their lives (**purpose**). A wide array of experiences, relationships, activities, and opportunities underlie each of these groupings.
- **The Basic Needs are a primary driver of adolescent development and can become tasks.** Tasks can be the vehicles for addressing (or not addressing) needs. How these tasks are attended to involves both an adolescent and the environment or context, because . . .

---

* Here I have expanded the conceptual models of Edward L. Deci and Richard Ryan of the University of Rochester (as cited in Richard M. Ryan and Edward L. Deci, "Self-Determination Theory and the Facilitation of Intrinsic Motivation, Social Development, and Well-Being," *American Psychologist* 55, no. 1 [2000]: 68–78, https://doi.org/10.1037/0003-066X.55.1.68) and of B. Bradford Brown of the University of Wisconsin (as cited in Institute of Medicine and National Research Council Committee on the Science of Adolescence, *The Science of Adolescent Risk-Taking: Workshop Report* [Washington, DC: National Academies Press, 2011]).

- **The Basic Needs are relationship-based.** We can work hard on belonging, but if the people in our world aren't welcoming, that need won't be met. Especially for young people, other people are critical in providing opportunities for these Basic Needs to be fulfilled because, again, the Basic Needs are relationship-based. I call relationships the swing-vote factor in development since they make the biggest difference. This recognition—that relationships are at the core of physical and mental health—has led the academic discipline of pediatrics to make a pivot away from just physical health toward relational health.[7]

- **We need to ask whether psychological needs are being met in young people's environments.** This is a huge point. All too often, we assess and judge young people—on, say, whether they're competent—as if they're solo players, neglecting the role of context: the environment in which adolescents become competent or not. Imagine the difference if educational settings assessed and then addressed whether the environment supports meeting adolescents' needs.

- **The Basic Needs can become internalized.** For example, if adolescents are in places and with people who enable them to act in increasingly autonomous or competent ways, they're more likely to feel autonomous or competent. The focus in the rest of the chapter, accordingly, is on how *we*—the people in adolescents' lives (or environments)—can meet their needs.

- **The Basic Needs tend to surface most strongly during transitions and/or in environments where they aren't being met.** Adolescence has many transitions, such as starting middle school, high school, or college and/or entering the workforce. Unsupportive environments might include a command-and-control situation where nothing adolescents do seems to matter.

Met or Unmet? Match or Mismatch? It's an Ongoing Process

More than half a century ago, Erik Erikson created one of the most durable frameworks for understanding development when he outlined psychosocial development as unfolding during a series of critical tasks over the life span.[8] While his theory outlines which needs are most important at certain life stages (e.g., for Erikson, developing basic trust is the task in infancy, identity is the task in adolescence), I don't think we find what he calls "lasting solutions"[9] in specific stages. For example, autonomy surfaces in toddlerhood, but it resurfaces during adolescence in new ways and will resurface repeatedly in adulthood. We are continually becoming—writing and revising the narratives of our lives.

My notion of a match/mismatch between what adolescents need and what society provides was inspired by a theory in psychology called person-environmental fit theory,[10] specifically research led by Jacquelynne Eccles of the University of California, Irvine, and her colleagues.[11] They began by asking:

Although most individuals pass through adolescence without excessively high levels of "storm and stress," many do experience difficulty. Why?[12]

In response, they suggested a hypothesis:

*That some of the negative psychological changes associated with adolescent development result from a **mismatch** [emphasis added] between the needs of developing adolescents and the opportunities afforded them by their social environments.*[13]

With the concept of match and mismatch in mind, let's begin our exploration of the Five Basic Needs with caring connections—the need to belong and to feel supported.

Need 1: Caring Connections: The Need for Belonging and Support

The need to belong involves feeling close, cared about, safe, and accepted for who you are. Support is feeling that you can rely on others for help, that they will be there for you when problems arise. When adolescents feel they belong and are supported, they can feel connected (caring connections).

The Need for Belonging

A few years ago (before the COVID-19 pandemic), I was hospitalized with a seemingly mysterious infection, put into isolation, and cut off from my family, friends, and life as I'd been living it. Suddenly, strangers—the hospital staff—became the center of my universe. I became driven by the need to be cared for and cared about, so I worked hard to belong. I asked staff questions to try to connect personally. One mentioned a call she'd overheard with my grandson, and I turned it into an opportunity to learn about her family. I asked the night nurse how she felt about working night shifts.

Like anyone in a new place, I needed to make sense of the hospital culture—its people and its hierarchy—and figure out how I might feel safe and fit in there. Even knowing I was only going to be there for a few days (luckily, the infection turned out to be not mysterious and easily treatable), I needed to feel I belonged.

SEEING THROUGH THE LENS OF BELONGING

Torrence, a California father I interviewed, told me he had lived his life with the mantra "If you want something different, you've got to do something different."

If we want adults and children to thrive, the something different is making belonging the lens through which we see and act. While this may be especially important for some children—those who are set apart because of what they look like, how they behave, the resources in their families' bank accounts, or not being seen as cool—it's not just about them but about everyone.

Businesses are seeing this shift, as a number of companies strive to understand what "inclusiveness" means and how to make it happen.[14] Education is shifting, too, and it is much needed.[15] A conversation I had with a seventh grader in Chicago shows why. He told me he knew from "the teacher's eyes" what kind of year he was going to have from the moment he entered the classroom on the first day of school:

> *I can tell from their eyes whether they like kids or not. I can tell from their eyes whether they like what they're teaching or not. I can tell from their eyes whether they want to be in that classroom or not.*

Even before interacting with a teacher, children can look at a teacher's eyes to gauge if a classroom is going to be a place where they can belong.

"BELONGING IS A BIG THING—I'M ALWAYS WORRYING ABOUT WHAT PEOPLE THINK OF ME"

When I asked Alice, mother of twelve-year-old Ingrid in Florida, about what she wants for her daughter and others her age, she said, "I think it's to learn to be happy with who they are."

Alice described how she helped Ingrid become comfortable with herself:

> By talking a lot to her to see if there's anything she doesn't seem to like about herself and to talk about it. I tell her not to worry too much about what other people think. If she enjoys something, it doesn't matter if it's cool or not—it's what she likes.

These words sound easy, but in reality, it's difficult for a young person "not to worry about what other people think" when their development primes them to be sensitive to the views of others and to where they belong. Ingrid said so:

> I feel like adults think that it's not hard to be our age because we have technology and stuff. But I think that's harder because it pushes us to be more self-conscious.
>
> At our age, there's a lot of stuff that hurts. With school and stuff, there's drama, but we don't really like to share our feelings because we've been kind of taught "Don't be a crybaby," so we kind of push our emotions down. That can make us moody.
>
> Then adults say, "Stop being such a teenager." But really, it's because we need someone to talk to.

Breakthrough Years Study Finding: Fifty-nine percent of adolescents report talking to their parents about what's important more than half of the time. Furthermore, talking more is associated with fewer reports of negative moods from adolescents. Our data show that Ingrid's insight is on target.

When I asked Ingrid about school "drama," she described several incidents, concluding:

It's about relationships—maybe someone hurt someone else's feelings by accident, and the other person took it the wrong way. It starts small—a little argument—then more people get involved. Then it becomes a big thing that everyone starts talking about.

Ingrid's description echoed the findings of a study we once conducted on young people and violence.[16] While adults thought of violence as "big aggressions" (fights, school shootings), we found that young people thought of violence as "small aggressions" (teasing, picking on others) because those could escalate into the big problems. When asked if they had one wish to stop the violence in their lives, the largest proportion of young people in our study wanted to stop the small aggressions—the everyday dramas.

The dramas Ingrid described were about belonging (who's included, who's excluded)—something adolescents' brains are very responsive to. She told me:

Belonging is a big thing because I'm very self-conscious, always worrying about what people think of me. Do people think I'm weird? Do people want to be my friend?

Ingrid's also an astute observer of the drive to fit in:

There're specific clothes people wear. People lose weight to fit in. They don't really like to be unique. They like to be just another short, blond, crop-top-wearing person.

And it's not only about clothes; twelve-year-old Brian told me:

I was in a new class last year. I didn't fit in because they were all taller than me and I'm short, so it made me feel bad because they wouldn't include me in a lot of stuff.

Despite books, articles, and efforts to curtail the pressure to conform to a certain look in adolescence, this tension is alive and well in Ingrid's and Brian's schools and very much on their and other adolescents' minds. A survey by Richard Weissbourd at Harvard University and his colleagues found that 80 percent of young people reported that their parents are most concerned about their children's academic achievement and happiness—much more so than being concerned about them having caring relationships with others.[17] But the Basic Need to belong is powerful. Ingrid continued:

Obviously I'm not going to be another short, blond, crop-top-wearing girl, but I'm definitely not going to be an outcast. I'm going to definitely try to fit in.

BELONGING VERSUS FITTING IN: HELPING ADOLESCENTS KNOW THE DIFFERENCE

Ingrid's statement demonstrates the difference between belonging and fitting in. When you fit in, you do what you have to do to meet others' expectations—even when it feels uncomfortable. When you belong, you feel as if you're accepted for yourself. Brené Brown writes:

Fitting in is about assessing a situation and becoming who you need to be to be accepted. Belonging . . . doesn't require us to change who we are; it requires us to be who we are.[18]

We can help adolescents move from wanting to fit in to wanting to feel welcome for who they are. When I asked Ingrid how she was handling this pressure, here's how she put it:

A lot of girls in my school dye their hair blond, get highlights. Everyone wears short sweaters, short shirts, tight jeans. There's a lot of pressure to be a specific look.
*   Most girls at my school look nothing like me. I'm tall and I can't change that. I'm not going to change the color of my hair. I'm not going to change the clothes I feel comfortable wearing. I'm not going to change my attitude toward things just to fit in. People will have to be friends with me for me—not if I dye my hair or wear short clothes or act a certain way.*

MATCH AND MISMATCH IN THE NEED FOR BELONGING?

We use many words to describe the psychological need to belong—to be "connected," "cared about," "safe," "bonded," "attached," "loved." In our Breakthrough Years survey, we asked a nationally representative group of adolescents:
In the last month, how often did you feel like . . . ?

1. *Your parent(s) and family make you feel like you belong*
2. *Your parent(s) and family make you feel like they really love you*

Then we asked these same questions about four other contexts—their friends, the people at school, the people in their out-of-school activities, and the people they connect with online. For these other four contexts, we changed the word "love" in the parent question to "made you feel like they really cared about you."

As you can see from the figure below, most adolescents feel they belong, especially in their families.* Taking a look at "often," which is measured as more than half the time, 56 percent of adolescents feel they belong online, 60 percent in school, 66 percent in out-of-school activities, 76 percent with their friends, and 88 percent with their families—somewhat heartening findings. We will see when we assess other needs that the relationships young people have online are the lowest in meeting all of their needs.

How Often Adolescents Report the Need for Belonging Is Met

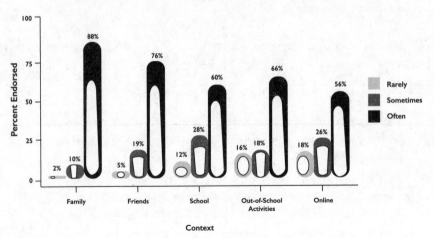

When you look at the arrows in the table on the following page, they reveal that when the adolescents in the Breakthrough Years study reported that the people in their lives made them feel they belonged, they reported better outcomes nine months later:

- More engagement in school
- A more positive view of their futures
- Being in positive moods (not negative moods)

---

* Adolescents answered each question on a five-point scale from "never" to "almost always." The answers for the two questions were summed, resulting in the following groups: "rarely" (2–4), "sometimes" (5–7), and "often" (8–10).

- Having less stress
- Having less conflict with their parents

If they felt they belonged in their school and out-of-school activities, they and their parents reported that they had better grades.

This is all the more impressive because we asked about belonging *before* the pandemic (never imagining that something like a pandemic would occur), but afterward we went back to the same nationally representative group and asked them to respond to the outcome questions again. With these data, we could assess how having the need for belonging—and the other needs—prior to the pandemic predicted a series of outcomes *during* the pandemic, nine months later.

Outcomes of Having the Need for Belonging Met

Belonging	Follow-Up Outcomes							
Context	School Engagement	Grades (P)	Grades (A)	Future	Negative Mood	Positive Mood	Stress	Conflict (A:P)
Family	↑			↑	↓	↑	↓	↓ : ↓
Friends				↑	↓	↑	↓	↓ :
School	↑		↑	↑	↓	↑	↓	↓ :
OSA	↑	↑	↑	↑	↓	↑	↓	:
Online				↑		↑		:

A = adolescent report, P = parent report, OSA = out-of-school activities. Arrows indicate the direction of an association (i.e., up arrow for promoting, down arrow for protecting), controlling for demographics. An empty cell indicates there is no statistically significant relationship. Significant relations are p-values < .0005, meaning these correlations are very reliable and unlikely to have occurred by chance.

WAYS TO PAY MORE ATTENTION TO THE BASIC NEED FOR BELONGING (AND WHY WE MAY NOT DO SO)

If we really valued belonging as a psychological need, parents would know that it matters. Some parents do, and rather than telling their kids to "stop being such a teenager" or "don't be a whiner" if they feel rejected by a friend, they listen, say they know how important that feels, and then help their adolescents make their own realistic plans to build friendships and to find places where they do belong.

If we really valued belonging, teachers would work to create a sense of belonging for every child in their classes, viewing it as foundational to learning, not a side issue or a distraction. Some teachers do this, and it can make all the difference to children's lives. A friend told me that she hated school when she was growing up. She didn't act out—she was just sad. Finally, her parents enrolled her in a different school. More than fifty years later, she remembers how the teacher introduced her to her new class, then seated her next to someone who, the teacher suggested, could help her settle in. Smart move: that student was an excellent student *and* popular. That afternoon, another classmate, also new, sat down beside her during gym and suggested they walk back to the locker room together. They're still friends today. One caring teacher and two welcoming students made all the difference.

There are a number of reasons we may pay less attention to belonging than we should:

- **Belonging may be seen as more important in infancy or early childhood than in the later years.**
  When infants become attached to the important adults in their lives, they gain a sense of safety and security that enables them to venture out, meet new people, and have new experiences.[19] Attachment in the early years is pretty well understood,[20] but it's less well accepted that the need for strong connections occurs in other settings beyond the family and persists throughout our lives.
- **Belonging may be seen as a side issue to learning.**
  The statement I hear most often is that this is a "soft issue," compared with grades and performance, but as Jaana Juvonen of UCLA and her collaborators have found in their studies,[21] children's and adolescents' grades and performance depend, in essential ways, on a foundation of belonging.
- **Belonging may be experienced less intensively, except in times of change.**
  Belonging tends to fade into the background when we feel safe in familiar surroundings—but this need can be sharply felt during the transitions of adolescence, such as beginning middle school (or junior high school) and high school. Diane, a mother of a twelve-year-old in Georgia, describes her experiences with her son:

In elementary school, there was a lot of hand-holding. In middle school, you're responsible for making it to class on time, turning in assignments. Your teacher may say on Monday, "This is due Friday," and may not speak of it again. You have to remember.

"On top of all this," she says, there's puberty, when young people are "trying to find where they fit in and figure out what they're going through, with their bodies changing. It's a lot to hit them all at one time, really."

Moving or changing schools can also arouse the need to belong. Following a move from New Jersey to South Carolina, Courtney, now fourteen, struggled to find her place:

I moved here in sixth grade and I didn't feel like I belonged. No one understood me because I was from New Jersey. I didn't know anyone and felt like everybody treated me different because I was from, like, the northern states.

Her father, Kevin, recalls Courtney had been successful in dance in her previous school but not in South Carolina:

She tried out for the dance team but wasn't part of the in-crowd because she didn't know a lot of the girls.

Kevin feels some kids blackballed her:

The girls on the team kind of put bugs in the coach's ear not to pick her— bad-mouthing her and things like that. She found out about it afterward and had to figure out how to deal with them in school—with them lying to her face saying they didn't do it. She couldn't confront them in a bad way because that would have affected her in school and in the future.

Kevin steered this problem into helping his daughter "read people who are being true" and look for friends she could trust:

She eventually weaned away from them. They were still saying they wanted to be her friend but she knew they weren't true friends.

Courtney decided to pursue a different sport and try to make other friends that way. "I think I handled it well," she says:

*I finally realized some people weren't my type of friends, so I dug deeper
into other things and found really good friends. I played volleyball and met
a lot of people. It took time!*

- **The need to belong can surface when young people don't fit the
  norm.**

It does take time for some, but for others it can be ongoing. Jessica,
fifteen, says:

*I'm multiracial. People used to think that was weird, so that made me feel
bad. I know that I love myself and I love my parents and I love where I
come from. But that's hard to deal with. My parents would come to school
events and the other kids would be like, "That's your dad! That's your
mom? Really?"*

Her mother, Gabrielle, says this continues:

*When we were in a small town, my daughter had a boyfriend and he was a
White boy. All of her biracial or Black friends—her friends of color—were
telling her, "You shouldn't date White boys because you're not White." They
were really trying to pressure her and she was, for a while, a little confused
on her identity: "Where do I fit in? I'm not White and I'm not Black."
There's not a lot of Black-and-White mixed kids in that rural community.
So she really struggled with that.*

*She stuck with him. She was like, "I'm not going to let other people
pressure me into not dating someone I like." Later, they broke up because
we moved. But her friends eventually realized she was going to be who she
was and kind of let it go.*

FOSTERING BELONGING: FINDING SUPPORTIVE PEOPLE

The dual challenge of adolescence is to fit in, then to belong where you can
stay true to yourself. That was the challenge twelve-year-old Ingrid faced
in not wanting to be another short, blond, crop-top-wearing girl. A drama
class became her ticket to becoming more comfortable with who she is by
pretending to be someone else, ironically enough. That's one of the true values of the arts—they enable us to explore our identities. Susan Magsamen,

founder and director of the International Center for Arts + Mind Lab at Johns Hopkins University and co-author of *Your Brain on Art*,[22] has found involvement in the arts in adolescence is very important in identity formation: "For getting to know who you are and how you feel and then building the ability to share it with confidence in the world—to have people know you by the way you express yourself."[23]

Ingrid didn't originally intend to take drama:

> *Me being in drama was an accident. I wanted to be in Beginning Art, but there was no space, so they put me in drama. It was a beginning drama class, full of people who didn't really like drama, just in it for the easy A, or maybe, like me, they wanted to do something else. But I walked into class that first day with an open mind, thinking this could be great, life-changing. And it was life-changing.*

It was life-changing because her teacher became a mentor:

> *It was the first year she was teaching at our school. She came from New York and was probably the most amazing teacher I've ever had. Our first unit was a monologue unit.*

Performing a monologue—memorizing the words and blocking the movements onstage—was frightening.

> *It was a big class with kids from older grades. As somebody who'd never performed before, I was terrified of doing anything in front of people.*

While Ingrid says she doesn't like opening up about her feelings with her family, she was able to talk with her teacher:

> *After being given the assignment, I went to my teacher and said, "Is there a way you could help me? I have a fear of doing anything in front of people." She said, "Of course." I came to her every day before school to practice my monologue. The first day, I was shaking, in front of just one person. I had no idea how I'd do it to a class of twenty kids from mostly eighth grade.*

Ingrid put in the practice to learn how to perform. Having a choice about which monologue to do probably helped, too. Our research shows that having choices affects school engagement:

I loved the monologue. I practiced a lot and made sure I could say that monologue forwards and backwards. Finally, when the unit was coming to an end, we had to perform in front of the class. I came extra early. I was sweating, shaking. I looked really scared, too. There were only three other girls in that class—everyone else was a boy. I don't know why that made me even more nervous, but it did. Then she called my name to go.

When I got up there, I'm like, "Whatever! It's a class full of people you don't know. They're eighth graders. They'll be gone next year. Just do it." Then I did it.

Ingrid was able to reframe her fear by taking a more distant or "far" perspective on it (almost as if she was taking a page from the research of Jennifer Silvers, described in chapter 1). She realized she wouldn't see these kids next year. In retrospect, overcoming this obstacle became a pivotal moment for her. Through that one experience, a combination of psychological needs was met. Ingrid felt she belonged in that class, she felt supported, respected, and had some autonomy while she was being challenged—all of which helped in shaping her identity. She says:

I got over my fear of acting in front of people that day.

But growth in adolescence, as in every phase of life, isn't a linear process. Although Ingrid felt more comfortable with herself while performing, she still struggled with fitting in and not going against the group. These feelings played out in her relationship with a new student from China.

Interestingly, another passion Ingrid discovered in her seventh-grade year was Chinese after her father both pushed and encouraged her to take Mandarin as her elective language. As she puts it, "I love everything Chinese. I love Chinese food, Chinese history."

But her enthusiasm turned more ambivalent regarding this new student. He always sat by himself in the lunchroom. She told me:

I don't understand what people have against Chinese kids. He doesn't really talk English very well, but it's not his fault. I see him sitting alone for the majority of the year.

School shouldn't be a place where you're uncomfortable or you're like, "Oh, I don't have any friends. Nobody really wants me here." It should be a place where you have friends to talk to, a place to learn, where you can count on people.

BEING ALL-IN TO CHANGE BELONGING

Ingrid captures the essence of belonging and support. I asked Ingrid:

What would make school more like what you want it to be for the Chinese boy who sits alone? Who could make that happen—the adults, the other kids?

Ingrid responded:

I don't think adults could do it. I think it's more the kids. They'd have to get over their snarky attitude and just accept him. He's a kid and he's human. He has feelings, too. How do you think he feels sitting all by himself, not having any friends to talk to, watching everyone else?

Ingrid has invited him to her table. "He has come a few times," she says. "Other times, I think he wants to sit alone":

I think he feels like an outcast because he doesn't really speak English really well. I think that's also part of why people aren't really accepting him. You can't really understand what he's saying sometimes. He seems really nice. I think if people gave him a chance, people would definitely feel better about themselves. It would benefit everyone. People would have more friends; he'd have friends.

As Ingrid spoke, I thought about the anticonflict intervention by Elizabeth Levy Paluck from Princeton University and her colleagues (chapter 2) where students from randomly selected middle schools in New Jersey were randomly assigned to take a public stance against conflict at their school.[24] Indeed, conflict decreased—more so if the group contained more students who were what the researchers call "social influencers."

In this study's definition, social influencers are the students whom more other students in their schools indicated that they "chose to spend time with." They are culture carriers—young people whom other classmates look to in order to determine what's acceptable behavior or not. In this experiment, it took both adults and students to bring about change; together, they were able to create a culture with much less student conflict.

With this in mind, I said to Ingrid, "Maybe there are ways of changing things that your classrmates could lead, working with adults—that's what would really change things."

The Need for Support

There have always been some kids sitting alone in the cafeteria, where no one helped them. Where they had no support. The way young people talk about support says it all:

Are you there for me?
Do you have my back?

Belonging doesn't happen by our efforts alone.

By definition, belonging is communal. It depends on how others behave toward us. Are they responsive, interested, engaged, willing to stick with us when we're struggling? Are they able to help us when things between us aren't going so well? Are they able to enable us to find our own solutions? "Support" encompasses these and more.

What do young people need in order to feel truly supported?

MATCH AND MISMATCH IN FEELING SUPPORTED?

In the Breakthrough Years study, we asked:

In the last month, how often did you feel like you could rely on your
parent(s) and family to help when you have a problem? *

We asked the same question regarding relationships with friends, the people at school, the people in out-of-school activities, and the people online.

As you see from the figure on the next page,** adolescents feel supported "most"—defined as more than half of the time—by their families (87 per-

---

* We originally included another item in this definition, and though it correlates with relying on others for help, it didn't make conceptual sense, so we have dropped it in these analyses. Currently, we are conducting studies on Basic Needs and have added other items to create a scale addressing the Basic Need for support. Because we only used one item in this measure, we did not assess the impact of support on adolescents' well-being.

** For this need, "rarely" was defined as an answer of "never" or "some of the time," "sometimes" as an answer of "about half of the time," and "often" as an answer of "most of the time" or "almost always."

cent) and least by their relationships online (41 percent). Next to families are friends (70 percent), while the people at school (60 percent) and in out-of-school activities (59 percent) are comparable. What's notable (and sad) to me are the percentages of young people who experience support sometimes or rarely at school and in out-of-school activities.

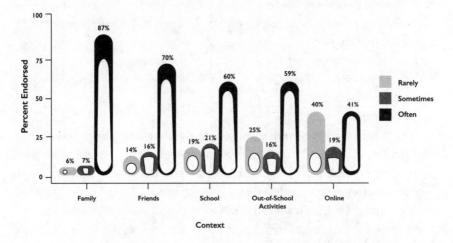

How Often Adolescents Report the Need for Support Is Met

SUPPORT FOSTERS "THE BEST KIND OF LEARNING"

Robert Pianta of the Center for Advanced Study of Teaching and Learning at the University of Virginia is adamant about the importance of supportive teacher-student relationships:

> Let me make really clear that when we talk about relationships that teachers have with children and the social and emotional aspects of a classroom environment—from almost every perspective we and others have been able to study those—they produce very real gains for students' achievement, and very real gains for students' social-emotional adjustment.[25]

Eric Ruzek, Pianta, and their colleagues at the University of Virginia took a unique approach in one of their studies of teacher support. The participants were sixty-eight middle and high school math, English, history, and science teachers from twelve schools in a mid-Atlantic state and 960 of their students.[26] While most studies rely on people reporting on what they're doing, feeling, and thinking (self-report), this study also included observed behavior, using forty-minute videos that the teachers recorded of teaching their classes and shared with the researchers at two-to-three-week intervals during the study.

The researchers assessed teachers' support for students in the videos as the presence of a positive climate, their sensitivity to students' cues, and their regard for students' perspectives. They assessed educational results by looking at student motivation and engagement.

Key Finding: When their teachers were observed to be more emotionally and socially supportive in this study, students reported becoming more motivated and more engaged as the year progressed.

But why?

Here's where the research team sought to add a new dimension to their inquiry. They wondered if student motivation and learning engagement were happening because teachers met the needs specified by Self-Determination Theory—autonomy, relatedness, and competence.

The study results did find that the increases in motivation and engagement over time were linked to students having more opportunities to be autonomous and to have better relationships with the other students. Competence wasn't significant in their analyses, possibly because their measure of students' sense of competence focused on social-emotional aspects and not instructional support. In my view, social, emotional, and cognitive competence go together!

Pianta also decries strictly separating elements of teachers' interactions with students into instructional and social-emotional support:

> One of the traps we get into in education is thinking of instruction and learning as the primary focus and of social and emotional relationships between teachers and students as a secondary, completely separate, touchy-feely thing that doesn't matter, or that it's nice to have but not essential. Our research and the research of others show that you have to have both good instructional interactions and good social-emotional interactions to produce the most meaningful learning![27]

It's a necessity, not a luxury.[28]

Building support can also build a sense of belonging. A meta-analysis by Kelly-Ann Allen of Monash University in Melbourne, Australia, and her

team of researchers, which combined the results of fifty-one individual studies including 67,378 students, found that having the support of parents,
teachers, and peers was strongly related to whether or not students felt they
belonged in schools.[29]

LAB ←→ LIFE: INTERVENTIONS ON BELONGING AND SUPPORT

When he was in high school in the early 1990s, Greg Walton, now of Stanford University, joined a student group called Students Educating Each
Other About Discrimination (SEED)[30]—not necessarily because he had an
interest at that time but "because my friend was going. He suggested it and
I tagged along."[31]

Walton continues:

> *The group made me really interested in the origins of inequality in*
> *American society.*

Despite many nonprofit and governmental initiatives aimed at reducing
the achievement gap between lower-income and higher-income students
and between Black and Brown students and White students, the "persistent
inequalities in educational achievement and life opportunities" became
clear to Walton. For him, it was a moment of grappling with the American
dream:

> *What was most powerful for me was coming to understand that these*
> *problems of inequality were so significant that it was a myth that any*
> *kid could succeed in America. It was just not true! Kids from poor*
> *backgrounds and kids from racial minority backgrounds did not have the*
> *same opportunities as other children.*

He wondered, "What's needed to make the American dream more of
a reality?" He found clues in the writing and research of Claude Steele of
Stanford University:

> *If somebody views you through the lens of a negative stereotype—if*
> *somebody thinks "You're the dumb girl" or "You're the White guy who*
> *can't jump" or "You're the Black person who's not smart at school," that*
> *poses a real threat in those settings that makes it harder to do well and*
> *engage with other people. That contributes to inequality.*[32]

He recalls the early Steele experiment[33] where White students performed better than Black students when a test was presented as a way to evaluate students' abilities, but when that same task was presented as challenging but *not* evaluative, there was no difference between Black and White students.

The recognition "that there are many different sources of inequality" led Walton to ask:

> Could you create school experiences that make it a psychologically safe environment for everybody? If you could, would you see changes in inequality?[34]

While he was well aware that "this approach wouldn't solve all of the problems of inequality, it would be a practical way to begin."

Walton explains why creating psychologically safe environments where students belonged and felt supported during adolescence could have cascading importance at the present time and in the future:

> As kids go into adolescence, they're beginning to build relationships and communities beyond their immediate family relationship. They're looking for communities of peers that they'll belong to. They're looking for helpful and trustworthy adults, mentors, and role models they can connect to.
>
> As they do that, they're trying to make sense of opportunities and whether or not those are opportunities they can pursue. They're especially attentive, then, to cues from peers and from adults that convey that they're included, respected, and valued—or that imply that they may not be.

In other words, transitions could be times when interventions on belonging and support could make a lasting difference. Walton focused on the transition to college and speculated that if young people worry about not belonging and being supported at college, why not change the narrative? Why not give students a new story to use, especially when challenges arise? The new story he envisioned is:

> It's normal to worry at first about whether you belong in college, but it gets better with time.

This can be seen as a way of addressing stereotype threats and as creating a growth mindset about belonging—that is, the feeling that you belong is something that grows and changes and it applies to transitions to middle school, high school, and to other new groups.

Belonging is important for all students but has special salience for students who are underrepresented in a group:

> *If you're going into an environment where your group is underrepresented, where there's maybe only one other person in the classroom who looks a little bit like you, where there's a negative stereotype about you, then that social reality—those facts—give you a particularly pernicious, negative interpretation of the normal worries and challenges that people have in a transition.*

MINDSET INTERVENTIONS

Walton's insights became the genesis for what's become a classic experiment and experimental process on how to change mindsets in ways that last—in this case, belonging and how belonging is linked to support.[35]

In the first phase of this experiment to test these ideas, led by Walton and Geoff Cohen, also of Stanford University, participants were randomly assigned to an intervention or a control group. In the intervention group, they were given a report said to contain the results of a survey of a diverse group of seniors at their college saying that they worried about belonging when they first got to school but grew more confident over time.[36]

The second phase of the experiment is called "saying is believing." Participants were asked to write about how their own college entry experiences were similar to the stories they'd read. Then they turned their essays into speeches, which were videotaped to help future students in their transition to college. In the control group, participants followed the same procedure of reading about a survey and responding, but the subject had nothing to do with belonging (it was about social and political attitudes).

The approach of making the people "helpers" rather than "the helped" is quite deliberate, as Walton explains:

> *I don't think anybody likes to be told "You need help." People are much more comfortable talking about how they try to achieve positive things.[37]*

In essence, when we help others, we help ourselves become the kind of people we want to be. Parenthetically, it can even improve grades. One large-scale study found that when high school students gave motivational advice (e.g., how to stop procrastinating) to younger students, they were more likely to have better grades than those in a control group.[38]

In the belonging experiment, the researchers assessed the impact of their approximately one-hour intervention when the students became seniors. First, they looked at whether the actual intervention was memorable and found it wasn't. While 79 percent remembered participating in the intervention, only 8 percent remembered the stories of the older students they'd read and only 14 percent thought the intervention had any direct effect on them.[39]

But comparing the participating students with the control group tells a different story. The intervention raised the scores of those who least felt they belonged—in this case Black students, sophomore to senior year, narrowing the achievement gap by 52 percent over these three years.[40] In later trials of the same experiment, students had lower dropout rates, were healthier, and were more confident that they belonged.[41]

This experiment took place in a "selective" college, and so the admitted students were very competent, but even their competence didn't protect them from the long-term toll of having their need for belonging go unmet.

So, what exactly was happening? It would be ridiculous, as Walton puts it, to think that the notion "you belong" remained in students' minds during these years.[42] Walton and his colleagues began to hypothesize about what was going on and came to see that it had to do with supportive relationships. He says:

> The social belonging intervention offers you a different way of making sense of the daily struggles that you're going through. When you have that way of making sense of challenges, you're better able to reach out to others to build relationships.

A follow-up study seven to eleven years after the intervention revealed that these positive changes continued.[43] At that time, the students in the intervention were more satisfied with their lives and more successful in their careers.

Walton wondered if their hypothesis about relationships remained correct. "We looked statistically to try to see why they're reporting these better life outcomes."[44]

> We asked: Is it because they got better grades in college that they're more empowered in their careers and in their lives? The answer is no. The students' GPA in college didn't correlate with those important life outcomes.

But yes, it was about supportive relationships:

What seems to be happening is that students in the intervention are telling us that they developed more significant mentor relationships in college—more mentor relationships with the faculty that extended after graduation, and it seems to be that those mentor relationships are what's empowering students' long-term success.

Key Finding: In this study, researchers found that the supportive relationships that students built were the vehicle for change.[45]

The lesson is that "**the subjective can become objective.**" In other words, a new way of thinking about the challenge of belonging set a self-reinforcing process into place for these students where they were more likely to reach out to others for emotional and practical support and mentoring, which ultimately improved their lives.[46]

Walton and his colleagues used the mindset process in a similar study of women in male-dominated college engineering programs and had similar positive results.[47]

Walton, Tim Wilson of the University of Virginia, and their colleagues call these "wise interventions,"[48] defined as those designed to address social problems in ways that can help people flourish by changing the way they make meaning or interpret what's happening to them. They compare making meaning to molding clay—ideas can be changed, especially when people are starting something new, experiencing a transition.

It's important that we understand how significant belonging and support are to positive development. A study conducted by Robert Sege of Tufts Medical Center and his colleagues found positive experiences can even counter the impact of adverse experiences, such as abuse or neglect. In a large state-based study, they found that if adults had six to seven positive experiences during childhood that co-occurred with adverse experiences, they were 72 percent less likely to be depressed or have poor mental health; if they had three to five such experiences, the likelihood dropped to 50 percent. These experiences were all about belonging and support, including how often the participants in the study felt they'd been able to talk to their families about their feelings, felt that their families stood by them in difficult times, felt a sense of belonging in school, and felt supported by friends.[49]

PROMOTING THE BASIC NEEDS FOR BELONGING AND SUPPORT

In the end, we—as adults—need to set the stage for needs to be met. To promote adolescents' need for **belonging**, we can:

- Recognize that belonging is a basic psychological need
- Do a reality check on ourselves to see if we are genuinely supporting young people's need to belong
- Let them know that the intensity of their feelings in adolescence might fade as they grow while acknowledging that these feelings are normal and matter a lot now
- Help them see that there's a difference between fitting in (where they conform) and belonging (where they become/are comfortable being themselves)
- Help them become the actors on their own stage by supporting them in their search to build friendships, pursue and discover shared interests, and find places where they do belong

While changing the narrative about belonging is a great starting point, in my view, it's not enough to assume that belonging will lead to support. To promote the need for **support**, we can:

- Make it clear that we all—adolescents and adults—need support to thrive
- Work to create environments that include actual real-life supports that help ensure adolescents' success

Need 2: Agency: The Need for Autonomy and Respect

Autonomy is feeling choiceful when you make decisions and when decisions are made about you by others as well as having support in figuring out how to make your own decisions. Respect is feeling that you, your ideas, your views, and your feelings are taken seriously. When adolescents are given some autonomy and treated with respect, they can become rightful owners of their own actions (agency).

The Need for Autonomy

Autonomy. People may glaze over or nod in agreement when you talk about belonging or support—but not autonomy. That word tends to elicit images of the my-way-or-the-highway adolescent. The rebellious adolescent. The independence-seeking, leaving-home-without-a-backward-glance, no-gratitude-for-all-the-nurturing-family-has-done adolescent.

In fact, we all need some autonomy throughout life. Decades of research have shown that when employees don't have some autonomy (the opportunity to make decisions about the tasks they do and how they do them), particularly in demanding jobs with little support, they're more at risk for stress and cardiovascular disease.[50]

The ongoing national studies of the workforce conducted by me and my organization have continued to find that employees with some autonomy (having a say about what happens on their job) are in better physical and mental health, more satisfied and engaged in their jobs, and more likely to remain with their employers.[51] I know this from my own life, too. When I've been in situations where I feel I've had little or no choice about what happens to me, I struggle against losing energy and hope.

Autonomy is, as Wendy Grolnick says, the opportunity to feel choice-ful.[52] And, as we'll see, autonomy is central to efforts to reduce bullying and smoking among adolescents.

A QUEST TO INSPIRE MOTIVATION

That quest has been central to David Yeager of the University of Texas, Austin, beginning when he was an early adolescent himself:

As a kid, summer camp is what I loved—the adventure, the friends, the learning new things, becoming an expert at archery. Growing up, I honestly thought the only job I'd have as an adult would be as a summer camp counselor. I wanted to become good at motivating teenagers in the same way I felt motivated at camp—and in the service work I had done.[53]

His journey first led to becoming a seventh-grade teacher:

From teaching, I learned that motivation is critical. You could make schoolwork easier or extra hard—but what really works is to make it meaningful.

He made his own teaching meaningful by focusing on a subject his students cared a lot about—bullying, fighting, conflict with other kids. Selecting conflict as a subject for study would be not only compelling for adolescents, he thought, but it would also help students better understand themselves and others. Using the book *The Outsiders*[54] in his curriculum, he didn't just ask students to read and discuss it.

> *As a way to get them to engage with the themes, not just the plot, I told them, "If you deeply understand this narrative, you could craft a conflict-training program for the younger kids in the school who seem to be getting in a lot of fights."*

That was their assignment—to create workshops for younger students. It involved writing persuasive essays, developing training exercises, presenting the information to their own classmates and critiquing each other, then finally presenting to the younger students.

Here Yeager is using the "saying is believing" principle in mindset research. The seventh graders in Yeager's class learned—genuinely learned—about preventing conflict and bullying by mastering the ideas from their schoolwork and then sharing them with younger students. They were the helpers, not those being helped, which, in turn, helped them learn.

CAN BULLYING BE REDUCED?

Yeager was one among many with a growing concern about bullying and youth violence, beginning as a teacher, then into graduate school and his career. During those years (and, tragically, still today), the nation was reeling from one incident of school shootings after another. By then, it had become apparent that harm accrues to those who are bullied *and* to those who bully. In response, states and school districts began mandating antibullying programs and implementing antibullying curricula.

Was this enough? Yeager wanted to know.

Gradually, evidence began to accumulate that while these programs seemed to work for students in elementary schools, they were less effective for older students.[55] In a meta-analysis of nineteen studies that included 350,000 students in grades one through thirteen in several Western nations, Yeager and his colleagues concluded:

Bullying appears to be effectively prevented in 7th grade and below. In 8th grade and beyond there is a sharp drop to an average of zero.[56]

In other words, antibullying programs weren't just less effective for these older students, they weren't effective at all. Yeager and his colleagues asked why.

While some speculated that it was too late—that bullying interventions need to start when children are young—the Yeager team didn't buy that. Instead, importantly, they put on an adolescent developmental lens to look at possible reasons. They found many, but key among them is that the antibullying programs tend to be didactic. They use "should" and "don't" language, as in "just say no to bullying." They often set forth adult rules and had students practice them.

AN INSIGHT FROM DEVELOPMENTAL
RESEARCH: THE BASIC NEED FOR AUTONOMY

The researchers concluded that the didactic nature of the antibullying programs would work against adolescents' need for feeling choiceful, for having some say in their own lives. In the words of Yeager and his team:

Indeed, developmental research finds that older adolescents (i.e., age 16), compared to younger children (i.e., age 8–10), increasingly invoke their right to make personal choices and not have them controlled by adults in school.[57]

What, then, would be effective? The researchers found insight in public health programs aimed to stop smoking. Originally, they, too, were didactic—telling adolescents what *not* to do—and were largely ineffective. Actually, they increased smoking! Yeager and his colleagues write:

In rigorous evaluations, more traditional direct injunctions from adults to "just say no" to smoking was found to ironically promote smoking.[58]

The Truth Initiative antismoking campaign took a different tack that the Yeager team found very promising. It depicted teens who didn't smoke as standing up to corporate executives in Big Tobacco who were trying to manipulate them into spending their money on cigarettes, getting hooked on tobacco, and then continuing to have to spend money to feed their smoking habit.

The Truth Initiative campaign saw dramatic reductions in smoking, whereas other campaigns had failed. Based on a nationally representative group of 8,904 adolescents ages twelve to seventeen surveyed annually from 1997 to 2004, an evaluation estimated the campaign prevented 450,000 adolescents nationwide from starting to smoke.[59]

The thing I find so fascinating about psychological needs is that we tend not to focus on them until problems arise. When we view young people's challenging behavior through a developmental lens, the needs are right there, critically important in whether solutions are effective or not.

AUTONOMY DOESN'T STAND ALONE: THE IMPORTANCE OF STRUCTURE

Autonomy isn't about letting young people do whatever they want to do. They, like all of us, need guidelines and limits. Wendy Grolnick defines structure as providing the information one needs to feel competent—in other words, clear expectations, rules, and consistency.[60]

One of Grolnick's studies that explored the relationship between autonomy and structure was conducted during the transition to middle school, an ideal time to see how these aspects fit together because it's a time of change.[61]

One consequence is that young people's motivation for learning tends to plummet—but, interestingly, this doesn't happen for everyone. Why? Grolnick had a hypothesis that prompted the study:

We figured that might be a time where structure in the home is really important.

The resulting 2015 study is unique in several ways. First, it followed a group of 160 students from sixth into seventh grade. Second, the measures of structure were created from students' real-life experiences with how their parents handled studying and homework.[62] Third, Grolnick and her colleagues didn't just ask if structure was there or not. They also looked at whether or not the structure was provided in a controlling or in an autonomy-supportive manner.[63]

By autonomy-supportive structure, these researchers mean that young people play a role in creating the rules and guidelines; that when problems arise, parents are understanding even if they disagree with their children; and that parents and children discuss the issue and problem-solve together, with adolescents having some say in resolving the problem.

Key Findings: The study found that when parents provided structure, especially in autonomy-supportive ways, the participating students were more motivated, felt more competent, and had better English grades, even when their prior feelings of competence and motivation as well as their grades were controlled for statistically.[64]

WHAT ABOUT BEING CONTROLLING IN UNSAFE NEIGHBORHOODS?

Understandably, some parents who fear for their child's safety can feel that being controlling—"just do what I say, no questions asked"—may best protect their children. But it's important to know that we can provide structure without being controlling, and we can be controlling without providing structure. These are two different ways of behaving.

To explore these nuances, Grolnick and her colleagues conducted a study of sixth graders and their mothers[65] in neighborhoods that varied in safety. They defined controlling behavior as behavior that "places pressure on children, solves problems for them, and disregards their perspectives and opinions."[66] Structure, on the other hand, is providing clear expectations, rules, and consistency.

Key Findings: Grolnick says, "Structure was important for all adolescents."[67] If anything, providing structure was more important in less-safe neighborhoods. Additionally, when mothers were controlling (based on children's reports), the children living in more dangerous neighborhoods (based on parents' reports) were more likely to experience depression and hostility.

These findings indicate that it's important to provide structure in both safe and less-safe neighborhoods and refrain from being controlling.[68]

In another study of supervised versus unsupervised time with sixth graders, Grolnick and her colleagues found that structure is particularly helpful during unsupervised time. The researchers write:

> *Many parents indicated that sixth grade was the first time they allowed*
> *their child to stay home alone or move about the neighborhood unattended.*
> *Thus, children may have been less certain about how to navigate this do*
> *main and so having clear structure would be particularly important.*[69]

PUTTING STRUCTURE AND AUTONOMY SUPPORT TOGETHER

In looking across Grolnick's studies, I can see how these different concepts— structure, control, and autonomy support—go together. When children are in unfamiliar, even dangerous situations, providing structure—that is, clear expectations, rules, and consistency—in positive, noncontrolling ways is key. Then, when these situations become more familiar and children become more adept in managing them, that's the time to provide structure in autonomy-supportive noncontrolling ways—that is, where young people play a role in creating the rules and guidelines.

Being controlling doesn't help children thrive in new or in more dangerous situations, but structure does and structure can be more or less autonomy-supportive. It's autonomy-supportive structure that facilitates motivation and other measures of adolescents' thriving.[70]

MATCH AND MISMATCH IN THE NEED FOR AUTONOMY?

In the Breakthrough Years study, we asked adolescents:

In the last month, how often did you feel like . . . ?

1. *You have choices when you and your parent(s) and family make*
   decisions
2. *Your parent(s) and family support you in figuring out how to make*
   your own decisions

As you can see from the figure on the next page,* young people experience

---

* Adolescents answered each question on a five-point scale from "never" to "almost always." The answers for the two questions were summed, resulting in the following groups: "rarely" (2–4), "sometimes" (5–7), and "often" (8–10).

the most autonomy (defined as more than half the time in our study) from their families (60 percent) and friends (61 percent). One might expect young people to experience more autonomy with friends, but since autonomy is really about making one's own decisions, this finding isn't surprising. Friends can be controlling at times, too, or adolescents may feel like they are going with the group rather than making their own decisions. All of these percentages show that there's lots of room for improvement.

How Often Adolescents Report the Need for Autonomy Is Met

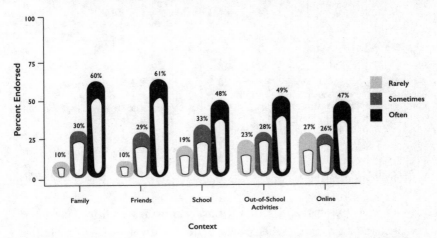

After surveying young people about how much autonomy support they had, we surveyed them about how they were doing nine months later during the pandemic. We could thus see whether having previous autonomy support made a difference later, during a time many experienced as turbulent.

The arrows in the table on the next page show that having autonomy support before the pandemic predicted later positive outcomes, except online, which makes sense since these are not in-person relationships. When young people are given choices and opportunities to solve their own problems, they are much more likely to imagine a better future for themselves, have less stress, and have more positive and fewer negative moods. Adolescents with more autonomy support at home have even less conflict with their parents, according to both parents and their adolescents.

Outcomes of Having the Need for Autonomy Met

Autonomy	Follow-Up Outcomes							
Context	School Engagement	Grades (A)	Grades (P)	Future	Negative Mood	Positive Mood	Stress	Conflict (A:P)
Family	↑			↑	↓	↑	↓	↓ : ↓
Friends				↑	↓	↑	↓	:
School	↑	↑		↑	↓	↑	↓	:
OSA	↑	↑	↑	↑	↓	↑	↓	:
Online				↑				:

A = adolescent report, P = parent report, OSA = out-of-school activities. Arrows indicate the direction of an association (i.e., up arrow for promoting, down arrow for protecting), controlling for demographics. An empty cell indicates there is no statistically significant relationship. Significant relations are p-values < .0005, meaning these correlations are very reliable and unlikely to have occurred by chance.

AUTONOMY AND STRUCTURE IN ACTION WITH A BIG DECISION

Providing autonomy and structure are mainstays of how Dakota and her husband have raised their three children—twelve-year-old Hanna, a fourteen-year-old son, and an eight-year-old daughter—in a coastal town in Maryland.

When children are little, Dakota says, they need more structure: "They might not know what the consequences of eating two candy bars are going to be with a little tummy." But they need increasing autonomy, too, so they can learn:

> You've got to let them start having some input so they can start thinking
> through what the consequences of their decisions are going to be. I try
> to give them practice so when I do turn them loose out of my house
> someday—even if they don't necessarily make what we might consider to
> be the right decision—they will have thought it through.

The most consequential decision their family faced recently was about middle school for Hanna. Students who do well in elementary school in their community receive an invitation to apply to a STEM middle school.

Once you apply, admission is through a lottery. Dakota's older son had qualified, applied, and been admitted. That decision was a "no-brainer" for him and the family because "he is all about that stuff." It wasn't as clear-cut for Hanna, whose passion is writing, not STEM. "From the time she could pick up a crayon, she was always making up her own stories," Dakota says.

Dakota and her husband wanted Hanna to make the decision herself because this school would be "a big part of her life":

> When that letter came, we said, "Hey, you're eligible to apply, do you want to do this?"

To help with the decision, Hanna's parents made a list of pros and cons for her. High on the pro side: educational quality—the quality of the courses was higher in the magnet school. On the con side: the fact that Hanna's close friends from grade school wouldn't be attending this school—although she'd still get to see them on the bus.

Dakota personally wanted her daughter to go to the magnet school.

> I was the first person in my family to go to college. I didn't grow up in an area where going to college was common. There was still a gender disparity—a belief that you're going to graduate from high school, get married right away, and have kids.

But Dakota's own parents had wanted more for their daughter:

> As my dad put it, he wanted me to have the choice between working with my brain or with my back. I grew up on a dairy farm, so I knew all about working with my back. I've tried to take that view with my kids. I want them to have choices.

Both Dakota and Hanna told me that fifth grade had been pivotal for Hanna, largely because of her teacher. This teacher had specific times she called "Freedom Times," when she told the students she wanted them to think about their motivation—what's behind what they want to do—and then do it, whether it was drawing, writing, reading, or something else. Hanna told me:

> In those times we learned more about ourselves and what we wanted to do because she'd have so many options for us.

This teacher provided clear expectations (structure) and choiceful times (autonomy). These helped Hanna see what motivated her and boosted her confidence.

What Hanna most wanted was to retain her sense of imagination. She'd heard that children begin to lose their imaginations as they grow older and she didn't want that to happen to her, so she focused on ways to keep fantasy strong in her life, which struck me as quite thoughtful:

> I read these books about magical characters. That really, really made me think more about what the world could be. You can go through a portal and all of a sudden, all your dreams could come true. I thought that was really cool because even though there's no evidence in the real world that supports that, it's still there for you to immerse yourself into.

Dakota and her husband shared their pros and cons list with Hanna and encouraged her to review and add to the list, and then tell them what she wanted to do. They did have a point of view, Dakota said: "You could tell which way we were leaning." So, was it a "real" choice? Dakota told me:

> Had Hanna said, "No, this is **not** something I really want to do," we wouldn't have made her go. It really was a matter of if she really wanted to do it and thought she could do well.

When I asked Hanna how much of a choice she felt she had, she told me that she wants to live up to her family's expectations.

> My father and my brother are really, really good at math. They can remember the equations; they love doing math. My little sister is showing signs of really liking math as well. I love language arts. My dad has really big expectations of having a family of mathematicians. So, of course you want to make your parents proud.

When I asked Hanna why making her parents proud mattered to her, she responded, "Well, because I care, because I look up to them." But Hanna had also been raised to make her own decisions.

> They didn't expect me to become what they are. They expected me to branch out and be my own person. When I showed signs of really liking to

write, they were like, "Oh, hey, this is something that you can really, really do." It made me feel like I had a choice to be what I wanted to be.

Hanna felt that the choice was real. That's important in meeting the Basic Need for autonomy. In the end, she chose to go to the STEM program *and* to keep up her writing and journaling.

Hanna's parents were providing autonomy-supportive structure in several ways:

- **Checking in on themselves.** Dakota was clear about her own expectations but managed them in a way that gave Hanna a choice.
- **Taking the child's view** by looking at the situation from her perspective.
- **Sharing reasons** when they made the list of pros and cons.
- **Providing a real choice.**
- **Problem-solving together.**

In giving Hanna this measure of autonomy, her parents were also meeting other Basic Needs—the need for beginning to figure out her identity and the need to gain competence. This is how psychological needs fit together and reinforce each other.

AUTONOMY DOESN'T STAND ALONE: THE IMPORTANCE OF INVOLVEMENT

Another aspect of their parenting stood out to me. These parents are involved in their children's lives. As Wendy Grolnick's research showed, **autonomy support, structure, and involvement go together in affecting motivation.**[71] From her studies on parental involvement, she has concluded:

The message to parents is that anything you do—any interest and activity you can provide around showing that school is important and that you have high expectations for your child—is really important.[72]

What about what's called "overinvolvement"? Here's where autonomy comes in. There's an essential distinction between being involved in controlling ways or being over-identified with your child (seeing their successes and failures as your own) versus being involved in autonomy-supportive ways. There never can be too much parental involvement if it is provided in an autonomy-supportive way, Grolnick says:

> *When involvement is high and autonomy support is high, it's great!*

PUTTING AUTONOMY INTO PRACTICE DAY-TO-DAY

Dakota used autonomy-supportive strategies when she helped Hanna at twelve make a decision about middle school, hoping that Hanna and her other children will make good decisions on their own someday.

That someday doesn't turn out to be in the far future for most parents. Take, for example, the time Dakota wasn't there to pick Hanna up from school to take her to dance class, as Hanna expected. Dakota had told Hanna that morning that the class was canceled, but Hanna didn't remember or hadn't heard. Hanna waited for her mother to show up, and when she didn't, Hanna decided to take the bus but couldn't find it.

Next, she tried to go back to the school for help, but there was no one in sight. The school was closing down, meaning that no students could get back inside. Hanna had to figure out what to do on her own, and she didn't have a cell phone.

A year or so before, her mother had walked her through a scenario: "If you ever need to get home by walking," and then had shown her the route to follow. So that's what Hanna decided to do:

> *I told myself, I know how to get home, but I was freaked out. The sun is setting. What if something happens? I don't have any way to contact anyone.*
>
> *I know this sounds really stupid for a twelve-year-old, but I hate walking. All my life, I was told that the streets in this area are very dangerous because there's no sidewalks.*
>
> *Half the time I was walking on the side of the road in the ditch. I had to, because I didn't feel comfortable walking by the side of the road where people could run me over.*

It was getting dark. Every time she came to a stoplight, she had to cross three lanes of traffic:

> *I had to stay calm. Otherwise, I was going to completely break down. So, I began to think about my characters that I write about. I just played little stories in my head while I walked down the road, just to keep myself calm.*

That's a very thoughtful way of managing a challenge. Meanwhile, when Hanna didn't get off the bus, Dakota ran back into the house and tried to call the school, but got no response. So she got in her car and began to drive toward school, still trying to reach someone at the school.

Twenty minutes after she should have arrived at home on the bus, Hanna turned a corner and saw her mom in the car.

> My mom was like, "What the heck happened to you?" I was in the seat, practically crying, and she kept saying, "What happened?" It took me forever to explain it because I was so emotionally distressed. She was scared and I was scared, but we both finally calmed down.

Helping Hanna learn how to solve problems for herself helped her manage her fear and figure out a solution as it will help her in the future. That's why autonomy is so crucial.

The Need for Respect

Repeatedly in our Breakthrough Years study, young people urged, demanded, even sometimes pleaded for respect:

> We matter.
>
> Treat us with respect.
>
> We are here, we are your future, please trust us and respect us.
>
> Respect us, we will respect you.

Now, maybe if you've argued with an adolescent, your response might be, "Respect has to be earned." Understandable. But research shows that respect is a two-way street. If we treat adolescents with respect, they'll likely treat us with respect. Or, in the words of one of the young people I just quoted, "Respect us, we will respect you." And vice versa.

Adolescents are primed to be sensitive to how they're treated, and treating them with respect can reduce behavior problems.

WHAT IS IT ABOUT RESPECT?

In 2018, David Yeager, Ron Dahl of the University of California, Berkeley, and Carol Dweck of Stanford University joined forces to write an article with a title that could be a parent's cry for help filtered through a science sensibility: "Why Interventions to Influence Adolescent Behavior Often Fail but Could Succeed."[73] Yeager and his team write:

> We propose the hypothesis that traditional interventions fail when they do not align with adolescents' **enhanced desire to feel respected and be accorded status** [emphasis added]; however, interventions that do align with this desire can motivate internalized, positive behavior change.[74]

You'll recall that Yeager focused on adolescents' need for autonomy to help explain why interventions on bullying fail or succeed. Autonomy is crucial, but so is respect.

Basic Needs are often mutually reinforcing. As Yeager, Dahl, and Dweck write:

> [I]ndividuals feel **respected** [emphasis added] and that they have high status when they are treated as though they are competent, have agency and autonomy, and are of potential value to the group.[75]

ARE ADOLESCENTS ESPECIALLY SENSITIVE TO STATUS AND RESPECT?

Have you ever given advice to a teen and had it rebuffed? Adolescents are on the lookout for whether someone is giving advice because "they think I'm a kid" and not competent and capable (i.e., a sign of disrespect) or whether "they're really trying to help me out." Yeager speaks from experience when he says:

> This can lead adolescents to overreact sometimes—to feel like a mom-suggestion like "Don't forget your coat" is an infringement.[76]

We can see clashes like this everywhere, once we look. And we need to look, because adolescents are seeing it everywhere. They're primed to do so. They're environmental detectors, like Geiger counters, except instead of scanning the environment to detect radiation, they're looking for signs of disrespect.

To explore why adolescents are especially sensitive to respect and status, Yeager, Dahl, and Dweck begin with biology and the many hormonal changes in puberty, with a focus on testosterone as an example. As we know, testosterone increases after puberty in both girls and boys. Although testosterone is typically seen as a hormone that heightens aggression, there's increasing evidence that it affects the desire to be respected and to earn status. The researchers write:

> A growing line of research in both humans and animals suggests that it [testosterone] increases the motivation to search for, learn about, and maintain status in one's social environment.[77]

Second, Yeager, Dahl, and Dweck turn to the research on social threat, reporting that adolescents tend to react particularly strongly to experiences that threaten their respect and their social status. For example, in experiments where young people have to give a last-minute speech to kids their age, middle adolescents (fifteen and older) typically show more of a cortisol or stress reaction than younger children.[78]

Third, the authors cite research showing that middle adolescents also react strongly to situations where they believe they're being disrespected. One has only to think of what a huge insult the word "diss" is among teenagers to see how important being respected is in their lives.

Key Finding: Evidence shows that adolescents' development primes them to be especially sensitive to whether or not they're treated with respect.

A NEW PERSPECTIVE: ADOLESCENTS ARE PRIMED TO BE ENVIRONMENTAL DETECTORS

Part of this priming is how strongly adolescents react to mistreatment—their detector-like sensibility. We could look at their reactions in a number of different ways. If fifteen-year-olds "overreact" (to use Yeager's word) to feelings of being disrespected by people at school, friends, or family, we could see this as a trait of those individuals: "They're overly sensitive." We could see it as hormonal: "They're a hormonal mess." Or as rude: "They've never learned manners."

The way we see situations like this determines the way we react to them. What we see is what we do.

I hope that the research on adolescent development helps all of us see their behavior in new ways. **Adolescents are primed to react like environmental**

detectors to how they're being treated. How else would they be able to go out into the world, encounter new people and new places, and make judgments about whether these situations are trustworthy—places where they can thrive or not? That doesn't mean that they should be disrespectful—it merely means that we should be attuned to *why* they care so much.

MATCH AND MISMATCH IN THE BASIC NEED FOR RESPECT?

In the Breakthrough Years study, we asked adolescents:
In the last month, how often did you feel like . . . ?

1. *Your parent(s) and family treat you with respect*
2. *Your parent(s) and family dismiss your ideas/do not take them seriously*

Then we asked the same questions about their friends, the people at school, the people in their out-of-school activities, and the people they connect with online.

Given how important respect is to adolescents, there is a lot of room for improving the match between what they need and what they experience. About six in ten "often" experience respect in these five settings, which we measured* as more than half of the time.

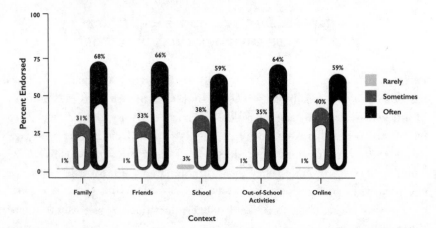

How Often Adolescents Report the Need for Respect Is Met

---

* Adolescents answered each question on a five-point scale from "never" to "almost always." The answers for the two questions were summed, resulting in the following groups: "rarely" (2–4), "sometimes" (5–7), and "often" (8–10).

You can also see from the table below—by looking at the arrows—that respect matters. If you'll recall, in the Breakthrough Years study, we asked adolescents about the frequency of having the psychological needs we've identified as basic being met (prepandemic); then we surveyed them again nine months later (during the pandemic) on outcomes, to see how they were doing. For every outcome except school engagement, being treated with respect was predictive of positive outcomes later. Adolescents who experienced more respect prepandemic were more hopeful about their futures, had more positive moods, and had better grades nine months later. They also had fewer bad moods, less stress, and fewer conflicts with their parents.

Outcomes of Having the Need for Respect Met

Respect	Follow-Up Outcomes							
Context	School Engagement	Grades (A)	Grades (P)	Future	Negative Mood	Positive Mood	Stress	Conflict (A:P)
Family		↑		↑	↓	↑	↓	↓ : ↓
Friends		↑	↑	↑	↓	↑	↓	↓ : ↓
School		↑		↑	↓	↑	↓	↓ : ↓
OSA		↑	↑	↑	↓	↑	↓	↓ :
Online		↑		↑				:

A = adolescent report, P = parent report, OSA = out-of-school activities. Arrows indicate the direction of an association (i.e., up arrow for promoting, down arrow for protecting), controlling for demographics. An empty cell indicates there is no statistically significant relationship. Significant relations are p-values < .0005, meaning these correlations are very reliable and unlikely to have occurred by chance.

DOES INCREASING RESPECTFUL INTERACTIONS PROMOTE POSITIVE BEHAVIOR CHANGE?

Having spent years looking at why interventions with adolescents do or don't work, Yeager, Dahl, and Dweck "argue that it may be possible to capitalize on adolescents' sensitivity to status and respect and redirect it toward positive behavior change."[79] One of the examples they cite that does honor adolescents' sensitivity to status and respect is an intervention on reducing misbehavior in schools led by Jason Okonofua of the University of California, Berkeley.

Just as parents can see misbehavior in different ways, so can teachers. Suppose adolescents keep getting up during class instruction to throw tissues into the wastebasket, walking by other students and disrupting them. This behavior isn't dangerous or violent; it isn't students fighting, yelling, or creating an uproar. But it's disruptive and annoying, and an example of the type of misbehavior that leads to school discipline.

Teachers can have different mental models for dealing with this type of misbehavior.[80] One is a relationship-based, respectful approach, where teachers view their role as building relationships of trust and respect with students. These teachers have a high standard for behavior (it's essential to note here that misbehavior is not okay), but they promote it through expecting the best and working with students to achieve it. When students misbehave, these teachers try to understand why and create a safe space for students to learn positive ways of behaving.

Another mental model is a punitive approach, exemplified by zero-tolerance policies. These teachers view their role as showing students that there are consequences for misbehavior and believe that students will learn this best by being punished for infractions, with punishments escalating for repeated misbehavior.

REFRAMING SCHOOL DISCIPLINE

Okonofua is attuned to differences in school discipline because he lived them, growing up in Memphis, Tennessee.

First, he saw that the way he was perceived and disciplined in school wasn't the same for his brothers. He excelled at school compared with them:

> I started seeing differences in those two tracks—in how students were treated and how students were allowed to behave.[81]

His family moved a lot, too, and as a Black student, he noticed that discipline was handled differently in the inner city and in the suburbs. The farther from the city his family lived and the Whiter the school population became, the less punitive and more relationship-based the discipline practices were.

Middle school was, he says, "the first time I really started thinking critically about how I was treated in my school environment." He told me about a time when he was in the cafeteria "and some kids were passing around flyers for a party that weekend."

He took the flyer he was handed, but before he'd even looked at it, the assistant principal took it away and sent him to the office. "She was walking around to everyone taking the flyers and telling them to go to the office."

Once there, he said, "The assistant principal told us we were all going to receive a one-day home suspension because the flyer had some profanity in it." The students were then told to sign an acknowledgment that they were being suspended. "Everyone signed off," he said, but "then she got to me":

> I said, "No. I'm not going to sign off on it. I would prefer to go back to my pre-calculus class," which was the highest-level math class that could be taken at the time.
>
> I told her, "I need to get back to work. I have nothing to do with this. I'm not a bad kid." She said, "Are you going to sign it or not?" I said, "No, I'm not going to sign it. Feel free to call my mom. She will agree with me."
>
> She said, "Okay, then, now it's a three-day board suspension for insubordination."

This approach is in keeping with a zero-tolerance approach. Okonofua was told to sign the three-day suspension paper. Again, he refused:

> I said, "No, I'm not going to sign it. Just let me go back to class. You have the wrong student. I'm not some bad kid. I've never been suspended."

That raised the temperature of the situation and is why some Black families may teach their children not to disagree but to accept a punishment even if it's unjust. The assistant principal responded:

> "Okay, then you can go to jail," and she called the school police officer to have me arrested.

Okonofua was fortunate. The school police officer knew him and his family. He took Okonofua aside and told him:

> "I don't know what you're doing here. You don't seem like one of the people I would be doing this to, but I have to do my job."

Okonofua had three days of home suspension—days he regretted because he liked his classes and didn't want to fall behind. Then he and his mother attended a court hearing:

The judge was going through a file that I later realized was mine. He had this weird look on his face. He's like, "You're Jason?"

"Yes."

He pulled out my report card, gave it to me, and said, "Is this your report card? You're taking these classes?"

"Yes."

"These are your grades?"

"Yes."

"Have you ever been in trouble before?" he asked.

"No."

He said, and I quote, "Get out of my office and tell your school to not send you here ever again!"

He explained to my mom that none of this ever happened according to my record—no arrest had ever happened, no suspension ever happened. He completely erased all of it, and that was the end of the story. I went back to school.

But it wasn't the end of the story. It was, in fact, the beginning. Okonofua realized that none of his efforts or accomplishments fully protected him. If there hadn't happened to be a police officer at the school who knew him, if his case hadn't happened to be assigned to a judge who looked at his record and believed in him, he could have drifted from being seen as an excellent student into being seen as a troublemaker. Just like that.

It literally went from nothing to a one-day suspension, a three-day suspension, then being arrested. Having those things on my record could have shaped the entire trajectory of my education.

He also learned what it felt like to be seen as a troublemaker, how helpless one feels when encountering the system. "Small things can become big things," he noticed. For some in his class, an experience like this could and did become the first step in the school-to-prison pipeline.

The summer after tenth grade, Okonofua had another experience that became a big deal in his life:

I was pulled out through a Rotary Foundation in Memphis to attend a prestigious prep school in the Northeast. They set this up for students like me to get enrichment classes and exposure to different types of learning.

The contrast was stunning:

I saw immediate differences between this prep school and all of the public schools I'd gone to in Memphis.

He describes his last school as jail-like:

It was surrounded by wire fences, with cameras in the hallways. On random days, there were metal detectors at the front door. At least one police officer always patrolled the hallways.

The prep school was like a club:

No wire fences. Everything was pleasant. In the school cafeteria, meals were given whenever we wanted them. There were no school uniforms. We had a dress code of slacks and an oxford button-down. All of the teachers and faculty were very welcoming. Everyone was pretty much in good spirits.

This contrast opened Okonofua's eyes to how context—that is, the environment—can shape students' behavior:

I didn't know it at the time, but the public schools felt more like a prison. At any given moment, everything could fall apart. If you did one thing wrong, you could end up in jail within an hour, versus this place where you were under the care of all these adults who were looking out for you. Just the feeling of knowing that people have your back, that people want to see you succeed, made a huge difference.

That sums up a respectful, supportive approach to discipline. More pertinent to what has become his life's work was the way Okonofua was expected to talk with adults. At his previous school, he was punished for trying to make a case for refusing a suspension. It was seen as talking back, even though his tone was respectful.

At his prep school, making a case was encouraged as a way for young people to learn how to navigate conversations with adults—how to figure out the point you want to make and frame your arguments convincingly. It was like writing a persuasive paper or making a compelling point in a debate. Okonofua was actually asked to join the debate club there. He said, "It's just two different contexts and they lead to different trajectories":

*That experience built a mission in me—a motivation to pinpoint how to
create the right context for students and then how to do that on the largest
scale possible.*

WHAT SUPPORTS RESPECTFUL DISCIPLINE (OR DOESN'T)?

After college at Northwestern University, Okonofua obtained his master's
and doctorate at Stanford University, working with Claude Steele, highly
admired for his research on stereotype threat, as well as Greg Walton, whom
you've met through his innovative research on belonging and support. There,
Okonofua's goal was to pinpoint how to create the right context for students
and create interventions exemplifying more respectful discipline. But first, he
needed to understand suspension better. He knew Black students were three
times more likely to be suspended, but why?[82]

One hypothesis at the time suggested that teachers might be responding
to misbehavior by Black and White children differently. Another suggested
that racial minority students might behave differently than White students
and therefore would be more likely to be suspended.

Okonofua began by exploring the first hypothesis, working with Jennifer
Eberhardt of Stanford, well known for her research on how implicit bias can
shape decision-making and its impact in the juvenile justice system.[83]

Across two experiments, the first with 57 K–12 teachers[84] and the second with 204, teachers read about typical student misbehavior. Okonofua
explains:

> *We had teachers from across the country read a series of misbehaviors.
> After reading about each incident, we asked teachers a series of questions:
> "How severe is this misbehavior? How hindered do you feel by this
> student? How irritated do you feel by this student? How severely do you
> want to discipline this student?" The first three questions we put together
> into what was called "How Troubled Teachers Felt."*[85]

One element the researchers looked at was based on a name change:

> *The misbehavior was either by a child with a stereotypical Black name, Darnell
> or Deshawn, or a child with a stereotypical White name, Jake or Greg.*

The behavior is exactly the same; only the student's name is different.
If teachers vary their response to a child with one name versus another, it

stands to reason that their response is influenced by assumptions about race/ethnicity. The researchers also asked follow-up questions to confirm that teachers did, in fact, assume that stereotypically Black names were associated with Black students. Another factor also mattered:

We'd looked at research on discipline and found that if teachers feel like this is going to be a consistent problem over time, they respond with more severe discipline. So, we set up the experiment to include multiple misbehaviors.

They selected misbehaviors that typically triggered school disciplinary action. One was the example I mentioned earlier: adolescents disrupting other students during class instruction by getting up to throw tissues into the wastebasket. This kind of classroom disturbance is one of the most common reasons students are disciplined.

Bias is more likely to affect decision-making when there's ambiguity about the situation:

This isn't sexual harassment, fighting in school, bringing weapons to school, or bringing drugs to school. It's something relatively minor in nature, but also something more subjective. Teachers have to decide, "Is this bad or not?"

The other example of misbehavior the researchers used was said to happen three days later with the same student:

This time, the student is sleeping in class. The teacher asks the student to raise his head and wake up. The student wakes up for a moment, and then falls back to sleep. This is something that would be classified as insubordination, which is the number one reason for children to be referred to the office across the country.

The researchers found that the order in which the misbehavior incidents (being disruptive or sleeping) were presented to teachers didn't affect the results. They also found that teachers responded similarly to the first misbehavior, regardless of whether a "Black" or "White" name was used. But that wasn't true when they read a second incident about this same student:

After the second incident, teachers responded to the same questions. This time, interesting effects emerged: teachers felt significantly more troubled by the misbehavior if it was by a child with a stereotypically Black name compared to a child with a stereotypically White name.

Similarly, they felt like they would want to discipline a student significantly more severely if the misbehavior was done by a student with a stereotypically Black name versus a student with a stereotypically White name.

The researchers also asked teachers to indicate the extent to which they thought the misbehavior was indicative of a pattern and found that teachers were more likely to see a pattern that would lead to suspension with students with stereotypically Black names and more likely to label the students with Black names as "troublemakers."

Key Finding: Differences in the way young people are disciplined in school are driven, in part, by stereotypes that can lead teachers to escalate their negative responses to Black students over the course of multiple teacher-to-student incidents. This response can get in the way of a more respectful or relationship-based approach toward students.

STEREOTYPING IS THE CULPRIT

Okonofua sees stereotypes as the "glue" that causes a teacher to piece together potentially unrelated ideas. I see stereotyping as not only the glue but also the culprit. Teachers—in fact, all of us—can make assumptions about others that stand in the way of providing respectful interactions. Although race is one key trigger, so are age, gender, and assumptions about young people who may stand apart from others because of factors such as the presence of adverse childhood experiences, a medical condition, or mental health concerns.

Christine Koh, a cognitive scientist turned accomplished parenting author, says she was helped to move beyond her childhood trauma by adults who didn't label her as traumatized. They helped her not because her family life was troubled but because they saw something of genuine value in her. That turned her life around.[86] In a focus group conducted by Shawn Ginwright of San Francisco State University with young men who'd had tough lives, one said it eloquently: "I am more than what happened to me. I'm not just my trauma."[87] Pamela Cantor, a physician and founder of Turnaround for

Children, has devoted her life to healing trauma; she says this is especially important since healing is affected by the way children are viewed:

> *The word "trauma" is a stigma to children who have it. No one wants to*
> *be taught by somebody where they feel labeled. This sets up a relationship*
> *that is deficit-oriented right from the start. What we all need to know is that*
> *trauma causes a disruption in our lives. What our kids need to know is that*
> *it can be fixed without stigma and without shame.*[88]

As the mother of an exuberant, active son, I had to be on alert for teachers stereotyping him as hyperactive or undisciplined (he was neither). When teachers appreciated him for who he was, he did beautifully in their classes. When they didn't, it was hard for him.

Stereotyping can block recognition of the humanity of children, leading to a punitive, take-no-prisoners approach to discipline.

LAB ←→ LIFE: CAN WE CHANGE LIVES BY CHANGING HOW WE VIEW AND APPROACH DISCIPLINE?

Driven by his mission to create better disciplinary experiences for students, Okonofua conducted a series of experiments with David Paunesku and Greg Walton, both of Stanford University.[89]

Adopting the wise intervention approach that Walton used in his belonging and support experiments you read about earlier, they focused on disciplinary mindsets—a relationship-based/respectful, empathic mindset versus a punitive mindset—and the approaches to discipline that emanate from these beliefs.

Their hypothesis was twofold:

- A punitive approach to misbehavior could incite already alienated students to become more rebellious and oppositional, engaging in more of the very behavior that punitive discipline has been established to prevent.
- A respectful approach could lead to compliance.

There was evidence for these hypotheses, as they write:

> *Much research shows that feeling respect for and being respected by*
> *authority figures can motivate people to follow rules enforced by those*

figures, especially in conflicts. If teachers convey this respect while disciplining students, this may improve students' behavior.[90]

Deep down, Walton* notes, teachers really want to help students:

Typically, people don't go into teaching to punish kids.[91]

Okonofua elaborates:

What we wanted to shift was the extent to which a teacher would view a child as a troublemaker—that label—because we knew that that label is what led to more severe discipline.[92]

Their first experiment looked at whether teachers' views of discipline could be changed. They randomly assigned thirty-nine teachers, kindergarten through twelfth grade, either to a punitive or a respectful/empathic relationship-based mindset group. In the first phase of the study, teachers in both groups were given prompts. In the relationship group, they read a brief article reminding them that good teacher-student relationships are essential for students to learn self-control. In the punitive group, the article stated that punishment for misbehavior was essential for teachers to maintain control of the classroom.

Next was the "saying is believing" phase, designed to reinforce one or the other approach teachers had just read about. Teachers in both groups were asked to write how that approach could help them maintain control of their classrooms.

Teachers were then asked how they'd respond to typical incidents of misbehavior, drawn from middle school disciplinary records, like a student disrupting the class by repeatedly throwing tissues in the wastebasket. "The effects," Walton reports, "were just hugely discrepant."[93]

When teachers were primed with punishing, they were very punitive. With the kids who were getting up and throwing tissues away, the teachers were threatening to send them to the principal, call their parents, give them detention. They were more likely to view those kids as troublemakers, a permanent label that—if it sticks in a teacher's mind—is not going to be helpful for future interactions.

---

* My interviews with Jason Okonofua and Greg Walton took place on different days and in different places, but since they felt like a conversation, I have written about them as such.

Teachers primed to have a more respectful approach responded quite differently. Okonofua says:

Teachers with this mindset were more likely to want to ask why the child was misbehaving in the first place, and they were much more likely to want to adjust the context to make it more conducive to better behavior.[94]

AN INTERVENTION DESIGNED TO CHANGE DISCIPLINE

Armed with this knowledge, the research team designed a wise intervention—something Okonofua had always wanted to do. They selected five middle schools from three California school districts. In all, their intervention included thirty-one math teachers who collectively taught 1,682 students. These teachers were randomly assigned to one of two groups. Okonofua says:

One group read about how technology is important for engaging students in the classroom. The other group read about how it's important to respect and value students' perspectives, especially when they misbehave.[95]

The article on respectful relationships discussed adolescent development and described how the changes adolescents are going through biologically and socially make them especially sensitive to unfair treatment and can cause them to react strongly. The article discouraged labeling students as troublemakers. It also noted that when teachers make students feel heard, understood, and respected, it shows students that school is fair and that they can succeed at school.[96] These ideas were reinforced through stories from students who'd written about how they felt when discipline was empathic and respectful.

In the next step of the intervention, teachers became the helpers, not the helped. Teachers were invited to incorporate the ideas they'd been reading about into materials for creating a teacher training initiative.

Walton says that the aspect of this study that he found most moving and powerful "is the way teachers wrote about how they wanted to think about and treat misbehaving students":

One teacher, for example, said that she always remembers that a child is the most precious thing in the world to somebody out there in the world and no matter what that child has done, she wants to remember that.

The intervention took forty-five minutes online. Okonofua describes a second online part that took about twenty-five minutes two months later:

> Teachers read stories from other teachers, thinking back to when they were in middle school and how they had craved support and trust from teachers. The stories concluded that now that they were teachers, they had to show this to their students.[97]

Both parts of this intervention were designed to reduce student suspension rates, and they did. In Walton's words:

> The basic finding was that students whose math teacher got the intervention were half as likely to be suspended over the course of the school year than the math teacher who got the control materials.[98]

Key Finding: The average suspension rate of the students in this study whose teachers had read about respectful relationships was 4.8 percent, compared with 9.6 percent for the students whose teachers had read about technology.[99] Importantly, Walton notes, it wasn't just math teachers who suspended students: "Even when kids were interacting with other adults in school who hadn't been part of the intervention, they were still less likely to get suspended."[100]

Okonofua and Walton wondered if these results could be replicated where they made predictions about the outcomes before the study was completed. In this study with sixty-six teachers across 5,822 students, their predictions were correct: the intervention reduced suspension rates over the school years, especially for Black and Hispanic students, cutting the racial disparity from 10.6 to 5.9 percentage points, a 45 percent drop.[101]

Okonofua and Walton speculate that having one teacher who is more empathic toward students—one teacher who can make students feel more like school is a place for them—can lead students to have a different mindset about the entire school environment. Indeed, in the new study, the reduction in suspension rates continued through the next year, when students interacted with teachers who had not received the intervention.

How students were treated the year before can have a lasting positive effect.

Teachers are in a high-stress job that itself doesn't get the respect it deserves. Walton says:

> *The tragedy of this circumstance is that teachers—in that stressful environment, in that craziness of trying to teach, in the pressures of trying to get kids' test scores up—can lose sight of who they want to be, and who they want to be in their interactions with children.*[102]

The same is true of us as parents. We didn't become parents to disrespect our children, yet in a red-hot moment or in the belief that it works, we can do just that. I am grateful to Jason Okonofua for turning his own life experience into a lifeline for others. He says:

> *What we tried to shift is how one views a troublemaker—period—which I think is a really promising direction that we're taking.*[103]

How we view our children is how we respond to them. If we respect them, they'll likely respect us.

PROMOTING THE BASIC NEED FOR AUTONOMY AND RESPECT

Over many years, studies have found that autonomy support is linked with children's growing ability to solve problems for themselves and more positive mental health.[104] But autonomy, support, structure, and adult involvement *together* help adolescents thrive. In helping meet the need for **autonomy**, we can:

- Check in on ourselves to understand our own expectations and how they color our response, so that we can be more intentional in our approach
- Take our child's point of view with an understanding of their capacities in mind
- Set doable limits and share the reasons why
- Provide choices where possible
- Problem-solve solutions together

Knowing that adolescents are environmental detectors, on the alert for whether they are respected, you need to be on the alert, too. In helping meet the need for **respect**, we can:

- Listen to what they say and what they do, understanding that behavior is a form of communication
- Look out for stereotypes (raging hormones, no impulse control, troublemakers, etc.) that might negatively affect the way we treat them
- Adopt a mental model that is focused on promoting skills, not punishing
- Resolve problems with adolescents in fair, consistent, and considerate ways
- Remember that respect breeds respect

Need 3: Mastery: The Need for Challenge and Competence

Challenge is feeling encouraged to do new or difficult things and that you can grow and learn. Competence is knowing that others think you can do things well and have confidence in your skills and abilities. When adolescents are encouraged to handle challenges in ways that develop competence, they can feel effective (mastery).

The Need for Challenge

Fifteen-year-old Dylan is deeply focused and completely lackadaisical, according to his mother, Nia. This is tripping him up in high school, especially in English class:

> The English teacher has them read a lot. Dylan's an avid reader, so he could tell you the entire synopsis of the book, but when the teacher had them write about the characters' motivation or to arrive at and support his conclusions about the book, he was writing two-sentence answers.

He's always been this way, Nia feels. When he was little, she'd read about child development ages and stages and he never fit. A milestone would say, "At this point, your child should be entertaining themselves for fifteen minutes," but he could go for an hour and a half stacking and unstacking blocks. Then he'd be deeply forgetful about other things:

> *We had a decision to make in third grade about whether he should go into an advanced academic program, and I took him to an educational psychologist. She said, "Basically, he's really high in certain things and super low in others." She also said, "People are going to misdiagnose him with ADHD, and I don't think that's it."*

It was tempting to put him into the advanced academic program, but they decided against it. Today, Dylan can tell you the entire story of Winston Churchill and World War II but can't remember a school assignment. "It's this interesting dichotomy," his mother notes.

At first glance, it seemed that when a challenge was of his own making, he'd pursue it relentlessly, but if a challenge was imposed by a teacher, he'd do as little as possible. So, were these motivational issues? Nia didn't fully understand, but came to the conclusion that something had to be done because his grades were slipping, fast.

Challenges in school go with the territory, as do challenges in life. The need to address and overcome them is linked to the need for mastery. Research by Barbara Schneider of Michigan State University adds immeasurably to our knowledge about challenges in school.

Schneider is deeply invested in improving equity,[105] a passion that was fueled by being hospitalized in her freshman year in high school and seeing for herself the ravaging effects that poverty had on some of the children who were hospitalized with her. She calls this a life-altering experience and has devoted herself to bringing about change. Education, she feels, is a lever for this kind of change, with engagement in learning as the force that can move that lever, but she finds engagement can be on the sidelines for schools in this country: "I think we've ignored what we can do to help young people feel more engaged and be more productive in school."

WHAT IS ENGAGEMENT?

I'll never forget the opening pages of the late Mihaly Csikszentmihalyi's book *Flow*,[106] where he details his discovery that happiness isn't something that happens by chance, nor something that money or power can buy, nor even something that can be directly sought—yet we all have moments when we feel exhilarated. Csikszentmihalyi, who grew up in Europe during World War II, realized how few adults in his life "were able to withstand the tragedies that war visited on them,"[107] which kindled his desire to understand what fosters a life worth living. He spent decades searching for what characterizes optimal experiences and found:

> *The best moments usually occur when a person's body or mind is stretched*
> *to its limits in a voluntary effort to accomplish something difficult and*
> *worthwhile. Optimal experience is something we make happen.*[108]

Note that Csikszentmihalyi mentions being "stretched" when accomplishing something "difficult and worthwhile." He writes, "In the long run optimal experiences add up to a sense of mastery," and that kind of moment "comes as close to what is usually meant by happiness as anything else we can conceivably imagine."[109]

Csikszentmihalyi's research clarifies engagement. These optimal experiences, periods of "flow," are close to what I see as the peak of engagement.

Key Finding: Optimal experiences include, but go beyond, being involved, enthusiastic, and committed (as engagement is typically defined in workplace research). They involve mastering challenge.

The story of promoting engagement is the story of promoting challenge. The two are inextricably linked:

- Without challenge, we don't stretch ourselves.
- Without challenge, we don't grow and change.
- Without challenge, we don't achieve mastery.

This is why I see challenge as a Basic Need that is part and parcel of mastery.

WE ARE BORN ENGAGED IN LEARNING

It was seeing the lack of engagement that led me to write my book *Mind in the Making.* I had asked young people in eight different parts of the country to talk to me about learning as a prelude to one of my youth voice studies, and I mostly got blank stares and silence in return. But when I asked them to talk to me about *not* learning, they couldn't stop interrupting each other, telling me about a "ridiculous" math teacher or horrible coach.

The fact is, children are born engaged in learning. Beyond the voluminous literature on this subject, there was no better example in my own life at that time than right next door. My neighbors had adopted eight-month-old twins from an orphanage in China. Despite their difficult beginnings, these babies' eyes were burning brightly as they tried to see, touch, and experience everything in this new place with these new people. Learning was a survival skill for them, as it is for all babies, and these twins were all-in, fully engaged. In contrast, the blank stares from the older students I was interviewing indicated that something in their experience had dimmed that engagement.

Unfortunately, the stories I was hearing from these students are typical. In *The Eight Myths of Student Engagement*, Jennifer Fredricks of Union College reports that 40 to 60 percent of students nationwide show signs of disengagement.[110]

Breakthrough Years Study Finding: Fifty-six percent of adolescents ages nine through nineteen were engaged or very engaged in learning in school prior to the pandemic. During the pandemic, that dropped to 33 percent.

If children are born learning but so many older children are disengaged, the question becomes: What are we doing in society to dim that fire for learning in school?

DEFINING THE FLOW AND FIRE TO CREATE A MODEL OF ENGAGEMENT IN LEARNING

Barbara Schneider's goal for her work has been to identify the key components of engagement, which taken together constitute optimal learning moments.[111] Like Csikszentmihalyi, she's focused on optimal experiences, in her case, **optimal learning moments**. Once defined, her goal has been to increase these moments because she, like I, was seeing too little of this kind of learning in her own studies of adolescents.

To pursue this, Schneider teamed up with Finnish researchers Katariina

Salmela-Aro and Jari Lavonen of the University of Helsinki as well as others to conduct an education study funded by the National Science Foundation. "In Finland, like the U.S.," Schneider says, "they're very worried about getting students more engaged in science and in taking more science courses." The overall goal of this research team isn't just increasing the number of future scientists, it's mainly about increasing the science literacy of all students.

The U.S.-Finnish team's research has been guided by a conceptual model of optimal learning culled from their and others' research. In this model, they hypothesized that the drivers of optimal learning moments are interests, skills, and challenge. Schneider says:

> These are three different dimensions that we can actually measure—and we can measure them multiple times. We get a really unique picture of when these optimal learning moments are occurring.[112]

Assessing **interest** gets more at the **emotional aspects** of engagement: students are going to be more engaged in learning content if they see value in learning it, if it seems useful, if they're interested in learning about it.

Assessing **skills** gets more at the **cognitive aspects** of engagement. The researchers define skills as the cognitive abilities that students believe they have in order to accomplish the specific tasks in their science curriculum—to take in, to retrieve, and to reassemble information.

For Schneider, it was important to include both the emotional and cognitive sides of engagement. She notes that girls may be very interested in science, but studies show they may lack confidence in their skills.[113] Addressing learning more holistically can help teachers level the learning playing field for all students.

Then there's assessing **challenge**. Schneider and her team define challenge as **the push within students to improve** their abilities beyond what they've previously learned. As she and her colleagues write:

> Challenge is the engine that propels interest and skills to new levels of capacity.[114]

Schneider says her team is continuing to try to refine their understanding of challenge, but they've seen that challenges often revolve around "something students don't know that piques their interest in such a way that they're going to have to figure it out. We think the excitement that occurs because they're trying to figure it out is critical in this whole process."[115]

Although Schneider defines challenge as a "push within students," my definition includes what adults can also do from the outside to help maintain or increase that inner fire by providing the right level of challenge and adjusting it to fit students' skills and needs.

The U.S.-Finnish model also includes **detractors** from these moments, like being confused or bored, or **enhancers**, like feeling happy and confident.

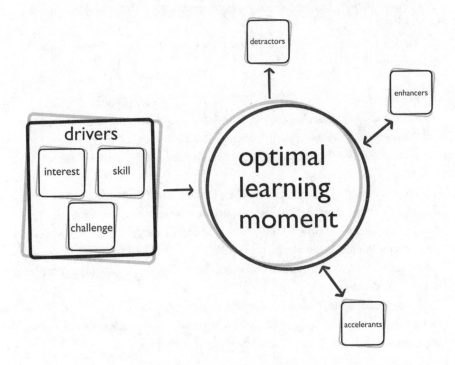

PINPOINTING THE CHALLENGE

When Dylan's grades began slipping, Nia decided to intervene. She didn't want to tell him what to do, but she wanted to try to determine what was going on:

> I asked him, "Have you gone to office hours? Have you talked to your teacher?" He hadn't and was just hugely frustrated. So I asked, "What if the three of us have a call?" He said, "Okay." So, we made an appointment. It was fascinating to hear her talk to him.

Nia doesn't want to be a helicopter parent, and she holds her son responsible for his schoolwork. So, when talking with teachers, similar to her approach with her son, she tries not to criticize, give instructions, or fix things. Without possibly knowing the label, she's being autonomy-supportive.

Nia finds asking questions can help get things unstuck, so she asked the teacher: "Could you give Dylan some examples of what you mean when you ask him to find examples of irony in the book?"

The teacher agreed to do this for Dylan and for all students, saying that when posting assignments, she'd include specific descriptions of what she's looking for.

The class had just read *All the Light We Cannot See* by Anthony Doerr.[116] Nia told me:

> *I knew if I said, "Dylan, walk me through the irony in that book," he could do it, spot-on. The teacher knew it, too, and said so on our call. She said, "Dylan, you are extraordinary at pointing out all the things I'm looking for. I know you've got them in your head. It's about putting them down on paper."*

That exchange between the teacher, Dylan, and Nia helped the three of them identify the specific challenge that Dylan was facing—getting his ideas down on paper. With other young people, it can be more difficult to pinpoint specific challenges, but walking through assignments and trying to figure out what goes wrong can provide clues. For others, help from learning specialists may be needed.

From the outside, it looked like Dylan didn't care—Nia described him as lackadaisical—but as he sees it, simply improving his grades was not motivating enough for him to want to tackle something so hard:

> *I thought it would be easier to describe the intricacies of the text than to [write them]. The concept of having to get a better grade based on how I describe these characters felt illogical to me.*

It wasn't about grades—it was about feeling competent.

GETTING THE CURRICULUM RIGHT

We've been talking about one student, Dylan. Barbara Schneider and her team's focus has been on classrooms of students—improving their experiences. They decided on project-based learning as their curricular approach because it contains the major elements of good science learning, including challenge. Students aren't just learning facts. They're doing real-world science, which project-based learning defines as (1) having a driving question that guides the activities, triggers students' interest, and connects these interests to the learning goals of the curriculum; (2) connecting project activities to core scientific knowledge while allowing the teacher to adjust the challenge level to students' skills; (3) supporting students' active involvement, thus modeling the active involvement of scientists; (4) involving teams of students collaborating to answer the driving question; (5) using technology; and (6) producing "artifacts" to demonstrate what the students have learned.[117]

Joseph Krajcik, of Michigan State University, an expert on STEM education and project-based learning, is a collaborator on this research. He has found that project-based learning is a very effective approach in engaging young people in learning rigorous subject matter and preparing them for the challenges of the world. That world (and its jobs), he says, will require the ability to find solutions to difficult problems and challenges, to make decisions, to collaborate, and to be innovative. Krajcik told me:

Having twenty-first-century skills is important for the future and important for right now, too![118]

In a unique twist, the study itself used a project-based design approach. The curriculum was co-created by teachers and researchers in a practice called Teacher-Researcher Partnerships.[119] In the study, teachers teach both their regular lessons and project-based learning lessons—both designed to meet state and national standards—so the learning in each could be compared. Teachers and researchers, together, are doing real-world science, asking: Can we identify the key elements of optimal learning moments, and can we increase the number of these engaging moments through project-based learning?

MEASURING WHAT MATTERS

To measure optimal learning moments, the U.S.-Finnish study team made several decisions:[120]

- Since a student may be engaged in one lesson but not another, they decided to measure engagement in terms of specific contexts—the classes students are in.
- Since feelings of engagement come and go, they decided to measure engagement as taking place in defined moments. They made this decision because they also know that engagement isn't always positive. Students

might be fully engaged in school, but also burned out and exhausted by the work.[121]

In order to take account of the context and the moment, the research team decided to use the experience sampling method that Csikszentmihalyi had pioneered, where young people randomly receive a beep on their phones during the day and are texted questions like: "Were you interested in what you were doing? Did you feel skilled in what you were doing? Did you feel challenged in what you were doing? How engaged are you?"[122]

I visited several schools participating in the U.S. portion of the experiment. The students in those classes seemed on fire with purposeful activity. In Washtenaw International High School in Ypsilanti, Michigan, I watched students learn a lesson about magnets, beginning with a spirited conversation about the use of magnets on high-speed trains. The students posed questions, but they weren't answered immediately, as is the norm in many schools. The point was to enable students to plan and conduct their own investigations to obtain answers, which has been found to maintain curiosity, promote challenge, and spur ongoing learning.[123] In fact, an active search for answers is what science is all about.

The U.S.-Finnish team is excited that their model is thus far effective—they can measure the components of optimal learning moments and they can increase them. With real joy, Schneider told me:[124]

> *It's working! What does that really mean? It means that we can change the state of learning—that there's an opportunity to make learning different so that some students, maybe all students, can become more engaged. We're making changes in how students learn science.*

Key Finding: Project-based learning practices can and do increase students' optimal learning moments and engagement.

HOW AND WHY ENGAGEMENT MATTERS

Jennifer Fredricks has studied engagement extensively[125] and has distilled the data revealing just how far engagement reaches into who we are. Her work aligns with workplace research where engagement is seen as a proxy for everything employers want in employees, including productivity. Fredricks explains:

- **Engagement is behavioral,** which includes actual involvement in classroom learning.
- **Engagement has an emotional component:** being interested in, excited by, and valuing learning.
- **These emotions are shaped by social experiences.** Fredricks finds that feelings of belonging are important for deeper learning.
- **And there's the cognitive component.** Fredricks says this is more than doing well academically; it's also making an effort to understand and master content and challenges.

The bottom line is that engagement matters for academic and nonacademic reasons. Fredricks and her colleagues write that "active engagement in school enhances the skills, competencies, and values that are critical to academic success."[126]

Key Findings: Studies find that when young people are engaged, they are more motivated,[127] have higher grades,[128] and are more likely to stay in school and to go to college. Students who are actively engaged are also more likely to have positive relationships with other students and less likely to get in trouble or to be depressed.[129]

OVERCOMING A CHALLENGE

Dylan's teacher had identified his problem—translating what he was thinking into written words. His teacher then used the technique of scaffolding. In education and parenting, scaffolding means providing just enough support so that students can meet the challenge but must still work to overcome it, thereby gaining experience in trying, succeeding, and learning from experience. The supports remain in place until children and adolescents gain the competence to do the tasks themselves. The teacher told Dylan, "I want you to try a few things. Try using Google Voice or Siri—where you speak and it writes down your words." Then she told him to read the words he'd dictated and edit them to more clearly express his ideas, to see if that helped him transition from holding the ideas in his mind to turning them into written words that expressed his thoughts.

Another wise thing this teacher did was to connect this scaffolding to something Dylan loved to do while removing a factor that might build in too much performance pressure too soon. In the meeting, she told Dylan, "To build your skill around translating what you think into what you write, take a chapter from any book you've read—you're clearly an avid reader—and use that to practice finding inference or irony." She didn't want him to learn this technique using a classroom assignment at first. She said to him, "Dylan, you're all about 'my grade, my grade, my grade.' I don't want you to worry about grades when you're learning this. I want you to practice this skill without the pressure of grades because you're struggling with this skill, and the pressure of grades might get in the way." Dylan found that this conversation made him more thoughtful about how he could articulate his thinking.

The family tried the teacher's suggestions. Nia told me that her husband has been helping Dylan practice this every night for three months.

> Last night, Dylan said to my husband, "Can I tell you what I think
> out loud and then write it myself?" He didn't feel he needed the step of
> dictating into a machine anymore. My husband said, "Sure." And Dylan
> did—he wrote five hundred words!

Before the intervention, Nia says, Dylan's engagement seemed to fade in and out:

> Sometimes he'd be like, "I don't care. I want to play my video games." He'd
> escape into games. When I questioned this, he'd say to me, "My gaming
> relaxes me and it gets me into the right space." I'd say, "You've got to
> own this, Dylan. It's your responsibility to do your best." Left to his own
> devices, he was so discouraged.

Dylan is a great example of the model of engagement we've been talking about. Learning began with his motivation. He was already motivated to read, and the teacher and the family built on this **interest** to help him gain the **skill** he needed. If he hadn't liked reading, the teacher would have had to find another way to spark his interest and motivation. The teacher also set the **challenge at just the right level**, so he could gradually move from where he was—able to talk about ideas in books—to writing them down.

Once this happened, he could see he *was* competent, and thus he became more confident in his skills and abilities. Nia sums it up:

> *It wasn't a ton of intervention that got him to a place where he started to see some success and to feel, "Okay, I've got this. I've got this." It built his confidence and his sense of competence, which increased his motivation.*

Dylan now sees he had a roadblock in skill development. From this intervention, he realized how he could write.

> *It takes more effort to turn my thinking into writing and she helped me understand that.*

And now that he sees he can succeed, he doesn't dismiss grades—actually, he hopes that he will get better grades! His experience illustrates how the need for challenge is intimately connected with the need for competence—which we'll talk about next.

MATCH AND MISMATCH IN MEETING THE NEED FOR CHALLENGE

In the Breakthrough Years study, we asked:
In the last month, how often did you feel like . . . ?

1. *Your parent(s) and family encourage you to do new and challenging things*
2. *Your parent(s) and family encourage you to grow and learn*

We asked the same question about friends, the people at school, the people in out-of-school activities, and the people online.

What interests me in the figure* on the next page is that 58 percent feel challenged to learn and grow often (more than half the time) at school and 51 percent feel that way in their out-of-school activities. That leaves a big space for improvement. While challenge may look and be experienced differently in each of these contexts, challenges need to be seen as opportunities for learning and growth.

---

* Adolescents answered each question on a five-point scale from "never" to "almost always." The answers for the two questions were summed, resulting in the following groups: "rarely" (2–4), "sometimes" (5–7), and "often" (8–10).

How Often Adolescents Report the Need for Challenge Is Met

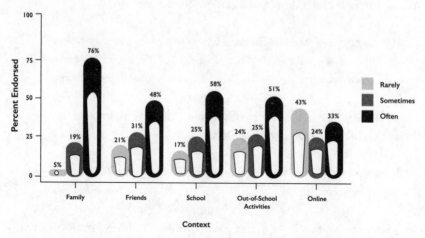

The percentage of young people who don't feel regularly challenged to grow and learn is all the more worrisome when you see how much it matters by looking at the arrows in the table below. The absence of positive outcomes from being challenged in school is surprising, but may reflect the fact that these were assessed during the pandemic, when so much about schooling had changed.

Outcomes of Having the Need for Challenge Met

Challenge	Follow-Up Outcomes							
Context	School Engage-ment	Grades (A)	Grades (P)	Future	Neg-ative Mood	Positive Mood	Stress	Conflict (A:P)
Family	↑	↑	↑	↑	↓	↑	↓	↓ :
Friends	↑	↑	↑	↑	↓	↑	↓	:
School				↑				:
OSA	↑	↑	↑	↑		↑	↓	:
Online								:

A = adolescent report, P = parent report, OSA = out-of-school activities. Arrows indicate the direction of an association (i.e., up arrow for promoting, down arrow for protecting), controlling for demographics. An empty cell indicates there is no statistically significant relationship. Significant relations are p-values < .0005, meaning these correlations are very reliable and unlikely to have occurred by chance.

The Need for Competence

I suspect many of us can sympathize with Dylan's struggle to express himself in writing and get good grades. But how many of us had a wise teacher like Dylan's, who tapped into his passion by allowing him to work on this skill using books he'd read for pleasure, not assigned books, and who removed the pressure to get good grades while he practiced? This teacher was trying to shift Dylan away from **performance goals** and toward **mastery goals**.

Here, we'll look at why mastery goals matter and at the differences between approach and avoidance goals. And we'll look at why social competence is also vital, especially during adolescence. Finally, we'll look at why actively building motivation and competence requires the right kinds of problem-solving, feedback, and praise.

COMPETENCE STARTS WITH MOTIVATION—BUT WHAT DOES THAT MEAN, EXACTLY?

Since its founding in 1896, the National Academies of Sciences, Engineering, and Medicine, an organization of some 2,400 top-flight scientists from multiple disciplines, has been tasked with bringing up-to-date valid knowledge to issues of major importance to society—like the science of learning. In 2000[130] and again in 2018,[131] they produced consensus volumes summarizing the best research on how people learn. Their 2018 report focuses on the pivotal role of motivation:

> To learn intentionally, people must want to learn and must see the value in accomplishing what is being asked of them.[132]

So that's where we'll begin in looking at the need to feel competent. The National Academies report concludes that children who are motivated to learn are more likely to be engaged in learning, to persist longer, and to do better in school and on achievement tests.[133]

According to Wendy Grolnick, adults spend only about 10 percent of our time intrinsically motivated (doing things because we find interest and pleasure in doing them).[134] So, what about the rest of the time, when we're extrinsically motivated?

First, it's essential to understand that not all extrinsic motivation is the same. Second, we need to know that autonomy is critical to successful motivation and that there are varying degrees of autonomy in the types of extrinsic motivation:[135]

- **External:** We do things to get rewards or avoid punishments and don't feel like we have a choice—people or circumstances outside of ourselves are telling us to do something.
- **Introjected:** This means the pressure to do something has become internalized; it's become our own pressure. We are doing something because we're pushing ourselves or because we would feel guilty if we didn't do it.
- **Identified:** This means we're doing things we're supposed to do be-cause we see the value in doing them. Think of bringing work home because we see the value in the work we do. It might not be fun, but we see it as important and feel choiceful in deciding to work at home.

When young people have to do things for extrinsic reasons, Grolnick says, we need to build on their need for autonomy by helping them see the purpose or value of the activity so they can still get behind it. We can do this by taking their perspectives, providing reasons for doing the activity, and not being controlling.[136] The more the adults in young people's lives can build on "identified motivation," the better they do. Grolnick summarizes some key findings from research based on Self-Determination Theory:

> If young people are more identified in what they're doing, they have better grades; they cope better; they're more competent; they use more optimal learning strategies; and they tend to drop out less from high school.[137]

THE POWER OF MOTIVATION

Natalie is a seventh grader in Boston. When she loves to do something—and she loves baking—her overall motivation comes from within:

> If I bake a cake and it turns out well, I'll be very excited and feel very confident about the next cake. That energy of doing well transfers to the energy I get when I'm making the next cake.

Doing well leads to feelings of confidence and competence—but Natalie has learned that these feelings don't always guarantee results:

I can get super confident and the next cake ends up not turning out as good as the last one.

Because she cares so much about baking, a flopped cake doesn't make her give up on herself:

Losing faith isn't a good thing to do. I think a lot of people try something and just stop if it doesn't work out. But you're not going to be good at something unless you work at it.

At school, though, her overall motivation is mostly extrinsic:

In seventh grade you have to work hard to get into a good public high school. I want to get into a good high school and a good college. I really want to be successful; I really want to have a good career.

Natalie's motivation at school is the "identified" type of extrinsic motivation. It indicates that her actions (trying to get good grades) are aligned with her longer-term values for the life she wants to lead.

But motivation linked to future success can sometimes feel like a "big wait,"[138] where some school tasks—in her case, learning algebra—don't seem clearly connected to what matters.

That makes Natalie feel anxious—"I feel I'm a very nervous person, and I get impatient." Here her motivation is "introjected." She feels a lot of pressure from others and from within, which makes her want to achieve things as fast as possible:

Teenagers have a lot of pressure. We feel pressured to get good grades. I worry: Am I going to get into a good school, get a good job? A few of my friends are saying, "I know exactly what I want to be when I grow up." It kind of makes me think, "Oh, my gosh. I might never find what I want to do for a living."
But I'm just in middle school.

"BUT I'M JUST IN MIDDLE SCHOOL": THE DOWNSIDES OF A FUTURE-FOCUSED CULTURE

A future-focused culture plays a part in the pressure Natalie feels. While a future-focused approach and language resonate with policymakers, professionals, the public, and families, it can take a toll on young people.

Children need to be ready for the next steps in their lives, but **an all-encompassing emphasis on the future can dim the power of the present.** I see some young people becoming too concerned about a faraway future, even thinking they should know what's typically unknowable, like what will motivate them in one to two decades. These comments from two sixteen-year-olds sum it up:

> *I feel as though everything is for the future. In middle school, everyone's pressuring you to be ready for high school. In high school, everyone's pressuring you to be ready for college. In college, everyone's pressuring you to be ready for life.*

And:

> *My parents are always saying: "Oh—when I was young," and "I wish I were young again." But when you're young, everyone's pressuring you to be older, and they don't let you enjoy it."*

As Natalie said: "But I'm just in middle school." How many hundreds of books have been written to help us, as adults, relearn that focusing on the present affects our overall well-being? We could course-correct ourselves and let our middle and high schoolers have time to be in the present, not just the future. And when we prepare them for the future, we need to give them real-world experiences with many different kinds of careers so that when they look ahead they are excited about the possibilities, not just afraid of a future that seems unknowable.

THE TYPE OF GOAL MATTERS, TOO: MASTERY GOALS AND PERFORMANCE GOALS

Natalie may not be aware of another differentiation that researchers make, between mastery goals (Natalie's goals when baking) and performance goals (her goals in school). Andrew Elliot of the University of Wisconsin, Madison, and Chris Hulleman of the University of Virginia write that **mastery goals focus on developing one's own competence,** whereas **performance goals focus on demonstrating competence and outperforming others.** Both are driven by the Basic Need for competence.[139]

GOING FOR IT VERSUS AVOIDING MESSING UP: APPROACH AND AVOIDANCE IN PURSUING GOALS

Researchers additionally differentiate between approach and avoidance motivation, too. Elliot and Hulleman define these as:

- **Approach:** striving to **reach success**
- **Avoidance:** striving to **avoid failure**

Key Findings: In general, studies show that mastery goals are linked with more positive developmental outcomes in young people, while performance goals are linked with more negative or mixed outcomes. Similarly, approach goals are linked with more positive developmental outcomes, while avoidance goals are linked with more negative outcomes.[140]

Canadian researchers Stéphane Duchesne and Simon Larose of Université Laval summarize this research more specifically, looking at how the goal types go together:

> *Mastery-approach goals have . . . been positively associated with . . .*
> *effort, perseverance, self-regulation, seeking help, peer satisfaction and*
> *performance. By contrast, mastery-avoidance and/or performance-*
> *avoidance goals have often been negatively related to these same indicators,*
> *and . . . positively correlated with disorganization in tasks, concerns,*
> *evaluative anxiety and loneliness.*[141]

In a two-year study that followed students from the eighth to tenth grades (from thirteen or fourteen years old to fifteen or sixteen years old), Duchesne and researcher Catherine Ratelle, also of Université Laval, suggest that "to facilitate social and emotional adjustment in high school, it appears important to encourage learning practices that move away from fearing "incompetence."[142]

Applying research to life is sometimes complicated, and Natalie is a telling example. She says grades (performance) are her most compelling motivation in school: "I want to get good grades. I *do*!" But she also says, "I won't be satisfied if I don't understand the thing that I'm learning to the full extent" (mastery). So she exhibits a mixture of performance and mastery goals.

Similarly, she combines approach and avoidance toward those goals. She told me she's largely motivated by avoidance: "I'll be fine if I don't get a perfect grade, but I don't want to get a really bad grade." She's noticed that if she concentrates on getting a perfect grade—being at the top of her class and showing the teacher how smart she is—she tends to rush or get very nervous. She fights her perfectionist tendencies by trying not to get bad grades or by improving her grades, which makes her feel more competent.

Her motivation also depends on how subjects are taught. Natalie says her math teacher is "really nice" but teaches math as a series of activities without sharing why they matter or taking time to ensure her students understand them. In math, Natalie is mainly motivated by fear of failure and by mastery:

> I get really stressed when I don't understand math, because I think it's all in my brain. I want my brain to understand it, if I am going to do well in this class.

Her history teacher's approach positively affects Natalie's motivation:

> She makes sure we understand what we're learning. If I'm stuck, she gives me multiple ways I can go about the problem and make sure that I understand.

CARING TEACHERS PER SE DON'T BUILD COMPETENCE

It's not enough to be a nice or caring teacher or a teacher who cares about the subject. When teachers also understand and apply their knowledge about how young people learn best, young people become more motivated to learn.

During the pandemic, a colleague from the Hunt Institute, Dan Wuori, and I interviewed experts on the lessons from COVID-19 for American education. Expert after expert we interviewed called for centering education on child development knowledge. For example, Beth Bye, commissioner of the Connecticut Office of Early Childhood, wishes she could inject knowledge of the phases of child development into all teachers, principals, and superintendents:[143]

> Look at three-year-olds as three-year-olds, not that they're going to be five-year-olds. And look at ten-year-olds as ten-year-olds. Who is more excited

than a ten-year-old? And high school students need to be treated like high
school students.

Bye says we adults are likely to forget about the salience of child development knowledge when we're hyperfocused on academic performance and neglect the importance of social and emotional competence. Another student, Brigid, could be a case study for how this neglect affects kids at school, as you'll see.

HELPING ADOLESCENTS BUILD SOCIAL COMPETENCE

Like Natalie, twelve-year-old Brigid describes herself as nervous:

I'm not clinically diagnosed with anxiety but I get anxious a lot and worry
about a lot of things.

Many wise observers of growing up today point to the rising tide of anxiety in young people. Lisa Damour, a clinical psychologist and author of the acclaimed *Under Pressure*[144] and *The Emotional Lives of Teenagers*,[145] points out that anxiety shouldn't necessarily be seen as bad—those feelings of fear, even dread, are essential to keep us safe and enable us to make course corrections.

But not when these feelings turn into unhealthy anxiety, meaning they aren't discussed or dealt with. Damour writes that anxiety and stress have become problematic, especially for girls. Among the reasons this is happening now, she says, are escalating pressures on girls about succeeding in school, fitting in with friends, and looking good compared with those in their lives and on social media. Because girls tend to hit puberty earlier, they also have to cope with grown-up-looking bodies while being inundated by messages that say women are mainly valued for their sex appeal.

Julie Lythcott-Haims, former dean of freshmen at Stanford University and author of the admired *How to Raise an Adult*, additionally points to the ways that young people are parented.[146] She says (and in the section on the need for autonomy we've seen in this chapter) that when parents "overparent"—that is, fix things for kids, prevent them from making mistakes, and solve problems for them—the results are anxious young people who don't know how to solve problems for themselves. Overparenting is different from parental involvement, which, as we've seen, reaps benefits for young people.

There are other factors, too, including the pandemic. The U.S. Surgeon

General's report *Protecting Youth Mental Health*[147] notes that a study of 80,000 youth globally found that depressive and anxiety symptoms doubled during the pandemic, with 25 percent of young people experiencing depressive symptoms and 20 percent experiencing anxiety symptoms.[148]

While Natalie's anxiety centers on schoolwork, Brigid's is about social competence in dealing with her group of friends—Regina, Elizabeth, and James:

> *I think part of why I struggle with anxiety is the friendships I've had. In sixth grade last year, I had a friend—Regina—who was really mean.*

Regina called people names and cheated at games, and if one of the friends dared to object, Regina would overreact, get really mad, and tell the group who her most favorite and least favorite friends were. The least favorite would get the silent treatment:

> *During the day, I was like, "I'll suck it up and I'll go with it." But at night, I'd think about everything she'd said to and about me. And I was like, "I need to do something." But there were so many complications, I didn't know what to do.*

Damour makes the crucial point that stress, like anxiety, isn't nessarily bad either;[149] it becomes unhealthy when we don't feel understood and when the stress exceeds what we feel we can manage because there are no supports and no solutions.[150] That's what Brigid was facing:

> *I talked to my mom. She was like, "Just talk to Regina and tell her how you feel."*

Brigid intensified her efforts to tell Regina how she felt or to ignore her:

> *Regina was like, "If it's not okay, then stop hanging out with me." So I'd ignore her, but then she'd get mad, like, "Why are you ignoring me?" It was really confusing.*

This dysfunctional situation affected Brigid's sense of social competence. She wondered if the mean things Regina said about her were true, and she didn't know what to do:

Probably two nights a week, I was crying in bed because I couldn't fall
asleep. I was so stressed about what was happening.

AN INTERVENTION THAT DIDN'T WORK

Eventually, Brigid says, adults took notice:

My mom and Elizabeth's mom finally realized how bad this was and talked
to my teacher about it. The teacher was like, "Some of your parents sent me
an email about how Regina's really not treating you guys well."

So I told the teacher everything that was happening, and even her—she
was like, "Just talk to Regina and stand up for yourself."

Her mother had suggested these strategies, but they had intensified the
situation. Now the teacher was giving advice that wasn't useful. In fact, the
intervention escalated the problem. When the teacher talked with Regina,
Regina got angry and flipped the blame by gaslighting Brigid:

Regina was like, "Well, the teacher talked to me and I think that it's about
you." And I was like, "Well, yes, sometimes I get very mad at you because
of how you treat us." She was like, "Well, why don't you just tell me?" I'm
like, "I do tell you, every time." And she's like, "No, you don't." I'm like,
"I do!"

When Brigid's mother asked her how the conversation with the teacher
about Regina had gone, Brigid told her:

"Well, it was kind of weird because she gave me the exact advice that
you give me." And my mom was like, "Well then, why don't you
do it?"

That bothered Brigid because that advice of standing up for herself, telling Regina how she felt, or ignoring her hadn't worked and had left her with
a sense of social incompetence. "It was complicated," she kept saying. "It
was confusing." "Maybe I'm a horrible friend," she said, then added, "Wait
a minute, it's not my fault."

This is affecting my mental health because I feel like the adults don't under-
stand what is happening.

MINDSETS MATTER IN BUILDING COMPETENCE

Mindsets, as we've discussed, are our core beliefs for making sense of the world and ourselves, including our competence. Carol Dweck has done game-changing research on mindsets.[151] With Daniel Molden of Northwestern University, she writes that mindsets about competence create "meaning systems" that lead us to different goals and strategies, which in turn can "result in different levels of interest, self-esteem, and competence, especially in the face of challenge or threat."[152]

Dweck's research has led her to identify two specific mindsets. People who give up in the face of a challenge and see themselves as not being capable or smart have a **fixed mindset**. They believe their abilities are inborn and set in stone, while people who see themselves as capable of improving have a **growth mindset**.[153] As you may remember, a growth mindset is the foundation for a Possibilities Mindset (which also stresses having the belief that you have the competence to change).

Knowing that a number of young people may have fixed mindsets about social situations, David Yeager and his colleagues wanted to do something about it.[154] Their goal was to change groups of young people's mindset about stressful interactions—the kind of interactions that Brigid and Regina were having. He explains:

> *Our theory was that if you think someone can never change, then no matter what you do, you'll never be able to overcome it. But if you think it's at least possible for people to change, then you can start imagining resources you could acquire that could help you overcome it.*[155]

In other words, it's possible to reframe your dealings with a difficult person from thinking it's impossible to seeing the situation as a challenge. Using the mindset intervention methodology, their team gave high school students information saying that if someone excludes or victimizes someone else, it's not that they're bad people whose personalities are fixed—they *can* change. Those students then read scientific stories and personal accounts from older students who reported changing. The next step involved students writing an essay where they persuade future students to have a growth mindset about people.

Key Findings: In experiments run by Yeager and his team, teaching adolescents that people can change encouraged the adolescents to see a stressor as a challenge they could overcome. Their physiological responses followed suit. Their blood vessels were less constricted when they learned people can change; their heart was more efficient and pumped more blood through the body.[156]

It is disheartening to feel you can't do anything about a problem, and so you tend to avoid it. Given this, Elliot and Hulleman write that striving for mastery-avoidance goals tends to be unhealthy. These goals have been found to be "predictors of anxiety, procrastination, and maladaptive forms of perfectionism."[157]

WISE FEEDBACK IN SUPPORTIVE CONTEXTS ALSO IMPROVES COMPETENCE

Brigid has an entirely different experience in ballet than she does in school, which illustrates how different contexts can meet the Basic Need for social competence. Ballet works for Brigid first because it's a place where she can express her feelings physically:

I may be feeling tired of all this stress. I ball it all up in dance.

Second, this ballet school has created a climate where students can say what they feel openly, honestly, and without judgment:

My ballet and dance friends are never going to get mad at me for what's happening because they're my friends and they love me and they know who I am.

Third is how feedback is provided—it's quite specific, identifying the exact changes that students need to make in order to improve. That helps Brigid take action to resolve a problem, something she's been unable to do with Regina. Ordinarily, she's a perfectionist:

I need to get everything right. When I usually get feedback, I beat myself up about it.

But in her ballet classes, corrections are presented as positives—given because teachers have high expectations about students' competence that they know students can meet. They also focus on the behavior, not the person. Brigid says:

> They're not like, "Oh, you're doing bad at this." A correction is more of you're doing good at this part but you need to fix this other thing.

In a series of additional studies, David Yeager and his colleagues tested the efficacy of "wise feedback" where competency is seen as a "given." In the first study, social studies students in the seventh grade wrote first-draft essays that were critiqued by teachers.[158] When their essays were returned with the teacher's comments, they included randomly assigned notes. Half of the students (the control group) received a note with a neutral statement ("I'm giving you these comments so that you'll have feedback on your paper"). The other half received a wise feedback note ("I'm giving you these comments because I have very high expectations and I know that you can reach them"). Only 17 percent of those in the control group revised their essay, compared with 72 percent of those who received the wise feedback.

In a second study, where everyone was required to submit revised essays, having received wise feedback improved the quality of their final drafts, indicating that students put more time and thought into their revisions. In addition, Yeager and his colleagues write:

> Effects were generally stronger among African American students than among White students, and particularly strong among African Americans who felt more mistrusting of school.[159]

Key finding: Providing feedback that includes expectations of success where competence is seen as a given can spur students to put more time and thought into their schoolwork.

THE POWER OF PRAISE (THE RIGHT KIND!)

Carol Dweck's mindset studies, described earlier, are among the best research on the impact of praise on competence. She has found that the children who develop a fixed mindset are likely to have been praised for their intelligence or their abilities, while those with a growth mindset have been praised for their effort or strategies.

Dweck has also found that **mindsets can be taught.** As one example, Dweck and her colleagues created a workshop for seventh graders. Since children's grades frequently decline in this grade, it was a promising time for intervening.[160] Dweck says:

> We divided the students into two groups: the control group got eight sessions of study skills; the experimental group got six sessions of study skills but two sessions on growth mindset.[161]

In these growth mindset sessions, the students learned that the brain gets stronger with use:

> They learned that every time they work hard, their brain forms new connections, and they also learned how to apply this to their schoolwork.

Importantly, the finding indicated that teaching good study skills is insufficient; the growth mindset content was necessary.

Key Finding: Dweck reports that the group that received study skills continued to show declining grades, possibly because they didn't have the motivation to put those study skills into practice. On the other hand, the group that received the study skills plus the growth mindset message showed a significant rebound in their grades.

The data from the teachers are particularly interesting. Dweck told me:

> We asked the teachers, "Did you notice any changes in your students?" The teachers didn't know what workshops the students were in—they didn't even know there were two different types of workshops. Yet they singled out three times as many students from the growth mindset workshop, reporting that they had noted remarkable changes in these children's study habits, in their turning in their homework on time, and in their asking for feedback from the teacher.[162]

Key Finding: These studies indicate that **process praise**—praising children on their effort (for example, "you spent a lot of time on this") and on their problem-solving strategies (for example, "you prioritized what was most important")—**is more effective** than praising children on their character (for example, "you are so smart").

New research by Dweck further clarifies the use of praise.[163] Process praise has many pluses. It avoids the problem of making children feel as if their abilities are unchangeable—that they're simply smart or clever or competent (i.e., a fixed mindset). It also suggests to young people that they can develop their abilities (i.e., a growth mindset). But process praise can be even more effective when we:

- **Connect process with outcomes and strategy**
  When parents or teachers repeatedly say "good job," thinking they're focusing on process, it becomes rote and meaningless. Similarly, "you tried hard" lacks specificity about what young people can do to achieve their goals or where specifically they placed their efforts. Dweck writes:

  > When students try hard but fail to progress, we can begin by appreciating their effort, but then we need to sit with them and say, "Show me what you've tried, and let's figure out what you can try next" or "Tell me exactly what your thought process was when you did it this way, and let's see if there are other ways that you can try."[164]

- **Remember that praise isn't just for when students struggle**
  Praise is for all students, both those who struggle and those who don't, and for all outcomes, whether the work is great or in need of improvement. Dweck writes that praise is important to help students take pride in their growing skills and understanding.

SOCIETAL PRAISE HAS AN EFFECT

Ariel, a twelve-year-old I interviewed, is an example of the impact that character praise can have, even when it's not from families. Ariel never wants to be wrong:

*I think that's one of my character flaws—well, no, I don't want to call
it that—it's just one of my personality traits, is that I'm afraid of being
wrong.*

I asked about this fear of failure, and Ariel said:

*Honestly, I think it's come at least partially from being told how intelligent
I am, if not from my parents, but from society as a whole—from most
people I talk to and who I show the work I've done to. They've said,
"Wow, you're really smart." And that gives me dopamine, and I don't want
the happy chemical to stop. So that means I can't be wrong because being
wrong means you're not intelligent.*

Ariel is pursuing questions of identity. The gender that Ariel was born
with didn't feel right, so among other subjects Ariel pursues is information
about gender, from reading the Bible to current psychology, including attending online lectures from universities. The stakes are too high to be wrong
about identity, Ariel says, even knowing that these perfectionist tendencies
aren't helpful.

MATCH AND MISMATCH IN MEETING THE
BASIC NEED FOR COMPETENCE

In the Breakthrough Years study, we asked:
In the last month, how often did you feel like . . . ?

1. *Your parent(s) and family make you feel that you do things well*
2. *Your parent(s) and family give you confidence in your skills and
   abilities*

We asked the same question about friends, the people at school, the people
in out-of-school activities, and the people online.

Almost eight in ten families are meeting adolescents' need for competence "often," which we define as more than half the time.* That number
drops to about six in ten when it comes to the people at school and in out-
of-school activities, and it drops further, to only half, with the people online.

---

* Adolescents answered each question on a five-point scale from "never" to "almost always." The
answers for the two questions were summed, resulting in the following groups: "rarely" (2–4),
"sometimes" (5–7), and "often" (8–10).

How Often Adolescents Report the Need for Competence Is Met

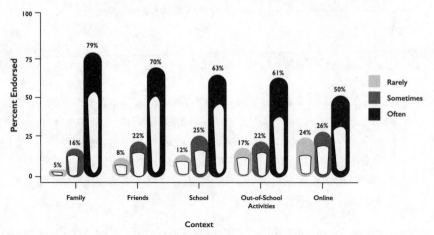

Having the need for competence met before the pandemic is linked to better outcomes during the pandemic. By looking at the arrows in the table below, we see that, with the exception of online, these young people are doing better in almost every outcome we measured.

Outcomes of Having the Need for Competence Met

Compe-tence	Follow-Up Outcomes							
Context	School Engage-ment	Grades (A)	Grades (P)	Future	Neg-ative Mood	Positive Mood	Stress	Conflict (A:P)
Family	↑	↑	↑	↑	↓	↑	↓	↓ : ↓
Friends	↑	↑		↑	↓	↑	↓	:
School	↑	↑	↑	↑	↓	↑	↓	:
OSA	↑	↑	↑	↑	↓	↑	↓	:
Online				↑				:

A = adolescent report, P = parent report, OSA = out-of-school activities. Arrows indicate the direction of an association (i.e., up arrow for promoting, down arrow for protecting), controlling for demographics. An empty cell indicates there is no statistically significant relationship. Significant relations are p-values < .0005, meaning these correlations are very reliable and unlikely to have occurred by chance.

LIGHT CAN DEFEAT DARK

Brigid left me with a concluding thought about how she copes:

Sometimes, I just sit and cry until I feel better and then I'm like, "Okay, you're a good person." I realize all the good things about myself. "You're cool. You have friends. You're smart. You're doing great in school and you're a good dancer."

I use that to cope with the fact that there are bad things in my life.

Have you ever seen Star Wars? *Do you know the light side is always going to defeat the dark? Dark can never defeat dark. Only light can defeat dark.*

I take all my light thoughts and I ball them up and throw them at my dark thoughts. I'm like, "You're not bad. You're a good person." That may be a little bit dramatic, but it helps.

With adolescents, identity—"who I am"—is usually at the center of that swirling ball of feelings and thoughts, as we saw with Brigid and Ariel.

PROMOTING THE BASIC NEED FOR CHALLENGE AND COMPETENCE

Meeting the need for **challenge** begins with understanding that challenge is a necessary part of learning. With this in mind, we can:

- Think about providing adolescents with engaging, real-world experiences that they care about
- Help them when they become stuck and ask questions about their challenges
- Scaffold what they need to learn onto something they care about

In the process, we're modeling how to address challenges—being curious, asking questions, and finding manageable ways to take on challenges. Our increasing skill and confidence in helping them address challenges foster these same qualities in them. It is a beautiful feedback loop as, together, we learn!

Core to meeting this need for competence is an understanding of adolescent development and the way in which Basic Needs play a role in positive development. It is also a recognition that competence involves academic competence and social competence, as well as other kinds of competence. And it means recognizing that adolescents are primed to explore, to try things out, and to look for meaning and purpose, and that motivation drives competence.

You can promote adolescents' need for **competence** when you:

- Align their motivation with their need for autonomy and their interests and values, emphasizing mastery (striving to gain skills and competencies), not just performance (demonstrating competence, outperforming others)
- Encourage a growth mindset, followed with actions they can take to address their challenges, thus also promoting a Possibilities Mindset
- Provide feedback and praise to adolescents that:
  - Emphasizes your trust in their ability to be successful
  - Is respectful and supportive
  - Is outcome-focused, strategic, and specific

Need 4: Identity: The Need to Explore Who I Am

Identity is being offered opportunities to explore what you are like, the groups you identify with, your goals and future roles, and the story you tell yourself about yourself. When adolescents can address questions about who they are, they can build their sense of identity (identity).

For some of us, there's a moment when we realize that we're the parent of an adolescent, even if for years we've heard the warning "Just wait!" We may notice that our child:

- Has thicker hair crowding out the silky fine hair on their body
- Is beginning to develop breasts or the shadow of a mustache
- Is whispering to friends so families can't hear
- Says "Mom" and "Dad" as two-syllable words: "Mo-ooM" and "Da-aaD"

- Says "You don't understand"
- Makes claims about their identity[165]

For Caroline, it happened when her ten-year-old daughter Anna told her to stop calling her a "guy." Caroline says:

The norm in our family and culture is to use "guys" or "you guys" to refer to people—male or female.

But Anna asked her to stop. Anna explains why:

I was thinking about the word "guy," and I was like, "I'm not a guy, so I don't want to be called that anymore." So, I told them.

This may seem like no big deal, but Caroline appreciated it as a defining moment in her life as a parent:

She doesn't accept that this is what her parents should call her and feels she can do something about it. I think it's neat that she's able to challenge the norm.

Caroline tried, but kept slipping up, reverting to a "forty-year-old habit," so she decided it would be easier if she created a new habit to replace the old one. Anna didn't like the word "kids" either, so Caroline selected a silly word:

I started calling Anna and her brother "chickens." If I say "guys," Anna says "chickens." We both laugh, and I remember.

This was an important moment for Anna in beginning to define her gender identity (which can vary in many ways, including timing and intensity, for different young people). It was also an important moment for Caroline: the first clue that she's now the parent of an adolescent and that adolescents need to explore fundamental questions of identity:

- Who am I?
- How did I come to be the person I am now?
- Who am I going to become?

THE TASK OF ADOLESCENCE

No discussion about the Basic Need for identity in adolescence would be right if it didn't begin with the work of the late Erik Erikson. Erikson, a Danish American psychologist and psychoanalyst, saw establishing an identity as *the* task of adolescence. He also saw it as a "normative crisis."[166] Erikson went through his own journey of self-identification,[167] searching for but never finding the identity of his biological father. A crucial step involved creating a new last name. When he and his wife came to the United States to escape the spread of Nazism, kids teased their sons about their surname, Homburger, taunting them with "Hamburger." He decided to adopt the Scandinavian tradition of naming the sons after the father; his wife and daughter adopted the new name, too. Erikson's biographer Lawrence Friedman writes that over and above a response to schoolyard taunts, Erikson was reinventing himself: "taking charge of his own life; . . . fathering himself as well as his two sons."[168]

Six decades after the first publication of his framework for understanding human development,[169] Erikson's theories have had well-deserved staying power for a number of reasons. First, he was unique for his times in recognizing the large role social context and culture play in shaping identity. The search for identity, he famously wrote, is "a process located in the core of the individual and yet also in the core of his communal culture."[170] Adults are instrumental in this development, as is membership in groups that are significant for a young person.

A second reason his work remains so influential is Erikson's recognition that the need for identity takes "center stage"[171] in adolescence.

Third, he saw that identity development involved exploration, experimentation, and trying on roles. Resolution, in his view, involved either a sense of identity or role confusion, though in some ways, his ongoing search for his own identity belies the idea that identity issues are resolved during adolescence. The need for identity is lifelong, though it is center stage in adolescence.

Returning to Caroline and Anna, I think the fact that Caroline was able to respond respectfully to Anna's request not to be called a "guy" and that she saw this as part of Anna's search for identity is a testament to Erik Erikson's original influence on our knowledge of child development. He brought home the importance of this need in some ways that continue to resonate today.

In general, identity exploration in adolescence tends to focus around three key levers: physical changes, societal changes/expectations, and cognitive changes.

A LEVER: THE PHYSICAL CHANGES OF PUBERTY

When adults are asked to recall how puberty felt—even for those long past these physical transformations—their memories collapse time and their emotions sound as intense as if these experiences were almost happening now. An adult woman says:

> At early puberty, I had no real idea of who I was, yet my body started changing in appalling ways. The eyes of my friends and people I wanted to be friends with became my mirror, making me want to be invisible.
>
> I was overly sensitive to any comment made about my looks. Plus, I measured myself by the stars in movie magazines . . . I think I hated my round shape, and even in junior high I dieted.
>
> Ah, those dreaded pimples that made the change all the more visible and made me want to shatter the mirror in my room. I was shrinking a little each day.

Another woman recalls:

> Terrified, mortified, I remember thinking that if I got thin enough no man would see me and look at me in that way, so there was refuge in the idea of invisibility through thinness.

Adolescents do feel like shrinking, according to a man:

> Hunching, closing in on ourselves—we are growing taller but becoming shorter/smaller at the same time.

Today, that mirror has been amplified by social media.[172] There's no shattering of the images that adolescents post of themselves online. They remain as permanent and visible records of their changing bodies, changing selves, whether they want them to or not. And there's little invisibility—others' comments are there for others to read.

Identity explorations are shaped by how our bodies change and how we and others react to those changes.

A LEVER: SOCIETAL CHANGES AND EXPECTATIONS

Then there are the societal changes that accompany the physical changes, such as moving into middle school or junior high school, high school, and beyond. These moves may involve other moves, too:

- From smaller to larger schools
- From a home-base classroom to many classes around the school
- From one classroom teacher who coordinates their assignments to teachers who don't know the homework other teachers are assigning
- From places where young people feel known to places where they might not feel known or may have to remake or adjust friend groups

As young people introduce themselves to new people in new classrooms and elsewhere, they call attention to how they see themselves and how they want others to see them.

In addition, the pressure of the future-focused culture that has been with them all along—as they got ready for preschool and elementary school—intensifies the pressure for them to make decisions about the interests they pursue, the courses they take, what they'll do in the future.

As they think about their future, they think about the kind of person they want to be.

"Overriding My Personality"

Noah, newly sixteen and living with his father in a bustling island community in the Pacific Northwest, has been thinking about his future and who he wants to be. He knows he doesn't want to be who he was. In his words, he's "trying to override my personality." His goal is to be mysterious, vague, and unpredictable. There's nobody in his life like this, but there are online personalities he sees as role models:

> I used to overspeak a lot, like run-on sentences when I was having a
> discussion but then I started thinking about how I could whittle it down to
> easily understandable and digestible words, adding in a certain amount of
> vagueness to those words.

To override his personality, he used the tactic of pausing before reacting to others in conversations:

Not a huge delay, but I'd definitely put a lot of thought into messages I'd send or things I'd say before I said them. I'd start responding with one word but that one word would be kind of a strange word, like one that isn't commonly used but carries on what was being talked about.

*Say somebody was talking to me about how they went surfing. I'd say, "Did you meet any big, **smooth** dolphins?" Just including the word "smooth" is surprising and fun to add in.*

I asked Noah how people respond. He said:

It was mostly positive but a few people thought I was acting a little less emotional or more robotic. But overall, it was fine.

This isn't playacting. It is very serious. Noah is exploring different ways to express himself because he wants to do something creative in the future:

If I am going to talk about something I'm actually looking forward to trying out in the future, it would be creating games or storytelling.

Puberty transforms our bodies. Noah talks about transforming his personality. In his mind and in reality, he has a perpetual audience. Recall that David Elkind of Tufts University says that adolescents anticipate what other people's responses to them are going to be; they react to what he calls "imaginary audiences."[173]

A LEVER: COGNITIVE CHANGES

A lot of brainpower underlies identity formation at this age. Adolescents can think about imaginary audiences because their cognitive capacities enable them to separate themselves from their own thoughts and feelings and analyze them, as if from afar.

Our understanding of cognitive development is rooted in the theories and research of a contemporary of Erikson's, the late Jean Piaget[174]—another giant in the field who, like Erikson, spawned many studies.

Key cognitive changes in adolescence include:

- **Abstract thinking:** the ability to think about concepts apart from concrete objects
- **Deductive reasoning:** assessing a theory by starting with a conclusion and testing what makes it true
- **Inductive reasoning:** combining specific facts to come to a general conclusion
- **Hypothetical thinking:** imagining different possibilities and exploring their consequences
- **Meaning-making:** more complexity in making sense of one's experiences
- **Autobiographical reasoning:** making meaning from specific episodes in one's life
- **Perspective-taking:** a deeper understanding of others' thoughts, feelings, likes, and dislikes, and how they differ from one's own
- **Metacognition:** thinking about how one thinks

Adolescents draw on these cognitive skills as they develop their sense of who they are.

THE THREE STRANDS OF IDENTITY DEVELOPMENT

Drawing on research and insights from Erikson and Northwestern University's Dan McAdams, I see adolescents as pursuing three questions in their search for identity:[175]

1. **What am I like/what are we like?**
   McAdams and his colleague Claudia Zapata-Gietl write that these questions represent the **"self as a social actor."** These identity questions are about the traits adolescents see in themselves, the traits others see in them, the roles they take, and the roles they're given.[176] "Others" include the people in the adolescent's immediate life and in the groups they belong to and identify with, such as groups based on where they live, their race or ethnicity, their religion, etc.[177]

2. **What do I do/what will I do?**
   McAdams and Zapata-Gietl call this facet in the search for identity the **"self as a motivated agent."** Applied to adolescents, it means defining themselves, in part, through the plans, goals, values, and commitments they make as they envision their lives in the future.[178]

3. **What story do I tell myself about myself?**
   The third strand involves seeking an "**internalized story of the self.**"
   As adolescents explore these questions, they're integrating the stories they hear about themselves and tell about themselves from the past, present, and anticipated future.[179]

If this sounds like intense and absorbing work, that's because it is—and, of course, it depends on how others meet adolescents' need for identity. Ultimately, these strands interweave and become the complex tapestry of who we are.

McAdams sees these strands emerging in sequence.[180] As he says:

> *You start out as an actor. Eventually you also become a motivated*
> *agent and an actor, and then layered over that is the story. All three are*
> *developing in adolescence.*[181]

It takes time. Indeed, in today's world, we can reexamine our goals and life choices throughout our adult lives, making new life choices and formulating new goals and projects as our life unfolds.

The Need to Explore What Am I Like / What Are We Like

It's a long way from India to Indiana. Nineteen-year-old Ishaan knows this well. His life as an Indian in India, where he was born and spent his early years, and his life as an Indian American now living in the United States are a study in contrasts.

In India, Ishaan says he felt "known" by his community from the time he was born.

> *When I was little, we lived in a small neighborhood in a city. We had*
> *neighbors my parents knew since they were kids. Through my dad's*
> *work—he's a doctor—every one of his friends came to our house. I grew up*
> *knowing everyone. There were many connecting villages outside the city, so*
> *my father's grandparents and ancestors always used to come, and I got to*
> *know the more rural village type of family, too.*

Ishaan says he was "talkative" and "outgoing" in India. When his family decided to come to America, he initially resisted:

I was seven. At first, I was like, "I don't want to leave all my friends and family." But there was something in the back of my mind that my parents were doing this for my family's benefit—to further my and my sister's future.

In addition to leaving the people he knew and the groups he felt part of, there were many other contrasts to adjust to. In India, he lived in a city; in Indiana, he lived in a small community. In India, everything was loud, teeming with activity; in Indiana, it was strangely quiet. In India, he had to wear a school uniform "so everyone would look the same and no one would feel like they were inferior to someone else"; in Indiana, people judged each other by what they wore. Ishaan wanted to fit in and initially saw clothes as his ticket:

I wanted to conform. I wanted the Nike shoes, the branded clothes others were wearing. But as I grew older—I would say in freshman year in high school—I didn't want to care about what others were doing. I wanted to be comfortable in my own body, so I started wearing clothes that were comfortable to me and made me feel happier inside.

Notice how often Ishaan uses the word "want"—he didn't want to care about what others were doing; he wanted to be comfortable in his own body. This word reflects a seeking that's normal in the process of identity development in the United States. It also reflects the fact that Ishaan's identity explorations were afflicted by bullying—something that shouldn't be normal for anyone, but sadly happens to about a fifth of twelve-to-eighteen-year-olds.[182]

In middle school, I had one of the roughest years of my life. I was bullied in sixth grade. Since I'm from India, they'd call me stereotypical names like "call center worker" or "you're a terrorist." That really affected me.

Although it hurt, he couldn't escape his feelings of still wanting to fit in:

I'd still try to conform because those people were always with me; they were my classmates. I wanted to be with them so I wouldn't be excluded from my school lifestyle.

Ishaan had been outgoing and talkative, but the bullying drove him inward:

When I got home at three p.m., I'd be like, "There's fourteen hours until I have to wake up to go to school." I was really reclusive. I'd stay in my bed and just do things by myself.

I wouldn't ask for anyone's help. I wouldn't tell my parents because they were working. I didn't want to bother them with my problems.

In not wanting to bother his family, Ishaan was modeling himself on his father, whom he saw as shielding his children from his worries and concerns.

Ishaan's identity explorations reveal how the communities we're in ("What are we like?") shape our behavior and sense of self ("What am I like?") and exemplify how psychology has come to view human development with an "I" and a "we" perspective.[183] As you'll see, they also reveal opportunities for how we can promote healthy identity formation in young people.

THE RIGHT CLIMATE FOR IDENTITY EXPLORATION: FEELING "TREASURED AND LOVED AND CAPABLE . . . SEEN AND HEARD"

Like Ishaan, Diane Hughes of New York University comes from a family of doctors. She thought she'd be a doctor, too, until her discovery in college that she didn't like physics and organic chemistry but instead liked community psychology, especially because it has a focus on social justice.[184] That was important to her because, as an African American woman, she'd grown up with her father's stories about living in the South and having to enter movie theaters through a side door and climb steep stairs to where the "colored" could sit, even though his own father was a well-respected surgeon in town.[185]

Hughes has dedicated her research to making a difference for all young people facing discrimination:

My work over my entire career has been embedded in this personal quest to address very small pieces of big questions about how to ensure that all children—and not just White children—can fly; that all children have an opportunity to feel like they're treasured and loved and capable, beautiful and optimistic and hopeful about their future; and for all children to feel like they're seen and heard.[186]

A number of her studies have focused on the kind of discrimination Ishaan experienced. He's far from alone. A recent nationally representative study of fifteen-to-twenty-four-year-olds by the Public Religion Research

Institute and MTV found that 71 to 81 percent of young people of color have witnessed or personally experienced discrimination because of their race, and 24 to 35 percent report being on the receiving end of discrimination.[187] Asians like Ishaan have the highest incidence of experiencing discrimination, at 35 percent. The percentages of White young people who've witnessed or personally experienced racial discrimination are lower than for other groups.

Decades of studies show that discrimination affects young people in multiple ways—negatively affecting their sleep, stress (including cortisol levels), relationships, mental health (including depression), academic engagement, and academic achievement.[188]

One study by Hughes and her colleagues is especially informative about discrimination's effects over time. They followed 226 young people from six public schools in New York City over six years, from the sixth through the eleventh grades, and found that discrimination increased in middle school and decreased in high school—similar to what Ishaan experienced. Although they found that "experiences of ethnic/racial discrimination are relatively infrequent among early adolescents, on average,"[189] the effects were pernicious—the same patterns we discussed in chapter 3.

Key Findings: Higher levels of discrimination in the sixth grade predicted poorer academic and psychological adjustment and more behavior problems by the end of eighth grade. On a positive note, the researchers found that if discrimination declined between eighth and eleventh grades, students were better adjusted psychologically and academically, though there was no effect on behavior problems.

Discrimination has clear effects on well-being—and when our well-being is under attack, the climate for identity exploration can be compromised. It's essential to note that while Ishaan was bullied for being Indian American and Hughes's research is about children of color, young people are picked on for a variety of reasons—for being short or tall, for being nerds or jocks, or (as we've discussed) for being teens. If we make this only about race/ethnicity, as crucial as this is, we are missing the essential problem. Kids of all races and backgrounds are picked on, and it hurts in ways that can affect their health and well-being now and in the future. It also can affect their identity explorations. For young people to ask themselves identity questions, the climate has to be right, inside and out, and they have to feel safe enough to explore and seek answers.

HELPING ADOLESCENTS FIND THE RIGHT FIT VERSUS FITTING IN

When Ishaan entered high school, there were lots of cliques: popular kids, quiet kids, basketball kids, geeks. He was still trying to fit in, but was beginning to experience his efforts as not feeling right:

During my first two years of high school, I was part of those cliques, part of the popular kids' group, which I didn't really fit in with because they'd always do things like go out and party, which I didn't like doing at all. I'd still do it just because those are the type of people I knew. Those were my friends, but . . .

His voice trailed off, and he paused briefly before continuing:

They'd go out partying, and they'd have different viewpoints on, say, politics or our society. I'd listen to them, but it just wasn't something that my values represent.

That led him, by junior year, to try to branch out, to meet other people. He turned to people who seemed more like him: the foreign exchange students and others. This led him to explorations that went beyond surface similarities:

There were some people that grew up in poor neighborhoods. Their family had been through divorces; they'd had family members who died; they'd had hardships. I grew up in an upper-middle-class family, so my parents provided everything for me. I didn't really have to do anything to live.
*   Just listening to the jobs they had—early, as kids—and what their parents had been through, I realized how other kids are different from me. At first, I only had a single perspective—my perspective—so knowing about others' perspectives made me more knowledgeable about myself and them.*

There was one similarity he cherished. The new friends he chose were open; they shared their stories, expressed their feelings. These felt like authentic relationships:

The people I met after branching out—they're the people that I believe are most genuine, that acted most genuinely towards me. They were being themselves and not what society wanted them to be. That's who I wanted to be or become. Through them, I believe I did become that.

Again we see Ishaan's focus on "wanting," but this time the striving goes beyond clothes; it goes beneath the surface to the kind of person he wants to become.

As I talked with adolescents about figuring out who they are and what they're like in relation to the communities they're in—the "I" and the "we" in identity development—I often heard about an internal process, a silent conversation young people have with themselves. It's what Ethan Kross calls "chatter": the voices in our minds, the way we talk to ourselves, and the way we listen to those voices.[190]

But . . .

- What if adolescents had more opportunities to turn this "identity chatter" from private to public?
- What if they had safe places for these opportunities, like the kind Ishaan found, where they could reflect on what they're like (and what they're not like—because exploring identities is as much about rejecting identities as it is about adopting them)?
- What if we could help them find supportive diverse groups, to provide a wider canvas for these explorations?

HELPING ADOLESCENTS SEE THAT PEOPLE CAN CHANGE

Ishaan had seen himself as outgoing and social as a child, but the bullying drove him inward, so he saw himself as "reclusive" and "uncommunicative" in sixth grade. By eighth grade, he began to find a path back to his outgoing self, through a reconnection with one of the bullies, Freddy. It was a turning point for him:

Freddy changed my life in a sense. He was one of the kids that bullied me in sixth grade. He'd taunt me for the clothes I was wearing or just anything that would come to his mind. We lived in the same neighborhood, but in eighth grade he started to get to know me.

Freddy had experienced a turning point of his own:

His mother and father were police officers, and they were really hard on
him as a kid. They told him what to do and didn't really give him the
freedom he wanted.

That hard time at home had spilled into school for Freddy, but by eighth
grade, Ishaan says, Freddy realized he didn't want to become the kind of
person his parents were—the kind of person he was becoming:

He was like, "I don't want to be a part of this. Through his own mindset,
he figured out that "whatever I'm doing is wrong." He apologized
to me.
    That mindset carried on to high school, and he's really grown as a per-
son, which has grown on me as well because it made me realize people can
change throughout their lives.

Do you remember the mindset experiment we discussed in the section
on competence—where David Yeager and his colleagues experimented
with giving high school students information that if someone excludes or
victimizes another person, it's not that they're bad people whose personalities are fixed—they can change?[191] Ishaan experienced this insight in real
life. Freddy changed, and that helped change Ishaan.

I was impressed, too, that Ishaan calls this a mindset, because the view
that people can or can't change is, indeed, a mindset. As you remember,
prompting young people to see the world this way, in Yeager's words,
"caused young people to see a stressor as a challenge they could overcome."[192]

Throughout high school, Ishaan and Freddy remained best friends.
Ishaan says that conversations with Freddy and with his other new friends
"opened my eyes to who I am." These self-discoveries happened in conversations where he and his friends asked each other what they were thinking
and feeling, and they cared about what the other said.

Feeling more comfortable and becoming more accepted by his peers
prompted Ishaan to reach out to some of his high school teachers, with
cascading results (similar to what happened in Greg Walton's experiments
on belonging and support):

I got to know teachers that were willing to go out of their way to help me
or listen to me, just in a friendly manner, which really helped me become
more talkative and myself.

Ishaan kept arriving at the same place: he felt most comfortable with himself when he paid attention to his feelings and thoughts, was emotionally open, and shared his feelings and thoughts with others.

A DYNAMIC PROCESS

But what felt like a safe harbor personally for Ishaan felt dissonant with his culture and with how he was raised, which seemed to value boys and men tamping down feelings. It was a dissonance Ishaan felt he needed to deal with.

Some of the research on identity development has focused on how adolescents explore possible identities and then begin to come to a resolution, a commitment. In a very simplified analogy, it might be akin to trying on different outfits and then deciding which outfit feels right.

In contrast, Deborah Rivas-Drake of the University of Michigan and Adriana Umaña-Taylor of Harvard University define identity exploration as more cyclical—a time when young people "pull together the information they have gathered from all of the significant social actors around them . . . and weave it together with their own ideas about their values, their beliefs, and their future goals."[193] In their view, the process is important for helping young people develop an "informed" understanding of their background, not just absorbing the information given to them:

> By actively engaging in identity exploration, adolescents gain a sense of
> ownership and confidence in this aspect of their identity . . . the ideal goal
> is to obtain a sense of clarity, or what is referred to as **resolution** about the
> identity.[194]

That resolution comes about through cycles of clarity and confusion, rather than being just a one-step process, though there can be key moments that move adolescents toward more clarity.

That was the case for Ishaan. By turns, he felt comfortable, confused, and conflicted about how he was different from his Indian background and how he was the same. His father, possibly understanding what was going on, suggested a literal exploration—a trip back to India when Ishaan was a freshman in high school:

> It was the first time I'd been back to India since moving here. My dad told
> me I should go on like a pilgrimage to different cities and villages he'd been

through as a kid. Talking to people from different regions of India made me feel more knowledgeable on being an Indian. I learned more about who I am and what being an Indian meant.

One incident was particularly clarifying:

I was on a tour in a secluded part of India. It mainly consists of deserts. A seventy- or eighty-year-old man pulled me aside and invited me to his house. I had a cup of chai tea and some roti, Indian bread, with him while he told me how he grew up and all the things he's been through.

There were many differences between this man's life and Ishaan's:

He had to do everything by himself. He started working when he was six, in the streets. That made me think of all the things I've had in my life, and it made me respect my parents even more because they didn't have to provide for me as much as they have.

Yet aspects of this man's life and his were the same:

We could joke about things that only we Indians would understand. We joked about politics and movie actors. Only people who've lived in this culture would think these things are funny.

I asked Ishaan how he reconciled being bullied for being an Indian and being proud to be Indian. He said:

I felt that the people that were bullying me for being Indian were wrong. They were only stereotyping me. They didn't take time out of their days to get to know the real me.

That journey back to India made me realize that I should be proud to be an Indian. Plus, being Indian wasn't something I could control—it's how I was born and raised.

A DYNAMIC PROCESS—AND THE MEDIA WEIGHS IN, TOO

Ishaan was not exploring his identity solo, or even just within his family, school, or community. There's the media, too—not just social media but movies and television, where views of the groups we're in affect our feelings about ourselves.

I heard about this from so many young people—they want to see people "like me" portrayed positively and as whole people, whether it is about being from one part of the country or another, or from one background or another. Max, a seventeen-year-old who identifies as trans, put it this way:

> There are so many stories about queer pain and suffering, and self-hatred as a result of being queer. Why aren't there more mainstream stories about all the happy, normal gay people?

BEGINNING TO RECONCILE THE DISSONANCE

Although he couldn't control the fact that he was born and raised Indian, Ishaan needed to find a way to be Indian on his own terms. That meant dealing with the disconnect he was feeling—that he was most comfortable expressing his feelings and thoughts in honest ways, but that wasn't in keeping with how he saw his father and the men in his life behaving:

> I just got tired of keeping things to myself. I wanted people to listen to my story or what I had to say or whatever I went through. I'd start talking to my friends or my mom.

He found that confiding in others gave him comfort, but doing things differently was also unsettling. As he explored, he read a lot of biographies on his own, of people like Winston Churchill and other historical figures. He gained particular insight from Princess Diana:

> When you think of princesses or princes or queens and kings, you just think of royalty and how they conduct themselves. But Princess Diana was different from all of them. She wanted to guide her own way and be herself in the monarchy. She did that by breaking a lot of cultural and social rules.

This exploration led Ishaan to another aspect of identity development— he's now more seriously pursuing questions of what he wants to do in the world.

The Need to Explore What I Do / What I Will Do

As we've seen, the framework developed by Dan McAdams for identity development looks at identity formation as a layered sequence of strands. This second strand is about the self as a motivated agent (striving), which McAdams sees as figuring out our identity through our goals, values, and life projects.

FROM "WHAT DO YOU WANT TO BE?" TO "WHAT DO YOU WANT TO DO?"

From the time they're little, children are asked:

What do you want to do when you grow up?

My daughter, Lara Galinsky, begins her book *Work on Purpose* with how this question made her feel as she grew up. She writes that as a young child, she'd say, "I want to be a teacher, a veterinarian, or a novelist," and felt proud to have an answer to this question that adults asked her. The older she got, the more this question filled her with dread:

It was a constant reminder that I had big decisions to make. I felt immense pressure to be . . . 100 percent certain of my goals, and in possession of a detailed, logical career path. Yet, I didn't even know where to start.[195]

Does this remind you of Natalie's anxiety in the section on the need for competence when she was confronted with the question "What do you want to do?" and responded, "But I am just in middle school"?

While my son was always certain he wanted to center his life on music (and in fact has his doctorate in music and directs an innovative performance ensemble), my daughter's path—like that of most young people—was less certain. In her final year in college, she began actively doing research on this, conducting many informational interviews and eventually moving into the new field of social entrepreneurship.

In her book, she suggests we ask children and adolescents questions about *being* first:

What kind of person do you want to be?

It does come first, developmentally. She's found, from working with hundreds of adult social entrepreneurs, that those who are the most fulfilled bring questions of being (often issues they've come to care about growing up) and doing together:

> I have come to believe that all those who build meaningful careers in social change have—whether consciously or unconsciously—synched what they feel strongly about with what they are good at. This alignment produces great impact.[196]

Ishaan, who has spent a lot of time thinking about the kind of person he wants to be, is now also thinking about what he wants to do:

> Most parents in India like my parents want their kids to be engineers, doctors, or lawyers. I am a major in political science and prelaw right now. It's just something that interested me.

In reading biographies, he realized that whatever job or profession he pursues, it will be only one facet of his life. He also has to continue to consider who he wants to be—a person who is in touch with his feelings. He will use all of these facets of himself to compose his life story:

> Reading and learning about the turmoil of others made me want to write my own story in a different way. I wanted to complete my story through releasing my true self and being who I am and showing people that I can try hard at doing what I do.

LAB ⟷ LIFE: ENCOURAGING REAL-WORLD EXPERIENCES WITH THE FUTURE: BALDWIN HIGH SCHOOL, BALDWIN, NEW YORK

This high school checks all of the achievement boxes, with a 98 percent graduation rate and selection as one of the top hundred schools in 2022 by *U.S. News and World Report*, but what sets it apart is the way it gives students real-world experiences that enable them to explore the world of work and what they might want to *do* in the future.[197] Within the New York State course requirements, the school uses electives (called "Academic Academies") to give students experience in building drones (STEM/engineering), in creating start-up companies (global business and entrepreneurship), in arguing legal cases (law and government), in creating websites for local employers (new media), in coming up with plans to reduce the food waste in their schools (medical and health sciences), and in conducting research on improving mental health (education). Through clubs, the school also provides students with the opportunity to create viable solutions to community problems, like finding free community resources for immigrant families, while working alongside community professionals who mentor them.

As one student said, "In school, you learn that your job is to get a job," but Baldwin makes that less daunting. Here, "we can find interests that bring a smile to our faces," one student said. This happens "at a time in our lives before we're locked into making career choices or selecting majors," another noted. Others added that they also learn how to take risks, put themselves out there, and network.

Superintendent Shari Camhi says that when she took this leadership job nine years ago, she was determined to work with students, teachers, and administrators to create new ways of learning that promote the skills students will need in the workforce—like collaboration, creativity, communication, and critical thinking—and to do so in ways that fully engage students and seed passions that will enable them to think about what they might like to do.

MATCH AND MISMATCH IN THE BASIC NEED FOR IDENTITY

In the Breakthrough Years study, we asked the nationally representative group of adolescents about the extent to which their Basic Need for identity was met. We asked:

In the last month, how often did you feel like . . . ?

1. *Your parent(s) and family help you figure out what really matters to you*
2. *Your parent(s) and family help you discover who you are*

In addition to parents and family, we asked the same questions about the other four main groups of people in their lives—their friends, the people at school, the people in out-of-school activities, and the people they connect with online.

How do you think the adolescents in your life would answer these questions?

You can see the findings below.* It's no surprise that families are most likely to meet this need "often" (more than half the time), and the people they met online are the least likely. Still, there's lots of room for positive change, especially given how pivotal the need for identity exploration is. For example, only 40 percent report that the people at school help them think about these issues often.

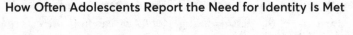

How Often Adolescents Report the Need for Identity Is Met

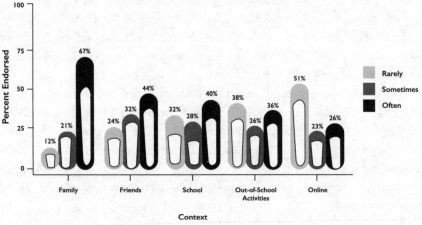

Having the need for identity met prior to the pandemic has made a difference during the pandemic. By looking at the arrows in the table on the next page, it's clear that the young people who have relationships in their families, in school and in out-of-school activities, and online that help them figure out who they are and what matters to them are much more likely to be engaged in school. Relationships in their families, with friends, and in school that prompt identity explorations are also linked to more positive views of their futures, to better moods, and to experiencing less stress.

---

* Adolescents answered each question on a five-point scale from "never" to "almost always." The answers for the two questions were summed, resulting in the following groups: "rarely" (2–4), "sometimes" (5–7), and "often" (8–10).

Outcomes of Having the Need for Identity Met

Identity	Follow-Up Outcomes							
Context	School Engage-ment	Grades (A)	Grades (P)	Future	Neg-ative Mood	Positive Mood	Stress	Conflict (A:P)
Family	↑			↑	↓	↑	↓	↓ : ↓
Friends				↑	↓	↑	↓	:
School	↑			↑	↓	↑	↓	:
OSA	↑			↑				:
Online	↑							:

A = adolescent report, P = parent report, OSA = out-of-school activities. Arrows indicate the direction of an association (i.e., up arrow for promoting, down arrow for protecting), controlling for demographics. An empty cell indicates there is no statistically significant relationship. Significant relations are p-values < .0005, meaning these correlations are very reliable and unlikely to have occurred by chance.

The Need to Explore What Story I Tell Myself About Myself

In a graduate class he was teaching in the 1980s, Dan McAdams posed this question to his students: "If you could see an identity—if you could picture it—what would it look like?"

> We tried all kinds of metaphors. "It might look like a house . . . like an archaeological site . . . like a circus."
>
> I eventually said, "No." I came around to the idea that if you could see it, identity would look like a story. It's a story that people have in their heads.
>
> Identity has a reconstructed past—the beginning; the middle where you are now; and the imagined future, an envisioned ending. There are themes; there're lots of different characters, and they could represent different parts of you.[198]

McAdams's fascinating conclusion matches, in essence, what neuroscientists such as Kenneth Norman of Princeton University are learning about how events are stored and retrieved from long-term memory. Our recollections are constructed through scripts and discrete events (think of a movie plot and scenes), like the way we tell stories.[199]

In the 1980s, when McAdams arrived at this conclusion, there was little research on life stories. He began by conducting research solo, without external funding, interviewing people about their life stories, developing a research protocol, and seeing how life stories fit into his other research as a personality psychologist. "Now," he says, "there are many people who study what we call narrative identity."[200]

McAdams's focus was on midlife and on studying Erik Erikson's notion of generativity: the adult's concern for and commitment to the well-being of future generations. It turns out our capacity for generativity is linked to the story we tell ourselves about who we are, including during adolescence. Here, we'll explore the roots of narrative identity, how it unfolds in adolescence, and what we can learn from studies of adults.

"YOU NEED A GOOD STORY": WHY NARRATIVE IDENTITY MATTERS

What makes a "good" story? For two decades, McAdams, his students, and a group of colleagues studied the stories of highly generative adults. Although their research is about adults, you can see that some of the recurring themes also occur in the stories of adolescents, like Anaya, whom we'll meet soon:

- **Exploratory:** the extent to which we explore and develop a rich self-understanding
- **Meaning-making:** the degree to which we learn something from an experience
- **Agency:** the degree to which we're able to achieve mastery and effect change in our own and others' lives
- **Communion:** the degree to which we're able to experience supportive relationships
- **Redemption:** the extent to which we overcome difficulties, turning negative events into positive ones
- **Contamination:** the degree to which a positive event turns negative and overwhelms or erases the positive effects[201]

You have probably noticed that these themes reflect many of the Basic Needs of adolescents, such as agency, mastery, support, and challenge. These needs are integral to our identity stories, and critical to our becoming generative adults.

HOW CHALLENGES SHAPE OUR STORY

McAdams and Kate McLean from Western Washington University write that for those who emerge strengthened from adversity, there's a two-step process. First, a person fully reflects on a negative experience:

> *thinking long and hard about what the experience felt like, how it came to be, what it may lead to, and what role the negative event may play in the person's overall life story.*

The second step involves figuring out how to turn a negative experience into a positive lesson:

> *The person articulates and commits the self to a positive resolution of the event. Research suggests that the first step is associated with personal growth; the second, with happiness.*[202]

Making Sense of a Challenge: The Story of Anaya

When asked about the story of her life, Anaya, now sixteen, begins with happy memories of the fifth grade, the beginning of middle school:

> *I had so many friends and it was so much fun. I remember fifth grade because it was one of the best years of my life.*

In seventh grade, Anaya's life went downhill quickly:

> *I got a tumor in my jaw. We caught it just before it turned cancerous. I had to have surgery.*

As you know, adolescents are primed to care deeply about where they stand with their friends, and the way they look is one important way of fitting in and belonging. Anaya's mind swirled with fears:

> *People were going to think I was ugly because my jaw was literally like out to here. They had to remove—I don't remember if it was a centimeter or an inch—I'm pretty sure it was an inch—around each part of the tumor to make sure all the cells were removed. I was so scared that I'd go back to school and everyone would hate me.*

Post-surgery, her mother tried to reassure her by telling her how beautiful she was, but Anaya knew it wasn't true. The proof came when she returned home from the hospital. Her little brother and sister took one look at her and hid upstairs. "I am the ugliest monster," she cried.

> *I was like, oh my God, even my own siblings don't recognize me. What will people in school think?*

Her first day back at school set off a panic attack and Anaya had to leave early. But, on the positive side, she realized none of her classmates had said anything mean or teased her. In fact, Anaya's best friend had organized their classmates to create a get-well card and a care package.

When she returned to school full-time, her classmates remained supportive, even when she felt she looked ridiculous, like the day she was laughing so hard in the cafeteria that she started drooling. "Here it comes," she thought. When one of the boys walked over, she expected him to say, "Anaya's such a baby—she's drooling." But he just handed her a napkin.

Anaya still wonders: Did her best friend alert people that "Anaya's scared about being in school, so be nice"? Or did they have compassion, thinking: "Anaya's had surgery—let me not be a horrible person"? Hearing this from Anaya makes me doubly sad for all of the young people who don't have these supportive relationships in school, like Ishaan and Brigid. Only 40 percent of adolescents in our study report having their need for identity met often (more than half the time) at school.

The surgery intensified Anaya's identity questions:

> *I really thought I was an ugly person. I'd look in the mirror for hours and be like, "Who is this person? Why do I look like this? Why did this happen to me?" I was really not happy.*
>
> *Not only was I not confident in myself, but I wasn't confident in what I was doing. I'd be scared to present a project when I'm normally really good at presenting things. I was scared to do new things, like, "Oh, I'm not good enough." I'd be scared to ask for my order at a drive-through or at a restaurant, because I wasn't confident in what I was saying.*

She had to have a second surgery the summer before eighth grade and returned to school that fall with missing teeth. But again, her friends didn't tease her. They asked questions about her missing teeth but were "nice" about it, the way most adolescents wish others would be.

In retrospect, Anaya sees that healing takes time. It took time for the swelling to go down and for her face to have a new normal look. In eighth grade, she had "not a real boyfriend, but a boyfriend in the ways eighth graders have boyfriends." He liked her and thought she was pretty, and her friends liked her, and that helped her like herself again.

I couldn't speed up the healing process. Going into freshman year, I still felt a little camera shy. Now in eleventh grade, my jaw looks almost the same almost on both sides. Sometimes I still look at myself, but it's not the same—I'm not hating who I see. It was self-reflection and self-growth that helped me heal.

I suspect that if researchers were coding Anaya's story of herself, they might say she was **exploring** in order to better understand herself, experiencing **communion**, and **making meaning**, looking for the lessons in her life experience. Her story might even be seen as somewhat **redemptive**, though certainly not as fully as the redemptive experiences that McAdams finds take place in midlife.

McAdams and others have found that narrative identity begins in early childhood, in the conversations parents have with their children to help them make sense of what happens to them.

FAMILY STORIES: THE FOUNDATION FOR OUR CHILDREN'S NARRATIVES

Robyn Fivush of Emory University has studied family stories for several decades. In taping conversations between parents and children, she's looked at how family stories—initially between mothers and preschoolers in her studies, and later with older children and their parents—shape children's narrative identities.

It turns out that certain factors are important for us to keep in mind.

The More Detail, the Better

Fivush and her colleagues found that the parents have different styles of recalling and making sense of the past: some are highly elaborative storytellers, some less so.[203] In a **highly elaborative** style, the parent:

- Discusses the past experience in rich detail
- Asks lots of open-ended questions, which the researchers call "wh" questions: *why, what, where,* or *who* ("What did you enjoy most about your visit with your friend?")

- Often repeats what the child says, thus encouraging the child to say more ("So, you and Saul both wanted to play video games.")
- As they go back and forth, provides feedback to the child, as well as more information
- Shows genuine interest in what the child is saying

Fivush and her colleagues have found that **children with elaborative parents tell more detailed, more complex, more cohesive stories about their own lives** than children of parents with a less elaborative style.

Beyond "How Was School Today?"

Fivush and her colleagues also taped dinnertime conversations with nine-through-twelve-year-olds and discovered that families don't just talk about what happened at school that day.[204] They tell history stories—about Mom or Dad growing up, or outrageous Uncle Bill—and the children know these stories because they've been told them again and again. She says:

> *The families that told more of these stories around the dinner table had children who had higher self-esteem, did better in school, had better social skills, and showed fewer problem behaviors.*

Being part of a storytelling family—which Fivush and Marshall Duke, also of Emory University, now assess by asking young people "20 Do You Know" questions about the family history they've learned through family stories[205]—predicts many positive outcomes for children when they become adolescents and adults, including "higher resilience, higher satisfaction, higher meaning and purpose in life."[206]

Gender Differences in Family Stories

Fivush and her colleagues have found that mothers are more elaborative than fathers, and that mothers and fathers are more elaborative with their daughters than with their sons.[207]

The impact of family stories can also differ for boys and girls. While family stories, in general, have a very positive impact, Kate McLean and her research team discovered in one study that in early adolescence boys who engage in trying to "make meaning" in telling personal stories have less positive outcomes (depression and self-esteem), but in late adolescence that reverses.[208] The researchers speculate this may be because young people in early adolescence are less adept at thinking abstractly or perhaps because these particular boys had especially disruptive events to process.

MAKING SENSE OF A DIFFICULT DIVORCE: THE STORY OF GIGI

Adolescents begin forming a more continuous sense of their identities[209] as they increasingly develop the cognitive capacity to think about themselves in abstract ways and thus become better able to deal with the complexities and contradictions in their life experiences.[210]

"The story of my life?" says sixteen-year-old Gigi. "Well, what I remember most is when my parents got divorced." She was going into fifth grade and it rocked her.

> *I wouldn't call it a shock because near the end there was always fighting and always having problems.*

The divorce made Gigi feel alone, different from her friends. Her relationships with each of her parents deteriorated:

> *Me and my dad were really on the fritz. I remember this like it was yesterday—he didn't talk to me and didn't come visit me.*

This conflicted with her view of what adults are supposed to be like—she was taking care of her father, rather than her father taking care of her:

> *I always found myself being the adult in our relationship. I thought it was really weird how a lot of other people's fathers gave them hugs and wished them a good day. Meanwhile, I was the one that had to text my father first. I had to communicate between my parents because they couldn't talk to each other without an argument. It was like I had to grow up faster than I wanted to because I had to take responsibility for this adult.*
>
> *My mother would cry at night because when my parents got divorced, she had no money. I was the one that hugged her when she was sobbing. My fifth-grade/sixth-grade self would hug her. I'd take care of my siblings. I'd make dinner. I'd do all of this stuff.*
>
> *I remember being in middle school and people telling me they're going on vacation and showing me what they had for dinner. We weren't financially*

stable when I was growing up. I remember a lot of times making sure my sib-
lings would eat before I did so they wouldn't be the ones that were hungry.

I just remember always being hungry. Until the past year, I remember
always eating more than I needed to because I didn't know when my next
meal would be.

The contrast with her friends was glaring:

A lot of my friends at the time were having a blast—having no
responsibility. I remember nights hearing my mother cry and I didn't know
what to do. I remember making sure my work was done, that I didn't cause
any problems so my mom didn't have more to worry about.

Gigi was overwhelmed, feeling that her parents didn't have a concept
of what it means to be an adult, especially when they sometimes called her
"immature." She also knew she was in way over her head. She wanted help
but hesitated for fear of upsetting her mother. It took a long time and lots of
courage, even desperation, for her to reach out to her grandmother.

Gigi's grandmother talked to her daughter, who promised she'd try. And
her mother did try, but when she slipped, she'd say to Gigi, "I'm sorry we
didn't understand that you were put in this situation, but sometimes we just
need to suck it up." Gigi reflects:

I don't blame my mom at all. I don't have hatred out for my mom because
I was hungry. She had three kids and she was by herself.

When my stepdad came into the picture, it was kind of like everything
got better. He was always talking to me about how he knows how I feel.

He would say, "I was a teenager once," but Gigi would respond, "Okay,
you might understand the general concept, but you don't know what I've
been through."

In learning about Gigi's story, it's easy to assume that divorce is bad for
children long-term; that's what research showed half a century ago. Over the
years—as studies have improved by having a greater number and more diverse families in their samples and by using more rigorous methodologies—
it's become evident that the impact of divorce is more nuanced. For some
children, divorce can eventually mean a change for the better—to less conflict between their parents, who become better able to co-parent. For others,
it can spiral into a worse situation. Research also shows that divorce isn't

simply one event—it is many events over time, and the way it's handled is what affects children the most.[211]

For Gigi, divorce led to poverty (which, of course, affects the children) and to her parents becoming people who needed care from their child. When her stepfather joined the family and the situation eased emotionally and financially, she began acting out her pent-up feelings. She stopped getting up for classes—not doing much but staying in bed or sneaking out to meet friends. Then the pandemic hit and she really didn't see a reason to get out of bed because there was only assigned homework, no virtual classes.

Her mom and stepfather punished her by taking away everything they could—her electronics, her rights to see or talk to her friends—for months on end, until there was little else to take away. That isolated her even more during the pandemic. Gigi says:

> It's not like I was out there doing drugs. I don't do drugs. I just wasn't doing the things I was supposed to. I wouldn't wake up on time. I wouldn't do my schoolwork. I didn't see the point.

The summer before her junior year, she began to turn around. As she describes it:

> I started being responsible. I stepped up. I did my chores every day and everything I had to do, no reminder. I made dinner sometimes. I made sure my siblings' homework was done, was driving myself to school every day, getting my work done, not doing anything bad. And I started working a part-time job [at a fast-food restaurant] twenty hours a week.

I asked Gigi to describe how she went from being someone who wouldn't get out of bed to someone who did everything she was supposed to, no reminders.

Her path toward recovery included therapy, so she had a way to look at the past and learn new coping skills. Her mother and stepfather also helped her transfer to a different school, where they hoped she'd connect more to learning.

It also included her friends, and that was pivotal. When they'd invite her to hang out during her difficult times and she'd have to say, "I can't," they'd say, "Gigi, what did you do this time?" She became tired of being a "terrible friend"—she missed others' birthday parties, yet her friends still made a big deal over her birthday and brought her gifts. She said to herself:

I need to grow up and stop refusing to do the things I'm supposed to so I can have the life that I want. I would look to my future and say, I can be this amazing person if I just give myself one more day.

Her siblings also affected her turnaround, she says:

One of the main things that got me through was my siblings. I'd look at my brother and say, "What is he going to do without his big sister? I have to be here for them."

Making art also helped, as it does for many people facing challenges.[212] Gigi paints, draws, and writes stories:

I have so many short stories in my computer or on pieces of paper. I'm writing my life—but not as myself. I have my characters live a life I want to live or do things I want to do.

When I asked her to describe herself, she said:

I'd call myself a pretender.

Most of the time, she says, she's pretending to be a bubbly, smiley, make-everyone-feel-better person, instead of the person she wants to be—the people she creates in her stories:

I would hope that someday I don't have to pretend anymore—that I can just be my full self. And when I call myself a pretender, I just mean that a lot of the time I still just don't feel like getting up out of bed.

Gigi says that in her hoped-for future:

I want to be able to wake up in the morning and say, "I'm so excited to live this day and be who I am."
    Traveling. I don't want to leave my family because I love them, but I really want to travel the world and see different cultures and different groups of people, hear new languages, and try foods I've never tried before.
    I want to wear a flowy hat on the beach or collect sand in a bottle. I want to be able to see the world and look out to what else is there.

Gigi is writing and painting the story of herself as she lives it. Like Anaya, she's trying to make sense of the challenges she has faced—the "reconstructed past," as Dan McAdams described—using them as a launching pad to be a different person. She is working on her "imagined future": who she wants to become, where she wants to go, what she wants to experience.

Gigi's story took me back to Mary Catherine Bateson's thought-provoking book *Composing a Life*,[213] where breakdowns can become breakthroughs. Gigi is literally composing her life. As Dan McAdams says, the stories we tell about ourselves not only help us make sense of our experiences but also affect how we live our lives.[214]

PROMOTING THE BASIC NEED FOR IDENTITY

It's crucial to understand identity development as a process: adolescents are exploring their identities as individuals and as members of groups, and determining how they're similar to and different from others. They're also figuring out what they want to be and do in the future. In helping them meet this Basic Need for **identity**, we can:

- **Intervene in addressing discrimination**—like bullying—when it surfaces by helping both the person bullied and the one doing the bullying. Intervening can dilute the negative impact on adolescents' well-being and help provide a climate that promotes identity exploration.
- **Give them opportunities to be with supportive groups** of people where they can turn their identity chatter from private to public—reflecting what they're like and, importantly, what they're not like.
- **Help them see that personalities aren't set in stone**—that people, including them, can change.
- **Help them begin to think about what they care about**, where their passions lie—and what first steps they want to take in doing what they want to do.

Developing a narrative identity—the story that adolescents tell themselves about themselves—is the way they seek to understand their experiences, determine how they handle the joys and sorrows of life, and shape their future. To help them **craft their story**, we can:

- **Understand that it takes time** for adolescents to explore and find meaning from positive and negative experiences. We can support them, but not overpromise, overpraise, or overprotect.
- **Share your favorite family stories**, including how these experiences affect who we are, what we do, and how we handle challenges.
- **Give adolescents tools to understand their past and their present and to dream of their future**, whether through conversations, help as needed, writing, creating art, or other forms of self-expression.

Need 5: Purpose: The Need for Purpose and to Contribute

Purpose is being provided opportunities to explore a life aim that is motivating and includes a commitment to something beyond the self. Contributing is having opportunities to do things to help others. When adolescents can explore what's meaningful to them and contribute to the greater good, they can begin to develop a sense of direction in their lives (purpose).

The Need for Purpose

Ishaan, the Indian American who was bullied in middle school for being Indian, found that reading biographies and learning about the turmoil of others made him want to write his own story in a different way. He told me:

> *I wanted to complete my story through releasing my true self and being who I am and showing people that I can try hard at doing what I do.*

Similarly, Gigi, at sixteen, moved beyond her parents' tumultuous divorce and began looking toward her future. She told me:

> *I want to be able to wake up and say, "I'm so excited to live this day and be who I am."*

These images of waking up with a sense of direction, of finding one's "true self," and of being able to "be who I am" reveal the Basic Needs of identity and purpose and how intertwined they are.

Many discussions about purpose begin with the book *Man's Search for Meaning*,[215] Viktor Frankl's harrowing yet inspiring account about the brutality of his life in four concentration camps during World War II, where his pregnant wife, his parents, and his brother were killed. While we can't avoid suffering in life, Frankl said, we do have a choice about how to deal with it. We can look beyond the suffering to seek meaning and find a life of purpose.

"The prisoner who lost faith in the future—his future—was doomed,"[216] he wrote; however, those who had faith could survive, he continued, quoting the German philosopher Friedrich Nietzsche: "He who has a *why* to live for can bear with almost any *how*."[217]

The search for the "why" begins in childhood, gains momentum in adolescence, and becomes a lifelong process of exploration, refinement, commitment, and change depending on the circumstances of our lives.

In adolescence, it's striking how a small moment can inspire a journey toward purpose for some people. The mystery, of course, is what those moments will be, when they will happen, and how we will see them manifest in a young person's life path. And the main question is: How can we help?

"THE PATH TO PURPOSE"

Bill Damon of Stanford University didn't have much sense of "a *why*"—of meaning or purpose—when he entered high school; now he's one of the leading researchers on purpose. Joining the school's newspaper freshman year was a pivotal moment for him:

> I was the definition of a mediocre student—I wasn't a bad student, but I got away with doing as little as I could without getting in trouble, and I did a pretty shoddy job of just about everything.
>   I actually found something I got interested in when I joined the school newspaper, which is why I always say that schools should be very careful before cutting extracurricular activities because that's where a lot of young people learn academic skills and gain motivation.[218]

Damon liked sports, so he was given a "low-level" assignment: covering a story about a group of Eastern European immigrant students who'd formed a soccer team and requested a practice match with his high school's junior varsity team. Soccer wasn't a popular sport in the United States then, so one of Damon's discoveries was that these immigrant students had amazing skills. But more than that, he recalls,[219] he was inspired by their gratitude for being in America—something foreign to his experience then:

> I'd never even thought about this. I was just assuming everything was easy in the world. These kids were refugees during the Hungarian Revolution and were saying things like, "My uncle got thrown in jail for carrying a sign."
>
> I remember they had sandwiches with green peppers and bacon fat. That was their lunch and these kids were so happy. They were much more joyful about their life than I or any of my friends. So I wrote this story for the school newspaper and predictably—probably—everyone went "Wow! This is really interesting."
>
> At that moment, something clicked: this could be a fun and useful thing to do—to find things out that can inform people about inspiring stuff. I think that stuck with me.[220]

We never know if or when pivotal moments of purpose like this will happen, and we should never underestimate the importance of this kind of diverse experience for young people because it can change their lives. This brief encounter with the immigrant students as the result of an extracurricular activity opened Damon's eyes to the world of cultural and historical understanding. Subsequently, he worked hard at school: "I was determined to learn the skills I needed to pursue this new purpose that I had discovered."[221]

When Stanford opened a Center on Adolescence, Damon applied and was hired as its inaugural director. His first visit to the center was memorable for what it said about adolescence research in the 1990s:

> The group there had decorated for my arrival and the decorations were posters lining the walls on both sides of the corridor.
>
> I walked down the gauntlet of these posters. One read something like, "Do you know that in the year 1998, 100,000 teenagers will kill another teenager?" Then the next one would say something like, "In the year 1998, 400,000 teenagers will become hopelessly addicted to some horrible substance like heroin." There was one about teenage pregnancy; one about kids flunking out of school.[222]

As we've discussed, the research on adolescence has had a bad-news bias. But Damon had forged a commitment to a focus on adolescents' assets, not their deficits, beginning right out of college when he served as an advisor to youth groups for the Bureau of Social Services in New York City and could see the potential in the young people he was working with. In fact, he went to graduate school "to make the case" that all young people have often-untapped potential—"a spark"—an approach that has coalesced under a Positive Youth Development framework (chapter 1) and the work of others, notably the Search Institute, which has been conducting and applying asset-based research for sixty years.[223]

Damon knew what he had to do right away when he got to Stanford:

I took down those posters.[224]

That was 1997. He's continued to shape the center accordingly ever since to focus on building strengths rather than looking at faults.

About two decades ago, he saw a convergence: that though his research has covered a wide range of topics, all of it was, in his words, "leading me to *one* master idea—the idea of purpose."

> *It's the idea that if people have a direction in life, IF they really have a sense of the kind of person they want to be—what they want to contribute to the world, what difference they want to make, what's important to them, and why it's important—that will give them energy in good times, resilience in bad times.*[225]

THE PATH TO PURPOSE IN ADOLESCENCE

Damon and his colleagues turned to study purpose, including conducting a national survey and interviews, to detect the patterns in the "path to purpose" (the title of his book) among twelve-to-twenty-two-year-olds.[226] They found four:

- **The disengaged:** young people who expressed no sense of purpose in their surveys or interviews. Some are apathetic; others are mainly focused on the here and now and are enjoying life.
- **The dreamers:** young people who have aspirations and dreams about their purpose but haven't done anything active to pursue those dreams.
- **The dabblers:** young people who've tried out purposeful activities but show no sustained signs of committing to these pursuits.
- **The purposeful:** young people who've found something meaningful to dedicate themselves to and sustain these interests; "they have a

clear sense of what they are trying to accomplish in the world and why."[227]

In the Path to Purpose study, one in five were purposeful, and at the other extreme, one in four were disengaged. Approximately another 25 percent were dreamers and 31 percent were dabblers. These percentages, of course, should be viewed as a moment in time. What these findings reveal is that meeting the Basic Need for purpose is a journey, not a destination.

Having a purpose isn't the same as having goals. Damon and his colleagues have worked hard to craft a clear definition of purpose:

Purpose is an enduring commitment to accomplish something that is meaningful to the self and of consequence to the world beyond the self.[228]

You can see that purpose is the answer to several questions: Why do I do what I do? Why does it matter? Why is it important to me and the world beyond me?

Thus, purpose over time:

- Involves having a far-reaching, long-lasting future-directed goal that provides **an overall sense of direction** in our lives
- Is a part of our search for personal meaning and is connected to what's **central in our identity**
- Is motivated by our **desire to make a positive difference** beyond ourselves
- Is directed at accomplishments **where we can make actual progress**

THE BENEFITS OF PURPOSE FOR ADULTS AND ADOLESCENTS

The benefits of having a sense of purpose in adolescence have been similarly studied, and the positives far outweigh the negatives, according to Heather Malin, a colleague of Bill Damon's at Stanford's Center on Adolescence.[229] Adolescents who have a greater sense of purpose are more likely to:

- Be in better health
- Be more optimistic about their futures
- Experience more positive emotions
- Be more engaged in school
- Have higher self-esteem

The one negative is that purposeful young people can be more stressed—perhaps because they use purpose as a way to manage adverse experiences, or perhaps because they have more going on in their lives.

Like Bill Damon, the path to purpose for Tony Burrow of Cornell University—another key leader in this field—wasn't a straight one. In college and graduate school, Burrow majored in developmental psychology, concentrating on issues of identity:

> *Over time, my mentors were like, "Tony, you don't have identity questions.*
> *You have purpose questions."*[230]

A number of Burrow's studies have investigated the benefits of purpose for adults, and they include experiencing fewer stress-related physical symptoms on stress-filled days[231] as well as improved financial well-being.[232]

In his studies of adolescents, Burrow classifies purpose as an asset for adolescents because it contributes to young people's "identity capital."[233] If you're more certain about who you are and where you want to go in life, you can interpret the good things and the bad things that happen to you in that light. It's like an investment (or a mindset) that enhances your life and protects you in rocky times.

In fact, Burrow told me, he has found that identity and purpose are tightly linked, even sequential:

> *Identity is an answer to the question of who you are; purpose is an answer*
> *to the question of where you are going. Purpose is more about what's*
> *ahead of you.*
> *You can't have a purpose fully until you know who you are.*[234]

It's clear to Burrow that purpose is a life aim, and as such, it affects the decisions we make:

> *Depending on their age or their linguistic toolkit, I may not go into a*
> *fifth-grade classroom and say, "What is your life aim?" I may ask that*
> *differently, but I'm really trying to get to the ultimate part of you that's*
> *organizing the other decisions you're making. That's getting really close to*
> *my sense of what we mean by purpose.*

Burrow finds that researchers haven't fully explored the extent to which the content of purpose matters. He and his colleagues cite studies showing that individuals with a sense of purpose are more likely to be healthy and have better well-being, "with overwhelming evidence signaling that when it comes to feeling purposeful, the more the better." "Yet," they write, "this compelling body of work has proceeded largely devoid of attention to purpose content."[235] Even the research that includes a focus on what types of purposes individuals pursue hasn't looked at whether different kinds of purposes relate to well-being; this calls for more research to better define it.

So, we know that purpose is notably important, but there's still much to learn.

UNDERSTANDING AND NOURISHING PURPOSE IN ADOLESCENCE

Like Ishaan, adolescents look for their "true self," and like Gigi, they want to "live this day and be who I am." They seek a sense of purpose in tandem with exploring their identity. They're very engaged with "this day"—the here and now—and also wondering about the future. Accordingly, I define purpose in adolescence as **a process of seeking,** an **exploration for a life aim** that:

- Is part of their search for **meaning** and what's central in their **identity**
- Gives them a sense of **direction**
- Is intrinsically **motivating**
- Is directed at their **future** but affects their goals and decisions **now**
- Is something they can **make progress** toward achieving
- Includes a commitment to something **beyond the self**

My daughter, Lara, has worked on purpose issues throughout her career and has repeatedly realized that there are a number of assumptions that stand in the way of seeking purpose.[236]

Here's how she puts it:

Assumption: Purpose is fixed.
   Finding: Purpose can change throughout your life.
Assumption: Happiness is more important than purpose.
   Finding: Purpose can bring happiness, but purpose can also come from a place of loss and challenge.
Assumption: Purpose must align with our careers.
   Finding: It can, but it doesn't have to.
Assumption: Purpose is a luxury.
   Finding: Everyone can have a purpose.

Assumption: You can only have one purpose.

   Finding: People can have one overarching purpose or more, and a purpose can have many different forms of expression.

Assumption: Purpose means creating social change.

   Finding: Purpose is beyond the self. That can mean creating social change, but it doesn't have to. It can mean contributing to the family or adding to knowledge, for example.

One assumption that my daughter, Tony Burrow, and I all find very disturbing is that adolescents should *find* their purpose. It's the wrong metaphor, Burrow says:

> The danger of saying "Find your purpose" is that it implies you have to
> find it, tell people about it, and never deviate.

Burrow has discovered through his studies that purpose is a "developmental process of exploration; it evolves and changes."

I worry about the term "find your purpose" because it can place inordinate pressure on young people—again, the weight of a future-focused culture—to have a clear map of their future. Furthermore, it implies that this is a solo act, which is both untrue and equally pressure-producing. As Larry Steinberg continues to point out, the plasticity of the brain during adolescence and into adulthood gives us biological time for pursuing interests that can lead to a sense of purpose.[237]

The Need to Contribute

Take a moment and think about these questions:

- What words best describe your family?
- What is most important to your family?
- What are your strengths as a family?
- What sayings best capture your family?

I've loved the idea of a family mission statement since I first read about it in Bruce Feiler's book *The Secrets of Happy Families*.[238] In arriving at this concept, Feiler was inspired by the wisdom of families and by management experts like Stephen Covey.[239] In his Happy Families Toolkit, he lists four family discussion questions (see above) that you can use to determine your family's core beliefs and create your own mission statement.[240]

It doesn't always take creating a mission statement, however, to think about our core parenting beliefs, something Ruth, mother of eighteen-year-old Emma, has been thinking about since before Emma was born. The first two of her beliefs—caring and connecting—draw on childhood values from her father:

> We call my father "the mayor" because wherever he goes, he talks to people.

Ruth's father didn't have a community growing up. His mother died when he was sixteen, and his father's new wife didn't want anything to do with the kids, so her father moved to an apartment as a late adolescent, where he took care of his younger sister. His father died soon afterward. Asking others about their stories, whether he's out shopping or with people he knows, Ruth says, became "his way of caring and connecting."

Ruth added curiosity to her other two values, drawing from her work in children's media: "When I think about writing for kids, the best stories are about characters that are curious, they care and they connect." Ruth wanted to instill those three values into Emma's life:

> I wanted her never to be afraid to ask questions. Everybody has a story, and it's okay to be curious about someone else's story because it's probably very different from your story.

Just before Ruth gave birth to Emma, her grandmother on her mother's side died:

> My grandmother's name was Ella and I named my daughter Emma after her. From the minute my daughter was born, Aunt G—my grandmother's sister—wanted to have this connection with her. We visited her every Friday at her residence facility. We fostered curiosity in Emma by asking Aunt G to tell us stories.

Ruth also wanted Emma to know the people at the residence facility where Aunt G lived, so they didn't just stay in her room during their visits.

Emma knew the people in the dining hall, the people at the front desk, the woman who cleaned my aunt's room. I think those kinds of experiences were really important so she could find her place in the world—and not be afraid of the world.

Emma, like her grandfather, treats interactions with people as opportunities to learn about them. She'd ask salespeople, "How was your holiday?" And, in keeping with their family values, curiosity, caring, and connecting led to contributing.

I use the word "contributing" intentionally. Ruth dislikes the term "giving back" or "charity" because it's a one-way street. By contributing, you both give and get.

Their family is Jewish, and one year, the California wildfires raged nearby during the High Holy Days. Their home was safe, but others were burning to the ground. At temple, their family heard stories about local firefighters working around the clock:

I'd made a brisket for the second night of Rosh Hashanah and we were going to have friends over, but Emma said, "Mom, why don't we give the firehouse our brisket because they're probably pretty hungry?" We sliced it up and brought it.

Initially Ruth suggested organizations where Emma might contribute. One was a working ranch for neurodiverse children. Emma helped the children there learn to take care of the animals:

Some of these kids had challenges socially. Through caring for the animals, they were able to come to understanding about compassion and connection.

As Emma grew up, she began taking the lead in finding her own ways to contribute. Through their temple, Emma heard about and got involved with Jewish World Watch:

It was an antigenocide organization and Emma realized that there were so many voices that weren't heard. She wanted to know their stories and make sure their voices were heard.

By promoting caring and connection through curiosity, Ruth helped Emma contribute in ways that strengthened herself and others.

Emma is not an anomaly. **Adolescents are primed to contribute**—and science confirms the importance of this Basic Need.

THE SCIENCE BEHIND CONTRIBUTING

Through his own research and also as the co-executive director of the Center for the Developing Adolescent, Andrew Fuligni of UCLA has concluded that the need to contribute has received much less attention than other psychological needs in adolescence. He attributes this, in part, to the fact that "teenagers get dismissed as supposedly selfish and irresponsible."[241] He sees the need to contribute as truly "fundamental."

Fuligni defines contributing as providing support, resources, or help toward a shared goal. In addition to being a need in its own right, this need builds on and promotes other Basic Needs, like autonomy, identity, caring connections, and purpose.[242] Fuligni says research shows that "one of the best ways to get a sense of purpose and meaning is through social contributions."[243]

Studies find that many adolescents are quite inclined to give something they value—like time or money—to someone else. According to Fuligni's review of experiments on contributing, adolescents are willing to give costly donations to friends between 50 and 75 percent of the time. They don't even have to know the person they're donating to—they'll donate to strangers at a loss to themselves between 30 and 50 percent of the time.[244]

Contributing doesn't only mean volunteering or donating money; it can be helping friends and family, as Emma did with Aunt G. When it comes to contributing to the family, other negative assumptions about adolescence kick in. Fuligni notes:

> There's been a belief in contemporary Western child development and developmental psychology that children should be protected—they shouldn't be asked to do too much and that helping the family might be a significant source of stress.[245]

That didn't ring true with what he and his colleagues were seeing in their study of over seven hundred adolescents from Asian, Latin American, and European backgrounds in the Los Angeles area. Led by Eva Telzer when she was a graduate student in Fuligni's lab, the team looked at how helping the family affected adolescents' well-being.[246] They asked adolescents to keep daily checklists reporting their events, activities, and moods for a fourteen-day period.

It turned out that helping the family wasn't uncommon: ninth graders helped their families on approximately 70 percent of the checklist days, averaging about an hour daily, with chores such as cleaning, cooking, and taking care of siblings being most frequent. While there were differences due to the students' background (Asian American and Latin American students helped more than European American students), there were no gender differences.

They also found that while helping the family did feel like a burden at times, students were happier on those days.[247] Fuligni says:

> *Helping conferred a sense of meaning and purpose that spilled over into positive well-being. It wasn't a huge effect, but it was very different than a lot of people would expect.*

That result, he said, "led us to start thinking—maybe we can see what this is doing in the developing adolescent brain."

In a follow-up study two years later, also led by Telzer, a small group of the same students played a donation game with real money in an fMRI scanner.[248] They were told they could win between $0 and $100 either for themselves or for their families. For each round of the game, students could either reject or accept the entire amount they were offered. There were four types of offers, as listed below (the dollar figures are examples, since the amounts varied):

Winning Rewards for Oneself	Making Donations to the Family
Noncostly: $2.00 for oneself, $0 for family	**Noncostly:** $0 for oneself, $2.00 for family
Costly: $2.00 for oneself, minus $1.00 for family	**Costly:** minus $1.00 for oneself, $2.00 for family

The researchers found that when adolescents made costly donations to their families, there were elevated levels of activation in the reward-related regions of their brains relative to a noncostly reward.

For adolescents who were more identified with their families and had reported being more fulfilled by helping them two years earlier, the activation in their reward-related regions was actually higher when they contributed to their family compared to gaining a reward for themselves.

The researchers found that this kind of decision-making isn't just engaging the reward-related regions of the brain.[249] Fuligni reports:

It's also engaging regions related to what is called mentalizing, which is thinking about the needs, wishes, and concerns of other people, and also to cognitive control-related regions.

We also saw functional connectivity between these regions. That was very compelling to us because it suggested a more mature level of processing.[250]

Studies find that adolescents and adults who contribute to others see increases in their physical and psychological health. There are also correlations with lower mortality rates, fewer health problems, and lower depression.[251]

Considering what a powerful force contributing is, are we providing enough opportunities for adolescents to contribute—for their benefit and for the benefit of their families, friends, and communities?

LAB ←→ LIFE: ENCOURAGING ADOLESCENTS TO ASK (THE "BIG") QUESTIONS: THE QUESTION PROJECT

When I discovered the QUESTion Project, I was intrigued. The notion of "quest" aligns with adolescents' drive to explore and QUEST becomes "question." Adolescents are full of questions—those they ask, and those they keep to themselves.

Would the QUESTion Project help bridge adolescents' inner and external worlds? Would it enable them to pursue their own questions?

When I spoke with Gerard Senehi, the creator of this project, he talked about how identity and purpose are typically addressed in education:

A lot of schools approach identity by nudging kids into labels and something static instead of creating the space for them to explore the unfolding of their identity.[252]

He feels the same about purpose, which can be reduced to asking young people what inspires them and nudging them toward a cause. Senehi wondered if there could be a structured process to help young people explore identity, purpose, and contributing together:

I took the approach of working two years with university and public high school students to identify the most important human questions—questions that can help students define who they are, make sense out of life, and give them a sense of direction and purpose.

He and his wife, Francesca Rusciani, set about creating a curriculum for university students including selecting an advisory board of respected figures. One day, as Senehi recalls, one of their advisors called, saying:

> *"I've arranged for you to go into a classroom in a public school in the Bronx tomorrow morning. You're going to do one session."*

It went so well that the principal of this high-performing school requested more, jumping at the opportunity to expand beyond "preparing students for college and career" to "preparing them for life."

As a result, Senehi and Rusciani, in an ongoing collaboration with public high school students, created eighty sessions—daily classes for a semester. They used a civic science approach, working in ongoing ways with the former students from the classes and the teachers to help them improve these lessons.

The QUESTion Project has served over twelve thousand high school students in public schools in New York City and Los Angeles. The curriculum consists of introductory sessions, five key overarching themes they call "pillars," and concluding sessions.

In the introduction classes, the students write a letter to themselves about what they want to get out of the class, which they seal and save until the end of the course. They also do a self-evaluation to chart their growth, and record their biggest questions. In the first pillar, students explore different aspects of who they are, with an emphasis on exploring the choice and agency they have to shape their own lives. Teachers are trained to support students not only to think about the topics covered but also to engage their humanity together. A student describes this:

> *I remember one day I had stated my opinion on a certain topic, and the teacher asked, "Why is that your opinion?" I was caught off guard. I embarrassingly responded with, "I don't know. I just do." The teacher didn't allow me to get away with such an answer and told me to look within myself and wonder what had led me to that opinion . . . No teacher has ever asked me to look within myself.*[253]

In the second pillar, Senehi says, "we aim for students to develop an authentic relationship to purpose."[254] In the third pillar, they bring in the concept of fearlessness as a way to strengthen the courage it takes for students to be themselves. In the fourth pillar, the students explore connectedness. In the fifth pillar, they consider how to look at their lives from a larger perspective and imagine the kind of society they want in the future. In the closing sessions, students reflect on the journey they've taken together and on some of their most important takeaways.

Senehi tells the story of talking to a group of students in California about the lessons learned from the class. One of the girls said that she had realized that she had been following a script, doing what she was supposed to do:

> But she also realized that *"I'm not supposed to know what life is about at this age. This is a time to explore and discover."*

Another student told him:

> It doesn't matter that I don't know **how** I'm going to have purpose in my life, but I now know I'm going to figure it out.[255]

I asked Senehi if there was pushback from parents that their children were having these deep discussions at school. He said there wasn't. Pushback comes, he feels, when adults try to impose a particular ideology— "leading kids to answers rather than creating the space for them to find answers."[256]

A 2022 evaluation of the QUESTion Project[257] validates this approach. This qualitative study of recent alumni, teachers, and principals, conducted by Heather Malin began with this question:

> How did we end up with a school system that purportedly prepares students for their future yet fails to support them in developing a sense of purpose for their lives?

The evaluation reveals that schools can provide this kind of support. Among the many benefits recent alumni reported are learning courage in the face of fear, becoming more open to the possibilities in their future, understanding that developing purpose is a process, feeling more responsible for their own choices, and becoming inspired to contribute to the world's improvement.

Edward Tom, the former principal of the Bronx Center for Science and Mathematics, where students take the QUESTion class, said his students used to be late to school, but now they're early because there's something at school that they can learn and give to others:

*That's a huge shift from some of the teenagers we're used to dealing
with—they come in and it's about receiving—about what you can give me.
I feel the kids who went through the QUESTion Project have shifted their
paradigm of thinking, and they begin asking themselves, "What can I give
others?"*[258]

FAMILY MISSION STATEMENTS

One Saturday morning, Bruce Feiler, his wife, and their children created
their mission statement together.[259] Gathering in their pajamas with popcorn,
s'mores, and a flip chart, they answered the questions about what they value
as a family and wrote their statement. It turned out to reflect much of what
adolescents need as part of their developmental journey:

- In writing "May our first word be adventure and our last word be
  love," their family acknowledged that the adolescent years are about
  exploring within their caring connections.
- In writing "We dream of lives of passion," they spoke to identity and
  purpose.
- And in writing "We help others to fly," they called out contributing.

What would your family's mission statement be?

MATCH AND MISMATCH IN THE BASIC NEED TO CONTRIBUTE

In our Breakthrough Years survey, we worded the questions about meeting
the need to contribute in a slightly different way than the wording for other
Basic Needs.
We asked:
How much do the following describe your parent(s) and family?

1. *Your parent(s) and family do things to help others.*
2. *You do things that help your parent(s) and family.*

We asked adolescents to what extent these statements described "us,"*
because we see contributing as being done either with or for others. We also

---

* Adolescents answered each question on a four-point scale from "does not describe us" to "describes
us very well." The answers for both questions were summed, resulting in the following groups: "not
us" (2–3), "kind of us" (4–6), "very much us" (7–8).

wanted the adolescents to reflect about their identity in answering these questions, which were posed regarding their family, their friends, the people at school, the people in their out-of-school activities, and the people they connect with online.

Perhaps because we experimented with different wording (we typically asked about how frequently needs were met), there are fewer adolescents who report that these statements sound "very much us," ranging from about two in five for family down to one in five for other relationships, except online, where it is one in ten.

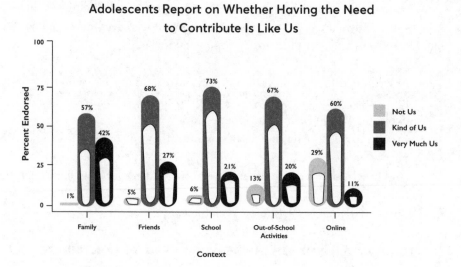

Adolescents Report on Whether Having the Need to Contribute Is Like Us

When the need to contribute was "very much us" prepandemic, adolescents were thriving in most of the outcomes we assessed during the pandemic. They reported being:

- More engaged in school
- More hopeful about their futures
- Experiencing more positive and fewer negative moods
- Having less stress

Interestingly, when their families meet the need for contributing, adolescents also report fewer conflicts.

Outcomes of Having the Need to Contribute Met

Contribute	Follow-Up Outcomes							
Context	School Engagement	Grades (A)	Grades (P)	Future	Negative Mood	Positive Mood	Stress	Conflict (A:P)
Family	↑			↑	↓	↑	↓	↓ :
Friends	↑	↑	↑	↑		↑	↓	:
School	↑	↑	↑	↑	↓	↑	↓	:
OSA	↑	↑		↑		↑	↓	:
Online		↑		↑		↑		:

A = adolescent report, P = parent report, OSA = out-of-school activities. Arrows indicate the direction of an association (i.e., up arrow for promoting, down arrow for protecting), controlling for demographics. When there is no statistically significant relationship between the need being met and the follow-up outcome, we leave the cell blank. Significant relations are p-values < .0005, which means these correlations are both very reliable and unlikely to have occurred by chance.

PROMOTING THE BASIC NEEDS FOR PURPOSE AND TO CONTRIBUTE

Rather than "finding purpose," it's useful to think of nourishing purpose in adolescence—of providing adolescents with experiences to explore and opportunities to find meaning. The research makes it clear that exploring purpose is a lifelong process and that this process doesn't happen alone; it happens in a dialogue with others. To promote the need for **purpose**, we can:

- Provide experiences that can open adolescents' eyes to new interests and new insights about life
- Remember that for adolescents, this is a time of exploration

Adolescents are primed to contribute—to give time, resources, and help to others in ways that benefit others and themselves. To promote the need to **contribute**, we can:

- Infuse opportunities to contribute into their everyday lives. It doesn't have to be volunteering—it can be sharing their thoughts in a class or helping their family or friends; it can be asking for or receiving help.

• Provide safe and welcoming opportunities for them to reflect by sharing their genuine questions of who they are, who they want to be, how they want to matter and contribute.

Rethinking Adolescence: From "How Are They Doing?" to "How Are We Doing?"

In December 2021, the surgeon general of the United States, Vivek Murthy, released an Advisory on Youth Mental Health,[260] where he wrote: "Mental health challenges in children, adolescents, and young adults are real and widespread. Even before the pandemic, an alarming number of young people struggled with feelings of helplessness, depression, and thoughts of suicide—and rates have increased over the past decade."[261] The 2023 release of data from the CDC's Youth Risk Behavior Survey shows that these worrisome trends continue to rise:

• In 2011, 28 percent of high school students reported experiencing persistent feelings of sadness or hopelessness. By 2021, 42 percent did (57 percent of females, 29 percent of males).[262]

These findings are scary, but equally scary to me were some of the public and private conversations about mental health issues that ensued.

In one community, for example, a group of educational leaders and I were discussing mental health challenges. These leaders felt they were on the road to solutions because they were conducting a survey of children on their sense of belonging and other social-emotional competencies at school.

"What are they going to do with the findings?" I asked.

"They'll know which kids to watch out for," one said.

"Are they going to rate kids on these?" I asked.

"Yes."

"So, kids are going to be graded on belonging as well as on English, math, and science?" That would be very troubling if belonging becomes one more thing for students to succeed or fail at.

It's crucially important to identify and support young people at risk. But if schools do assessments, they should also focus on the extent to which the classroom environment—the contexts children are in—helps children feel they belong, feel supported, and feel competent. The environment is crucial because the mental health issues noted above aren't happening solely because of a student's traits or skills. Students are part of peer groups, families, and communities. So at the meeting I said that if they do this survey, it would be important that the results not be used to grade children or their teachers but only to figure out what works and what can be improved.

And that's been the trouble with how we approach Basic Needs like belonging or competence. If we approach them through an individualistic lens, these needs are likely to be seen as residing in the individual, apart from the environment these individuals are in. It would be like judging children on how hungry they are, without looking at whether their environment provides access to food.

When we fail to understand the role of context in meeting needs, we are leaving this critical process up to chance, lucky coincidence, or happenstance:

- It was happenstance that researcher Jason Okonofua was sent to a private school where he could have his need for respect met and see, firsthand, what the lack or presence of respect can do for young people.
- It was happenstance the teenager who bullied Ishaan turned his life around and showed Ishaan that identity isn't fixed and unchangeable.
- It was happenstance that researcher William Damon was given an assignment to write a story for his high school newspaper on a Hungarian soccer team that led him on the path toward purpose.

Lucky coincidences like these do seem to shape our lives—but why not increase the odds with intention? If we recognize that adolescents have Basic Needs, we should provide opportunities for these needs to be met. If we find ways to systematically create and maintain those environments, we will have a lot more people like those you've met in these chapters who are thriving.

Let's rethink adolescence and move from seeing needs as just internal to seeing them as internal drives that need external opportunities— opportunities we can provide—to be fulfilled. Then, we will shift from asking "How are the kids doing?" to "How are we doing?"

5

MESSAGE 5: WE ARE DRAWN TO LEARN LIFE AND LEARNING SKILLS

Adolescents in the Breakthrough Years study wrote to tell us about *how* they're learning and want to learn.

They want us to know they're learners:

We like to learn.
—Sixteen-year-old boy

Give us more opportunities to learn.
—Seventeen-year-old boy

They learn from life—especially from us. Not just from what we say but importantly from what we do:

We are watching u.
—Thirteen-year-old boy

We can hear you when you think we're not listening.
—Ten-year-old girl

We do hear what you all are saying, but we also see how you are behaving.
—Fifteen-year-old girl

You have to help us learn the right way by showing us—not just telling us.
—Nine-year-old girl

They say they're exploring and want back-and-forth interactions about what they're learning:

That we think and need more exploration.
—Twelve-year-old boy

We need to try more new things.
    —Ten-year-old girl

We like to be interactive learners. We are often scared and overwhelmed by school and life.
    —Eleven-year-old boy

They want what they learn to be useful:

We don't use half the stuff we learn in school. Why do we have to keep taking these classes to graduate?
    —Fourteen-year-old boy

Help us learn in a way we understand. Ask us our opinion and LISTEN TO US PLEASE!!!
    —Thirteen-year-old girl

They want to learn to make decisions. Some say they want more guidance; others say they want less:

Let us be more independent and make our own decisions. We need to learn to find our own way.
    —Fifteen-year-old boy

Encourage us and help us, but let us think for ourselves.
    —Thirteen-year-old girl

We are just learning and need direction.
    —Twelve-year-old girl

They write of learning from making mistakes and from difficult experiences:

Learning takes time and failing is a part of it.
    —Seventeen-year-old girl

That we are people, learning, and sometimes we will mess up, but give us a chance, we are the leaders of the future
    —Seventeen-year-old boy

Learning, they say, is about the knowledge and the skills to live their lives:

We are a generation of very lucky people, but also one that is kind of lost in terms of what direction we should go in life.
     —Fourteen-year-old girl

The school system is outdated, they tell us what to do instead of helping us with our future.
     —Eleven-year-old boy

We see everything. It's okay to be sad and not to hide tears. Being brave means letting kids see how to live life. Even when daddy goes to live in heaven.
     —Ten-year-old girl

Breakthrough Years Study Finding: Twenty-seven percent of adolescents ask adults to help them learn useful things in the ways they learn best.

In this chapter, we'll look at a set of foundational skills—executive function skills—that are instrumental to school and life success. We'll then turn to another set of skills that are based on these foundational skills. I call them Life and Learning Skills because they're essential for living well, including setting and achieving goals, understanding the perspective of others, communicating and collaborating, problem-solving, and taking on challenges. These skills can help adolescents be the learners they want to be and get the most out of what they are learning.

In chapter 4, we saw that meeting adolescents' basic psychological needs is important to their well-being—in school and in their lives. So, how do needs and skills fit together?

A separate study conducted for the book gave us an opportunity to address this question. It was a study of problem-solving and executive functioning of 223 students in the sixth, ninth, and twelfth grades in twenty-two schools in six states across the United States.

Unlike our surveys, this study included behavioral measures where adolescents performed a series of cognitive assessments after completing an abbreviated questionnaire that roughly matched the baseline survey. The timed tasks included a general measure of executive function skills as well as measures of verbal fluency, cognitive flexibility, reflection, problem-solving/planning, and processing speed.

Overall, we found that students who had better cognitive skills *and* whose needs were met reported less perceived stress and better grades than those with less proficient skills and lower need satisfaction. So, we need both—environments that meet Basic Needs and opportunities to develop Life and Learning Skills.

Reflections on Message 5

Think about a time when you faced a challenging situation but felt you handled it well. What skill did you use, and how did it help you?

I think we need to see the importance of skills in our own lives before we can fully understand this from our children's vantage point. Here are a few of the stories I've heard in my talks to adults.

A mother **reflects** on what she wants her son to learn from being sent to the principal's office and then **uses all of the self-control she can muster** to let her son advocate for himself:

When I picked up my son from school on Friday, he told me he was sent to the middle school principal's office because he was accused of something he didn't do. The principal! That's a big deal. My son was confused about why it happened and really upset. My temptation was to become a momma bear and call the teacher. It took all the control I could gather not to do that. In looking at this from my son's viewpoint, I could see that he was feeling disempowered by what happened. If I called the teacher, I would disempower him more. I wanted him to learn self-advocacy, so I asked him questions about how he wanted to handle it. He decided to write the teacher a letter saying he was confused. The teacher ended up believing him, but even if she hadn't, he would have been doing the hard work himself—I wouldn't be doing it for him.

A graphic designer has learned to **think flexibly:**

I've learned that when I get stuck with a project, I need to step back and stop trying to solve it. When I can take lots of small pieces of paper and try out different ideas, when I can let myself explore possibilities, I can usually come up with a solution to the design problem.

Using what you know became the route for a parent faced with eldercare challenges:

I was facing a family problem taking care of a parent who is getting old and my solution became to enroll people to help me. I asked my brother to take turns with me, I asked another friend to help me with a budget, and another friend to help restructure the space. I found someone in the community who we could pay to help a little, too. I realized that that's how life works. No one does anything alone but most people, including myself, are really bad at asking for help. I found that if I didn't ask for too much, most people were honored to be asked.

Wondering became a way to make a threatening work situation more manageable:

I used to leave meetings and say to myself "they just don't get it" about whatever I was trying to communicate. It was always someone else's fault. I realized that I was talking without listening. Now I've learned to ask questions—authentic questions—that are in search of real answers. Since I began doing this, I'm not saying "they don't get it" as much.

Whether we're having trouble communicating, are dealing with eldercare, feel stuck in a work project, or are coping with a child sent to the principal's office, we need skills we can call forth and count on. And if you're like most of the adults we talked with, you probably learned your most valuable skills by trial and error as a grown-up. Just think how empowering it would be if we learned and practiced Life and Learning Skills like these in a more intentional way while growing up.

Foundational Executive Function Skills

While people may know that belonging, identity, and competence are important—but just not see them as basic psychological needs—I find there's even less awareness about the science behind foundational executive function skills and the Life and Learning Skills based on them.

Philip David Zelazo of the University of Minnesota, who was featured earlier, says that executive function skills are best seen as a "broad umbrella concept," because they're defined behaviorally in terms of what people do.[1] These "top-down neurocognitive processes"[2] involve managing emotions, thoughts, and behavior to achieve goals.[3] They call on the cognitive control parts of the brain, including the prefrontal cortex, which we've talked about frequently.

Zelazo elaborates on the importance of executive function skills:

Executive function skills provide a foundation for learning deliberately
and for adapting to life's challenges. Whenever we want to do something
deliberately—we want to pursue a goal—we need to rely on these attention
regulation skills. In fact, I would say, everything that we want to do deliber-
ately and intentionally requires executive function skills for success.[4]

WHAT'S UNDER THE "UMBRELLA"? THE FOUR COMPONENTS OF FOUNDATIONAL EXECUTIVE FUNCTION SKILLS

If I continue with Zelazo's analogy, the umbrella itself would be **focus**, because executive function skills are attention-regulation skills.[5] When we're trying to achieve a goal or solve a problem, we need to focus attention on it, just as when we're out in a storm, the umbrella has to be open to keep us dry.[6]

Under the umbrella are four component skills: **cognitive flexibility, working memory, inhibitory control**, and **reflection**. These skills enable us to:

- **Think flexibly:** Consider alternative perspectives in response to changing circumstances (cognitive flexibility)
- **Use what you know:** Keep information in mind so it can be used (working memory)
- **Use self-control:** Resist automatic and impulsive behaviors (inhibitory control) so you can engage in goal-directed reasoning and problem-solving and persist in reaching goals[7]
- **Reflect:** Notice challenges, pause, step back, consider options, and put things into context before responding (reflection)[8]

These four component skills are the building blocks of the Life and Learning Skills we'll discuss later.

EXECUTIVE FUNCTION SKILLS ARE PREDICTIVE OF SUCCESS

Increasing attention has been paid to the foundational executive function skills because studies across many disciplines show that people with better executive function skills are more likely to succeed in almost every way.

Adele Diamond and Daphne Ling of the University of British Columbia have reviewed the impact of having these foundational executive function skills across studies that met strict criteria for scientific rigor. Here—in their words—is a summary of the findings:

> *EFs are predictive of achievement, health, wealth, and quality of life throughout life, often more so than IQ or socioeconomic status. They are more critical for school readiness than IQ or entry-level reading or math. They are predictive of success throughout the school years from preschool through university (often more so than IQ).*
>
> *The importance of strong EFs does not stop in childhood. There is abundant evidence that EFs are crucial for success in getting and keeping a job as well as career advancement, making and keeping friends, marital harmony, staying out of jail and resisting substance abuse. Adults with better EFs also report they are happier and have a better quality of life.*[9]

EARLY CHILDHOOD AND ADOLESCENCE—PRIME TIMES FOR THE DEVELOPMENT OF EF SKILLS

Children aren't born with executive function skills, but they are born with the capacity to learn them. As the Harvard Center on the Developing Child says, genes provide blueprints, but the environments children are in leave lasting signatures on those blueprints.[10]

Executive function skills grow rapidly in the early childhood and adolescent years. The Harvard Center points out that the development of EF skills corresponds to the development of the prefrontal cortex. In the early years, this development is formative, "as relevant circuits emerge, mature, and forge critical interconnections." In adolescence and early adulthood, these "circuits are then refined and made more efficient."[11]

Two major changes in the brain during the adolescent years explain why adolescence is a prime time for the development of these foundational skills. First, the prefrontal regions—regions central to executive function—develop significantly. Second, there's improved connectivity within and between the outer cortical regions (areas linked to cognitive control) and inner cortical regions (areas linked to emotional responses, rewards, and learning).[12]

Executive function skills improve rapidly in adolescence, and on emotionally "sunny" days, according to Jennifer Silvers at UCLA, adolescents can use these skills as well as adults or even outperform them. But on emotionally "stormy" days, it can be a different story. Silvers compares the developing connections between the prefrontal and subcortical regions to newly paved roads. When a storm of strong emotion comes in, the cement can get wet and things can get messy.

Notice that I use the word "can." In fact, adolescence is a critical time for gaining these skills, which can buffer adolescents against difficulties throughout their lives.[13]

LEARNING TO THINK FLEXIBLY: COGNITIVE FLEXIBILITY

Jack, now seventeen, describes his childhood self as being intrigued by newness while holding tightly to sameness. He told me:

I've always been curious about things, but when I was younger, I was opposed to any change. It was just something I couldn't cope with.

Newness could set him off:

At six or seven, if my mom painted the front door a different color, I'd pitch a fit. It would be days of me trying to not talk to her, which didn't work because she was my mom and I'm six. I struggled with "going with the flow" and grasping change in any area of my life.

Despite his wish to keep things constant, things kept changing. When he was in elementary school, his parents divorced, leading to more changes in his family life. Eventually, he reached what he sees as a tipping point:

I realized pushing back was making everything more difficult for me and the people around me.

He began telling himself, "I'm just going to go with it—just one time." It didn't always work, but he kept trying: "I'm going to go with it one more time." Gradually, he realized he could begin to loosen up.

One step at a time is a sophisticated strategy, requiring the cognitive flexibility to venture into the unknown. Jack saw the move out of his childhood home at age thirteen as a test:

> *I'd lived there since I was three. I was so connected to my toys, my old things. But I was finally at a place where I made myself let it all go. I gave away stuff, we sold stuff, and I cut a lot of the emotional attachment to the things around me. As life moves on, you can't hold on to everything. That move and getting rid of my old stuff helped me start fresh.*

He gave away more than his mother expected because he realized that even if he parted with these childhood possessions, they didn't go away:

> *It's not like I forgot about that house or those memories. I still have them, built into who I am. I can let things come and go, and I'll have more space to grow.*

I asked Jack what helped him become more flexible. He told me it was realizing he had to learn to get along with the new people in his parents' lives.

> *My mom has a long-term boyfriend. I refer to him as my stepdad. My dad remarried and had a baby with his new wife.*

He said he was a genuine "a-hole" to his stepdad for years, doing things like trying to pit his mother against his stepdad or poking at him, but his stepdad didn't usually fall into those traps; he kept inviting Jack to do things together:

> *He continued reaching out, even when I continued saying no. I'm so, so grateful he did that.*

Eventually, Jack came to terms with the fact that "I can't pretend this is a temporary thing. When somebody's living in your home, you have to learn to work with and live with them."

In retrospect, Jack feels that all four of his parents took a helpful approach. They made him aware of the issue, telling him when he pitched a fit, "You don't like things to change. We understand that." But they also made it clear that he was holding *himself* back: "You can figure it out," he recalls his mother saying.

This is the essence of the autonomy-supportive approach we've been discussing: adults don't try to resolve things for children, but rather engage children in learning to come up with their own solutions, as they are developmentally able to do so. That promotes practice in thinking flexibly and other executive function skills. Bonus: when adolescents have a say in solving problems for themselves, they're more likely to work hard at their resolutions and stick with them!

Working to figure it out has helped shape Jack into the person he is today. As Erasmus University neuroscientist Eveline Crone notes, cognitive flexibility helps us learn to adapt to a changing world.[14] Jack says he's become more capable of thinking on his feet, a skill he's especially needed in the jobs he's had. What was a liability is becoming an asset!

USE WHAT YOU KNOW: WORKING MEMORY

Working memory is defined as holding information in our minds while we work with it in trying to solve a problem or make plans to reach a goal. We rely on working memory for everything from tackling a global crisis to making our breakfast.

As a student leader working toward responsible gun use, Marco has a lot to keep track of. This issue is "very personal" for him:

As a child, I did undergo a domestic violence incident where my biological father was an irresponsible gun owner and he used that for several years to traumatize my family.

Eventually, with the help of other family members and law enforcement, Marco's family physically escaped his father, but there was no escaping the psychological effects, which Marco says have shaped his life.

In high school, there was an incident of gun violence at his school. Some of his classmates turned to Students Demand Action, a grassroots organization of student leaders—high school through college—working to promote responsible gun use. Marco's SAT tutor suggested that he might like to attend a meeting to "see what this organization is about." Marco says:

I realized there was a movement that could provide support for someone like me and I could help other potential survivors.

Marco joined and ultimately founded a leadership academy on gun safety in his city. He sometimes finds his schedule overwhelming; it includes school, homework, and his involvement in Students Demand Action. Keeping track of everything is beyond what he can keep in his mind all at once—Eveline Crone refers to this phenomenon as "out of sight, out of mind"[15]—so he uses his working memory in a proactive way to write to-do lists. These lists then scaffold and support his memory so he doesn't get overwhelmed.

> *I leverage a number of tools and technology, including a paper agenda where I write down my to-do lists daily and check off things when they're done. I think that really helps.*

Given all of the information surrounding us in our daily lives, how do we improve our memory skills? Daniel Willingham of the University of Virginia, a leading memory researcher, uses the catchy phrase "memory is as thinking does." This means that what becomes "stored in memory is quite specific to what you think about when you encounter the material."[16]

To illustrate, he shares a classic 1969 experiment by Thomas Hyde and James Jenkins[17] where students listened to a list of words, one word every two seconds. One group of students was asked to rate whether the word made them think of pleasant or unpleasant things; another group was asked to count the number of times the letter *E* appeared in the word. If you think about how unpleasant or pleasant the word "garbage" is, you're more likely to remember the word later than if you think about how many *E*s it has. When asked to give advice to students about improving their recall, Willingham says, focus on the meaning of what you're trying to remember.[18] The late Kurt Fisher of Harvard University also made the crucial point that we remember what we care about:

> *One of the most beneficial things that brain research has done is—it's made it very hard for us to split cognition from emotion. For example, the areas of the brain most involved in memory—the quintessential cognitive function—are strongly tied to the emotion areas.*[19]

USE SELF-CONTROL: INHIBITORY CONTROL

"Stopping in time" is the clever way Eveline Crone describes inhibitory control.[20] We've been talking about this skill throughout the book because it's the basis for saying no to temptation, delaying gratification, and resisting distractions.

This is the skill that Sarah, a junior in high school, finds herself needing, especially as she manages the demands of being a competitive athlete in track along with the demands of the rest of her life. To maintain her motivation, Sarah sets goals. At first, it was to make the team in high school, then to compete in different meets; now it's running in the nationals and eventually making a college team.

"Sometimes," Sarah says, "you don't realize a goal is within reach until you get a little closer. Maybe winning nationals doesn't seem possible for me right now, but sometime in the future I might realize that it's a possibility for me."

There have been many obstacles in her path toward the finish line, and Sarah has to use self-control to keep going. During the school year, she finds herself saying no to hanging out with her friends because she has to rest, practice, or participate in a meet.

During summer, when there are no races and she sees less of her teammates, she finds "it's hard to run on my own—to stick to the plan." In response, she tries to hold her goals for later in the season in mind. She tells herself, "I'll be running with my teammates soon. They're counting on me to put in the work now." This is an example of how her working memory interacts with her inhibitory control to help her achieve her goals.

Having the social support of her friends and teammates also helps her keep up her training regime. So does reframing setbacks: "If I run a bad race, I might be upset," she says. But she's realized that the best way to cope is to try to learn from these experiences: "Maybe I went out too fast or didn't save enough energy." It also helps to remember her long-term goals:

> There's been moments where I just feel like I can't do this anymore. But I just have to remind myself that there'll be moments when I'll feel better—this is just a low point. I remind myself that this is what I'm working toward and this is what I want.

REFLECT

Reflection refers to slowing down, pausing, stepping back to notice challenges, considering options, and putting things into perspective before responding.[21] It involves thinking about—monitoring, if you will—your own thinking. Zelazo sees reflection as intentional attention.[22]

Although I think reflection should be seen as a foundational executive function skill, it isn't typically viewed that way, possibly because it calls on the brain's default mode network (DMN), centered in the midline and inferior parietal regions, not the cognitive control network. The DMN supports internally directed or self-generated thought such as reflection, future thinking, perspective-taking, mind-wandering, and more abstract thought.

To make executive functions work, we need to monitor them, to learn from our mistakes, and often to pause before we try to use self-control. That's where reflection comes in. As we reflect, we toggle between networks. Mary Helen Immordino-Yang of the University of Southern California describes this process like a ball game. There's **in-play**, when you're in the midst of a ball game, thinking on your feet about achieving your goal of winning (that's the more outward-facing executive control network), and **out-play**, which is like a time-out—a brief pause when you're reflecting on strategies to try when the game starts again (that's the more inward-facing default mode network).[23]

Pursuing goals can be hard and requires reflection. Sarah finds she needs breaks so she can refresh her stamina. Marco finds he needs step-back times to remember why he's working so hard as an activist. He has moments of doubt when he wonders if it's worth it, but he finds that if he takes his moments of doubt seriously and takes breaks, he can remind himself of what he wants the future to look like.

WHAT ARE (AND AREN'T) EXECUTIVE FUNCTION SKILLS?

I've had a lot of experience talking about foundational executive function skills and the Life and Learning Skills based on them because they've been central to my work for the past two decades. So, I'll ask you the questions I usually ask the audience when I speak:

Have you heard about executive function skills?

In some groups, a lot of people have heard of them; in others, fewer have.

If you've heard of them, what are they?

I hear confusion in the replies, including some definitions that are sort of but not quite right.

- A top official in the Department of Education called them noncognitive or soft skills. Lots of people say that.
- A large group of parents at an event hosted by a school district said that executive function skills are all about kids being quiet, sitting still, and listening to what teachers say.
- A corporate colleague said that executive function skills sound like an executive in a pinstriped suit bossing you around in your brain.

We've talked about how EF skills are "top-down neurocognitive processes"[24] that involve managing emotions, thoughts, and behavior to achieve goals.[25] So here's why the definitions I hear frequently are a little off.

First, EF skills are not noncognitive or soft skills. That's probably said because they differ from academic content, like English or math or science. EF skills are mostly centered in the cognitive control parts of the brain, including the prefrontal cortex. It's better to think of them as neurocognitive skills that pull together our cognitive, social, and emotional capacities to achieve goals.

Second, executive function skills aren't just compliance skills (be quiet, sit still, listen to the teacher). In a 2016 report for the Department of Education, Zelazo, Clancy Blair of New York University, and Michael Willoughby of the Research Triangle Institute write:

Executive function (EF) skills are the attention-regulation skills that make it possible to sustain attention, keep goals and information in mind, refrain from responding immediately, resist distraction, tolerate frustration, consider the consequences of different behaviors, reflect on past experiences, and plan for the future.[26]

You can see that these skills are central to learning in school and learning in general. They do matter when we are trying to sit still and listen (sustaining attention, resisting distractions, tolerating frustration), but they are so much more. For example, think about keeping goals and information in our minds, refraining from responding immediately, considering the consequences of different behaviors, reflecting on past experiences, and planning for the future. Interestingly, too, we often learn these skills from physical activity, not from sitting still.

As for the analogy of an executive in a pinstriped suit bossing you around in your brain, that's not so bad, though "bossing" isn't right—*you* are in the driver's seat, coordinating what you think, feel, and do to meet a goal. A better analogy, coined by the Harvard Center on the Developing Child and the Frameworks Institute, is that of an air traffic controller at a busy airport, managing the arrivals and departures of dozens of planes on multiple runways.[27] They use this analogy because foundational executive function skills enable us to "focus on multiple streams of information at the same time, monitor errors, make decisions in light of available information, revise plans as necessary, and resist the urge to let frustration lead to hasty actions." Others use the analogy of an orchestra conductor, which is also a good description.[28]

IMPROVING FOUNDATIONAL EXECUTIVE FUNCTION SKILLS

Adele Diamond cautions that foundational executive function skills take practice. To promote the skill of **thinking flexibly (cognitive flexibility)**, we can:

- **Provide constructive feedback.** Jack's parents were wise in telling him how his behavior was hurting him. We can say, "You have a choice in how you respond to change. If you fight against it, it can make things harder for you than if you find a way to manage it." Eveline Crone writes: "It appears that adolescents' brains are more attuned to encouragement and confirmation and less well equipped to deal with punishment and rejection,"[29] so presenting this feedback in constructive ways is key.
- **Share perspectives.** We can help young people think flexibly when they hear an alternative perspective on a situation and/or how a variety of different people would handle it.
- **Notice when adolescents manage change well.** When we see our children being flexible, we can call attention to it: "You couldn't get together with Zach today and I know how disappointed you were, but you bounced back when you made another plan." This noticing is a form of process praise and helps children think more intentionally about why this skill matters and how they can improve it.

As they note in their book with writer Peter Brown titled *Make It Stick*, researchers Henry Roediger and Mark McDaniel of Washington

University in St. Louis have found that remembering is an acquired skill, and that some of the most effective strategies are counterintuitive.[30] We can use some of their lessons to promote using what you know (**working and longer-term memory**) by helping adolescents learn to:

- **Make an effort.** People aren't necessarily good judges of what they'll remember. They may think that if they don't have to put much effort into remembering something, it'll stick. Not necessarily so. Memories tend to be more durable if we're learning something that's hard and if we put more effort into remembering.
- **Quiz themselves.** Rereading text and underlining passages from that text are the most frequent ways people try to remember, but they're among the least effective. It is more effective to put the text aside and repeat what they've learned to themselves.
- **Space out practice times.** Cramming isn't very effective either; spacing out practice is. We can help our children create schedules that provide space in between practice times.
- **Use different approaches to remembering.** There's no such thing as a one-and-only "learning style." Learning through a combination of approaches—not just learning visually, for instance—creates more durable memories.
- **Get to the essence.** We can help our kids try to identify the general principle from what they're learning and apply it to how they can use this knowledge in the future.
- **Make connections.** Intentionally connecting something they're learning to something they already know is a useful strategy.
- **Teach others.** Telling others about what they've learned is a very useful strategy for "making it stick." So be available for discussions about what your children are learning.

We can promote **self-control (inhibitory control)** in our adolescents when we:

- **Stay goal-focused.** Ensure that adolescents think about their own goals. Sarah says, "My life would be weird if I didn't have running in it." Not all adolescents will be as dedicated as Sarah is, but their lives would be better if they could think about what *they* care about, what *they* want to achieve. That's the foundation on which using self-control is built.

- **Reframe setbacks.** Help them see setbacks as necessary steps in reaching goals.
- **Help them make plans for overcoming obstacles.** It's easier for adolescents to say no or yes if they've thought about scenarios in advance and what they're going to do about them: "IF a party gets too wild for me, THEN I am going to find a safe way to get home."
- **Ensure that there is support.** We can do what's hard when we're around people who help us. That's true for young people, too. Encourage relationships that help adolescents reach their goals. It's much easier to resist temptation and distraction with the support of others.

We can promote **reflection** when we:

- **Make reflection an everyday practice for young people.** Daniel Siegel, author of *Brainstorm*, uses the phrase "time-in," which he defines as a time to focus on one's inner subjective experience—the "life of our own mind."[31] He suggests taking a minute a day, ten minutes a day, or a few minutes throughout the day for time-in.
- **Don't answer their questions right away.** Give young people a chance to answer their own questions—they'll learn more that way.
- **Invite adolescents to think about what they've learned when they make a mistake.** Rather than telling young people what you think of as the right answer, you can invite them to figure out what went wrong and how they might do things differently next time.
- **Help them pause if they're angry or upset.** It may sound like a cliché, but helping young people learn to step back by taking deep breaths or counting to ten really is effective. Pausing before acting is essential to managing our emotions, resisting distraction, turning away from temptation, and not going on autopilot.

Life and Learning Skill 1: Setting Goals

Setting goals involves thinking about your future, then motivating your-self to make achievable plans to turn this future into reality.

Michele Borba writes in her must-read book *Thrivers* that we're raising a generation of strivers, not thrivers:

> *We've told them that if they strive for more—more likes, better grades, more accolades—they'd be happy. But these young Strivers aren't happy . . . and what's more they aren't thriving.*[32]

Like Borba, learning and thriving are the goals I seek. I see the answers in meeting Basic Needs *and* in promoting Life and Learning Skills—skills based on foundational executive functions, skills that, in study after study, are linked to life success, to thriving; skills that we can learn ourselves and promote in our kids.

EF skills involve managing emotions, thoughts, and behavior to achieve goals. So by its very nature, setting goals is a Life and Learning Skill that calls on the component executive function skills. When you set and work toward goals, you need to:

- Use what you know to explore your dreams and desires—what do you really want to accomplish (**working memory**)
- Figure out whether the goals you have are realistic and how they can be achieved (**reflection**)
- Think flexibly and respond to changing circumstances as you pursue goals (**cognitive flexibility**)
- Stay the course, resisting temptations and distractions and addressing obstacles (**inhibitory control**)

GOALS, THEN STRATEGIES

The uneasy dread of Sunday evenings was in the air—when the week ahead, with its unrelenting to-do list, reared up.

Zoey was at her mother's kitchen table with her son Asa. "It's time to go home," she told him. "We need to leave so we don't get caught in traffic."

"Five more minutes," her ten-year-old responded, not looking up. He was playing a game on his grandmother's phone, fingers flying, probably steering an avatar through a dangerous obstacle course.

"It's always five more minutes. Then five more minutes. We *have* to go."

From the moment Asa first held a phone in his hand about seven years ago (given to him during an interminable plane ride), Zoey says, he was transfixed and she was worried. She hated hearing him beg: "phone, phone." "Cell phone executives won't let their own kids use them," she told her mother. "Why should I let them ruin my child?"

The more Zoey hated her son playing games on other people's phones, the more Asa wanted to. She knew technology was a lifeline to friends and school during the pandemic, but she worried about the overall impact of playing these games.

So she tried what other parents try. Parental control apps on electronics. No screen time on weekdays except for homework and limited amounts on weekends. Staying busy with outdoor adventures. She found a teenager to teach him Java so he could create his own Minecraft characters. She found an online class in video-making and he began making clever live-action videos and animations. Being a media creator was better than being a passive consumer—but still she worried.

On this Sunday, the more heated Zoey became, the more Asa retreated, ignoring her—fingers racing as his avatars fled danger, like fleeing a mother trying to wrest him from his fantasy world.

Zoey slumped down, head in hands. "I never thought it would be like this," she told her mother. "I don't see my friends in constant wars about screen time. This is just too hard." She knew things had to change.

She had access to Mind in the Making training and had tried WOOP there, a tool for creating change developed by Gabriele Oettingen of New York University and the University of Hamburg, but she hadn't stuck with it. The fear that technology was harming her son's brain overrode all. She had to figure out if that fear was real and why it bothered her so much:

I have a deeply held belief that the type of media he likes, and his relationship to it, isn't healthy or good for him. I don't appreciate this kind of media because I didn't grow up with it. I also know these things are built to connect to a part of our brain that requires automatic reactions—

dopamine hits—and that's addicting. It's part of the gamification of
everything, which doesn't encourage pleasure in the process but reduces
everything to winning.

Zoey veered between wanting to give up and sticking to her beliefs. "What if I just gave him limitless access?" she wondered at one point. "Would he get sick of it?" But "I might be feeding the beast. I can't risk it."

That Sunday night ended with Zoey yanking the phone away, something she didn't want to do because she was trying to teach Asa to give it up himself. Asa pitched a fit.

More battles followed.

Zoey began to realize that something stronger was blocking her forward movement on this issue—and it, too, was media-influenced: her own expectations of idyllic parenting. Those TV ads showing kids and parents gazing into each other's eyes . . . she'd had that, but it seemed more marred since the phone had entered their lives. Or the ads showing cheeky-but-nice kids and their parents at the dinner table enjoying mac and cheese and conversation. And in real life, she saw that children Asa's age did gaming, but handed over the phone or the iPad without a fit when their parents said "time's up."

Zoey wondered: "Are my parenting expectations realistic?"

I've found for years that expectations stand between us and becoming the parents and people we want to be.[33] We may not even be aware of them—but if we're feeling stuck, sad, disappointed, angry, even depressed, often there's a hidden expectation, and shining a light on it can open up the process of change.

With a friend, Zoey decided to retry the WOOP technique.

WOOP is an acronym (Wish, Outcome, Obstacle, Plan). It's an evidence-based tool for turning **dreams about the future into doing** and is the result of more than two decades of research by Gabriele Oettingen and her colleagues. We use WOOP in our Mind in the Making training because we've found that it's one of the best distillations of research on the first Life and Learning Skill: setting goals.

RETHINKING POSITIVE THINKING

Gabriele Oettingen's latest book is *Rethinking Positive Thinking: Inside the New Science of Motivation.*[34] Oettingen's work is rooted in a question that emerged during her growing-up years in Germany after World War II:

I was interested in hope and what strategies—what way of thinking—is responsible for people to live a constructive life.[35]

To her surprise, Oettingen found that having positive thoughts and fantasies about a desired future, like weight loss, grades, or hip replacement recovery, led to less positive outcomes for people who were trying to achieve that desired future.[36] Why? As Oettingen has observed in her experimental work, energy is needed to fulfill wishes, but people who focus on positive thoughts about the future relax instead. How, then, might we seek to make wishes come true? That led to the four-step process that ultimately became WOOP.

STEP ONE: MAKE A WISH THAT'S DEAR TO YOUR HEART

Generating a wish differs from setting a goal. Fantasizing about wishes is a powerful form of **exploring**. As we know, exploring is a gateway to learning for adolescents—in fact, for all of us.[37] Wishes can then be refined into goals.

A wish engages both our **social-emotional and cognitive** capacities. As we've discussed, uniting these capacities is the most powerful engine for change we have.

Finally, Oettingen says that generating a wish *you* really want to come true "reflects a need": either a physiological need, like the need for food, shelter, water, and/or the kind of basic psychological needs we've been talking about in this book, like the need to belong, to feel competent, and to have autonomy and meaning or purpose in life.[38]

1. **Does your wish fulfill a need?**
   Needs are motivating, so if you are trying this research-based strategy for behavior change as an adult, ask yourself what wish you have that is dear to your heart. That will put you in touch with your unfulfilled needs.[39] When Zoey retried WOOP, her initial wish was that parenting would be easy. The need behind that wish was to be respected by her son.

2. **Is your wish based on an expectation—and if so, is this expectation realistic?**
   I've added this aspect to the WOOP process. In implementing WOOP, we've found expectations can be like a rug you trip on. It's best to step back, uncover the expectation, and ask if it's realistic.

Parental growth comes from reconciling expectations with reality in one of two ways:[40]

- **If it's a realistic expectation, then change yourself to live up to it.**
  For example, "I don't want to talk to my children the way my parents talked to me" is a realistic expectation. Yet some parents hear themselves repeating words they resented when they were children. Parental growth comes from finding ways to pause in the heat of the moment and think about what we want to communicate, and then using more supportive words.
- **If it's an unrealistic expectation, then change the expectation to better fit with reality.**
  An example is "Most working parents don't struggle with routines like getting everyone ready for school and work on time. I am the only one." Here, parental growth comes from saying, "That's unrealistic. Transitions can be hard," and then dealing with the problem without the overlay of an unrealistic expectation triggering negative feelings.

Zoey's expectation was both unrealistic and realistic. When friends posted images on social media of picture-perfect children loving their homework, she knew that wasn't the whole story, but she still wrestled with thoughts like, "I bet that child's too busy doing math to pitch fits about playing games on the phone."

Zoey could see that most parents have moments of difficulty—if not with screen time, then with something else. She decided to revise her image of conflict-free parenting because it was causing anguish that wasn't helpful. So every time that expectation reared up, she vowed to pause and remind herself that growth only comes from dealing with challenges.

Through this process, Zoey's second try at a wish was: "I wish Asa would listen to me."

3. **Is your wish about something *you* have control over?**
   There was still some fine-tuning for Zoey to do. The main problem with her wish is that for WOOP to be effective, the wish has to be something *we* can control. We can't control what others think and feel; we can only control our own reactions. We can't make others listen; we can only create an environment where listening to each other becomes more possible.

Shawn Bryant of YesToECE, and a Mind in the Making trainer who uses WOOP in daily life, described a similar challenge. During the pandemic, his four nephews—thirteen-year-old twins, a sixteen-year-old, and an eighteen-year-old—stayed with him on weekdays because he worked at home and could oversee them, while his brother had to leave home for work.

"The teenagers," as he calls them, left Shawn's kitchen a mess. "There were always dishes in the sink."[41] He'd been nagging them—"clean up, clean up"—but that wasn't working.

So he tried WOOP.

"At the heart of WOOP," he says, "is to take action yourself and promote action in others." He felt this could happen if he became a role model for cleaning up:

Literally, my wish was to model washing the dishes after cooking.

He also determined that he could create an environment that promoted cleaning up:

My plan was to put an attractive sign over the sink about how nice it is to wash the dishes for the next person.

He saw this approach as more promising than nagging:

Without modeling it, demonstrating it, embodying it, it was just talk.

As his nephews began doing the dishes regularly, Shawn would take a photo of the clean sink and text it to them all as a thank-you. To encourage taking turns, he tried the following language:

"You know what? I did the dishes yesterday, on Tuesday. Can someone volunteer to do the dishes today for all of us to keep the kitchen clean?" In the beginning, I'd get silence. Then I said, "I think if we all pick a day, it'll work really well and no one will feel like, 'Oh, I'm doing the dinner dishes every day.'"

That worked better, he says. "There's only one who really doesn't like doing dishes. He kind of rinses them and puts them in the dishwasher, but I'm fine with that because they're not in the sink."

By changing himself and the environment, Shawn promoted change in others.

Similarly, Zoey's third try at selecting a wish for WOOP was about something she had control over:

My wish is to have a deeper understanding of Asa—not just about screen time, but of Asa.

She felt an urgency to try to understand him better as he moved into adolescence. She could already see that "his need for autonomy and his need to make his own decisions have grown."

4. Is your wish challenging but feasible?

Oettingen has found that having a wish that deeply motivates us isn't enough:

The wish should also be a bit challenging. If it's easy and effortless, you just need positive thinking to go for wish fulfillment.[42]

And it needs to be feasible. When we use WOOP for Mind in the Making, we ask participants to rate how likely they are to achieve their wish, and to consider making another wish if it's not too likely. That happened to Barb Lunnemann of Save the Children.[43] She's also a Mind in the Making trainer and, like Shawn, uses WOOP in her own life.

Her wish: to have a clean basement. By clean, she meant organized, so "I can easily find things whenever I need to." She also meant that "the stuff I'm never going to use is gone."

But she didn't think cleaning up the basement was feasible—it was overwhelming and all too easy to put off.

She realized that if she narrowed her wish into smaller, more feasible tasks, she had a better chance of realizing it.

First task: dish towels.

My mom left me probably three hundred dish towels that she'd made out of flour sacks or old sheets, or bought on sale. I thought, "What am I going to do with all these dish towels?" Yes, my mom did all this work, but they aren't really something that I want or need.

Narrowing her wish into a feasible goal worked. She found a charity and donated them. She felt good that her mother's dish towels would be in the hands of people who wanted them, not stashed away in her basement. And she was on her way to an organized basement.

STEP TWO: VISUALIZE THE OUTCOME OF FULFILLING YOUR WISH

To maintain your motivation and positive energy, Oettingen has found it's important to visualize the outcome of fulfilling your wish, to imagine how you'll feel or what will happen. Zoey envisioned the outcome of trying to better understand Asa:

> More calmness, less conflict, more peace, and probably a deeper apprecia-tion of his autonomy and freedom.

STEP THREE: DETERMINE THE
OBSTACLE IN YOU THAT COULD HOLD YOU BACK

Oettingen's next research question was how to help people maintain the energy from visualizing the outcome "to go all the way to wish fulfillment, even if wish fulfillment is challenging." That took years of scientific experimentation:

> We came up with a strategy we called "Mental Contrasting." Instead of indulging in positive fantasies and daydreams, you switch gears and say: "What is it in me that holds me back from fulfilling my wish? What stops me? What is my main inner obstacle?"[44]

It's easy to see others as the obstacle—partner, children, parents, boss, co-workers. "We all nourish these external excuses—it's a way of keeping the status quo," Oettingen says. "Asking about an 'obstacle in me' helps people get rid of the external excuses. I can't really change others, but I can change me."

Oettingen and her team tested whether this process could maintain people's commitment to change.[45] I was able to observe some college-age students going through this experiment. When asked to think about a wish that was very important to her, one student wrote: "Being closer to my mother."

When prompted to write down the outcome of fulfilling her wish, she wrote: "My mother and I don't have a good relationship. I feel if I got to know her better, I would feel better about my life."

This woman was in the experimental group (the Mental Contrasting

Group), but other students were assigned to a control group (the Indulging Group), where participants were only instructed to write down positive outcomes (i.e., step two above), not to think about and write down obstacles (i.e., step three). This student listed her "impulsiveness" as an obstacle.

The researchers then measured blood pressure as an indicator of people feeling energized in both groups. Oettingen reports:

> The blood pressure of the participants in the Mental Contrasting Group
> who expected to be able to overcome the critical obstacle went up, and
> their commitment went up as well, more so than in the Indulging Group.[46]

The increase was comparable to the rise in blood pressure after drinking a cup of coffee! Oettingen summarizes the power of this process:

> Fantasizing about the desired future gives people's action a direction. Then
> switching gears and understanding what their inner obstacle is gives people
> the energy to overcome that obstacle and attain the desired future.

Zoey first thought of the obstacle as being in Asa—his meltdowns when he comes off playing games on the phone. But the obstacle had to be in her, not her son, so she revised it:

> The obstacle is my frustration when he throws an epic meltdown. It's like
> someone coming off of drugs.

Another obstacle was the pressure of her job and taking care of Asa:

> When I'm busy—and I'm constantly busy—I tend to give Asa more screen
> time, and he knows that. I need to deal with my frustration when work
> pressure piles up.

STEP FOUR: MAKE A PLAN

Oettingen knew that people like Zoey, Barb, and Shawn need specific strategies for overcoming obstacles. She discovered the strategy that she was looking for in the work of her husband, Peter Gollwitzer of New York University. Called "Implementation Intentions" in the scientific literature,[47] it's basically an "if-then" process: *if* a given obstacle occurs, *then* that person will implement a specific behavior intended to overcome it.

If Barb found herself making excuses to avoid dealing with the basement, then she'd tell herself, "I just have to do at least three things." It worked. "Sometimes that would keep me going for a couple of hours. Or, after finishing those three things, it would give me an opportunity to take a break."

Zoey's plan was to deal with her own frustration when Asa fought about screen time. She was aware of many strategies for dealing with frustration and had tried a number of them, but when work pressures piled up (and they did), it was too much. She decided that she needed help, that she should find a coach to help her.

In terms of having a "deeper understanding" of Asa, Zoey had to listen to him without judgment. She and her partner decided to use dinnertime to ask open-ended questions of each family member and listen and respond to the answers. She saw that the more they listened, the more he talked. The outcomes she wished for—more calmness, less conflict, more peace, and a deeper appreciation of her son's autonomy and freedom—were beginning to happen.

ENCOURAGING GOAL SETTING IN OTHERS

Given the fact that we can't set goals for others, only ourselves, Zoey asked Asa to come up with his own plan for giving up the phone when phone time was over. She told him she hated the conflicts they got into and wanted a better way to handle the "time's up" challenge. She'd experimented with setting timers and giving warnings ("five more minutes till time's up"), but they hadn't resolved this issue; she wanted something that would work for both of them. Asa joked that his plan would be "just one more time of five minutes," but Zoey joked back that she suspected that a onetime extension would become a bottomless pit—five more minutes multiplying into lots of five more minutes. So, Asa said his plan was to make a plan *before* he got phone time—a plan of something he wanted to do when the time was up.

"But what if that doesn't work?" Zoey said, raising the obstacle part of the goal-setting process.

"It will work," Asa said, "because I promise it will."

"Okay, then let's try it," Zoey said. It did work . . . sort of. Asa still struggled. Zoey began to feel that his struggle was tied to larger learning issues. He was having trouble with transitions in school that had nothing to do with screen time. It was hard for him to switch to new tasks, to deal with mistakes, and he became easily frustrated.

Zoey took her concerns to the school. She made a list of what she thought he needed to learn—dealing with transitions, planning and organizing schoolwork over longer periods of time (assignments and homework), time management (moving from getting stuff done as fast as possible to doing things well), dealing with distractions, and tackling schoolwork that was a stretch for him. Asa's teacher agreed that these were holding him back and that his motivation was dropping, but she didn't think that the school had a role in "teaching study skills."

Zoey was very irritated and so was I in listening to her story—it's like so many stories I've heard for years. The skills Asa needed to learn are executive function skills and are foundational to learning in school and life. School leaders ought to reframe this issue—not as nice-to-have "study" skills but as essential-to-have Life and Learning Skills—and ought to promote them throughout children's and adolescents' schooling.

Zoey felt she had to do something before Asa's resolve declined more. Her challenge was twofold. She knew she wasn't the right person to help him with these skills because she tended to get frustrated by his frustrations.

After a search, she found a former teacher who was working as a tutor while in graduate school. The organization he works for specializes in helping children gain EF skills.

It was two months into Asa's work with the tutor when I spoke with her. The tutor had begun his work with Asa by talking to him about his goals for himself, his passions, and his interests. When Asa gets frustrated, the tutor can help connect the relevancy of the frustrating task to Asa's passions.

In this first session, the tutor also asked Asa to tell him what a great school would be like. The tutor could then use this as the "ground" from which he built their work together. The sessions were then organized around:

- **Roses and thorns.** Asa begins each weekly session sharing the things that were positive and exciting during the week and things that weren't.
- **Agenda.** Then the tutor shares an agenda with the list of activities they will do together. Asa's job is to prioritize the order of the activities and estimate how long each will take, thus strengthening his organizational skills.
- **Activities.** These include writing time where he is asked a fun question ("What made you laugh this week?") to write about. Other activities include book club, where they discuss the books Asa is

reading, and help with homework. This work focuses on the challenges that Asa is facing.

- **Reflection.** Here is where the tutor helps Asa fulfill the goal he set for himself—to deal with the hard times at school more successfully. He takes the thorns Asa tells him about and turns them into similar problem-solving scenarios for the following week. Asa's role is to suggest solutions for other kids who might face these problems, too. Together, they compile Asa's solutions into a written "toolbox" for everyday solutions to everyday learning problems.

With this approach, the tutor is addressing Zoey's challenges. He's helping her son learn to set his own goals and come up with viable strategies for addressing them. These are techniques that Zoey is now using at home with Asa.

Already there is some progress: a little less frustration over mistakes, more concrete strategies for addressing schoolwork. The biggest return from the tutoring so far: Asa asked for a watch for Christmas: He wanted to be the timekeeper so he can help others in his family manage their time. On a family holiday after Christmas, he did just that. He's becoming the helper, not just the person being helped.

PROMOTING MAKING WISHES, SETTING GOALS, AND STRATEGIES: WOOP IN A NUTSHELL

Here is the way we use WOOP in our training.*[48] You can find the steps on the WOOP app and on the website that Oettingen and her team created: https://woopmylife.org.

Now, let's begin:

1. **Wish (W)**

    Take a moment to step back and relax.

    Make a wish. Make sure this wish is important to you—dear to your heart. Write it down in a few words: _____.

    Then ask yourself each of the following questions, and circle Yes or No for each:

---

* This application of WOOP was created by Gabriele Oettingen with the Mind in the Making team in 2015 and updated for the book.

- Is it based on a realistic expectation?   Yes   No
- Is it something *you* have control over?   Yes   No
- Is it a little challenging but feasible?   Yes   No

If you've answered no to any of these questions, think about re-vising your wish and write down this new wish in just a few words: _____.

Now, on a scale of 1 to 7, rate how likely you think you are to achieve this goal, with 7 being very likely and 1 being not likely at all.

   1   2   3   4   5   6   7

If you rated the likelihood as a 4 or less, you may want to consider another wish. It's important that you believe you can fulfill your wish even if it's challenging.

What is your wish now? Write it down in a few words: _____.

2. **Outcome (O)**

What would be the best outcome or the best thing about fulfilling your wish? It can be an emotion, a positive result, or the way other people will feel about you. Write it down: _____.

And now, imagine the best outcome. Let your mind go; feel the best outcome in your mind.

3. **Obstacle (O)**

What is the obstacle *within you* that prevents you from fulfilling your wish? What is it in you that stops you from tackling your wish and experiencing the outcome? Write it down: _____.

Again, it's important to take the time and leisure to imagine this obstacle fully.

4. **Plan (P)**

What action can you take to overcome your obstacle? What can you do? Name an action you can take or a thought you can think when the obstacle occurs, and write it down: _____.

And now form an if-then plan.

In other words, *if* obstacle _____ occurs, *then* I will _____ [act in the specified way] to overcome the obstacle.

Life and Learning Skill 2: Perspective-Taking

Perspective-taking involves understanding what others think and feel, then understanding the similarities and difference between their perspective and yours. It builds on empathy toward compassion—feeling *for* others—as well as a cognitive understanding of others' perspectives.

When Zane was in eighth grade, Ben asked to join his friend group. "We had a little clique," Zane, now seventeen and a senior in a midwestern high school, told me. These seven or eight friends have been together since grade school.

Zane says that since his group likes to read books, watch movies, and play video games, they were probably seen as nerds. The kids in the jock group thought they were cooler than Zane's group. That became a baseline by which Zane's friends judged themselves:

I think there was that questioning of, "Do I think I'm not cool? No! I think I'm pretty cool." I don't think anyone wants to be like, "I'm un-fun or I'm un-cool, or I don't have status in life."

Ben's request prompted many conversations among Zane's friends. Ben was new to the school, but the group had accepted other new kids. Ben sometimes acted needy and obnoxious, but that, too, wasn't viewed as a sufficient reason for rejection, for Zane at least. It came down to the fact that the games Ben liked were ones the group had played when they were younger, not the ones they were playing now, so the group decided to say no to Ben.

As adolescents move into the wider world, it's developmentally necessary for them to try to figure out where they fit in, belong, and rank in relation to others. Having someone who wasn't up on the best games wouldn't be fun and might make the friends feel uncool.

Perhaps it's tempting to feel judgmental or dismissive about this situation among middle schoolers, but the need for status—feeling good about oneself and being respected—affects us at any age.

Zane was initially in favor of including Ben:

I like to think of myself as an inclusive person. I don't like the idea of keeping someone out when it would bring fun for them and not really any negative drawbacks for us, except having to—what—endure a different perspective.

"Did you talk about this rejection with Ben?" I asked. Yes, he said, describing it as a "forced conversation" instigated by his parents. During this conversation, Zane began to realize that some of Ben's obnoxious behavior came from not having good friends at school. Ben hadn't reached out to others because he was set on belonging to this group, and the rejection was painful. This perspective slightly shifted Zane's view of him.

Momentarily, Zane recalls, he became "more hesitant," but ended up deciding not to push back against the group's decision, which was based on not wanting to be "stuck in the past." "Let's move on," he agreed.

As he got older, Zane became interested in how people make decisions. While canvassing for a statehouse primary election in his district, he'd assumed two candidates from the same party would agree on most issues . . . but found out that was not so. He'd assumed people in his district might have similar political opinions . . . but found out that was not so. Was a position inherently right or wrong? What affected people's views and votes?

Ben found other friends, but in senior year, he approached the group again. They were studying for finals, making college decisions, planning a getaway—and figuring out what to do about Ben.

Underlying this drama of acceptance and rejection are two very human tendencies: our propensity to use stories to explain our world and, as part of that, to sort people into us versus them; and our use of an essential Life and Learning Skill—perspective-taking.

THE STORIES WE TELL

Jonathan Gottschall of Washington & Jefferson College studies the science of stories. At a conference on learning and the brain, he showed a film he refers to as "one of the earliest and most important experiments in the science of storytelling."[49]

Made in 1944, it's a simple, primitive ninety-second silent animated if-then depicting four shapes.[50] A small triangle, a big triangle, and a small circle move around a rectangle. One side of the rectangle opens and closes, and sometimes the other shapes move inside or outside, poking at and circling each other. At the end, the small triangle and the small circle move off-screen. The large triangle then moves in and out of the rectangle, poking at its sides until it breaks apart.

Gottschall asked the audience the question that the original researchers, Fritz Heider and Marianne Simmel, asked: "Will you please tell us what you saw?" Then he asked, "Did you see a story?" Close to 100 percent raised their hands.[51] About 70 percent by his estimate raised their hands, agreeing that they saw the characters as human; about 25 percent saw the triangles as males and the circle as a female. Finally, Gottschall asked, "Who saw the big triangle as the bad guy?" About 50 percent did.

The specific stories people saw varied. Some saw a love story, as Gottschall and I did. Others saw playground bullying. One reported seeing the smaller shapes as intruders and the big triangle as protecting his property. In the original study, in its replications, and at this conference, only a few saw the animation as just shapes, moving around, which is what they really are.[52] Gottschall sees this as one piece of evidence among many for his thesis—we are storytellers!

Did you notice that the plot in this experiment follows a classic story structure: victim, villain, hero; conflict and resolution? This, Gottschall says, is "how human beings make meaning. We see wildness . . . chaos in the world. We impose this structure . . . to make it orderly and meaningful."[53] As he writes in his book, "We learn most and best through stories."[54] His research explains something to me that I'd never fully understood—why actors and celebrities are paid much more than others in societally important jobs like teachers. Storytellers are highly valued by society and accordingly command top salaries.

It's important, Gottschall noted in his speech, that although our stories may share a basic structure, we don't all see the exact same story.[55] To understand each other's stories, we must take each other's perspectives.

THE LIFE AND LEARNING SKILL OF PERSPECTIVE-TAKING

I define perspective-taking as understanding the similarities and differences between what we think and feel and what others think and feel. As with all of the essential Life and Learning Skills, perspective-taking brings together your social, emotional, and cognitive capacities, is typically goal-driven, and calls on the four components of foundational executive function skills. You need to:

- Use self-control to inhibit your own perspective in order to understand someone else's (**inhibitory control**)

- Think flexibly, switching between your own and others' viewpoints (**cognitive flexibility**)
- Use what you know to balance your prior knowledge and your understanding of the current situation to piece together what's happening (**working memory**)
- **Reflect**, as you ponder the meaning of your experiences.

Adam Galinsky* of Columbia Business School has studied perspective-taking for more than two decades. He halfway jokes that his interest in the subject arose because his twin brother was bigger, stronger, and faster, and "I had to be a good perspective-taker so he didn't beat the crap out of me."[56]

THE IMPACT OF PERSPECTIVE-TAKING

"Perspective-taking," Galinsky says, "is one of our most important skills as human beings":

All over the world—it doesn't matter how old you are, what industry you're in, or how smart you are—if you're not a good perspective taker, you're not going to get good outcomes in life for yourself and for other people.

The late Peter Drucker, celebrated as the father of modern management, called perspective-taking an "outside-in perspective"—seeing things as a customer would see them—and deemed it responsible for launching the most successful new businesses.[57] Look up best inventions for any year and you'll see inventions that you—the customer—may have wished existed, like the most recent winners—making text audible, hands-free shoes, multilingual meetings made easy, a computer notebook you can repair, and reusable shipping boxes.[58]

In the Breakthrough Years study interviews I conducted for the book, young people told me they want adults to listen more than they talk, and to listen with their "when-I-was-a-child" mind, not just their "now-I'm-an-adult" mind. That's the essence of perspective-taking.

According to Galinsky, perspective-taking enables us to:

- Understand others' expectations
- Think less stereotypically

---

* We've established that Adam and my husband, Norman, are not related, though we wish we were—we would happily claim each other as family.

- Have better relationships, especially in a diverse world
- Communicate effectively
- Manage conflict constructively
- Plan for the future

Much of the research underlying perspective-taking in children is called theory of mind research: children are creating theories—that is, stories—about what others are thinking.

MEASURING PERSPECTIVE-TAKING

Studies in the 1980s by Alison Gopnik at the University of California, Berkeley, and others have shown that infants develop a theory of mind, the ability to understand others' perspectives, beginning around eighteen months old and developing into the early and later childhood years.[59] For long afterward, the scientific community seemed to conclude that perspective-taking was pretty well-formed during those years.

Neuroscientist Iroise Dumontheil of the University of London was not convinced.[60] Her research on adolescents' social development indicated that this skill was continuing to develop but there wasn't a good way to measure it. Eventually, Dumontheil and her colleagues settled on the Director Task. In contrast to tasks used with young children, which all typically developing adolescents and adults are able to do without difficulty, the Director Task isn't easy, even for adults. This means it allows researchers to test whether the skill of perspective-taking continues to develop after childhood with better precision.

To understand the Director Task, picture a bookcase where each shelf is divided into squares.[61] Some are open—see-through from front to back. Others are closed off by a gray panel in the back.

The experiment takes place on a computer screen.

Dumontheil describes the introduction to the experiment:[62]

We show participants the shelves, with the director standing behind the shelves. We then tell participants the director is going to ask them to move objects in the shelves, however, importantly, the director has a different viewpoint from them.

We then show them the view from the other side of the shelves—what the director sees. The participant can see that some shelves have these gray

*panels at the back, which means that the director can't see all the objects
on the shelves. We tell participants they have to take this into account when
following the director's instructions.*

To confirm that the participants understand that the director has a different perspective, the experimenter asks: "Can you show me an object that
the director *can* see?" And: "Can you show me an object that the director
cannot see?" All of the participants can do this easily, even as young as age
seven.

Then the experiment begins. In the "critical trial," the director (a recorded voice) might ask the participant to move the small glasses to the
left. The director wouldn't be able to see the smallest glasses on the bottom row (called a distractor object) because a gray panel is blocking his
view, so the participant needs to move glasses on the second row from
the bottom.

This task requires participants to use theory of mind skills (to think
about the director's perspective and which objects are visible to him, as he
wouldn't ask them to move an object he doesn't know is there) and executive function skills (to inhibit the response of wanting to move the smallest
glasses from their own perspective).

There are also control trials where this complexity is removed because
the distractor object is replaced by a completely different object—for example, a truck rather than glasses. In this case, both the director and the
participant can see all of the glasses.

In the next part of the experiment (which is key, I think), participants are
told that the director had to leave the room. They receive the same instructions as in the first part of the experiment from a recorded voice, but with
no director visibly present. In these instructions, they were told to move objects only in the clear slots and that they should ignore objects in slots with
a gray background. In other words, instead of having to take the director's
perspective into account, participants had to follow the rule of ignoring all
objects in slots with a gray background.

In this study of 177 females between ages seven and twenty-seven, Dumontheil and her colleagues found that in the no-director condition where
they only had to ignore all objects in the gray slots, fourteen-to-seventeen-
year-olds were as accurate as adults. But when there was a director—a
person—giving the directions in the task, adolescents made more mistakes
than adults. Simply having to take the perspective of someone else makes

this task more difficult.[63] The Life and Learning Skill of perspective-taking continues to develop during adolescence and beyond.

In later work, it was found that adolescents who performed better on this task (i.e., more frequently took into account the director's perspective) reported more prosocial behavior[64] and showed greater trust in response to positive social behavior and a stronger reaction to negative social behavior in a multiround financial trust game.[65] This shows that performance on the Director Task picks up aspects of the development of social cognitive skills that are relevant to everyday social behavior.

The results of these studies help explain Zane's problem-solving process about Ben. Although Zane wanted to be inclusive in middle school and understood that Ben's occasional difficult behavior was a result of his trying too hard to fit in, he had more trouble putting together multiple perspectives—his own, Ben's, and his friends'—in this emotional situation. It was a skill he had, but the emotions and the social pull to be cool by not playing last year's (now uncool) games took precedence in his problem-solving.

Zane's high school "self" now cringes a bit looking back on his middle school "self." He feels as if he was playing a simplistic role:

> I feel I was pretty close to this portrayal of nerds in the media, and that's a negative portrayal.

As children gain facility in thinking about their own thinking processes (metacognition), their narratives tend to become more complex. Even so, we continue to want to sort people into in-groups and out-groups—"us versus them" groups. Jonathan Gottschall writes about this limitation of stories as a primary tool for making sense of ourselves and our world:

> Yes, stories typically have moral dimensions that reinforce prosocial behavior. But in their monotonous obsession with plots of villainy and justice, they gratify and reinforce our instincts for savage retribution and moral sanctimony.[66]

It wasn't savage retribution in Zane's case, but it would help if media creators were less prone to stereotyping young people. That's the goal of the newly formed Center for Scholars & Storytellers at UCLA. Yalda Uhls, a psychologist and former movie executive at MGM and Sony, founded the center to be a "bridge between the siloed worlds of researchers, content creators, and young people." Her intent is that media produce more stories that help young people thrive and less media that stereotypes adolescents.[67]

By senior year, when Ben again asked to join the group, Zane was more committedly in favor of inclusion:

> I'm like, "Anyone who wants to be friends, why not?" Maybe I don't play the same games as Ben, but that doesn't mean I need to.

The other members of the group agreed, Zane told me. Ben was also included in the senior trip the friends were planning.

What changed?

Adolescents engage in teenism—but like adults, they can move beyond it.

Zane's shift began with rejecting a two-dimensional portrayal of himself as a nerd:

> No, I'm not as simplistic or obnoxious or boring as the media portrays me to be.

If you're worried about being seen as obnoxious, it's hard to want to associate with someone seen as even more obnoxious than you. But now, Zane realizes that media depictions of teenagers are "simplified stereotypes about what high school's supposed to be like." Growing up has brought a fuller assessment: "You see a person can be complex."

This insight didn't happen simply because Zane got older. His life experiences have shown him that people don't fit into neat labels. For example, nerds:

> You get a perspective from the media that kids who like video games a lot don't go out, don't do meaningful stuff like community service, or have life goals. They just play video games.

He began to see that this wasn't true about him or his friends. Neither was the portrayal of jocks, who were seen as self-involved or dumb. In reality, he says, the kids who play sports in his school volunteer at the supermarket, bagging groceries for people needing help.

Similarly, he can now look at Ben in more holistic ways and see Ben's more redeeming and engaging traits.

As a middle schooler, it's more difficult to break people down into complex beings. I now try to see people for who they truly are. That you're not defined by this specific group you're in, or that there isn't cool and uncool.

Zane is using the skill of perspective-taking, seeing that he isn't fully defined by the kids he hangs out with and doesn't have to like everything about his friends. His "we/they" grouping of people has loosened up. His thinking has become more multidimensional.

As the Breakthrough Years study reveals, many adolescents feel that stereotypes constrain them. So I asked Zane if this understanding could be prompted earlier. He thought it could if young people had more experiences with others who are different, and opportunities to "see that you're not as limited as the media and your own perception of yourself see you as being."

He also thinks social media plays a role in creating and sustaining two-dimensional views:

Social media encourages a very simple, limited perspective. The point of social media is "I want to get my thoughts out to anyone who'll listen." So, you do generic things to get followers or likes—"I'll flaunt my wealth because people want to be wealthy."

What experiences have prompted Zane to question his perspectives of himself and others?

First, **reflection is a family value.** Zane told me that when he was applying to college and making his selection, his parents didn't tell him what to think or do. They asked questions that helped him clarify his own decision-making criteria, like "What appeals to you about this school?"

Second, a **part of every day in high school is structured to promote a deeper understanding among students.** They have an advisory process—a small student group that meets for ten minutes every morning and for forty-five minutes weekly, not to do homework but to get to know others beyond their friendship groups. The advisors ask questions like "What do you think your best memory from high school will be?" Or "What were your takeaways from the school assembly?" Zane says these discussions help him "unpack stuff" and "to understand other kids personally."

In addition, **some of his classes are designed to help students think about different perspectives on societal issues.** In his World Religion class, for example, representatives from different religions visit and answer students' questions. Zane has become interested in their perspectives—whether religious leaders believe in absolute or situational morality (e.g., do they believe that abortion is always wrong, or that it's permissible in certain situations and if so, what situations?).

It's also **the responsibility of society to prompt less stereotypical thinking in young people**—a mantle that the Center for Scholars & Storytellers at UCLA is picking up and helping to carry.

PERSPECTIVE-TAKING REDUCES STEREOTYPING

Adam Galinsky has found that stereotypical thinking can be reduced in intentional ways. His insights on this came when he was a graduate student at Princeton University. There was a culture of political correctness then, he says, and students were bending over backward to never, ever act in any prejudicial or discriminatory way.[68] He was casting about for a dissertation topic when an article was published reporting a downside to how political correctness was being self-enforced. This study found that actively trying to suppress any stereotypical or prejudicial thoughts made things worse.

"Yes," he said to himself. "If we tell someone, 'Don't think about a white bear,' all they can think about is white bears." Was there another way? he wondered. Would perspective-taking make a difference?

In an experiment conducted for his dissertation, Galinsky and Gordon Moskovitz, now of Lehigh University, divided thirty-seven college-age study participants into three groups. They were asked to look at a photograph of an elderly man sitting on a chair near a newspaper stand and write an essay about a day in his life.[69]

To one group, Galinsky explains,

we said, "While you write your essay, suppress any stereotypic thoughts about the person."

To the second group,

we said, "While you write the essay, imagine that you are that person. Go through your day as if you're looking at the world through their eyes and in their shoes."[70]

The study participants in the third (control) group received no instructions beyond writing about a typical day in the life of the elderly man.

After a series of other tasks, the participants in all of the groups were shown a photograph of an African American teen and asked to write an essay about a typical day in his life, with no other instructions.

The researchers analyzed the essays' content, finding that young people who had been asked to imagine they were the person they were writing about—that is, the perspective-takers—"wrote less stereotypical essays about 'the day in the life' than the people in the control condition."

In a second experiment in this series, with eighty-seven undergraduates, the researchers found that perspective-takers saw more of themselves in the people in the photographs than those in the suppression group.

In a third experiment, with forty undergraduates, the researchers conclude that trying to suppress feelings of difference actually increases bias (in-group and out-group thinking), while perspective-taking diminishes it. Although suppression helped people avoid stereotyping in their essays, it increased their implicit bias afterward.[71]

NOT ALL PERSPECTIVE-TAKING IS ALIKE (BUT THEY ALL CAN WORK TOGETHER)

Jason Chein of Temple University has been looking at differences in types of perspective-taking with his colleague Nora Newcomb, also of Temple University.

There's **more cognitively based** perspective-taking (I say "more" because I think we can never fully dissociate cognition and emotion). As Chein described it to me, he said:

> It would be me trying to understand what do you, Ellen, sitting there looking at me, believe about the world, about me? What's in your mind? What do you understand?[72]

This is the kind of perspective-taking seen in a compelling experiment called Crayons and Paper Clips with preschool-aged children by Alison Gopnik. Children were shown a box of crayons. When they opened it, they saw there were paper clips—not crayons—inside. They were then asked what others might think when they saw the unopened box. Younger preschoolers were more likely to say "paper clips"—thinking that what they know now, others would know—while older preschoolers were more likely to say "crayons."[73]

Thinking that others know what we know doesn't end in the preschool years. I am sure you can think of times when this has happened with adolescents and adults.

A second type of perspective-taking is **more emotionally based**. Chein continued:

This focuses on empathy, emotion, mentalizing. So, Ellen, what do I know about how you feel? What emotions might you be experiencing?

And there's "a third form of perspective-taking," too:

Spatial perspective-taking. What is my mental model of what you see from your perspective, from where you're sitting?

This type is captured in the Director Task.

Brain analyses are showing these types of perspective-taking are supported by different brain regions.

THE IMPORTANCE OF HOLISTIC PERSPECTIVE-TAKING

But these differences shouldn't mean that the different types of perspective-taking don't work together. At best, they can and do!

I'll never forget a session I helped to arrange where Admiral Mike Mullen, retired chair of the Joint Chiefs of Staff and a member of my board of directors at Families and Work Institute at the time, answered questions from young people at the Aspen Institute Ideas Festival. When asked, "What leadership skill is important to you?" he talked about perspective-taking.

He said that when he was preparing for a trip to a country, like Afghanistan, he didn't want the usual briefing about historical events. He wanted a better understanding of the people he would meet—what they might think, what they might feel, how they might view the events, people, and places in their lives. Only by having this holistic understanding, he continued, would he be able to try to understand the people he was meeting and look for ways to resolve conflicts peacefully, not through military force.

Galinsky has come to a similar conclusion from his studies:[74]

We find that empathy without cognitive perspective-taking leads to what I call the "doormat effect." You become a doormat. You just give and give and give.

The other effect—which I haven't studied as much experimentally but have thought a lot about—is what I call the "bully effect." What bullies are really good at is understanding someone's perspective and knowing their

*weakness, and then targeting that weakness and not feeling any compassion
for the person.*

Cognitive and emotional perspective-taking go together for the best results, Galinsky says:

*We need both heart and mind to connect to understand someone else. We
also need a sufficient amount of self-focus, where we're not sacrificing our
own perspective completely.*

A PATH FORWARD FOR ZANE

As he sought to understand himself and others, Zane's path forward has
become clearer. When he enters college, he plans to study decision-making
in politics. He doesn't want to go into politics, but international relations is
a possibility. The question that intrigues Zane is:

*How can we take different perspectives from different parts of the world
and get them to cooperate?*

He also has dreams for changing how social media affects young people's
perspectives of themselves and others. It's natural, he says, for young people to
try to understand others and what's going on around them. But social media
can impede that for various reasons. First, it can preclude personal contact:

*It can be hard to talk to someone who doesn't have any classes with
you—to stop sitting with your friends at lunch and go over to their table
and actually sit with them. It's easy to go, "I'll just open my phone, go to
the app, follow them, and then see about their life there."*

Second, he believes that social media limits our view of life because
what's on social media is a curated life—"the life they want to put on the
internet" in hopes of being popular.

Zane believes that some young people will emerge and lead the charge
for change against some of these social media downsides. But, he continues,
he already sees his friends taking charge of their use of social media, like
giving up Instagram and Snapchat or creating their own nonpublic online
discussion groups where they can more honestly share their angst and joys
about graduating from high school. By making these changes, Zane says, he

and his friends feel less stressed, more confident, and more open to different perspectives.

Zane's view—that young people who use social media a lot and those who don't seem different—aligns with a 2023 study conducted by Eva Telzer of the University of North Carolina, Chapel Hill. She and her colleagues found that the frequency of checking social media is actually associated with longitudinal brain changes.[75] The brains of those who checked frequently were "becoming more and more sensitive to social feedback over time," Telzer reports.[76] While the study established a strong correlation between social media use and a greater sensitivity to social feedback, Telzer adds, the findings don't reveal which is causing the other.

Zane isn't waiting for more research results. He thinks that change should happen soon and that young people should help drive it:

> There always is a push among kids to confront the issues in society, and to do better.

It's already happening in small and larger ways. For example, Logan Lane, a seventeen-year-old in Brooklyn, has been in the news for making the decision to ditch her smartphone and to found a group of like-minded young people they've named the Luddite Club.[77] On a larger scale, a group called Tech(nically) Politics was co-founded by Alicia Kopans and Emma Lembke, who as teens fell prey to endless hours of scrolling through the perfectly curated lives of others, to counting "likes" to measure their self-worth, and to eating disorders and mental health challenges.[78] Now in college, they joined forces with other young people to guide the laws governing the way the internet affects young people.[79] Their solution is sharing adolescents' real stories about the negative impact of the internet with lawmakers across the country. Already their advocacy has helped pass a California law requiring safeguards to reduce risks for those under eighteen.[80]

PROMOTING PERSPECTIVE-TAKING

Regarding perspective-taking as a skill, I expect adolescents and adults will think of many opportunities to improve it. Here are some:

- At the end of the school day, you can ask how the teacher's day was. Why do you think that? What were the clues?

- When you are watching a movie, you can select a character in the movie and ask what you think that person is thinking and feeling. What do you think they'll do next? Why?
- When you are with family, you can ask each person for their perspective on a favorite family story and see how similar or different their takes are. Then try to figure out why.
- When you are watching a world event, you can ask what various world leaders might have been thinking when they made a certain decision. Why would they think that way?
- When your adolescent has a disagreement with a friend, you can try to speculate why the friend might act that way. Come up with several ideas and then talk about how realistic each idea is.

Life and Learning Skill 3: Communicating and Collaborating

Communicating is understanding yourself and what you want to say while simultaneously understanding others by thinking about how your communication is likely to be received and making adjustments so it can be best heard. Collaborating is considering multiple perspectives—yours and others'—in order to work and live together and to resolve conflicts that arise.

AN EXPERIMENT: NAME THESE TUNES

Try this experiment with the adolescent in your life. Select three familiar tunes (like "Happy Birthday" or "Twinkle, Twinkle Little Star") that you can tap out with your fingers.

Before tapping, try to guess how many people in an audience of a hundred listeners would be able to name these tunes if they heard your tapping amplified in a recital hall.

Do you think your child will be able to guess correctly?

Now, sitting back-to-back, ask your child to name each tune you tap.

Okay, go!

Did your child guess the tunes? My kids rarely did when we played this game.

Now switch, with you being the one to name the tune they tap out.

In the original experiment, by Stanford University graduate student Elizabeth Newton in 1990,[81] most tappers showed "substantial overconfidence," estimating that "half the listeners" (fifty out of a hundred) would guess correctly. But "listeners were only able to identify two out of one hundred fifty tunes." What's going on?

In this section of the book, we'll talk about what is going on—why communication can become miscommunication and the cognitive predispositions that can cause it. We'll move on to the Life and Learning Skill of collaborating, which depends heavily on communicating, and talk about handling conflicts. Finally, we'll look at how school disciplinary practices can promote the development of this skill.

THE LIFE AND LEARNING SKILL OF COMMUNICATING

Communicating involves two processes—understanding yourself and what you want to say (in words, behavior, or forms of art) and, simultaneously, understanding others by thinking about how your communication is likely to be received and making adjustments so it can be best heard.

Communicating, so defined, calls on the building blocks of foundational executive function skills:

- Paying attention to yourself and others in figuring out what you want to say and how it will be heard (**reflection**)
- Using what you know to draw on what you've learned about similar situations while balancing events in the moment (**working memory**)
- Thinking flexibly and changing your behavior if miscommunications occur (**cognitive flexibility** and **inhibitory control**)

It also builds on the first and second Life and Learning Skills, of having goals for the communication and understanding the perspectives of others.

While there's not much research on communication as an executive function–based skill, there are scores of studies on effective communication, especially in the workplace, where it's seen as a key to job success.[82] In the National Association of Colleges and Employers job outlook yearly surveys, communicating is typically among the top skills that employers report seeking in new hires.[83]

WHAT'S GOING ON: WHY WE MISCOMMUNICATE

Studies have found that there are obstacles, even cognitive predispositions, that can obstruct our understanding of others, impeding effective communication.

The Curse of Knowledge

Once we know something, that knowledge can blind us to what others might not know. That's what was happening when you assumed someone else would know the tune you were tapping. It's what was happening in the experiment I described in the last section on perspective-taking, where young children who learned that a closed crayon box really had paper clips inside would then believe that others would think the same. It's also what's happening when we as adults, with our extensive experience, might not be able to appreciate how our adolescent sees the world. This cognitive bias, called the curse of knowledge, affects our ability to communicate.

Ships Passing in the Night

"Ships passing in the night" is a term that Adam Galinsky uses to indicate when two people who are communicating *think* they're adopting each other's perspectives but don't fully understand what the other thinks and feels, and so they miscommunicate.[84] As parents, we might assume we know what our kids mean when they ask a question, and so we jump into responding without finding out more.

This happened to me sometimes when my teenage daughter would say she wanted to do something she was actually ambivalent about. She'd say (often defiantly), "I want to go to the party the senior kids are having" or "I want to spend the night at this new friend's house" or "I want to pierce my nose." I'd fall into the trap of answering her defiance with defiance—until I realized she was ambivalent. When I learned to pause and ask her to tell me more, to tell me the pluses and minuses, she'd open up about her worries:

- The senior boys are charging for the party; it's a moneymaking scheme. I feel like we're being scammed.
- I don't know my friend's parents, so I'd really rather you pick me up, but it'll be late.
- If I pierce my nose and leave it in for more than a year, I'll have a scar for life, which I don't want.

By asking questions, I could understand more, and our communication was better.

Misunderstanding Meanings

A friend got a text from her son about the dinner they had: "This low key slaps."

While confused about what low-key slapping might mean, she figured it was positive because he asked her to make it again! Later, she found out that the phrase meant the initial dinner was better than he had expected.

It's easy to misunderstand the emotional meaning of words, especially in texts or emails. I remember responding to an email from a colleague in all caps because I felt strongly about it, and she thought I was angry at her—not the emphasis I'd intended.

THE GOLDEN OR PLATINUM RULE?

The Golden Rule is: "In everything, do to others what you would have them do to you" (Matthew 7:12). This rule is essential to ethical conduct for religions around the world, but in today's world, a slight modification helps.

"Treat others as *you* want to be treated" makes the assumption that others are just like you, but that's not necessarily true, even when they share your background and culture.

Since we aren't clones, the Platinum Rule (taken from a book of the same name by Tony Alessandra and Michael J. O'Connor)[85] works better: "Treat others the way *they* want to be treated."

The underlying principle needs to remain as treating others with respect, but the specifics rely on effective perspective-taking. For example, when Adam Galinsky participated in an American Field Service program at age seventeen and lived abroad, he remembers learning that finishing the food you were served means different things in different countries. In some countries, leaving food on your plate is "a sign of respect. It says you got enough to eat." In other countries, the custom is to "eat everything on your plate because it's a sign of disrespect to leave it. It says the food wasn't very good."[86]

"I WANT HONEST COMMUNICATION."

Jane, a single mother in Florida, vowed not to communicate with her daughter Lissy the way she was communicated to when she was growing up.

If I said something to my mother she didn't want to hear, she'd cut me off. I'd be iced out for days. I felt I could never do anything right. I didn't want my daughter growing up feeling that way. I want honest communication between us.

Soon after Lissy's birth, Jane left her husband, an actor, who was later diagnosed with bipolar disorder. Unlike her mother, who could sever relationships swiftly, Jane didn't want to harm her child's relationship with her ex-husband even though he could be erratic and hurtful before his diagnosis, and especially before he got on medications that helped him manage his moods.

Jane hadn't learned to communicate growing up but wanted do better. It involved three changes she learned she needed to make.

First, she needed to learn how to listen, because she'd never been listened to. So, if Lissy missed a homework assignment, Jane had to refrain from making a snap judgment but listen to what had gone wrong.

Second, she needed to learn how to talk about her former husband without burdening her daughter, especially if he didn't show up for a planned visit or was harsh. Once he was diagnosed, she realized she could describe his behavior within the context of the bipolar disorder without disparaging him. She didn't want Lissy to think his behavior was her fault, so she focused on what they could do to make the visits better rather than on what he did wrong.

The third thing she had to learn was the most difficult. She says, "I'm not a yeller, because my mother was," but "I don't know how to talk about my feelings."

If I'm angry with my daughter, it's hard for me to talk about it. I was punished for expressing my feelings. Lissy wants to talk.

I've had to learn that it's safe to express my feelings to her. But I might need time to express them in the way I want to. I might say, "Give me an hour and then we'll talk."

Through using these guideposts—listening without judgment, focusing on solutions, and serving as a role model in her honesty while being careful not to burden Lissy with her anger—Jane was developing the skill of communicating. But there was more to learn when she began to see that there was something not quite right about the way her daughter was eating. Or not eating.

Lissy was skipping meals or eating foods with few to no calories, so Jane asked her to weigh herself. Lissy agreed.

So, I was like, "Okay, well, that's too low."

Lissy seemed worried, too, and was willing to talk with her doctor, but her doctor dismissed their concerns, saying, "You're fine. You're the perfect weight. Just keep doing what you're doing."

Jane wasn't sure that was right and noticed that Lissy continued to avoid eating. Jane asked her to weigh herself again.

She'd lost weight, and then again a few days after that—and I was like, "Okay, this is definitely a problem."

Through friends, Jane found a treatment center for anorexia. Lissy, surprisingly, agreed to go. Jane wonders why:

At the treatment center, they have parent groups. A lot of parents said their kids wouldn't admit there was an issue. With Lissy, her friend had also noticed and said things to her, so when I began to talk about it, I think she must have been ready.

A bigger incentive was that Lissy has dreams for her life. Like her father, she wants to be an actor, but she wants to be a healthy one.

She knows she really needs to deal with her eating issues so that she can do her acting, go to college, and do the things she wants to do in life. To do that, you have to be healthy.

Although the honest communication they'd worked hard to establish also contributed to Lissy's willingness to talk with her mother and seek treatment, Jane began to realize that she'd been contributing to Lissy's problem. While she was careful about how she talked about Lissy's father, she hadn't been careful about sharing her own worries about overeating.

I've had weight issues, so I was always watching what I was eating; counting calories.

Jane had to ease up and stop saying her overeating was making her fat. She also had to make it clear that her weight problems were not Lissy's weight problems.

I finally said to her, "Look, we have almost the same issue—just the opposite sides of the coin. You're going to always have to be careful not to eat too little, and I'm always going to have to be careful not to eat too much. It's going to be something we deal with for a good part of our lives. Hopefully, over time, it'll get better."

Jane is thinking about the next steps in their lives and believes communicating will be central in Lissy's life as it's been in hers:

Lissy's not always going to be living with me. She'll go to college; have a roommate; have to learn how to get along with people who are different, with different upbringings and outlooks. The more you can talk about things, the better.

THE LIFE AND LEARNING SKILL OF COLLABORATING

Getting along with people involves communicating as well as collaborating. This Life and Learning Skill includes considering multiple perspectives—yours and others'—in order to work and live together and to resolve conflicts that arise.

Like the other skills, collaboration is based on the components of the foundational executive function skills. It includes:

- Setting goals for the kind of relationships you want to have (**goal setting**)
- Paying attention to yourself and others when conflicts arise (**perspective-taking** and **reflection**)
- Using what you know to recall what you've learned from dealing with similar situations while considering information about the current moment (**working memory**)
- Communicating, and modifying your behavior as necessary (**cognitive flexibility** and **inhibitory control**)

AN EXPERIMENT: DRAW AN E

Here's another experiment to try with your adolescent.

Stand or sit facing each other. Ask your child to use the index finger of their dominant hand to draw a capital *E* on their forehead as quickly as possible.

What does their *E* look like **to you**? Does it look like an *E*, or is it backward: ꓱ?

If they drew the *E* so you can read it (an ꓱ from their perspective), they're other-focused—taking your perspective. If they drew it so it was self-focused (*E*), it would look backward to you.

Do you think the power dynamics between the two of you had any effect on the *E* they drew?

"THERE'S SOMETHING ABOUT POWER!"

I suspect we've all had experiences where people more powerful than us make decisions that seem clueless—a doctor, our child's teacher, our boss.

Were they simply oblivious? Or did power in some ways blind them to your perspective?

That's the question that a classic *E* experiment by Adam Galinsky and Joe Magee of New York University explored.[87] In the experiment, the researchers randomly assigned fifty-seven college-age participants to "high power" and "low power" conditions, where power meant controlling the ability of another person to get what they want or being placed in a position where they depended on someone else. For the two conditions, some were asked to remember and write about an incident where they had power over someone else (high power) or someone else had power over them (low power).[88] Next:

> We told the people in the high-power condition, "Here are seven lottery tickets. You get to divide them up between you and another person. You can take as many as you want, or you can give some to the other people."
>
> This is called the "Dictator Game." This person dictates what everyone gets, including themselves. The other person was told, "You are dependent on this other person and they're going to decide how many, if any, lottery tickets you're going to get."[89]

The prize was an iPod.

It turns out power mattered. A lot. After the Dictator Game, the participants were asked to do the *E*-on-the-forehead task described above. The participants randomly assigned to the high-power condition were almost three times more likely to draw the self-focused *E* than those randomly assigned to the low-power condition. As Galinsky told me, "There's something about power!"

In another study, he and his colleagues found that feeling more powerful (this time in terms of social status) is linked to lower activation in the prefrontal cortex and the cingulate cortex, parts of the brain linked to thinking about others.[90]

Galinsky says:

What's really interesting is that power reduces perspective-taking![91]

Notice Galinsky talks about priming their study participants to feel powerful by recalling a time when they had power. Power is a position (you have greater authority or status) and an attitude (you feel in charge). Both can affect the extent to which you consider multiple perspectives in order to work together.

CAN TOGETHERNESS IMPROVE COOPERATION AND COLLABORATION?

In the 1950s, the late Harvard psychologist Gordon Allport developed an influential theory called "contact theory," which holds that increasing the personal contact among groups that historically don't get along can reduce tensions.[92] Thomas Pettigrew, a doctoral student then working with Allport, writes that they suspected contact alone wasn't sufficient. Allport and Pettigrew thought four key factors could reduce group conflict and prejudice: (1) equivalent status or power in the situation (there's power again, playing a role); (2) the support of a respected authority; (3) shared common goals; and (4) cooperation—doing things together, not just talking.[93]

Contact theory, by different names, has permeated workplace culture. A number of business leaders believe employees can't really collaborate unless they're literally working side by side, a proposition that was difficult to uphold during the pandemic and in the global economy where teams can work in different parts of the world. That view has underpinned years of resistance to workplace flexibility. But studies have increasingly found that working side by side isn't enough to reduce conflict or to promote collaboration, nor does working flexibly preclude good co-worker relationships.[94]

What *is* enough?

In 2006, Pettigrew and Linda Tropp of Boston College assembled 713 independent samples from 515 studies and discovered that, overall, contact theory works, writing: "Intergroup contact typically reduces intergroup prejudice." *But* the story is more complex. They found that the four factors aren't always necessary to reduce conflict, and the factors don't seem to function independently but rather operate together.[95]

At age thirteen, Sarah-Anne had few of these four factors going for her in school. As the one Jewish student in her class in a largely Catholic and Protestant inner-city school in New Jersey, she was repeatedly bullied. It was about religion, her mother, Eleanor, told me:

She had probably ten out of twenty-five kids attacking her verbally, asking, "What's wrong with you that you don't believe what we do?"

Her father, Richard, added:

They told her, "You're going to hell."

Sarah-Anne stood her ground. "That's not what I believe," she told them, but that didn't stop the conflict. When Sarah-Anne tried making friends with one of the girls in her class, another girl tried to stop it and, according to Eleanor, got verbally abusive:

The first time it became an issue, both girls got punished, which was appropriate. The second time, I kind of put my foot down with the school. They called in the other girl's mother. The other girl was basically given a very strict verbal warning to stay away from my daughter.

Two weeks and two days later, the abuse and conflict reignited in gym class. The other girl shoved Sarah-Anne.

My daughter shoved her back. She's like, "I'm done." That afternoon, this girl and a friend of hers made Nazi jokes. Let's just say both of those girls were suspended.

Sarah-Anne didn't show any emotion in school, but when she got home, her sadness was profound. Eleanor says, "I worry about my daughter because she's a very sensitive soul, but I will say, it was nice to see that she has a very strong backbone, too. She stood her ground every single time."

But she often felt she didn't belong. Her father told me:

She made a very sad kind of "I'm so lonely" comment. It was this very isolated feeling, like, "Everyone else around me has their own language and I'm the only one speaking in this particular way, who looks like this, who believes this."

Her parents decided to enroll her in a Jewish Sunday school. Sarah-Anne's spirits improved. According to Richard:

She was surrounded by people who look like her, talk like her, have the same beliefs. She was part of a larger group, and that was very reassuring to her.

Here's a situation where contact clearly wasn't enough (as I've found it isn't in workplace studies). Although Sarah-Anne acted as if she felt powerful, she was one against many. The school would react to incidents but wasn't proactive in helping kids from different backgrounds learn to connect and collaborate. They used traditional exclusionary discipline—calling the parents in, separating the kids, and suspension. Discipline wasn't about teaching (as in the original meaning of the word). It was about punishing.

HIGH CONFLICT

Incidents like this can escalate and can become what journalist Amanda Ripley calls "high conflict," which she's found is a mysterious force that causes us to lie awake at night, obsessed about the situation. It's quite different from good conflict, which can spur us to think better and be better. Here's how Ripley describes high conflict in her book of the same name:

When conflict escalates past a certain point, the conflict itself takes charge. The original facts and forces that led to the dispute fade into the background. The us-versus-them dynamic takes over.[96]

That's what was beginning to happen with Sarah-Anne and her classmates. "Us versus them" was taking over, and cooperation and collaboration became less possible. The little things in conflict can become big things. It would take leadership in the school or among the parents to turn this situation around.

Ripley herself grew up monitoring conflict. Although she lived in a home she describes as filled with food, love, and second chances, her mother struggled with depression and anxiety that could easily escalate to anger and blame. Ripley recalls that she'd sit on the stairs of her house monitoring her parents' fights while her brother drowned them out with his Star Wars action figures. Ripley now reflects that she'd hoped listening would help her better understand what was happening and maybe even prevent it. Her book does just that—helps us understand the nature of conflict and how to de-escalate it. Included are strategies to reduce conflict and improve communication and collaboration. You will see later in this chapter that a number of these strategies are central in the research on self-control:[97]

- **Avoid the fire-starters**—the conflict triggers. That's what Sarah-Anne's school did when they prohibited contact between her and the girl who was attacking her. It was, however, a short-lived solution because these students remained in the same class.
- **Make changes to the situation to lessen its emotional power.** Perhaps the teachers might have worked with the two girls to make a list of things they could agree to talk about that wouldn't set them off.
- **Practice rhythmic breathing.** This practice is central to an evidence-based curriculum for schools and parents created by actress and extraordinary children's advocate Goldie Hawn and launched in 2003 for children in pre-K through eighth grade (it is currently being piloted for high school students). Called MindUp, its purpose, as Hawn writes, is to "help kids learn how to self-regulate their emotions, become more resilient and learn about how their brain works to give them a road map out of despair and into a more positive mindset."

    Working with neuroscientists, teachers, positive psychologists, and mindfulness experts, more than seven million children in forty-eight countries worldwide have participated in MindUp. They now also have a program for teachers.[98] A key feature of their programs, "Brain Break," entails practicing mindfulness and breathing techniques.[99]
- **Use distraction.** That means intentionally focusing your attention on something else during the conflict. That's hard to do during the heat of the moment, but it can be very helpful even later, if you can't get the conflict out of your mind.[100]
- **Reappraise the situation.** This involves reframing how you think about the situation, similar to Jennifer Silvers's studies discussed earlier in the book. Sarah-Anne's parents tried to help her do this by explaining that the other girls hadn't learned to deal with conflict. Her mother says: "We ended up having a whole conversation about ignorance." The other kids' parents and the teachers were not actively teaching the students how

to deal with people from different cultures, so Eleanor told Sarah-Anne that those other kids only knew how to be reactive, not proactive.

- **Go to the balcony.** With psychological distancing,[101] you step back and imagine you're viewing the situation from afar, from a place of calm self-control. When my young kids had public outbursts, I'd imagine I was acting in a television show and being filmed. It helped me handle the meltdown much more calmly. This involves pretending and is a very constructive technique for taking on challenges.
- **Use perspective-taking.** Imagining how the other person sees this situation can build understanding. Pettigrew and Tropp suggest that perspective-taking is a promising factor in reducing conflict and that new studies should look at it.[102]

In 2018, Elizabeth Paluck of Princeton University and her colleagues conducted a ten-years-later reevaluation of the Pettigrew and Tropp conclusions with much more explicit criteria.[103] They assembled studies of contact theory that randomly assigned people to experimental or control conditions and that measured the impact of the experiment over time. In all, they found twenty-seven studies—and, interestingly, most of them involved young people from middle school into the college years.

In sum, they found that contact between in-groups and out-groups can reduce conflict and prejudice, but that some kinds of prejudice are more easily diminished than others. As the authors write, "Contact seems to work especially well as a strategy for reducing prejudice toward people with mental or physical disabilities."[104]

THE POWER OF CURIOSITY

Megan Price of the Center for Applied Insight Conflict Resolution takes a different tack in approaching conflict and collaboration—one she's learned alongside her father, Jamie Price, a noted scholar on peace. They have looked at how the mind responds to conflict.

Research has shown that conflict is a matter of defending against a feeling of threat.[105]

Stress, as we discussed in chapter 1, is a cascading process. When the amygdala registers threat, the hypothalamus releases adrenaline into our blood so that we can defend ourselves.[106] Our heart rate rises, we breathe faster, and our senses become heightened. This response makes it possible for us to defend ourselves against the threat by **fighting** (being aggressive), **taking flight** (getting away from the threat), **freezing** (deflecting attention from ourselves), or **fawning** (groveling or sucking up).[107]

Next, cortisol is released so we can continue to defend ourselves, though it inhibits our ability to think clearly. A number of cognitive biases can ensue:[108]

- **Tunnel vision,** where we focus on one key aspect of the threat, unable to focus on other information
- **Selective perception,** where we pay attention only to information that we see as confirming our understanding of the threat, to the exclusion of information that may cast our conclusions into doubt
- **Confirmation bias,** where we become convinced that what we believe is true and erect barricades against anything that might discredit our conclusions
- **Egocentricity,** where we discount others' points of view
- **Attribution bias,** where we attribute the problem to another person (they're at fault, they're jerks)
- **Enemy images,** where we generalize about the perpetrator's traits, despite insufficient evidence

These biases can become self-fulfilling prophecies, where the more we expect someone to react in negative ways, the more likely it is that they will.

How can we transcend these cognitive blockages that push us into opposing corners, where we dig in and get increasingly divided—us versus them?[109] That's not only true of the partisan divide in this country; it's true of the divide that Sarah-Anne experienced in her school. Despite everything her parents and teachers said, Sarah-Anne and her classmates were becoming entrenched in an us-versus-them divide, where the solutions seemed to be fight (as Sarah-Anne did) or flight (the teacher-imposed restriction against contact between the disputing students).

In wondering about how to reduce these tendencies, Price found an answer in wondering itself: curiosity. She's found that *if* **we can become curious about how our minds work when we engage in conflict,** *then* **new possibilities for weakening the us-versus-them divide can emerge.**[110]

It does sound simple, even simplistic. Can you really use this to address international problems like disputes between nations, national problems like the partisan divide, and local problems like the decision-making of police or of teachers and kids in classroom conflict? Can you really promote more co-operation with curiosity?

Price says yes. She says that what separates this approach, called the Insight approach, from others is that it is grounded in an understanding of how we use our minds to make decisions in conflict. Curiosity can improve how we make decisions and can change how the brain responds to conflict by activating the brain's reward centers.[111] This is similar to the insight I had in developing the Possibilities Mindset—that being curious and wondering open us up to bringing about change in our own behavior.

As Price defines it, curiosity is the desire to know. She writes:

> It has been recognized over the years as a common, innate human characteristic, one that compels us to ask questions (both implicitly and explicitly), seek knowledge, gain understanding and make appropriate decisions.[112]

Ultimately, Price concludes, curiosity is part of our exploratory nature. Just as our response to threat is necessary for survival, so, too, is exploring.

And who is more exploratory than adolescents?

Most of Price's work has been with the police, especially how to help them deal differently with those split-second decision moments when they are faced with conflict in the course of their duties. Will they increase their power by chasing or shooting, or will they ask questions?[113] Price says that they teach police to be strategically curious:

> We teach officers to ask strategic questions that get into the thought process of the person who they're dealing with. What is the citizen hoping to achieve by doing what they're doing? What are they worried is going to happen? We find that getting curious works extraordinarily well to not only de-escalate or prevent escalation, but to break down boundaries and barriers to understanding.[114]

That could be a textbook definition of perspective-taking, communication, and collaboration.

Price says that police respond to this approach very positively because it connects to their reasons for joining the police force—their purpose—in the first place: typically to improve their communities. This is similar to the rationale Jason Okonofua and Greg Walton used with teachers (see the section on the need for respect in chapter 4), where the researchers connected teachers' discipline practices to their original reasons for becoming teachers.

It feels to me as if adolescents would be ideal for this kind of intervention—given their desire to explore, understand, and make the world a better place. Price wanted to find out, too, so she worked with a school in the District of Columbia that was rife with violence and conflict, to see if this approach could work in one school. If it worked, could it be a model for "the persistent, contemporary problem of the school-to-prison pipeline, where kids who are punished for misbehavior through suspension and expulsion are overwhelmingly ending up in the juvenile justice system without future prospects for success?"[115]

It's "a heavy lift," Price writes, to "[shift] away from decades-long use of exclusionary discipline."[116] For adults who've grown up in a culture of punitive discipline, it's easy to slip back. As Price continues:

> It takes broad buy-in from staff, many of whom believe in the effectiveness of strict punishments for misbehavior and rely on sending kids out to maintain order in their classrooms.

Price found that calling attention to adult decision-making had a profound impact. It's what teachers found especially useful and what they reflected on after the intervention was over. As Price writes:

> When we become curious . . . we generate insights into how we and others are using our minds, allowing ourselves and others to improve our performances and imagine possibilities for acting that enhance the probability of finding creative solutions to our troubles rather than destructive ones.[117]

No wonder her approach is called the Insight approach!

FROM CURIOSITY TO COMPASSION

Empathy—feeling what others feel, whether it's joy or pain—is often viewed as the bedrock of collaboration, but it's not that clear-cut. Sharing the suffering of others can be depleting and stressful, resulting in burnout and withdrawal from others.

There is, however, another emotion that builds on empathy but is a much surer bridge to collaboration, and that's compassion. Tania Singer of the

Max Planck Society in Berlin, Germany, and Olga Klimecki of the University of Geneva in Switzerland define compassion as feelings of warmth, concern, and care for others and a strong motivation to improve others' well-being.[118]

Singer has conducted a number of studies to differentiate these feelings and to intervene to see how they work. In one study with Klimecki and others, adult participants received one day of empathy, compassion, or memory training (the control group).[119] In the empathy training, participants were guided to visualize a person (beginning with themselves, then someone they knew, then a stranger, and then all humanity) who was suffering and to respond by saying things to themselves like "I share your suffering." In contrast, participants in the compassion training were guided to relate to the pain of the same sequence of people with loving-kindness. Afterward, all three groups were shown videos of human suffering while their brains were scanned. The researchers found that those who received empathic training felt more negative and their scans showed activations in the anterior insula and anterior midcingulate cortex— regions associated with empathy for pain. Those who received compassion training experienced more positive emotions, and their scans revealed activations of a nonoverlapping network, including the ventral striatum and medial orbitofrontal cortex. These networks are associated with positive emotions, reward, and social connections.

In a longer and larger study, Singer and her colleagues trained adult participants for twenty to thirty minutes a day over nine months on presence (aimed at attention and mindfulness), affect (aimed at emotional compassion and gratitude), and perspective (aimed at a cognitive understanding of one's own and others' perspectives).[120] This training uniquely involved meditations and practicing what participants had learned in pairs of two.

Their findings show that it matters what you practice. Following the presence module, participants had improved attention skills and abilities to focus on the present moment. Additionally, there were brain changes in attention-relevant brain areas. After the affect module, participants were more compassionate and prosocial, and there were brain changes in limbic and paralimbic networks associated with empathy and compassion. In the perspective module, participants became better at understanding others. In the modules that included applying what they learned to real-life circumstances and practicing their responses in pairs, participants experienced a lower biological reaction to a stressful situation.[121] Although Singer's studies are of adults, her findings, as well as those by Richie Davidson and his team at the University of Wisconsin,[122] make it clear to me that if we want to foster collaboration among adolescents, we need to **cultivate both compassion *and* a cognitive under-**

standing of the perspectives of others. Importantly, compassion strengthens the capacity to forgive, Singer says, adding that there is nothing weak about this; it is the most courageous way of being in the world.[123]

PROMOTING COMMUNICATING AND COLLABORATING

We can promote the Life and Learning Skill of **communicating** when we help adolescents:

- Think about what they want to communicate and then consider how others will understand their point of view.
- Understand the biases that can be roadblocks to communication. Are they assuming that others will know what they know (the curse of knowledge), understand what they mean (ships passing in the night), or want what they want (the platinum rule)? How can they include others' perspectives in their communicating?

We can help young people become more adept at **collaborating** when we help them:

- Wonder what the people working with them want to achieve. What are their goals and how are they different from or similar to their own goals?
- Become curious if they run into conflict with others. What seems to be the threat to themselves and to others? How then can they turn that threat into a challenge and find ways to resolve it?
- Become curious about some of the cognitive biases that might impede their own work with others, like only paying attention to information that confirms their understanding (confirmation bias), blaming others without looking at their own role (attribution bias), or dividing the world into us and them without trying to work together (enemy images).
- Feel compassion for the issues that others face.

All of us have a **choice** in how we communicate and collaborate with others. Seeing challenges as opportunities to build better Life and Learning Skills helps us make choices that work better for us *and* for our children.

Life and Learning Skill 4: Problem-Solving: Meaning-Making, Creative Thinking, Relational Reasoning, and Critical Thinking

Problem-solving has four steps, each involving executive function–based skills: (1) meaning-making, or making sense of the decision in both concrete and abstract ways; (2) creative thinking, or thinking of options that are novel and useful; (3) relational reasoning, or seeing the connections in all information being considered; and (4) critical thinking, or searching for valid and accurate information, weighing the pros and cons, and solving the problem.

The opening lines in Robert Frost's iconic poem "The Road Not Taken" are: "Two roads diverged in a yellow wood, / And sorry I could not travel both."[124]

It's an everyday image. You're out walking, come to a fork in the road, and have to decide which way to turn, which route to take. It may seem like a small decision. You're just out for a walk, and the two roads in the Frost poem look similar—both seem traveled about the same.

I discovered this poem in an English class as a teenager, and once I'd read it, I've never forgotten it. In the poem's closing words, the poet looks back at the decision of which road to take, writing: "I took the road less traveled by." It was a decision that "made all the difference."

When I first came upon this poem, making big decisions seemed mysterious, scary, possibly because the process and the consequences were unknowns. What courses should I take in high school? Which group of kids should I hang out with? How do I know if I'm in love? What does it mean to have a serious boyfriend versus meeting lots of different people? Should I study for a test or have fun with friends? What college should I go to? What should I major in? How do I know which road to travel? Each of these decisions we make and the problems we solve accrue to the life we ultimately have. They can—sometimes do—make "all the difference."

Problem-solving is a Life and Learning Skill, and there's a science behind it. In this section, we'll look at this science, beginning with how we make sense of problems (meaning-making), come up with options (creative thinking), reason about these options (relational thinking), weigh their pluses and minuses (critical thinking), and eventually resolve the problem. The more we understand this science, the more we can help adolescents learn to become better problem-solvers.

"SHOULD I LEAVE OR SHOULD I STAY?"

Brooke had a big problem to solve in ninth grade—should she leave the dance studio she'd attended since she was three years old and follow her longtime teacher to a different studio, or should she stay? Her teacher's quitting was sudden and surprising:

> She told us she eventually wanted to become a physical therapist. Her son was going to an expensive university, so she was like, "I need to make more money now to change careers."

What's more, Brooke's friends from the studio—twenty-five of them—decided to follow their teacher: "They were like, 'Come with us.'"

Brooke had just enrolled in a new high school and didn't have many friends there yet. Now, unexpectedly, she was faced with losing her dance friends:

> I had this dilemma!! Should I leave? Should I stay?
>
> Should I stay true to the studio I've been at since I was three? Or follow this teacher who I trust with my life?

Her parents decided to leave the choice to her:

> It was the first big decision I had to make by myself, and it was scary.
>
> My mom was like, "I'm supporting you, whatever you want to do."
> Having her support, no matter what I decided, was important because everyone was telling me different things.

Brooke also realized that figuring this out could be a growth opportunity. Although her parents weren't "super-controlling," they'd taken a hand in most of her major life decisions until now.

Brooke stepped back and began looking at the options more carefully. First, she looked at her relationship with her dance teacher and began to realize that while her teacher cared about her, she had never really given Brooke opportunities to excel:

I was kind of in the shadows. I didn't get a lot of attention from her. Maybe because the other dancers were a little older than me, I never had a chance to be in front of the dances or anything.

Conversely, she realized she had a long-lasting connection with the studio owner. She could also put herself into the owner's shoes:

I'd been there for twelve years. I felt loyal to her. She did play a huge part in my growing up. Because everyone was leaving her, she was losing so much money.

She also began thinking about the nature of lasting friendship:

Are these friends really good friends for me? Are they going to be lifelong people in my life? Or would I rather have this role model who's a woman, a boss, running an entire studio? Would I rather leave that for these people who really aren't always that great to me? Am I just depending on them for friendship, or do I actually like them?

While her mother didn't solve the problem for Brooke, she'd asked Brooke questions that took her out of the here and now and prompted her to think about belonging:

My mother was like, "Where do you feel like you belong? Where do you feel like you're going to feel at home for the next four years?" It really made me think, "Who do I want to be with for the rest of my high school career? Which people are healthy for me?"

Brooke began to see that maybe because her dance friends were older or maybe because of their personalities, "at the end of the day, they thought they were better than me and kind of looked down on me. I don't think it was intentional but it was happening."

The Life and Learning Skill of Meaning-Making

Problem-Solving

MEANING-MAKING
Identifying and defining the problem

Mary Helen Immordino-Yang studies meaning-making, which is the first step in problem-solving. One major question has driven her work:

We're really interested in understanding how adolescents come to understand and make sense out of the things that they learn, witness and experience.[125]

That's the essence of **meaning-making**—making sense of experience—and it's essential to problem-solving. The way young people understand a situation is basic to how they respond to it.

For a 2017 *NOVA* TV special on her research, Immordino-Yang demonstrated a key facet of her methodology, which involves showing very short film clips to adolescents about other adolescents and asking how they react. In her actual studies, the film clips depict adolescents who aren't famous, but for TV, Immordino-Yang used the well-known story of Malala Yousafzai, the Pakistani teenager who stood up against a Taliban edict forbidding girls from receiving an education.[126] She begins by telling each study participant—in the *NOVA* special, a girl named Isela—about the video they will be seeing: that it's about a twelve-year-old in Pakistan whose city was taken over by a group called the Taliban. Then Isela watches a one-minute clip. Afterward, Immordino-Yang follows a scripted protocol and their exchange is videotaped:[127]

I look down and say, "How does her story make you feel?" I tell them and
show them I'm writing it down. I'm standardizing my behavior so they
don't worry about what I'm thinking or doing.[128]

Isela reacts emotionally. "This story makes me feel upset," she says. She
summarizes what she saw—that Malala wanted to be a doctor and continue her education—and Isela feels sad knowing Malala's journey will be
so difficult.[129]

Then Isela pauses before shifting to talking about her own life and beyond, telling Immordino-Yang:

It makes me think about my own journey in education—how I want to go
to college and hopefully be a scientist someday and even more. I guess what
really hits me is how not everyone is able to get this chance to go forward
with their life and get an education or do what they want to do with their
life. I mean, it's not right.

That pause is key—it's the gateway between here-and-now, concrete
thinking and abstract thinking. Immordino-Yang calls these **two categories**
of meaning-making.

In this case, the **here-and-now meaning-making** makes Isela sad, especially knowing that because education is prohibited for girls in Pakistan,
Malala's journey won't be easy.

When she moves into more **abstract* meaning-making**, Isela's thinking is
qualitatively and cognitively different. She talks about a society that prevents
some people from learning, and it inspires her to work harder. Immordino-
Yang further explains:

All of a sudden, Isela gets this awareness that this has deeper meaning than
just Malala and her. It's about how the world is and how the world could
be. These complex abstractions aren't actually said in the story, and are
instead Isela's inferring about the broader systems-level meaning of the
story.

Do you see the parallels with Brooke's meaning-making? Initially, Brooke
focused on the here and now, the immediate dilemma: staying at the dance
studio with the owner or moving to a new studio with her friends and

---

* Immordino-Yang calls this "transcendent" thinking because it involves transcending the current
situation and making deep meaning about oneself and the social world.

teacher. Then she, too, paused, and moved to a more abstract interpretation about whom she'd like to be friends with, what kind of behavior inspires feelings of belonging and loyalty, and what kind of future opportunities she might have under each scenario.

These two categories of meaning-making affect adolescents' brain development in different ways, as brain scanning studies reveal.

THE BRAIN BASIS FOR MEANING-MAKING

The protocol used with Isela for the TV show demonstrates the protocol used in an ongoing USC study following sixty-five adolescents, who were ages fourteen to eighteen at the study's beginning. They come from neighborhoods in Los Angeles where families are largely immigrants and low-income. They are doing well in school and have stable home situations.[130]

At the onset of this longitudinal study, the participants spent a day in the lab, where they were interviewed about their experiences at home and school, their identities, and their hopes for their futures. They were given standardized tests, including an IQ test. As demonstrated in the *NOVA* episode, the study participants were told stories of real teenagers from around the world, then shown a one-minute video clip depicting each story, followed by being invited to express how they think and feel about the story.[131] In all, there were forty such stories.

Then, says Immordino-Yang:

> *We moved them into the fMRI scanner and had them watch five-second reminders of the crux of each story. They are given a few seconds to think about the story and then, using a button, report how strongly they felt about it. They watch those twice in two different scanner runs for statistical validity.*[132]

After viewing a reminder of each story in the scanner, they were asked how emotionally engaged they were in the story:

> *We conduct Resting State Connectivity and other scans allowing us to look at cortex thickness and how that's changing over time. We're also measuring heart rate, microscopic amounts of sweating on the bottoms of people's feet, breathing, and chest volume changes.*[133]

FIVE STANDOUT FINDINGS ABOUT MEANING-MAKING

In looking at this research from Immordino-Yang's articles, speeches, and my interviews with her, I see five findings that have important implications for adolescent development.

First, this research elevates **the significance of storytelling in adolescent development.** In an article for educators, Immordino-Yang and Douglas Knecht of Bank Street College write that the fundamental premise of this work is that people "construct *narratives* about the world and their experiences in it." In effect, "people tell themselves stories about who they and others are, how the world works and why."[134] This research takes the kind of storytelling and the search for a narrative identity we've explored in the research of Dan McAdams of Northwestern University and investigates its impact on brain development during adolescence and beyond.

A second standout finding is that **different brain networks are involved in different types of meaning-making.** That may not sound like a big deal, but you'll see that it becomes a big deal as adolescents grow up.

When participants talk in a **concrete way** about what they've seen and felt, their **Executive Control Network (ECN)** is activated. "They're **outwardly focused, engaged in the here and now.**"[135] They're **noticing, responding,** and **reacting** to things, which takes executive function and involves the fundamental EF skills of working memory, cognitive flexibility, and inhibitory control.

When the issue in the story matters to the participants (i.e., they are emotionally engaged), their executive function network links to the **Salience Network (SN):**

> Among these are the brain regions that tell you when you have a stomachache or that your heart is pounding after running up the stairs, and those that make you feel a jolt of arousal when you notice something you care about . . . The SN weighs the relevance and perceived importance and urgency of information to facilitate further thinking.[136]

Then there's that spontaneous **pause.** Study participants (adults, too, in other studies) tend to avert or close their eyes, might say "um" and "ah" a lot, and speak more slowly as they move from the concrete meaning of the event into deeper meaning-making.

At that time, their **Default Mode Network (DMN)** becomes activated.

This kind of meaning-making is **inwardly focused** and involves more **abstract thinking;** the participants **reflect,** thinking about what inspires them and about their own psychological capabilities.[137]

> *The DMN is activated when reflecting, imagining hypothetical or possible future scenarios, remembering the past, and processing morally relevant information. It is important for conceptual understanding, reading comprehension, creativity, nonlinear and "out-of-the-box" thinking, for constructing a sense of self, and for feeling inspired.*[138]

To get a clearer idea about how these thought processes affect adolescent development, the researchers control for factors that might affect the results, such as the adolescents' IQ, age, and gender, as well as their family's socioeconomic status, including their parents' educational level.[139] Interestingly enough, these demographic factors don't affect meaning-making.

A third standout finding: **adolescents are capable of both types of meaning-making.** "It's not like you have that abstract head-in-the-clouds kid and a concrete-empathic kid," Immordino-Yang says.[140] Kids can do both, and both are important in their lives and their learning.

Furthermore, each type of meaning-making affects their development in different ways.

Key Findings: The more participants in this study talked concretely in the interviews, the more likely they were to have good relationships with peers and teachers. The more they talked abstractly, the more creative and thoughtful they were in understanding and reasoning about complex issues.

A fourth finding of importance: **emotional engagement drives complex thinking.** As you know, emotion and reason are often considered competing forces—but these studies indicate otherwise. **Emotion is, in fact, the driver of deep thinking.** Immordino-Yang concludes: "Emotion organizes brain activity when thinking abstractly and deeply."

The fifth finding is particularly noteworthy. When the research team went back two years later to the study participants, who were now sixteen to twenty years old, Rebecca Gotlieb, Immordino-Yang, and their team found that abstract thinking is, in fact, a brain builder.[141] The more adolescents talked abstractly, the more they grew the connectivity between the Executive Control Network and the Default Mode Network.

Key Finding: The growth in the coordination between these networks "predicted better personal and scholarly outcomes in young adulthood."[142] A subsequent study found that this neural growth also predicted stronger identity development, which then predicted greater life satisfaction (the participants' satisfaction with themselves and their relationships) five years after the initial data collection. The authors write: "Ultimately, transcendent thinking may be to the adolescent mind and brain what exercise is to the body: most people can exercise, but only those who do will reap the benefits."[143]

To work toward ensuring that more adolescents have opportunities to build their minds and brains, Immordino-Yang and her team evaluated an eight-week storytelling program, Sages and Seekers.[144] The program, which takes places in neighborhood gathering places, was so named because high school students (seekers) select an older person in their seventies (sages) to work with and then share stories in response to prompts like: "What is the best advice you have ever received?" "Who has been the greatest influence in your life?" "What quality do you value most in your friends?" and "Do you have any regrets so far in life?" An evaluation showed that sharing stories increased transcendent meaning-making in the adolescents, resulting in more sense of purpose in their own lives.[145]

Who knew that when your children toggle between concrete and abstract thinking, as Brooke did in figuring out whether to stay or leave her dance studio, it's building their brains? It may seem mundane, but it's not at all. It's another way that problem-solving and decision-making can make "all the difference." Immordino-Yang underlines this point, saying it's not what they decide but how they go about deciding that matters most.

The Life and Learning Skill of Creative Thinking: From "What Is" to "What Might Be"

Problem-Solving

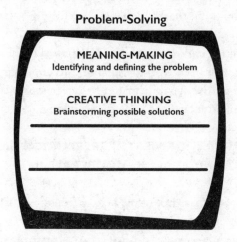

MEANING-MAKING
Identifying and defining the problem

CREATIVE THINKING
Brainstorming possible solutions

In figuring out what to do, Brooke engaged in concrete and abstract thinking, which led her to something else—thinking creatively. She thought beyond the confines of *what is* to *what might be*. If she stayed at the studio, she might have the opportunity to become a leader:

> *I was the oldest one at the studio at the time when everyone left. We had twenty-five people who were older than me that left. I was just scared to step into that leadership role because it kind of was a huge change from what I'd been doing.*

In the process of problem-solving, Brooke began thinking creatively and thus brainstorming possible solutions. Like meaning-making, creative thinking is a Life and Learning Skill that's integral to good problem-solving.

Creativity is defined as thinking what's new or novel and at the same time useful. Roger Beaty, who studies the psychology and neuroscience of creativity at Penn State University, says that this definition is widely accepted:

> *The first paragraph on every paper about creativity says creativity is novelty and usefulness and/or appropriateness, effectiveness.*[146]

Unless, perhaps, you're thinking about abstract art, but abstract art can be useful, too (my husband's intent as an artist has always been to promote a meditative healing state, and there is growing literature on the connections between art and well-being).[147] Eveline Crone describes "novel" thinking as out-of-the box thinking that's doable or applicable[148]—which is just what Brooke was doing.

Creative thinking calls on executive function skills. To disassemble and recombine ideas, you need **working memory**; to come up with novel ideas, you are using **cognitive flexibility**; and to reject the status quo, you need **inhibitory control**. You also need abstract thinking.

INSPIRATION MEETS PERSPIRATION: HOW INSIGHT AND ANALYSIS COOPERATE IN CREATIVITY

When you saw the phrase "out of the box" (Crone's words), did you think of a sudden moment of inspiration? That's a typical view of creativity—as an aha moment and something geniuses do. Robert Weisberg of Temple University has spent years questioning those notions through a meticulous series of studies.[149]

AN EXPERIMENT: THE NINE-DOT PROBLEM

Here's an experiment Weisberg and Jason Chein (whom you met in the section on perspective-taking) conducted that you and your adolescent can try together. On a piece of paper, draw three rows of three dots to look like this:

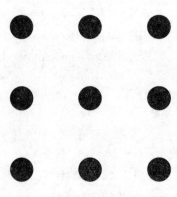

(You can repeat this grid on several pieces of paper so that you can try again if you don't get it right away.)

Now, with a pencil or pen, draw a line through each of these dots using only straight lines—no curves or crossing lines. Once you begin, you can't lift the pencil or pen from the page.

Did you or your child solve it?

If you are like me, I made an X-like figure but missed the sides. Other people try an N or a Z.

Chein says he's watched many people do this experiment,[150] and typically they struggle:

> You can make a hundred attempts and still might not solve the problem. Normally what happens is that something hits you. You'll see the problem in a different light. You'll have an inspiration and you'll solve the problem.[151]

Is this insight or analysis?

Chein, Weisberg, and their team used the example of the marrying man problem to illustrate a leap of mind:

> A man in our town has married twenty women from the town. Bigamy is illegal here, and yet this man has broken no law. Explain.[152]

Most people get the problem wrong until they reinterpret the word "marrying," not as meaning "he has been married to twenty women" but as meaning he's a clergymember who has officiated at these women's marriages. Then they "see" the solution.

To solve the Nine Dot problem by **analysis**, you'd work steadily toward a solution by trying alternatives. To use **insight**, the answer would come to you as an aha moment outside of your consciousness.

Here's a hint at the solution. You need to draw lines outside the implicit box that the three rows of dots create.

Yet Chein and Weisberg have found that even giving people this hint doesn't always help. They suspected that "a critical component . . . is *lookahead*—the person's ability to imagine in WM [working memory] the result of carrying out various moves."[153]

Key Finding: In these experiments, young people with better spatial working memories—that is, who were able to hold spatial solutions in their working memories—were more likely to figure out solutions to the Nine Dot problem and to do it faster.

Oh yes—the solutions. Here are some:

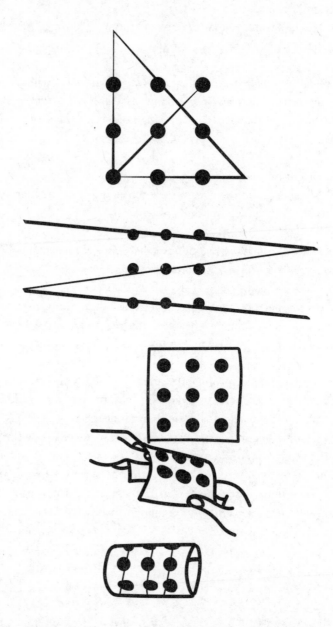

If you solved this problem, did you do it step by step, or was it a flash, a creative moment? Even if you did it in a flash, your spatial working memory skills played a role in your arriving at a solution.

That's spatial working memory. What about verbal working memory?

AN EXPERIMENT: COMPOUND REMOTE ASSOCIATE (CRA) PROBLEMS

"Compound remote associate (CRA) problems" is a mouthful, but you may have played games similar to this experiment. The experimenter selects three words. Here's your task and your adolescent's: think of one word that would go with all three of them, before or after the word, to make up a compound.

Example: If I say "aid," "rubber," and "wagon," what would the fourth word be?

It's "band" ("Band-Aid," "rubber band," and "bandwagon").

Okay, now try this out yourself or with your child. Here are three words from their study: "teeth," "arrest," "start." Can you think of a fourth word that goes with these three?

It's not so easy, Chein says.[154] The researchers had the undergraduate participants "think aloud," sharing their thoughts as they went about solving the compound word puzzle.[155] They found that even when the solution seems to arrive as a creative act, participants' prior skill in verbal working memory and attention control predicted how well they solved these word problems.

Key Finding: The study concludes that we usually think of reaching conclusions by insight or by analysis,[156] implying "an either/or stance toward problem solving," but it is really a both/and.[157]

And the solution to the problem I gave you is "false": as in "false teeth," "false arrest," and "false start."

"THERE IS NO CREATIVITY REGION": THE BRAIN BASIS OF CREATIVITY

Roger Beaty has been interested in creativity since adolescence, wanting to understand how his own creative processes as a musician worked.[158]

In college, I took a class on creativity and problem-solving innovation with Robert Weisberg. It was transformative for me to discover that you could actually study creativity with scientific methods. You could study famous creators all the way down to the normal creative thoughts people have in daily life that help them solve problems.

Although we tend to associate creativity with "famous creators," Beaty, like Weisberg, emphasizes the importance of creative thinking in daily life, like figuring out how to solve a challenging problem.

Beaty knew that looking at specific parts of the brain wouldn't answer his questions about the brain processes underlying creativity and "what characteristics distinguish more versus less creative people":

*I wasn't satisfied with the conventional fMRI activation type of studies— like studies showing one area lighting up or another. **There is no creativity region.***

That's an important statement! People have searched for a creativity region for ages. Even the misguided right-brain/left-brain theories—now known as an inaccurate neuromyth—were an attempt to pinpoint one specific creativity place in the brain. Beaty knew, however, that different areas of the brain contribute in different ways to creative thinking. His search: to find what those areas are and how they work together.

He began small, as most neuroscientists do. While still in graduate school in 2015, he and his team gave twenty-five college-age participants a creative thinking task, scanning them as they responded.

Since it was a "very small sample and a modest correlation," they then "essentially did the same study with six times that sample size." They also "used a different approach to search throughout the whole brain." The goal: "to see if we could not just correlate a few regions together, but find a pattern across the whole brain that was predictive of creativity."[159]

Beaty says that's all he did for months—scanning.

AN EXPERIMENT: THE ALTERNATIVE USES TASK

One task Beaty uses to measure creative (or divergent) thinking is the Alternative Uses Task (AUT).[160] Try it yourself or with your adolescent the way Beaty uses it.

Imagine a sock. Now take two minutes and think of as many uses for it as you can. Write down your ideas.

Beaty reports:

> For the sock, one participant suggested using it to warm your feet . . . while another participant suggested using it as a water filtration system.[161]

Want to keep going? Try it with nearby objects—a cup, a pen, or a paper clip. It's fun with kids! The AUT works well for two reasons: first, because anyone can be an expert in the common uses of everyday objects—yet it also asks you to go beyond what you already know to think of novel or original uses—and, second, because the type of thinking assessed by the AUT is moderately predictive of people's creative achievements in the arts and sciences.[162]

In a follow-up study using the AUT both in the scanner and afterward, Beaty and his colleagues trained raters to assess the creativity, cleverness, and uncommonness of the answers of the 163 study participants, who were primarily undergraduate and graduate students.[163]

If you were rating yourself on the AUT, how would you say you did?

HIGH-CREATIVE NETWORKS

In order to analyze the fMRI scans, Beaty told me, they used a relatively new "machine learning" tool called connectome prediction modeling, which enabled them to see whole brain networks. As in the pilot study, three networks showed up: the Default Mode Network (DMN), the Executive Control Network (ECN), and the Salience Network (SN).[164]

Sound familiar? Yes, these are the same three networks that are important in the Immordino-Yang studies.

Key Finding: According to Beaty's results, creative thinking begins when we draw on our imaginations (DMN). When an idea comes up that seems promising (detected by the SN), we switch over to do a reality check (using the ECN) on its effectiveness and perhaps elaborate on it or discard it.

As Immordino-Yang also found, the DMN and the ECN aren't "on" at the same time. In fact, they tend to work in opposition—that's central to these findings.

Key Finding: To be a creative thinker, you need both idea generation and idea evaluation. The stronger the connections among these networks, the more creative the person's ideas are. Beaty and his team called this brain profile "high-creative networks," compared to "low-creative networks," which have fewer connections.

Could they predict how creative individuals are simply by looking at the connections in their brain networks—like a doctor can diagnose an illness by looking at X-rays, MRIs, or blood work (based on an accumulation of data about scores of people)?

They reached out to scholars in Austria and China who collectively had three datasets that included brain scans and creativity assessments. Despite the differences in the populations, they found "robust" correlations, indicating that a person's capacity to generate original ideas can be reliably predicted from the strength of their brain's functional connectivity. This indicates that "creative thinking ability is characterized by a distinct brain connectivity profile."[165]

TRAINING CREATIVITY?

So, one might wonder, can we begin to figure out what kind of life experiences build better connections among these networks? Beaty's first step was to collaborate with Solange Denervaud on a study comparing the brain networks of children educated in Montessori programs and those in traditional school programs in Switzerland. Denervaud, a former Montessori teacher and now a postdoctoral fellow at Lausanne University Hospital, had collected data on sixty-seven children from ages five through fourteen in Montessori and traditional school settings. The groups were comparable in age, gender, and background characteristics, including socioeconomic status and intelligence.[166] In the study, the children completed two tests of their nonverbal creativity thinking:[167]

- **Convergent thinking**—that is, thinking of a single creative solution to a problem (selecting three abstract shapes out of eight and making a drawing combining these shapes)

- **Divergent thinking**—that is, thinking of ideas that differ from each other (making as many drawings as they could from one abstract form)

In addition, they completed a **verbal fluency** test, asked to name as many animals as they could think of in sixty seconds.

A semantic network analysis of the children's responses to the verbal fluency test enabled the researchers to depict how the animals were likely organized in the children's memories.

> **Key Findings:** Montessori-educated children tended to have a more "flexible" semantic network structure, meaning that they tended to exhibit more connections and shorter paths between animal concepts compared to children who received a traditional education. Montessori-educated children also had higher scores on the two creative thinking tests.

The researchers speculate that, in contrast with the teacher-directed learning found in traditional education,

specific teaching practices found in Montessori classes may foster higher creativity skills, such as the error-and-trial approach (children need to solve problems by and for themselves), the peer-peer tutoring in multi-age classes (higher social diversity, different points of view), the multisensory didactic material (using more than two senses to learn and later create), the absence of time pressure (uninterrupted three working hours), and the project-based learning (self-directed exploration).[168]

However, they suspect that it may be a combination of those factors or other or unknown factors that "enable children to access and train their creative abilities."[169] As always, more studies are needed, and I know I can't wait to see what they find!

ADOLESCENCE: A TIME OF CREATIVITY

Adolescents can be uniquely creative. As Eveline Crone says: "Anyone with an iPad knows that a fifteen-year-old can figure it out much quicker than an adult."[170] She's basing this statement on a study she conducted with Sietske Kleibeuker and Carsten De Dreu, both working with her at Leiden University at the time. The researchers divided ninety-eight participants into four age groups—twelve-to-thirteen-year-olds, fifteen-to-sixteen-year-olds, eighteen-to-nineteen-year-olds, and twenty-five-to-thirty-year-olds—and administered a battery of tests gauging creative insight and divergent thinking.[171]

They found that the mid-adolescents (fifteen-to-sixteen-year-olds) were the best performers on a divergent thinking task that tapped into visual-spatial thinking where participants have to find as many matching pictures as they can (a measure that doesn't rely on verbal or prior knowledge, where, as expected, the older you are, the more you know).

To test the accuracy of this finding, they used other measures and continued to find that mid-adolescents outperformed adults. Their next step was a scanning study, where they found that "adolescents showed more prefrontal cortex activity and had more solutions."[172]

Key Finding: Adolescents can outperform adults in tasks calling for creative thinking. Crone says, "This is completely different compared to what we'd seen in the executive functions literature where adolescents show less activity compared to adults."

As you know, the findings that adults show more prefrontal cortex activity in most EF studies have led to the conclusion that adolescents' prefrontal cortexes are less well-developed than those of adults. But Crone recognizes that the issue may be **experience**, not maturity. Crone explains it this way. She says that if the task is to get from A to B, adults will probably be better at it than younger people because we've done that kind of thing a lot. But adolescents can think outside the box and can come up with a different route—a path "less traveled." Crone says that while experience is often an advantage, sometimes it's not:

> It's beneficial for adolescents that they don't always take those paths that go from A to B!

Given her lab's experience with successfully and quickly training executive function skills like working memory and inhibitory control, they thought, "We can train creativity." In a two-week study, they gave fifteen- and sixteen-year-olds practice on the Alternative Uses Task and other nonverbal tasks in comparison with a group that received practice on rule-switching.

Unfortunately, practice, practice, and more practice didn't work as well as expected,[173] though there were hints of promise in the findings. Crone remains committed:

> I haven't given up. Maybe it's just not possible to improve creativity in
> a short amount of time. We know executive functions are important for
> creativity but creativity is something extra.[174]

ORIGINALS IN ACTION

Adam Grant, of the Wharton School of Business and author of the book *Originals*, told me:

> We live in a world where—pretty soon—if you're not creative, you're
> not going to have a job. We're getting to a point where almost anything
> that can be done in a predictable, repeatable way will be pretty easy
> to automate or outsource. So far, we don't have machines that are that
> brilliant at creativity. Even if we did, I don't think people would value it in
> the same way.[175]

Studies on the development or training of creativity (like those conducted by Roger Beaty and Eveline Crone) continue, but in the meantime, I also find Adam Grant's research-based suggestions both unexpected (or should I say *original*) and very useful.

Grant is himself an original, a respected researcher at Wharton and translator of research—but that didn't come without setbacks. He begins his book by telling how he passed up an opportunity to invest in Warby Parker, the online glasses store, only to watch the start-up company become a stunning business success.[176] And he told me about another missed opportunity: he created an internet network at Harvard, a Facebook, before Facebook existed.

When Grant applied to Harvard and was accepted, he told me, he didn't know anyone. "I was going to be moving halfway across the country and was afraid I'd have no friends":

> At the time, America Online [AOL] was how everyone used the internet.
> I searched to see if I could find other students who'd be joining the same

entering class. I found a few and emailed them. I was like, "Hey, we're going to be classmates. It would be great to connect."[177]

It started with fifteen or twenty future classmates in January. By April, there were a hundred people in the network, then two hundred. But he says, "When we got to college, we disbanded the group."

The Harvard Crimson would go on to write an article about how we were the first online social network at Harvard. A few years later, Mark Zuckerberg started Facebook in the dorm next door.

Does he regret this?

I don't think we'd have ever created Facebook. I wasn't a coder. I didn't have the vision for what this could become, but I don't think the co-founders of Facebook did, either.

He does have second thoughts, though:

You have teenagers with really exciting ideas—they just don't see quite how to pursue them or don't realize how promising their ideas are and give up on them too soon. That's where a lot of creativity goes to die. So, I hope that no one follows in those footsteps because I've regretted it ever since.

Grant's missed personal opportunity has become our opportunity, in one sense, because he's worked hard to ensure that adolescents can turn their promising ideas into action. He finds that rather than narrowly "training" creative thinking, our overall approach to parenting and teaching can help adolescents become more adept in thinking creatively in problem-solving:

- **Don't push adolescents to specialize—encourage more than one interest.**

Grant sees that many of the parents he comes into contact with are fearful that their children will fall off the high-achievement track. In response, they encourage their children to specialize.

To the contrary, Grant says it's important to "encourage your kids to pursue different hobbies and interests." Among the evidence he cites[178] is a study showing that Nobel Prize–winning scientists between 1901 and 2005 were significantly more likely than their peers to have artistic hobbies.[179]

- **Don't think all practice is the same—encourage practice that's engaging.**

Children who grow up to do well in their fields aren't necessarily the high achievers in grade school or middle school.[180] What matters most are relationships (an enduring theme song from research). It's the coach, teacher, or parent who makes the learning and practice engaging and fun.

- **Don't make practice rote—provide opportunities for positive risk-taking.**

Grant has an apt statement: "Practice makes perfect, but it doesn't make new."[181]

You can spend hours or years trying to learn how to play a perfect Mozart sonata, but you never learn how to write your own. You can master the rules of chess, but never learn how to create your own game.

- **Don't hide differences from children—help them learn to argue with ideas, not people.**

In an op-ed, Grant writes:

The skill to get hot without getting mad—to have a good argument that doesn't become personal—is critical in life . . . We want to give kids a stable home, so we stop siblings from quarreling and we have our own arguments behind closed doors. Yet if kids never get exposed to disagreement, we'll end up limiting their creativity.[182]

- **Don't become rule-bound—help adolescents learn to solve problems for themselves.**

What's important, according to a number of studies, is that adults are more autonomy-supportive—they explain the rules as well as talk about the impact that breaching those rules would have on others,[183] and they emphasize values: **kids aren't helping out, they are being helpers;** they aren't sharing, they are being sharers.[184] Grant says:

> *You see that lots of creative kids are raised by parents who do discipline their children, but they don't do it with extreme forms of punishment. They do it with explanations; they ask their kids to reflect on why that behavior was wrong. How did it hurt other people?*[185]

When these approaches are used, children and adolescents can learn to become creative thinkers in solving problems.

That was the intent of Brooke's parents in leaving the decision of whether to stay or leave her dance studio up to her, but that didn't mean they were uninvolved. They asked questions that helped her move from feeling like a victim to seeing possibilities in various if-then scenarios. She began to realize that *if* she followed her teacher, *then* it might be more of the same—she might remain in the background as she'd always been.

However, *if* she stayed, *then* she'd be the oldest and could step into a leadership role. She was only in the ninth grade, and being the oldest and being a leader were intimidating. "I was scared," she said. "It was a huge change from what I'd been doing." She began to see new and creative possibilities in her dilemma.

The Life and Learning Skill of Relational Reasoning

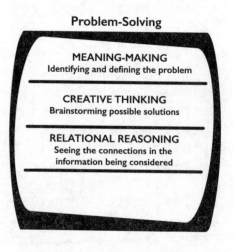

Problem-Solving

MEANING-MAKING
Identifying and defining the problem

CREATIVE THINKING
Brainstorming possible solutions

RELATIONAL REASONING
Seeing the connections in the
information being considered

In the Life and Learning Skill of problem-solving, the third step is relational reasoning.

Silvia Bunge and Elena Lieb of the University of California, Berkeley, define relational reasoning as "the ability to compare or integrate the relations among disparate pieces of information":

> *Relational reasoning is conceptualized as an all-purpose cognitive ability that enables us to compare the magnitudes of two fractions, derive logical conclusions from a set of premises, understand the analogies used to teach scientific concepts, and more.*[186]

These examples are academic—fractions, logical conclusions from a premise, analogies in science—and this skill is often studied in an academic context, but it also applies to **making connections among different pieces of information in life.**

Bunge's research has focused on relational reasoning because it is an influential predictor of school and life achievement and because it can be improved.[187]

EXPERIMENTS IN RELATIONAL REASONING

Why don't you try these nonverbal examples of relational reasoning that come from the Raven's Progressive Matrices Task for yourself or with your adolescent? These are tasks used to measure general intelligence and abstract reasoning.[188] On REL-0, can you or they find the match?

REL-0

find match

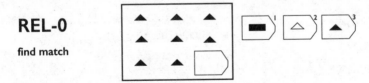

Did you or they find it? It is 3.

On REL-1, can you or they find the match using either horizontal or vertical information?

REL-I

horizontal OR vertical

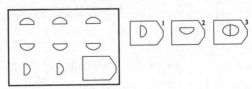

The answer is 1.

Now try to combine horizontal and vertical information. Can you or they find the match?

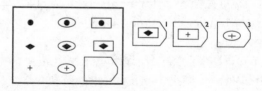

REL-2

integrate
horizontal AND vertical

The answer is 2.

When you were doing this last matrix problem, you were using relational reasoning because you were integrating both horizontal and vertical information.

A major question in the research on relational reasoning is how to improve it.[189] When Allyson Mackey was a graduate student with Bunge at Berkeley, she suggested they look at whether preparation for the Law School Admission Test (LSAT) was an avenue toward improvements in relational reasoning. She'd been conducting school-based research when an experience in one school shook her and initially led her to momentarily contemplate dropping out of her graduate school program and going to law school—but eventually led to a study:

> I was waiting for a parent to pick up their kids. He was shot on the way over. I had this panic that science was going to be too slow—that these kids' lives can change so dramatically, so quickly. I started thinking about going into policy instead.

She got an LSAT prep test and began studying:

> I noticed that the LSAT problems were very similar to the kinds of reasoning problems we do in the lab.

In fact, about two-thirds of the LSAT focuses explicitly on teaching strategies for improving reasoning.[190] That insight led Mackey to the realization that science was in fact her path forward—that she could accomplish more for children that way.

Perhaps, she thought, their research team at Berkeley could test how practicing for the LSAT might affect the brain. If there were effects—and there well might be, since interventions can be powerful during adolescence—

perhaps their findings on young people in their twenties could become a platform for intervening with younger adolescents (in middle school and high school).

In one of their first studies, they compared prelaw students who enrolled in an LSAT preparation course (which includes seventy hours of reasoning instruction) with a group of well-matched students on age, IQ, gender, and other factors who hadn't taken the course yet, so they could ensure that any changes they found weren't simply due to maturation.[191]

When we learn, individual pieces of information accumulate in the parietal lobes—a part of the brain that processes sensory experiences from the external world. That information then is sent forward to the frontal lobes in order to integrate it. Mackey's team hypothesized that when students learn to reason better, the integration would be faster, thus changing the structure and function of those connections.[192]

To test this hypothesis, they used an MRI tool called Diffusion Tensor Imaging that allows scientists to tag water molecules in the brain and see how they disperse.

Mackey and her colleagues did find that as students learned to reason better during the LSAT training, their brains also changed.

This was an important finding in and of itself, but *how* the brain changed was equally important. Much of the time we use the left hemisphere of the brain to reason, but when reasoning gets difficult, we recruit the right hemisphere.*

Key Finding: After the LSAT prep course, students had stronger connections between the left and the right prefrontal cortex and between the left and the right parietal cortex.

This fits with the theme you've been hearing about in study after study: adolescence is a prime time for creating better connections among parts of the brain. Mackey says that adolescents are building a more organized brain to tackle harder problems in the future.

---

* This is another indication that the idea that the right brain is for creative thinking and the left brain is for reasoning is a myth. We use both hemispheres for reasoning. And, as I wrote in the section on creative thinking, there is no creative region of the brain.

AN EXPERIMENT IN RELATIONAL REASONING IN MIDDLE SCHOOL

In order to further understand how we learn relational reasoning, Mackey created a real-world experiment[193] in a new middle school in Boston. Wanting to incorporate psychology and neuroscience into its curriculum, the school had asked Mackey if the kids could play "brain games" for twenty minutes a day.[194]

The research team narrowed the games to card games that promoted working memory, processing speed, task switching (where the rules change), and relational reasoning. The control group played games that promoted typing and knowledge of geography.

Key Finding: The study found that students playing these games for just twenty minutes a day improved significantly more on their cognitive skills than the control group, but both groups improved a lot.

Perhaps the overall improvements relate to the fact that this school incorporated the science of learning into their overall curriculum. The research team did find, interestingly, that the students in the experimental group who showed the biggest cognitive gains also made the biggest gains in math. That wasn't true for the control group, giving Mackey confidence that the games could improve relational reasoning in ways that could be applied to other learning.

Her long-term goal is to create school programs that can improve both cognitive skills and academics. To that end, it might be better if these skills were promoted within everyday school learning, in specific subjects or throughout the school day, not just as stand-alone games.[195]

Here again, you'll recognize a theme—that executive function–based Life and Learning Skills are best learned in everyday situations where there are opportunities to notice and improve these skills and to reflect on what you're learning.[196]

The Life and Learning Skill of Critical Thinking

Relational reasoning is a building block of critical thinking, which is the search for valid and accurate knowledge to inform problem-solving.[197]

Problem-Solving

MEANING-MAKING
Identifying and defining the problem

CREATIVE THINKING
Brainstorming possible solutions

RELATIONAL REASONING
Seeing the connections in the
information being considered

CRITICAL THINKING
Searching for valid information,
weighing pros and cons, making a decision

Allyson Mackey and her colleagues note that critical-analytic thinking is important in assessing the validity of arguments, particularly those that stand in contrast with one's own beliefs or biases.[198]

Like all the skills that go into problem-solving, critical thinking calls on the foundational executive function skills—you use what you know (**working memory**), think flexibly (**cognitive flexibility**), reflect (**reflection**), and use self-control to stop yourself from going on autopilot (**inhibitory control**). It also calls on the Default Mode Network, as you'll see.

CRITICAL THINKING ISN'T ALWAYS RATIONAL: FRAMING MATTERS

It's easy to see critical thinking just in terms of rational cognition, but it isn't, as the research of Rosa Li of the University of North Carolina, Chapel Hill, makes clear in an experiment about gambling. Try out the task that Li uses—for yourself or with an adolescent.

If you were given $20 and then offered the following options, which choice would you make?[199]

1. Keep half of the $20 for sure.
or
2. Flip a coin. Heads: you keep all $20. Tails: you lose all $20.

If you're like most people, you'd choose the first option—to keep half of the $20.

Here's a second scenario for you or your child:

You still have $20. Which choice would you make?

1. Lose half of the $20 for sure.

or

2. Flip a coin. Heads: you keep all $20. Tails: you lose all $20.

Which did you choose?

Again, if you're like most people, you'd select the second option—to gamble with the flip of a coin.

If you stop and think about it, these two scenarios are the same. Option 1 of both scenarios leaves you with half the money; option 2 leaves the decision to a coin toss. We can think of option 2 in each scenario as a 50 percent chance to lose nothing ($0) and a 50 percent chance to lose $20. The difference is the **framing**. One is a win or gain scenario; the other is a loss scenario. We react to those frames differently, as Li explains:

> If you frame something as a loss, it tends to push people to be more willing
> to take risks, whereas if you frame something as a gain, they tend to be a
> little less willing to take those risks.[200]

Can this be explained as emotion overriding reason—it feels good to win and bad to lose, so we make irrational decisions and don't use critical thinking? Li suspected it may not be that simple.[201] As she told me:

> Neuroscientists like to say that the brain activity that you see in some
> studies is only the tip of the iceberg. There's a whole iceberg underneath the
> water.[202]

Li wanted to explore what was under the water. She and her colleagues hypothesized that the framing effect itself acts as a decision-making shortcut: since we like to win, we adopt winning as an overall strategy, reducing our cognitive load by saving us the time and energy of fully reasoning about every decision.

To test this idea, she and her colleagues selected a large (for a scanning study) sample—143 people ages eighteen through thirty-one, with a mean age of 21.9. These older adolescents and young adults were scanned while engaging in 126 trials of the kind of gambling game you or your adolescent just played. The researchers then compared their findings with over eight thousand neuroimaging studies, using a tool called Neurosynth. With this tool, they aren't just looking at isolated brain regions but examining the whole brain.[203]

Key Finding: This study found that when choices were framed as losses, the Executive Control Network was activated; when choices were framed as winning, the Default Mode Network (the network we use for abstract thinking, reflecting, imagining) was activated. Winning is a less effortful choice to make.

Li explains:

In some ways, individuals are not really thinking all the way through the decision process. They're going with the choice that seems like the right answer. They're spending less time and cognitive effort on that decision.[204]

Importantly, this study shows that **we can't just view decision-making as reason versus emotion. What matters more is how problems are framed and how engaged people are in the problem-solving process itself.**

Brooke originally saw her decision as being about loss—she was losing her friends and her teacher. But through the deeper meaning-making she did, she began looking at what she might gain as well. If she stayed, she could become a leader.

CRITICAL THINKING ISN'T JUST RATIONAL: VALUES MATTER

These findings fit with the model for understanding adolescent decision-making developed by Jennifer Pfeifer and Elliot Berkman of the University of Oregon. Like Li, they take a whole-brain approach. They posit that adolescents make decisions and solve problems based on weighing various options by how they stack up against their values about who they are and who they want to become. Problem-solving is about adolescents' search for identity.[205]

A DECISION

When we look at Brooke's process, it becomes clear that she considered her options in light of who she wanted to become—a leader. That clinched her decision to stay at the studio and to act like a leader by volunteering to work with classes of younger students and by connecting with their parents.

She also had an idea of what kind of leader she wanted to be. She saw leaders taking good-cop/bad-cop roles. Bad cops took advantage of opportunities for self-serving reasons; good cops worked on behalf of the people they served.

> *I definitely wanted to be a good cop. When I was assisting dance classes—if they were really young—I'd try to connect with their parents and ask how many siblings they had, how are they growing up? For kids closer to me, I made a personal connection with all of the kids on the dance team because I wanted them all to look up to me and know that I care about them.*

She didn't want the younger students to feel in the shadows as she had felt when she was a younger student. Furthermore, when she had to correct the way they were dancing, she wanted the students to know that she was doing so to help them, not to criticize them.

And, in a telling example of applying what's she learned to a new situation (far transfer), her view of herself as a leader began to spill out beyond dance. It helped her manage some of the tough situations she faced in high school, especially when a classmate—someone she once dated—was killed in a car accident at the end of junior year:

> *It was a few days after school ended. That was hard because we weren't all together. So immediately, when we found out—my friends and I—we had consecutive sleepovers. But we didn't sleep. It felt like the world wasn't moving.*
>
> *We all decided to do something—to start making friendship bracelets for everyone. We stayed up multiple nights making hundreds of bracelets for his family and friends and then for the entire senior class.*

Brooke and her friends also organized a memorial service for their classmate where his teachers spoke about him. She says that was "super hard, but we got through it."

During those days after the death, there was a dance recital. Should she go or not? She decided it was important for the younger students to see her. When she arrived, everyone reached out to her to comfort her and let her know they were there for her. Brooke says, "I knew then I was becoming a leader!"

As she thinks about her life during high school, Brooke is grateful her parents gave her the responsibility for deciding whether to leave or stay at her dance studio in the ninth grade.

When I was a teen myself, problem-solving seemed mysterious, but science is shining a light on how it works. When our adolescents come to a fork in the road, we can help them make more intentional decisions. Whether they take the road less traveled or not, young people can begin to make decisions and solve problems that can make all the difference.

PROMOTING PROBLEM-SOLVING

To promote problem-solving in adolescents, we can:

- **See problem-solving as a skill and give young people opportunities to learn it.** Brooke says it well: "Decision-making is a skill you learn through making your own decisions. It bothers me when parents make all the decisions for their kids in high school. They need to learn that skill on their own. You're going to have to make decisions in life—so it's important to learn how to do it!"
- **Ask questions that prompt meaning-making about problem-solving.** In these questions, ask how a situation makes them feel now (in the here and now) and in the future. In this way, we'll be building connections in their brains that will enable more abstract thinking.
- **Prompt creative thinking.** Help young people brainstorm lots of solutions to a problem.
- **Prompt relational reasoning and critical thinking.** Help them evaluate the pros and cons of the various options. Can they assess what about a loss might actually be a gain? How do the options fit with their values?

Life and Learning Skill 5: Taking on Challenges

Taking on challenges goes beyond coping and being resilient. It includes taking steps—including using self-control strategies—to try what's hard and reach your goals. In a world that's constantly changing, we need young people who can both manage and surmount challenges.

Kelly's mental health challenges began surfacing—suddenly, surprisingly—in eighth grade, though in retrospect, her mother, Kate, could see some clues. "She was an open, communicative kid," Kate recalls four years later. "We'd always had a really good relationship, with little animosity or conflict. She always talked to me about what was going on. Which is why it was so shocking."

> There was a set of girls in elementary school and through middle school that was her core group. I thought they were a pretty good, solid set of girlfriends. They'd have sleepovers, go ice-skating, whatever. Looking back, I can remember some conversation about somebody not making her feel good about herself or questioning what she was wearing, or what she looked like.

Kate had read about adolescent girls and chalked up Kelly's comments as normal, fitting into the patterns outlined in *Queen Bees and Wannabes*, Rosalind Wiseman's wise and compelling book helping parents help their daughters survive cliques, gossip, and dating.[206]

> I really thought I was giving her good advice about encouraging her to stand up for herself and push back. But it turns out—and I really didn't know this—she was internalizing this a lot more deeply than I think she let on. In eighth grade, she started showing some signs of OCD [obsessive-compulsive disorder]—needing to have things arranged a certain way or a certain sequence of things she had to do.

Finally, Kelly told her mother, "This feels like it's starting to get in the way of my life and I want to get help."

They did find a therapist and tried to unravel what was going on, but as they were doing so, Kelly began expressing deep-seated insecurities, lack of self-confidence, and thoughts of suicide. Then she began having panic attacks about going to school; she couldn't face seeing those girls.

Megan Gunnar of the University of Minnesota says all children face challenges: "A childhood that had no stress in it wouldn't prepare you for adulthood."[207] As parents, she says, "we need to help our children manage challenges, not protect them completely."

But how do we help adolescents with serious challenges—like mental health problems, taking drugs, drinking, or dropping out literally or figuratively from school? Parents and researchers have found strategies that can help children take on challenges. That's what we'll explore here, beginning with mental health.

FACING MENTAL HEALTH CHALLENGES: A PARENT'S JOURNEY

Through her job, Kate knew about social service systems, but it was different when it was her own child. She was faced with trying to find the right help, whether to use medication (and if so, what kind), how to deal with the school when her daughter refused to go, and then how to protect her daughter from harming herself:

> We were really struggling to keep her in school. The school system was both helpful and unhelpful. We spent a lot of time in counseling, but also a lot of time getting called into school, trying to figure out what was going on. I kept telling them, "We're stepping up her interventions; we're trying to get her more help."

There was no road map. Kate didn't know how to figure out what might come next or the likely results of any action she might take. Even the terminology used to describe Kelly's behavior was new and confusing. And the systems seemed unfathomable. What was the right kind and level of care? How much did it cost? What was covered by insurance and what wasn't?

"WE WERE NOT ABLE TO KEEP HER SAFE. WE JUST COULDN'T."

At home, Kate and her husband, Jay, were doing all they could to try to keep Kelly from harming herself:

We locked up everything sharp—even the backs of earrings—knives, tools,
all the medicine, all the pills. Kelly slept on a mattress in our room, or one of
us slept in her room. It was twenty-four-hour surveillance. She was never alone.

Despite all of this, Kelly moved from cutting herself to a serious attempt
at suicide four months after they initially sought help. Kate and Jay decided
they couldn't protect her at home anymore and made the heartbreaking
decision to put her in a nearby inpatient facility:

They kept her in for almost four weeks. She was put in an adolescent unit,
even though she was only thirteen. She basically learned a lot of other tricks
for how to commit suicide while she was there.

Kelly learned other things as an inpatient, too. She went from being communicative to being closed off. Kate and Jay visited every night and Kelly
often refused to see them. Then she was discharged.
She spent the next two months in and out of a series of local facilities:

She'd come out; then she'd either attempt suicide again or have suicidal
thoughts and need to be hospitalized. We were basically popping in and out
of facilities.

During these hospitalizations, the doctors began to try medication. Kate
says, "They literally throw the kitchen sink of medications at you."

When your kid has a mental health issue and needs a medication, it's a
chemistry experiment. It's not like a diagnosis equals a clear medical path.
They don't know because everybody's body reacts differently.

There was also no continuity of care. Each time Kelly went into a facility,
there was a different psychiatrist in charge, and each had a slightly different
diagnosis and a slightly different treatment plan. It became a catch-22: Kate
and her husband knew they couldn't keep Kelly safe at home, yet the treatment seemed more and more traumatizing.

She was getting worse, not better. She developed a psychosis, which
happens a lot with kids who have severe anxiety. She had psychotic
*tendencies. We were not able to keep her safe. We just **couldn't**.*

Kate didn't know what else to do, so she turned to what had helped when her children were little—she asked lots of other parents for help.

Through parent word of mouth, I heard about a residential facility. It was one of the very few that (a) had beds for thirteen-year-olds and (b) took insurance.

They applied to this facility and several others. Knowing it might take a month or more for a space to open up, Kate worried that they couldn't keep their daughter alive during the wait, so they kept her in local inpatient facilities.

One Friday, six months after the crisis began, Kate got a call at work from the doctor where Kelly was being treated. He told her there was nothing more they could do and they were releasing her that evening. Kate panicked. "You need to give me time to figure out a step-down plan because that's what you do in health care." For Kate, it was like her daughter was having a heart attack, yet they were putting her out on the street.

She returned to her work meeting, still shaking, when her phone rang again:

It was a call from a number I didn't recognize. I left the meeting and took the call because at this stage, you have to take calls from any number that pops up. It was the residential facility I'd been hoping would take Kelly. They said, "We have somebody who left early. Can you be here on Monday morning?"

That evening, Kate and Jay drove to the inpatient facility, checked Kelly out, told her about the move to a residential facility, and went home to pack. On Monday, they were on a plane to this place nine hundred miles away. "And this was a kid who'd never even been to sleepaway camp."

When young people face difficulties with friends, most of this turbulence doesn't set off serious mental health issues, as happened with Kelly. It is known, however, that the majority of serious mental health illnesses do have their initial onset during the teen and early adult years.[208] The plasticity of the developing brain during adolescence renders these years both a time of opportunity and of vulnerability.[209]

Although it's human nature to want to search for a single cause—a bad guy, if you will, like genes—decades of research have shown that it's a combination of factors that shape the mental health of a young person. Think of concentric circles, with the individual in the center (their biology and psychology), surrounded by a circle of family and close relationships, which in turn is surrounded by a circle of community (encompassing relationships with peers, teachers, mentors, and the supports and pressures therein). The community circle is then surrounded by the circle of the environment (think, for example, of neighborhood safety and environmental health). Finally, the outer ring is the society.[210] All of these, in various combinations, affect the well-being of us and our children.

There is a new science of epigenetics that counters the traditional view that heredity is unchanging, proving instead that we can't separate out the influences of genetics and the environment on an individual's health and well-being.[211] Even with environmental factors, there's typically no one single cause, like social media or parents. Relationships are what I call the swing-vote factor. Here, they include the important people in all of these concentric circles or systems that converge to affect mental health.

If we are to optimize the mental health of young people, then we need to promote strong relationships in these systems. This is becoming increasingly urgent. In December 2021, the surgeon general of the United States issued an advisory—a call to arms—to protect youth mental health because the effects of life today on mental health have been "devastating" for adolescents.[212] As we've discussed, recent data from the Centers for Disease Control and Prevention (CDC) reveal that:[213]

- Forty-two percent of high school students said they'd experienced such persistent feelings of sadness or hopelessness in the past year that they couldn't participate in their regular activities, up from 28 percent in 2011. That's more than two in five students—a *huge* number!
- About one in five students (22 percent) reported having seriously considered attempting suicide in 2021, up from 16 percent in 2011.
- In 2021, almost one in five (18 percent) reported making a suicide plan in the past year, a large increase since 2011, when it was 13 percent.
- In 2021, 10 percent of high school students attempted suicide, compared with 8 percent in 2011.

The CDC data indicate that girls are disproportionally experiencing mental health challenges. For example, in 2021, 57 percent of girls reported persistent feelings of sadness or hopelessness, compared with 29 percent of boys, and 30 percent of girls seriously considered suicide, compared with 14 percent of boys.

Breakthrough Years Study Finding: When we assessed stress during the pandemic in our Breakthrough Years study, we found, not surprisingly, that girls reported greater stress than boys, controlling for other demographics. **However, when adolescents reported that their basic psychological needs had been met nine months earlier in each of the contexts we assessed (with families, friends, school, out-of-school activities, and online), the differences in stress between females and males disappeared!** This important finding suggests that when there are differences between boys and girls, it's crucial to pay attention to and address the level of support that adolescents receive in all their social relationships.

WHAT IS TAKING ON CHALLENGES?

When I write about the Life and Learning Skills to help us and our children take on challenges, I must preface this by saying how inadequate it feels. It's like trying to fortify a car and assuming all will go well, without taking into account the fact that the terrain may be unnavigable, desolate, or dangerous. Managing challenge as individuals must be a part of the picture, but work toward improving societal systems that support learning and thriving must continue in tandem.

Much attention has been given to the concept of resilience, but I don't think it goes far enough. To me, resilience is **coping** with what happens. **Taking on challenges goes beyond coping and includes taking steps to try what's hard.** In a world that's constantly changing, we need young people who can address and overcome challenges.

Taking on challenges is **goal-directed,** as are all executive function–based Life and Learning Skills. It calls on the other foundational EF skills, as it is centered on figuring out what you want to accomplish and how you can do so. It's also centered on self-regulation—**managing your attention, thoughts, emotions, and behavior to achieve these goals.** In many ways, then, taking on challenges is about self-control.

Angela Duckworth, of the University of Pennsylvania and co-founder of the Character Lab, defines self-control as **"the capacity to align your present actions, and your feelings and thoughts, with tomorrow's intentions and** goals."[214] That's such a beautiful definition because it emphasizes the gap between what we do right now and what we want to do in the future, and the necessity of reconciling our present and future selves. She knows that working to resolve these conflicts is essential because self-control is highly predictive of academic, financial, and personal success, including better relationships with others as well as health and well-being.[215] But it's a struggle. Duckworth says, "Honestly, I think every human being struggles with this conflict."

Duckworth saw this conflict firsthand when she worked with kids during college, as a tutor and a teacher in a summer school. She recalls:

> *What frustrated me, in part, was that I wasn't able to do more for these kids. I could see what they were capable of, but they weren't necessarily achieving that under my guidance.*[216]

While she had a number of jobs after college, her heart was in teaching because she believes it is the way forward for society, so she worked as a math teacher in the public schools in New York, San Francisco, and Philadelphia:

> *As a teacher, I saw failures of self-control daily in my classroom. At the time, I didn't know self-control was one of the most widely studied topics in psychology; I didn't know about executive function. All I knew is that the kids in my classroom authentically, genuinely wanted what was best for them. They actually wanted to go home and study and do their homework—but then they'd come back the next morning and it wasn't done.*

This dissonance prompted Duckworth to become a psychologist. She wanted to know more, to be able to do more to help young people succeed.

Duckworth and Larry Steinberg of Temple University argue that when you unpack self-control, it comes down to two distinct yet competing psychological processes: a conflict between what we do on purpose (like managing our behavior to achieve goals) versus our more impulsive tendencies (like succumbing to the lure of immediate rewards).[217] She says:

> *It's a conflict between blurting something out in a conversation or keeping quiet. It's about: "Should I have this piece of chocolate cake or an apple?"*[218]

One of the next steps in her quest to help young people learn self-control was to work with James Gross of Stanford University, who's well known for his pioneering research on emotional regulation. Duckworth was drawn to the Gross model of self-control because it explains how impulses go from something feeble and small into something irresistible. By understanding this process, Duckworth felt, researchers could develop more targeted interventions that "help kids develop more self-control in their lives." And not just kids. These strategies can help us all, even in situations like what Kate was facing.

GETTING A HANDLE ON OURSELVES: THE PROCESS MODEL OF SELF-CONTROL

Duckworth, Tamar Szabó Gendler of Yale University, and Gross organized Gross's Process Model into a sequence of five strategies.[219] As is often the case with academic research, the names of these strategies don't quite roll off the tongue.

1. **Situation selection.** This involves deliberatively choosing to be in places or with people who facilitate self-control and help us achieve our goals. For students, it can mean choosing to study in the library rather than at home, or finding friends who have more self-control to serve as role models.
2. **Situation modification.** Since we can't always choose our circumstances, sometimes we have to adjust the circumstances we're in. These strategies entail purposefully changing the physical or social situation to reinforce self-control. For example, we can turn our cell phones off or put them out of sight.
3. **Attention deployment.** Sometimes we face temptation where there are no possibilities of choosing or changing the circumstances. In these situations, we exercise self-control by how we focus our attention. If we're having trouble focusing, we can turn away from others trying to talk with us. Or if we're trying to control our tempers, we can move away from a hot conflict, breathe deeply, or count to one hundred.
4. **Cognitive change.** Cognitive change strategies come into play when there are no possibilities of choosing or changing our circumstances. We can use self-control by changing the way we think about the situation. For example, we can view mistakes as opportunities to

learn; break a large task into more discrete, more doable, smaller tasks; or step back and view the situation from afar, using a fly-on-the-wall or an on-the-balcony perspective.

5. **Response modulation.** The final strategy is necessary when a temptation is present and there's no possibility of avoiding it. I and others call it the **willpower** approach. We call on kids to use willpower when we tell them to "calm down," "pay attention," or "don't blow up." This strategy can work, but in the words of the researchers, it's "an unpleasant experience," and "the least effective and least efficient of all self-control strategies."[220]

You can see that there's a continuum of strategies, from changing our external circumstances to changing the way we pay attention to (or frame) challenges to simply confronting the immediate challenge. You can also see that the earlier one intervenes in this process, the higher the likelihood of success. Conversely, the later one intervenes, the more effort it takes to bring about change.

The researchers then wondered how these strategies played out in real life and if they could be taught. Duckworth, Gross, and their team conducted several investigations.[221] In one study, they asked 577 high school students to write about a specific incident where they used self-control—what they tried to do and what actually happened. Duckworth reports:

When asked what they did spontaneously—on their own—they actually named all of the strategies that are in the Process Model![222]

That was wonderfully confirming, especially since to their knowledge, this is the "first naturalistic study of self-control in the everyday lives of high school students."[223]

For the next series of experiments, the team created an intervention.[224] All of the 126 high school students in this experiment were asked to set an academic goal and make plans to achieve it. In one intervention, participants were told about the strategy of "situation modification"—for example, of "removing temptations from sight rather than trying to resist them directly." They watched an animated video about relevant research, heard from an expert, and were asked to practice this strategy. A second intervention group followed the same process, but the strategy for this group was the willpower approach. The control group simply set a study goal.

Key Finding: Students who learned situation modification were much more successful in accomplishing their goals than the willpower group and the control groups.

Duckworth knows that self-control and grit (which is a cousin of self-control because it involves the passion and perseverance to achieve long-term goals) aren't silver bullets.[225] But she also knows that self-control strategies can help young people manage the challenges in their lives. It's a skill that can be taught, she says, and it should be!

SELF-CONTROL IN ACTION: STRATEGIES THAT WORK

As Duckworth noted, high school students spontaneously mentioned all of the strategies in the Process Model when asked how they managed challenges. Similarly, when I asked Kate about how she managed Kelly's mental health challenges, she, too, identified these strategies.

Using Situation Selection

The strategy that turned the corner for Kate was situation selection—finding a good residential facility for Kelly. When they arrived, Kate and Jay told the doctor that they were panicked about signs of psychosis, but the doctor put their fears into perspective:

> The doctor was like, "Oh no, we see this all the time. She's not psychotic. This is a sign of the anxiety. It'll go away once we get the anxiety under control."

The facility used a combination of therapies (which relied on cognitive change), food, and nutrition, and they tested and then adjusted Kelly's medication. These therapies included cognitive behavioral therapy, which helped Kelly recognize and change distortions in her thinking, and dialectical behavior therapy, which helped her focus on changing her behavior by learning coping and emotional regulation skills. Kelly also had exposure therapy:

> Exposure therapy helped Kelly deal with social anxiety and feeling judged all the time. They'd go into a local high school and she'd have to walk around and talk to people or ask them a question she thought was stupid.

Kelly stayed at the residential facility for nine weeks. When she returned, her family could see that in some respects she was better, but in others she wasn't:

> *It was a challenge—she still had to come back to her life. Every day, she still had to walk back into what felt like a burning building [school] and see the people who were making her insecure.*

Once home, Kate had to again find the right therapist for Kelly (a situation selection strategy), and that was a trial-and-error process. Kate found that traditional therapy didn't work as well. Kelly would have episodes where she was inconsolable:

> *The system isn't structured well for helping you deal with that kind of crisis. In the residential facility, you are all-in. At home, you have to wait until three or four o'clock for an appointment with your therapist.*

Eventually, she landed on the right kind of therapy, albeit a costly one—a therapist who provides phone and online support in real time.

> *In adolescence, if you've got somebody with a mental health issue, those roller-coaster moods go way up high and way down really fast. It's super helpful to have in-the-moment support.*

Promoting a Growth and Possibilities Mindset

The therapist who ultimately worked best "isn't into just talk therapy," Kate said. Other therapists had let Kelly talk about whatever was on her mind and didn't push her to deal with her tough issues, but this one challenges her. He also understands adolescent development and helps Kelly understand it, too. For example, when she's sure things will never be different, he tells her she's growing and changing and what she feels today won't be the same as what she may feel in the future (just as Jennifer Silvers's mother told her daughter in chapter 1). In addition, this therapist helps Kelly have a growth mindset and thus a Possibilities Mindset, meaning that she's learning that change is possible and that she has the efficacy to make it happen.

School: Experimenting with Situation Modification

When Kelly returned to the same school and the same kids, each step forward seemed to lead to two steps backward.

Kate could see that the kids in Kelly's class got niched into groups and didn't know how to leave them, even when being categorized that way was unhealthy for them—because leaving meant sitting alone in the lunchroom or having no one to be with after school or on weekends. This school, like many schools, saw learning as academic and did little to try to create a social environment where a diverse group of adolescents could feel that they belonged and mattered.

COVID turned out to be a blessing for Kelly. For a year and a half, she didn't have to go into that building with its three thousand students; she could do online classes with her laptop's camera off. Her grades improved, and when in-person classes started again, there'd been enough of a break that Kelly herself was able to craft the social environment she needed, a situation modification strategy. She stopped seeing her old friends, found one friend a year younger (that's all you need, says Kate), and joined a club, which she now helps run, on youth mental health: Our Minds Matter.

Using a Cognitive Change Strategy

For her own part, Kate found she had to change her mental model of Kelly's illness. At first, she saw it like a physical illness—describing it like a heart attack. When you think that way, Kate realized, then you believe that if you "do X, Y, and Z, the person will get better." But that was not helpful. She realized, "I needed to learn to validate her, not to try to fix things for her":

> On the good side, I'm much more validating; much more attuned to Kelly's feelings. We're still very close but in some ways I'm like, I can't be your therapist right now. You need to talk to him.

On the bad side, she says, she's struggled to give her other daughter the time and attention she needs:

> Kelly takes up a lot of space in our family. A lot of things can trigger her. It's a challenge trying to make sure that my other kid gets some amount of balanced support. It's not perfect, but we're trying.

The Importance of Finding Support (for Everyone)

None of us can take on challenges without having support for ourselves. Kate has learned that she needs to find other people besides just her husband to support her:

If I start telling him what I'm worried about, then he just has more to worry about and vice versa.

Kate has seen her friends' marriages break up over their children's mental health problems and has concluded that it is hard to lean on your partner 100 percent because they're going through the same situation but worrying about different things:

I try to find a support system that I can lean on for when I get angry at this illness. It helps to have some people who are slightly removed who can just listen to how you're processing your emotions, who're not so wrapped up with her and our family.

DRUGS, DRINKING, AND ALMOST DROPPING OUT OF SCHOOL: AN ADOLESCENT'S JOURNEY

Kelly's problems surfaced in eighth grade and, by chance, so did Nina's. She's adopted, which was the first thing she told me:

Before I was adopted, my mom was kind of nervous about being a single woman considering adopting. Must have been so scary. Sometimes when she had doubts, she'd go to the park and sit under this massive tree. It's the biggest tree in the park; super old and beautiful.

Ever since, that's become our tree. We go there all the time—sit there, have picnics, and talk. We do everything under that tree. I am grateful to that tree for my existence.

Nina had an extremely close relationship with her mom, Laura, as she grew up—considered her her best friend—though sometimes she felt as if she had to be more grown-up than she was:

This may have halted my sense of identity a bit because I needed to be somebody I wasn't. I needed to be there to talk to her about work, about finances, about the family and how everyone's doing.

As an adoptee from Eastern Europe, Nina was focused on figuring out who she was, but this intensified in the eighth grade, precipitated by a family crisis. Laura, who had been a very present parent, was suddenly absent "through no fault of her own," Nina says. Laura's sister became ill and died, and Laura had a lot on her plate, including caring for her sister's children.

> *I really acted out. At first, I just craved attention because my mom was really busy, and she wasn't paying attention to me.*

Nina had always been responsible, very grown-up, but that finally became too much:

> *I was like, "You know what? I'm just going to party." I was sneaking out of the house, drinking, doing lots of drugs. I was even drinking at school. Then I began skipping school. I started having sex at a really young age.*

In retrospect, Nina sees this as a way of exploring her identity:

> *I was really doing this, I guess, to figure out what felt right for me. It became a way of trying to find my sense of identity, trying to be different than how I had been because I'd been so responsible for so long.*

Nina says that she got a boyfriend who introduced her to a lot of "bad people," and things spiraled further down. Her grades plunged, too.

The first wake-up call for Laura, Nina told me, was literally a call from a teacher in her public school who said Nina was failing her class. "What is going on?" the teacher asked Laura, who hadn't known but jumped into action—asking friends, seeking resources, having Nina tested. They discovered Nina had attention deficit hyperactivity disorder (ADHD), which contributed to her behavior.

Even though Laura was back, present, Nina says she wasn't ready to stop partying:

> *I didn't take any responsibility for what I was doing. I was blaming everybody for having not been there or having done something to me.*

She also saw partying as an escape from being the responsible one. The second wake-up call was worse. Nina took too many pills:

I ended up in the hospital and almost overdosed.

This began to happen repeatedly. Skipping school also became routine. Laura would take Nina to school; Nina would wait till her mom left, then turn around and leave.

The third wake-up call was an intervention staged by the school. It was a threatening intervention, and though it did help in this case because Nina cared deeply about her mother, I can't recommend it in general, because I strongly expect it would cause a lot of kids to get into even more trouble.

The school told Nina that she was missing too much school and told Laura she wasn't able to ensure her daughter stayed at school:

> *They said if I didn't start going back to school, get better grades, and not do as many drugs, they'd put me into foster care. They told us, "We can take you away from your mom. We can put you in a drug house, a sub-stance abuse facility." They did give us a chance to turn things around.*

SELF-CONTROL IN ACTION: REALIZING THE CONSEQUENCES AND ENVISIONING THE FUTURE

It was the look on Laura's face that got to Nina:

> *It was how she looked when we were told about foster care that did it. I realized I did not want to lose my mom and she did not want to lose me. That was when I realized it's not just me being impacted by this. It's somebody else. It's the best person in the world who's being impacted by my actions, really negatively. She's crying. I'm doing this to her.*

Discipline practices are generally based on consequences—usually imposed by parents ("if you do this, then that will happen"). Nina hadn't cared about consequences that affected her, but she did care about affecting her mother. Martin Hoffman calls this other-oriented discipline, where you clearly see or are shown how your behavior affects others.[226]

The idea of "foster care" brought Nina's future into focus. She realized there was a gap between who she was and who she wanted to become, and that she was going to have to do something different to become this future self. She realized she had a lot to live for:

*I had a future. I had this privilege. I had opportunities. I could really do
something with my life.*

In other words, Nina reframed how she saw her challenge—using a cognitive change strategy.

PSYCHOLOGICAL DISTANCING

The cognitive change strategy of psychological distancing is quite useful
in situations like this, as the research of Ethan Kross of the University of
Michigan demonstrates. When Kross was growing up and something went
wrong, his father would ask him to try to understand and get to the bottom
of his feelings. Kross found this introspective strategy personally helpful, but
when he got to college and began studying psychology, he found that studies
on introspection showed the exact opposite:

*Those studies showed that when something bad happens and you ask
a person to try to figure out why they're feeling the way they are, their
attempts to work through their problems often make them feel worse. I
found that puzzling.*[227]

For a number of years, Kross experimented with chipping away at this
puzzle,[228] which led him down different pathways; but ultimately he discovered self-distancing—that is, looking at what's going on as if you're on
a balcony, looking down on your situation from afar. In a series of studies,
Kross and his research team tested this concept. For example, they asked undergraduate students to think of a painful experience in one of two ways:[229]

- Make sense of this experience as you usually would

or

- Step back and adopt a fly-on-the-wall perspective

Kross says:

*We found that giving people that psychological space was like giving them
a mental timeout. It allowed them **not** to get stuck in all the negative things*

that happened to them, but instead to focus on the broader context, and make sense of the event.[230]

Does this remind you of meaning-making in the here and now, and then in a more abstract context in the research of Mary Helen Immordino-Yang? Does it also remind you of asking young people to take a near or far perspective in the research of Jennifer Silvers? Both of these techniques draw on the same psychological strategy: self-distancing. However, although self-distancing is useful, it poses a challenge because it takes considerable time, effort, and energy to implement.

Kross began looking for a self-distancing strategy that would be easier to implement. He told me that he and his team "stumbled on an idea"—a very simple one. They found if people think about themselves either by name ("What would Ellen do?") or as a non-first-person pronoun ("What would she do?"), it helped calm their high emotions.

The researchers tested this idea first in the lab. They gave undergraduates a task of preparing for a speech to land their dream job—a stressful task! Some were told to use first-person pronouns ("I," "me," "my") as much as possible in preparing. Others were told to use their own names and other non-first-person pronouns.

Key Finding: Participants who were using their own name were rated as having delivered more persuasive speeches and reported less anxiety.

Follow-up brain studies revealed that psychological distancing leads to less activation of the cognitive control executive function circuitry than thinking of yourself in the first person.[231] That's good news. As Kross concludes, it's "a relatively effortless self-control tool."[232] Psychiatrist and author Daniel Siegel adds an important word of caution about this approach—*excessive* distancing can lead to detachment, to feeling that "these aren't really my feelings." He reminds us to stay balanced. When we distance, we also need to stay connected with our sensations, thoughts, and feelings.[233]

PROVIDING SOCIAL AND ACADEMIC SUPPORT AT SCHOOL

Whereas Kate and Kelly had more of a struggle with their public school, Laura's and Nina's experiences were generally more productive. Laura helped make changes in Nina's school to make it work better for her (a situation modification strategy) by getting her an IEP (an Individualized Education Program, required by law to help students manage disabilities) for ADHD.

At first, Nina says, Laura closely monitored her:

> She'd ask, "How are your grades? How is everything?" She'd want to watch me do my homework. Once I got my IEP, I had a teacher who helped me do that for myself. She actually talked to my mom and said, "Hey, you need to stop. Once you stop, she'll be able to do it on her own." And my mom did.

That's the same lesson Kate learned—validate, but don't try to fix things.

REDEFINING EXPECTATIONS: BEST ≠ PERFECT

Nina sees that her mother is "the best mother ever," primarily because she's open about her mistakes and works to correct them, just as Nina does. That's something my mother always did with me and for which I am deeply grateful. She saw both of us as learning and growing.

Nina also says that Laura really listens—she's someone kids want to be around.

> All of my friends are like, "My mom is great, but Nina's is better." Literally, my friends come over to hang out with my mom.

The most important lesson from these years of turmoil is a crucial one—**best is *not* perfect.** Nina says:

> I think she always thought that I was this perfect little kid, and I was—well, I tried to be for a while—a perfect little kid. Now she's realized that I am a whole different person, and she learned to love me like that.

Nina and her mother talk about these years of turmoil. She told me:

> My mom learned a lot about herself as a mom and her responsibility for me and I learned a lot about myself. I don't think other moms and daughters should have to go through that and it could have been handled a lot better, but ultimately, I'm so grateful.

When it was time for Nina to write a college essay, she wrote about the massive tree in the park.

That tree is the reason why I exist. It's the thing that keeps me going. It's a metaphor for growth. I want to use my experiences to empower me over the course of my life—to become a behavioral economist so I can help people in low-income communities make better decisions about their lives.

Similarly, as much as Kate would never wish mental health issues on anyone, she realizes that this experience has shaped Kelly:

She wants to be a teacher. She might want to work with special needs kids. She will be a much stronger person, dealing with stuff that I didn't deal with until my twenties or thirties. She sees the world so much more clearly and she's learning skills that can help her get through the hard stuff and still find a reason to get up in the morning, go be her best self, and help the world.

LEANING INTO STRESS

On these pages, I've written about adolescents like Nina and Kelly with serious mental health issues. But what about the majority of adolescents who face everyday stresses, like breakups of important relationships, rejections, academic pressures, or learning difficulties? There is a huge need for an approach that prevents this type of everyday stress from spiraling into crisis.

Our societal response to record-high mental health challenges seems to be to lean away from stress. According to Jeremy Jamieson of the University of Rochester, David Yeager of the University of Texas, Austin (introduced earlier), and their colleagues, "Conventional thinking portrays stress as mostly a bad thing to be avoided or kept at bay." They call this a "stress-avoidance" mentality, which, they write, "ignores the reality that elevated levels of stress are a normal and, in many ways, even a desirable feature of adolescence."[234]

Whether we **lean into** or lean away from everyday stress matters. If we go back to Megan Gunnar's definition of stress as a time when the demands on our bodies—or **our expectations of those demands**—exceed our ability to handle them,[235] we can see the pivotal role that perception plays. If we think stress is to be avoided, we act one way, but if we understand that feeling stressed in difficult situations can be positive, we act differently.

Over the past years, Jamieson and his colleagues have been experimenting with an approach they call **stress optimization**. This approach helps people reframe stress not as distress—not as a threat—but as a **challenge**.[236] It is for precisely this reason that I have called this skill "taking on challenge," versus coping or being resilient. I, like Jamieson, see it as proactive, not reactive.

Avery, a mother of three from Arizona, has come to embrace a proactive approach to stress out of necessity. As a parent, she is mostly on her own because her husband is on the road for work for long stretches of time. She's found that if a sink gets damaged and the repair is too expensive, she is capable of learning how to plumb in a new sink herself.

She's adopted this approach with Parker, now seventeen. At nine months, Parker climbed out of her walker and has been on the move ever since, climbing onto everything, doing what Avery calls "thrill-seeking," which sometimes feels heart-stoppingly scary.

> *She was my first one so I couldn't understand why she was acting this way. I couldn't stop her, even if I tried. She lived in her own world. I called it Parker's world.*

As she grew, Parker began to feel that her world was different from other kids' worlds. By the time she was eight or nine, she recalls:

> *I was not paying attention in school and everything felt boring. I couldn't focus very well and I just . . . It was really hard doing anything with school and writing. That's pretty much it. That began to affect me a lot.*

So, Avery took Parker to a series of doctors who eventually diagnosed her with attention deficit disorder and put her on medication. The first medication made her jittery; the next one made her feel like a zombie.

Parker says, "I wasn't me anymore." Avery says, "Parker's world went away."

The third try worked better, especially when they reduced the dosage. Avery's learned to join into Parker's world and help her recognize how she functions best. Parker describes some of her strategies:

> *If I have to take notes at school, I draw pictures so I can remember what they're talking about. I also get to listen to music in school. Because I have so many things going through my head, it's easier to concentrate on what I'm doing when something is playing.*

Parker's world involves facing challenges:

I think seeing the challenge is definitely a first step. You have to face it straight on, and think what ways you could do it, and different ways you can challenge yourself.

Sometimes, it doesn't work:

You have to give yourself a break if you can't actually do something and know that it's not your strong suit. But then you can try to find someone to help, like with math.

Their life isn't without challenges, like the time Parker cut a hole in the trampoline to remove rocks that had been sitting on top of it. After being furious, Avery looked at her child's head poking out of the middle of the trampoline and saw it as a perfect portrayal of Parker's world. Parker is very grateful that her mom responds this way and encourages her do things that interest her:

I'm glad she let me be myself because I wouldn't be me today if she didn't let me be myself.

In a series of six ingenious experiments, Yeager, Jamieson, and their colleagues joined forces to create a thirty-minute online intervention that tests the type of approach that Avery has learned to use with Parker and her other kids. This stress-optimization intervention is anchored in James Gross's cognitive change strategy of **altering the way we think about stressful situations**[237] by targeting two mindsets. The first is a growth mindset that presents normal but challenging stressors (taking a test, giving a speech, keeping up with coursework) not as dangers to be avoided but as opportunities for learning and self-improvement. The second is a "stress-can-be-enhancing" mindset, which focuses on learning that the physical symptoms of stress (racing heart, being out of breath, feeling anxious) can be positive because they are our body's way of mobilizing energy to reach a goal. These two mindsets go together—both are necessary to equip adolescents to take on challenges in a lasting way.

With more than four thousand high school and college-age students across the six experiments, the research team tested their approach, comparing those who received the intervention with control groups. In one experiment, for instance, eighth-through-twelfth-grade students were asked to imagine that the instructor of their most stressful class had assigned a very demanding assignment but they had only two days to complete it before presenting their work to their classmates. In another, students actually took a timed quiz. In still another, students participated in the Trier Social Stress Test (which you may remember from Gunnar's research), where college students were asked to give a speech about their personal strengths and weaknesses in front of two peer evaluators who were trained to provide negative nonverbal feedback (such as frowning, sighing, and crossing their arms) and no positive verbal or nonverbal feedback. Afterward, the students were asked to do mental math (counting backward from 996 by sevens). The outcomes of the various experiments that the researchers assessed included cardiovascular reactivity, daily cortisol levels, academic success, anxiety during the pandemic lockdowns, and self-regard—how good or bad the students felt about themselves, which is a precursor of anxiety and depression.

The study results indicate that this thirty-minute self-administered online training helping adolescents see that they *can* grow and learn from stress and that they *can* reframe their physical stress reactions from a threat into a challenge was effective.

The researchers' hope for this intervention is that it could become a scalable, low-cost treatment to prevent the everyday stresses of adolescence from adding to our mental health crisis. They also hope it helps reframe the public conversation about adolescents, from viewing adolescents as vulnerable to seeing them as capable:

> Our studies suggest that we might not teach adolescents that they are too fragile to overcome difficult struggles, but that we might, instead, provide them with the resources and guidance that they need to unleash their skills and creativity in addressing big problems.[238]

Those words could not express my hopes for *The Breakthrough Years* any better!

PROMOTING TAKING ON CHALLENGES

To promote the Life and Learning Skill of Taking on Challenges, we can help our children learn a number of strategies for managing their emotions, behavior, and attitudes. The strategies that help them can help us, too.

- **Setting goals for what you want to achieve.** Life and Learning Skills are always goal driven, so managing challenges is always more effective if we know why this will help—when we want to change.
- **Have a Possibilities Mindset.** Even when the going got extremely rough, Kate and Laura didn't give up on their children. And they found ways to help their children not give up on themselves and recognize that things, and they, can change.
- **Try to find the right place or the right people.** We all need support when there are challenges—people who provide support, who aren't judgmental, and who can help us say what we feel and see what we are doing in new ways. That's what help is all about.
- **Change our expectations.** Changing the way we think about a challenge—such as seeing that mistakes are opportunities to learn or that a parent or a child can't be perfect—is a ticket to better managing challenges.
- **Use self-distancing strategies.** When we think of ourselves from a distance, in the third person or by name, we can handle challenges with less effort.
- **Turning struggles into opportunities.** Both Kelly and Nina turned their mental health challenges into opportunities to contribute to make the world a better place for people like themselves. We can do this, too, when faced with the inevitable challenges that life brings.

Executive Function and Life and Learning Skills in Programs

Most of the adolescents you've met so far in this chapter struggled with or worked on improving their executive function and Life and Learning Skills on their own, with their families, or with the help of tutors/therapists. Some of them were told that it's not the role of schools to help promote these skills. But suppose—*just suppose*—it was the role of programs in school and in out-of-school activities. Given how essential these skills are to success in school and life, it seems shortsighted, self-defeating, even foolish to draw a line around these skills, concluding they're beyond the scope of the programs that we entrust our children's learning to. That's a view I am working hard to change. In the meantime, however, what should parents and professionals seek in programs that may already exist? What are some promising practices?

WHAT TO LOOK FOR

Fortunately, there are sound scientific guideposts in research reviews of interventions conducted by Adele Diamond and Daphne Ling. Diamond and Ling set high scientific standards for the interventions they included in the first of their comprehensive reviews, published in 2016. The interventions they included:[239]

- Were published in a **peer-reviewed journal** in English.
- Showed **causal effects.** Causality is a big deliverable. For example, if a study simply compares two groups of students—let's say, those who were in orchestras and those who weren't—and concludes that students in orchestras have better executive function skills, that's a correlational finding, not a causal one. You wouldn't know from this finding whether the orchestra students in this study just happened to have more "get-up-and-go" (to quote neuroscientist Michael Gazzaniga)[240] or whether something about being in orchestra actually improved their cognitive skills.
- Included a **comparison group.** To show causal effects, you need to show that an intervention creates an improvement over time by presenting evidence that a comparable population that was randomly assigned to a group without the intervention doesn't change.[241]
- Examined **longer-term effects**—that is, the improvement lasts for a measurable amount of time and not just immediately after (e.g., an hour after the intervention).
- Demonstrated **transfer**—that is, shows effects beyond improvements on the immediate task. Diamond and Ling write: "We were interested in . . . improvement in a basic cognitive ability that generalized at least to similar tasks."[242]

They found 84 interventions meeting these strict criteria in 2016, and in 2020 they published a second review—the largest one of EF skills ever conducted—that includes 179 studies from 193 papers.[243]

In their 2020 review, Diamond and Ling predicted that activities that will most successfully improve executive function skills will contain *all* of these elements:

- *They will tax EFs, continually challenging them in new and different ways.*
- *They will be personally meaningful and relevant, inspiring [participants'] deep commitment and emotional investment . . . to the activity and perhaps also to one another.*
- *They will have a mentor or guide who firmly believes in the [activity's] efficacy . . . and is supportive (sincerely cares about and believes steadfastly in the individual participants).*
- *They will provide joy, reduce feelings of stress and loneliness, and inspire self-confidence and pride.*[244]

Six Principles for Promoting Executive Function Skills

Drawing on Diamond's and Ling's reviews and conclusions, we've built on their predictions* to arrive at six principles for promoting skills. These principles are a lens that we can use to judge whether programs are effectively promoting EF and Life and Learning Skills.

PRINCIPLE 1: A GOAL-DIRECTED, WHOLE-PERSON APPROACH

The program is goal-directed, informed by child development knowledge, and has an asset-based and whole-person approach (calls upon social, emotional, and cognitive capacities to pursue goals) that helps children and adolescents become self-directed, engaged learners.

Since we use executive function skills to achieve our goals, programs that improve these skills need to be fashioned around goals *for* young people. It's critical these goals be informed by child development knowledge and the science of learning.

Further, it's critical that program goals be asset- or strength-based—in other words, they build on and extend what children and adolescents do well rather than focus on what's "wrong" with them.

Since EF skills are goal-centered, program aims should include helping young people learn to set *their own* goals—in other words, to become self-

---

* Very special thanks to Phil Zelazo of the University of Minnesota, Deb Leong of Tools of the Mind, and Erin Ramsey of the Families and Work Institute for discussions that led to the formulation of these principles.

directed, engaged learners, masters of their own intentional learning, as Deb Leong of Tools of the Mind, an EF curriculum for younger children, puts it.[245]

PRINCIPLE 2: STEADFAST, WELL-FOUNDED BELIEF IN THE PROGRAM

The people facilitating the program deeply believe in and care about the efficacy of the program and in the children and adolescents they serve.

Study after study finds that relationships are what I call the swing-vote factor. As Diamond and Ling write: "A deeply caring relationship between the trainer and the children produces the best outcomes."[246]

PRINCIPLE 3: GENUINE COMMITMENT TO CREATING A COMMUNITY OF LEARNERS

The people facilitating the program are ongoing learners themselves and see their role as helping children learn, inspiring a commitment and investment in learning, and serving as role models.

In my own studies, I've found that the best teachers are ongoing learners themselves—learning about the children, about the subjects, about themselves and how they can improve.[247] That intentionality, that drive to learn what the children are learning, is linked to better-quality learning experiences for children.

PRINCIPLE 4: INTENTIONALITY IN MEETING THE NEEDS OF ALL

The people in the program—facilitators and students alike—work intentionally to create environments where Basic Needs (like belonging, support, autonomy, respect, competence, challenge, identity, and purpose) are met and positive mindsets are fostered.

Diamond and Ling call out the importance of addressing developmental needs—writing, for example, about the importance of "social belonging"[248] and support. They emphasize, "It is not enough to usually be supportive. It is an important principle that one negative act, such as humiliating someone, can override the benefit of scores of positive ones."[249] They further predict that autonomy matters, noting:

Having input (even about something as trivial as the order in which things are done) has been consistently shown to produce more engagement in the activity and more improvement.[250]

Diamond and Ling write about right-sized or doable challenges, stating, "It helps people to believe in themselves and to feel proud and self-confident if they are given challenges that are do-able but push their limits (so they can see for themselves that they are capable)."[251] They further also emphasize the importance of mindsets, stating, "Our expectations about whether or not we can do something have a huge effect on whether we succeed."[252]

PRINCIPLE 5: A RELEVANT, CHALLENGING, AND REFLECTIVE LEARNING ENVIRONMENT

The activities are meaningful, real-world activities that provide opportunities to become aware of, use, reflect on, and practice executive function skills and Life and Learning Skills in new and different ways.

Studies have found, in general, that programs that train one specific skill may lead to specific improvements on that skill in that context but don't necessarily affect the skill use in other contexts (i.e., far transfer). Real-world activities that enable ongoing practice and varied use lead to "better long-term performance."[253]

In addition, young people need opportunities to reflect on these skills and their own learning. Zelazo says young people need "discussion about what has been learned, what it's good for, and how it can be applied to new situations."[254] This includes providing time for pausing and reflecting,[255] learning to monitor their own progress,[256] and sharing their learnings with others.[257]

PRINCIPLE 6: PRIORITIZING WELL-BEING

The program, its people, and its activities promote the well-being of all involved, providing times of joy, reducing feelings of stress and loneliness, and inspiring self-confidence, pride, and compassion.

Diamond and Ling predict that whether people are "emotionally invested in an activity that requires EFs may be key to whether that activity improves EFs";[258] in other words, people need to find meaning in that activity.

Similarly, they state that "there is some evidence that EF benefits from any activity may be proportional to how much joy that activity instills." In fact, meaning and joy are essential in their predictions about promoting executive function skills.[259] They point out that activities that bring joy stimulate dopamine production, which affects the prefrontal cortex, which, as we know, is central to executive function skills. Activities that bring joy also activate the nucleus accumbens, key to feeling pleasure and to the willingness to persevere in the face of challenge. Conversely, stress stimulates the release of cortisol and other neurotransmitters that can negatively affect the prefrontal cortex and are linked with impairment of executive functions.[260]

Executive function skills also depend on eating well, exercising, managing stress, and sleeping well.[261] Indeed, exercising and managing stress can directly improve executive function skills. In *Altered Traits*,[262] Daniel Goleman (also author of the best-seller *Emotional Intelligence*)[263] and Richard J. Davidson of the University of Wisconsin lay out the science of how meditation can affect these skills, too—improving attention and concentration, lessening mind-wandering, and increasing inhibitory control.[264]

In their extensive review, Diamond and Ling ask: Which will matter more—the type of program, or the way it's done? They predict—hands down—that it's not what you do but how you do it that matters most.[265]

Executive Function / Life and Learning Skills in Schools

Since I strongly believe that it's not enough to ask young people to work on these skills on their own and I believe that we need to infuse these skills into programs, I conclude this chapter with two examples of school programs that promote Life and Learning Skills using the six principles I've just outlined (references to these principles are in bold font in the descriptions).

LAB ←→ LIFE: MOUNTAIN VIEW HIGH SCHOOL

Mountain View High School in Centreville, Virginia, has been honored by the Virginia General Assembly as one of the best schools in the state. It's received a Fairfax County Board of Supervisors' resolution, recognizing Mountain View for academic excellence, the *Washington Post* Agnes Meyer Award for Outstanding Teachers, and every other award Fairfax County offers,[266] which is especially impressive because its 180 students have been placed there or chosen to go there because they aren't making it in their regular high schools.

A Teacher-Created Course on EF Skills

Principal Joe Thompson finds that for the most part in Fairfax County, high school teachers expect "someone else"—parents or grade school/middle school teachers—to teach executive function and Life and Learning Skills: they say teachers don't have time, claim the school's too big, or give lots of other reasons why it's not the teachers' responsibility. From his experience, Thompson thinks it *is* the school's job at every level—not only for the students in his school but for all students. He also thinks such a course shouldn't be one more thing for teachers to jam into a tight schedule— "another rock in my knapsack," as it's been called in the business world; it should be part of all learning. So he and a group of teachers have created a course called Success Prep.

> We were concerned about how to make this course enmeshed in the curriculum, day-to-day. I want to see it in every classroom, in the hallways, and everywhere that we talk to students.[267]

The members of the team drafted individual lessons (based on an earlier course they'd created), which were reviewed and revised by a working group. They then piloted the course with students and made revisions again. Their goal has been to create a course that could be taught by teachers, counselors, and others in any school. As such, it is posted online (www.efintheclassroom .net) as a free course for any school to use.[268]

Students take the course on their computers either virtually or in the classroom group. Jeff Jones, one of the program's architects and a teacher of Active Physics, says:

> Students who are shy or want to say something privately are responding through the computer. We can respond to them privately as well.[269]

Success Prep is a yearlong, county-approved, credit-bearing course. Every single teacher at Mountain View teaches this course and every single student takes it during third period, with the focus on EF in the first semester and on social-emotional learning in the second semester.

The course slide deck begins with teachers-only slides inviting teachers to "set a positive tone, provide a sense of recognition, create an emotionally safe place, communicate respect, let students know they matter and are welcome." In other words, teachers are encouraged to meet **students' basic psychological needs** for belonging, respect, and support.

To describe the course, I use the module on planning as an example. The first slides in this module are designed to **engage them with a relevant and emotional challenge.** They are asked, for example, what they think when someone asks them to complete a school project, with response choices depicted as clever memes:

- I have no idea what I'm doing (a dog flying a plane).
- Wing it (a cartoon bird).
- Help (a name tag that says "Help").
- I have a plan (Star Trek image).

The next slide asks which of these memes represents how they'd feel if someone asked them to plan a party. Jones says:

We want them to see that they may actually have a strength they hadn't realized—it just hasn't been applied towards school.

This activity represents an **asset- or strength-based approach.** It assumes adolescents have capabilities that teachers can build on—versus fixing their deficits. Molly Flatley, Special Education department chair and one of the program creators, says that for years students have been told to "pay attention, do better"—but if the students haven't learned the skills to do so, these words have little meaning. Mountain View's goal is to thread these skills throughout the curriculum in ways that show students "you *can* do this."

The next slides portray the "selling point" or **motivation** for learning to plan. Students are asked to think about whether they'd like to work hard now for little in return later. Obviously they wouldn't. Through some other exercises, the students learn that planning is a time-saver.

Next, students are shown that planning is a skill they can use outside school. They're prompted to think about the planning necessary for a football play or to win a video game. As Jones says, "Planning is knowing what to do before you do it."

After making the business case for planning (it saves time *and* effort), students engage in **reflective writing exercises.** They're asked, "What is your reaction when a teacher gives you a long-term project?" Then, "What's your reaction if a friend tells you your favorite band is coming to play a show in two months?" A third question prompts them to compare the difference between their answers. Jones says:

> Do they have more to say about getting concert tickets in advance than about having to get their term paper done? We ask them to highlight the differences between the two.

Students are then asked: "Is there any part of your life where you'd like to improve your planning skills? Why?" This aims to **foster students' responsibility** to develop and use this skill. Jones says:

> We're not going to make them better planners just by talking about planning. They're going to have to put some effort in themselves. We can make them aware of what might need improvement or what they can do to improve, but the work ends up being theirs!

English teacher and co-creator Tim McElroy says that the overarching goal of Success Prep is to have students become more independent—**to become self-directed, engaged learners.**

Throughout the deck, teachers can select activities to illustrate key points. Jones explains:

> Basically, teachers can tailor activities to their classroom because classrooms are very different. An English 12 classroom looks nothing like my Active Physics classroom.

There's a poster in every classroom—which students photograph on their phones—depicting the EF skills in the course: (1) working memory, (2) response inhibition, (3) emotional control, (4) sustained attention, (5) task initiation, (6) planning, (7) organization, (8) time management, (9) flexibility, (10) metacognition, and (11) goal-directed persistence. There's also an introductory lesson on mindset. The selection of these specific EF skills was inspired by the book *Smart but Scattered*.[270]

On Mondays, there's an overview of the skill of the week, like the lesson just described on planning. On Tuesdays, students focus on thinking errors—self-defeating patterns such as blaming others, feeling entitled, feeling like a victim, etc. Administrative tasks take place on Wednesdays and mentoring on EF skills happens on Thursdays.

On Fridays, there's a review, which the teachers see as time to **pause and reflect**. After the week on planning, for example, students are asked, "Did you take the time to make a plan to do something at school?" Students write about this situation, how satisfied they were with their ability to plan, and whether planning helped them be more efficient. Teachers also tie each skill to resilience. Students are asked to remember that resilience is the ability to recover from challenges. Their aim is to show students, as Jones says, that

> *if you want to be tough mentally, physically—to be able to get back up and keep going and deal with the challenges of life—planning (or whatever skill we're working on) will help you do that. The wrap-up is: we're doing this because we want you to get better at life, not just school!*

Executive Functioning:
How we think about our thinking

WORKING MEMORY

The ability to hold information in your head while you do something with it.

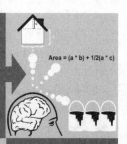

$Area = (a * b) + 1/2(a * c)$

RESPONSE INHIBITION

The ability to think before acting.

EMOTIONAL CONTROL

The ability to manage emotions.

SUSTAINED ATTENTION

The ability to maintain attention to a task.

TASK INITIATION

The ability to begin a task.

PLANNING

The ability to see the individual steps in an assignment and sequence them.

ORGANIZATION

The ability to keep track of information and materials.

TIME MANAGEMENT

The ability to effectively manage your time.

FLEXIBILITY

The ability to switch activities or accept different ways to do something.

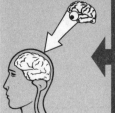

METACOGNITION

The ability to think about your thinking.

GOAL-DIRECTED PERSISTENCE

The ability to keep working toward a goal.

Illustration: Peter Garvey

Gauging Success

Principal Joe Thompson says he steers away from assessing students' EF skills:

> *The easy answer would be that we could have the students self-assess on their skill level, and then get feedback from teachers, but I think that's a trap.*

I believe Thompson's caution is well placed though an external evaluation might be helpful. **Teachers do see progress.** Disciplinary violations have gone down in the two years since they've implemented Success Prep. Learning outcomes have improved, too. And the language of EF has become everyday language. A student who's stuck may say, "Whoa. I'm stuck on an escalator"—the analogy used to teach about cognitive flexibility—and then work to become unstuck.

Kim Dockery, the former chief academic officer of the Fairfax County Public Schools, says when she attends graduation at Mountain View High School every year, she often runs into assistant principals from other Fairfax schools. They've come to see students who didn't make it in their school graduate from Mountain View. They tell Dockery, "I don't know why we didn't do this in our schools. We could have succeeded with this or that student. We could have done this, but we didn't."

LAB ←→ LIFE: EL EDUCATION

A number of years ago, science teacher Aurora Kurshner brought a project to her high school students at the Springfield, Massachusetts, Renaissance School; the project was to conduct a professional water-quality assessment of a local pond that had been fenced off from the public for environmental reasons. Students were asked to answer this question: What would it take for Loon Pond to be reopened as a public recreation area? One student, Danielle Cassista, recalls being both skeptical and inspired when she first heard of the pond project:

> *What do they expect us to do? We're fifteen-year-old students. They were depending on us to decide if this pond was suitable or not. It was kind of empowering.*[271]

Kurshner said this project offered her students the opportunity to learn scientific content in ways that met rigorous state educational standards while providing a community service. They had to learn how to read environmental standards, research primary sources, conduct field research, analyze the data, write up findings, and present them to their school and the mayor (which ultimately contributed to the reopening of the pond). Through this project and their daily classroom work, the students learned many skills—which they call life skills, representing a second way, a holistic way, of incorporating Life and Learning Skills into a whole program approach.

Springfield Renaissance School, rated as the number one public high school in Springfield,[272] is one of the more than 150 schools nationwide in the EL (originally Expeditionary Learning) Education network of high-achieving elementary, middle, and high schools in thirty-five states and serving sixty thousand students.

To understand EL Education and its approach to Life and Learning Skills, it's important to begin with the visionary behind it, Ron Berger. When he was growing up, school was a place where he protected himself at all costs:

I navigated school feeling like I was carrying things I'd never want others in the school to know. I think many of us have those kinds of things—home or personal situations.[273]

Although Berger's family was caring, "with lots of love for the world," his mother struggled with mental health issues. As an adult, he became a sixth-grade teacher in a rural community in Massachusetts, where he recognized there were lots of kids like him:

I taught kids for more than twenty-five years. I could see kids holding the pain I remember in myself. I know you can't really dive into school with heart if you feel like you're always protecting yourself.

That experience ultimately led him to help create EL Education, as did his own experiences as an adult with Outward Bound, where he saw the difference that this kind of experience can make.

Once adolescents got on an Outward Bound trip, it changed them into a better person.[274]

As a sixth-grade teacher, he had created Outward Bound types of experiences for his students. On the first day of school, he'd tell his students to come to school the next day with their oldest clothes because they were going to go cave exploring:

*"You're going to be scared to death. You're going to be in total darkness.
You're going to support each other, because in the dark, you're not going to
know if it's your friend or not or if that person is cool or not. You're just going
to be giving them a hand and they're going to be giving you a hand. We're
going to get out. We're going to feel like Indiana Jones at the end of this day."*

Think about all of the Life and Learning Skills students are learning in
positive risk experiences like this!

Cave exploring became the impetus for what EL Education calls Crew,
a structure they create in all their schools where all students support each
other, where no one *really* gets left out or left behind. As Berger says, that's
the big message: everyone gets to the top of the mountain, together.

EL Education was created by winning a 1991 federal competition for a
new vision of schools. This proposal was co-submitted by the Harvard Graduate School of Education (where Berger was teaching) with Harvard's developmental psychologist Howard Gardner and by Outward Bound USA.[275]
Out of eight hundred applicants, eleven won the $1 million prize, including
EL Education, launching with ten schools.

Learning Tailored to Developmental Abilities

In many ways, an EL Education school looks like most schools. In a high
school English class, students discuss books they've read; in science class,
they conduct experiments. But it's different. If the students are working
on longer-term "expeditionary projects" like Loon Pond, the book they're
reading might be about water resources. The science experiments might be
about water purity. Those students would be going out and testing water,
interviewing local citizens, and preparing a presentation on how to combat
pollution and open the pond as a community resource. Their learning would
be in the service of contributing to their community.

This approach to learning can be contrasted with workshop models—
learning where teachers show students how to do something, practice it with
students, and then give assignments where students practice on their own.
Instead, EL Learning espouses a model they call Workshop 2.0, where they
implement Five *E*s: Engage, Explore, Explain, Extend, and Evaluate.[276] Teachers engage students by beginning with a challenging problem. Berger explains:

*Instead of students coming into class and the teacher giving them a
lesson using an algorithm, they come into math class and there's a really
intriguing, challenging problem on the board.*[277]

As you can see, a school set up this way makes **exploring—one of the most important ways that adolescents learn—the gateway for learning** the content their school is required to teach and the state standards students are required to meet. Standards and exploratory learning go together.

Taking positive risks is critically important to adolescents and to learning in general. Positive risks are built into the EL Education approach. This is key to Berger:

> *If you can't take risks in your English class, in your mathematics class, in your art class, you can't learn. Learning comes from risk-taking.*[278]

In EL Education schools, every class does expeditionary projects one to three times a year. They're tied to building students' character by **doing good for others in their community (i.e., contributing)**—which, as you know, is a need adolescents have.

Typically, adults try to motivate adolescents by saying that doing well in their academic subjects will help them get a job, make money, support themselves, and live a good life in the future. But **doing good for oneself and for others in the here and now** is seen as the **motivator for learning** in this program.

With its approach to learning and to expeditionary projects, the EL Education curriculum **melds social-emotional *and* cognitive learning as the means for learning content.** Nor is theirs a values-neutral approach. Berger continues:

> *We feel that courage, compassion, respect, and responsibility are not neutral. We **don't** say we want you to have good communication skills. We do say we want you to have good communication skills in service of being a citizen who stands up for what's right, who stands up for the rights of all people, who accepts and values all people.*[279]

Promoting Life and Learning Skills in the service of values really resonates, especially with adolescents, because they're acutely aware of authenticity and fairness.

Each school goes through a precise process of identifying for themselves the characteristics they seek to instill as they create "a portrait of a graduate" of their school. Thus, **the adults and students in each school grapple with defining their values and Life and Learning Skills, and in doing so, they "own"** them: they are *their* values, *their* skills.

For example, Polaris, a charter school in Chicago serving 450 students from kindergarten through the eighth grade, concluded that their mission is "to educate students to be self-motivated, creative, critical thinkers, with the ultimate goal of shaping lifelong learners and citizens with a strong sense of personal and civic responsibility."[280] Polaris created a five-point star depicting these values. Their website shows five students, each wearing a T-shirt that states their values as nouns.

There are commonalities across the network. In all EL Education schools, for example, **being a self-directed, engaged learner who contributes to the greater good** is the ultimate goal.

Student voice is embedded into their curriculum and culture. For example, parent-teacher conferences are student-led from the early childhood years through high school. Gabriela,[281] a seventh grader at WHEELS, a pre-K–12 public school in New York City, shows her dad examples of her work during the conference, explaining that she's learned to organize essays into paragraphs she can support with evidence from primary sources. She also discusses HOWL, the Habits of Work and Learning—the Life and Learning Skills that she's gained in doing her schoolwork.

Collaboration is embedded throughout the program. The structure designed for this, as I mentioned earlier, is Crew.[282] The name comes from the sport of rowing. You have to row together to get anywhere. Berger elaborates:

> We thought, "What if school was like a team sport, not an individual sport? What if everyone was looking out for each other in school?"
>
> Your job in Crew is to get everyone to the top of the mountain or onto the ocean or down the river. There's no credit getting out ahead of other people. The idea of Crew is that you're looking out for the other person as much as you're looking out for one's self.[283]

Crew is a time for honest academic and personal conversations in **asset-based ways**. If a student hasn't completed their homework, the other students would be expected to hold this student accountable, but say, "What's the matter and how can we help you?"

I see Crew as providing a **structure where the Basic Needs of students and adults are met**. For example, Hunter, an eighth grader at Meadow Glen Middle School in Lexington, South Carolina, talks about the need for challenge when he says that in Crew students are "pushed to where you're not in your comfort zone, you're in a little bit of a stretch zone."[284]

EL Education sees Life and Learning Skills as the tools students need to master knowledge and develop character. They are promoted **through real-world activities that continually exercise students' abilities to use skills in new and different ways.** Additionally, children and adolescents are coached to reflect on and name the skills they use: "I showed critical thinking here, I showed resilience there."[285]

Belief in the effectiveness of their program and in the children is made explicit at EL Education. Ron Berger calls on teachers "to believe in the genius in each child."[286] As an example, Berger recounted the story of a math teacher who didn't want to do Crew, telling Berger that he was hired to be a math teacher, not a psychologist. Berger responded that he'd heard the teacher was wonderful at math, but disabused him of the notion that he had been hired to teach. He said, "We didn't actually hire you to teach. We hired you to help kids learn." He continued:

> *Crew is the place to figure out why your students aren't thriving at math, why they're afraid to take risks, why they're afraid to raise their hand in class and ask you questions, why they're afraid to put their work on the board.*[287]
>
> *So we want to work with you because we know you're a great math teacher and we need you to be a great Crew leader.*[288]

EL Education has created a system for learning that's designed to help every child thrive and learn Life and Learning Skills, including those students who are like Ron Berger once was—feeling the need to protect themselves. Berger wants schools to be places where the rewards of coming together to learn far outweigh what students might have been trying to achieve by staying hidden in their shells.

Rethinking Adolescence: From Skills That Benefit Us to Skills That Benefit Us *and* Others

I've been involved in sharing information about Life and Learning Skills for children, adolescents, and adults for two decades. This has provided more than enough opportunities to see how this knowledge can be used . . . and abused. Which leads me to end by sharing my enthusiasm for skills with five strong caveats.

1. **It's essential that Life and Learning Skills *and* the context in which they're learned be seen as inextricably connected.** The analogy of a car says it all—if we only ensure that a car drives well, that car still won't go far if the roads are rutted or blocked. That's why the concepts of meeting Basic Needs and promoting Life and Learning Skills must go hand in hand. Adolescents can best learn Life and Learning Skills when they are in environments where they feel they belong, are supported, are treated with respect, and are given the agency to make appropriate decisions.

2. **We need to expand beyond foundational executive function skills to Life and Learning Skills.** As we saw in the research, a number of the efforts to train executive function skills have failed to create "far transfer"—the learners weren't able to apply what they learned to new situations. I believe that's partly because some of these EF trainings were directed narrowly at foundational EF skills, like working memory, inhibitory control, and cognitive flexibility. The comprehensive review by Adele Diamond and Daphne Ling of the University of British Columbia tells us the activities that successfully improve these skills continually challenge learners in new ways, are personally meaningful, are relevant, produce joy, and inspire self-confidence and pride.[289] That's why I focus on promoting Life and Learning Skills based on EF skills—they provide the real-life context for developing our competencies.

3. **Promoting Life and Learning Skills needs to provide opportunities to learn *and* to reflect.** Studies show that providing time for people to pay attention to what and how they are learning—time for reflection—is critical for these skills to become a useful part of our lives.[290] As Deb Leong of Tools of the Mind says, this kind of intentional learning enables us to get better at learning itself.[291]

4. **Measuring Life and Learning Skills and EF skills must not become one more thing for kids to be graded on.** At a research conference a number of years ago, I went to a session on EF skills where some of the scientists called for EF skills to be measured in schools. A few of us—including some leading scholars of EF—gathered afterward to further express our concerns. I—we—agree that we need good measures of Life and Learning Skills and we are working on that, but the results should be used to inform and improve adults' teaching practices—not to grade or judge young people.

5. **Promoting Life and Learning Skills should be viewed and used for the benefit of each of us *and* all of us.** I'll always remember a conversation I had close to two decades ago—just about when I began talking about EF-based Life and Learning Skills as a missing piece of the puzzle in closing the achievement and opportunity gap. "Yes," said my colleague, "but these skills can be used for good or for ill." My colleague talked about a relative who was a great perspective-taker but who used this skill to figure people out so that he could manipulate and scam them. We all probably know someone like that. This is why we must think about how Life and Learning Skills can be used to help each of us *and* all of us.

Recall that adolescents—and adults, too—have a basic human need to contribute to helping others, to making the world a better place. Andrew Fuligni of UCLA writes, "The expansion of adolescents' social world and the approaching transition to adulthood arguably create a fundamental need for youths to apply and develop their capacity to make contributions to others"[292]—whether those others are family, friends, neighbors, or the larger world. During adolescence, the psychological and physical health benefits of contributing to others are manifold.[293]

Our culture is very individually focused. Parents say they value caring, but young people don't see it happening. The researchers in Harvard's Making Caring Common project found that about 80 percent of the young people reported that their parents are more concerned about their achievement or happiness than their caring for others.[294] Yet, ironically, people who do things to benefit others are often happier.

Which is why, when we promote Life and Learning Skills, we need to emphasize how they can benefit each of us *and* all of us.

CONCLUSION

A Letter to My Grandson

You were two years old in the summer of 2015 when I began this book. Now you're an early adolescent yourself. Over these years, I've had privileges few of us will ever have—to deeply explore this transition from childhood to adulthood—adolescence.

Unique among those privileges was talking with young people themselves, asking them what their hopes and dreams were for a book about adolescents, asking them what I should ask researchers when I interviewed them.

You were with me on one of those trips—to Colorado—where I interviewed seventeen high school students who'd been selected to spend a week at the Aspen Ideas Festival participating in the Bezos Scholars leadership program. I know you don't remember what one of the students said to me. He said:

Look at us!

That's because you were too busy looking at a menacing stuffed mountain lion at the lodge where we'd assembled for dinner. But I will never forget that student's words. He spoke about this group of young people, defying stereotypes of teenagers; he spoke about their passion to bring about change. He repeated:

Look at us—we're not what comes to mind when you ask an American adult to think of the typical teenager.

At the time, you barely reached the top of the legs of the young man who was speaking. Now, you'd be close to his shoulder height. Now, you could look him in the eyes and understand the meaning of his words because you've had experiences of how young people are treated. The other evening you went to get ice cream by yourself and people kept pushing past you in line; no one would wait on you. You said, "It's because I'm a kid."

Over the years, as I've listened to the voices of young people and pursued these studies, my thoughts were always on you.

I am like every grandparent, parent, professional—anyone—who reads this book. I always have that special person or people in mind. For me, that's *you*! I am always asking myself: What are my hopes for you? What have I learned that can make a difference in your life—in you, the emerging adolescent I care most about?

I hope you retain the joy you were born with. I think about that week in Aspen and I can see how you were bursting with joy in every photograph I took of you as you reached up and touched that forbidding stuffed mountain lion, climbed on a pool table and created mayhem with the balls, and raced over the hills, often faster than we could run. In fact, in most of the photographs of you throughout these years, you are joyous. Of course, there were tears, as dark and turbulent as the smiles were bright. I hope the world and the schools you attend don't take away the passion you have for life.

I hope you keep your sense of adventure. When we go for walks then and now, I joke that if there's a stone wall to walk on, a massive boulder to jump from, or a tall tree to climb, you'll be there—running, jumping, and climbing. I remember going to a parents' night at your school when you were in kindergarten. Everyone was out on the deck, standing around the high climbing structures. Other parents gasped as you reached the top and, hand over hand, got to the other side. Now, you love rock climbing gyms.

As you enter the teen years, some may label your energy as sensation-seeking. But I hope that's not seen negatively. I hope you live in a world where people are less likely to disparage teenagers, where adults understand that having a sense of adventure is positive, where they help you develop your passion to explore into learning adventures and positive risks.

I understand your sense of adventure. My love for adventure looks different on the surface, but it's the same underneath. It has felt as scary and thrilling for me to leave the comfort of the work I've done for years and embark on understanding adolescence as it is for you to be on the top of that tall climbing structure at your school.

I hope your psychological needs are met. I hope you go to schools and are in groups where adults understand that all of us—children, adolescents, adults—have basic psychological needs and that it's our job as adults to create environments where meeting those needs is not a nice-to-do but a must-do. I hope that meeting these needs is seen as being as important as meeting our biological needs for food, water, and shelter.

As a biracial child, you have the kind of stop-in-your-tracks looks where people literally stop you on the street to admire you—the way you insist on wearing your hair, the way you present yourself, your style. But I know that as you become more of a teen, you might not seem as alluring as you were as a little child. You might even seem scary to some people. I know the road won't always be easy, but I hope that the adults in your life make you feel you belong—that we make every child, no matter their race, background, abilities, and disabilities—feel they belong and are cared for and cared about. I hope they give you and others genuine opportunities to explore your identities. Meeting psychological needs is key to your future—to all of our children's future—and thus to our own future as well.

I hope you always have something you want to learn about. My mother, at close to one hundred, said, "When you stop learning, you stop living." She was the epitome of her own philosophy, leaving a job she'd never much liked in her late seventies, becoming an art critic for her hometown paper, helping to found an art museum, reading for the blind. In fact, the book club in our hometown is named after her, more than a decade and a half after her death. She was always learning.

The biographies and autobiographies I devoured as a child and adolescent—especially the ones I remember—told the stories of people who overcame all manner of hardships in their lives because they had a sense of purpose, a sense of something they wanted to know more about so they could do more about it. While lots of parents worry about spelling or math or science proficiency, I am most concerned about your being strongly motivated to learn. You've always been that way—and I hope the pressures to succeed and achieve in our culture don't diminish it.

I hope you gain Life and Learning Skills and you use them to help yourself and help others. I have realized in my own adventures that these skills help us in innumerable ways. Over the years, I've wondered why. Is it because they help us set goals and then work to achieve those goals? Is it because they help us better understand the world in which we live? Is it because they help us make sounder, well-reasoned decisions and tackle things that are hard? It is all of those things, but it's more. Gaining Life and Learning Skills helps us understand how we learn so we can become masters of our own self-directed, engaged learning.

I hope you gain that mastery. **I hope you use these skills to serve yourself and others.**

Most of all, I hope that if you ever, as an adolescent, tell adults to "look at us," it will be because you know that they—the adults in your life and beyond—understand you and appreciate these years as the breakthrough years that they truly are.

ACKNOWLEDGMENTS

I've always looked at my work as a journey where the adventure is not scaling the highest peaks or exploring new lands but asking and seeking answers to questions:

- Questions that have no easy answers, that are often demanding and difficult but that matter
- Questions that I think will help *me* if I can find answers
- Questions that I think will help *others* if I can find answers

In the journey to research and write *The Breakthrough Years*, there are so many people who have not only traveled with me but have also made this journey possible.

I am deeply grateful for the adolescents and their parents who shared their lives, their challenges and triumphs, and fears and hopes with me. Not only did you make this journey possible, you lit the way with your insights and wisdom.

I am also deeply grateful for my editor, Lee Oglesby. When we first met, she told me she'd come to Flatiron to change some of the conversations in publishing, and I knew she would be perfect for this book because my goal, similarly, is to change the conversations about adolescents. Little did I know then just how truly perfect Lee would be. She has take-your-breath-away editing skills, an artist with words and ideas. She's helped me create the book I wanted to write and for that, I am forever thankful.

I am also so thankful for my publisher, Bob Miller. I love to tell the story of how we met at a publication event for the book *The World According to Mister Rogers*, honoring my dear friend the late Fred Rogers. I knew then and there I wanted to work with Bob and was thrilled when he made an offer for my book *Mind in the Making* at HarperCollins. I followed Bob to his founding of Flatiron, where we began exploring the possibilities of writing two books—one on adults and one on adolescents. On February 7, 2015, Bob wrote me, suggesting that the book on adolescence should be first—so that's the birthdate of this book. Bob combines the qualities of an ideal publisher from the past with one who is reinventing the future of publishing today. It is an honor and a privilege to work with him.

Everyone else at Flatiron has been a joy to work with. Editorial assistants Ruben Reyes and Mary Retta have helped enormously with the details of publishing. I am so impressed by the skills of the production team—production editor Frances Sayers, copy editors Sue Warga and Sarajane Herman, proofreaders Melanie Gold, Peter Kranitz, and Rima Weinberg, and indexer Katherine Etzel. A very special thanks to the audio producer, Katy Robitzski. Marlena Bittner, the executive director of publicity, has brought her keen insight and knowledge to introducing *The Breakthrough Years* to the world, as have publicist Chris Smith and marketer Katherine Turro. The book designers Sue Walsh and Lisa Amoroso created a look and feel for the book that I truly love!

And Toni Sciarra Poynter! I can never thank her enough. Toni was my editor for *Ask the Children* and my brilliant editorial consultant for *Mind in the Making* and *The Breakthrough Years*. She is my first, middle, and last reader and a superb editor. Every conversation with Toni brings awesome insight and joy. I look forward to having conversations with Toni forever, and I am deeply grateful to her for so enriching my life and work.

How lucky am I that Jim Levine is my literary agent and has been my dear friend for years. We met over books—Jim was writing a book for fathers, and I was writing a book on childcare. Then we worked together at Bank Street College, and at the Families and Work Institute. Now we have come back together over books. Jim has that truly rare talent for seeking and finding unique ideas that make a difference. It's no exaggeration to say that without Jim—without his probing questions, his superb ability to synthesize and to deeply care—that my life as an author and researcher would have been very different.

One person has taken this entire journey with me—Brandon Almy. In September 2014, as I was exploring the ideas of an adult and an adolescent book, I asked Phil Zelazo of the University of Minnesota if he could recommend a graduate student to work with me. Without hesitation, he recommended Brandon, and Brandon and I have worked together ever since—through his master's, doctoral and postdoc studies, and the launching of his career as a pediatric neuropsychologist. He thinks of this book as his other dissertation—this one for the adults in adolescents' lives—and it truly is! From conducting literature reviews to designing studies, analyzing data and writing up findings, and fact-checking, Brandon has been there—contributing his brilliance, compassion, competence, can-do attitude, and skills as an incisive researcher and communicator.

The other person on this entire journey has been the inestimable Phil Zelazo. He is a scholar of the highest order, world-renowned for identifying the critical importance of executive function skills for learning, for defining and measuring these skills (including creating gold standard measures), and for creating wise interventions. The two words that keep coming to mind about Phil are "generative" and "generous." He has encyclopedic knowledge across many academic fields but remains a rigorous seeker of knowledge. I could not be more grateful for his help, including in designing the studies, discussing the findings, and reading the entire book. I am even more grateful to be working with Phil now—to translate our knowledge into action in the Center for Civic Science at the University of Minnesota. Thanks, too, for two of his graduate students—Louise Zhuang and Destany Calma-Birling—who have joined our team.

Two other people joined the journey in 2016—Lisa Rinehart and Jennifer Hamblett of Mighty Egg Productions, both immensely gifted and passionate visual storytellers. We took trips to the labs of thirty-four researchers together and from this came a series of you-are-there videos of their research. There is nothing better than discussing research with them—they bring the originality of exceptional filmmakers and the knowledge of parenting, and the results are works of art and science.

And Jackie and Mike Bezos! There are almost no words for how much they have brought to this journey. There is no one who is more creative in her ways of seeing and saying than Jackie—her statements become memorable mottoes, her ideas become life-changing projects. And Mike is deeply thoughtful and astute—his just-right questions, great kindness, and inspiring vision make everyone who has the pleasure of knowing him far better than they were before. Both Jackie's and Mike's unshakable commitment to children—their children, my children, all of our children—has been a gift to the world. Many thanks, too, to my former colleagues at the Bezos Family Foundation—your unique wisdom and talent have added immeasurably to my work on adolescence—especially Megan Wyatt, Chris Plutte, Jody Rosensweig, Francis Icasiano, Elyse Rowe, Lis Stevens, Kelsey Berg, and Linda Shockley. Thank you too to the wise Angela Griffin.

Very, very special thanks go to our team at Families and Work Institute. Year in, year out, you demonstrate off-the-charts courage in following your beliefs, committing yourself to making the world a better place, and creating studies and projects with consummate skill. Marline Griffith, endnote compiler, fact-checker, proofer, and organizer extraordinaire, your laugh changes every room you are in, and your ability to take on challenges guides us. I am so grateful to have worked on this book with you from day one. Jennie Portnof, your artistry and design made all of the data in the book more compelling, and your deep insight added depth to every concept in the book. Erin Ramsey, when you say something, everyone stops to listen—and bingo, your words become not-to-be-forgotten quotes. And when you do something, you lead the way with energy and abundance. Very special thanks to Sara Wolman from Lightbulb Learning Lab for finding just the right way to express some of our concepts; to the bright shining star Kyle Zimmer and First Book for partnering with us to create materials; to Mind in the Making trainers; Shawn Bryant of YestoECE and Barb Lunnemann of Save the Children for your thoughtful help; and to Sam Peterson and Alberto Jimenez, as recent adolescents, for being such excellent interns. Gratitude always to Robert and Marisol DeLeon for the "fantastic" attitude you bring to travel.

I had the honor of working with two extraordinary research teams on the studies conducted for the book. I am so grateful to Larry Osborn, Randall Thomas, and Yifei Liu of Ipsos for your work on the nationally representative studies and to Helene Jennings and Kate Flynn of ICF for your work on the behavioral study.

I also want to thank the board of directors of Families and Work Institute. Our board calls FWI a "treasure," but they are the real treasures. Special thanks to our board chair, Mike Carey, and to Ted Childs for being my mentors. Mike, your knowledge of how to bring about change is visionary, and Ted: you are a game changer in everything you do—always working for a kinder and more just world. Kind and visionary are apt descriptions of our board—Mike, Ted, and Ken Barrett, Deb Dagit, Ellen Marram, Pat Miller, Chris Morena, Stephanie Mudick, and Judy Woodruff. You also made this book possible with your support of the baseline study and I am forever appreciative.

Thanks, too, to the lawyers who have overseen all things literary and legal—Steve Sheppard, Brenda Ulrich, David Erb, and Gray Coleman.

Because research and writing are adventures, there are times when the path forward is rocky and uncertain, when grayness blankets everything. I am blessed to have a very special group of friends and colleagues who helped me see the path ahead and its possibilities: Karen Diamond, my college roommate, who voiced the questions that framed this journey; Penny Armstrong, who makes me laugh over our high school antics; Susan Magsamen: what a thrill to be writing books at the same time; Michael Levine, the smartest and most caring colleague; Ralph Smith, who connects me to what I value most; Mort Sherman, who has been instrumental in creating the future of education; Debbie Bergeron and Yasmina Vinci, the best partners in turning research to action; Dan Wuori, who shares my desire to make the pandemic a turning point in education; Shelley Waters Boots, always at the center of improving the lives of adolescents; Elaine Zimmerman, a poet in life; Lauren Behsudi, beyond creative and thoughtful; Susan Leger Ferrero, the epitome of abundant joy; and Alice Wilder, the best in children's media.

Thank you to the dazzling and brilliant Tiffany Shlain and Goldie Hawn. I am so proud that your film on adolescents and my book will come into the world together.

In these pages, who have met the adolescence researchers who also lit the path forward. The deepest thanks to Nick Allen, Roger Beaty, Elliot Berkman, Tony Burrow, Jason Chein, Eveline Crone, Ron Dahl, Bill Damon, Angela Duckworth, Iroise Dumontheil, Phil Fisher, Jenn Fredricks, Andrew Fuligni, Adam Galinsky, Adriana Galván, Adam Grant, Wendy Grolnick, Megan Gunnar, Berna Güroğlu, Rick Huganir, Mary Helen Immordino-Yang, Ethan Kross, Rich Lerner, Rosa Li, Bea Luna, Dan McAdams, Allyson Mackey, Kate Mills, Velma McBride Murry, Gabriele Oettingen, Jason Okonofua, Jiska Peper, Sabine Peters, Jenn Pfeifer, Megan Price, Yang Qu, Barbara Schneider, Jen Silvers, Larry Steinberg, Ahna Suleiman, Eva Telzer, Melina Uncapher, Greg Walton, David Yeager, and Phil Zelazo.

I have also called on the expertise of many other researchers and thought leaders over these years. I am so grateful for the wisdom of Ron Berger, Linda Burch, Beth Bye, Shari Camhi, Pam Cantor, Stephanie Carlson, Adele Diamond, John Dugan, Carol Dweck, Tony Earls, the late Kurt Fisher, Ken Ginsburg, Alison Gopnik, Diane Hughes, the late Jerry Kagan, Joe Krajcik, Jessica Lahey, Deb Leong, Susan Magsamen, and Andy Meltzoff. Thanks, too, to the Mountain View School team and colleagues—Kim Dockery, Molly Flatley, Pete Garvey, Jeff Jones, Tim McElroy, and Joe Thompson; Kyle Kastler, Bob Pianta, Karen Pittman, David Rose, Dan Siegel, Gerard Senehi, and Henry Shepherd; Jack Shonkoff, the late Dan Stern, Ed Tronick, and Judy Warner.

Finally, thanks to my family—to my gifted and loving sister, Sally Ruth May, her daughter, my beloved niece, Sasha Rau, and my cousin Kristin Loeb, who was invaluable in helping with the audiobook.

Enduring thanks with forever love to Norman, who has helped us live the life and create the work we most want to. I am so blessed that my children found life partners who are such good, good people—the loving and creative Valerie and the loving and spell-blindingly fascinating Ibi.

Most of all, I thank my children, Philip and Lara. Of everything in my life, I am the most proud of them—for the caring, contributing, and exceptional adults they are. And my grandchildren: Antonio, as a college student, you worked with me in the summer of 2015, setting up and participating in interviews. This book has your marks all over it. We are so happy you found the beautiful Kaitlyn. And Zai: all I can say is that my happiness meter hits 1,000 when I hear your voice or see you. This book is for you and your generation.

APPENDIX 1: BREAKTHROUGH YEARS STUDY

CIVIC SCIENCE

I began as I always do, listening to the voices of the people who would be the subjects of the study, but via the scientific process I use—civic science—they become the co-creators. Civic science highlights scientists' responsibility as citizens to use science to assess and respond to problems faced by citizens, to draw on their life experience and wisdom, and to collaborate throughout the scientific process.

FOCUS GROUPS/INTERVIEWS

When I began *The Breakthrough Years* in 2015, I conducted focus groups/ interviews with thirty-eight adolescents, ages fourteen to eighteen, from around the country and other parts of the world, asking them what they wanted to know about their development and what questions I should ask researchers.

From the get-go, their answers were unexpected. For example, they suggested I look into why adolescents are seen so negatively, including suggesting I ask researchers what words they would use to describe the stereotypical adolescent and the typical adolescents they study. In fact, there's not much research on how adolescents are viewed by society—so had I simply followed the science of adolescence, this wouldn't be the unique book it is.

INTERVIEWS WITH ADOLESCENCE RESEARCHERS

In all, I interviewed more than forty-five leading adolescence researchers in-depth. In addition, I and my team conducted three studies.

NATIONALLY REPRESENTATIVE STUDIES

Brandon Almy and Philip Zelazo of the University of Minnesota and I created a quantitative online survey. It was reviewed by ten leading researchers and baseline data were collected between November 22, 2019, and January 9, 2020, by the research firm Ipsos with a nationally representative sample of 1,666 adolescents (nine-to-eighteen-year-olds)* and their parents.

---

* We began the survey with nine-year-olds because that age marks the time when some young people, especially girls, begin to enter puberty.

A follow-up study of 1,115 of the same adolescents and parents was conducted between August 14 and 31, 2020, to see how these young people and their parents were doing during the pandemic.

QUALITATIVE INTERVIEWS

In 2020, in between the baseline and follow-up study, I interviewed fifty-six parents and fifty-two of their adolescents who had volunteered for follow-up interviews from this sample. This was a critical step in the civic science approach—gaining feedback on what we'd found in the other studies and posing new questions, such as "What are the most important parenting skills/strategies?" In 2021 and 2022, I conducted a second round of interviews with twenty adolescents and some of their parents through posting a request on social media.

BEHAVIORAL STUDY OF EXECUTIVE FUNCTION AND DECISION-MAKING

Our team also designed a behavioral study that included an assessment of executive function and decision-making skills. It was conducted with 223 young people (sixth, ninth, and twelfth graders) in nine schools in six states (Kentucky, New Jersey, Arizona, Washington, Virginia, and Missouri) by the research firm ICF between November 21, 2019, and January 9, 2020.

APPENDIX 2: RESEARCHERS INTERVIEWED

Nicholas Allen, Ph.D., Ann Swindells Professor and director of the Center for Digital Mental Health, University of Oregon.

Roger E. Beaty, Ph.D., assistant professor of psychology and principal investigator at the Cognitive Neuroscience of Creativity Lab, Pennsylvania State University.

Elliot T. Berkman, Ph.D., associate dean of the natural sciences and professor of psychology, University of Oregon; co-director of the Center for Translational Neuroscience, University of Oregon.

Anthony Burrow, Ph.D., Ferris Family Associate Professor of life course studies, department of psychology, Cornell University; director of the Bronfenbrenner Center for Translational Research, Cornell University.

Jason Chein, Ph.D., professor of psychology and neuroscience, Temple University; director of Temple University Brain Research & Imaging Center.

Eveline Crone, Ph.D., professor of developmental neuroscience in society and director of SYNC lab (Society, Youth and Neuroscience Connected), Erasmus University, Rotterdam, the Netherlands.

Ronald E. Dahl, M.D., director of the Institute of Human Development, University of California, Berkeley; distinguished professor, School of Public Health, University of California, Berkeley; founding director, Center for the Developing Adolescent.

William Damon, Ph.D., director of the Stanford Center on Adolescence and professor of education at Stanford University; senior fellow, Hoover Institution.

Angela Duckworth, Ph.D., Rosa Lee and Egbert Chang Professor at the University of Pennsylvania; faculty co-director of the Penn-Wharton Behavior Change for Good Initiative; faculty co-director of Wharton People Analytics; co-founder, chief scientist, and board member of Character Lab.

Iroise Dumontheil, Ph.D., professor of cognitive neuroscience, department of psychological sciences, Birkbeck, University of London.

Philip A. Fisher, Ph.D., Excellence in Learning Professor, Graduate School of Education, Stanford University.

Jennifer Fredricks, Ph.D., professor of psychology, Union College.

Andrew J. Fuligni, Ph.D., professor, department of psychiatry and biobehavioral sciences, and professor, department of psychology, UCLA; senior scientist, Jane and Terry Semel Institute for Neuroscience and Human Behavior,

UCLA; director, Adolescent Development Lab, UCLA; co-executive director, UCLA Center for the Developing Adolescent.

Adam Galinsky, Ph.D., vice dean for diversity, equity, and inclusion and Paul Calello Professor of Leadership and Ethics, Columbia Business School.

Adriana Galván, Ph.D., dean, undergraduate education, and professor of psychology, UCLA; director of the Developmental Neuroscience Lab, UCLA; co-executive director, UCLA Center for the Developing Adolescent.

Adam Grant, Ph.D., organizational psychologist at the Wharton School; author of *Hidden Potential* and *Think Again*.

Wendy S. Grolnick, Ph.D., professor of psychology, Clark University.

Megan R. Gunnar, Ph.D., Regents Professor; Distinguished McKnight University Professor; member of the Academy of Distinguished Teachers, University of Minnesota.

Berna Güroğlu, Ph.D., professor, neuroscience of social relations, developmental and educational psychology unit, Institute of Psychology, Leiden University, the Netherlands.

Richard L. Huganir, Ph.D., Bloomberg Distinguished Professor of Neuroscience and Psychological and Brain Sciences; director, the Solomon H. Snyder Department of Neuroscience, Johns Hopkins University School of Medicine.

Mary Helen Immordino-Yang, Ed.D., Fahmy and Donna Attallah Chair in Humanistic Psychology; director, USC Center for Affective Neuroscience, Development, Learning and Education (CANDLE); professor of education, psychology, and neuroscience, Brain and Creativity Institute, Rossier School of Education, University of Southern California.

Ethan Kross, Ph.D., professor of psychology, University of Michigan; professor of management and organizations, Ross School of Business, University of Michigan; director of Emotion & Self-Control Lab.

Richard M. Lerner, Ph.D., professor, Elliot-Pearson Department of Child Study and Human Development; Bergstrom Chair in Applied Developmental Science; and director, Institute for Applied Research in Youth Development, Tufts University.

Rosa Li, Ph.D., teaching assistant professor, department of psychology and neuroscience, University of North Carolina, Chapel Hill.

Beatriz Luna, Ph.D., Distinguished Staunton Professor of Psychiatry and Pediatrics, professor of psychology, scientific director of the Magnetic Resonance Research Center; acting past president and founder of the Flux Society for Developmental Cognitive Neuroscience; editor in chief of the journal

Developmental Cognitive Neuroscience, Laboratory of Neurocognitive Development, Western Psychiatric Hospital, University of Pittsburgh Medical Center.

Allyson Mackey, Ph.D., associate professor, department of psychology, University of Pennsylvania; principal investigator, the Changing Brain Lab, University of Pennsylvania.

Dan P. McAdams, Ph.D., Henry Wade Rogers Professor of Psychology, professor of human development and social policy, Northwestern University.

Kate Mills, Ph.D., associate professor, department of psychology, University of Oregon.

Velma McBride Murry, Ph.D., Lois Audrey Betts Chair, associate provost, Office of Research & Innovation, University Distinguished Professor, departments of health policy and human and organizational development, Vanderbilt University.

Gabriele Oettingen, Ph.D., professor of psychology, New York University.

Jason Okonofua, Ph.D., assistant professor of psychology, University of California, Berkeley.

Jiska Peper, Ph.D., assistant professor in the development and educational psychology unit of the Institute of Psychology, Leiden University, the Netherlands; Science2share, Utrecht, the Netherlands.

Sabine Peters, Ph.D., scientific reseacher, Institute for Social Research, The Hague, Netherlands.

Jennifer Pfeifer, Ph.D., professor, department of psychology, University of Oregon; director, Developmental Social Neuroscience Lab, University of Oregon; co-director, Center for Translational Neuroscience, University of Oregon; associate dean for research and scholarship, College of Arts and Sciences, University of Oregon; co-director, National Scientific Council on Adolescence.

Megan Price, Ph.D., director, Center for Applied Insight Conflict Resolution.

Yang Qu, Ph.D., assistant professor, Human Development and Social Policy, Northwestern University; faculty associate, Institute for Policy Research, Northwestern University.

Barbara Schneider, Ph.D., John A. Hannah University Distinguished Professor in the College of Education and the department of sociology, Michigan State University.

Jennifer Silvers, Ph.D., associate professor, department of psychology; Bernice Wenzel and Wendell Jeffrey Term Endowed Chair in developmental neuroscience, UCLA.

Laurence Steinberg, Ph.D., Distinguished University Professor; the Laura H. Carnell Professor of Psychology; professor of psychology, Temple University.

Ahna Ballonoff Suleiman, Dr.PH., independent adolescent development and youth engagement consultant.

Eva H. Telzer, Ph.D., professor of psychology and neuroscience, University of North Carolina, Chapel Hill; co-director of the Winston National Center on Technology Use, Brain and Psychological Development; director, Developmental Social Neuroscience Lab at University of North Carolina, Chapel Hill.

Melina Uncapher, Ph.D., chief of research and development, AERDF (Advanced Education Research and Development Fund); founder and scientific director of EF+M (an AERDF program).

Gregory M. Walton, Ph.D., professor, department of psychology, Stanford University; Michael Forman University Fellow in Undergraduate Education, Stanford University.

David Yeager, Ph.D., Raymond Dickson Centennial Professor of Psychology, University of Texas, Austin.

Philip David Zelazo, Ph.D., Nancy M. and John E. Lindahl Professor, Institute of Child Development, University of Minnesota.

Of these interviews, thirty-four were conducted as virtual field trips to the labs of the researchers, with their experiments filmed by Lisa Rinehart and Jennifer Hamblett of Mighty Egg Productions. In addition, other interviews were conducted with thought leaders in this and other related fields, and I draw on other interviews I have conducted over the years for *Mind in the Making* and *Ask the Children*.

NOTES

Introduction

1. Richard M. Lerner and Laurence Steinberg, "The Scientific Study of Adolescent Development: Historical and Contemporary Perspectives," in *Handbook of Adolescent Psychology: Individual Bases of Adolescent Development*, ed. Richard M. Lerner and Laurence Steinberg (New York: John Wiley, 2009), 3–14, https://doi.org/10.1002/9780470479193.adlpsy001002.

2. Granville S. Hall, *Adolescence: Its Psychology and Its Relations to Physiology, Anthropology, Sociology, Sex, Crime, Religion, and Education*, 2 vols. (New York: Appleton, 1904).

3. National Academies of Sciences, Engineering, and Medicine, *The Promise of Adolescence: Realizing Opportunity for All Youth* (Washington, DC: National Academies Press, 2019), https://doi.org/10.17226/25388.

4. Lerner and Steinberg, "The Scientific Study of Adolescent Development."

5. National Academies of Sciences, Engineering, and Medicine, *The Promise of Adolescence*, 1.

6. Ibid., 59, 11, 35.

7. Adele Diamond and Daphne S. Ling, "Conclusions About Interventions, Programs, and Approaches for Improving Executive Functions That Appear Justified and Those That, Despite Much Hype, Do Not," *Developmental Cognitive Neuroscience* 18 (April 2016): 34–48, https://doi.org/10.1016/j.dcn.2015.11.005.

8. Jennifer Silvers, interview by Ellen Galinsky, May 5, 2017.

9. National Academies of Sciences, Engineering, and Medicine, *The Promise of Adolescence*.

10. Laurence Steinberg, *Age of Opportunity: Lessons from the New Science of Adolescence* (Boston: Houghton Mifflin Harcourt, 2014).

11. "Youth Risk Behavior Survey: Data Summary and Trends Report, 2011–2021," Centers for Disease Control and Prevention, 2023, https://www.cdc.gov/healthyyouth/data/yrbs/pdf/YRBS_Data-Summary-Trends_Report2023_508.pdf.

12. National Academies of Sciences, Engineering, and Medicine, *The Promise of Adolescence*, 44.

13. National Assessment of Educational Progress, "NAEP Long-Term Trend Assessment Results: Reading and Mathematics Scores Decline During COVID-19 Pandemic," The Nation's Report Card, accessed August 31, 2023, https://www.nationsreportcard.gov/highlights/ltt/2022/.

14. Annie Bernier, Stephanie M. Carlson, and Natasha Whipple, "From External Regulation to Self-Regulation: Early Parenting Precursors of Young Children's Executive Functioning," *Child Development* 81 (February 2010): 326–339, https://doi.org/10.1111/j.1467-8624.2009.01397.x; Rebecca Distefano et al., "Autonomy-Supportive Parenting and Associations with Child and Parent Executive Function," *Journal of Applied Developmental Psychology* 58 (July–September 2018): 77–85, https://doi.org/10.1016/j.appdev.2018.04.007; Alyssa S. Meuwissen and Stephanie M. Carlson, "An Experimental Study of the Effects of Autonomy Support on Preschoolers' Self-Regulation," *Journal of Applied Developmental Psychology* 60 (January 2019): 11–23, https://doi.org/10.1016/j.appdev.2018.10.001.

15. Wendy S. Grolnick et al., "Parental Provision of Academic Structure and the Transition to Middle School," *Journal of Research on Adolescence* 25, no. 4 (2015): 668–684, https://doi.org/10.1111/jora.12161.

16. Carol S. Dweck and David S. Yeager, "Mindsets: A View from Two Eras," *Perspectives on Psychological Science* 14, no. 3 (February 2019): 481–496, https://doi.org/10.1177/1745691618804166; Albert Bandura, "Self-Efficacy: Toward a Unifying

Theory of Behavioral Change," *Psychological Review* 84, no. 2 (1977): 191–215, https://doi.org/10.1037/0033-295X.84.2.191.

17. David R. Williams et al., "Perceived Discrimination, Race and Health in South Africa," *Social Science and Medicine* 67, no. 3 (2008): 441–452, https://doi.org/10.1016/j.socscimed.2008.03.021.

18. Andrew Fuligni, interview by Ellen Galinsky, May 4, 2017; Angelina Majeno et al., "Discrimination and Sleep Difficulties During Adolescence: The Mediating Roles of Loneliness and Perceived Stress," *Journal of Youth and Adolescence* 47 (2018): 135–147, https://doi.org/10.1007/s10964-017-0755-8; Virginia W. Huynh et al., "Everyday Discrimination and Diurnal Cortisol During Adolescence," *Hormones and Behavior* 80 (April 2016): 76–81, https://doi.org/10.1016/j.yhbeh.2016.01.009.

19. Richard M. Ryan and Edward L. Deci, "Self-Determination Theory and the Facilitation of Intrinsic Motivation, Social Development, and Well-Being," *American Psychologist* 55, no. 1 (2000): 68–78, https://doi.org/10.1037/0003-066X.55.1.68; B. Bradford Brown of the University of Wisconsin as cited in Institute of Medicine and National Research Council Committee on the Science of Adolescence, *The Science of Adolescent Risk-Taking: Workshop Report* (Washington, DC: National Academies Press, 2011).

20. Richard M. Ryan and Edward L. Deci, "Brick by Brick: The Origins, Development, and Future of Self-Determination Theory," in *Advances in Motivation Science*, ed. A. J. Elliot (Cambridge, MA: Elsevier Academic Press, 2019), 111–156, https://psycnet.apa.org/doi/10.1016/bs.adms.2019.01.001.

21. Emily C. Hanno et al., "Developmental Trajectories of Children's Behavioral Health and Family Well-Being Prior to and Through the COVID-19 Pandemic," paper presented at the 2023 Society for Research in Child Development (SRCD) Biennial Meeting, Salt Lake City, Utah, March 23–25, 2023; Emily C. Hanno et al., "Changes in Children's Behavioral Health and Family Well-Being During the COVID-19 Pandemic," *Journal of Developmental and Behavioral Pediatrics* 43, no. 3 (April 2022): 168–175, https://doi.org/10.1097/DBP.0000000000001010.

1. Message 1: Understand Our Development

1. Patrick Healy and Lulu Garcia-Navarro, "12 Teenagers on What Adults Don't Get About Their Lives," *New York Times*, March 24, 2022, https://www.nytimes.com/2022/03/24/opinion/teenagers-america.html.

2. Lawrence J. Stone and Joseph Church, *Childhood and Adolescence: A Psychology of the Growing Person* (New York: Random House, 1973), 425.

3. Granville S. Hall, *Adolescence: Its Psychology and Its Relations to Physiology, Anthropology, Sociology, Sex, Crime, Religion, and Education*, 2 vols. (New York: Appleton, 1904).

4. Laurence Steinberg, "A Social Neuroscience Perspective on Adolescent Risk-Taking," *Developmental Review* 28, no. 1 (March 2008): 78–106, https://www.doi.org/10.1016/j.dr.2007.08.002; Laurence Steinberg, "A Dual Systems Model of Adolescent Risk-Taking," *Developmental Psychobiology* 52, no. 3 (March 2010): 216–224, https://www.doi.org/10.1002/dev.20445.

5. Elizabeth P. Shulman et al., "The Dual Systems Model: Review, Reappraisal, and Reaffirmation," *Developmental Cognitive Neuroscience* 17 (February 2016): 103–117, https://www.doi.org/10.1016/j.dcn.2015.12.010.

6. B. J. Casey, Rebecca M. Jones, and Leah Somerville, "Braking and Accelerating of the Adolescent Brain," *Journal of Research on Adolescence* 21, no. 1 (February 2011): 21–33, https://doi.org/10.1111/j.1532-7795.2010.00712.x.

7. Laurence Steinberg et al., "Around the World, Adolescence Is a Time of Heightened Sensation Seeking and Immature Self-Regulation," *Developmental Science* 21, no. 2 (March 2018): e12532, https://www.doi.org/10.1111/desc.12532.

8. Daniel Busso et al., "One Half of the Story: Media Framing of Adolescent Development," Research Report, FrameWorks Institute, December 2018, 8, https://www.frameworksinstitute.org/publication/one-half-of-the-story/.

9. Ibid., 16.

10. Ibid., 14.
11. Jennifer Silvers, interview by Ellen Galinsky, May 5, 2017.
12. Kevin N. Ochsner and James J. Gross, "The Cognitive Control of Emotion," *Trends in Cognitive Sciences* 9, no. 5 (May 2005): 242–249, https://doi.org/10.1016/j.tics .2005.03.010; Walter Mischel, *The Marshmallow Test: Why Self-Control Is the Engine of Success* (New York: Little, Brown, 2014).
13. Jennifer Silvers, interview by Ellen Galinsky, May 5, 2017.
14. Ibid.
15. Jason T. Buhle et al., "Cognitive Reappraisal of Emotion: A Meta-Analysis of Human Neuroimaging Studies," *Cerebral Cortex* 24, no. 11 (June 2013): 2981–2990, https:// doi.org/10.1093/cercor/bht154.
16. Jennifer Silvers, interview by Ellen Galinsky, May 5, 2017.
17. Jennifer Silvers et al., "Concurrent and Lasting Effects of Emotion Regulation on Amygdala Response in Adolescence and Young Adulthood," *Developmental Science* 18, no. 5 (September 2015): 771–784, https://doi.org/10.1111/desc.12260.
18. Jennifer Silvers, interview by Ellen Galinsky, May 5, 2017.
19. Silvers et al., "Concurrent and Lasting Effects of Emotion Regulation."
20. Peter J. Lang, Margaret M. Bradley, and Bruce M. Cuthbert, *International Affective Picture System (IAPS): Instruction Manual and Affective Ratings, Technical Report* (Gainesville: University of Florida, 2001).
21. Jennifer Silvers, interview by Ellen Galinsky, May 5, 2017.
22. Jennifer Silvers et al., "Age-Related Differences in Emotional Reactivity, Regulation, and Rejection Sensitivity in Adolescence," *Emotion* 12, no. 6 (December 2012): 1235–1247, https://doi.org/10.1037/a0028297.
23. Ronald E. Dahl, interview by Ellen Galinsky, October 11, 2016.
24. National Academies of Sciences, Engineering, and Medicine, *The Promise of Adolescence: Realizing Opportunity for All Youth* (Washington, DC: National Academies Press, 2019), 43, https://doi.org/10.17226/25388.
25. Ibid., 59.
26. Richard Huganir, interview by Ellen Galinsky, September 8, 2017.
27. Beatriz Luna, interview by Ellen Galinsky, August 30, 2019.
28. Jennifer Silvers, interview by Ellen Galinsky, May 5, 2017.
29. "National Parent Survey Report," Zero to Three, June 6, 2016, https://www .zerotothree.org/resources/1425-national-parent-survey-report.
30. Adriana Galván, interview by Ellen Galinsky, May 3, 2017.
31. Adriana Galván, "Insight into the Teenage Brain," TEDxYouth, California Institute of Technology, Pasadena, February 12, 2013, https://www.youtube.com/watch?v =LWUkW4s3XxY.
32. Ibid.
33. Adriana Galván and Kristine M. McGlennen, "Enhanced Striatal Sensitivity to Aversive Reinforcement in Adolescents Versus Adults," *Journal of Cognitive Neuroscience* 25, no. 2 (2013): 284–296, https://doi.org/10.1162/jocn_a_00326.
34. Adriana Galván et al., "Earlier Development of the Accumbens Relative to Orbitofrontal Cortex Might Underlie Risk-Taking Behavior in Adolescents," *Journal of Neuroscience* 26, no. 25 (June 21, 2006): 6885–6892, https://doi.org/10.1523 /JNEUROSCI.106206.2006.
35. Adriana Galván, interview by Ellen Galinsky, May 3, 2017.
36. Ronald E. Dahl, interview by Ellen Galinsky, October 11, 2016; Ronald E. Dahl, email message to Ellen Galinsky, August 31, 2022.
37. Wendy S. Grolnick, email message to Ellen Galinsky, September 2, 2022.
38. John A. Bargh, Peter M. Gollwitzer, and Gabriele Oettingen, "Motivation," in *Handbook of Social Psychology*, 5th ed., ed. Susan T. Fiske, Daniel T. Gilbert, and Gardner Lindzey (New York: John Wiley and Sons, 2018), 268.
39. National Scientific Council on the Developing Child, "Understanding Motivation: Building the Brain Architecture That Supports Learning, Health, and Community Participation," Working Paper 14, Center on the Developing Child at Harvard University, December 2018, 1, https://developingchild.harvard.edu/resources

/understanding-motivation-building-the-brain-architecture-that-supports-learning
-health-and-community-participation/.

40. Adriana Galván, interview by Ellen Galinsky, May 3, 2017.
41. Daniel Romer, Valerie F. Reyna, and Theodore D. Satterthwaite, "Beyond Stereotypes of Adolescent Risk Taking: Placing the Adolescent Brain in Developmental Context," *Developmental Cognitive Neuroscience* 27 (October 2017): 21, https://doi.org/10 .1016/j.dcn.2017.07.007.
42. Juliet Y. Davidow et al., "An Upside to Reward Sensitivity: The Hippocampus Supports Enhanced Reinforcement Learning in Adolescence," *Neuron* 92, no. 1 (2016): 93–99, https://doi.org/10.1016/j.neuron.2016.08.031.
43. Adriana Galván, interview by Ellen Galinsky, May 3, 2017.
44. Wendy S. Grolnick, interview by Ellen Galinsky, October 27, 2017; Wendy S. Grolnick, email message to Ellen Galinsky, September 5, 2022.
45. Gabriele Oettingen, interview by Ellen Galinsky, October 23, 2015; Gabriele Oettingen, email message to Ellen Galinsky, September 4, 2022.
46. National Scientific Council on the Developing Child, "Understanding Motivation," 3.
47. Stacey D. Espinet, Jacob E. Anderson, and Philip D. Zelazo, "Reflection Training Improves Executive Function in Preschool-Age Children: Behavioral and Neural Effects," *Developmental Cognitive Neuroscience* 4 (April 2013): 3–15, https://doi.org /10.1016/j.dcn.2012.11.009.
48. Philip David Zelazo, interview by Ellen Galinsky, June 11, 2014.
49. Linda Wilbrecht, "Your Twelve-Year-Old Isn't Just Sprouting New Hair but Is Also Forming (and Being Formed by) New Neural Connections," in *Think Tank: Forty Neuroscientists Explore the Biological Roots of Human Experience*, ed. David J. Linden (New Haven, CT: Yale University Press, 2018), 46.
50. Adriana Galván, interview by Ellen Galinsky, May 3, 2017.
51. Laurence Steinberg, interview by Ellen Galinsky, October 3, 2017.
52. Laurence Steinberg, *Age of Opportunity: Lessons from the New Science of Adolescence* (Boston: Houghton Mifflin Harcourt, 2014).
53. Laurence Steinberg, interview by Ellen Galinsky, October 3, 2017.
54. Ibid.
55. Margo Gardner and Laurence Steinberg, "Peer Influence on Risk Taking, Risk Preference, and Risky Decision Making in Adolescence and Adulthood: An Experimental Study," *Developmental Psychology* 41, no. 4 (July 2005): 625–635, https://doi.org/10 .1037/0012-1649.41.4.625.
56. Laurence Steinberg, interview by Ellen Galinsky, October 3, 2017.
57. Jason M. Chein et al., "Peers Increase Adolescent Risk Taking by Enhancing Activity in the Brain's Reward Circuitry," *Developmental Science* 14, no. 2 (December 2010): F1–F10, https://doi.org/10.1111/j.1467-7687.2010.01035.x.
58. Laurence Steinberg, "A Dual Systems Model of Adolescent Risk-Taking," *Developmental Psychology* 52, no. 3 (April 2010): 216–224, https://doi.org/10.1002/dev.20445; Leah H. Somerville, Rebecca M. Jones, and B. J. Casey, "A Time of Change: Behavioral and Neural Correlates of Adolescent Sensitivity to Appetitive and Aversive Environmental Cues," *Brain and Cognition* 72, no. 1 (February 2010): 124–133, https://doi.org /10.1016/j.bandc.2009.07.003; Elizabeth P. Shulman et al., "The Dual Systems Model: Review, Reappraisal, and Reaffirmation," *Developmental Cognitive Neuroscience* 17 (February 2016): 103–117, https://doi.org/10.1016/j.dcn.2015.12.010.
59. Laurence Steinberg, interview by Ellen Galinsky, October 3, 2017.
60. Steinberg et al., "Around the World, Adolescence Is a Time of Heightened Sensation Seeking and Immature Self-Regulation."
61. Eveline A. Crone and Ronald E. Dahl, "Understanding Adolescence as a Period of Social-Affective Engagement and Goal Flexibility," *Nature Reviews Neuroscience* 13, no. 9 (September 2012): 636–650, https://doi.org/10.1038/nrn3313; Jennifer H. Pfeifer and Nicholas B. Allen, "Arrested Development? Reconsidering Dual-Systems Models of Brain Function in Adolescence and Disorders," *Trends in Cognitive Sciences* 16, no. 6 (May 2012): 322–329, https://doi.org/10.1016/j.tics.2012.04.011; Romer, Reyna, and Satterthwaite, "Beyond Stereotypes of Adolescent Risk Taking."

62. Jennifer H. Pfeifer and Nicholas B. Allen, "The Audacity of Specificity: Moving Adolescent Developmental Neuroscience Towards More Powerful Scientific Paradigms and Translatable Models," *Developmental Cognitive Neuroscience* 17 (February 2016): 131–137, https://doi.org/10.1016/j.dcn.2015.12.012; Romer et al., "Beyond Stereotypes of Adolescent Risk Taking."

63. Steinberg, *Age of Opportunity: Lessons from the New Science of Adolescence.*

64. B. J. Casey and Kristina Caudle, "The Teenage Brain: Self Control," *Current Directions in Psychological Science* 22 (April 2013): 82, https://doi.org/10.1177 /0963721413480170; Carl C. Bell and Dominica F. McBride, "Affect Regulation and Prevention of Risky Behaviors," *Journal of the American Medical Association* 304, no. 5 (2010): 565, https://doi.org/10.1001/jama.2010.1058.

65. Wilbrecht, "Your Twelve-Year-Old Isn't Just Sprouting New Hair but Is Also Forming (and Being Formed by) New Neural Connections," 45.

66. Philip David Zelazo, interview by Ellen Galinsky, June 26, 2017.

67. Philip David Zelazo and Stephanie M. Carlson, "Hot and Cool Executive Function in Childhood and Adolescence: Development and Plasticity," *Child Development Perspectives* 6, no. 4 (December 2012): 354–360, https://doi.org/10.1111/j.1750-8606 .2012.00246.x.

68. Angela Prencipe et al., "Development of Hot and Cool Executive Function During the Transition to Adolescence," *Journal of Experimental Child Psychology* 108, no. 3 (March 2011): 621–637, https://doi.org/10.1016/j.jecp.2010.09.008.

69. Philip David Zelazo, interview by Ellen Galinsky, June 26, 2017.

70. Sarah-Jayne Blakemore, *Inventing Ourselves: The Secret Life of the Teenage Brain* (New York: PublicAffairs, 2018).

71. Ibid., 134.

72. Kathryn L. Mills et al., "The Developmental Mismatch in Structural Brain Maturation During Adolescence," *Developmental Neuroscience* 36, nos. 3–4 (2014): 147–160, https://doi.org/10.1159/000362328.

73. Kathryn L. Mills, interview by Ellen Galinsky, July 8, 2019.

74. Ibid.

75. Blakemore, *Inventing Ourselves*, 139.

76. Wim Meeus et al., "On Imbalance of Impulse Control and Sensation Seeking and Adolescent Risk: An Intra-Individual Developmental Test of the Dual Systems and Maturational Imbalance Models," *Journal of Youth and Adolescence* 50 (2021): 827–840, https://doi.org/10.1007/s10964-021-01419-x.

77. David. S. Yeager et al., "Declines in Efficacy of Anti-Bullying Programs Among Older Adolescents: Theory and a Three-Level Meta-Analysis," *Journal of Applied Developmental Psychology* 37 (March–April 2015): 37, https://doi.org/10.1016/j.appdev .2014.11.005; Matthew C. Farrelly et al., "Sustaining 'Truth': Changes in Youth Tobacco Attitudes and Smoking Intentions After 3 Years of a National Antismoking Campaign," *Health Education Research* 24, no. 1 (February 2009): 42–48, https://doi .org/10.1093/her/cym087; Matthew C. Farrelly et al., "The Influence of the National Truth Campaign on Smoking Initiation," *American Journal of Preventive Medicine* 36, no. 5 (May 2009): 379–384, https://doi.org/10.1016/j.amepre.2009.01.019.

78. Sibel Altikulaç et al., "The Teenage Brain: Public Perceptions of Neurocognitive Development During Adolescence," *Journal of Cognitive Neuroscience* 31, no. 3 (March 2019): 339–359, https://doi.org/10.1162/jocn_a_01332.

79. Steve Farkas et al., *Kids These Days: What Americans Really Think About the Next Generation* (New York: Public Agenda, 1997), https://www.ojp.gov/ncjrs /virtual-library/abstracts/kids-these-days-what-americans-really-think-about-next -generation.

80. Adolescents were asked how often they had experienced the following feelings in the past month: good, bad, happy, sad, afraid, brave, angry, calm, worried, joyful, and lonely. Adapted from Ed Diener, Derrick Wirtz, and William Tov, "New Measures of Well-Being: Flourishing and Positive and Negative Feelings," *Social Indicators Research* 39 (January 2010): 247–266.

81. Adolescents were asked how often they had felt the following way in the last month:

(1) You were unable to control the important things in your life. (2) You were confident about your ability to handle your personal problems. (3) Things were going your way. (4) Difficulties were piling up so high that you could not overcome them. (5) You felt nervous and stressed. Adapted from Sheldon Cohen, Tom Kamarck, and Robin Mermelstein, "A Global Measure of Perceived Stress," *Journal of Health and Social Behavior* 24 (December 1983): 386–396, https://doi.org/10.2307/2136404.

82. Adolescents were asked if the following statements applied to them (yes/no): (1) I keep trying as many different possibilities as are necessary to succeed at my goal. (2) I think about exactly how I can best accomplish what I want to. (3) For important things, I pay attention to whether I need to devote more time or effort. (4) When something doesn't work as well as usual, I look at how others do it. (5) I consider exactly what is important to me in setting goals for myself. Adapted from Steinunn Gestsdóttir and Richard M. Lerner, "Intentional Self-Regulation and Positive Youth Development in Early Adolescence: Findings from the 4-H Study of Positive Youth Development," *Developmental Psychology* 43, no. 2 (2007): 508–521, https://doi.org/10.1037/0012-1649.43.2.508.

83. Adolescents were asked how often they have experienced the following in the last month: (1) At school, I feel like I have a lot of energy. (2) I can continue studying for long periods of time. (3) I feel like going to school when I get up in the morning. (4) I am enthusiastic about my studies. (5) The work I do for school inspires me. (6) I find my schoolwork full of meaning and purpose. (7) I feel happy when I am working intensively at schoolwork. (8) When I am studying at school, I forget everything else around me. (9) Time flies when I am studying. Adapted from Katariina Salmela-Aro and Katja Upadaya, "The Schoolwork Engagement Inventory: Energy, Dedication and Absorption (EDA)," *European Journal of Psychological Assessment* 28, no. 1 (2012): 60–67, https://doi.org/10.1027/1015-5759/a000091.

84. Adolescents were asked how often they did the following during school hours: (1) I came to class prepared. (2) I followed directions. (3) I got to work right away instead of waiting around until the last minute. (4) I paid attention, even when there were distractions. (5) I stayed focused when doing independent work. Daeun Park et al., "A Tripartite Taxonomy of Character: Evidence for Intrapersonal, Interpersonal, and Intellectual Competencies in Children," *Contemporary Educational Psychology* 48 (October 2017): 16–27, https://doi.org/10.1016/j.cedpsych.2016.08.001.

85. Richard M. Lerner, interview by Ellen Galinsky, October 26, 2017.

86. Karen Pittman, interview by Ellen Galinsky, June 30, 2006.

87. Karen Pittman, email to Ellen Galinsky, February 2, 2023.

88. Richard M. Lerner, interview by Ellen Galinsky, October 26, 2017; Richard M. Lerner et al., "Positive Youth Development, Participation in Community Youth Development Programs, and Community Contributions of Fifth-Grade Adolescents: Findings from the First Wave of the 4-H Study of Positive Youth Development," *Journal of Early Adolescence* 25, no. 1 (2005): 17–71, https://doi.org/10.1177/0272431604272461; Edmond P. Bowers et al., "The Five Cs Model of Positive Youth Development: A Longitudinal Analysis of Confirmatory Factor Structure and Measurement Invariance," *Journal of Youth and Adolescence* 39, no. 7 (2010): 720–735, https://doi.org/10.1007/s10964-010-9530-9; Richard M. Lerner with Roberta Israeloff, *The Good Teen: Rescuing Adolescence from the Myths of the Storm and Stress Years* (New York: Three Rivers Press, 2007).

89. Richard M. Lerner, interview by Ellen Galinsky, October 26, 2017; Richard M. Lerner, email to Ellen Galinsky, February 4, 2023.

90. Lerner and Israeloff, *The Good Teen*, 35.

91. Richard M. Lerner et al., "Promoting Positive Youth Development in the Face of Contextual Change and Challenges: The Roles of Individual Strengths and Ecological Assets," *New Directions for Youth Development* 135 (Fall 2012): 119–128, https://doi.org/10.1002/yd.20034.

92. Richard M. Lerner, interview by Ellen Galinsky, October 26, 2017.

93. Lerner et al., "Promoting Positive Youth Development in the Face of Contextual Change and Challenges."

94. Richard M. Lerner et al., "The Positive Development of Youth: Comprehensive Findings from the 4-H Study of Positive Youth Development," December 2013, https://dunn .extension.wisc.edu/files/2018/04/4-H-Study-of-Positive-Youth-Development-Full -Report.pdf; Richard M. Lerner et al., "Individual and Contextual Bases of Thriving in Adolescence: Findings from the 4-H Study of Positive Youth Development," *Journal of Adolescence* 34, no. 6 (December 2011): 1107–1114, https://doi.org/10.1016/j .adolescence.2011.08.001; Edmond P. Bowers et al., "Special Issue Introduction: Thriving Across the Adolescent Years: A View of the Issue," *Journal of Youth and Adolescence* 43, no. 6 (June 2014): 859–868, https://doi.org/10.1007/s10964-014-0117-8.

95. Richard M. Lerner, interview by Ellen Galinsky, October 26, 2017; Richard M., Lerner, email to Ellen Galinsky, February 4, 2023.

96. Richard M. Lerner, "Taking the Boy Out of Brooklyn: Time, Place, and People in the Development of a Developmental Scientist," in *The Developmental Science of Adolescence: History Through Autobiography*, ed. Richard M. Lerner et al. (New York: Psychology Press, 2014), 277–308.

97. Andrew J. Fuligni, interview by Ellen Galinsky, May 4, 2017; Andrew J. Fuligni, email message to Ellen Galinsky, September 7, 2022.

98. Jennifer Silvers, interview by Ellen Galinsky, May 5, 2017.

99. Gabriele Oettingen, interview by Ellen Galinsky, October 17, 2016; Gabriele Oettingen, email message to Ellen Galinsky, September 4, 2022; Gabriele Oettingen, *Rethinking Positive Thinking: Inside the New Science of Motivation* (New York: Penguin Random House, 2014); "How Can I Practice WOOP?," WOOP My Life, accessed May 2022, https://woopmylife.org/en/practice.

2. Message 2: Listen and Talk *with* Us, Not *at* Us

1. Jennifer H. Pfeifer, interview by Ellen Galinsky, September 7, 2016.

2. Annie Murphy Paul, *The Extended Mind: The Power of Thinking Outside the Brain* (Boston: Houghton Mifflin Harcourt, 2021), 9.

3. Ibid., 17.

4. Daniel Stern, interview by Ellen Galinsky, October 12, 2001.

5. Ahna Suleiman and Ronald E. Dahl, "Parent-Child Relationships in the Puberty Years: Insights from Developmental Neuroscience," *Family Relations* 68, no. 3 (July 2019): 279, https://doi.org/10.1111/fare.12360.

6. Ibid., 281.

7. Eva H. Telzer, interview by Ellen Galinsky, July 17, 2017.

8. Ibid.

9. Eva H. Telzer, Nicholas T. Ichien, and Yang Qu, "Mothers Know Best: Redirecting Adolescent Reward Sensitivity Toward Safe Behavior During Risk Taking," *Social Cognitive and Affective Neuroscience* 10, no. 10 (October 2015): 1383–1391, https:// doi.org/10.1093/scan/nsv026.

10. Eva H. Telzer, interview by Ellen Galinsky, July 19, 2017.

11. Ibid.

12. Telzer et al., "Mothers Know Best," 1389.

13. João F. Guassi Moreira and Eva H. Telzer, "Mother Still Knows Best: Maternal Influence Uniquely Modulates Adolescent Reward Sensitivity During Risk Taking," *Developmental Science* 21, no. 1 (January 2018): e12484, https://doi.org/10.1111 /desc.12484.

14. Yang Qu et al., "Buffering Effect of Positive Parent-Child Relationships on Adolescent Risk Taking: A Longitudinal Neuroimaging Investigation," *Developmental Cognitive Neuroscience* 15 (October 2015): 26–34, https://doi.org/10.1016/j.dcn .2015.08.005.

15. Eva H. Telzer, interview by Ellen Galinsky, July 19, 2017.

16. Will M. Aklin et al., "Evaluation of Behavioral Measures of Risk Taking Propensity with Inner City Adolescents," *Behaviour Research and Therapy* 43, no. 2 (February 2005): 215–228, https://doi.org/10.1016/j.brat.2003.12.007; Carl W. Lejuez et al.,

"Evaluation of the Balloon Analogue Risk Task (BART) as a Predictor of Adolescent Real-World Risk-Taking Behaviours," *Journal of Adolescence* 26, no. 4 (August 2003): 475–479, https://doi.org/10.1016/S0140-1971(03)00036-8.

17. Qu et al., "Buffering Effect of Positive Parent-Child Relationships."

18. Eva H. Telzer, interview by Ellen Galinsky, July 19, 2017.

19. Ethan M. McCormick, Yang Qu, and Eva H. Telzer, "Adolescent Neurodevelopment of Cognitive Control and Risk-Taking in Negative Family Contexts," *Neuro-Image* 124, part A (October 2015): 989–996, https://doi.org/10.1016/j.neuroimage.2015.09.063.

20. Judith Warner, *And Then They Stopped Talking to Me: Making Sense of Middle School* (New York: Crown, 2020), 10.

21. Ibid., xi.

22. Judith Warner, interview by Ellen Galinsky, May 15, 2020.

23. Nicholas B. Allen, interview by Ellen Galinsky, September 7, 2016.

24. Orli S. Schwartz et al., "Parental Behaviors During Family Interactions Predict Changes in Depression and Anxiety Symptoms During Adolescence," *Journal of Abnormal Child Psychology* 40, no. 1 (January 2012): 59–71, https://doi.org/10.1007/s10802-011-9542-2; Sarah Whittle et al., "Positive Parenting Predicts the Development of Adolescent Brain Structure: A Longitudinal Study," *Developmental Cognitive Neuroscience* 8 (April 2014): 7–17, https://doi.org/10.1016/j.dcn.2013.10.006.

25. Nicholas B. Allen, interview by Ellen Galinsky, September 7, 2016.

26. Sarah Whittle et al., "Role of Positive Parenting in the Association Between Neighborhood Social Disadvantage and Brain Development Across Adolescence," *JAMA Psychiatry* 74, no. 8 (2017): 824–832, https://doi.org/10.1001/jamapsychiatry.2017.1558.

27. Nicholas B. Allen, interview by Ellen Galinsky, September 7, 2016.

28. Jessica Lahey, *The Gift of Failure: How the Best Parents Learn to Let Go So Their Children Can Succeed* (New York: Harper, 2016).

29. Jessica Lahey, interview by Ellen Galinsky, June 6, 2020.

30. Ellen Galinsky, *The Six Stages of Parenthood* (Cambridge, MA: Da Capo Press, 1987).

31. Velma McBride Murry, interview by Ellen Galinsky, June 12, 2020.

32. Thomas G. Gordon, *Parent Effectiveness Training* (New York: Harmony Books, 2019).

33. Kenneth R. Ginsburg, interview by Ellen Galinsky, August 17, 2021; Kenneth R. Ginsburg, email message to Ellen Galinsky, February 4, 2023.

34. Kenneth R. Ginsburg, *Congrats—You're Having a Teen! Strengthen Your Family and Raise a Good Person* (Itasca, IL: American Academy of Pediatrics, 2022), 179.

35. Kenneth R. Ginsburg, interview by Ellen Galinsky, August 17, 2021; Kenneth R. Ginsburg, email message to Ellen Galinsky, February 4, 2023.

36. National Academies of Sciences, Engineering, and Medicine, *The Promise of Adolescence: Realizing Opportunity for All Youth* (Washington, DC: National Academies Press, 2019), 11, https://doi.org/10.17226/25388; Gene H. Brody et al., "Protective Prevention Effects on the Association of Poverty with Brain Development," *JAMA Pediatrics* 171, no. 1 (January 2017): 46–52, https://doi.org/10.1001/jamapediatrics.2016.2988.

37. National Academies of Sciences, Engineering, and Medicine, *The Promise of Adolescence*, 70.

38. Megan R. Gunnar, interview by Ellen Galinsky, September 26, 2001.

39. Megan R. Gunnar, interview by Ellen Galinsky, July 27, 2017.

40. Megan R. Gunnar et al., "Neonatal Stress Reactivity: Predictions to Later Emotional Temperament," *Child Development* 66, no. 1 (1995): 1–13; Mary C. Larson et al., "Dampening of the Cortisol Response to Handling at 3 Months in Human Infants and Its Relation to Sleep, Circadian Cortisol Activity, and Behavioral Distress," *Developmental Psychobiology* 33, no. 4 (1998): 327–337; Erikson Institute, *Early Development and the Brain: Teaching Resources for Educators*, ed. Linda Gilkerson and Rebecca Klein (Washington, DC: Zero to Three Press, 2008).

41. Megan R. Gunnar, email message to Ellen Galinsky, February 14, 2023.

42. Megan R. Gunnar, interview by Ellen Galinsky, July 27, 2017.

43. Nicole B. Perry et al., "Associations Between Stress Reactivity and Behavior Problems for Previously Institutionalized Youth Across Puberty," *Development and Psychopathology* 32, no. 5 (December 2020): 1854, https://doi.org/10.1017/S0954579420001297.

44. Megan R. Gunnar, email message to Ellen Galinsky, May 10, 2019.

45. Esther Landhuis, "Puberty Can Repair the Brain's Stress Responses After Hardship Early in Life: Adolescence Could Be a Time to Reset the System That Helps People Cope with Stress," *Science News*, August 28, 2020, https://www.sciencenews.org/article/puberty-teens-brain-stress-responses-early-trauma.

46. Megan R. Gunnar, email message to Ellen Galinsky, May 10, 2019.

47. Nicole B. Perry et al., "Cortisol Reactivity and Socially Anxious Behavior in Previously Institutionalized Youth," *Research on Child and Adolescent Psychopathology* 50, no. 3 (March 2022): 375–385, https://doi.org/10.1007/s10802-021-00862-5.

48. Carrie E. DePasquale et al., "Cortisol and Parenting Predict Pathways to Disinhibited Social Engagement and Social Functioning in Previously Institutionalized Children," *Journal of Abnormal Child Psychology* 48 (March 2020): 797–808, https://doi.org/10.1007/s10802-020-00633-8.

49. Kalsea J. Koss, Jamie M. Lawler, and Megan R. Gunnar, "Early Adversity and Children's Regulatory Deficits: Does Postadoption Parenting Facilitate Recovery in Postinstitutionalized Children?," *Development and Psychopathology* 32, no. 3 (August 2020): 879–896, https://doi.org/10.1017/S0954579419001226.

50. Perry et al., "Cortisol Reactivity and Socially Anxious Behavior in Previously Institutionalized Youth."

51. Ibid.

52. Ibid.

53. Koss, Lawler, and Gunnar, "Early Adversity and Children's Regulatory Deficits."

54. Megan R. Gunnar, email message to Ellen Galinsky, May 10, 2019.

55. Megan R. Gunnar et al., "Pubertal Stress Recalibration Reverses the Effects of Early Life Stress in Postinstitutionalized Children," *Proceedings of the National Academy of Sciences* 116, no. 48 (November 2019): 23985, https://doi.org/10.1073/pnas.1909699116; Andrew P. Allen et al., "The Trier Social Stress Test: Principles and Practice," *Neurobiology of Stress* 6 (2016): 113–126, https://doi.org/10.1016/j.ynstr.2016.11.001.

56. Megan R. Gunnar, email message to Ellen Galinsky, May 10, 2019.

57. Ibid.

58. Megan R. Gunnar, interview by Ellen Galinsky, October 25, 2021.

59. Perry et al., "Associations Between Stress Reactivity and Behavior Problems," 1854–1863.

60. Philip Fisher, interview by Ellen Galinsky, July 10, 2017.

61. National Scientific Council on the Developing Child, "Young Children Develop in an Environment of Relationships," Working Paper No. 1, Center on the Developing Child at Harvard University, 2004, https://developingchild.harvard.edu/resources/WP1/.

62. Nicole R. Giuliani et al., "A Preliminary Study Investigating Maternal Neurocognitive Mechanisms Underlying a Child-Supportive Parenting Intervention," *Frontiers in Behavioral Neuroscience* 13, no. 16 (2019): https://doi.org/10.3389/fnbeh.2019.00016.

63. Ibid.

64. Philip Fisher, interview by Ellen Galinsky, July 10, 2017.

65. National Academies of Sciences, Engineering, and Medicine, *The Promise of Adolescence*; Brody et al., "Protective Prevention Effects on the Association of Poverty with Brain Development."

66. Velma McBride Murry, "Adolescent Development," Adolescent Virtual Speaking

Series, Bezos Family Foundation, September 18, 2020; Velma McBride Murry, email message to Ellen Galinsky, February 16, 2023.

67. Velma McBride Murry, "Adolescent Development: Recovery and Repair," Adolescent Virtual Speaking Series, Bezos Family Foundation, March 2, 2021; Velma McBride Murry, email message to Ellen Galinsky, February 16, 2023.

68. Murry, "Adolescent Development" (2020).

69. Velma McBride Murry et al., "Intervention Induced Changes in Perceptions of Parenting and Risk Opportunities Among Rural African Americans," *Journal of Child and Family Studies* 23, no. 2 (February 2014): 422–436, https://doi.org/10.1007 /s10826-013-9714-5; Murry, email message to Ellen Galinsky, February 16, 2023.

70. Velma McBride Murry, interview by Ellen Galinsky, October 15, 2021.

71. Gene H. Brody et al., "The Strong African American Families Program: Translating Research into Prevention Programming," *Child Development* 75, no. 3 (2004): 900–917, https://doi.org/10.1111/j.1467-8624.2004.00713.x.

72. Gene H. Brody et al., "A Family-Centered Prevention Ameliorates the Associations of Low Self-Control During Childhood with Employment Income and Poverty Status in Young African American Adults," *Journal of Child Psychology and Psychiatry* 61, no. 4 (2020): 425–435, https://doi.org/10.1111/jcpp.13139; Murry et al., "Intervention Induced Changes"; Velma McBride Murry et al., "Longitudinal Study of the Cascading Effects of Racial Discrimination on Parenting and Adjustment Among African American Youth," *Attachment and Human Development* 24, no. 3 (2022): 322–338, https://doi.org/10.1080/14616734.2021.1976926.

73. Brody et al., "Protective Prevention Effects on the Association of Poverty with Brain Development."

74. Ibid.

75. Gregory E. Miller et al., "A Family-Oriented Psychosocial Intervention Reduces Inflammation in Low-SES African American Youth," *Proceedings of the National Academy of Sciences* 111, no. 31 (2014): 11287–11292, https://doi.org/10.1073 /pnas.1406578111; Gene H. Brody et al., "Family-Centered Prevention Ameliorates the Association Between Adverse Childhood Experiences and Prediabetes Status in Young Black Adults," *Preventive Medicine* 100 (2017): 117–122, https://doi.org/10 .1016/j.ypmed.2017.04.017. See also National Academies of Sciences, Engineering, and Medicine, *The Promise of Adolescence*, 91–92.

76. Dan Hurley, "Scientist at Work—Felton Earls; On Crime as Science (A Neighborhood at a Time)," *New York Times*, January 6, 2004, https://www.nytimes.com/2004/01/06 /science/scientist-at-work-felton-earls-on-crime-as-science-a-neighbor-at-a-time.html.

77. Felton Earls, interview by Ellen Galinsky, October 18, 2001.

78. Robert J. Sampson, Stephen W. Raudenbush, and Felton Earls, "Neighborhoods and Violent Crime: A Multilevel Study of Collective Efficacy," *Science* 277, no. 5328 (August 1997): 918–924, https://doi.org/10.1126/science.277.5328.918.

79. Felton Earls and Stephen L. Buka, "Project on Human Development in Chicago Neighborhoods," Research and Technical Report, National Institute of Justice, March 1997; Felton Earls and Mary Carlson, *Voice, Choice, and Action: The Potential of Young Citizens to Heal Democracy* (Cambridge, MA: Harvard University Press, 2020).

80. Sampson, Raudenbush, and Earls, "Neighborhoods and Violent Crime."

81. Felton Earls, interview by Ellen Galinsky, October 18, 2001.

82. Robert J. Sampson, Stephen W. Raudenbush, and Felton Earls, "Neighborhood Collective Efficacy—Does It Help Reduce Violence?," National Institute of Justice, last modified April 1998, https://www.ojp.gov/pdffiles1/nij/184377NCJRS.pdf.

83. Sampson, Raudenbush, and Earls, "Neighborhoods and Violent Crime," 923.

84. Ibid.

85. Earls and Buka, "Project on Human Development in Chicago Neighborhoods."

86. Velma McBride Murry, interview by Ellen Galinsky, October 15, 2021.

87. Murry, "Adolescent Development: Recovery and Repair" (2021); Murry, email message to Ellen Galinsky, February 16, 2023.

88. Stephanie M. Carlson, interview by Ellen Galinsky, September 15, 2017. Some of

the studies Carlson is referring to are summarized in an article we wrote as well as in the studies listed. See Ellen Galinsky et al., "Civic Science for Public Use: Mind in the Making and Vroom," *Child Development* 88 (July 2017): 1409–1418, https://doi .org/10.1111/cdev.12892. See also Brenna Hassinger-Das et al., "Domain-General Mediators of the Relation Between Kindergarten Number Sense and First-Grade Mathematics Achievement," *Journal of Experimental Child Psychology* 118 (February 2014): 78–92, https://doi.org/10.1016/j.jecp.2013.09.008; Megan M. McClelland et al., "Relations Between Preschool Attention Span-Persistence and Age 25 Educa-tional Outcomes," *Early Childhood Research Quarterly* 28 (April 2013): 314–324, https://doi.org/10.1016/j.ecresq.2012.07.008; Terrie E. Moffitt et al., "A Gradient of Childhood Self-Control Predicts Health, Wealth, and Public Safety," *Proceedings of the National Academy of Sciences* 108 (February 2011): 2696, https://doi.org/10.1073 /pnas.1010076108.

89. Moffitt et al., "A Gradient of Childhood Self-Control."
90. Annie Bernier, Stephanie M. Carlson, and Natasha Whipple, "From External Regu-lation to Self-Regulation: Early Parenting Precursors of Young Children's Executive Functioning," *Child Development* 81 (February 2010): 326–339, https://doi.org/10 .1111/j.1467-8624.2009.01397.x.
91. Stephanie M. Carlson, interview by Ellen Galinsky, September 15, 2017.
92. Julie C. Laurin and Mireille Joussemet, "Parental Autonomy-Supportive Practices and Toddlers' Rule Internalization: A Prospective Observational Study," *Motiva-tion and Emotion* 41, no. 5 (2017): 562–575, https://doi.org/10.1007/s11031-017 -9627-5.
93. Rebecca Distefano et al., "Autonomy-Supportive Parenting and Associations with Child and Parent Executive Function," *Journal of Applied Developmental Psychol-ogy* 58 (July–September 2018): 78, https://doi.org/10.1016/j.appdev.2018.04.007.
94. Ibid., 77.
95. Alyssa S. Meuwissen and Stephanie M. Carlson, "An Experimental Study of the Effects of Autonomy Support on Preschoolers' Self-Regulation," *Journal of Applied Developmental Psychology* 60 (January 2019): 11–23, https://doi.org/10.1016/j .appdev.2018.10.001.
96. Edward L. Deci and Richard M. Ryan, *Intrinsic Motivation and Self-Determination in Human Behavior* (New York: Plenum, 1985).
97. Wendy S. Grolnick, interview by Ellen Galinsky, October 27, 2017.
98. Richard M. Ryan and Edward L. Deci, "Self-Determination Theory and the Facil-itation of Intrinsic Motivation, Social Development, and Well-Being," *American Psychologist* 55, no. 1 (2000): 68–78, https://doi.org/10.1037/0003-066X.55.1.68.
99. Wendy S. Grolnick, "Meeting Development Needs," Adolescent Virtual Speaking Series, Bezos Family Foundation, October 13, 2020.
100. Wendy S. Grolnick, interview by Ellen Galinsky, October 27, 2017; Grolnick, "Meeting Development Needs"; Wendy S. Grolnick, email message to Ellen Galinsky, February 4, 2023.
101. Grolnick, "Meeting Development Needs."
102. Ibid.
103. Wendy S. Grolnick et al., "Antecedents and Consequences of Mothers' Autonomy Support: An Experimental Investigation," *Developmental Psychology* 38, no. 1 (Feb-ruary 2002): 143, https://doi.org/10.1037/0012-1649.38.1.143.
104. Wendy S. Grolnick, email message to Ellen Galinsky, February 4, 2023.
105. Wendy S. Grolnick, interview by Lisa Rinehart, November 5, 2019.
106. Wendy S. Grolnick, interview by Ellen Galinsky, October 27, 2017; Wendy S. Grolnick, email message to Ellen Galinsky, February 4, 2023.
107. Katherine Reynolds Lewis, *The Good News About Bad Behavior: Why Kids Are Less Disciplined Than Ever—and What to Do About It* (New York: PublicAffairs, 2018), 5.
108. Ellen Galinsky, *The Six Stages of Parenthood* (Cambridge, MA: Da Capo Press, 1987).
109. Maya L. Rosen et al., "Promoting Youth Mental Health During the COVID-19

Pandemic: A Longitudinal Study," *PloS One* 16, no. 8 (August 2021): e0255294, https://doi.org/10.1371/journal.pone.0255294.

110. Daniel J. Siegel, interview by Ellen Galinsky, July 18, 2023.

111. Edward Z. Tronick, *The Neurobehavioral and Social-Emotional Development of the Infant* (New York: W. W. Norton, 2007).

112. Edward Z. Tronick, email message to Ellen Galinsky, August 26, 2009.

113. Carol S. Dweck and David S. Yeager, "Mindsets: A View from Two Eras," *Perspectives on Psychological Science* 14, no. 3 (2019): 481–496, https://doi.org/10.1177/1745691618804166; Albert Bandura, "Self-Efficacy: Toward a Unifying Theory of Behavioral Change," *Psychological Review* 84, no. 2 (1977): 191–215, https://doi.org/10.1037/0033-295X.84.2.191.

114. Murry et al., "Intervention Induced Changes in Perceptions of Parenting and Risk Opportunities Among Rural African Americans," 429; Larissa G. Duncan et al., "A Model of Mindful Parenting: Implications for Parent-Child Relationships and Prevention Research," *Clinical Child and Family Psychology Review* 12, no. 3 (2009): 255–270, https://doi.org/10.1007/s10567-009-0046-3.

115. Jennifer H. Pfeifer, interview by Ellen Galinsky, July 8, 2019.

116. Shannon J. Peake et al., "Risk-Taking and Social Exclusion in Adolescence: Behavioral and Neural Evidence of Peer Influences on Decision-Making," *NeuroImage* 82 (November 2013): 23–34, https://doi.org/10.1016/j.neuroimage.2013.05.061.

117. Jennifer H. Pfeifer, interview by Ellen Galinsky, September 7, 2016.

118. Kipling D. Williams, Christopher K. T. Cheung, and Wilma Choi, "Cyberostracism: Effects of Being Ignored over the Internet," *Journal of Personality and Social Psychology* 79, no. 5 (November 2000): 748–762, https://doi.org/10.1037//0022-3514.79.5.748; Kipling D. Williams, "Ostracism," *Annual Review of Psychology* 58, no. 1 (January 2007): 425, https://doi.org/10.1146/annurev.psych.58.110405.085641.

119. Jack L. Andrews et al., "Expectations of Social Consequences Impact Anticipated Involvement in Health-Risk Behavior During Adolescence," *Journal of Research on Adolescence* 30, no. 4 (2020): 1008–1024, https://doi.org/10.1111/jora.12576.

120. Eva H. Telzer et al., "The Quality of Adolescents' Peer Relationships Modulates Neural Sensitivity to Risk Taking," *Social Cognitive and Affective Neuroscience* 10, no. 3 (March 2015): 389, https://doi.org/10.1093/scan/nsu064.

121. Ibid.

122. Eveline A. Crone, interview by Ellen Galinsky, September 1, 2017.

123. "Youth Risk Behavior Survey: Data Summary and Trends Report, 2011–2021," Centers for Disease Control and Prevention, 2023, https://www.cdc.gov/healthyyouth/data/yrbs/pdf/yrbs_data-summary-trends_report2023_508.pdf.

124. Ahna Suleiman et al., "Becoming a Sexual Being: The 'Elephant in the Room' of Adolescent Brain Development," *Developmental Cognitive Neuroscience* 25 (2017): 209–220, https://doi.org/10.1016/j.dcn.2016.09.004.

125. Ahna Suleiman, interview by Ellen Galinsky, October 11, 2016.

126. Kathy T. Do, Ethan M. McCormick, and Eva H. Telzer, "Neural Sensitivity to Conflicting Attitudes Supports Greater Conformity Toward Positive over Negative Influence in Early Adolescence," *Developmental Cognitive Neuroscience* 45 (October 2020): art. 100837, https://doi.org/10.1016/j.dcn.2020.100837.

127. Jack P. Shonkoff, interview by Ellen Galinsky and Dan Wuori, April 19, 2021.

128. Eva H. Telzer et al., "Neurobiological Sensitivity to Social Rewards and Punishments Moderates Link Between Peer Norms and Adolescent Risk Taking," *Child Development* 92, no. 2 (March 2021): 741, https://doi.org/10.1111/cdev.13466.

129. Ibid.

130. Kathy T. Do, Mitchell J. Prinstein, and Eva H. Telzer, "Neurobiological Susceptibility to Peer Influence in Adolescence," in *The Oxford Handbook of Developmental Cognitive Neuroscience*, ed. Kathrin Cohen Kadosh, online ed. (New York: Oxford University Press, 2020), https://doi.org/10.1093/oxfordhb/9780198827474.013.27.

131. Eva H. Telzer, "Parenting and Peer Relationships/Positive Risks," Adolescent Virtual Speaking Series, Bezos Family Foundation, February 11, 2021.

132. W. Thomas Boyce, *The Orchid and the Dandelion: Why Sensitive Children Face Challenges and How All Can Thrive* (New York: Vintage Books, 2020).

133. Jerome Kagan, "Temperament and the Reactions to Unfamiliarity," *Child Development* 68, no. 1 (1997): 139–143; Jerome Kagan, interview with Ellen Galinsky, February 20, 2003.

134. Jay Belsky, "Your Kid Is Probably Not an 'Orchid' or a 'Dandelion'—But Could Be Both," *Scientific American*, March 15, 2022, https://www.scientificamerican.com /article/your-kid-is-probably-not-an-orchid-or-a-dandelion-but-could-be-both/.

135. Ronald E. Dahl, "Adolescent Brain Development: A Period of Vulnerabilities and Opportunities. Keynote Address," *Annals of the New York Academy of Sciences* 1021, no. 1 (2004): 1–22, https://doi.org/10.1196/annals.1308.001.

136. Simon Ciranka and Wouter van den Bos, "Adolescent Risk-Taking in the Context of Exploration and Social Influence," *Developmental Review* 61, no. 2 (2021): 100979, https://psycnet.apa.org/doi/10.1016/j.dr.2021.100979.

137. Natasha Duell and Laurence Steinberg, "Positive Risk Taking in Adolescence," *Child Development Perspectives* 13, no. 1 (March 2019): 48–52, https://doi.org/10.1111 /cdep.12310.

138. Adriana Galván, conversation with Ellen Galinsky, March 23, 2019.

139. Daniel J. Siegel, *Brainstorm: The Power and Purpose of the Teenage Brain* (New York: Penguin, 2013), 109.

140. Ronald E. Dahl, interview by Ellen Galinsky, October 11, 2017; Ronald E. Dahl, email message to Ellen Galinsky, January 24, 2023.

141. Jeffrey M. Spielberg et al., "Exciting Fear in Adolescence: Does Pubertal Development Alter Threat Processing?," *Developmental Cognitive Neuroscience* 8 (April 2014): 87, https://doi.org/10.1016/j.dcn.2014.01.004.

142. Valerie F. Reyna and Frank Farley, "Risk and Rationality in Adolescent Decision-Making: Implications for Theory, Practice, and Public Policy," *Psychological Science in the Public Interest* 7, no. 1 (2006): 1–44, https://doi.org/10.1111/j.1529-1006 .2006.00026.x.

143. Abigail A. Baird, Jonathan A. Fugelsang, and Craig Bennett, "What Were You Thinking? An fMRI Study of Adolescent Decision Making," ResearchGate, January 2005, https://www.researchgate.net/profile/A_Baird/publication/268048958 _What_were_you_thinking_An_fMRI_study_of_adolescent_decision_making /links/551a85680cf244e9a45882a5/What-were-you-thinking-An-fMRI-study-of -adolescent-decision-making.pdf.

144. Ronald E. Dahl, interview by Ellen Galinsky, October 11, 2017.

145. Spielberg et al., "Exciting Fear in Adolescence."

146. Ronald E. Dahl, interview by Ellen Galinsky, October 11, 2017.

147. Duell and Steinberg, "Positive Risk Taking in Adolescence," 49.

148. "Courage Is Resistance to Fear, Mastery of Fear, Not Absence of Fear: Mark Twain? Apocryphal?," Quote Investigator, November 26, 2019, https://quoteinvestigator.com /2019/11/26/courage-fear/.

149. Ronald E. Dahl, interview by Ellen Galinsky, October 11, 2017.

150. Eveline A. Crone, interview by Ellen Galinsky, September 1, 2017.

151. Barbara R. Braams et al., "Longitudinal Changes in Adolescent Risk-Taking: A Comprehensive Study of Neural Responses to Rewards, Pubertal Development, and Risk-Taking Behavior," *Journal of Neuroscience* 35, no. 18 (May 2015): 7226–7238, https://doi.org/10.1523/JNEUROSCI.4764-14.2015.

152. Ronald E. Dahl, interview by Ellen Galinsky, October 11, 2017; Ronald E. Dahl, email message to Ellen Galinsky, January 24, 2023.

153. Ronald E. Dahl, interview by Ellen Galinsky, October 11, 2017; David S. Yeager, Ronald E. Dahl, and Carol S. Dweck, "Why Interventions to Influence Adolescent Behavior Often Fail but Could Succeed," *Perspectives on Psychological Science* 13, no. 1 (2018): 101–122, https://doi.org/10.1177/1745691617722620.

154. "Youth Risk Behavior Surveillance System (YRBSS)," Centers for Disease Control and Prevention, accessed August 30, 2021, https://www.cdc.gov/healthyyouth/data /yrbs/index.htm.

155. "United States, High School Youth Risk Behavior Survey, 2017," Centers for Disease Control and Prevention, accessed February 26, 2023, https://nccd.cdc.gov /Youthonline/App/Results.aspx?TT=A&OUT=0&SID=HS&QID=QQ&LID=XX &YID=2017&LID2=&YID2=&COL=S&ROW1=N&ROW2=N&HT=QQ&LCT =LL&FS=S1&FR=R1&FG=G1&FA=A1&FI=I1&FP=P1&FSL=S1&FRL=R1&FGL =G1&FAL=A1&FIL=I1&FPL=P1&PV=&TST=False&C1=&C2=&QP=G&DP=1 &VA=CI&CS=Y&SYID=&EYID=&SC=DEFAULT&SO=ASC.

156. "Youth Risk Behavior Survey: Data Summary and Trends Report, 2011–2021."

157. Daniel Romer, Valerie F. Reyna, and Theodore D. Satterthwaite, "Beyond Stereotypes of Adolescent Risk Taking: Placing the Adolescent Brain in Developmental Context," *Developmental Cognitive Neuroscience* 27 (October 2017): 19–34, https://doi.org/10 .1016/j.dcn.2017.07.007.

158. Eveline A. Crone, interview by Ellen Galinsky, September 1, 2017.

159. Jennifer H. Pfeifer and Nicholas B. Allen, "Arrested Development? Reconsidering Dual-Systems Models of Brain Function in Adolescence and Disorders," *Trends in Cognitive Sciences* 16, no. 6 (June 2012): 322, https://doi.org/10.1016/j.tics.2012.04 .011.

160. Jennifer H. Pfeifer, interview by Ellen Galinsky, July 8, 2019.

161. Jennifer H. Pfeifer, interview by Ellen Galinsky, April 19, 2019.

162. Jennifer H. Pfeifer, interview by Ellen Galinsky, July 8, 2019.

163. Ibid.

164. Jennifer H. Pfeifer and Elliot T. Berkman, "The Development of Self and Identity in Adolescence: Neural Evidence and Implications for a Value-Based Choice Perspective on Motivated Behavior," *Child Development Perspectives* 12, no. 3 (September 2018): 160, https://doi.org/10.111/cdep.12279.

165. Elliot T. Berkman, interview by Ellen Galinsky, July 9, 2019.

166. Duell and Steinberg, "Positive Risk Taking in Adolescence," 48–52.

167. Ibid., 49.

168. Natasha Duell and Laurence Steinberg, "Differential Correlates of Positive and Negative Risk-Taking in Adolescence," *Journal of Youth and Adolescence* 49, no. 6 (June 2020): 1162–1178, https://doi.org/10.1007/s10964-020-01237-7.

169. "Adolescents Who Take Positive Risks Tend to Be Less Impulsive, More Connected to School, Suggests NIH-Funded Study," National Institutes of Health, May 22, 2020, https://www.nichd.nih.gov/newsroom/news/052220-adolescents-risk-taking.

170. Eva H. Telzer, "Dopaminergic Reward Sensitivity Can Promote Adolescent Health: A New Perspective on the Mechanism of Ventral Striatum Activation," *Developmental Cognitive Neuroscience* 17 (2016): 57–67, https://doi.org/10.1016/j.dcn.2015.10 .010; Eva H. Telzer et al., "Ventral Striatum Activation to Prosocial Rewards Predicts Longitudinal Declines in Adolescent Risk Taking," *Developmental Cognitive Neuroscience* 3 (2013): 45–52, https://doi.org/10.1016/j.dcn.2012.08.004.

171. Eva H. Telzer, "Parenting and Peer Relationships/Positive Risks," Adolescent Virtual Speaking Series, Bezos Family Foundation, February 11, 2021.

172. Neeltje E. Blankenstein et al., "Behavioral and Neural Pathways Supporting the Development of Prosocial and Risk-Taking Behavior Across Adolescence," *Child Development* 91, no. 3 (2020): e665–e681, https://psycnet.apa.org/doi/10.1111/cdev .13292.

173. Eva H. Telzer, "The Developing Adolescent Brain," Adolescent Virtual Speaking Series, Bezos Family Foundation, September 18, 2020.

174. Katie Fitzgerald, "The Aspen Challenge at the Aspen Ideas Festival Opening Remarks," July 6, 2017, https://www.youtube.com/watch?v=GjPJg0QlUPA.

175. Ibid.

176. "How It Works," Aspen Challenge, accessed August 30, 2021, https://aspenchallenge .org/about/how-it-works/.

177. "Louisville Aspen Challenge Gives Us Hope," Aspen Challenge, accessed August 20, 2021, https://aspenchallenge.org/louisville-aspen-challenge-gives-us-hope/.

178. John D. Dugan, S. Patterson, and K. C. Skendall, *The Power of Youth: A 5-Year Analysis of the Impact of Aspen Challenge* (Washington, DC: Aspen Institute, 2022).

179. "Louisville Aspen Challenge Gives Us Hope."

180. Emily A. Vogels, Risa Gelles-Watnick, and Navid Massarat, "Teens, Social Media and Technology 2022," Pew Research Center, August 10, 2022, https://www.pewresearch .org/internet/2022/08/10/teens-social-media-and-technology-2022/.

181. "The Common Sense Census: Media Use by Tweens and Teens," Common Sense Media, 2021, https://www.commonsensemedia.org/sites/default/files/research/report /8-18-census-integrated-report-final-web_0.pdf.

182. Mitchell J. Prinstein, Jacqueline Nesi, and Eva H. Telzer, "Commentary: An Updated Agenda for the Study of Digital Media Use and Adolescent Development—Future Directions Following Odgers & Jensen (2020)," *Journal of Child Psychology and Psychiatry* 61, no. 3 (2020): 350, https: doi.org/10.1111/jcpp.13219.

183. Kristen Purcell et al., "How Teens Do Research in the Digital World," Pew Research Center, November 1, 2012, https://www.pewresearch.org/internet/2012/11/01/how -teens-do-research-in-the-digital-world/.

184. Nellie Bowles, "Now Some Families Are Hiring Coaches to Help Them Raise Phone-Free Children," *New York Times*, June 6, 2019, https://www.nytimes.com/2019/07 /06/style/parenting-coaches-screen-time-phones.html?searchResultPosition=1.

185. Diane Sawyer, "Screentime," ABC, accessed May 4, 2019, https://abc.go.com/movies -and-specials/screentime-diane-sawyer-reporting.

186. National Academies of Sciences, Engineering, and Medicine, *The Promise of Adolescence*, 40.

187. Amy Orben and Andrew K. Przybylski, "Screens, Teens, and Psychological Well-Being: Evidence from Three Time-Use-Diary Studies," *Psychological Science* 30, no. 5 (May 2019): 693, https://doi.org/10.1177/0956797619830329; Amy Orben and Andrew K. Przybylski, "The Association Between Adolescent Well-Being and Digital Technology Use," *Nature Human Behaviour* 3, no. 2 (February 2019): 177–178, https://doi.org/10.1038/s41562-018-0506-1.

188. Orben and Przybylski, "The Association Between Adolescent Well-Being and Digital Technology Use."

189. Vivek Murthy, "Social Media and Youth Mental Health: The U.S. Surgeon General's Advisory," U.S. Health and Human Services, accessed May 28, 2023, 4, https:// www.hhs.gov/sites/default/files/sg-youth-mental-health-social-media-advisory.pdf.

190. Eva H. Telzer, interview by Ellen Galinsky, July 21, 2022.

191. Jacqueline Nesi, Eva H. Telzer, and Mitchell J. Prinstein, "Adolescent Development in the Digital Media Context," *Psychological Inquiry* 31, no. 3 (2020): 229, https://doi .org/10.1080/1047840x.2020.1820219.

192. Ibid.

193. "Facebook Knows Instagram Is Toxic for Teen Girls, Company Documents Show," *Wall Street Journal*, September 14, 2021, https://www.wsj.com/articles /facebook-knows-instagram-is-toxic-for-teen-girls-company-documents-show -11631620739.

194. Logan Lane, "The Teenager Leading the Smartphone Liberation Movement," interview by Lulu Garcia-Navarro, *New York Times*, February 2, 2023, https://www .nytimes.com/2023/02/02/opinion/teen-luddite-smartphones.html?showTranscript=1.

195. David Elkind and Robert Bowen, "Imaginary Audience Behavior in Children and Adolescents," *Developmental Psychology* 15, no. 1 (1979): 38–44, https://doi.org/10 .1037/0012-1649.15.1.38.

196. Nesi, Telzer, and Prinstein, "Adolescent Development in Digital Media Context," 230.

197. Vogels, Gelles-Watnick, and Massarat, "Teens, Social Media and Technology 2022."

198. Christopher J. Bryan, David S. Yeager, and Cintia P. Hinojosa, "A Values-Alignment Intervention Protects Adolescents from the Effects of Food Marketing," *Nature Human Behaviour* 3, no. 6 (2019): 596–603, https://doi.org/10.1038/s41562-019 -0586-6.

199. Nandita Vijayakumar et al., "Getting to Know Me Better: An fMRI Study of Intimate and Superficial Self-Disclosure to Friends During Adolescence," *Journal of Personality and Social Psychology* 118, no. 5 (2020): 885–899, https://doi.org/10.1037

/pspa0000182; Nandita Vijayakumar and Jennifer H. Pfeifer, "Self-Disclosure During Adolescence: Exploring the Means, Targets, and Types of Personal Exchanges," *Current Opinion in Psychology* 31 (2020): 135–140, https://doi.org/10.1016/j.copsyc .2019.08.005.

200. Jennifer H. Pfeifer, interview by Ellen Galinsky, July 9, 2019.
201. Yeager, Dahl, and Dweck, "Why Interventions to Influence Adolescent Behavior Often Fail but Could Succeed," 101–122.
202. Nesi, Telzer, and Prinstein, "Adolescent Development in Digital Media Context," 230.
203. Eva H. Telzer, interview by Ellen Galinsky, July 21, 2022.
204. Prinstein, Nesi, and Telzer, "Commentary: An Updated Agenda for the Study of Digital Media Use and Adolescent Development—Future Directions Following Odgers & Jensen (2020)," 350.
205. Ethan Kross, interview by Ellen Galinsky, January 17, 2018.
206. Ibid.
207. Ethan Kross, "Facebook Use Predicts Declines in Subjective Well-Being in Young Adults," *PLoS ONE* 8, no. 8 (August 14, 2013): e69841, https://doi.org/10.10.1371 /journal.pone.0069841.
208. Ethan Kross, interview by Ellen Galinsky, January 17, 2018.
209. Philippe Verduyn et al., "Passive Facebook Usage Undermines Affective Well-Being: Experimental and Longitudinal Evidence," *Journal of Experimental Psychology: General* 144, no. 2 (2015): 480–488, https://doi.org/10.1037/xge0000057.
210. Ibid., 484.
211. Ethan Kross, interview by Ellen Galinsky, January 17, 2018.
212. "Youth Risk Behavior Survey: Data Summary and Trends Report, 2011–2021."
213. Jean M. Twenge, *iGen: Why Today's Super-Connected Kids Are Growing Up Less Rebellious, More Tolerant, Less Happy—and Completely Unprepared for Adulthood—and What That Means for the Rest of Us* (New York: Atria Books, 2017).
214. Greg Lukianoff and Jonathan Haidt, *The Coddling of the American Mind: How Good Intentions and Bad Ideas Are Setting Up a Generation for Failure* (New York: Penguin, 2018).
215. Jacqueline Nesi, "Does Social Media Cause Teen Mental Health Issues?," Techno Sapiens, posted January 30, 2023, https://technosapiens.substack.com/p/does-social -media-cause-teen-mental.
216. Patti M. Valenburg, Adrian Meier, and Ine Beyens, "Social Media Use and Its Impact on Adolescent Mental Health: An Umbrella Review of the Evidence," *Current Opinion in Psychology* 44 (April 2022): 58–68, https://doi.org/10.1016/j.copsyc.2021.08.017.
217. Murthy, "Social Media and Youth Mental Health: The U.S. Surgeon General's Advisory," 4.
218. "Health Advisory on Social Media Use in Adolescence," American Psychological Association, accessed June 1, 2023, 3, https://www.apa.org/topics/social-media-internet /health-advisory-adolescent-social-media-use.
219. Ibid., 7.
220. Ellen Galinsky, *Ask the Children: The Breakthrough Study That Reveals How to Succeed at Work and Parenting* (New York: Quill, 2000).
221. Eva H. Telzer, interview by Ellen Galinsky, July 22, 2022.
222. Betsy Sparrow, Jenny Liu, and Daniel M. Wegner, "Google Effects on Memory: Cognitive Consequences of Having Information at Our Fingertips," *Science* 333, no. 6043 (July 2011): 776–778, http://doi.org/10.1026/science.1207745.
223. Ibid., 777.
224. Kathryn L. Mills, "Effects of Internet Use on the Adolescent Brain: Despite Popular Claims, Experimental Evidence Remains Scarce," *Trends in Cognitive Sciences* 18, no. 8 (August 2014): 385–387, https://doi.org/10.1016/j.tics.2014.04.011; Kathryn L. Mills, "Possible Effects of Internet Use on Cognitive Development in Adolescence," *Media and Communication* 4, no. 3 (June 2016): 4–12, https://doi.org/10.17645/mac .v4i3.516.
225. Kathryn L. Mills, interview by Ellen Galinsky, July 9, 2019.

226. Victoria Rideout and Michael B. Robb, *Social Media, Social Life: Teens Reveal Their Experiences* (San Francisco: Common Sense Media, 2018).

227. Melina R. Uncapher, interview by Ellen Galinsky, February 20, 2020; Melina R. Uncapher, email to Ellen Galinsky, March 11, 2023.

228. Melina R. Uncapher, "How Can Learning Engineering Be Applied in Schools?," keynote presentation, LearnLaunch Across Boundaries Conference, Boston, January 31, 2019, https://www.youtube.com/watch?v=__GbwKCV-GY.

229. Melina R. Uncapher, Monica K. Thieu, and Anthony D. Wagner, "Media Multitasking and Memory: Differences in Working Memory and Long-Term Memory," *Psychonomic Bulletin and Review* 23, no. 3 (2016): 483–490, https://doi.org/10.3758/s13423-015-0907-3.

230. Melina R. Uncapher et al., "Media Multitasking and Cognitive, Psychological, Neural, and Learning Differences," *Pediatrics* 140, suppl. 2 (November 2017): S62–S66, https://doi.org/10.1542/peds.2016-1758D.

231. Melina R. Uncapher and Anthony Wagner, "Minds and Brains of Media Multitaskers: Current Findings and Future Directions," *Proceedings of the National Academy of Sciences* 115, no. 40 (October 2018): 9889–9896, https://doi.org/10.1073/pnas.1611612115.

232. Uncapher, "How Can Learning Engineering Be Applied in Schools?"

233. John David Lorentz et al., "Media Multitasking, Executive Function, and Academic Achievement in Middle Childhood," poster, International Mind Brain and Education Society Conference, Los Angeles, September 28, 2018.

234. "About Us," Advanced Education Research and Development Fund, accessed September 15, 2022, https://aerdf.org/about-us/.

235. Laura M. Padilla-Walker et al., "The Protective Role of Parental Media Monitoring Style from Early to Late Adolescence," *Journal of Youth and Adolescence* 47, no. 2 (2018): 445–459, https://doi.org/10.1007/s10964-017-0722-4.

236. Ibid., 455.

237. James P. Steyer, *The Other Parent: The Inside Story of Media's Effect on Children* (New York: Atria Books, 2002).

238. Linda Burch, interview by Ellen Galinsky, August 11, 2021.

239. "About Us," Common Sense Media, accessed September 12, 2022, https://www.commonsensemedia.org.

240. Linda Burch, interview by Ellen Galinsky, August 11, 2021; Linda Burch, email message to Ellen Galinsky, February 21, 2023.

241. Linda Burch, email message to Ellen Galinsky, February 21, 2023.

242. "Health Advisory on Social Media Use in Adolescence," 3.

243. Murthy, "Social Media and Youth Mental Health: The U.S. Surgeon General's Advisory."

244. Tiffany Shlain, *24/6: The Power of Unplugging One Day a Week* (New York: Gallery Books, 2019).

245. Ellen Galinsky et al., *Leaders in a Global Economy: A Study of Executive Women and Men* (New York: Families and Work Institute, 2003).

246. Elizabeth Levy Paluck, Hana Shepherd, and Peter M. Aronow, "Changing Climates of Conflict: A Social Network Experiment in 56 Schools," *Proceedings of the National Academy of Sciences* 113, no. 3 (January 2016): 566, https://doi.org/10.1073/pnas.1514483113.

247. Sharon Brody and Paul Connearney, "What the 'Designated Driver' Campaign Could Teach Us About How to Handle the Pandemic," WBUR, February 7, 2021, https://www.wbur.org/news/2021/02/07/designated-driver-coronavirus-pandemic-public-health-campaign.

248. "Center for Health Communication," Harvard University, accessed September 1, 2021, https://www.hsph.harvard.edu/chc/.

249. Paluck, Shepherd, and Aronow, "Changing Climates of Conflict."

250. Elizabeth Levy Paluck and Hana Shepherd, "The Salience of Social Referents: A Field Experiment on Collective Norms and Harassment Behavior in a School Social

Network," *Journal of Personality and Social Psychology* 103, no. 6 (September 2012): 899–915, https://doi.org/10.1030/a0030015.

251. Paluck, Shepherd, and Aronow, "Changing Climates of Conflict."

252. "Students with Influence over Peers Reduce School Bullying by 30 Percent," *Science Daily*, January 4, 2016, https://www.sciencedaily.com/releases/2016/01/160104163206.htm.

253. Ibid.

254. Paluck, Shepherd, and Aronow, "Changing Climates of Conflict."

255. Ibid.

256. Hope Shinderman, email message to Ellen Galinsky, December 22, 2021.

257. Walter Mischel, *The Marshmallow Test: Why Self-Control Is the Engine of Success* (New York: Little, Brown, 2014).

258. Ellen Galinsky, *Mind in the Making: The Seven Essential Life Skills Every Child Needs* (New York: HarperStudio, 2010), 64; Walter Mischel, interview by Hank O'Karma, June 8, 2006.

259. Celeste Kidd, Holly Palmeri, and Richard N. Aslin, "Rational Snacking: Young Children's Decision-Making on the Marshmallow Task Is Moderated by Beliefs About Environmental Reliability," *Cognition* 126 (October 2012): 109–114, https://doi.org/10.1016/j.cognition.2012.08.004.

3. Message 3: Don't Stereotype Us

1. Andrew N. Meltzoff, interview by Ellen Galinsky, February 25, 2015.

2. Andrew N. Meltzoff, "'Like Me': A Foundation for Social Cognition," *Developmental Science* 10, no. 1 (2007): 126–134, https://doi.org/10.1111/j.1467-7687.2007.00574.x.

3. Peter J. Marshall and Andrew N. Meltzoff, "Neural Mirroring Systems: Exploring the EEG Mu Rhythm in Human Infancy," *Developmental Cognitive Neuroscience* 1, no. 2 (April 2011): 110–123, https://doi.org/10.1016/j.dcn.2010.09.001; Peter J. Marshall, Thomas Young, and Andrew N. Meltzoff, "Neural Correlates of Action Observation and Execution in 14-Month-Old Infants: An Event-Related EEG Desynchronization Study," *Developmental Science* 14, no. 3 (May 2011): 474–480, https://doi.org/10.1111/j.1467-7687.2010.00991.x.

4. Andrew N. Meltzoff, interview by Ellen Galinsky, February 25, 2015; Andrew N. Meltzoff, email message to Ellen Galinsky, February 15, 2013.

5. Yair Bar-Haim et al., "Nature and Nurture in Own-Race Face Processing," *Psychological Science* 17, no. 2 (February 2006): 159–163, https://doi.org/10.1111/j.1467-9280.2006.01679.x; Chelsea Derlan Williams et al., "A Lifespan Model of Ethnic-Racial Identity," *Research in Human Development* 17, no. 2–3 (2020): 105–106, https://doi.org/10.1080/15427609.2020.1831882.

6. Naiqi G. Xiao et al., "Older but Not Younger Infants Associate Own-Race Faces with Happy Music and Other-Race Faces with Sad Music," *Developmental Science* 21, no. 2 (March 2018): e12537l, https://doi.org/10.1111/desc.12537; Naiqi G. Xiao et al., "Infants Rely More on Gaze Cues from Own-Race Than Other-Race Adults for Learning Under Uncertainty," *Child Development* 89, no. 3 (May/June 2018): e229–e244, https://doi.org/10.1111/cdev.12798.

7. Andrew N. Meltzoff, interview by Ellen Galinsky, January 17, 2017.

8. Allison L. Skinner, Andrew N. Meltzoff, and Kristina R. Olson, "'Catching' Social Bias: Exposure to Biased Nonverbal Signals Creates Social Bias in Preschool Children," *Psychological Science* 28 (December 2016): 216–224, https://doi.org/10.1177/0956797616678930.

9. Andrew N. Meltzoff, interview by Ellen Galinsky, January 17, 2017; Andrew N. Meltzoff, email message to Ellen Galinsky, February 15, 2013.

10. Allison Master, Sapna Cheryan, and Andrew N. Meltzoff, "Social Group Membership Increases STEM Engagement Among Preschoolers," *Developmental Psychology* 53, no. 2 (September 2016): 201–209, http://dx.doi.org/10.1037/dev0000195; Allison Master and Andrew N. Meltzoff, "Cultural Stereotypes and Sense of Belonging

Contribute to Gender Gaps in STEM," *International Journal of Gender, Science and Technology* 12 (April 23, 2020): 152–198, https://genderandset.open.ac.uk/index .php/genderandset/article/view/674; Skinner, Meltzoff, and Olson, "'Catching' Social Bias."

11. Andrew N. Meltzoff, interview by Ellen Galinsky, January 17, 2017; Andrew N. Meltzoff, email message to Ellen Galinsky, February 15, 2013.

12. Isabel Wilkerson, *Caste: The Origins of Our Discontents* (New York: Penguin Random House, 2020), 17.

13. Ibid.

14. Ibid.

15. Ibid., 18.

16. James M. Jones, *Prejudice and Racism* (Reading, MA: Addison-Wesley, 1972), 117.

17. "Stereotype," American Psychological Association, accessed January 6, 2022, https:// dictionary.apa.org/stereotype.

18. Charles Young, "Kennedy Visit Marked States Centennial," *Charleston Gazette-Mail*, June 20, 2013, https://www.wvgazettemail.com/news/kennedy-visit-marked-states -centennial/article_3b3bcfc4-9d4f-58cd-9758-b6ca0965fc00.html.

19. "Stereotype."

20. Christy M. Buchanan and Grayson N. Holmbeck, "Measuring Beliefs About Adolescent Personality and Behavior," *Journal of Youth and Adolescence* 27 (October 1998): 609–629, https://doi.org/10.1023/A:1022835107795.

21. Christy M. Buchanan and Johna L. Hughes, "Construction of Social Reality During Early Adolescence: Can Expecting Storm and Stress Increase Storm and Stress?," *Journal of Research on Adolescence* 19, no. 2 (May 2009): 261–285, https://doi.org /10.1111/j.1532-7795.2009.00596.x.

22. Yang Qu, interview by Ellen Galinsky, March 12, 2020; Yang Qu, email message to Ellen Galinsky, February 14, 2023.

23. Yang Qu et al., "Conceptions of Adolescence: Implications for Differences in Engagement in School over Early Adolescence in the United States and China," *Journal of Youth and Adolescence* 45 (July 2016): 1512–1526, https://doi.org/10.1007/s10964 -016-0492-4.

24. Yang Qu, interview by Ellen Galinsky, March 12, 2020.

25. Qu et al., "Conceptions of Adolescence."

26. Yang Qu, interview by Ellen Galinsky, July 15, 2018.

27. Qu et al., "Conceptions of Adolescence."

28. Ibid., 1523.

29. Yang Qu, interview by Ellen Galinsky, March 12, 2020.

30. Yang Qu et al., "Youth's Conceptions of Adolescence Predict Longitudinal Changes in Prefrontal Cortex Activation and Risk Taking During Adolescence," *Child Development* 89, no. 3 (May 2018): 773–783, https://doi.org/10.1111/cdev.13017.

31. Yang Qu, interview by Ellen Galinsky, March 12, 2020.

32. Yang Qu, Eva M. Pomerantz, and Guohong Wu, "Countering Youth's Negative Stereotypes of Teens Fosters Constructive Behavior," *Child Development* 91, no. 1 (January–February 2020): 197–213, https://doi.org/10.1111/cdev.13156.

33. Joshua Aronson, Carrie B. Fried, and Catherine Good, "Reducing the Effects of Stereotype Threat on African American College Students by Shaping Theories of Intelligence," *Journal of Experimental Social Psychology* 38, no. 2 (March 2002): 113–125, https://doi.org/10.1006/jesp.2001.1491; Gregory M. Walton, "The New Science of Wise Psychological Interventions," *Current Directions in Psychological Science* 23, no. 1 (February 2014): 73–82, https://doi.org/10.1177/0963721413512856.

34. Yang Qu, email message to Ellen Galinsky, February 14, 2023.

35. Qu, Pomerantz, and Wu, "Countering Youth's Negative Stereotypes."

36. Cari Gillen-O'Neel, Diane N. Ruble, and Andrew J. Fuligni, "Ethnic Stigma, Academic Anxiety, and Intrinsic Motivation in Middle Childhood," *Child Development* 82, no. 5 (August 2011): 1470–1485, https://doi.org/10.1111/j.1467–8624.2011.01621.x.

37. Virginia W. Huynh and Andrew J. Fuligni, "Discrimination Hurts: The Academic,

Psychological, and Physical Well-Being of Adolescents," *Journal of Research on Adolescence* 20, no. 4 (2010): 916–941, https://doi.org/10.1111/j.1532-7795.2010.00670.x.

38. Ibid.

39. Andrew J. Fuligni, interview by Lisa Rinehart, August 21, 2018.

40. Andrew J. Fuligni, interview by Ellen Galinsky, May 4, 2017.

41. Huynh and Fuligni, "Discrimination Hurts."

42. Andrew J. Fuligni, interview by Ellen Galinsky, May 4, 2017.

43. David R. Williams et al., "Perceived Discrimination, Race and Health in South Africa," *Social Science and Medicine* 67, no. 3 (2008): 441–452, https://doi.org/10.1016/j.socscimed.2008.03.021.

44. Virginia W. Huynh et al., "Everyday Discrimination and Diurnal Cortisol During Adolescence," *Hormones and Behavior* 80 (April 2016): 76–81, https://doi.org/10.1016/j.yhbeh.2016.01.009.

45. Andrew J. Fuligni, interview by Ellen Galinsky, May 4, 2017.

46. Ibid.

47. Huynh et al., "Everyday Discrimination and Diurnal Cortisol During Adolescence."

48. Andrew J. Fuligni, interview by Ellen Galinsky, May 4, 2017.

49. Huynh et al., "Everyday Discrimination and Diurnal Cortisol During Adolescence," 79.

50. Ibid.

51. Andrew J. Fuligni, interview by Ellen Galinsky, May 4, 2017.

52. Huynh et al., "Everyday Discrimination and Diurnal Cortisol During Adolescence," 76–81.

53. Andrew J. Fuligni, interview by Ellen Galinsky, May 4, 2017.

54. Graham H. Diering et al., "Homer1a Drives Homeostatic Scaling-Down of Excitatory Synapses During Sleep," *Science* 355, no. 6324 (2017): 511–515, https://doi.org/10.1126/science.aai8355.

55. Richard Huganir, interview by Ellen Galinsky, September 8, 2017.

56. Andrew J. Fuligni, interview by Lisa Rinehart, August 21, 2018.

57. Angelina Majeno et al., "Discrimination and Sleep Difficulties During Adolescence: The Mediating Roles of Loneliness and Perceived Stress," *Journal of Youth and Adolescence* 47 (2018): 136, https://doi.org/10.1007/s10964-017-0755-8.

58. Andrew J. Fuligni, interview by Lisa Rinehart, August 21, 2018.

59. "Discrimination Can Compromise Health During Adolescence," Adolescent Development Lab at UCLA, 2018, http://adolescence.semel.ucla.edu/article/2018/4/1/discrimination-and-health-risk-during-adolescence.

60. Tracy R. Whitaker and Cudore L. Snell, "Parenting While Powerless: Consequences of 'The Talk,'" *Journal of Human Behavior in the Social Environment* 26, no. 3–4 (2016): 303–309, https://doi.org/10.1080/10911359.2015.1127736.

61. Williams et al., "Perceived Discrimination, Race and Health in South Africa," 441–452.

62. Xiao et al., "Infants Rely More on Gaze Cues from Own-Race Than Other-Race Adults for Learning Under Uncertainty," e229–e244.

63. Meltzoff, "'Like Me': A Foundation for Social Cognition," 126–134.

64. Skinner, Meltzoff, and Olson, "'Catching' Social Bias: Exposure to Biased Nonverbal Signals Creates Social Bias in Preschool Children," 216–224.

65. Master, Cheryan, and Meltzoff, "Social Group Membership Increases STEM Engagement Among Preschoolers," 201–209; Master and Meltzoff, "Cultural Stereotypes and Sense of Belonging Contribute to Gender Gaps in STEM," 152–198.

66. David Rose, "Deeper Learning for EVERY Student: Neuroscience, Technology, and Universal Design for Learning," keynote speech, Learning and the Brain Conference, Boston, November 23, 2019; David Rose, briefing for the Bezos Family Foundation, June 22, 2021; David Rose, email message to Ellen Galinsky, February 15, 2023.

67. Wim Meeus et al., "On Imbalance of Impulse Control and Sensation Seeking and Adolescent Risk: An Intra-individual Developmental Test of the Dual Systems and Maturational Imbalance Models," *Journal of Youth and Adolescence* 50 (2021): 827–840, https://doi.org/10.1007/s10964-021-01419-x.

68. Sarah-Jayne Blakemore, *Inventing Ourselves: The Secret Life of the Teenage Brain* (New York: PublicAffairs, 2018), 139.
69. Richard M. Lerner, "Adolescent Development," Adolescent Virtual Speaking Series, Bezos Family Foundation, September 18, 2020.

4. Message 4: We Are Trying to Understand Ourselves and Our Needs

1. Leo Lionni, *Fish Is Fish* (New York: Knopf Books for Young Readers, 1970).
2. Wendy S. Grolnick, "Meeting Development Needs," Adolescent Virtual Speaking Series, Bezos Family Foundation, October 13, 2020.
3. Richard M. Ryan and Edward L. Deci, *Self-Determination Theory: Basic Psychological Needs in Motivation, Development, and Wellness* (New York: Guilford Press, 2017). This book describes decades of research on Self-Determination Theory and the role it has played in parenting, social development, and mental health research.
4. Richard M. Ryan and Edward L. Deci, "Self-Determination Theory and the Facilitation of Intrinsic Motivation, Social Development, and Well-Being," *American Psychologist* 55, no. 1 (2000): 68–78, https://doi.org/10.1037/0003-066X.55.1.68; Institute of Medicine and National Research Council Committee on the Science of Adolescence, *The Science of Adolescent Risk-Taking: Workshop Report* (Washington, DC: National Academies Press, 2011).
5. Richard M. Ryan and Edward L. Deci, "Brick by Brick: The Origins, Development, and Future of Self-Determination Theory," in *Advances in Motivation Science*, ed. A. J. Elliot (Cambridge, MA: Elsevier Academic Press, 2019), 111–156, https://psycnet.apa.org/doi/10.1016/bs.adms.2019.01.001.
6. Wendy S. Grolnick, interview by Ellen Galinsky, October 27, 2017.
7. Andrew Garner et al., "Preventing Childhood Toxic Stress: Partnering with Families and Communities to Promote Relational Health," *Pediatrics* 148, no. 2 (2021): e2021052582, https://doi.org/10.1542/peds.2021-052582; David Willis, "Advancing a Family-Centered Community Health System: A Community Agenda Focused on Child Health Care, Early Relationships, and Equity," Center for the Study of Social Policy, accessed February 28, 2023, https://cssp.org/resource/advancing-a-fcchs/.
8. Erik H. Erikson, *Identity and the Life Cycle* (New York: W. W. Norton, 1980).
9. Ibid., 87.
10. David E. Hunt, "Person-Environment Interaction: A Challenge Found Wanting Before It Was Tried," *Review of Educational Research* 45, no. 2 (June 1975): 209–230, https://doi.org/10.2307/1170054.
11. Jacquelynne S. Eccles et al., "Development During Adolescence: The Impact of Stage-Environment Fit on Young Adolescents' Experiences in Schools and in Families," *American Psychologist* 48, no. 2 (1993): 90, https://doi.org/10.1037/0003-066X.48.2.90.
12. Ibid.
13. Ibid.
14. Lynn Shore, Jeanette Cleveland, and Diana R. Sanchez, "Inclusive Workplaces: A Review and Model," *Human Resource Management Review* 28, no. 2 (July 2017): 177, https://doi.org/10.1016/j.hrmr.2017.07.003; Roy F. Baumeister and Mark R. Leary, "The Need to Belong: Desire for Interpersonal Attachments as a Fundamental Human Motivation," *Psychological Bulletin* 117, no. 3 (1995): 497, https://doi.org/10.1037/00332909.117.3.497; "Diversity, Inclusion, Belonging and Equity Toolkit," Harvard University, accessed September 26, 2022, https://edib.harvard.edu/diversity-inclusion-belonging-equity-toolkit; Ipshita Pal, Ellen Galinsky, and Stacy Kim, "Employee Health and Well-Being After a Crisis—Reimagining the Role of Workplace Inclusion," *Community, Work and Family* 25, no. 1 (2022): 30–62, https://doi.org/10.1080/13668803.2021.1987859.
15. Kelly-Ann Allen et al., "What Schools Need to Know About Fostering School Belonging: A Meta-Analysis," *Educational Psychology Review* 30, no. 1 (2018): 1–34, https://doi.org/10.1007/s10648-016-9389-8; Jessica P. Montoro et al., "Coping

with Discrimination from Peers and Adults: Implications for Adolescents' School Belonging," *Journal of Youth and Adolescence* 50, no. 1 (2021): 126–143, doi:10.1007/s10964-020-01360-5.

16. Ellen Galinsky and Kimberlee Salmond, *Youth and Violence: Students Speak Out for a More Civil Society* (New York: Families and Work Institute, 2002), https://cdn .sanity.io/files/ow8usu72/production/fc1cdf43e2ee4f396097ee12ebff187bdc26b2f6 .pdf.

17. "The Children We Mean to Raise: The Real Messages Adults Are Sending About Values," Making Caring Common Project of the Harvard Graduate School of Education, July 2014, https://static1.squarespace.com/static/5b7c56e255b02c683659fe43/t /5bae774424a694b5feb2b05f/1538160453604/report-children-raise.pdf.

18. Brené Brown, *The Gifts of Imperfection: Let Go of Who You Think You're Supposed to Be and Embrace Who You Are* (Center City, MN: Hazelden, 2010), 25.

19. John Bowlby, *Attachment and Loss*, vol. 1, *Attachment*, 2nd ed. (New York: Basic Books, 1969); Mary D. Salter Ainsworth et al., *Patterns of Attachment: A Psychological Study of the Strange Situation* (Hillsdale, NJ: Erlbaum, 1978); L. Alan Sroufe, "Attachment and Development: A Prospective, Longitudinal Study from Birth to Adulthood," *Attachment and Human Development* 7, no. 4 (August 16, 2006): 349–367, https://doi.org/10.1080/14616730500365928; Marianne S. Wolff and Marinus H. van Ijzendoorn, "Sensitivity and Attachment: A Meta-Analysis of Parental Antecedents of Infant Attachment," *Child Development* 68 (1997): 571–591, https://doi.org/10.1111/j.1467-8624.1997.tb04218.x; Leah Matas, Richard Arend, and L. Alan Sroufe, "Continuity of Adaptation in the Second Year: The Relationship Between Quality Attachment and Later Competence," *Child Development* 49, no. 3 (September 1978): 547–556, https://doi.org/10.2307/1128221.

20. DYG Inc., "What Grown-Ups Understand About Child Development: A National Benchmark Survey," Civitas Initiative and Brio Corp., 2000, https://eric.ed.gov/?id =ED448909.

21. Jaana Juvonen et al., "Promoting Social Inclusion in Educational Settings: Challenges and Opportunities," *Educational Psychologist* 54, no. 4 (2019): 263, https://doi.org /10.1080/00461520.2019.1655645.

22. Susan Magsamen and Ivy Ross, *Your Brain on Art: How the Arts Transform Us* (New York: Random House, 2023).

23. Susan Magsamen, interview by Ellen Galinsky, April 22, 2022.

24. Elizabeth Levy Paluck, Hana Shepherd, and Peter M. Aronow, "Changing Climates of Conflict: A Social Network Experiment in 56 Schools," *Proceedings of the National Academy of Sciences* 113, no. 3 (January 2016): 566–571, https://doi.org/10 .1073/pnas.1514483113.

25. Robert Pianta, interview by Amy McCampbell, August 3, 2006; Robert Pianta, email message to Ellen Galinsky, February 2, 2023.

26. Erik A. Ruzek et al., "How Teacher Emotional Support Motivates Students: The Mediating Roles of Perceived Peer Relatedness, Autonomy Support, and Competence," *Learning and Instruction* 42 (April 2016): 95–103, https://doi.org/10.1016/j .learninstruc.2016.01.004.

27. Robert Pianta, interview by Amy McCampbell, August 3, 2006; Robert Pianta, email message to Ellen Galinsky, February 2, 2023.

28. Juvonen et al., "Promoting Social Inclusion in Educational Settings," 250. These researchers make the point that meeting needs is a necessity.

29. Allen et al., "What Schools Need to Know About Fostering School Belonging."

30. Miguel E. Thornton et al., "Students Educating Each Other About Discrimination (SEED)," Ann Arbor (MI) Public Schools, 1993, https://eric.ed.gov/?id=ED376223.

31. Gregory M. Walton, interview by Ellen Galinsky, January 11, 2017.

32. Claude M. Steele, "Thin Ice: 'Stereotype Threat' and Black College Students," *Atlantic Monthly*, August 1999, 44–47, 50–54.

33. Claude M. Steele and Joshua Aronson, "Stereotype Threat and the Intellectual Test Performance of African Americans," *Journal of Personality and Social Psychology* 69, no. 5 (November 1995): 797–811, https://doi.org/10.1037//0022-3514.69.5.797.

34. Gregory M. Walton, interview by Ellen Galinsky, January 11, 2017.
35. Gregory M. Walton and Geoffrey L. Cohen, "A Brief Social-Belonging Intervention Improves Academic and Health Outcomes of Minority Students," *Science* 331, no. 6023 (March 2011): 1447–1451, https://doi.org/10.1126/science.1198364; Gregory M. Walton, email message to Ellen Galinsky, February 16, 2023.
36. Walton and Cohen, "A Brief Social-Belonging Intervention," 1448.
37. Gregory M. Walton, interview by Ellen Galinsky, January 11, 2017.
38. Lauren Eskreis-Winkler et al., "A Large-Scale Field Experiment Shows Giving Advice Improves Academic Outcomes for the Advisor," *Proceedings of the National Academy of Sciences* 116, no. 30 (July 2019): 14808–14810, https://doi.org/10.1073/pnas.1908779116.
39. Walton and Cohen, "A Brief Social-Belonging Intervention."
40. Ibid.
41. David S. Yeager et al., "Teaching a Lay Theory Before College Narrows Achievement Gaps at Scale," *Proceedings of the National Academy of Sciences* 113, no. 24 (May 2016): E3341–E3348, https://doi.org/10.1073/pnas.1524360113; Mary Murphy et al., "A Customized Belonging Intervention Improves Retention of Socially Disadvantaged Students at a Broad-Access University," *Science Advances* 6, no. 29 (2020): https://www.science.org/doi/10.1126/sciadv.aba4677.
42. Gregory M. Walton, interview by Ellen Galinsky, January 11, 2017; Gregory M. Walton, email message to Ellen Galinsky, February 16, 2023.
43. Shannon T. Brady et al., "A Brief Social-Belonging Intervention in College Improves Adult Outcomes for Black Americans," *Science Advances* 6, no. 18 (2020): eaay3689, https://doi.org/10.1126/sciadv.aay3689.
44. Gregory M. Walton, interview by Ellen Galinsky, January 11, 2017.
45. Ibid.
46. Dushiyanthini (Toni) Kenthirarajah and Gregory M. Walton, "How Brief Social-Psychological Interventions Can Cause Enduring Effects," in *Emerging Trends in the Social and Behavioral Sciences*, ed. Robert A. Scott and Stephen Michael Kosslyn (Hoboken, NJ: John Wiley and Sons, 2015).
47. Gregory M. Walton et al., "Two Brief Interventions to Mitigate a 'Chilly Climate' Transform Women's Experience, Relationships, and Achievement in Engineering," *Journal of Educational Psychology* 107, no. 2 (2015): 470, https://doi.org/10.1037/a0037461.
48. Gregory M. Walton and Timothy D. Wilson, "Wise Interventions: Psychological Remedies for Social and Personal Problems," *Psychological Review* 125, no. 5 (2018): 617–655, https://doi.org/10.1037/rev0000115.
49. Christina Bethel et al., "Positive Childhood Experiences and Adult Mental and Relational Health in a Statewide Sample: Associates Across Adverse Childhood Experiences Levels," *JAMA Pediatrics* 173, no. 11 (September 2019): e193007, https://doi.org/10.1001/jamapediatrics.2019.3007.
50. Robert A. Karasek, "Job Demands, Job Decision Latitude, and Mental Strain: Implications for Job Redesign," *Administrative Science Quarterly* 24, no. 2 (1979): 285–308, https://doi.org/10.2307/2392498; Sean M. Collins, Robert A. Karasek, and Kevin Costas, "Job Strain and Autonomic Indices of Cardiovascular Disease Risk," *American Journal of Industrial Medicine* 48, no. 3 (2005): 182–193, doi:10.1002/AJIM.20204.
51. Ellen Galinsky, J. T. Bond, and Dana E. Friedman, *The Changing Workforce: Highlights from the National Study* (New York: Families and Work Institute, 1993); J. T. Bond, Ellen Galinsky, and Jennifer Swanberg, *The 1997 National Study of the Changing Workforce* (New York: Families and Work Institute, 1997); J. T. Bond et al., *Highlights of the National Study of the Changing Workforce* (New York: Families and Work Institute, 2003); Kerstin Aumann and Ellen Galinsky, *The State of Health in the American Workforce: Does Having an Effective Workplace Matter?* (New York: Families and Work Institute, 2009).
52. Wendy S. Grolnick, interview by Ellen Galinsky, October 27, 2017.
53. David S. Yeager, interview by Ellen Galinsky, April 4, 2017.
54. S. E. Hinton, *The Outsiders* (New York: Penguin, 1967).

55. David S. Yeager et al., "Declines in Efficacy of Anti-Bullying Programs Among Older Adolescents: Theory and a Three-Level Meta-Analysis," *Journal of Applied Developmental Psychology* 37 (March–April 2015): 37, https://doi.org/10.1016/j.appdev .2014.11.005.

56. Ibid., 36.

57. Ibid., 42.

58. Ibid.

59. Matthew C. Farrelly et al., "Sustaining 'Truth': Changes in Youth Tobacco Attitudes and Smoking Intentions After 3 Years of a National Antismoking Campaign," *Health Education Research* 24, no. 1 (February 2009): 42–48, https://doi.org/10.1093/her /cym087; Matthew C. Farrelly et al., "The Influence of the National Truth Campaign on Smoking Initiation," *American Journal of Preventive Medicine* 36, no. 5 (May 2009): 379–384, https://doi.org/10.1016/j.amepre.2009.01.019.

60. Wendy S. Grolnick et al., "Parental Provision of Academic Structure and the Transition to Middle School," *Journal of Research on Adolescence* 25, no. 4 (2015): 668, https://doi.org/10.1111/jora.12161.

61. Wendy S. Grolnick, interview with Ellen Galinsky, October 27, 2017.

62. Melanie S. Farkas and Wendy S. Grolnick, "Examining the Components and Concomitants of Parental Structure in the Academic Domain," *Motivation and Emotion* 34, no. 3 (September 2010): 266–279, https://doi.org/10.1007/s11031 -010-9176-7.

63. Grolnick et al., "Parental Provision of Academic Structure," 668–684.

64. Ibid.

65. Madeline R. Levitt, Wendy S. Grolnick, and Jacquelyn N. Raftery-Helmer, "Maternal Control and Children's Internalizing and Externalizing Symptoms in the Context of Neighbourhood Safety: Moderating and Mediating Models," *Journal of Family Studies* 28, no. 4 (November 2020): 1543–1565, https://doi.org/10.1080/13229400 .2020.1845779.

66. Rachel E. Lerner and Wendy S. Grolnick, "Maternal Involvement and Children's Academic Motivation and Achievement: The Roles of Maternal Autonomy Support and Children's Affect," *Motivation and Emotion* 44, no. 3 (June 2020): 378, https:// doi.org/10.1007/s11031-019-09813-6.

67. Wendy S. Grolnick, email message to Ellen Galinsky, February 2, 2021.

68. Levitt, Grolnick, and Raftery-Helmer, "Maternal Control and Children's Internalizing and Externalizing Symptoms," 19.

69. Wendy S. Grolnick et al., "Parental Provision of Structure: Implementation and Correlates in Three Domains," *Merrill-Palmer Quarterly* 60, no. 3. (July 2014): 377–378, https://doi.org/10.1353/mpq.2014.0016.

70. Wendy S. Grolnick, email message to Ellen Galinsky, February 2, 2021.

71. Lerner and Grolnick, "Maternal Involvement and Children's Academic Motivation and Achievement."

72. Wendy S. Grolnick, interview by Ellen Galinsky, October 27, 2017; Wendy S. Grolnick, email message to Ellen Galinsky, February 4, 2023.

73. David S. Yeager, Ronald E. Dahl, and Carol S. Dweck, "Why Interventions to Influence Adolescent Behavior Often Fail but Could Succeed," *Perspectives on Psychological Science* 13, no. 1 (January 2018): 101–122, https://doi.org/10.1177 /1745691617722620.

74. Ibid., 101.

75. Ibid., 104.

76. David S. Yeager, interview by Ellen Galinsky, April 4, 2017.

77. Yeager, Dahl, and Dweck, "Why Interventions to Influence Adolescent Behavior Often Fail but Could Succeed," 104.

78. Megan R. Gunnar et al., "Developmental Changes in Hypothalamus-Pituitary-Adrenal Activity over the Transition to Adolescence: Normative Changes and Associations with Puberty," *Development and Psychopathology* 21, no. 1 (January 2009): 69–85, https://doi.org/10.1017/S0954579409000054.

79. Yeager, Dahl, and Dweck, "Why Interventions to Influence Adolescent Behavior Often Fail but Could Succeed," 106.
80. Jason A. Okonofua, interview by Ellen Galinsky, January 10, 2017.
81. Ibid.
82. "The Transformed CRDC: Data Summary," Office for Civil Rights, accessed March 23, 2012, https://www2.ed.gov/about/offices/list/ocr/data.html?src=rt, cited in Jason A. Okonofua and Jennifer L. Eberhardt, "Two Strikes: Race and the Disciplining of Young Students," *Psychological Science* 26, no. 5 (May 2015): 617–624, https://doi.org/10.1177/0956797615570365.
83. "About Jennifer Lynn Eberhardt," Stanford University, accessed November 28, 2021, https://web.stanford.edu/~eberhard/about-jennifer-eberhardt.html.
84. Okonofua and Eberhardt, "Two Strikes."
85. Jason A. Okonofua, interview by Ellen Galinsky, January 10, 2017.
86. Christine Koh, "The Adults Who Saved Me + What You Need to Know About ACEs," May 6, 2019, https://www.christinekoh.com/blog/2019/5/the-adults-who -saved-me-what-you-need-to-know-about-aces.
87. Shawn Ginwright, "The Future of Healing: Shifting From Trauma Informed Care to Healing Centered Engagement," Medium, May 31, 2018, https://ginwright.medium .com/the-future-of-healing-shifting-from-trauma-informed-care-to-healing-centered -engagement-634f557ce69c.
88. Pamela Cantor, interview by Ellen Galinsky and Dan Wuori, July 26, 2021.
89. Jason A. Okonofua, David Paunesku, and Gregory M. Walton, "Brief Intervention to Encourage Empathic Discipline Cuts Suspension Rates in Half Among Adolescents," *Proceedings of the National Academy of Sciences* 113, no. 19 (May 2016): 5221, https://doi.org/10.1073/pnas.1523698113.
90. Ibid.
91. Gregory M. Walton, interview by Ellen Galinsky, January 11, 2017.
92. Jason A. Okonofua, interview by Ellen Galinsky, January 10, 2017.
93. Gregory M. Walton, interview by Ellen Galinsky, January 11, 2017.
94. Jason A. Okonofua, interview by Ellen Galinsky, January 10, 2017.
95. Ibid.
96. Okonofua, Paunesku, and Walton, "Brief Intervention to Encourage Empathic Discipline," 5221–5226.
97. Jason A. Okonofua, interview by Ellen Galinsky, January 10, 2017.
98. Gregory M. Walton, interview by Ellen Galinsky, January 11, 2017.
99. Okonofua, Paunesku, and Walton, "Brief Intervention to Encourage Empathic Discipline," 5221–5226.
100. Gregory M. Walton, interview by Ellen Galinsky, January 11, 2017.
101. Jason A. Okonofua et al., "A Scalable Empathic-Mindset Intervention Reduces Group Disparities in School Suspensions," *Science Advances* 8, no. 12 (2022): eabj0691, https://10.1126/sciadv.abj0691.
102. Gregory M. Walton, interview by Ellen Galinsky, January 11, 2017.
103. Jason A. Okonofua, interview by Ellen Galinsky, January 10, 2017.
104. Martin Pinquart, "Associations of Parenting Styles and Dimensions with Academic Achievement in Children and Adolescents: A Meta-Analysis," *Educational Psychology Review* 28, no. 3 (2016): 475–493, https://psycnet.apa.org/doi/10.1007 /s10648-015-9338-y; Martin Pinquart, "Associations of Parenting Dimensions and Styles with Internalizing Symptoms in Children and Adolescents: A Meta-Analysis," *Marriage and Family Review* 53, no. 7 (2017): 613–640, https://doi.org/10.1080 /01494929.2016.1247761; Martin Pinquart, "Associations of Parenting Dimensions and Styles with Externalizing Problems of Children and Adolescents: An Updated Meta-Analysis," *Developmental Psychology* 53, no. 5 (2017): 873, https://doi.org/10 .1037/dev0000295.
105. Barbara Schneider, interview by Ellen Galinsky, April 20, 2017.
106. Mihaly Csikszentmihalyi, *Flow: The Psychology of Optimal Experience* (New York: Harper Perennial, 2008).

107. Mihaly Csikszentmihalyi, "Flow, the Secret to Happiness," TED, February 2004, https://www.ted.com/talks/mihaly_csikszentmihalyi_flow_the_secret_to_happiness ?language=en#t-20282.
108. Csikszentmihalyi, *Flow*, 3.
109. Ibid., 4.
110. Jennifer A. Fredricks, *Eight Myths of Student Engagement: Creating Classrooms of Deep Learning* (Thousand Oaks, CA: Corwin, 2014).
111. Barbara Schneider et al., "Investigating Optimal Learning Moments in U.S. and Finnish Science Classes," *Journal of Research in Science Teaching* 53, no. 3 (March 2016): 400–421, https://doi.org/10.1002/tea.21306.
112. Barbara Schneider, interview by Ellen Galinsky, April 20, 2017.
113. Schneider et al., "Investigating Optimal Learning Moments."
114. Ibid., 403.
115. Barbara Schneider, interview by Ellen Galinsky, April 20, 2017.
116. Anthony Doerr, *All the Light We Cannot See* (New York: Scribner, 2014).
117. Kalle Juuti et al., "A Teacher–Researcher Partnership for Professional Learning: Co-Designing Project-Based Learning Units to Increase Student Engagement in Science Classes," *Journal of Science Teacher Education* 32, no. 4 (March 2021): 1–17, https://doi.org/10.1080/1046560X.2021.1872207.
118. Joseph Krajcik, interview by Ellen Galinsky, April 20, 2017.
119. Juuti et al., "A Teacher–Researcher Partnership for Professional Learning."
120. Barbara Schneider, interview by Ellen Galinsky, April 20, 2017.
121. Katariina Salmela-Aro et al., "Integrating the Light and Dark Sides of Student Engagement Using Person-Oriented and Situation-Specific Approaches," *Learning and Instruction* 43, no. 3 (January 2016): 61–70, https://doi.org/10.1016/j.learninstruc.2016.01.001.
122. Barbara Schneider, interview by Ellen Galinsky, April 20, 2017.
123. Janna Inkinen et al., "High School Students' Situational Engagement Associated with Scientific Practices in Designed Science Learning Situations," *Science Education* 104, no. 4 (February 2020): 667–692, https://doi.org/10.1002/sce.21570.
124. Barbara Schneider, interview by Ellen Galinsky, April 20, 2017.
125. Jennifer A. Fredricks, interview by Ellen Galinsky, June 9, 2017; Jennifer A. Fredricks, Phyllis C. Blumenfeld, and Alison H. Paris, "Potential of the Concept, State of the Evidence," *Review of Educational Research* 74, no. 1 (March 1, 2004): 59–109, https://doi.org/10.3102/00346543074001059; Fredricks, *Eight Myths of Student Engagement*; Jennifer A. Fredricks et al., "What Matters for Urban Adolescents' Engagement and Disengagement in School: A Mixed-Methods Study," *Journal of Adolescent Research* 34, no. 5 (September 2019): 491–527, https://doi.org/10.1177/0743558419830638.
126. Fredricks et al., "What Matters for Urban Adolescents' Engagement and Disengagement," 492.
127. Johnmarshall Reeve, "A Self-Determination Theory Perspective on Student Engagement," in *Handbook of Research on Student Engagement*, ed. Sandra L. Christenson, Amy L. Reschly, and Cathy Wylie (Boston: Springer, 2012), 149–172, https://doi.org/10.1007/978-1-4614-2018-7_7.
128. Yibing Li and Richard M. Lerner, "Trajectories of School Engagement During Adolescence: Implications for Grades, Depression, Delinquency, and Substance Use," *Developmental Psychology* 47, no. 1 (2011): 233–247, https://doi.org/10.1037/a0021307.
129. Ibid.
130. National Research Council, *How People Learn: Brain, Mind, Experience, and School: Expanded Edition* (Washington, DC: National Academies Press, 2000), https://doi.org/10.17226/9853.
131. National Academies of Sciences, Engineering, and Medicine, *How People Learn II: Learners, Contexts, and Cultures* (Washington, DC: National Academies Press, 2018), https://doi.org/10.17226/24783.

132. Ibid., 5.
133. Ibid., 109.
134. Wendy S. Grolnick, "Meeting Development Needs," Adolescent Virtual Speaking Series, Bezos Family Foundation, October 13, 2020.
135. Ibid.; Wendy S. Grolnick, interview by Ellen Galinsky, October 27, 2017; Wendy S. Grolnick, email message to Ellen Galinsky, February 4, 2023.
136. Wendy S. Grolnick, email message to Ellen Galinsky, September 5, 2022.
137. Wendy S. Grolnick, interview by Ellen Galinsky, October 27, 2017; Wendy S. Grolnick, briefing for the Bezos Family Foundation, October 12, 2020; Ryan and Deci, *Self-Determination Theory*; Deci, "Brick by Brick," 111–156.
138. Joseph P. Allen and Claudia Worrell Allen, "The Big Wait," *Educational Leadership: Journal of the Department of Supervision and Curriculum Development, N.E.A.* 68, no. 1 (September 2010): 22–26.
139. Andrew J. Elliot and Chris S. Hulleman, "Achievement Goals," in *Handbook of Competence and Motivation: Theory and Application*, 2nd ed., ed. Andrew J. Elliot, Carol S. Dweck, and David S. Yeager (New York: Guilford Press, 2017), 43–60.
140. Ibid.
141. Stéphane Duchesne and Simon Larose, "Academic Competence and Achievement Goals: Self-Pressure and Disruptive Behaviors as Mediators," *Learning and Individual Differences* 68 (December 2018): 42, https://doi.org/10.1016/J.LINDIF.2018.09.008.
142. Stéphane Duchesne and Catherine F. Ratelle, "Achievement Goals, Motivation, and Social and Emotional Adjustment in High School: A Longitudinal Mediation Test," *Educational Psychology: An International Journal of Experimental Educational Psychology* 40, no. 8 (June 2020): 1046, https://doi.org/10.1080/01443410.2020.1778641.
143. Beth Bye, interview by Ellen Galinsky and Dan Wuori, April 15, 2021.
144. Lisa Damour, *Under Pressure: Confronting the Epidemic of Stress and Anxiety in Girls* (New York: Ballantine Books, 2019).
145. Lisa Damour, *The Emotional Lives of Teenagers: Raising Connected, Capable, and Compassionate Adolescents* (New York: Ballantine Books, 2023).
146. Julie Lythcott-Haims, *How to Raise an Adult: Break Free of the Overparenting Trap and Prepare Your Kid for Success* (New York: St. Martin's Griffin, 2016).
147. Office of the Surgeon General, *Protecting Youth Mental Health: The U.S. Surgeon General's Advisory 2021*, U.S. Department of Health and Human Services, https://www.hhs.gov/sites/default/files/surgeon-general-youth-mental-health-advisory.pdf.
148. Nicole Racine et al., "Global Prevalence of Depressive and Anxiety Symptoms in Children and Adolescents During COVID-19: A Meta-Analysis," *JAMA Pediatrics* 175, no. 11 (2021): 1142–1150, https://doi.org/10.1001/jamapediatrics.2021.2482.
149. Damour, *Under Pressure* and *The Emotional Lives of Teenagers*.
150. Richard S. Lazarus and Susan Folkman, *Stress, Appraisal, and Coping* (New York: Springer, 1984); Robert Karasek, "Low Social Control and Physiological Deregulation—The Stress-Disequilibrium Theory, Towards a New Demand-Control Model," *Scandinavian Journal of Work, Environment and Health Supplements* 6, no. 6 (January 2008): 117–135, https://www.sjweh.fi/show_abstract.php?abstract_id=1259.
151. Carol S. Dweck, *Mindset: The New Psychology of Success* (New York: Ballantine Books, 2007).
152. Carol S. Dweck and Daniel C. Molden, "Mindsets: Their Impact on Competence Motivation and Acquisition," in *Handbook of Competence and Motivation: Theory and Application*, 2nd ed., ed. Andrew J. Elliot, Carol S. Dweck, and David S. Yeager (New York: Guilford Press, 2017), 135.
153. Carol S. Dweck, *Self-Theories: Their Role in Motivation, Personality, and Development* (Philadelphia: Psychology Press, 1999).
154. David S. Yeager, Hae Yeon Lee, and Jeremy P. Jamieson, "How to Improve Adolescent Stress Responses: Insights from Integrating Implicit Theories of Personality and

Biopsychosocial Models," *Psychological Science* 27, no. 8 (August 2016): 1078–1091, https://doi.org/10.1177/0956797616649604.

155. David S. Yeager, interview by Ellen Galinsky, April 4, 2017.

156. Yeager, Lee, and Jamieson, "How to Improve Adolescent Stress Responses."

157. Elliot and Hulleman, "Achievement Goals," 47.

158. David S. Yeager et al., "Breaking the Cycle of Mistrust: Wise Interventions to Provide Critical Feedback Across the Racial Divide," *Journal of Experimental Psychology: General* 143, no. 2 (2017): 804–824, https://doi.org/10.1037/a0033906.

159. Ibid., 804.

160. Lisa S. Blackwell, Kali H. Trzesniewski, and Carol Sorich Dweck, "Implicit Theories of Intelligence Predict Achievement Across an Adolescent Transition: A Longitudinal Study and an Intervention," *Child Development* 78, no. 1 (2007): 246–263, https://doi.org/10.1111/j.1467-8624.2007.00995.x.

161. Carol Dweck, interview by Ellen Galinsky, April 17, 2008, reported in Ellen Galinsky, *Mind in the Making: The Seven Essential Life Skills Every Child Needs* (New York: HarperStudio, 2010), 295–296.

162. Carol Dweck, interview by Ellen Galinsky, April 17, 2008.

163. Carol S. Dweck, "Praise the Effort, Not the Outcome? Think Again," Student Experience Research Network, March 23, 2016, https://studentexperiencenetwork.org /praise-the-effort-not-the-outcome-think-again/#.

164. Ibid.

165. Ellen Galinsky, *The Six Stages of Parenthood* (Boston: A Merloyd Lawrence Book, 1987).

166. Erik H. Erikson, *Childhood and Society* (New York: W. W. Norton, 1963), 147–174.

167. Sue Erikson Bloland, *In the Shadow of Fame: A Memoir by the Daughter of Erik H. Erikson* (New York: Penguin Books, 2006).

168. Lawrence J. Friedman, *Identity's Architect: A Biography of Erik H. Erikson* (New York: Scribner, 1999), 147.

169. Kate C. McLean and Moin Syed, "The Field of Identity Development Needs an Identity: An Introduction to the *Handbook of Identity Development*," in *Oxford Handbook of Identity Development*, ed. Kate C. McLean and Moin Syed (New York: Oxford University Press, 2015), 1–10; Erikson, *Childhood and Society*; Erik H. Erikson, *Identity and the Life Cycle* (New York: W. W. Norton, 1980); Erik H. Erikson, *Identity: Youth and Crisis* (New York: W. W. Norton, 1968).

170. Erik H. Erikson, *Gandhi's Truth: On the Origins of Militant Nonviolence* (New York: W. W. Norton, 1969), 265–266.

171. McLean and Syed, "The Field of Identity Development Needs an Identity," 4.

172. Jacqueline Nesi, Sophia Choukas-Bradley, and Mitchell J. Prinstein, "Transformation of Adolescent Peer Relations in the Social Media Context: Part 1—A Theoretical Framework and Application to Dyadic Peer Relationships," *Clinical Child Family Psychology Review* 21, no. 3 (September 2018): 267–294, https://doi.org/10.1007 /s10576-018-0261-x.

173. David Elkind, "Egocentrism in Adolescence," in *Readings in Developmental Psychology*, 2nd ed., ed. Judith Krieger Gardner and Ed Gardner (Boston: Little, Brown, 1967), 383–390; David Elkind, "Egocentrism in Adolescence," *Child Development* 38, no. 4 (1967): 1025–1033.

174. Jean Piaget, *Science of Education and the Psychology of the Child* (New York: Viking Press, 1970).

175. Dan P. McAdams and Claudia Zapata-Gietl, "Three Strands of Identity Development Across the Human Life Course: Reading Erik Erikson in Full," in *The Oxford Handbook of Identity Development*, ed. Kate C. McLean and Moin Syed (New York: Oxford University Press, 2015), 81–94.

176. Ibid., 83.

177. Erikson, *Identity: Youth and Crisis*, 23.

178. McAdams and Zapata-Gietl, "Three Strands of Identity Development," 83.

179. Ibid., 89.

180. McAdams and Zapata-Gietl, "Three Strands of Identity Development," 83; Dan P. McAdams and Bradley D. Olson, "Personality Development: Continuity and Change over the Life Course," *Annual Review of Psychology* 61 (January 2010): 517–542, https://doi.org/10.1146/annurev.psych.093008.100507.

181. Dan P. McAdams, interview by Ellen Galinsky, June 7, 2021.

182. "Student Reports of Bullying: Results from the 2017 School Crime Supplement to the National Crime Victimization Survey," National Center for Educational Statistics, July 2019, https://nces.ed.gov/pubs2019/2019054.pdf; "Youth Risk Behavior Survey: Data Summary and Trends Report, 2011–2021," Centers for Disease Control and Prevention, 2023, https://www.cdc.gov/healthyyouth/data/yrbs/pdf/YRBS_Data -Summary-Trends_Report2023_508.pdf.

183. Diane Hughes, "Context Matters—Parenting and Peer Relationships, Positive Risk," Adolescent Virtual Speaking Series, Bezos Family Foundation, February 11, 2021.

184. "How Did I Get Here: My Journey to Developmental Science," YouTube, posted by Society for Research in Child Development, January 10, 2020, https://www.youtube .com/watch?v=KZgCjlCf6cs.

185. Diane Hughes, "Teaching Race to Children and Adolescents," webinar, University-Based Child and Family Policy Consortium, in collaboration with SRCD, March 13, 2017, https://www.srcd.org/event/teaching-race-children-and-adolescents.

186. Hughes, "Context Matters."

187. Robert P. Jones et al., "Diversity, Division, Discrimination: The State of Young America," PRRI, January 2018, https://www.prri.org/wp-content/uploads/2018/01/PRRI -MTV-Survey-Report-FINAfL.pdf.

188. Hughes, "Context Matters"; Nancy Gagnier, "Talking to Children About Racism with Dr. Diane Hughes," Community Coalition on Race, September 1, 2020, https:// www.communitycoalitiononrace.org/talking_to_children_about_racism; Iheoma U. Iruka et al., "Effects of Racism on Child Development: Advancing Antiracist Developmental Science," *Annual Review of Developmental Psychology* 4, no. 1 (2022): 109–132, https://doi.org/10.1146/annurev-devpsych-121020-031339.

189. Diane Hughes et al., "Trajectories of Discrimination Across Adolescence: Associations with Academic, Psychological, and Behavioral Outcomes," *Child Development* 87, no. 5 (September–October 2016): 1348, https://doi.org/10.1111/cdev.12591.

190. Ethan Kross, *Chatter* (New York: Crown, 2021).

191. Yeager, Lee, and Jamieson, "How to Improve Adolescent Stress Responses," 1078–1091.

192. David S. Yeager, interview by Ellen Galinsky, April 4, 2017.

193. Deborah Rivas-Drake and Adriana J. Umaña-Taylor, *Below the Surface: Talking with Teens About Race, Ethnicity, and Identity* (Princeton, NJ: Princeton University Press, 2019), 54.

194. Ibid., 55 (the word "resolution" is italicized in the original).

195. Lara Galinsky with Kelly Nuxoll, *Work on Purpose* (New York: Echoing Green, 2011), 6.

196. Ibid., 8.

197. Shari Camhi, "The Road to Future-Driven Learning in Baldwin Union Free School District," Future-Driven Learning Summit, School Superintendents Association (AASA), Baldwin, New York, March 1–3, 2023.

198. Dan P. McAdams, interview by Ellen Galinsky, June 7, 2021.

199. Christopher Baldassano et al., "Discovering Event Structure in Continuous Narrative Perception and Memory," *Neuron* 95, no. 3 (August 2017): 709–721.e5, https://doi .org/10.1016/j.neuron.2017.06.041; James Somers, "The Science of Mind Reading," *New Yorker*, December 6, 2021, https://www.newyorker.com/magazine/2021/12/06 /the-science-of-mind-reading.

200. Dan P. McAdams, interview by Ellen Galinsky, June 7, 2021.

201. Dan P. McAdams and Kate C. McLean, "Narrative Identity," *Current Directions in Psychological Science* 22, no. 3 (June 2013): 234, https://doi.org/10.1177 /0963721413475622.

202. Ibid.

203. Robyn Fivush and Fayne A. Fromhoff, "Style and Structure in Mother-Child Conver-
     sations About the Past," *Discourse Processes* 11, no. 3 (1988): 337–355, https://
     doi.org/10.1080/01638538809544707; Robyn Fivush, Catherine A. Haden, and
     Elaine Reese, "Elaborating on Elaborations: Role of Maternal Reminiscing Style in
     Cognitive and Socioemotional Development," *Child Development* 77, no. 6 (2006):
     1568–1588, http://www.jstor.org/stable/4139261.
204. FamilySearch, "The Science Behind Family Stories (Robyn Fivush Live)," You-
     Tube, posted December 9, 2020, https://www.youtube.com/watch?v=VCCll
     VY4460&list=PLGng78LVGBHFHc43LeCqkdJ5O0Zmv7v_U&index=3; Jennifer G.
     Bohanek et al., "Narrative Interaction in Family Dinnertime Conversations," *Merrill-
     Palmer Quarterly* 55, no. 4 (October 2009): 488–515, https://doi.org/10.1353/mpq
     .0.0031.
205. Marshall P. Duke, Amber Lazarus, and Robyn Fivush, "Knowledge of Family History
     as a Clinically Useful Index of Psychological Well-Being and Prognosis: A Brief
     Report," *Psychotherapy Theory, Research, Practice, Training* 45, no. 2 (June 2008):
     268–272, https://doi.org/10.1037/0033-3204.45.2.268.
206. "The Science Behind Family Stories."
207. Robyn Fivush and Widaad Zaman, "Gendered Narrative Voices: Sociocultural and
     Feminist Approaches to Emerging Identity in Childhood and Adolescence," in *The
     Oxford Handbook of Identity Development*, ed. Kate C. McLean and Moin Syed
     (New York: Oxford University Press, 2015), 33–52.
208. Kate C. McLean, Andrea V. Breen, and Marc Fournier, "Constructing the Self in
     Early, Middle, and Late Adolescent Boys: Narrative Identity, Individuation, and Well-
     Being," *Journal of Research on Adolescence* 20, no. 1 (February 2010): 166–187,
     https://doi.org/10.1111/j.1532-7795.2009.00633.x.
209. Fivush and Zaman, "Gendered Narrative Voices."
210. McAdams and McLean, "Narrative Identity."
211. Joan B. Kelly, "Risk and Protective Factors Associated with Child and Adolescent
     Adjustment Following Separation and Divorce: Social Science Applications," in
     Parenting Plan Evaluations: Applied Research for the Family Court, ed. Kathryn
     Kuehnle and Leslie Drozd (New York: Oxford University Press, 2012), 49–84, https://
     doi.org/10.1093/med:psych/9780199754021.003.0003.
212. "The NeuroArts Blueprint: Advancing the Science of Arts, Health, and Wellbeing
     Initiative," NeuroArts Blueprint, November 2021, https://neuroartsblueprint.org/wp
     -content/uploads/2021/11/NeuroArtsBlue_ExSumReport_FinalOnline_spreads_v32
     .pdf.
213. Mary Catherine Bateson, *Composing a Life* (New York: Grove Press, 2001).
214. Dan P. McAdams, "Personal Narratives and the Life Story," in *Handbook of Person-
     ality: Theory and Research*, ed. Oliver P. John, Richard W. Robins, and Lawrence A.
     Pervin (New York: Guilford Press, 2008), 242–262.
215. Viktor E. Frankl, *Man's Search for Meaning* (Boston: Beacon Press, 2017).
216. Ibid., 77.
217. Ibid., 80.
218. William Damon, interview by Ellen Galinsky, March 15, 2015.
219. William Damon, "My Research Life and Times," in *The Developmental Science of
     Adolescence: History Through Autobiography*, ed. Richard M. Lerner et al. (New
     York: Psychology Press, 2014), 104.
220. William Damon, interview by Ellen Galinsky, March 15, 2015.
221. Damon, "My Research Life and Times," 104.
222. William Damon, interview by Ellen Galinsky, March 15, 2015.
223. "About," Search Institute, accessed September 28, 2022, https://searchinstitute.org
     /about.
224. William Damon, interview by Ellen Galinsky, March 15, 2015.
225. Ibid.
226. William Damon, *The Path to Purpose: How Young People Find Their Calling in Life*
     (New York: Free Press, 2008).
227. Ibid., 59–60.

228. William Damon, Jenni Menon, and Kendall Cotton Bronk, "The Development of Purpose During Adolescence," *Applied Developmental Science* 7, no. 3 (July 2003): 121, https://doi.org/10.1207/S1532480XADS0703_2.

229. Heather Malin, *Teaching for Purpose: Preparing Students for Lives of Meaning* (Cambridge, MA: Harvard Education Press, 2018), 59–61.

230. Anthony Burrow, interview by Ellen Galinsky, July 2, 2021.

231. Patrick L. Hill et al., "Sense of Purpose Moderates the Associations Between Daily Stressors and Daily Well-Being," *Annals of Behavioral Medicine* 52, no. 8 (2018): 724–729, https://doi.org/10.1093/abm/kax039.

232. Patrick L. Hill et al., "The Value of a Purposeful Life: Sense of Purpose Predicts Greater Income and Net Worth," *Journal of Research in Personality* 65 (December 2016): 41, https://doi.org/10.1016/j.jrp.2016.07.003.

233. Anthony L. Burrow and Patrick Hill, "Purpose as a Form of Identity Capital for Positive Youth Adjustment," *Developmental Psychology* 47, no. 4 (July 2011): 1196–1206, https://doi.org/10.1037/a0023818.

234. Anthony Burrow, interview by Ellen Galinsky, July 2, 2021.

235. Anthony L. Burrow et al., "Are All Purposes Worth Having? Integrating Content and Strength in Purpose Research," *Human Development* 65, no. 2 (June 2021): 101, https://doi.org/10.1159/000515176.

236. Lara Galinsky, "Core Principles," The Genuine, accessed January 7, 2021, https://thegenuine.org/core-principles.

237. Laurence Steinberg, *Age of Opportunity: Lessons from the New Science of Adolescence* (Boston: Houghton Mifflin Harcourt, 2014).

238. Bruce Feiler, *The Secrets of Happy Families: Everything You Need to Improve Your Mornings, Rethink Family Dinner, Fight Smarter, Go Out and Play, and Much More* (New York: William Morrow, 2013).

239. Stephen R. Covey, *The 7 Habits of Highly Effective Families: Creating a Nurturing Family in a Turbulent World* (New York: St. Martin's Griffin, 1997).

240. Bruce Feiler, "The Happy Families Toolkit: Everything You Need to Improve Your Mornings, Rethink Family Dinner, Fight Smarter, Go Out and Play, and Much More," October 2019, https://www.brucefeiler.com/wp-content/uploads/2019/10/Happy-Families-Toolkit-1.pdf.

241. Andrew J. Fuligni, "Adolescents Have a Fundamental Need to Contribute," The Conversation, February 15, 2019, https://theconversation.com/adolescents-have-a-fundamental-need-to-contribute-110424.

242. Andrew J. Fuligni, "The Need to Contribute During Adolescence," *Perspectives on Psychological Science* 14, no. 3 (May 2019): 331, https://doi.org/10.1177/1745691618805437.

243. Andrew J. Fuligni, interview by Ellen Galinsky, May 4, 2017.

244. Fuligni, "Adolescents Have a Fundamental Need to Contribute."

245. Andrew J. Fuligni, interview by Ellen Galinsky, May 4, 2017.

246. Eva H. Telzer and Andrew J. Fuligni, "Daily Family Assistance and the Psychological Well-Being of Adolescents from Latin American, Asian, and European Backgrounds," *Developmental Psychology* 45, no. 4 (July 2009): 1177–1189, https://doi.org/10.1037/a0014728.

247. Andrew J. Fuligni, interview by Ellen Galinsky, May 4, 2017.

248. Eva H. Telzer et al., "Gaining While Giving: An fMRI Study of the Rewards of Family Assistance Among White and Latino Youth," *Social Neuroscience* 5, nos. 5–6 (October 2010): 508–518, https//doi.org/10.1080/17470911003687913.

249. Eva H. Telzer et al., "Neural Regions Associated with Self Control and Mentalizing Are Recruited During Prosocial Behaviors Towards the Family," *NeuroImage* 58, no. 1 (September 2011): 242–249, https://doi.org/10.1016/neuroimage.2011.06.013.

250. Andrew J. Fuligni, interview by Ellen Galinsky, May 4, 2017.

251. Fuligni, "Adolescents Have a Fundamental Need to Contribute."

252. Gerard Senehi, interview by Ellen Galinsky, December 28, 2021; Gerard Senehi, email message to Ellen Galinsky, February 10, 2023.

253. Letter to Gerard Senehi from a student, "The Beauty That Is the QUESTion Project," sent to Ellen Galinsky, December 29, 2021.
254. Gerard Senehi, interview by Ellen Galinsky, December 28, 2021; Gerard Senehi, email message to Ellen Galinsky, February 10, 2023.
255. Gerard Senehi, email message to Ellen Galinsky, February 13, 2023.
256. Gerard Senehi, interview by Ellen Galinsky, December 28, 2021; Gerard Senehi, email message to Ellen Galinsky, February 10, 2023.
257. Heather Malin, "A Qualitative Impact Study of the QUESTion Project," Summary Report, Stanford Center for Adolescence, 2022.
258. "The QUESTion Project at BCSM, South Bronx," Open Future Institute, accessed January 17, 2023, https://openfutureinstitute.org/the-question-project-at-bcsm-south -bronx/.
259. Feiler, "The Happy Families Toolkit."
260. "Protecting Youth Mental Health: The U.S. Surgeon General's Advisory, 2021," U.S. Department of Health and Human Services, 2021, https://www.hhs.gov/sites/default /files/surgeon-general-youth-mental-health-advisory.pdf.
261. "U.S. Surgeon General Issues Advisory on Youth Mental Health Crisis Further Exposed by COVID-19 Pandemic," U.S. Department of Health and Human Services, December 7, 2021, https://www.hhs.gov/about/news/2021/12/07/us-surgeon -general-issues-advisory-on-youth-mental-health-crisis-further-exposed-by-covid-19 -pandemic.html.
262. "Youth Risk Behavior Survey: Data Summary and Trends Report, 2011–2021."

5. Message 5: We Are Drawn to Learn Life and Learning Skills

1. Philip David Zelazo, interview by Ellen Galinsky, December 8, 2008.
2. Philip David Zelazo and Stephanie M. Carlson, "Hot and Cool Executive Function in Childhood and Adolescence: Development and Plasticity," *Child Development Perspectives* 6, no. 4 (December 2012): 354–360, https://doi.org/10.1111/j.1750-8606 .2012.00246.x.
3. Akira Miyake et al., "The Unity and Diversity of Executive Functions and Their Contributions to Complex 'Frontal Lobe' Tasks: A Latent Variable Analysis," *Cognitive Psychology* 41, no. 1 (August 2000): 49–100, https://doi.org/10.1006/cogp.1999.0734.
4. Philip David Zelazo, interview by Ellen Galinsky, June 26, 2017.
5. Ellen Galinsky et al., "Civic Science for Public Use: Mind in the Making and Vroom," *Child Development* 88 (July 2017): 1410, https://doi.org/10.1111/cdev.12892.
6. Ibid.
7. Ibid.; Stephanie M. Carlson, Philip David Zelazo, and Susan Faja, "Executive Function," in *The Oxford Handbook of Developmental Psychology*, vol. 1, *Body and mind*, ed. Philip David Zelazo (New York: Oxford University Press, 2013), 706–743; Susan E. Gathercole et al., "Working Memory Skills and Educational Attainment: Evidence from National Curriculum Assessments at 7 and 14 Years of Age," *Applied Cognitive Psychology* 18, no. 1 (2004): 1–16, https://doi.org/10.1002/acp.934; Megan M. McClelland et al., "Self-Regulation: The Integration of Cognition and Emotion," in *Handbook of Life-Span Human Development: Cognition, Biology and Methods*, ed. Willis F. Overton and Richard Lerner (Hoboken, NJ: Wiley, 2010), 1: 509–553; M. Rosario Rueda et al., "Training, Maturation, and Genetic Influences on the Development of Executive Attention," *Proceedings of the National Academy of Sciences* 102, no. 41 (October 2005): 14931–14936.
8. Philip David Zelazo, Clancy B. Blair, and Michael T. Willoughby, *Executive Function: Implications for Education*, NCER 2017–2000 (Washington, DC: National Center for Education Research, Institute of Education Sciences, U.S. Department of Education, 2016), 6.
9. Adele Diamond and Daphne S. Ling, "Conclusions About Interventions, Programs, and Approaches for Improving Executive Functions That Appear Justified and Those That, Despite Much Hype, Do Not," *Developmental Cognitive Neuroscience* 18 (April 2016): 35, https://doi.org/10.1016/j.dcn.2015.11.005.

10. National Scientific Council on the Developing Child, "Building the Brain's 'Air Traffic Control' System: How Early Experiences Shape the Development of Executive Function," Working Paper No. 11, Center on the Developing Child at Harvard University, February 2011, https://developingchild.harvard.edu/resources/building-the-brains-air -traffic-control-system-how-early-experiences-shape-the-development-of-executive -function/.

11. Ibid., 4.

12. National Academies of Sciences, Engineering, and Medicine, *The Promise of Adolescence: Realizing Opportunity for All Youth* (Washington, DC: National Academies Press, 2019), https://doi.org/10.17226/25388.

13. Jennifer Silvers, interview by Ellen Galinsky, May 5, 2017.

14. Eveline A. Crone, *The Adolescent Brain: Changes in Learning, Decision-Making and Social Relations* (London: Routledge, 2017), 33.

15. Ibid., 25.

16. Daniel T. Willingham, "Ask the Cognitive Scientist: Students Remember . . . What They Think About," American Federation of Teachers, Summer 2003, https://www .aft.org/periodical/american-educator/summer-2003/ask-cognitive-scientist-students -rememberwhat; Daniel T. Willingham, *Why Students Don't Like School*, 2nd ed. (Hoboken, NJ: Jossey-Bass, 2021).

17. Thomas S. Hyde and James J. Jenkins, "Differential Effects of Incidental Tasks on the Organization of Recall of a List of Highly Associated Words," *Journal of Experimental Psychology* 82, no. 3 (1969): 472–482, https://doi.org/10.1037/h0028372.

18. Daniel Willingham, "Knowledge and Practice: The Real Keys to Critical Thinking," presentation at the Learning and the Brain Conference, Boston, Massachusetts, November 24, 2019, https://www.youtube.com/watch?v=mEOLYaoqcQQ; "Daniel Willingham's Top Tips for Students to Improve Their Memory," YouTube, posted by TesWorld, September 9, 2015, https://www.youtube.com/watch?v=mEOLYaoqcQQ.

19. Kurt Fischer, interview by Ellen Galinsky, August 31, 2006.

20. Crone, *The Adolescent Brain*, 29.

21. Zelazo, Blair, and Willoughby, *Executive Function*, 6.

22. Philip David Zelazo, interview by Ellen Galinsky, June 7, 2021.

23. Mary Helen Immordino-Yang, interview by Ellen Galinsky, April 3, 2022.

24. Zelazo and Carlson, "Hot and Cool Executive Function in Childhood and Adolescence."

25. Miyake et al., "The Unity and Diversity of Executive Functions."

26. Zelazo, Blair, and Willoughby, *Executive Function*.

27. National Scientific Council on the Developing Child, "Building the Brain's 'Air Traffic Control' System," 1.

28. Jennifer Silvers, interview by Ellen Galinsky, May 5, 2017.

29. Crone, *The Adolescent Brain*, 35.

30. Peter C. Brown, Henry L. Roediger III, and Mark A. McDaniel, *Make It Stick: The Science of Successful Learning* (Cambridge, MA: Belknap Press of Harvard University Press, 2014).

31. Daniel J. Siegel, *Brainstorm: The Power and Purpose of the Teenage Brain* (New York: Penguin, 2013), 113.

32. Michele Borba, *Thrivers: The Surprising Reasons Why Some Kids Struggle and Others Shine* (New York: G. P. Putnam's Sons, 2021).

33. Ellen Galinsky, *The Six Stages of Parenthood* (Cambridge, MA: Da Capo Press, 1987).

34. Gabriele Oettingen, *Rethinking Positive Thinking: Inside the New Science of Motivation* (New York: Penguin Random House, 2014).

35. Gabriele Oettingen, interview by Ellen Galinsky, October 17, 2016.

36. Gabriele Oettingen, email message to Ellen Galinsky, February 15, 2023.

37. Oettingen, *Rethinking Positive Thinking*, 36.

38. Ibid., 27.

39. Gabriele Oettingen, email message to Ellen Galinsky, February 15, 2023.

40. Galinsky, *The Six Stages of Parenthood*.
41. Shawn Bryant, interview by Ellen Galinsky, February 4, 2022.
42. Gabriele Oettingen, interview by Ellen Galinsky, October 17, 2016; Gabriele Oettingen, email message to Ellen Galinsky, February 15, 2023.
43. Barb Lunnemann, interview by Ellen Galinsky, February 4, 2022.
44. Gabriele Oettingen, interview by Ellen Galinsky, October 17, 2016; Gabriele Oettingen, email message to Ellen Galinsky, February 15, 2023.
45. Gabriele Oettingen et al., "Mental Contrasting and Goal Commitment: The Mediating Role of Energization," *Personality and Social Psychology Bulletin* 35, no. 5 (February 2009): 609, https://doi.org/10.1177/0146167208330856; Peter M. Gollwitzer and Gabriele Oettingen, "Goal Attainment," in *The Oxford Handbook of Human Motivation*, 2nd ed., ed. Richard M. Ryan (New York: Oxford University Press, 2019), 247–268.
46. Gabriele Oettingen, email message to Ellen Galinsky, February 15, 2023.
47. Peter M. Gollwitzer, "Implementation Intentions: Strong Effects of Simple Plans," *American Psychologist* 54, no. 7 (1999): 493–503, https://doi.org/10.1037/0003-066X.54.7.493; Peter M. Gollwitzer and Gabriele Oettingen, "Implementation Intentions," in *Encyclopedia of Behavioral Medicine*, ed. Marc Gellman and J. Rick Turner (New York: Springer Verlag, 2013), 1043–1048.
48. Gabriele Oettingen, email message to Ellen Galinsky, February 15, 2023.
49. Jonathan Gottschall, "The Story Paradox: How Stories Can Affect Our Brains, Bind Us Together or Circumvent Rational Thought," presentation at the Learning and the Brain Conference, New York, April 3, 2022.
50. Fritz Heider and Marianne Simmel, "Animation" (1944), YouTube, posted by Kenjirou, July 26, 2010, https://www.youtube.com/watch?v=VTNmLt7QX8E.
51. Gottschall, "The Story Paradox."
52. Fritz Heider and Marianne Simmel, "An Experimental Study in Apparent Behavior," *American Journal of Psychology* 57, no. 2 (1944): 243–259, https://doi.org/10.2307/1416950; Adrianna Ratajska, Matt I. Brown, and Christopher F. Chabris, "Attributing Social Meaning to Animated Shapes: A New Experimental Study of Apparent Behavior," *American Journal of Psychology* 133, no. 3 (January 2020): 295–312, https://doi.org/10.5406/amerjpsyc.133.3.0295; Ami Klin, "Attributing Social Meaning to Ambiguous Visual Stimuli in Higher-Functioning Autism and Asperger Syndrome: The Social Attribution Task," *Journal of Child Psychology and Psychiatry* 41, no. 7 (2000): 831–846, https://doi.org/10.1111/1469-7610.00671.
53. Gottschall, "The Story Paradox."
54. Jonathan Gottschall, *The Story Paradox: How Our Love of Storytelling Builds Societies and Tears Them Down* (New York: Basic Books, 2021), 27.
55. Gottschall, "The Story Paradox."
56. Adam Galinsky, interview by Ellen Galinsky, December 9, 2016.
57. Elizabeth Haas Edersheim, *The Definitive Drucker* (New York: McGraw-Hill, 2007), 45.
58. "The Best Innovations of 2021: 100 Innovations Changing How We Live," *Time*, https://time.com/collection/best-inventions-2021/.
59. Betty M. Repacholi and Alison Gopnik, "Early Reasoning About Desires: Evidence from 14- and 18-Month-Olds," *Developmental Psychology* 33, no. 1 (1997): 12–21, https://doi.org/10.1037/0012-1649.33.1.12; Alison Gopnik and Janet W. Astington, "Children's Understanding of Representational Change and Its Relation to the Understanding of False Belief and the Appearance-Reality Distinction," *Child Development* 59, no. 1 (1988): 26–37, https://doi.org/10.1111/j.1467-8624.1988.tb03192.x; Alison Gopnik and Virginia Slaughter, "Young Children's Understanding of Changes in Their Mental States," *Child Development* 62, no. 1 (1991): 98–110, https://doi.org/10.1111/j.1467-8624.1991.tb01517.x.
60. Iroise Dumontheil, interview by Ellen Galinsky, September 21, 2017.
61. Iroise Dumontheil, Ian A. Apperly, and Sarah-Jayne Blakemore, "Online Usage of Theory of Mind Continues to Develop in Late Adolescence," *Developmental Science* 13, no. 2 (2010): 331–338, https://doi.org/10.1111/j.1467-7687.2009.00888.x.

62. Iroise Dumontheil, interview by Ellen Galinsky, September 21, 2017; Iroise Dumontheil, email message to Ellen Galinsky, January 28, 2023.

63. Dumontheil, Apperly, and Blakemore, "Online Usage of Theory of Mind."

64. Christian K. Tamnes et al., "Social Perspective Taking Is Associated with Self-Reported Prosocial Behavior and Regional Cortical Thickness Across Adolescence," *Developmental Psychology* 54, no. 9 (2018): 1745–1757, https://doi.org/10.1037/dev0000541.

65. Anne-Kathrin J. Fett et al., "Trust and Social Reciprocity in Adolescence: A Matter of Perspective-Taking," *Journal of Adolescence* 37, no. 2 (2014): 175–184, https://doi.org/10.1016/j.adolescence.2013.11.011.

66. Gottschall, *The Story Paradox*, 13.

67. "About Us," Center for Scholars and Storytellers, accessed September 30, 2022, https://www.scholarsandstorytellers.com/.

68. Adam Galinsky, interview by Ellen Galinsky, December 9, 2016.

69. Adam D. Galinsky and Gordon B. Moskowitz, "Perspective-Taking: Decreasing Stereotype Expression, Stereotype Accessibility, and In-Group Favoritism," *Journal of Personality and Social Psychology* 78, no. 4 (2000): 708–724, https://doi.org/10.1037/0022-3514.78.4.708.

70. Adam Galinsky, interview by Ellen Galinsky, December 9, 2016.

71. Adam Galinsky, interview by Ellen Galinsky, December 9, 2016; Adam Galinsky, email message to Ellen Galinsky, February 21, 2023.

72. Jason Chein, interview by Ellen Galinsky, April 22, 2022.

73. Gopnik and Astington, "Children's Understanding of Representational Change"; Gopnik and Slaughter, "Young Children's Understanding of Changes in Their Mental State"; Alison Gopnik, interview by Ellen Galinsky, November 29, 2001.

74. Adam Galinsky, interview by Ellen Galinsky, December 9, 2016; Adam Galinsky, email message to Ellen Galinsky, February 21, 2023.

75. Maria T. Maza et al., "Association of Habitual Checking Behaviors on Social Media with Longitudinal Functional Brain Development," *JAMA Pediatrics* 177, no. 2 (2023):160–167, https://doi.org/10.1001/jamapediatrics.2022.4924.

76. Madeline Holcombe, "For Adolescents, Social Media Might Be a Brain-Changer, Researchers Say," CNN, January 4, 2023, https://www.cnn.com/2023/01/03/health/social-media-checking-teen-development-wellness/index.html.

77. Logan Lane, "The Teenager Leading the Smartphone Liberation Movement," interview by Lulu Garcia-Navarro, *New York Times*, February 2, 2023, https://www.nytimes.com/2023/02/02/opinion/teen-luddite-smartphones.html?showTranscript=1.

78. Brit McCandless Farmer, "Meet the Teens Lobbying to Regulate Social Media," CBS News, December 11, 2022, https://www.cbsnews.com/news/social-media-regulation-lobby-60-minutes-2022-11/.

79. "About," Tech(nically) Politics, accessed January 17, 2023, https://www.technicallypolitics.org.

80. Farmer, "Meet the Teens Lobbying to Regulate Social Media."

81. Elizabeth L. Newton, "The Rocky Road from Actions to Intentions," Ph.D. diss., Stanford University, 1990, ix.

82. Mike Allen, ed., *The SAGE Encyclopedia of Communication Research Methods*, 4 vols. (Thousand Oaks, CA: SAGE Publications, 2017), https://dx.doi.org/10.4135/9781483381411.

83. "The Attributes Employers Want to See on College Students' Resumes," National Association of Colleges and Employers, accessed June 12, 2023, https://www.naceweb.org/talent-acquisition/candidate-selection/as-their-focus-on-gpa-fades-employers-seek-key-skills-on-college-grads-resumes/.

84. Adam Galinsky, interview by Ellen Galinsky, December 9, 2016.

85. Tony Alessandra and Michael J. O'Connor, *The Platinum Rule: Discover the Four Basic Business Personalities and How They Can Lead You to Success* (New York: Grand Central Publishing, 1998).

86. Adam Galinsky, interview by Ellen Galinsky, December 9, 2016.

87. Adam Galinsky and Maurice Schweitzer, *Friend and Foe* (New York: Crown Business, 2015), 51.

88. Adam Galinsky et al., "Power and Perspectives Not Taken," *Psychological Science* 17, no. 12 (December 2006): 1068–1074, https://doi.org/10.1111/j.1467-9280.2006.01824.x.

89. Adam Galinsky, interview by Ellen Galinsky, December 9, 2016.

90. Keely A. Muscatell et al., "Social Status Modulates Neural Activity in the Mentalizing Network," *NeuroImage* 60, no. 3 (April 2012): 1771–1777, https://doi.org/10.1016/j.neuroimage.2012.01.080.

91. Adam Galinsky, interview by Ellen Galinsky, December 9, 2016.

92. Gordon W. Allport, *The Nature of Prejudice* (Cambridge, MA: Addison-Wesley, 1954).

93. Thomas F. Pettigrew, "Advancing Intergroup Contact Theory: Comments on the Issue's Articles," *Journal of Social Issues* 77, no. 1 (2021): 258–273, https://doi.org/10.1111/josi.12423.

94. Stacy S. Kim, Ellen Galinsky, and Ipshita Pal, "One Kind Word: Flexibility in the Time of COVID-19," Families and Work Institute, April 2020, https://cdn.sanity.io/files/ow8usu72/production/e09f06cb1ed14ae25da4753f60a942668f9dc269.pdf.

95. Thomas F. Pettigrew and Linda R. Tropp, "A Meta-Analytic Test of Intergroup Contact Theory," *Journal of Personality and Social Psychology* 90, no. 5 (May 2006): 766, https://doi.org/10.1037/0022-3514.90.5.751.

96. Amanda Ripley, *High Conflict: Why We Get Trapped and How We Get Out* (New York: Simon and Schuster, 2021), 9.

97. Ibid., 188–189.

98. Goldie Hawn, conversation with Ellen Galinsky, May 13, 2022.

99. "The MindUP Program," MindUP, accessed June 2022, https://mindup.org/mindup-program/.

100. Ripley, *High Conflict*, 189–191.

101. Rachel E. White and Stephanie M. Carlson, "What Would Batman Do? Self-Distancing Improves Executive Function in Young Children," *Developmental Science* 19, no. 3 (2016): 419–426, https://doi.org/10.1111/desc.12314.

102. Pettigrew and Tropp, "A Meta-Analytic Test of Intergroup Contact Theory," 751–783.

103. Elizabeth Levy Paluck, Seth A. Green, and Donald P. Green, "The Contact Hypothesis Re-Evaluated," *Behavioural Public Policy* 3, no. 2 (2019): 129–158, https://doi.org/10.1017/bpp.2018.25.

104. Ibid., 153.

105. Megan Price, interview by Ellen Galinsky, April 26, 2022.

106. Megan Price, "Change Through Curiosity in the Insight Approach to Conflict," *Revista de Mediación* 11, no. 1 (2018): e3, 1–7.

107. Megan Price and Jamie Price, "Insight Policing and the Role of the Civilian in Police Accountability," *Clearinghouse Review*, August 2015, 4.

108. Megan Price, "When Students Misbehave: Student Discipline from the Insight Approach," Ph.D. diss., George Mason University, 2016.

109. Megan Price, conversation about the Insight approach with Ellen Galinsky and others, March 31, 2022.

110. Price, "Change Through Curiosity in the Insight Approach to Conflict."

111. Megan Price, email message to Ellen Galinsky, February 11, 2023.

112. Price, "Change Through Curiosity in the Insight Approach to Conflict," 2.

113. Megan Price, email message to Ellen Galinsky, February 11, 2023.

114. Megan Price, conversation about the Insight approach with Ellen Galinsky and others, March 31, 2022; Megan Price, email message to Ellen Galinsky, February 11, 2023.

115. Price, "When Students Misbehave," x.

116. Ibid., 26.

117. Ibid., 108.

118. Tania Singer and Olga M. Klimecki, "Empathy and Compassion," *Current Biology* 24, no. 18 (September 2014): R875–R878, https://doi.org/10.1016/j.cub.2014.06 .054.

119. Olga M. Klimecki et al., "Differential Pattern of Functional Brain Plasticity After Compassion and Empathy Training," *Social Cognitive and Affective Neuroscience* 9, no. 6 (June 2014): 873–879, https://doi.org/10.1093/scan/nst060.

120. Fynn-Mathis Trautwein et al., "Differential Benefits of Mental Training Types for Attention, Compassion, and Theory of Mind," *Cognition* 194 (2020): Article 104039, https://doi.org/10.1016/j.cognition.2019.104039.

121. Tania Singer and Veronika Engert, "It Matters What You Practice: Differential Training Effects on Subjective Experience, Behavior, Brain and Body in the ReSource Project," *Current Opinion in Psychology* 28 (August 2019): 151–158, https://doi.org /10.1016/j.copsyc.2018.12.005; Malvika Godara et al., "Investigating Differential Effects of Socio-Emotional and Mindfulness-Based Online Interventions on Mental Health, Resilience and Social Capacities During the COVID-19 Pandemic: The Study Protocol," *PloS One* 16, no. 11 (November 2021): e0256323, https://doi.org/10 .1371/journal.pone.0256323.

122. Helen Y. Weng et al., "Compassion Training Alters Altruism and Neural Responses to Suffering," *Psychological Science* 24, no. 7 (May 2013): 1171–1180, https://doi .org/10.1177/0956797612469537.

123. The Compassionate Mind Foundation, "Interview with Tania Singer: Creating a Compassionate World," YouTube, posted March 10, 2023, https://www.youtube.com /watch?v=lbWG2ItNtsk.

124. Robert Frost and Louis Untermeyer, *The Road Not Taken: A Selection of Robert Frost's Poems* (New York: Henry Holt, 1991).

125. Mary Helen Immordino-Yang, "Learning and the Brain," Adolescent Virtual Speaking Series, Bezos Family Foundation, December 9, 2020.

126. *NOVA*, "School of the Future: How Can the Science of Learning Help Us Rethink the Future of Education for All Children?," PBS, aired September 14, 2016.

127. Rebecca Gotlieb, Xiao-Fei Yang, and Mary Helen Immordino-Yang, "Default and Executive Networks' Roles in Diverse Adolescents' Emotionally Engaged Construals of Complex Social Issues," *Social Cognitive and Affective Neuroscience* 17, no. 4 (2022): 421–429, https://doi.org/10.1093/scan/nsab108.

128. Mary Helen Immordino-Yang, interview by Ellen Galinsky, April 3, 2022.

129. Mary Helen Immordino-Yang, "Building Meaning Builds Teens' Brains," Harvard Graduate School of Education, Next Level Lab Distinguished Speaker Series, April 13, 2022; Gotlieb, Yang, and Immordino-Yang, "Default and Executive Networks' Roles."

130. Immordino-Yang, "Building Meaning Builds Teens' Brains"; Gotlieb, Yang, and Immordino-Yang, "Default and Executive Networks' Roles."

131. Mary Helen Immordino-Yang, email message to Ellen Galinsky, February 14, 2023.

132. Mary Helen Immordino-Yang, interview by Ellen Galinsky, April 3, 2022; Gotlieb, Yang, and Immordino-Yang, "Default and Executive Networks' Roles."

133. Immordino-Yang, "Building Meaning Builds Teens' Brains"; Mary Helen Immordino-Yang, email message to Ellen Galinsky, February 14, 2023.

134. Mary Helen Immordino-Yang and Douglas R. Knecht, "Building Meaning Builds Teens' Brains," ASCD, May 1, 2020, https://www.ascd.org/el/articles/building -meaning-builds-teens-brains.

135. Mary Helen Immordino-Yang, interview by Ellen Galinsky, April 3, 2022.

136. Immordino-Yang and Knecht, "Building Meaning Builds Teens' Brains."

137. Immordino-Yang, "Building Meaning Builds Teens' Brains"; Xiao-Fe Yang et al., "Looking Up to Virtue: Averting Gaze Facilitates Moral Construals via Posteromedial Activations," *Social Cognitive and Affective Neuroscience* 13, no. 11 (November 2018): 1131–1139, https://doi.org/10.1093/scan/nsy081.

138. Immordino-Yang and Knecht, "Building Meaning Builds Teens' Brains"; Mary Helen Immordino-Yang, email message to Ellen Galinsky, February 14, 2023.

139. Immordino-Yang and Knecht, "Building Meaning Builds Teens' Brains"; Immordino-Yang, email message to Ellen Galinsky, February 14, 2023.

140. Mary Helen Immordino-Yang, interview by Ellen Galinsky, April 3, 2022.

141. Immordino-Yang, "Building Meaning Builds Teens' Brains."

142. Immordino-Yang and Knecht, "Building Meaning Builds Teens' Brains"; Mary Helen Immordino-Yang, email message to Ellen Galinsky, February 14, 2023.

143. Rebecca Gotlieb, Xiao-Fei Yang, and Mary Helen Immordino-Yang, "Diverse Adolescents' Transcendent Thinking Predicts Young Adult Psychosocial Outcomes via Brain Network Development," *PsyArXiv* (May 2023): 11, https://doi.org/10.31234/osf.io/cj6an.

144. "About Us," *Sages and Seekers*, accessed October 23, 2023, https://www.sagesandseekers.org/about.html.

145. Rodrigo Riveros et al., "Sages and Seekers: The Development of Diverse Adolescents' Transcendent Thinking and Purpose Through an Intergenerational Storytelling Program," *PsyArXiv* (June 1), https://doi.org/10.31234/osf.io/5e4bu.

146. Roger E. Beaty, interview by Ellen Galinsky, June 29, 2022.

147. Susan Magsamen and Ivy Ross, *Your Brain on Art: How the Arts Transform Us* (New York: Random House, 2023).

148. Eveline A. Crone, interview by Ellen Galinsky, September 1, 2017.

149. Robert W. Weisberg, *Creativity: Genius and Other Myths* (New York: W. H. Freeman, 1986).

150. Jason M. Chein et al., "Working Memory and Insight in the Nine-Dot Problem," *Memory and Cognition* 38, no. 7 (2010): 883–892, https://doi.org/10.3758/MC.38.7.883.

151. Jason M. Chein, interview by Ellen Galinsky, April 22, 2022.

152. Chein et al., "Working Memory and Insight in the Nine-Dot Problem," 883.

153. Ibid., 884.

154. Jason M. Chein, interview by Ellen Galinsky, April 22, 2022; Jason Chein, email message to Ellen Galinsky, February 20, 2023.

155. Jason M. Chein and Robert W. Weisberg, "Working Memory and Insight in Verbal Problems: Analysis of Compound Remote Associates," *Memory and Cognition* 42, no. 1 (January 2014): 67–83, https://doi.org/10.3578/s13421-013-0343-4.

156. Ibid., 78.

157. Ibid., 79.

158. Roger E. Beaty, interview by Ellen Galinsky, June 29, 2022.

159. Ibid.

160. Joy Paul Guilford et al., *Alternative Uses Manual* (Orange, CA: Sheridan Supply Company, 1960).

161. Roger E. Beaty, "New Study Reveals Why Some People Are More Creative Than Others," *Interalia Magazine*, March 2018, https://www.interaliamag.org/articles/roger-beaty-new-study-reveals-people-creative-others/.

162. Roger E. Beaty et al., "Robust Prediction of Individual Creative Ability from Brain Functional Connectivity," *Proceedings of the National Academy of Sciences* 115, no. 5 (January 2018): 1087–1092, https://doi.org/10.1073/pnas.1713532115.

163. Ibid.

164. Beaty, "New Study Reveals Why Some People Are More Creative"; Roger E. Beaty, interview by Ellen Galinsky, June 29, 2022.

165. Beaty et al., "Robust Prediction of Individual Creative Ability," 1087.

166. Roger E. Beaty, interview by Ellen Galinsky, June 29, 2022.

167. Solange Denervaud et al., "Education Shapes the Structure of Semantic Memory and Impacts Creative Thinking," *npj Science of Learning* 6, no. 35 (2021): 1–7, https://doi.org/10.1038/s41539-021-00113-8.

168. Ibid., 4.

169. Ibid.

170. Eveline A. Crone, interview by Ellen Galinsky, September 1, 2017.

171. Sietske W. Kleibeuker, Carsten K.W. De Dreu, and Eveline A. Crone, "The Develop-

ment of Creative Cognition Across Adolescence: Distinct Trajectories for Insight and Divergent Thinking," *Developmental Science* 16, no. 1 (2013): 2–12, https://doi.org/10.1111/j.1467-7687.2012.01176.x.

172. Eveline A. Crone, interview by Ellen Galinsky, September 1, 2017.

173. Sietske W. Kleibeuker et al., "Training in the Adolescent Brain: An fMRI Training Study on Divergent Thinking," *Developmental Psychology* 53, no. 2 (February 2017): 353–365, https://doi.org/10.1037/dev0000239; Claire E. Stevenson et al., "Training Creative Cognition: Adolescence as a Flexible Period for Improving Creativity," *Frontiers in Human Neuroscience* 8 (2014): 827, http://dx.doi.org/10.3389/fnhum.2014.00827.

174. Eveline A. Crone, interview by Ellen Galinsky, September 1, 2017.

175. Adam Grant, interview by Ellen Galinsky, November 29, 2017.

176. Adam Grant, *Originals: How Non-Conformists Move the World* (New York: Viking, 2016).

177. Adam Grant, interview by Ellen Galinsky, November 29, 2017.

178. Grant, *Originals*, 46–47; Robert Root-Bernstein et al., "Arts Foster Scientific Success: Avocations of Nobel, National Academy, Royal Society, and Sigma Xi Members," *Journal of Psychology of Science and Technology* 1, no. 2 (2008): 51–63, https://doi.org/10.1891/1939-7054.1.2.51.

179. Adam Grant, interview by Ellen Galinsky, November 29, 2017.

180. Ellen Winner, "Child Prodigies and Adult Genius: A Weak Link," in *The Wiley Handbook of Genius*, ed. Dean Keith Simonton (Malden, MA: Wiley-Blackwell, 2014), https://onlinelibrary.wiley.com/doi/10.1002/9781118367377.ch15.

181. Adam Grant, interview by Ellen Galinsky, November 29, 2017.

182. Adam Grant, "Kids, Would You Please Start Fighting?," *New York Times*, November 4, 2017, https://www.nytimes.com/2017/11/04/opinion/sunday/kids-would-you-please-start-fighting.html.

183. Martin L. Hoffman, "Parent Discipline and the Child's Consideration for Others," *Child Development* 34, no. 3 (1963): 573–588, https://doi.org/10.2307/1126753.

184. Christopher J. Bryan, Allison Master, and Gregory M. Walton, "'Helping' Versus 'Being a Helper': Invoking the Self to Increase Helping in Young Children," *Child Development* 85, no. 5 (2014): 1836–1842, https://doi.org/10.1111/cdev.12244.

185. Adam Grant, interview by Ellen Galinsky, November 29, 2017.

186. Silvia A. Bunge and Elena R. Leib, "How Does Education Hone Reasoning Ability?," *Current Directions in Psychological Science* 29, no. 2 (2020): 167, https://doi.org/10.1177/0963721419898818.

187. Ibid., 167–173.

188. Eveline A. Crone et al., "Neurocognitive Development of Relational Reasoning," *Developmental Science* 12, no. 1 (2009): 55–66, https://doi.org/10.1111/j.1467-7687.2008.00743.x.

189. Bunge and Leib, "How Does Education Hone Reasoning Ability?"

190. Ibid.

191. Allyson P. Mackey, Alison T. Miller Singley, and Silvia Bunge, "Intensive Reasoning Training Alters Patterns of Brain Connectivity at Rest," *Journal of Neuroscience* 33, no. 11 (2013): 4796–4803, https://doi.org/10.1523/JNEUROSCI.4141-12.2013.

192. Allyson P. Mackey, interview by Ellen Galinsky, November 30, 2017.

193. Allyson P. Mackey et al., "A Pilot Study of Classroom-Based Cognitive Skill Instruction: Effects on Cognition and Academic Performance," *Mind, Brain, and Education* 11, no. 2 (2017): 85–95, https://doi.org/10.1111/mbe.12138.

194. Allyson P. Mackey, interview by Ellen Galinsky, November 30, 2017.

195. Mackey et al., "A Pilot Study of Classroom-Based Cognitive Skill Instruction."

196. Allyson P. Mackey, interview by Ellen Galinsky, November 30, 2017.

197. Ibid.

198. Donald J. Bolger et al., "The Role and Sources of Individual Differences in Critical-Analytic Thinking: A Capsule Overview," *Educational Psychology Review* 26, no. 4 (2014): 496, https://psycnet.apa.org/doi/10.1007/s10648-014-9279-x.

199. "Mental Shortcuts, Not Emotion, Guide Irrational Decisions," *Neuroscience News*,

March 31, 2017, https://neurosciencenews.com/irrational-decisions-mental-shortcuts
-6319/.

200. Rosa Li, interview by Ellen Galinsky, June 27, 2022; Rosa Li, email message to Ellen Galinsky, February 7, 2023.

201. Rosa Li et al., "Reason's Enemy Is Not Emotion: Engagement of Cognitive Control Networks Explains Biases in Gain/Loss Framing," *Journal of Neuroscience* 37, no. 13 (March 2017): 3588–3598, https://doi.org/10.1523/JNEUROSCI.3486-16.2017.

202. Rosa Li, interview by Ellen Galinsky, June 27, 2022.

203. Li et al., "Reason's Enemy Is Not Emotion."

204. Rosa Li, interview by Ellen Galinsky, June 27, 2022.

205. Jennifer Pfeifer, interview by Ellen Galinsky, July 8, 2019.

206. Rosalind Weisman, *Queen Bees and Wannabes: Helping Your Daughter Survive Cliques, Gossip, Boyfriends, and the New Realities of Girl World* (New York: Harmony Books, 2009, 2016).

207. Megan Gunnar, interview by Ellen Galinsky, September 26, 2001.

208. National Academies of Sciences, Engineering, and Medicine, *The Promise of Adolescence: Realizing Opportunity for All Youth* (Washington, DC: National Academies Press, 2019), 44, https://doi.org/10.17226/25388.

209. Laurence Steinberg, *Age of Opportunity: Lessons from the New Science of Adolescence* (New York: Houghton Mifflin Harcourt, 2014).

210. Office of the Surgeon General, *Protecting Youth Mental Health: The U.S. Surgeon General's Advisory* (Washington, DC: U.S. Department of Health and Human Services, 2021), https://www.hhs.gov/sites/default/files/surgeon-general-youth-mental -health-advisory.pdf.

211. National Academies of Sciences, Engineering, and Medicine, *The Promise of Adolescence*, 59.

212. Office of the Surgeon General, *Protecting Youth Mental Health: The U.S. Surgeon General's Advisory*, 3.

213. "Youth Risk Behavior Survey: Data Summary and Trends Report, 2011–2021," Centers for Disease Control and Prevention, 2023, https://www.cdc.gov/healthyyouth/data /yrbs/pdf/YRBS_Data-Summary-Trends_Report2023_508.pdf.

214. Angela L. Duckworth, interview by Ellen Galinsky, October 6, 2017.

215. Angela L. Duckworth, Tamar Szabó Gendler, and James J. Gross, "Self-Control in School-Age Children," *Educational Psychologist* 49, no. 3 (2014): 199–217, https:// doi.org/10.1080/00461520.2014.926225.

216. Angela L. Duckworth, interview by Ellen Galinsky, October 6, 2017.

217. Angela L. Duckworth and Laurence Steinberg, "Unpacking Self-Control," *Child Development Perspectives* 9, no. 1 (2015): 32–37, https://doi.org/10.1111/cdep.12107.

218. Angela L. Duckworth, interview by Ellen Galinsky, October 6, 2017.

219. Duckworth, Gendler, and Gross, "Self-Control in School-Age Children."

220. Ibid., 211.

221. Angela L. Duckworth et al., "A Stitch in Time: Strategic Self-Control in High School and College Students," *Journal of Educational Psychology* 108, no. 3 (2016): 329–341, https://doi.org/10.1037/edu0000062.

222. Angela L. Duckworth, interview by Ellen Galinsky, October 6, 2017.

223. Duckworth et al., "A Stitch in Time."

224. Ibid.

225. Angela L. Duckworth, interview by Ellen Galinsky, October 6, 2017.

226. Martin L. Hoffman, "Parent Discipline and the Child's Consideration for Others," *Child Development* 34, no. 3 (1963): 573–588, https://doi.org/10.2307/1126753.

227. Ethan Kross, interview by Ellen Galinsky, January 17, 2018; Ethan Kross, email message to Ellen Galinsky, February 1, 2023.

228. Jiyoung Park, Ozlem Ayduk, and Ethan Kross, "Stepping Back to Move Forward: Expressive Writing Promotes Self-Distancing," *Emotion* 16, no. 3 (October 2016): 349, https://doi.org/10.1037/emo0000121; Rachel E. White, Ethan Kross, and Angela L. Duckworth, "Spontaneous Self-Distancing and Adaptive Self-Reflection

Across Adolescence," *Child Development* 86, no. 4 (2015): 1272–1281, https://doi .org/10.1111/cdev.12370.

229. Ethan Kross et al., "Self-Talk as a Regulatory Mechanism: How You Do It Matters," *Journal of Personality and Social Psychology* 106, no. 2 (2014): 304, https://doi.org /10.1037/a0035173.

230. Ethan Kross, interview by Ellen Galinsky, January 17, 2018.

231. Jason S. Moser et al., "Third-Person Self-Talk Facilitates Emotion Regulation Without Engaging Cognitive Control: Converging Evidence from ERP and fMRI," *Scientific Reports* 7, no. 4519 (July 2017): https://doi.org/10.1038/s41598-017-04047-3.

232. Ethan Kross, interview by Ellen Galinsky, January 17, 2018.

233. Daniel J. Siegel, interview by Ellen Galinsky, July 20, 2023.

234. David Yeager et al., "A Synergistic Mindsets Intervention Protects Adolescents from Stress," *Nature* 607 (July 2022): 512, https://doi.org/10.1038/s41586-022 -04907-7.

235. Megan R. Gunnar, interview by Ellen Galinsky, September 26, 2001.

236. Jeremy P. Jamieson et al., "Optimizing Stress Responses with Reappraisal and Mindset Interventions: An Integrated Model," *Anxiety, Stress & Coping* 31, no. 3 (February 2018): 245–261, https://doi.org/10.1080/10615806.2018.1442615.

237. David Yeager et al., "A Synergistic Mindsets Intervention," 512.

238. Ibid., 519.

239. Diamond and Ling, "Conclusions About Interventions, Programs, and Approaches," 34–48.

240. Michael Gazzaniga, interview by Ellen Galinsky, April 21, 2009.

241. Diamond and Ling, "Conclusions About Interventions, Programs, and Approaches."

242. Ibid., 35.

243. Adele Diamond and Daphne S. Ling, "Review of the Evidence on, and Fundamental Questions About, Efforts to Improve Executive Functions, Including Working Memory," in *Cognitive and Working Memory Training: Perspectives from Psychology, Neuroscience, and Human Development*, eds. Jared M. Novick et al. (Oxford Scholarship online, 2020), 1–572, https: //doi.org/10.1093/oso/9780199974467.001.0001.

244. Ibid., 501.

245. Deb Leong, email message to Ellen Galinsky, February 21, 2022.

246. Diamond and Ling, "Review of the Evidence," 506.

247. Susan Kontos et al., *Quality in Family Child Care and Relative Care* (New York: Teachers College Press, 1995).

248. Diamond and Ling, "Review of the Evidence," 511.

249. Ibid., 508.

250. Ibid., 505.

251. Ibid., 509.

252. Ibid.

253. Ibid., 502.

254. Philip David Zelazo, interview by Ellen Galinsky, February 12, 2022.

255. Stacey D. Espinet, Jacob E. Anderson, and Philip David Zelazo, "Reflection Training Improves Executive Function in Preschool-Age Children: Behavioral and Neural Effects," *Development Cognitive Neuroscience* 4 (April 2013): 3–15, https://doi.org /10.1016/j.dcn.2012.11.009.

256. Lauren V. Hadley, Frantzy Acluche, and Nicolas Chevalier, "Encouraging Performance Monitoring Promotes Proactive Control in Children," *Developmental Science* 23, no. 1 (January 2020): e12861, https://doi.org/10.1111/desc.12861.

257. Yusuke Moriguchi et al., "Teaching Others Rule-Use Improves Executive Function and Prefrontal Activations in Young Children," *Frontiers of Psychology* 6 (June 2015): art. 894, https://doi.org/10.3389/fpsyg.2015.00894.

258. Diamond and Ling, "Review of the Evidence," 503.

259. Ibid., 501.

260. Ibid., 504.

261. Adele Diamond, interview by Ellen Galinsky, October 4, 2008.

262. Daniel Goleman and Richard J. Davidson, *Altered Traits: Science Reveals How Meditation Changes Your Mind, Brain, and Body* (New York: Avery, 2017), 17.

263. Daniel Goleman, *Emotional Intelligence: Why It Can Matter More Than IQ* (New York: Bantam Books, 1995).

264. Goleman and Davidson, *Altered Traits*, 138–140.

265. Diamond and Ling, "Review of the Evidence," 512–513.

266. "About," Mountain View High School, accessed February 2022, https://mountainviewhs.fcps.edu/about.

267. Mountain View EF Team and Kim Dockery, interview by Ellen Galinsky, February 14, 2022 (Mountain View EF Team: Joe Thompson, Tim McElroy, Molly Flatley, Pete Garvey, and Jeff Jones).

268. "Practical Classroom Lessons for Building Resilient Minds," Executive Function in the Classroom, http://www.efintheclassroom.net/.

269. Mountain View EF Team and Kim Dockery, interview by Ellen Galinsky, February 14, 2022.

270. Peg Dawson and Richard Guare, *Smart but Scattered* (New York: Guilford Press, 2009).

271. "Water Quality and the Future Use of Loon Pond: Illuminating Standards Video Series," EL Education, https://modelsofexcellence.eleducation.org/resources/water-quality-and-future-use-loon-pond-illuminating-standards-video.

272. "High Schools in Springfield Public Schools District," *U.S. News and World Report*, https://www.usnews.com/education/best-high-schools/massachusetts/districts/springfield-public-schools-107767.

273. Ron Berger, interview by Ellen Galinsky, February 16, 2022.

274. Ron Berger, interview by Ellen Galinsky, February 7, 2022.

275. "History," EL Education, https://eleducation.org/who-we-are/history.

276. Ron Berger et al., *Learning That Lasts: Challenging, Engaging, and Empowering Students with Deeper Instruction* (San Francisco: Jossey-Bass, 2016).

277. Ron Berger, interview by Ellen Galinsky, February 16, 2022.

278. Ron Berger, interview by Ellen Galinsky, February 7, 2022.

279. Ron Berger, interview by Ellen Galinsky, February 7, 2022.

280. "About Us," Polaris Charter Academy, https://www.pcachicago.org/about/.

281. "Middle School Student-Led Conference," EL Education, https://eleducation.org/resources/middle-school-student-led-conference.

282. "The Power of Crew—Short Version," EL Education, https://eleducation.org/resources/the-power-of-Crew-short-version.

283. Ron Berger, interview by Ellen Galinsky, February 7, 2022.

284. "Identity and Belonging in Crew," EL Education, https://eleducation.org/resources/identity-and-belonging-in-Crew.

285. Ron Berger, interview by Ellen Galinsky, February 7, 2022.

286. Ibid.

287. Ron Berger, interview by Ellen Galinsky, February 16, 2022.

288. Ron Berger, interview by Ellen Galinsky, February 7, 2022.

289. Diamond and Ling, "Review of the Evidence."

290. Espinet, Anderson, and Zelazo, "Reflection Training Improves Executive Function"; Joan Paul Pozuelos et al., "Metacognitive Scaffolding Boosts Cognitive and Neural Benefits Following Executive Attention Training in Children," *Developmental Science* 22, no. 2 (2019): e12756, https://doi.org/10.1111/desc.12756; Loren Marie Marulis, Sara T. Baker, and David Whitebread, "Integrating Metacognition and Executive Function to Enhance Young Children's Perception of and Agency in Their Learning," *Early Childhood Research Quarterly* 50, part 2 (2020): 46–54, https://doi.org/10.1016/j.ecresq.2018.12.017; Hadley, Acluche, and Chevalier, "Encouraging Performance Monitoring Promotes Proactive Control in Children," e12861; Moriguchi et al., "Teaching Others Rule-Use."

291. Deb Leong, email message to Ellen Galinsky, February 21, 2022.

292. Fuligni, "The Need to Contribute During Adolescence," 332.

293. Ibid.

294. Making Caring Common Project, "The Children We Mean to Raise: The Real Messages Adults Are Sending About Values," Harvard Graduate School of Education, July 2014, https://mcc.gse.harvard.edu/reports/children-mean-raise; https://static1
.squarespace.com/static/5b7c56e255b02c683659fe43/t/5bae774424a694b5feb2b05f
/1538160453604/report-children-raise.pdf.

INDEX

ABOUT THE AUTHOR

ELLEN GALINSKY is the author of the bestselling *Mind in the Making*, president of Families and Work Institute, and a former chief science officer of the Bezos Family Foundation. She is a recipient of a lifetime achievement award from the Work and Family Researchers Network and serves as its elected president.